LAW, LIFE, AND GOVERNMENT AT RED RIVER

VOLUME 1

Rupert's Land Record Society Series
Jennifer S.H. Brown, Editor

1 The English River Book
A North West Company Journal and Account Book of 1786
Edited by Harry W. Duckworth

2 A Country So Interesting
The Hudson's Bay Company and Two Centuries of Mapping, 1670–1870
Richard I. Ruggles

3 Arctic Artist
The Journal and Paintings of George Back, Midshipman with Franklin, 1819–1822
Edited by C. Stuart Houston
Commentary by I.S. MacLaren

4 Ellen Smallboy
Glimpses of a Cree Woman's Life
Regina Flannery

5 Voices from Hudson Bay
Cree Stories from York Factory
Compiled and edited by Flora Beardy and Robert Coutts

6 North of Athabasca
Slave Lake and Mackenzie River Documents of the North West Company, 1800–1821
Edited with an Introduction by Lloyd Keith

7 From Barrow to Boothia
The Arctic Journal of Chief Factor Peter Warren Dease, 1836–1839
Edited and annotated by William Barr

8 My First Years in the Fur Trade
The Journals of 1802–1804
George Nelson
Edited by Laura Peers and Theresa Schenck

9 The Spirit Lives in the Mind
Omushkego Stories, Lives, and Dreams
Louis Bird
Edited and Compiled by Susan Elaine Gray

10 Memories, Myths, and Dreams of an Ojibwe Leader
William Berens as told to A. Irving Hallowell
Edited and with Introductions by Jennifer S.H. Brown and Susan Elaine Gray

11 Letters from Rupert's Land, 1826–1840
James Hargrave of the Hudson's Bay Company
Edited by Helen E. Ross

12 Treaty No. 9
Making the Agreement to Share the Land in Far Northern Ontario in 1905
John S. Long

13 Law, Life, and Government at Red River
Volume 1: Settlement and Governance, 1812–1872
Dale Gibson

14 Law, Life, and Government at Red River
Volume 2: General Quarterly Court of Assiniboia, Annotated Records, 1844–1872
Dale Gibson

Law, Life, and Government at Red River

Volume 1
Settlement and Governance, 1812–1872

DALE GIBSON

McGill-Queen's University Press
Montreal & Kingston · London · Chicago
and
The Osgoode Society for Canadian Legal History
Toronto

© McGill-Queen's University Press 2015

ISBN 978-0-7735-4521-2 (cloth)
ISBN 978-0-7735-4522-9 (paper)
ISBN 978-0-7735-9706-8 (ePDF)

Legal deposit third quarter 2015
Bibliothèque nationale du Québec

Printed in Canada on acid-free paper that is 100% ancient forest free (100% post-consumer recycled), processed chlorine free

This publication was supported in part with funds from the 2014 Wilson Prize for Publishing Canadian History awarded to McGill-Queen's University Press by the L.R. Wilson Institute for Canadian History at McMaster University.

McGill-Queen's University Press acknowledges the support of the Canada Council for the Arts for our publishing program. We also acknowledge the financial support of the Government of Canada through the Canada Book Fund for our publishing activities.

Library and Archives Canada Cataloguing in Publication

Gibson, Dale, author
Law, life, and government at Red River / Dale Gibson.

(Rupert's Land Record Society series ; 13–14)
Includes bibliographical references and indexes.
Contents: Volume 1. Settlement and governance, 1812–1872 – Volume 2. General Quarterly Court of Assiniboia, annotated records, 1844–1872.
Issued in print and electronic formats.
ISBN 978-0-7735-4521-2 (v. 1 : bound). – ISBN 978-0-7735-4522-9 (v. 1 : paperback).– ISBN 978-0-7735-4563-2 (v. 2 : bound). – ISBN 978-0-7735-9706-8 (v. 1 : ePDF).– ISBN 978-0-7735-9707-5 (v. 2 : ePDF)

1. Law – Red River Settlement – History – Sources. 2. Courts – Red River Settlement – History – Sources. 3. Community life – Red River Settlement – History – Sources. 4. Red River Settlement – Politics and government. 5. Red River Settlement – History. I. Osgoode Society for Canadian Legal History, issuing body II. Title. III. Title: Settlement and governance, 1812–1872. IV. Title: General Quarterly Court of Assiniboia, annotated records, 1844–1872. V. Series: Rupert's Land Record Society series ; 13–14

KEM165.G528 2015 349.7127'43 C2015-901759-9
KF345.G52 2015 C2015-901760-2

Typeset by Jay Tee Graphics Ltd. in 10.5/13 Baskerville

Contents

Acknowledgments

However many hours are spent in solitary study and composition, scholarship is an essentially collaborative art. My debt begins with Lee Gibson, who introduced me to the joys of probing the past, and with whom my early historical research and writing were shared. It was Judge Roy St George Stubbs, who laboured long and almost alone at first on the barren plains of western Canadian legal history, who introduced me to the Quarterly Court of Assiniboia and some of the unforgettable people who sat on its bench and in its dock and witness box.

Leslie Hoffman was the first person to begin work on the current project – back in 1990–93 – by transcribing volumes A, B, and C of the court records in electronic form. When volume D was recently discovered, Leslie agreed to transcribe that also, and did so with remarkable dispatch. Her contribution – astonishingly accurate given that she was working from photocopies of microfilm the first time and from amateur photographs the second – is the bedrock of this book, and I am deeply indebted to her.

A change of residence, and of professional preoccupations, necessitated my putting the project aside even before Leslie had finished transcribing the first three volumes. When I was finally able, a few years ago, to turn my attention to the quarterly courts once more, I was heartily encouraged to do so by Dr DeLloyd Guth, director of the Legal History Project in the Faculty of Law at the University of Manitoba, in whose custody the transcripts had remained. And DeLloyd did much more than offer encouragement. It was he who proposed a collaboration between the Faculty of Law and the Centre for Rupert's Land Studies at the University of Winnipeg, and he and his assistant Sue Law provided much other practical help in the early stages of the revived project. DeLloyd also made a number of valuable research contributions, some of which are specifically noted hereafter. Although both he and I had hoped he would be able to contribute even more than he did, circumstances disappointed us in that respect. I am nevertheless warmly grateful to DeLloyd for being at my side when he could.

I offer my sincere thanks to the Social Sciences and Humanities Research Council of Canada – that vital enabler of humane studies in this country – for making it financially possible for me to travel to Winnipeg for the purpose of mining the mother lode of western Canadian historical resources that lies, still too little exploited, in the Archives of Manitoba, as well as to engage Sally Nystrom and Jo-anne Desanges to assist in that work. Sally and I met at neighbouring microfilm readers at the archives shortly after I resumed work on the project. After we had chatted briefly about our respective research, and had turned back to our work at hand, Sally suddenly asked, her eyes glued to a document she was examining, "You interested in an axe murder?" It was not long before she was a key member of the Quarterly Court team – knowledgeable, energetic, diplomatic, loyal, and uncommonly resourceful. This study would have been significantly less worthy without Sally Nystrom's labours. Jo-anne's gleaning, paraphrasing, and translation of French-language materials, all infused with her enthusiasm for "meurtre et brouhaha," have also enriched the project.

Almost the totality of the study derives, directly or indirectly, from the incredibly rich and uniquely important holdings of the Archives of Manitoba and Hudson's Bay Company Archives, a combined resource that is too little known, too little appreciated, and too little supported by Manitobans and Canadians. I am extremely grateful to the staff of those connected institutions, as well as of the allied Legislative Library of Manitoba, for innumerable services and kindnesses. Although they are far too numerous to list here, there are two who must not go unrecognized. In 1988 former Hudson's Bay Company archivist Dr Shirlee-Anne Smith made available the photocopies from which most of Leslie Hoffman's first transcriptions were made; and, when occasionally cornered while conducting private research during more recent years, Dr Smith generously and invaluably answered off-beat questions from Sally and me. The other person who cannot be left unmentioned is one of the Archive of Manitoba's most valuable human resources: archivist Chris Kotecki. Wonderfully familiar with the holdings of both archives, as well as with the territory and times they illumine, and invariably friendly and helpful, Chris enriches the value of every researcher's visit to the treasures he and his colleagues curate. It was a hunch on Chris's part, for instance, that led to the recent discovery of the fourth volume of General Quarterly Court records.

Dr Jennifer Brown, director emerita of the Centre for Rupert's Land Studies, has been an enthusiastic and helpful supporter of this project ever since the University of Winnipeg became involved in it. Among Jennifer's many contributions was to attract the interest of David Malaher, one of the centre's longest-standing and most enthusiastic supporters, whose splendid maps adorn volume 1. Jennifer's then colleague at the centre, Anne Lindsay, went far beyond the call of duty with her valuable insights and suggestions. The folks at McGill-Queen's University Press dealt calmly, imaginatively, and skilfully with the problem of the manuscript's length, as well as providing their usual essential editing and publishing services. Those at the press with whom I had the pleasure to work directly were acquisitions editor Jacqueline Mason, managing editor Ryan Van Huijstee, and Robert Lewis, whose meticulous copy editing improved the final product appreciably. The effort, prowess, and ingenuity of my Edmonton assistant, Lorie Huising, who has been making my professional life easier for many years, were responsible for bringing this work to a conclusion sooner than would otherwise have been the case. The final contributor to the project was the admirable indexer Judy Dunlop, whose enthusiasm for her mysterious art has been a joy to witness.

My wife, Sandra Anderson, has not only graciously put up with my fixation on the nineteenth-century prairies for too much of the twenty-first century, but has also subjected the entire manuscript to eagle-eyed scrutiny, made innumerable valuable suggestions, and saved me from many gaucheries.

And, from beginning to end, there has been that indispensable company of collaborators, the most directly pertinent of whom are listed in the Bibliography, to whose timeless previous scholarship I dare to offer this addendum and in whose invisible companionship I have constantly delighted these past several years.

Thank you all.

Dale Gibson
Edmonton, Alberta
31 March 2015

Foreword

The General Quarterly Court of Assiniboia can justly be called the first "British" court in western Canada. Although there were predecessor institutions and judicial arrangements for hearing criminal and civil cases, the establishment of the Quarterly Court in the 1830s put the administration of justice in the Red River region on a firm and regularized footing. Professor Dale Gibson's comprehensive history of the court weaves together the legal history of the Red River Settlement and its social, economic, and political history. At the centre of this book sits the complete court proceedings of the General Quarterly Court from 1844 until 1872, which are examined in detail and in context to provide a compelling narrative of the administration of substantial rather than formal justice in a Hudson's Bay Company community. The buffalo hunt, frontier business arrangements, and settlement ferries come and go in the court records, coexisting with the minutiae of everyday life and relations among European, Métis, and Aboriginal peoples. This is a unique and extremely valuable account of law and courts on the frontier, which were administered usually without lawyers but never without law.

The purpose of the Osgoode Society for Canadian Legal History is to encourage research and writing on the history of Canadian law. The society, which was incorporated in 1979 and is registered as a charity, was founded at the initiative of the Honourable R. Roy McMurtry and officials of the Law Society of Upper Canada. The society seeks to stimulate the study of legal history in Canada by supporting researchers, collecting oral histories, and publishing volumes that contribute to legal-historical scholarship in Canada. It has published ninety books on the courts, the judiciary, and the legal profession, as well as on the history of crime and punishment, women and law, law and economy, the legal treatment of ethnic minorities, and famous cases and significant trials in all areas of the law.

Current directors of the Osgoode Society for Canadian Legal History are Robert Armstrong, Kenneth Binks, Susan Binnie, David Chernos, J. Douglas Ewart, Violet French, Martin Friedland, Philip Girard, William Kaplan, C. Ian Kyer, Virginia MacLean, Patricia McMahon, R. Roy McMurtry, Madeleine Meilleur, Janet Minor, Dana Peebles, Paul Perell, Jim Phillips, Paul Reinhardt, William Ross, Paul Schabas, Robert Sharpe, Alex Smith, Lorne Sossin, Mary Stokes, and Michael Tulloch.

The annual report and information about membership may be obtained by writing to the Osgoode Society for Canadian Legal History, Osgoode Hall, 130 Queen Street West, Toronto, Ontario, M5H 2N6 (telephone: 416-947-3321; e-mail: mmacfarl@lsuc.on.ca; website: http://www.osgoodesociety.ca).

R. Roy McMurtry
President

Jim Phillips
Editor-in-chief

Preface

One late afternoon in November or December 1857 visiting artist William Henry Edward Napier, standing in the Red River Settlement slightly south of where Winnipeg's Portage Avenue and Main Street now intersect, painted a quick, charming watercolour sketch of what he saw farther to the south.[1] A pink sky announces the approach of dusk. In the foreground, two men are talking – perhaps bargaining, possibly arguing. Behind them stands an empty horse-drawn sled, and behind that is the colourful home of Andrew McDermot, the settlement's most prominent, and wealthiest, independent businessman. McDermot himself might be one of the conversing men. Watching from beside his fence is what appears to be an Aboriginal family. Someone is driving a dogsled past the end of the fence. In the distance, grey on the horizon, are the formidable walls of Upper Fort Garry, the commercial and governmental headquarters of the Hudson's Bay Company, and – a little outside the fort walls, enclosed by a wooden stockade of its own – the combined courthouse and jail of the District of Assiniboia. The latter is the only such facility in north-central North America.

This book is about the pioneer community – the first in what is now western Canada – of which the McDermot property and the scattering of other rude residences out of sight behind the artist's back were a part. It deals with the establishment of the settlement, its development through much of the nineteenth century, and its ambivalent relationship with the legal and governmental institutions represented by the grey walls in Napier's sketch. You could say it's a book about links between the foreground and the background of the painting.

Red River was largely a community without lawyers, although not without law, during most of the period examined; and that fact had interesting consequences. It was also a company community. The Hudson's Bay Company (HBC) was not only the primary employer; it was also – by virtue of its 1670 royal charter – both the owner and the governor of this entire part of the world until, 200 years later, the area was absorbed by the fledgling Dominion of Canada.

The rulers spoke a different language and practised a different religion than most of those they ruled; and the latter, while generally inured to that fact, resented the disadvantage at which it put them in their relations with officialdom. They also resented the fact that few of their number were ever allowed to enter the governing ranks; and the majority of them thought their rulers had no right to own the land or to govern the community. Democratic urges, fuelled by developments in the United States and the Canadas, grew more insistent over time. The HBC fur-trading monopoly, which the charter also purported to bestow, was a source of continual hostility among those who felt entitled to share the natural bounties of the land. Yet most residents of the settlement were willing participants, most of the time, in a legal and governmental system that everyone knew could not function without their cooperation.

The book was prompted by the author's fascination with a unique collection of court records, extending from 1844 to 1872, that chronicle the work of the General Quarterly Court of Assiniboia – the senior division of the earliest British judicial system west of Toronto – and the vicissitudes of frontier life that brought inhabitants of the HBC territories into conflict with each other and with the law. With a very few exceptions, those records – and the hundreds of dramatic, everyday, poignant, mean-spirited, uplifting, humorous, tragic, informative, human stories they tell – had never been published; and I believed that the insights they provide into the legal, political, and social history of the Canadian midwest ought to be made more widely available.

Two major obstacles stood in the way. First, although the court records are extensive, and therefore expensive to publish in full, they would convey a distorted picture if merely "cherry-picked" for sensational trials, as some previous accounts have done. Second, a full appreciation of the records' contents and significance requires considerable background knowledge on the reader's part: an understanding of the highly unusual privately owned but publicly endorsed legal-governmental system that produced them and of the rapidly evolving, one-of-a-kind, wilderness community it served.

Such contextual data are vital; law cannot be satisfactorily understood in isolation. To know – to even speculate intelligently about – what court documents signify, one must be aware of many other things. Who were the judges and jurors whose decisions they record? What laws did those adjudicators apply (or ignore in favour of other norms)? What governmental structures and political factors produced or shaped the law? What legal challenges did the laws themselves face? How did judicial bodies within and beyond the jurisdiction relate to each other? Was there effective law enforcement machinery to support the courts? Who were the advocates – amateur, semi-professional, and professional – who represented those who came before the courts? What were the back stories of particular cases, which the official records often fail to disclose, but of which everyone in the courtroom had usually heard? Were there significant sequels? What demographic, social, economic, and political forces underlay all the foregoing factors? Yet, adding all that data to an already large body of official records would exacerbate the problem of length.

The solution devised to deal with these twin difficulties has been to publish the book in two volumes. The background story – essentially a retelling of Red River history from a legal and governmental perspective, including discussions of key cases – is presented, along with a glossary, bibliography, and index, in this volume; and the complete official records, containing the courtroom narratives, extensive explanatory notes and commentaries, and an index by case number, are published in a second volume.

Although it is hoped that volume 1 will be of interest independently of the volume 2 court records, it was written as a backdrop for the records themselves. It is in those records where Red River comes alive: from the first case, in which Mrs Smith climbs from her husband's bed into that of the hired man across the room, to one of the last, where three alleged participants in Manitoba's only-ever armed foreign invasion are tried for treason. In between those cases are hundreds of other little-known frontier dramas: a public assassination that resulted in the settlement's first and only hanging; a courthouse siege by more than 250 armed men determined to prevent an unpopular trial; the torrid love affair between the settlement's first lady and a dashing military officer that caused most of the community to take sides and Red River's first professional judge to be dismissed; the conviction of a respected cleric for attempted abortion; the cheating of justice by a future Manitoba lieutenant governor; and the private tragedies of unwed mothers prosecuted for infanticide. Discussion of the socio-political context with which volume 1 is chiefly concerned also extends into volume 2, where case accounts are copiously annotated and often followed by longer commentaries providing background information about the cases in question and related matters.

Those volume 2 records, preserving over 600 case accounts in four large leather-bound books housed in the Archives of Manitoba (one volume of which was not recognized as such until this project began), have had only rare public exposure. A handful of politically significant cases have occasionally been discussed by historians; but this uniquely revealing window on everyday life in the first major community in the British American northwest has never before been thrown entirely open.

Conventions and Abbreviations

The format, spelling, capitalization, and punctuation are wildly inconsistent in the original court records and other documents reproduced or quoted herein. Capitalization and spelling display few discernible patterns, and punctuation – when there is any – is idiosyncratic. Although accents are occasionally added to French expressions, the anglophone clerks who penned most of the documents were usually ignorant of proper French usage. Names pose especially difficult problems. Not only are they spelled in widely differing ways by different hands, but it is not uncommon for the same person's name to be given varied spellings by the same hand within a single document. Indian[1] names involve special problems.

Those problems have been dealt with herein by a hybrid approach lying somewhere between reproducing the original text as is and adopting modern conventions. My rationale is that the primary purpose of publishing these court records and related documents is to advance knowledge and understanding of their contents, not to record the inconsistent capitalization practices of the era or the variable spelling prowess of those who penned them. Where clarity was not affected, however, it seemed preferable to preserve the original form. Particular components of this approach are explained below.

EDITORIAL INTRUSIONS

Where considered desirable in the interests of clarity to insert additions or comments within reproduced or quoted text, such have been placed between brackets and kept as brief as possible.

STYLE

Punctuation is modern. Format, spacing, and paragraphing are generally in accordance with the original documents, but changes have been made where desirable for clarity, emphasis, or efficient use of space. The more generous capitalization of the era has been mostly retained in the court records and in quotations from other original documents.

SPELLING AND ACCENTING

Modern spelling and accenting have been used in transcribed documents, except for words that were commonly spelled differently at the time than they now are (gaol, shew, expence, etc.), where the original is retained. Because original spellings varied between English and US models (shifting gradually toward American usages over time), the originals are generally followed in that respect too; although inconsistencies within particular documents are usually made uniform.

QUOTATION MARKS

In the court records, the testimony of witnesses was often recorded in the first-person, apparently verbatim, but the use of quotation marks was infrequent and inconsistent. In this transcription, quotation marks are added where the context suggests it is appropriate to do so. Where a quotation occurs within another, it is enclosed in inverted commas.

PAGINATION AND NUMBERING OF VOLUMES AND CASES

The court records are contained in four volumes. Each original volume is internally paginated, but the volumes themselves are not numbered or otherwise sequentially identified. For this transcription, the volumes have been designated "A" (November 1844 to August 1851), "B" (November 1851 to February 1863), "C" (February 1863 to May 1872), and "D" (May 1871 to August 1872: civil cases only).[2] The original internal pagination has been retained, with the addition of appropriate alphabetical prefixes.

Cases were not numbered sequentially in the original records – except in volume D. For this transcription it has been thought useful to do so throughout, from case 1 in November 1844 (page [A]1) to case 685 in

August 1872 (page [D]185). This means that volume D contains two sets of case numbers: the original ones and those added herein. Cases were sometimes adjourned from one court session to another, and where that occurred each court appearance is identified by the same case number but with a sequential alphabetical suffix: case 455a, case 455b, and so on. In the final court session reported in volume C, some accused persons faced two or more charges with respect to the same alleged conduct (rape and indecent assault, for example). In those situations, the separate charges are indicated by sequentially numbered suffixes in parentheses: case 495(1), case 495(2), case 495(3), and so on.

NAMES

Many persons referred to in the court records are known to historians by names with commonly accepted spellings. In such cases, if the identifications are certain, the accepted versions are preferred to spellings used in the records. Even where the particular individual is not known to history but bears a name commonly spelled a particular way, that spelling has been adopted. Where a name is spelled in more than one way within a given case, a single spelling is adopted: usually the first one that appears. For French names, modern accenting is used throughout.

Indian names were written in two different ways in the original documents: either broken into hyphen-separated syllables corresponding to the syllabic alphabet; or written in run-on fashion. The latter method has been followed consistently herein.

RACIAL/ETHNIC IDENTIFIERS

At the time of writing, certain racial and ethnic identifiers are considered by some to be impolite or "politically incorrect." "Indian" and "Halfbreed" are among the avoided expressions. Those terms were in common use at Red River, and in the original documents reproduced or quoted from herein, during the entire time under study. The former indicated a person of Aboriginal blood, without other known genetic identity; and the latter referred to someone of mixed Aboriginal and other blood. A further, linguistic-cultural, distinction was made between "French Halfbreeds" and "English Halfbreeds." It would have been nonsensical to avoid the same usages herein.

The expressions "Aboriginal" and "Métis" (the latter term having come into widespread use about 1869) are also employed where historically appropriate. It is impossible to pinpoint the moment when the population previously called "French Halfbreeds" began to be known as "Métis." Although the term had undoubtedly been used well before the 1869 uprising led by Louis Riel Jr brought it into general use among anglophones as well as francophones, that year has been chosen to adopt it herein. In more recent times, "Métis" has also been applied, sometimes without an accented *e*, to the group called "English Halfbreeds" in this book. Since that usage did not prevail during the times discussed, it is not used here. The French and English mixed-blood populations are referred to collectively as "Halfbreeds." "Aboriginal" embraces all Indians and Halfbreeds (as well as Inuit, although members of that group do not figure in this account).

ENGLISH MONEY

English currency was in common use at Red River during most of the period covered, although other currencies occasionally showed up. The units were the pound sterling, or "quid" (£); the shilling, or "bob" (/), of which there were twenty in every pound; and the penny (d) of which there were twelve in every shilling.

A further subdivision was the farthing, worth one-quarter of a penny, which was never referred to in the court records, but was mentioned in a newspaper account of a March 1860 trial that was never officially recorded, in which the court awarded one farthing in damages to signify its contempt for the claim.[3] A conventional, but unofficial, denomination sometimes referred to at the time, but not employed in court records, was the guinea. A guinea was a kind of "baker's dozen" pound sterling – a monetary sum equivalent to 21 shillings – in which lawyers were traditionally paid. There were no official banknotes or coins in guinea denominations, and no symbol is known to the author.

In the court records, pounds, shillings, and pence are designated in various and sometimes confusing ways, often separated by dots or slashes. The convention adopted herein, unless the context demands otherwise, is to express sums in English currency as in the following example: £12.00.04 (12 pounds, 0 shillings, 4 pence).

ERRORS, GAPS, AND REPETITIONS

These are treated variously. Obvious spelling and accenting errors and clearly unintended repetitions are corrected without comment. Other types of errors and gaps, whether obvious or suspected, are flagged and sometimes commented upon in brackets.

ABBREVIATIONS IN ORIGINALS

Ampersands, ditto marks, and other abbreviations – which were common in the originals – have usually been retained, if internally consistent and compatible with prevailing practices. Where necessary, explanations enclosed in brackets are provided.

ABBREVIATIONS USED HEREIN

" ditto. See do.
ABC Archives of British Columbia
AM Archives of Manitoba
do. ditto. Used in the court records and other original documents, interchangeably with a single quotation mark ("), to indicate a repetition of the word or figure immediately above it.
HBC Hudson's Bay Company
HBCA Hudson's Bay Company Archives (housed in AM)
JP justice of the peace
LAC Library and Archives Canada
MAN *Manitoban* newspaper (suffix shows date; e.g., MAN701015 for *Manitoban,* 15 October 1870)
MET *Le Métis* newspaper (suffix shows date; e.g., MET710527 for *Le Métis,* 27 May 1871)
NN *New Nation* newspaper (suffix shows date; e.g., NN700107 for *New Nation,* 7 January 1870)
NW *Nor'-Wester* newspaper (suffix shows date; e.g., NW591228 for *Nor'-Wester,* 28 December 1859)
NWC North West Company
QC Queen's Counsel. See Glossary.
qv Literally, a Latin abbreviation for "which see." Used herein to indicate that the word preceding it is defined in the Glossary.
sic Such. An assurance that a word or expression quoted from a document or other statement is accurately quoted.
viz. Namely. Used in the court records and other original documents to introduce a list of specific names or items comprising a group or collective entity.

Figures

LAW, LIFE, AND GOVERNMENT AT RED RIVER

VOLUME 1

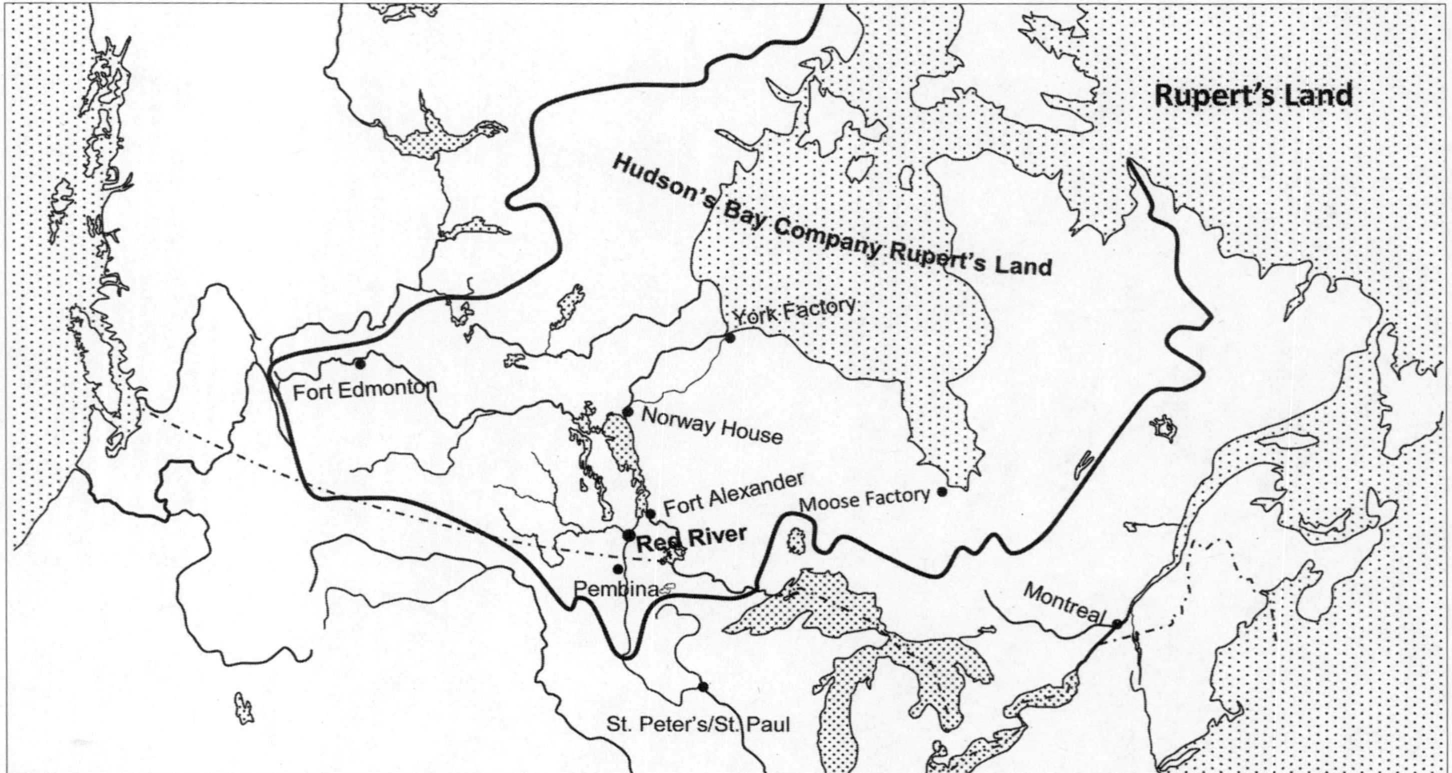
Rupert's Land
Hudson's Bay Company Rupert's Land
York Factory
Fort Edmonton
Norway House
Fort Alexander
Moose Factory
Red River
Pembina
Montreal
St. Peter's/St. Paul

Figure 1.1

1

Origins, 1670–1821

North-central North America, bordered by the Great Lakes on the east, the Rocky Mountains on the west, Hudson Bay and the Arctic Ocean on the north, and the Mississippi-Missouri watershed on the south, is traversed by a network of great waterways, a major hub of which is the juncture of the Red and Assiniboine Rivers at what is now Winnipeg, Manitoba. Until the late seventeenth century, this vast expanse of prairie, forest, tundra, and ice was home to none but Aboriginal peoples and profusely abundant wildlife. Then came European trader-explorers: French from the east and Scots from Great Britain via Hudson Bay. In the early nineteenth century, commercial, cultural, and legal conflicts between those two groups of newcomers, exacerbated by a controversial attempt to create a settlement called Red River in the area surrounding the forks of the Red and Assiniboine, were severe and sometimes bloody.

Peace was eventually restored by an 1821 merger of the former trade rivals that ensured Red River's survival and future growth. To serve the burgeoning settlement, a unique form of governance and judicature began to evolve. Before the commercial rivals merged, two distinct and competing legal systems were in operation, but amalgamation gave priority to one of those, based on political and legal powers bestowed upon the Hudson's Bay Company by royal charter. Governmental and legal arrangements were initially rudimentary, but a start had been made.

ASSINIBOIA'S BIRTH AND TURBULENT INFANCY[1]

The Red River ("of the North," some add to distinguish it from its southern namesakes) rises in the United States, not far north of the headwaters of the Mississippi River, and flows northward to Lake Winnipeg. Roughly half-way between the Canadian-American border and Lake

Winnipeg, it is joined from the west by the Assiniboine River. The junction of the Red and Assiniboine was a transportation hub from time immemorial. Lake Winnipeg gave Aboriginal travellers and early European explorers access to waterways leading to Hudson Bay, the Great Lakes, and the Rocky Mountains. The Assiniboine penetrated the northwest plains and provided, via portage to Lake Manitoba, another route to the mountains. The Mississippi-Missouri river system carried canoes to the heart of the continent and as far south as the Gulf of Mexico.

The same waterways later served the fur traders. The Hudson's Bay Company (HBC), established by English royal charter in 1670,[2] initially made only passive use of them, installing itself on the shores of Hudson Bay and inviting Aboriginal trappers to bring their skins to the bay for sale. Montreal-based traders – the North West Company (NWC) and its predecessors and rivals – took a different approach, pushing actively west and north from the Great Lakes in search of commercial opportunities, and eventually establishing a network of inland trading posts across an area that included much of what we now call the prairie provinces of Canada and beyond.

Although the activities of the HBC and the NWC came into little direct contact at first, the westward and northward expansion of the latter's operations made an eventual collision inevitable. HBC authorities claimed the NWC was intruding illegally into territories the older company owned, and over which its charter had granted it exclusive trading rights. NWC officials thought otherwise, and plausible legal arguments supported the positions of both companies. The charter that Charles II granted to the HBC in 1670 purported to bestow upon it "the sole trade and commerce,"[3] along with many other rights, over "Rupert's Land," a vast area comprising all lands drained by lakes and rivers flowing ultimately into Hudson Bay. This included much of the area that, by the fourth quarter of the eighteenth century, was considered by the NWC to be its sole domain because it got there first. Moreover, the NWC's lawyers pointed out, by the time Charles II granted the HBC charter with its purported trade monopoly, Parliament had outlawed all monopolies that Parliament itself did not either grant or confirm.

About the time the NWC completed its occupation of the area, the HBC began to probe south and west from its bases on Hudson Bay, and to establish hinterland posts in order to prevent the NWC from undermining its sources of fur. The subsequent rivalry between HBC and NWC traders, although vigorous and not always friendly, was mostly peaceful at the outset. That changed dramatically in the early nineteenth century, however, and hostilities at the forks of the Red and Assiniboine Rivers were especially bitter.

A Scottish nobleman – Thomas Douglas, Earl of Selkirk – became a major HBC shareholder in 1808. Along with two brothers-in-law, both also shareholders, Selkirk became a member of the company's governing committee in 1810. That enabled him to take a major new step in a philanthropic and commercial enterprise in which he had been passionately engaged for some time: resettling Scottish and Irish crofters displaced by sheep-raising "clearances"[4] to frontier settlements in British North America. He had already established settlements in Prince Edward Island and Upper Canada, and now proposed that the HBC cede him territory in Rupert's Land for the site of a third such colony. On 12 June 1811 the HBC conveyed to Lord Selkirk, for a price of "10 shillings ... and ... divers good and other valuable causes and consideration," 116,000 square miles of land centred on the junction of the Red and Assiniboine Rivers.[5] The grant embraced most of modern Manitoba south of about the middle of Lake Winnipeg and much more. At the meeting of those rivers – the heart of that sprawling domain – Selkirk's Red River Settlement was established.

Although the granted territory, officially called Assiniboia,[6] was no longer a major source of furs, its access to seemingly limitless herds of plains buffalo, from which was produced pemmican,[7] the fur trade's most staple food, made it "the principal source of provisions for the northwest fur trade."[8] Also, of course, it straddled the hub of the competing NWC's transportation network. If Selkirk's chief interest in Assiniboia was charitable, the HBC's motivation in agreeing to the scheme was commercial; and that gave the NWC cause for nervousness.

At first, however, the Norwesters' establishment at what is now called the Forks reacted kindly to the arrival of the bedraggled Selkirk pilgrims. The initial group, just nineteen in all, appeared in August 1812. It was joined by a larger second wave in late October and a third in 1813. They might all have perished without advice and material assistance from the NWC traders, the local Indians,[9] and a community of French Halfbreed[10] buffalo hunters located at Pembina, just south of the 49th parallel. Trouble began in 1814, when Selkirk's rigid local governor, Miles Macdonell, began to exert his authority in ways the Norwesters resented. First he served eviction notices on those in charge of NWC establishments. Although this was a mere legal formality, intended to prevent prescriptive ownership rights arising from unchallenged long-term occupation by the NWC, it predictably angered those upon whom the notices were served. Then Governor Macdonell unwisely decreed, ostensibly to preserve scarce food supplies for local consumption, that no pemmican was to be exported from Assiniboia.

The Norwesters, annoyed by the eviction notices, were outraged by the pemmican order since their entire fur trade operation, like that of the HBC, was fuelled by prairie pemmican. In early 1815, therefore, NWC personnel arrested Macdonell and his sheriff, burned the settlement, and forced the settlers to flee to Jack River at the north end of Lake Winnipeg. The settlers soon rallied, struck back at their opponents, and re-established the colony under a new governor, Robert Semple. But the trouble had only begun.

On 19 June 1816, after a spring and early summer in which the NWC fort at Red River was burned on Semple's orders and the HBC post at Brandon House was captured and sacked by an NWC force of Canadians,[11] Halfbreeds, and Indians, a mounted party of about sixty men, mostly Halfbreeds and Indians, was spotted crossing the prairie behind the settlement's Fort Douglas stronghold. Fearing that this might be the same group that had attacked Brandon House, Governor Semple set out on foot with some twenty-five men to investigate. Heading north, he intercepted the procession at a place called Seven Oaks, 2 or 3 miles north of the fort.

The leader of the passersby was Cuthbert Grant, a bold and charismatic young man destined for a prominent place in Métis and Red River history. The first person Semple encountered, however, was a Canadian, with whom he began to argue, and whose saddle or gun he grabbed. A shot was fired, and Semple was wounded in the thigh. A general fusillade followed, in which Semple and his men, on foot and inexperienced in warfare, were no match for their more numerous mounted opponents. It was later said that Cuthbert Grant tried to restrain his men but failed. When the battle was over, Governor Semple, shot a second time, lay dead among nineteen slain comrades. Only one of Grant's men was killed. A few of the victors, allegedly Indians, stripped and mutilated their victims. Following the bloodshed, the settlers were once more driven out of Red River. Cuthbert Grant seized Fort Douglas on behalf of the NWC, and the exiled settlers again took sanctuary at Jack River.

Lord Selkirk had been in Montreal preparing for a journey to Red River while most of these events were taking place. Notified of the 1815 expulsion and re-establishment, but as yet unaware of the Seven Oaks tragedy, Selkirk determined to provide military protection for the settlers. A regiment of predominantly Swiss mercenary soldiers, known as de Meurons, was in Lower Canada, having just completed service in the War of 1812–14, and was about to be disbanded. Selkirk hired about sixty of them to accompany and precede him to Red River. After learning en route of the Red River bloodbath, Selkirk and his troops seized NWC establishments along the way. Using a commission as a magistrate of Lower Canada he had acquired before leaving Montreal, Selkirk interrogated NWC personnel, sent anyone he suspected of wrongdoing to Montreal for trial, and ignored warrants directed against himself by magistrates sympathetic to the NWC. In January 1817 the de Meurons easily recaptured Red River, and the exiled settlers returned once more.

Lord Selkirk was able to restore order and confidence to the beleaguered community. A new local governor – former sheriff Alexander Macdonell – was designated. The settlers who returned after exile were granted perpetual rent-free title, and lands were set aside for churches and schools. De Meurons troops who wanted to stay were settled on the east side of the Red, across from the Forks. And a treaty was negotiated with local Indians that granted Selkirk a 6 mile circle centred on the Forks, along with 2 mile strips along both sides of the Red and Assiniboine Rivers.[12] Selkirk's presence and decisive leadership at Red River that summer ensured the settlement's survival; and when he left in September 1817, it was with justified confidence in the future of the little colony.

It was not long, however, before Selkirk's vigilante actions against NWC personnel and property had serious negative personal consequences. British colonial secretary Lord Bathurst was outraged that a peer of the realm had taken a private army to Rupert's Land, seized NWC property, imprisoned NWC officers, and refused to respect warrants issued against him by other magistrates. An official investigation condemned both sides. Subsequent civil and criminal legal proceedings were hugely costly, and concluded much less favourably to Selkirk and the HBC than they had expected. That legal maelstrom,[13] along with failing health, darkened the three remaining years of Lord Selkirk's life.

By 1820 it had long been obvious that it was in the interests of all concerned to end the caustic commercial rivalry between the two fur trade companies. The NWC was in poor shape financially, and the HBC had also suffered serious economic damage during the years of wasteful conflict. Lord Selkirk, who had been an obstacle to rapprochement, was out of the picture by then: in dire financial straits himself, Red River's founder was dying of consumption, and his estate would soon reconvey Assiniboia to the Hudson's Bay Company. The British government exerted heavy pressure on both parties to resolve their differences,[14] and negotiations began between Edward Ellice for the HBC and William McGillivray for the NWC. In early 1821 a deal was struck by which the former rivals amalgamated under the name of the older company and took steps to restructure the governance of Rupert's Land and Assiniboia.[15]

GOVERNMENTAL RECONSTRUCTION

One of the most powerful levers employed by Lord Bathurst to bring the fur trade rivals together had been a statute called the Fur Trade Regulation Act of 1821,[16] which called for, among other things, an elaborate – and expensive – new judicial system based in Canada to administer justice in Rupert's Land. Although that institution was initially to function alongside company tribunals, it might well displace them in future, and there was little doubt that the companies would be required to contribute to its cost. With the commercial hatchets buried and a united company formed after the 1821 merger, the HBC's next task was to forestall, if possible, the implementation of the new legislation. To that end, the governance structures of Rupert's Land and Assiniboia were swiftly reorganized in a manner that the new company hoped would win back the confidence of the Colonial Office and satisfy it that the new measures were not needed. A meeting of the HBC General Court on 29 May 1822 enacted a package of resolutions that:[17]

- Created a new Council of Rupert's Land[18] with two governors (the dynamic junior of whom, George Simpson, would soon eclipse his senior colleague, William Williams, and become the primary power in Rupert's Land for almost the next four decades)[19] and two sheriffs.
- Created a new Council of Ossiniboia (later Assiniboia) with a governor, Andrew Bulger, and a sheriff. Ossiniboia, defined as the area granted by the HBC to Lord Selkirk, was later reconveyed to the company by Selkirk's estate.
- Authorized the new governors and councils to administer justice in accordance with the HBC charter.
- Empowered the governors to "enroll and arm such members of the Company's servants and other male inhabitants of the ages from 18 to 45 as they may from time to time deem expedient for the defence and protection of the settlements and of the lives and properties of the inhabitants."[20]

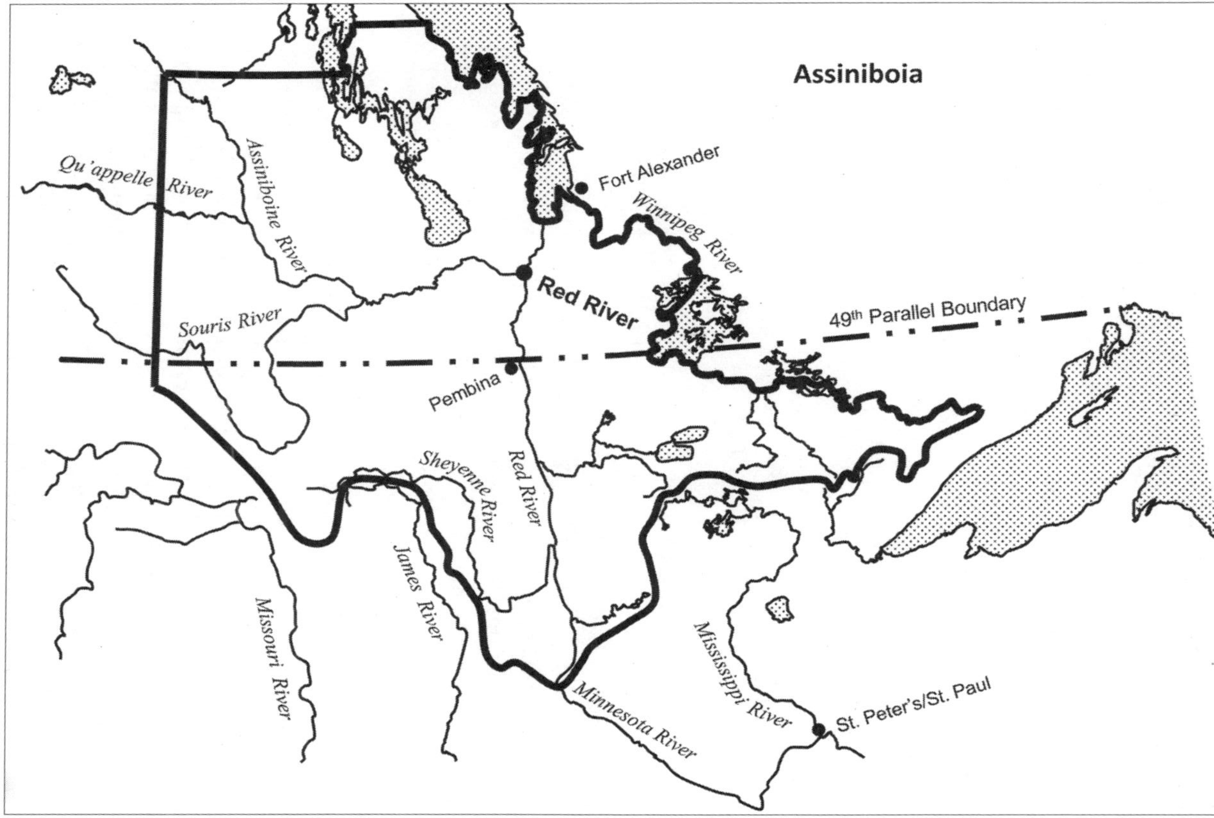

Assiniboia
Qu'appelle River
Assiniboine River
Fort Alexander
Winnipeg River
Red River
Souris River
49th Parallel Boundary
Pembina
Sheyenne River
Red River
James River
Missouri River
Mississippi River
Minnesota River
St. Peter's/St. Paul

Figure 1.2

Those resolutions were immediately dispatched by the company to Colonial Secretary Lord Bathurst, who replied two days later that "His Majesty does not deem it expedient to issue an immediate commission under the ... [Fur Trade Regulation Act], and until His Majesty shall constitute courts and justices under the said Act, the ... [HBC resolutions of 29 May] appear well calculated to preserve the peace and good government of that part of North America under the jurisdiction of the Hudson's Bay Company."[21] The new courts contemplated by the new statute would *never* be appointed. Perhaps Lord Bathurst never seriously considered doing so; he may merely have bandied the possibility about as an inducement to improve the company's own judicial arrangements. At any rate, the judiciary of Rupert's Land remained in HBC hands, with a rarely used alternative recourse to British and Canadian courts, until November 1869.

ADMINISTERING JUSTICE IN THE WILDERNESS[22]

The HBC charter bestowed upon any "Governor and Council" appointed by the company to govern a particular part of Rupert's Land the power "to judge all persons belonging to the ... Governor and Company, or that shall live under them, in all causes, whether civil or criminal, according to the laws of this kingdom, and to execute justice accordingly."[23] Such governors and their councils could only govern and adjudicate collaboratively – neither could do so without the other.

Although it is not known how frequently the adjudicative power of a governor and council was exercised throughout the lonely reaches of HBC territory during the 200 years the power existed, there is plenty of evidence that it was exercised – sometimes in dramatic fashion – whenever company officials considered it appropriate to do so. Robert Baker has documented several cases in which serious criminal charges against HBC employees were formally tried by governors and councils at establishments on Hudson Bay in the late seventeenth and early eighteenth centuries.[24] Two of them involved Albany Post men who, when England and France were at war and the company was competing intensely with French fur traders, were charged with mutiny, apparently for aiding the French. Both cases involved trials, guilty verdicts, and punishments of imprisonment, lashing, and deportation.[25] At York Fort in 1715, another employee was tried and found guilty of a variety of offences, ranging from theft and slander to "abusing the natives here by lying with a woman of this country."[26]

Probably the most drastic recorded early adjudication under the authority of the HBC charter occurred in March 1755, after the governor of Albany Factory on James Bay learned that Henley House, a company post, had been raided by Indians and that five HBC employees had been killed. An investigation produced evidence implicating two Indian men, who happened to be present at Albany at the time. The accused men were tried separately in the presence of twenty-one HBC officers and employees. The examination was conducted in Cree, with English translation for the observers. Guilt being established to the satisfaction of the questioners and observers, a meeting of the governor and council was convened, which brought down a formal verdict of guilt and imposed a sentence of death. It was then decided to report these findings to the governor and council at Moose Factory, a more senior post – before proceeding further. When, on 21 June 1755, Albany was informed that the senior governor and council had approved the decision, the convicted murderers were forthwith executed.[27]

Crime in the wilderness did not often lend itself to such relatively orderly forms of "due process," however. Where no governor and council were available, or when other considerations were thought to render resort to judicial procedures impracticable, they were ignored in favour of immediate and direct action. The nonfatal stabbing of a Red Lake officer while visiting Lake Manitoba in 1800, for example, was dealt with by simply carrying the alleged perpetrator off and peremptorily hanging him.[28] The mere threat of punishment could sometimes also be effective, as an entry in the *Norway House Post Journal* by Chief Factor Donald Ross in March 1833 attests: "Got the last of our fish hauled from Jack River. Having discovered that Old M [illegible name] has been stealing some of them, I got him taken down here, and gave him a good fright by exhibiting a pair of handcuffs – which the old fellow acknowledged he deserved to wear, but begged hard for mercy and, on [his] promising to behave honestly for the future, I allowed him to depart."[29]

There were times, on the other hand, when any firm response to crime – judicial or otherwise – was simply considered impossible. The killing in 1794 of three HBC employees in the Edmonton House area was dealt with, two years later, by merely reprimanding the Indians thought to be responsible (in the presence of the local master of the rival NWC post for greater effect) and accepting presents from them in compensation.[30] In 1807, an officer of the same post,[31] who also felt unable to punish the slaying of an employee, explained the considerations that had to be taken into account in such situations:

> A small canoe of freemen arrived, who brought us the disagreeable intelligence of the death of William Walker, who was killed by a party of Stone Indians ... [T]hey had long secretly determined on this kind of revenge [for discipline imposed by another company officer], and [thought] that all white men were equally satisfactory objects for their vengeance. This kind of unbounded resentment is an universal characteristic of all the natives in these parts ...
>
> I feel myself extremely at a loss how to act in so disagreeable an affair. At first, abhorrence of the deed awakens a desire of revenge; but on cool reflection it appears more prudent for us to settle the matter without shedding blood, yet with all the dignity in our power, for it will be impossible for us to obtain possession of the murderers (and indiscriminate vengeance, tho their own method, is repugnant to our ideas, particularly, as the present crime seems to have arisen from the hasty resentment of a few inconsiderate young villains). And, judging from probabilities, it appears impossible for us to ... [punish] it with advantage: they are numerous and almost independent of us, and we are often obliged, in pursuit of the trade and for our own subsistence, to disburse ourselves and travel in such small numbers as to be often in their power. It may however, and very naturally, be thought that if such crimes may be committed with impunity they will be often repeated. Experience, however, (here) does not confirm this conclusion, for this is not the first unfortunate circumstance of the kind that has happened to us, or our opponents, and they had no future effect.[32]

The charter alternatives to trial by local governor and council were "to transmit the party, together with [the charge and evidence of] the offence, to such other [place] ... where there shall be a Governor and Council ... or into this Kingdom of England."[33] Those fallbacks were rarely convenient; and although the first was occasionally resorted to, the option of holding trials in England was ruled out in 1804 when, the first time it was attempted, the English court in question denied that it had jurisdiction. In that case, HBC solicitors approached London barrister J. Gurney for an opinion as to whether London's Bow Street magistrates had the authority to try an NWC employee called Oiseaux du Plau, who was being held prisoner in an HBC ship moored in the Thames. He had been arrested in Rupert's Land on a charge of stealing furs from an HBC trader there and had been brought to England for trial in accordance with the company charter. The barrister's opinion was in the affirmative, provided that a witness to the crime had accompanied the accused man to England in order to give evidence, as was apparently the case.[34] But when du Plau was brought before the magistrates, they refused to try the man.[35] Their reasons were not made clear. No further efforts seem ever to have been made to clarify the matter, however, and the option of a trial in Britain was apparently abandoned.

The request that the HBC's solicitors prepared for barrister Gurney's opinion contained an interesting observation about the incidence of serious crime in Rupert's Land: "From the rigour of the climate, but few persons ... [reside] within the territories, and those few are the Company's servants, whose demeanour is peaceable, so that there has been no establishment of any [permanent] court of justice whatsoever by the Company within Hudson's Bay." However, a later document – a draft of an apparently never-submitted petition to the attorney general concerning jurisdiction over crimes in Rupert's Land[36] – presented a much less complacent view: "There has never been any court of judicature at Hudson's Bay ... Many cases of robbery, & even some of murder, have heretofore occurred in which the offenders have escaped punishment." Whatever estimate of its prevalence one accepted, no one denied that crime did occur in the HBC's territories from time to time and that there were no generally applicable means of administering justice.

Although the foregoing memorial alleged that the charter's juridical authority extended only to HBC employees, an interpretation that the NWC often asserted, the generally accepted view among lawyers was that it applied to all manner of legal disputes, and to the conduct of everyone, regardless of employer or race, while present in Rupert's Land. The HBC rarely saw any advantage, however, in making its judicial services available to its trade rivals or to Aboriginal persons or groups as a means for them to settle their internecine disputes. For a long time, therefore, the charter's adjudicative powers were exercised only in situations where HBC interests were somehow involved.

The unfairness of such selective administration of charter justice was illustrated by an 1802 case. An altercation between an employee of the NWC and one of the rival XY Company[37] ended in the death of one at the hands of the other. The accused killer, Joseph Lamothe of the XY Company, claimed to have acted in self-defence. His NWC captors, lacking any legal authority to conduct a hearing themselves, transported him and a witness to Montreal for trial. But what jurisdiction did the courts of Lower Canada have? The trial was postponed while the chief justice consulted provincial authorities, who in turn consulted

British authorities. Before the matter could be resolved at those levels, Lamothe had disappeared.[38] As a consequence of this unsatisfactory series of events, the British Parliament enacted the Canada Jurisdiction Act of 1803, which explicitly authorized Canadian courts to deal with criminal cases arising in the "Indian Territories."[39] Unfortunately, as will be seen in the next section, uncertainty about the meaning of the term "Indian Territories" caused much confusion.

The establishment of Lord Selkirk's Red River Settlement at the junction of the Red and Assiniboine Rivers in 1812 brought increased urgency to the need for improved juridical arrangements.[40] Miles Macdonell, the first leader of the new colony and a career soldier, proposed that the settlement's first judicial apparatus should be based on the law with which he was most familiar: martial law. In May 1812, even before arriving at Red River, Macdonell wrote to Selkirk, pointing out that "[w]e must have some kind of judicature in the colony," and expressing the opinion that the best kind of judicial arrangement to establish first would be one based on martial law.[41] Selkirk agreed that a judiciary was needed, but he hoped that martial law could be avoided. In its place, he arranged that Macdonell be appointed as the local governor under the HBC charter, as well as a magistrate under the 1803 Canada Jurisdiction Act.[42] To assist him in carrying out those unfamiliar responsibilities, Macdonell was equipped with copies of two reliable and compendious legal treatises: Sir William Blackstone's *Commentaries on the Laws of England* and Richard Burn's *Justice of the Peace*.

Although Lord Selkirk had hoped that the HBC would supplement those ponderous general authorities with simpler and more specific legal guidelines to assist the governor, such would not be forthcoming for quite some time. To fill the gap, Selkirk wrote Macdonell a long rambling letter in June 1813, offering personal advice. His suggestions, if short on legal authority, were generally long on common sense: appoint a council, sheriff, and constables as soon as possible in order to bring the HBC charter authority into effect; employ juries for important cases; avoid, if possible, punishments more severe than imprisonment; in difficult murder cases, send the accused and witnesses to England for trial; be "impartial and temperate"; and show greater concern for "essential principles" than for "form."[43] As we have seen, however, one part of Lord Selkirk's advice – to serve formal eviction notices on NWC officers with respect to any property that company had occupied long enough to be near acquiring legal rights by prescription – had sown the seeds of future trouble.

In early 1814 the HBC finally sent Governor Macdonell some concise but relatively detailed instructions about his judicial responsibilities,[44] but they do not seem to have had much impact. Macdonell's judicial performance – what there was of it – was unimpressive. Failing for some reason to appoint a council during his first eighteen months in Assiniboia, the governor was obliged, when faced with the first case requiring adjudication, to fall back on his questionable authority[45] as magistrate under the Canada Jurisdiction Act. The case involved a charge of theft by one settler family from another, and regrettably Governor Macdonell and the trader-magistrate at York Factory who laid the initial charge failed to see eye-to-eye about the matter, each believing the assertions of a different family. The case ended inconclusively.[46]

Although he did eventually establish a council and appoint a sheriff and constable as authorized by the charter, Macdonell did not have much opportunity to exercise his charter powers before he and his sheriff were, as mentioned earlier, arrested by NWC officers (also Canada Jurisdiction Act magistrates) in answer to Macdonell's eviction and pemmican edicts, and carried off to Montreal for trial while the other settlers were chased into exile at Jack River.

About the same time Miles Macdonell was being transported eastward under NWC arrest, HBC lawyers in London were preparing a complete code of laws for Rupert's Land – a much more elaborate document than the "Instructions Relative to Judicial Proceedings" they had sent out previously. In his reply to Macdonell's initial martial law suggestion, Lord Selkirk had implied that if the governor would just be patient, the settlement's judicial needs would soon be met. "It is intended by the directors," he said, "to send out full instructions on this head ... but it requires so much consideration to draw these up correctly that they cannot be ready this year."[47] As he would have been aware, company lawyers were working on a very ambitious legislative project.

Worldwide, the codification of contemporary laws was at an early stage of development. The first of the Napoleonic Codes had been promulgated in 1804, but work on that massive project was still in progress, and similar treatment of the common law[48] for England was as yet only a futuristic notion touted by reformers like Jeremy Bentham. Nevertheless, sometime between August 1814 and May 1815, lawyers engaged by the HBC produced a comprehensive code of basic criminal and civil[49] legal principles, both substantive and procedural, for use within the company's territories – particularly in Lord Selkirk's District of Assiniboia. It was a conservative codification, in the sense that it drew its authority exclusively from the existing HBC charter and its content largely from existing English law. It eschewed the "precise practice or rules" of particular English courts in favour of "general principles," however, and even adopted a few small reforms in the interests of accommodating local conditions and needs.[50] As a concise compendium of common law principles and procedures for application by nonlawyers in a remote community, it was a commendable, indeed remarkable, accomplishment.

All that seems to have survived of that code is an oversized handwritten document of 105 pages – an obviously incomplete and tentative first draft.[51] It is known, however, that a next-to-final printed version was later sent to London barristers G. Holroyd and J. Scarlett to ascertain its compliance with the HBC charter and other legal requirements. Those gentlemen approved it, subject to slight revisions, on 13 May 1815,[52] and the company's solicitors submitted it to the colonial secretary and to the Law Officers of the Crown for approval later that month.[53] Government endorsement was never granted.[54]

Even after it was evident that the government would not bless the proposed code of laws anytime soon, HBC governor Joseph Berens told Colonial Secretary Bathurst he remained hopeful that this would eventually happen. Meanwhile, he wrote, because "the circumstances of the colony" required that "adequate provision for the administration of justice between man & man should be made without delay," the company had directed local authorities "to try & determine according to the laws of England all causes which may arise." He was still hopeful "that we may yet be enabled to transmit to Hudson's Bay the opinion of His Majesty's Attorney & Solicitor General" in support of the code.[55] But that never occurred.

Why the government was unwilling to place its imprimatur on the code is not difficult to imagine. Whether or not the HBC agreed to Selkirk's settlement because it would hamper the NWC's commercial activities at Red River, the HBC unquestionably looked eagerly upon the prospect of a government-endorsed legal code, bristling with powers of arrest, seizure, and imprisonment that the company's sheriff and constables could deploy against the NWC and others whenever needed. With Rupert's Land then in a state of virtual war between the trade rivals, no government wishing to preserve an appearance of impartiality would have approved a legal code that originated with, and would be enforced by, one of the rivals.

Why was the HBC, for its part, so anxious to obtain governmental endorsement? Why did it not simply enact the code itself, relying on its express authority under the company charter to make laws supplemental to but not inconsistent with the laws of England? It probably realized that without the authority of a power higher than that of a private entrepreneur, the code would be disdained by the local population. As the events of 1815–17 had shown, where a government lacks strong police support, its laws are obeyed only if respected by those to whom they apply.

This concern for public acceptance was reflected in an interesting scheme for adjudicating civil disputes sent to Assiniboia governor Alexander Macdonell by the company's London authorities in 1818 for implementation "till the establishment of a [still hoped-for] legal judicature."[56] It was suggested that, because the losing party in a case adjudicated by the governor and council might treat his loss as a "pretext ... to accuse his superiors of partiality or favouritism, or to say that his case had not been fairly judged," it would be "desirable," until such time as a "legal" system was in place, to establish "some regular plan for deciding differences between the settlers by arbitration." "Whenever," the proposal went on, "the parties can be induced to agree upon one or two of their neighbours to judge between them, that will be the best and simplest way. But when the parties are unreasonable and intractable, it may have a good effect to call them before something like a regular court." Although this proposed tribunal would be "something like" a legally authorized court, and might even have the assistance of "ordinary, unconcerned settlers" assembled "in the manner of" a jury, it would *not* include the governor and his council, whose involvement was required by the charter to give legal validity to judicial proceedings. Its express object would be to decide disputes between private parties in an *unofficial* manner that avoided the appearance of being under HBC auspices. The most interesting feature of the scheme was the method by which it was to be made enforceable:

> Such a tribunal as this having no legal authority to enforce its decisions, it may be advisable ... to make both parties publicly give a solemn promise to abide by the decision. If any individual should either break this promise, or obstinately refuse to give it, there is a punishment which may be held over him, as to the legality of which no doubt can be entertained viz.: that he should be 'sent to Coventry.'[57] When this is effectually done it is no slight punishment, even in a civilized country; but in a situation like yours it would be doubly severe. The individual who refuses to submit to the judgment of his

> neighbours has no right to expect that his neighbours should assist and protect him. [T]hey have a right to say that he must defend himself by his own efforts; that he is fair game to anyone, black or white, who is not afraid to make a prey of him; and that if his property be stolen, or even his life endangered, it is no concern of theirs to repel or to punish the aggression.

There is no evidence that this remarkable proposed experiment in desert island justice was ever attempted. Nor, on the other hand,is there any evidence that Governor Macdonell ever assembled his council to administer justice in accordance with the HBC charter.[58] Macdonell does not seem, in fact, to have done much of anything other than enjoy a hedonistic existence in the company of cronies and sycophants. The years immediately following the HBC's failed attempt to revolutionize the legal system of Rupert's Land by codification thus appear to have been judicially barren.

A quarter-century would pass before another large-scale attempt was made to codify the settlement's laws, and that experiment also failed.[59] For the remaining years of the HBC's suzerainty, Assiniboia authorities who sought to administer justice at Red River had no authority for doing so that they could not find within the four corners of the company charter.

LEGAL CHALLENGES TO THE HBC CHARTER, COURTS, AND LAWS

Although the storm of litigation that followed Lord Selkirk's 1817 expedition to Red River is not of direct concern to this account, we cannot ignore numerous other legal disputes that raised some of the same issues, and would continue to bedevil the administration of justice in Rupert's Land until the area was finally annexed to Canada.

J.M. Bumsted has observed that the settlement "lacked a proper political dimension, which meant that a history of Red River could not be hung on ... either a political or constitutional narrative."[60] In fact, the problem was not so much a *lack* of legal structure as a disagreement about the competing claims of *several different* legal structures. While HBC and Assiniboia authorities relied on powers conferred by the charter Charles II of England had granted to the company in 1670,[61] their opponents disputed the validity of those powers, arguing that they were trumped by other, overriding jurisdictions or edicts. They contended, variously, that the jurisdictional claims of France, the Aboriginal inhabitants of Rupert's Land, and Canada overruled those based on the HBC charter; that even if England had the right to bestow the disputed powers they could only have been enacted by Parliament, not by the King alone; and that even if the charter were valid, its alleged purview – in particular, its asserted application to the entirety of the Hudson Bay drainage basin and every human being within it, and its alleged bestowal of local law-making powers – could not be reasonably derived from its language.

In the author's view, the answers to those various challenges are as follows:

1 Any challenges to HBC authority based on prior occupation of Rupert's Land by representatives of France were defeated by French concessions to England in the Treaty of Utrecht, 1713 and in the Treaty of Paris, 1763.
2 Although the HBC charter ignored the prior rights of the Aboriginal population of Rupert's Land, that oversight was arguably remedied, so far as *territorial* rights in Assiniboia were concerned, by Lord Selkirk's 1817 treaty with the Indians of Assiniboia and did not, in any case, derogate from the charter power to *govern* everyone in Rupert's Land, including Indians.
3 Although the courts of Upper and Lower Canada had the power under British statutes enacted in 1803 and 1821 to adjudicate legal disputes originating in Rupert's Land, that power was *concurrent* with the authority of the charter-based courts of Rupert's Land, and was only rarely thought practical to exercise.
4 King Charles II had the legal authority, as part of his royal prerogative powers, to convey private ownership of Crown lands and to legislate unilaterally for the government of newly acquired territories. That is not to say that *every* power purported to be granted by the 1670 charter had been within the prerogative authority of King Charles at the time. The power that the HBC cherished most – its alleged trade monopoly within the granted territories – was invalid. Parliament had long manifested its disapproval of royally bestowed privileges to engage in exclusive trade and had, in 1624, enacted the Statute of Monopolies, decreeing, with just a few exceptions, that only Parliament itself could grant such monopolies. Although the company and the courts of Assiniboia tried very hard to enforce this illegal monopoly, and did so successfully for many years, they were, as will be seen,

ultimately unable to uphold it in face of determined opposition by a large majority of the population.

5 Apart from the fur trade monopoly, all other major aspects of Red River's laws and its legal and governmental infrastructure during the years chiefly examined by this study – 1835 to 1872 – were fundamentally sound, if rudimentary. There is no legally persuasive reason to doubt the general validity of the HBC charter or of the governmental and judicial authority it bestowed. An unbroken chain of legality connected the original 1670 grant and the powers upon which the Hudson's Bay Company and its local institutions relied to govern and adjudicate during the years when the General Quarterly Court of Assiniboia functioned.

2

Colony without Court, 1822–34

Once a base for observing and interfering with commercial rivals, the Red River Settlement now served the Hudson's Bay Company in other ways: as a home for employees made redundant by the merger or who would retire in future years, as a source of pemmican and agricultural produce for the fur trade, and as a field headquarters for the company's far-flung Rupert's Land operations. Fort Garry, constructed at the confluence of the Red and Assiniboine immediately after the merger, became, and remained for the next fifty years, the economic and governmental centre of British north-central North America. Red River remained a tiny, tense, racially and religiously mixed, socially brutish community all but lost in an uncaring wilderness. A devastating flood in 1826 broke the hearts of old and new settlers alike, but most of them stubbornly rebuilt their homes and got on with their hard lives. By 1834 the settlement was considerably larger and more prosperous.

The justice system improved after 1822, most markedly by demonstrating that the rule of law applied to even the company that owned, governed, and judged the country. But liquor-induced violence remained difficult to keep in hand; resentment of the community's rulers smouldered and occasionally flared among the Halfbreed majority; and the entire population was increasingly apprehensive of possible depredations from nomadic Sioux.

EXPANDING SETTLEMENT

There was no doubt now that the Red River Settlement was a permanent fixture, destined for future growth. The de Meuron mercenary troops brought by Lord Selkirk in 1817 had settled on the east side of the Red opposite the Forks, and European immigration continued after Selkirk's death in April 1820. In the autumn of 1821, 170 Swiss,

Figure 2.1 Sir George Simpson. As the HBC's North American governor-in-chief, he oversaw Red River's governance from 1820 to 1860. The legal system he created in 1835 served the community until 1872.

recruited by agents of the Selkirk estate, arrived to settle among their countrymen along and beyond what came to be called German Street (now Taché Avenue). Although both new and old Swiss contingents were sources of more trouble than benefit to the community – eventually causing the cessation of overseas recruiting[1] – another, more stable, source of population growth was the rising tide of fur trade retirees and their families, many made redundant by the joinder of the former fur trade rivals.

Those superannuated employees, their families, and families abandoned by men who chose not to settle down, were soon the object of a not altogether altruistic training scheme approved by the HBC's London

Governor and Committee. Because "those people form a burden which cannot be got rid of without expense, and ... [could] become dangerous to the peace of the country and safety of the trading posts," North American governor George Simpson was informed, "it will ... be prudent and economical to incur some expense in placing ... [them at Red River,] where they may maintain themselves and be civilized and instructed in religion."[2] Families with male parents were to be settled on "small allotments of 20 or 25 acres" and given assistance in the form of clothing, tools, seeds, ammunition, and labour "until they can reap a crop." Orphans were to be placed in a new "school of industry."[3] Newly arrived Bishop J.N. Provencher and his colleague Father S.J. Dumoulin, who had established a mission across the Red River from the Forks in 1818, would provide the contemplated "instruct[ion] in religion" for Catholics; and Anglican pastor John West, who had set up a church and school on the west side of the river in 1820–21, would do the same for Protestants.

Nicholas Garry, dispatched to Red River in the autumn of 1821 to oversee the local implementation of the corporate merger, and after whom a large new establishment built at the Forks in 1822 was named, estimated the settlement's population at 919, distributed as follows: 221 Scottish, 65 de Meurons, 133 French Canadians, and 500 Halfbreeds, the latter residing chiefly at or near Pembina.[4] A census taken in the spring of 1822 placed the total at 1,271.[5] Although there may be additional explanations for the discrepancy between those figures, the population was on the rise. Later in 1822 the first influx of former employees, families, and orphans arrived, taking up residence primarily along the west bank of the Red north of the Assiniboine, between the Selkirk Settlers' allotments and the St Andrew's Rapids. They boosted Red River's population by about 600.[6] The foregoing figures did not purport to include Indians, but there was a large, and growing, permanent Aboriginal population in the area. The 1822 census included an unexplained figure of 681, which one historian speculated might refer to Indians.[7]

The large French Halfbreed population in the Pembina area was a concern to the company because of the potential threat they were thought to pose to its firmly asserted fur trade monopoly. The HBC trading post just north of the international boundary near Pembina was closed in 1822,[8] and, to reduce the risk that the Halfbreeds of the area, lacking that commercial outlet, would take their furs to American traders, Simpson prevailed upon Bishop Provencher to persuade them to move north. Provencher succeeded, in 1823, in bringing a large proportion of Pembina Halfbreeds to the settlement, where the following year Cuthbert Grant – again at Simpson's behest – induced them to join him in taking up large land allotments provided by the HBC on the Assiniboine River at the White Horse Plains (modern St François Xavier). The area would be known as Grantown for a time,[9] and Cuthbert Grant would remain the acknowledged Halfbreed leader for many years. The importance to Red River, and to Rupert's Land generally, of Grant's influence over that large segment of the community resulted in his appointment in 1828 as the HBC's "Warden of the Plains," a kind of free-ranging sheriff, at an annual salary of £200.[10]

EARLY LAWLESSNESS AND OFFICIAL INDOLENCE

Red River's diverse new population, much of it unused to settled ways and agricultural pursuits, was not an easy community to manage. George Simpson's early impressions were not flattering:

> Red River at present, I am sorry to say, assumes more the appearance of a receptacle for freebooters and infamous characters ... [T]here is no law, order, or regularity. [E]very man is his own master, and the strongest and most desperate is he who succeeds best ... [T]he well disposed feel themselves in continual danger. The population is now getting very considerable, and such a mass of renegades and malcontents ... are not to be constrained without the assistance of civil and military power ... I therefore conceive it indispensably necessary for its future welfare that a code of laws should be made, magistrates appointed, constables sworn in, and a small military establishment provided to give effect to the civil authorities.[11]

The settlement was not entirely without "civil authorities." Alexander Macdonell, who originally came to Red River in 1815 as Governor Semple's sheriff, had been made governor of Assiniboia after Semple's death; and he, together with the Council of Assiniboia, had the legal authority to exercise the governmental and juridical powers bestowed by the HBC charter. The problem was that Macdonell was doing nothing to employ those powers – or to perform many of his other duties. Simpson's September 1821 letter went on to report that "Mr. MacDonnell, I am concerned to say, is extremely despised and held in contempt by every person connected with the place ... [H]e is accused of partiality, dishonesty, untruth, drunkenness – in short, a total dereliction of every moral and honourable feeling."[12] Although the 1822 census discloses that there were three law books in the settlement at the time,[13] a legal dictionary having been added to the two tomes the first governor brought, there is no indication that they were ever put to use while this indolent and dissolute governor was in office.

IMPROVING GOVERNMENTAL AND JUDICIAL ARRANGEMENTS

In March 1822 Macdonell was replaced as governor by Andrew Bulger,[14] a Newfoundland-born career soldier with experience in the maritime colonies, the Canadas, and the upper Mississippi during the War of 1812–14. Then, on 29 May 1822, the HBC General Court enacted the large package of resolutions that restructured and restaffed the governments of Rupert's Land and Assiniboia in the manner described earlier.[15]

When he arrived in the tiny colony that summer, Andrew Bulger may have been optimistic. If so, his attitude turned quickly to dismay after observing local conditions. By 25 July he was writing to Selkirk's executor to say he had already begun to "repent" his decision to undertake Assiniboia's leadership, which had required him to give up "a comfortable situation for a wretched subsistence, a life of slavery, and exposure to the insults and threats of some of the most worthless of God's creatures, in one of the most miserable countries on the face of the earth."[16]

In another communication, Bulger bemoaned his powerlessness to protect his subjects from rampant lawlessness. There was, he said, an "absence of all power, either to correct the evil which is among ourselves, or to ward off the danger with which we are menaced from [hostile Sioux] without. By far the greater part of our population," he continued, "are sunk in vice and depravity, and daring enough to despise our laws, and openly defy our magistrates," while most of "the well-disposed part of the community" were unwilling to act as magistrates from fear of "endangering their persons and property."[17] Being unable to raise the local militia he was authorized to recruit, Bulger called in vain for an external military force to be sent to Red River, and warned in a third letter that "I tremble for the consequences ... when there is no gaol, no magistrate, and no power to restrain ... [the] evil propensities [of] the great majority of the settlers."[18] Being "quite sick of living among such people," as he put it in that third letter, he had already announced he would be resigning at the end of his first year of service rather than remaining the three years originally contemplated.[19]

Nevertheless, despite ill health and his aversion to Red River, Andrew Bulger made serious and successful efforts to govern and to curb lawlessness during that year. In early December, when the newly appointed members of the Council of Assiniboia were finally resident in the settlement, he began meeting with them. The minutes of what appears to have been the council's first meeting record that it resolved to report to London certain "circumstances which have of late occurred in the colony," one of which was, in E.H. Oliver's words, "the punishment of an Indian for attempted murder."[20] Later that month, Bulger wrote to Selkirk's executor urgently requesting that the British government provide troops and courts, that a market be found for surplus Red River grain, and that settlers be relieved of an HBC embargo on the purchase of the skins and meat of moose and deer for personal use.[21] Although the troops and courts were not forthcoming, and export markets lay far in the future, efforts were made to comply with the other requests.[22]

In the absence of external courts, Bulger did not hesitate to exert his own judicial authority under the HBC charter and British legislation. In January 1823, having received a complaint from settler Pierre Perronne that persons in Pembina to whom he had entrusted goods for safekeeping had refused to return them, Bulger examined the plaintiff under oath and issued a warrant to one John Allez, presumably an ad hoc constable, to proceed to Pembina and recover the property.[23] In February, learning that John Dubach, a discontented Swiss immigrant, was disposing of property with a view to leaving the settlement via the United States, Bulger interrogated the man under oath and convened a meeting of the Assiniboia council to determine whether Dubach and other Swiss who were acting similarly "should be arrested and detained for the debt which they owe to the Earl of Selkirk's estate." The council decided that it would be "very unwise" to do so because such action "might be deemed arbitrary or illegal" in the settlement.[24] At the end of March 1823 Bulger appointed residents Donald Murray and Donald McKay as constables, with authority to "command and require all persons whomsoever to be aiding and assisting to the said constables to preserve the peace."[25]

ESTABLISHING THE RULE OF LAW

Andrew Bulger's most serious judicial challenge arose from a complaint by an HBC employee assaulted on the job, and seriously injured, by a company clerk under whom he was working. When Bulger attempted to pursue the matter judicially, he was warned off by John Clarke, the company's local chief factor, on the ground that Assiniboia authorities had no jurisdiction over HBC operations or employees. Clarke, a rough and ready fur trade veteran, had arrived at Red River to take up the position of chief factor not long after Bulger came, and tension between the men, representing the commercial and civil authorities respectively, emerged early. For instance, it was Clarke's edict prohibiting the purchase by settlers of big game skins and meat from Indians that Bulger successfully appealed to London.[26] Another dispute involved land allocations for retired company employees. Bulger wrote to Clarke in April 1823 explaining that although the Council of Rupert's Land had called for lots "not exceeding 30 acres," such lots "will be insufficient for a family" since, in the area designated for the lots, they would include considerable swamp. He proposed, instead, that the retirees be given 48 acre lots, "which I dare say the Honourable Committee would not think too much, if you sanction the measure."[27] Clarke's flat refusal and accompanying suggestion that Bulger was remiss in not resolving the matter sooner himself, prompted a testy response from the governor.[28]

Neither man was in a cooperative mood when the case of alleged employee assault arose on 2 May 1823. Bulger was working in the settlement store when two men appeared. One wore a bloody bandage on his head, and the other asked, "Is the Captain [Bulger] here? We understand that justice is to be found here ... This man has been almost killed by that murderer. This is the third [time] this year that he has [been] used in the same manner." The alleged assailant was a clerk of Clarke's called Pensonant.[29] Taken aback by this request to prosecute a member of the chief factor's staff, Bulger stalled. He asked the two men to wait for an hour and retired to his room to decide whether to get involved. Concluding that it was "his bounden duty ... to guard the life of even the meanest individual in the District," he summoned the Council of Assiniboia to meet the following morning and told the complainants to return then. John Clarke was informed in writing of Bulger's decision to refer the complaint to the council.

Clarke's response was adamant. He sent an emissary to Bulger disputing the authority of the governor and council to deal with such matters, and refusing to allow any HBC employee to appear before the council in the affair. Bulger responded by proposing that if Clarke would put his objections in writing, the council would stay proceedings and refer the question to the Governor and Committee in London. Ignoring that proposed compromise, Clarke reiterated in writing his position that the "internal affairs" of the company, which he defined as civil or criminal matters "where both parties belong to the Company,"[30] were completely beyond the governor and council's competence. Then *he* proposed a compromise: he would allow the council to deal with the dispute if he, as the company's representative, were present to "assist" in the proceedings. Since such an arrangement would likely tip the balance in favour of the accused clerk, and would certainly undermine the council's judicial independence, Bulger and the council refused. They then sent a copy of Clarke's letter and a statement of their opposing views to the company's Governor and Committee, and they suspended the charges against Pensonant until the jurisdictional question – which amounted to whether the rule of law prevailed in Assiniboia – was settled in London.

Less than three weeks later, well before the Pensonant material could even have reached London, the issue it raised concerning the respective authority of the settlement's public and commercial administrations was decisively resolved by the Governor and Committee in a different context. In a letter to North American governor Simpson concerning Bulger's *earlier* complaints about Clarke's actions, the Governor and Committee decreed that in all governmental and legal matters the chief factor and his staff were subject to the authority of the Assiniboia governor and council.[31] After castigating the chief factor for other incidents in which he had taken the law into his own hands, the Governor and Committee observed that "Mr. Clarke seems to have totally misconceived his rights and powers as Chief Factor, and to have considered himself not only independent of Governor Bulger in matters relating to the trade, but superior to him in authority ... Mr. Clarke was sent to Red River in the expectation that ... he might render essential assistance to Mr. Bulger ... without injury to the trade. We cannot conceive, therefore, how he should have thought himself justified in slighting and disregarding the authority of Mr. Bulger." In future, they ordained, "The chief factors, the chief traders and servants of the Company within the District [of Assiniboia] are to consider themselves under the authority of the Governor, and to conform [to] and obey all orders that may be issued by the said Governor and his Council ... It is necessary to put an end to all doubt as to the supreme authority in the District to prevent disputes for the future ... [F]or the purpose of municipal regulations and the preservation of the peace of the District [of Assiniboia] ... the supreme authority in case of dispute or emergency is vested in the Governor and Council of Assiniboia."

The principle of the law's supremacy had been established. History seems to have lost track, however, of whether Pensonant was ever tried for the alleged assault.

As a matter of practice, the line between the company's commercial and governmental roles in Rupert's Land would often blur again in the future. J.M. Bumsted sees the appointment of an HBC chief factor as governor of Assiniboia in 1825, and the subsequent appointment of several other HBC career officers to that position, as "ending the fiction that Red River and the Company were separate entities."[32] But the sovereignty of the Assiniboia governor and council in governmental and juridical matters was much more than a fiction; it was a legal principle that was never repudiated. Nor was it ever *generally* abandoned even in practice. For the most part, Assiniboia's legal and governmental authorities carried out their responsibilities as they thought best; and their decisions were seldom challenged or interfered with. Yet the fact that for many years the governors of Assiniboia would be HBC personnel, plus the reality that it would always be the company that appointed the governors and members of the council and courts, meant that Assiniboia's theoretical independence from the company would, indeed, *occasionally* be little more than a fiction – and that it would *always* be suspect. The extent of the settlement's actual independence would nevertheless increase – albeit gradually – over time. Like most democratic accretions to the British political tradition, it evolved slowly and in response to extralegal factors: some subtle, others dramatic.

POLICE, LAND REGISTRY, LOCAL LEGISLATION

Robert P. Pelly, a cousin of HBC governor John Henry Pelly, replaced Andrew Bulger as governor of the settlement in 1823.[33] Although his two-year administration was comparatively uneventful, and J.M. Bumsted says it was, in general, "not a great success,"[34] the legal system underwent considerable further development under his leadership. A "strong police force" was established early in Pelly's regime, consisting of "twenty [paid] regular constables and two bailiffs" and "about fifty special constables who do duty gratuitously." All were under the command of new chief factor Donald McKenzie as "High Constable."[35] Early in 1825 Assiniboia's first land registry was established.[36] And in 1832, while Chief Factor McKenzie was also governor, the Council of Assiniboia exercised its legislative powers for the first time, enacting local laws concerning open fires, stray animals, statutory labour, public fairs, and horse theft.[37]

CRIMINAL PROSECUTION OF INDIANS

The previously mentioned punishment of an Indian for attempting to draw a knife during an altercation with Governor Bulger in December 1822[38] was consistent with the general rule in other parts of Rupert's Land and British North America: ignore intra-Indian conflict and treat crimes by Indians against whites as matters for peremptory punishment or retaliation rather than for legal prosecution.[39] But the legal system's formal engagement with Natives could not be delayed for long. In the spring of 1824 Governor Bulger's replacement, Robert P. Pelly, had an encounter with intra-Indian crime, and his response might be considered a half-step toward engagement. A Saulteau man was accused of murdering an old woman of his own tribe in order to pass off her scalp as that of a rival Sioux warrior. Red River historian Alexander Ross takes up the story:

> This savage deed was soon noised abroad, and the public voice was loud for bringing the murderer to punishment. At length, therefore, he was brought before the Governor, who was attended on the occasion by some of his officials, so as to form a little court. Having listened with attention to the charges, this sapient gentleman, judging it less troublesome to overlook the crime than to punish the murderer, transferred the case to a higher and more impartial tribunal than his own in these words: "Tell him," he said to the interpreter, "that he has manifested a disposition subversive of all order, and that if he should not be punished in this world, he is sure to be punished in the next."[40]

It is not altogether clear from Ross's account whether the "little court" – which could only have been the Council of Assiniboia – convicted the accused man and Governor Pelly subsequently granted him clemency; or the governor, after learning the circumstances, simply declined to prosecute the matter. Neither response would have been surprising. What was new was that Pelly chose to take official notice of a crime between Indians in the first place.

Although Governor Pelly may not have been aware of it when he acted as he did, there had been a watershed decision on this topic by an Upper Canada court in August 1822. The case, *R. v. Shawanakiskie*,[41] was very similar to the one Pelly was faced with. An Indian man was convicted of murdering a woman of his own tribe in the town of Amherstberg, and was sentenced to death. The trial judge, cautioned by defence counsel that legal opinions differed concerning the amenability of Indians to prosecution for crimes that did not involve Europeans, stayed execution of the sentence until the matter could be referred to the lieutenant governor. The lieutenant governor submitted the question to Colonial Secretary Lord Bathurst, who in turn passed it on to Home Secretary Sir Robert Peel. After seeking the opinion of the attorney general, Peel ruled on 13 February 1826 that "the conviction ... was proper; and that no valid objection exists against the jurisdiction of the court before which the said Shawanakiskie was tried." A warrant for the accused's execution was issued but with discretion on the part of local authorities to exercise clemency if appropriate. The ultimate fate of Shawanakiskie is not known.

When Indian crime affected the white population, the rule of law was still not much in evidence – at least not in remoter parts of Rupert's Land. Governor Simpson wrote to the company's London headquarters in August 1832 about what he called "one of the most horrible massacres ever heard of in ... the country."[42] In January, he wrote, a family group of seventeen Rupert's River Indians had visited Hannah Bay, a small HBC goose-hunting outpost on Hudson Bay about 40 miles from Moose Factory. After enjoying the hospitality of Post Master William Corrigal and his wife, staff, and their families, the visitors killed and mutilated everyone except two boys – ten persons in all – and carried off most of the post's provisions. The boys, who escaped the assassins, fled to Moose Factory, where they reported the crime to veteran chief factor John George McTavish. Although an immediately dispatched search party was unable to find the suspects, two of them showed up at Moose Factory toward the end of March, were arrested, confessed after interrogation, and agreed to lead another HBC party to their alleged accomplices. "Forthwith" after the others were located, the six adult males of the group (whether including the informers is uncertain) were executed – "the only punishment," Simpson said, "which could serve the ends of justice and deter others from the like crimes." There is no reference in the report to any trial, and it is unlikely that the only court with power to conduct such a trial – grossly overweight Governor McTavish and his council – had accompanied the search party into the bush. While Simpson's report that "[t]he great part of the stolen property was recovered" suggests that members of this party had probably committed the crime, only a trial could have determined whether *every* man executed was equally guilty.[43]

GROWTH, DEVASTATION, RECONSTRUCTION

The years under the reign of Governor–Chief Factor Donald McKenzie were eventful ones, during which Red River grew impressively. Alexander Ross, who settled there at the beginning of McKenzie's governorship and would remain for the next three decades, noted that even McKenzie's first year, 1825, was "one of great enterprise among the colonists ... No less than forty-two new houses had been built within a few months. Strings of fencing were made, enclosures formed, and a stirring industry manifested on every side."[44]

The following winter was hard, however. A poor fall buffalo hunt, followed by profuse snowfalls, caused severe scarcities in the settlement; and before spring arrived the Company's inability to provide as many relief supplies as the destitute demanded led to serious unrest among the rarely content Swiss community. Many Halfbreeds were similarly affected. Violent self-help measures, such as breaking into storehouses of the company and of the well-to-do, were threatened and sometimes carried out. There was even talk of capturing Fort Garry.[45] McKenzie managed to quell the Halfbreed threat through the good offices of Bishop Provencher, however.[46]

Then a devastating flood displaced all else. The 1826 flood,[47] the first to strike the settlement, and the greatest inundation ever experienced since then, virtually wiped out the community. It began with a tsunami, released at 2:00 PM on 5 May by a sudden collapse of barricading ice. The resulting torrent carried away forty-seven houses in the first half-hour. Before the waters began to recede, most of the remaining dwellings were gone, or were hopelessly damaged. Fort Garry, built on the highest ground in the vicinity of the Forks, stood under 11.5 feet of water, and a high percentage of the community's livestock had perished.

Although the flood swept away many recent improvements, it also cleansed the settlement of its worse malcontents. For most of the already discontented de Meurons and other Swiss residents, the flood was a final straw, and about 250 of them moved to the United States that summer.[48] Although that sudden and substantial a population loss was a blow to the community, the exodus was soon more than replaced by a steady flow of newcomers. In that same year alone, some 150 francophones – company retirees and their families – settled at St Boniface,[49] largely on land vacated by the departed Swiss. They and the remaining settlers quickly turned to rebuilding "their cheerless farms," Ross tells us, and by the following year, "a new era in the Settlement had commenced."[50]

Year	Population*	Increase	Acres cultivated	Increase
1831	2,417		2,152	
1832	2,751	334	2,631	479
1833	2,982	231	3,237	606
Total increase		565		1,085

* Population figures do not appear to include resident Indians

By 1830 not only was the settlement entirely rebuilt,[51] but construction of an imposing new HBC edifice – Lower Fort Garry (the "Stone Fort") just below the St Andrew's Rapids at the north end of the settlement – had also been authorized, as had the establishment of an experimental farm nearby. The new fort was to be the home of newly married George Simpson, now in sole control of the company's North American operations, when he arrived at Red River with his British bride, Frances. The couple would remain in residence from 1830 to 1833, when Simpson shifted his permanent base of operations back to Montreal.[52]

An indication of the community's growth during Simpson's residency may be gleaned from census data for the period, presented here in a brief table.[53]

New churches were providing improved schooling for the children of the settlement, and in 1832 Reverend David Jones established the Red River Academy, an Anglican institution of advanced education for the children of company officers and other members of the Red River elite.[54] That same year, Reverend William Cockran established, with a handful of Saulteaux families, an Indian agricultural village, called St Peter's, on the lower Red River north of the new Stone Fort.[55]

Even the customarily pessimistic Simpson occasionally sounded upbeat chords. In a report to London in July 1834, Simpson remarked, "I have the satisfaction to say that I found the Settlement in a healthy state, the prospects of a crop very favourable, and ... the whole state and appearance of things bearing ample evidence of ... excellent management."[56] The contrast with Simpson's 1821 impressions is striking.[57]

STORM CLOUDS

Alexander Christie, another tough HBC chief factor, was appointed governor of Assiniboia in 1833, when Donald McKenzie retired from company service following a dispute with Simpson. Christie held the position for the next six years, and would serve a second term from 1844 to 1848.

It was during his first term that storm clouds of settler resentment began to gather that would cause serious difficulties during his second term. After the distractions of flood survival and reconstruction subsided, the Halfbreed discontent exposed during the famine-stricken spring of 1826 began to resurface, along with new complaints.[58] It seemed to some, for example, that recent HBC hiring policies, which relied heavily on temporary labour and favoured Scottish immigrants for permanent positions, were seriously reducing employment opportunities for Halfbreeds. The company's refusal to pay the increased prices that Halfbreed buffalo hunters were now asking for pemmican made matters worse, and the company's determination to maintain exclusive control over the fur trade rankled with many. Tensions grew.

Then, late in 1834, a violent altercation between HBC clerk Thomas Simpson, the cousin of Governor-in-Chief George Simpson, and a French Halfbreed employee named Antoine Larocque fanned the smouldering Halfbreed discontent into flames.[59] Larocque came to Simpson at Fort Garry to request payment of a portion of his salary – perhaps an advance. Simpson arrogantly denied the request, and angry words led to a physical scuffle that ended with Simpson striking the employee on the head with a fireplace poker. Bleeding from the blow, Larocque fled Fort Garry and reported the assault to his relatives and friends. Before long, a large proportion of the settlement's male French Halfbreeds descended on Fort Garry. The demonstrators came to demand that Thomas Simpson be punished, and finding the fort's gates locked against them only heightened their anger. Governor Christie, Sheriff Ross, and others eventually brokered a settlement that gave Larocque his wages, and mollified the demonstrators with tobacco and a keg of rum.

The Larocque affair illustrated what settlement authorities had long known: law and order at Red River was at the sufferance of the Halfbreeds, who collectively constituted a great preponderance of the population. Nor were Halfbreeds the only perceived threat to peace. The Sioux, whose sporadic visits to Red River and frequent skirmishes with both Halfbreeds and Saulteaux were a constant source of nervousness, were also thought to pose an ongoing risk to the settlement.

Governor-in-Chief Simpson and his young wife returned to England in the summer of 1833. Frances Simpson's health was poor, and she had come to hate Red River – in part, perhaps, because of the sudden death of their first child in April 1832. She would never return to Rupert's Land. Her husband was back at Red River in 1834, however;

and what he observed and was told about the mood of the Halfbreeds, and settlers' fears of the Sioux, gave him much cause for concern.

Those concerns reinforced Simpson's long-held opinion that a stronger protective force for the settlement was sorely needed. Red River's minimal police force would be no match for a serious uprising by either the Halfbreed or the Indian populations. In July 1834, therefore, even before the Larocque disturbance, he wrote to London proposing a major strengthening of Red River's law enforcement powers.[60] And while improved police protection was the governor-in-chief's primary goal, a major by-product of his reforms would be the first formal judicial system in north-central North America.

3

Court without Judge, 1835–38

A historic meeting of the Council of Assiniboia and other local leaders on 12 February 1835 brought about an almost complete restructuring of the Red River Settlement's justice system, centred on a new two-tiered judicial body called the Quarterly Court of Assiniboia that would serve the settlement until the end of Hudson's Bay Company rule and beyond. At first the court functioned – quite effectively – without a legally trained judge.

Law enforcement was greatly improved by a large, salaried, Volunteer Mounted Constabulary Corps under the command of Sheriff Alexander Ross. But settlement authorities remained nervous about increasing Halfbreed restiveness. After news of the 1837–38 uprisings in Upper and Lower Canada demanding responsible government reached the settlement, Assiniboia's French Halfbreeds began singing Canadian protest songs.

POLICING

Governor-in-Chief Simpson's 1834 letter to HBC officials in London seeking strengthened police protection at Red River had begun by describing a recent visit of Sioux warriors, led by their famous chief "Terre Qui Brûle."[1] Although the delegation had peaceful objectives, the situation became suddenly dangerous when "Cuthbert Grant ... in a fit of inebriety ... galloped [into Fort Garry] with a party of Saulteaux." The Sioux and Saulteaux were long-time enemies, and Grant's French Halfbreeds were historic allies of the Saulteaux. Disaster was averted by Governor Christie's diplomacy, backed up by a hastily mustered force of English Halfbreed and Scottish settlers, but Simpson stressed that it had been a close call: "[I]t required ... much ... to restrain the Scotch, who were eager for an opportunity of punishing the Saulteaux for many insults they had received at their hands ... and ... the Scotch had neither forgotten nor forgiven Cuthbert Grant for the part he acted in the lamentable occurrences of the year 1816."[2]

Having illustrated the precariousness of law and order at Red River, Simpson's letter came to the point:

> [A] necessity ... exists of ... a more powerful force for the protection of the Settlement from a foreign enemy – likewise for maintaining good order at home – than the inefficient police we now have, amounting only to 30 men ... [A] militia or volunteer corps should be raised for the defence and protection of the colony ... This corps, I think, should consist of one hundred men, 50 horse and 50 foot, including the officers, the officers to render their services gratuitously, but the privates to have the same pay and allowances as ... [British] soldiery for the time they may be on duty – say, in all, 30 days of the year – with a suit of regimentals to the whole corps, officers and privates, once in three years.[3]

To meet this expense, he recommended a 5 per cent duty on imports from England to the settlement, which he estimated would yield £500 annually – enough to pay for the construction and maintenance of roads, bridges, and other public works as well as for the expanded police force.[4]

London's approval, in a letter dated 4 March 1835,[5] was subject to two conditions. To offset the customs duty, which would be chiefly borne by the company as the colony's main importer, retail prices must be raised by the same percentage, thus passing the cost on to consumers. And implementation of the scheme should be delayed pending further company consideration of its details "unless ... you find the emergency very urgent."

Still rattled by the hostile public reaction to his kinsman Thomas Simpson's treatment of Antoine Larocque, the governor-in-chief did consider the situation urgent – so much so that he began recruiting and swearing in members of the new force even before the approval letter was written. Oaths of office include many sworn in February.[6] He did seek *local* authorization, however – for both the new police force and other, more extensive, reforms.

BIRTH OF A JUSTICE SYSTEM

On 12 February 1835 Governor Simpson convened an extraordinary meeting of the Council of Assiniboia. It was a conspicuous affair attended by many other members of the Red River establishment.[7] Besides Simpson, local governor Alexander Christie and his eight-man council, and two members of the Council of Rupert's Land, attendees included, by special request to "assist with their advice," Bishop J.N. Provencher, newly appointed sheriff of Assiniboia Alexander Ross,[8] native-born settlement physician Dr John Bunn,[9] HBC veteran Donald Ross, and wealthy HBC critic Andrew McDermot.

As governor-in-chief, Simpson had the right to preside over the Council of Assiniboia whenever present, and he asserted that privilege on this occasion, opening the proceedings with an address calling for a major reshaping of Red River's government and judicature. "Gentlemen," he began,

> The population of this colony is become so great, amounting to about 5,000 souls,[10] that the personal influence of the Governor and Council, and the little more than nominal support afforded by the police, which, together with the good feeling of the public, have heretofore been its principal safeguard, are no longer sufficient to maintain the tranquility and good government of the Settlement – so that although rights of property have of late been frequently invaded and other serious offences been committed,[11] I am concerned to say we are under the necessity of allowing them to pass unnoticed because we really have not the means at command of enforcing obedience and due respect of the law.
>
> Under such circumstances, it must be evident to one and all of you that it is quite impossible society can be held together – that the time is at length arrived when it becomes necessary to put the administration of justice on a more firm and regular footing than heretofore, and that immediate steps ought to be taken to guard against dangers from abroad or difficulties at home, for the maintenance of good order and tranquility, and for the security and protection of lives and property. Towards these important ends I therefore beg to propose the following resolutions, which I trust will receive your favourable consideration.

Thirteen detailed resolutions were then presented, all of which were adopted by the council without apparent amendment or dissent.[12] First came the means of paying for the improvements: a customs duty of 7.5 per cent on all imports and exports other than personal effects, not just

5 per cent on English imports as first proposed. Following that were resolutions authorizing

- Appointment of a receiver and custodian of import and export duties.
- Construction of a courthouse-jail within the walls of Upper Fort Garry.
- Creation of a public works committee to manage the construction of the courthouse-jail and other public works (the company providing a "liberal grant of £300 ... in aid of public works").[13]
- Disbanding of the existing police force and its replacement on 1 April 1835 by the new "Volunteer Corps," consisting of Commanding Officer Alexander Ross, one sergeant major (Angus Matheson), four sergeants (John Bird, J.P. Bourke, William Shaw, and Bostonnais Pangman), and fifty-four privates. Salaries for a maximum of twenty-eight days' annual service were set at £20 for the commander, £12 for the sergeant major, £10 for the sergeants, and £6 for the privates, plus a per diem sum for additional service and a food allowance for days on duty. Rules and regulations for the "discipline and good government of the Corps" were to be developed and submitted to the next meeting of the council for approval.

The most important resolutions from the perspective of the present study were two that radically restructured the settlement's judicial arrangements. Resolution 8 observed that the colony was now too big to have most of its judicial needs met by "one magistrate."[14] Resolution 9 therefore divided the settlement into four districts for judicial and policing purposes: White Horse Plain District (along the Assiniboine River from modern St François Xavier downstream to Sturgeon Creek in modern St James), Upper District (from the southern end of the settlement on the Red River downstream to the Forks), Middle District (from Sturgeon Creek on the Assiniboine down to modern Middlechurch on the Red), and Lower District (from Middlechurch down to the northern extremity of the settlement).[15]

For each district, the resolution continued, "[A] magistrate or justice of the peace [shall] be appointed, who shall attend at places to be hereinafter determined for the purpose of hearing and deciding on cases of petty offence, and of debts under 40 [shillings]." Such court sittings were to be held quarterly, commencing 1 June 1835, but on different Mondays in each district to permit the same constables, two of whom were to attend each sitting, to serve every magistrate. Of the four magistrates appointed by the resolution,[16] not one was of French origin, and only one – Cuthbert Grant for the White Horse Plain – carried any Aboriginal blood. Grant was also French-speaking. This staffing differed sharply from the list of possible appointees in a document thought to reflect Simpson's early scheme for the courts, which contemplated French Halfbreed and/or Canadian magistrates in two of the four districts.[17]

These district-based courts – commonly referred to as "Courts of Petty Sessions" or "Petty Courts" – were not the only ones established at this time. Of greatest significance to the present study is the following passage, almost buried in Resolution 9: "[A]nd ... a General Court of the Governor and Council shall be held at the Governor's residence on the last Thursday of every quarter, at which the said magistrates shall attend, when cases of a more serious nature, cases of debt exceeding 40 [shillings], and all appeal cases from the decision of the justices of peace, shall be examined into."[18]

In law, the General Quarterly Court of Assiniboia was not really new; it was the same "Court of the Governor and Council" for which the HBC charter had made provision since 1670. Only its name, the regularity of its sittings, and the additional presence of magistrates were new. Those novel features gave the body a new prominence and prestige, however, as did its placement at the apex of the entirely unprecedented body of permanent local courts. What was most significant about the resolutions of February 1835, in fact, was that they established for the first time an integrated *system* of courts and related infrastructure. Law and order had ceased to be an ad hoc matter in the settlement. A *justice system* was now in place.

After that, cases of lesser import – constituting most of Red River's civil and criminal litigation – would be dealt with by the petty courts. The General Court would deal only with situations of unusual seriousness and with those rare cases in which petty court decisions were appealed. Regrettably, the only surviving records of petty courts are few and fragmentary. The records of the General Quarterly Court of Assiniboia, however, have survived intact for the period from November 1844 to May 1872, and it is they that will be the principal focus of this study.

Two somewhat connected questions arise concerning this pivotal session of the Council of Assiniboia: (1) Where did the council get the legal authority to create these new arrangements? (2) Why were the HBC's London authorities apparently so minimally involved in their creation? As for the first question, although the HBC charter conferred authority *explicitly* in respect of only judicial and executive functions, it can also be reasonably *inferred* for legislative powers. The answer to the second question has several elements. One is that the company was a commercial corporation – among the world's largest – with complex business issues to attend to and little time or resources to devote to noncommercial matters. Another is that Red River's distant wilderness location made management from London extremely difficult, and Lord Selkirk's estate was about to hand that task back to the HBC. Allowing the local governor and council to undertake the estate's former functions – under Governor-in-Chief Simpson's watchful eye, of course – made good operational sense. Underlying all the company's dealings with Assiniboia, too, was a rudimentary awareness of the colony's quasi independence and growing restlessness. While the London office would continue to take a great interest in Red River affairs – sometimes benevolent, sometimes self-serving – there was also a grudging understanding as increasing discontent surfaced locally that Assiniboia must be accorded a degree of supervised autonomy.

FIRST SITTINGS

Little is known about the initial sessions – in June 1835 – of either the magistrates' petty courts or the General Quarterly Court.[19] There is nothing, however, to suggest that the first hearings did not proceed satisfactorily. Simpson reported to London on 10 June that "[t]he Settlement is now in a more tranquil state than it has been for the past 12 months."[20]

It is possible that the General Court did not sit before the second quarter of 1836. Alexander Ross stated, "The first petty jury was empanelled on the 28th day of April 1836."[21] Since the General Court commonly sat with juries, and the petty courts never did, this may mean that the senior tribunal was not called upon to convene until then. Although the resolutions of 1835 said nothing about juries, Governor Bulger's 1822 instructions had called for juries in civil and criminal cases,[22] and rules adopted for the General Court in July 1839 required it to employ juries in all criminal cases, and in civil cases involving more than £10.[23] Perhaps, therefore, if the General Court did not sit with a jury before the second quarter of 1836, it did not sit at all before that date. It seems more likely, though, that Ross's observation means only that the General Court opted to sit without juries until April 1836.

One difficulty that arose early for Red River's courts can be inferred from a public notice by Governor Christie in April 1836: "[C]ourts will take no cognizance of ... any bargains or agreements ... [unless] made either before a magistrate, in writing, or in the presence of two unexceptional witnesses." Apparently, the courts were finding it difficult – as their modern counterparts still do – to decide which of two contradictory but equally credible parties to believe. The partial solution announced by Christie – that all agreements be either written or made in the presence of a magistrate or two disinterested witnesses – would no doubt simplify the work of the courts, but it lacked any legal authority. Christie signed the notice in his commercial capacity as chief factor of the company; but even if acting as governor of Assiniboia, he had no power to legislate without the concurrence of his council, and there is no evidence that the Council of Assiniboia even met at that time.[24] In any event, the HBC charter required that local laws not be "contrary or repugnant"[25] to English law, and English common law recognized and enforced verbal, unwitnessed contracts. Also, one wonders, quite apart from its legality, how workable a requirement of written or witnessed contracts could be in a frontier settlement of mostly illiterate inhabitants. It is not known how long the policy operated or what impact, if any, it had on business practices or litigation;[26] but it was probably short-lived and insignificant.

If the courts' first year of operation was successful, the second year began riotously. Alexander Ross told the story:

> [O]n the 28th day of April, 1836 ... a man named Louis St. Denis, a French Canadian, ... had been tried, convicted of theft, and, besides some further punishment, sentenced to be publicly flogged; which sentence was carried into effect on that day. The police being all in attendance, the utmost order was maintained till the close of the scene, when the popular excitement assumed a somewhat threatening aspect. The unusual spectacle of a white man being stripped and flogged before the public gaze had raised a spirit of indignation against the poor flogger. His task being accomplished, he no sooner stepped outside the ring, or police circle, when one fellow called out: "Bourreau, Bourreau";[27] another threw a chip at him; a third improved upon the example by throwing mud, while the bystanders, with one voice, called aloud: "Stone him! Stone him!" The poor frightened German, for such he was, ran, as he probably thought, for his life, and had not gone many yards before he stumbled and fell headlong into a hole, which gave rise to an uproarious burst of laughter, mingled with hisses. Here, however, the police interfered,

> and the bespattered official, being dragged out of the pit, was locked up in the Fort till the people dispersed.[28]

The next time the court imposed a sentence of flogging, no one was willing to inflict the punishment publicly: "On this occasion, therefore, the flogging took place within the prison walls, the official being masked, and for further security, locked up till dusk, when he was dismissed unknown."[29] Such disorderliness appears, however, to have been the exception rather than the rule.

In February 1837 the council took an important step forward by recognizing the admissibility of Indian testimony: "Resolved ... [t]hat the evidence of an Indian be considered valid, and be admitted as such in all courts of this Settlement."[30] This measure seems to have been a concomitant to legislation, to be discussed below, prohibiting the sale of liquor to Indians. Also enacted in February 1837 was a requirement that "any councillor being a party to a case brought forward for the decision of the [General] Court shall leave his seat as councillor while such case is under consideration."[31] It would be interesting to know the circumstances that prompted that enactment.

COURT IMPROVEMENTS

In June 1837 the council made several major amendments to the court system.[32] The four judicial districts were reduced to three: the former White Horse Plain District on the upper Assiniboine River became the new Upper District; the Middle District was expanded to include the upper reaches of the Red River (former Upper District); and the Lower District was extended to take in the Kildonan area occupied by the Selkirk Settlers, which had formerly been part of the Middle District.

The makeup of the petty courts was also changed importantly. Instead of a sole magistrate as previously, *panels* of three magistrates were required for every trial. Two resident magistrates were appointed for each of the three districts, meaning that at least one magistrate in any given case would have to reside beyond the district where the case arose. Although the reasons for those changes were not explained in the minutes, it seems likely that the use of single judges had raised perceptions of bias in some situations and had resulted in courts being unavailable when magistrates were absent or indisposed.

Other improvements included raising the civil jurisdiction of the petty courts from a maximum of £2 to a maximum of £5, perhaps because the

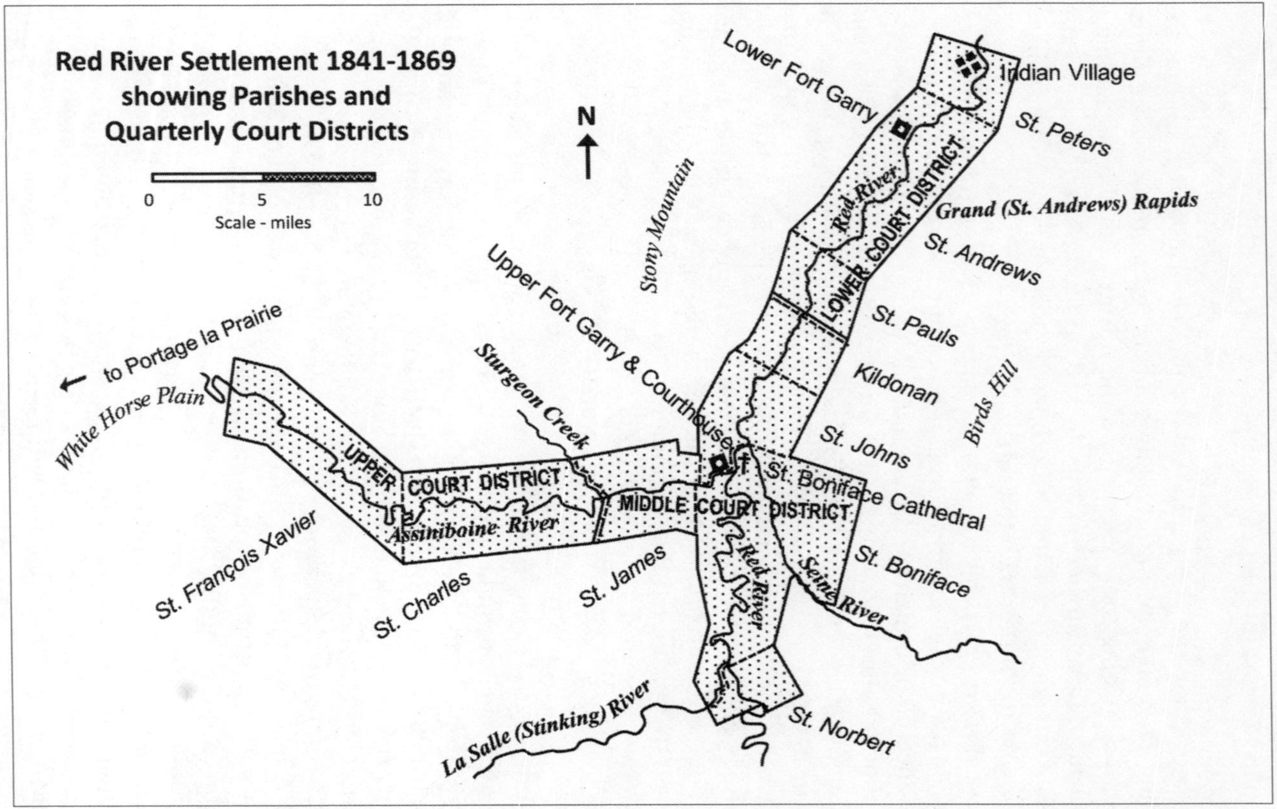
Red River Settlement 1841-1869
showing Parishes and
Quarterly Court Districts
0
5
10
Scale - miles
N
Lower Fort Garry
Indian Village
St. Peters
Red River
LOWER COURT DISTRICT
Grand (St. Andrews) Rapids
St. Andrews
St. Pauls
Kildonan
Birds Hill
St. Johns
Stony Mountain
Upper Fort Garry & Courthouse
to Portage la Prairie
White Horse Plain
Sturgeon Creek
UPPER COURT DISTRICT
Assiniboine River
MIDDLE COURT DISTRICT
St. Boniface Cathedral
St. Boniface
Seine River
Red River
St. François Xavier
St. Charles
St. James
La Salle (Stinking) River
St. Norbert

Figure 3.1

General Court was getting more cases than it could comfortably handle. The General Court was required to sit with at least four magistrates, and it was stipulated – contrary to charter requirements – that the HBC's principal commercial representative at Red River could sit on the court in place of the governor of Assiniboia. It was also decided to provide the police with more effective firearms than in the past and to purchase new law books for the magistrates: three copies each of Richard Burn's *Justice of the Peace* and the *Magistrates' Manual*.

These improvements were all condescendingly approved by the Governor and Committee in London as an "answer [for] all immediate necessary purposes, as a temporary measure"; but notice was given that "we have it in contemplation to establish as early as convenient a more regular and effectual administration of justice [the appointment of a full-time professional judge] which cannot fail of being productive of salutary advantages to all classes."[33] Little did they know.

In the opinion of Sheriff Alexander Ross at least, these were years in which justice was administered effectively at Red River despite the lack of sophisticated legal machinery: "During all this period ... [the laws] worked remarkably well, and gave general satisfaction, *without the aid of lawyers* ... [I]n no instance were the decisions of magistrates questioned or disobeyed; no collision of interests or parties disturbed the peace. So much confidence was placed in the simple and straightforward course pursued, that the good will of the people always backed and strengthened the hands of justice. Thus peace and order were thoroughly maintained throughout every part of the Settlement; the laws were respected, and life and property was everywhere secure."[34]

REVISED LAWS

The next time the Council of Assiniboia met after its creation of Red River's new justice system was two and a half months later on 30 April 1835.[35] Its task on that occasion was to examine the local laws of Assiniboia, originally passed on 4 May 1832, and to make any revisions deemed necessary.[36] The composition of the council that day included two men who had previously been present only as invitees, Dr John Bunn and Sheriff–Police Commandant Alexander Ross, as well as Warden of the Plains Cuthbert Grant, who had not been previously present at all. The formal appointments of Dr Bunn – the first Halfbreed on the council – and Sheriff Ross were not made by the London authorities until the following March,[37] and Grant would not be so appointed until March

1839.[38] Yet all three appear to have participated fully, if informally, at this and subsequent meetings.

It is interesting to compare the 1832 Assiniboia laws with the revised versions adopted at this meeting. With just two exceptions, the topics addressed by the two sets of laws were identical: open fires, stray pigs, stray stallions, and horse theft. And every revision was less severe in penalty than the original – perhaps because the magistrates were not willing to enforce unduly harsh restrictions in a community where, as Sheriff Ross put it, "crimes and misdemeanours had so long been committed with impunity."[39] Only two topics dealt with by the 1832 law were not addressed by the 1835 revision, and presumably remained in force unaltered: a requirement that all land occupants give, annually, either 3 shillings or three days' labour "towards the improvement of roads and bridges"; and a provision that public fairs be held twice a year.

In June 1836 new measures were enacted by the council to remove perceived inefficiencies in the organization of the police force. At that same session, the sale of beer to Indians – a problem that was to plague the settlement and the courts for years to come – was prohibited.[40] In February 1837 the council added an informer provision to the latter prohibition, ordaining that anyone who reported an offence would receive, on conviction, half of the fine paid. At its June 1837 session, the Council of Assiniboia (now expanded to add Bishop Provencher to the two Protestant clerics it already included) made the major amendments to the judicial system outlined above.[41]

GOVERNOR SIMPSON'S CONTINUING CONCERNS

Although Alexander Ross's glowing description of the juridical tranquility prevailing in the Red River Settlement during the courts' lawyerless years was likely true in large measure, it must be remembered that it was written more than a decade after the event, at a time when the settlement was still smarting from the consequences of its first lawyer's ill-advised actions. There is no way of knowing whether Sheriff Ross felt quite so positive about Red River's experiment in lay justice while the experiment was underway.

Certainly, Governor-in-Chief George Simpson was not so sanguine. In February 1837 Simpson wrote to HBC governor J.H. Pelly, "[I]t is no longer safe to trust the peace of the Settlement solely to the goodwill of the inhabitants. I therefore consider it highly necessary to the security of lives and property that a court of justice for the trial of civil and criminal cases with an efficient police to support the civil power should be established there without delay."[42] Given that it was only two years since the Council of Assiniboia had established, at his instigation, a new court system and police force for Red River, and even less than two years since he had reported the settlement to be in a "tranquil state,"[43] something serious must have occurred in the meantime. In fact, there had been several events that the governor-in-chief perceived as ominous portents.

In the summer of 1836, while Simpson was in residence, Red River had a large visitation of Sioux from the plains – a much larger and more menacing contingent than any in the past. Ross tells us that on this occasion the visitors, 250 strong, split up, leaving 180 "in ambush" while 70 proceeded to Fort Garry.[44] While the "very friendly manner" in which the delegation was received defused any possible violent intentions, and the Sioux left peaceably, the incident was enough to unsettle Simpson, who was always anxious about the potential for harm when Indians, or Halfbreeds, acted in concert.

In August of that same year, the company's Halfbreed tripmen (boat crews) went on strike, refusing to make a second trip to York Factory as their contracts obliged them to do.[45] That dispute was settled by negotiation, but Warden of the Plains Cuthbert Grant was nevertheless dispatched to accompany the boats to York and guard against further disruptions. Then, in December, an American adventurer calling himself "General" James Dickson arrived at Red River in command of a small group of mounted and armed men he styled the "Indian Liberating Army."[46] Dickson was a man of comic appearance but somewhat menacing demeanour. Simpson described his face as "covered with huge whiskers and mustachios, and seamed with saber wounds." Dickson's dream was to establish an independent state for Aboriginals in California. His immediate mission was to recruit Halfbreeds for his "cavalry," and he contacted Cuthbert Grant with the latter goal in view. When Dickson departed from Red River early in 1837, he left empty-handed; but the prospect of a renegade army composed of Indians and Halfbreeds roaming the prairies on some future occasion under the command of freelancers like Dickson was distressing to Governor Simpson.

Even after Simpson's letter of February 1837 was written, other developments continued to fuel his concerns about law and order at Red River and in Rupert's Land generally. One was his perennial nervousness about the increasing numbers of Indians being attracted to the Red River area. A decision of the Council of Rupert's Land at its 1837 annual meeting to cease hiring Indians as tripmen "as a means of discouraging the migration of Indians to the Settlement[,] which has of late years taken place to a dangerous extent,"[47] was not a sufficient deterrent in Simpson's mind; and he wrote to Assiniboia governor Christie on 20 February 1838, calling for a similar ban to be applied also to the crews of all private carriers working under contract for the company.[48] In the same letter he blamed this "dangerous migration" in part on the encouragement that the Catholic and Protestant missions gave Indians to settle near trading posts, but chiefly on liquor supplied to Indians by private traders.

Another cause for concern was the complex and costly legal aftermath of an infamous massacre. Sometime in 1835 or 1836 eleven Indians – men, women, and children – were brutally murdered at remote Fort Norman on the Mackenzie River by Baptiste Cadien and two others, all Halfbreeds in the company's employ.[49] The accused men were placed under arrest by HBC officers in the area and transported to York Factory on Hudson Bay. London was then consulted as to what should be done next. An "eminent counsel" was retained, who thought it would be wise to pass the question on to the attorneys general of Upper and Lower Canada, with the request that one of them should prosecute the prisoners.

Simpson, who was by that time in Montreal about to begin his long annual canoe journey to Rupert's Land, was instructed to act on the advice of Canadian authorities. He in turn ordered the York Factory staff to transport Cadien, in irons, along with an accomplice-witness called Jourdain, to Lower Canada by canoe and to send the other accomplice, one Creole Lagrasse, to the same place by ship via England. His hope, apparently successful, was that Lagrasse could be persuaded to turn King's evidence.[50] After being detained in London over the winter of 1837–38,[51] Lagrasse eventually reached Lower Canada and testified at the trial of Cadien, who was convicted and sentenced to death at Trois Rivières in March 1838. He was subsequently released on bail, however, because "a question has arisen as to the legality of the sentence." When the HBC protested the release, Cadien was returned to custody, and his sentence was commuted to "transportation" (banishment) for life to Australia.[52] As those tortuous and extremely expensive steps slowly unfolded, George Simpson must often have thought that a better way was needed for dealing with serious crimes committed in the far corners of Rupert's Land.

Throughout the winter of 1837–38, which Simpson spent in London, he received distressing reports of the French Canadian uprising in Lower Canada, where he had primarily resided since establishing the HBC's North American headquarters at Lachine in 1826. Louis-Joseph Papineau was leading a rebellion demanding democratically responsible government. In Upper Canada, William Lyon Mackenzie was heading a counterpart insurrection. George Simpson, a social and political conservative, had long supported the English party in Lower Canada, and he abhorred Papineau's aims and actions.[53] The French Halfbreeds of Rupert's Land, on the other hand, greeted the news of Papineau's uprising with an enthusiasm captured in the following account by Alexander Ross: "The Papineau rebellion, which broke out in Canada about this time, and the echo of which soon reached us, added fresh fuel to the spirit of disaffection. The Canadians of Red River sighed for the success of their brethren's cause. Patriotic songs were chanted on every side in praise of Papineau. In the plains, the Halfbreeds made a flag called the Papineau standard, which was waved in triumph for years, and the rebels' deeds extolled to the skies."[54]

SEEKING BETTER SAFEGUARDS

Even before the latter events, steps were being taken at Governor Simpson's instigation that he and the HBC management hoped would strengthen the ability of Assiniboia authorities to meet such threats to law and order. Chief among them was a plan to buttress the justice system by stronger law enforcement and a legally trained judge. On 10 February 1837, little more than a week after receiving Simpson's letter of concern, HBC governor Pelly wrote to Colonial Secretary Lord Glenelg in a similar vein but with greater particularity: "[I]t will soon be necessary to have the assistance of a person of competent legal knowledge as ... [judge], with other requisite officers, so as to form a more regular court of justice. It will also be necessary to provide a sufficient military or police force to support the civil power."[55]

Why did Pelly choose to communicate with the colonial secretary about Red River's need for a legally trained judge and stronger protective force rather than just urging company officers to get on with the job? He probably hoped to persuade the government to undertake the responsibility and some of the cost; but if that was his aim, he was disappointed. When he next wrote to Lord Glenelg on the subject, nine months later, Pelly seemed resigned to the fact that the HBC would receive no public assistance in its efforts to strengthen law and order in the settlement. His letter pointed out the great expense the government had avoided by the company's establishment of legal machinery similar to that called for in the Canada Jurisdiction Act of 1821. He also described "General" Dickson's attempts to recruit a Halfbreed army at Red River the previous winter in order to illustrate the risks the colony faced and went on to state, with an air of resignation, that the estimated £5,000 annual expenditure needed to "establish a more regular form of government and administration of the laws than heretofore ... will be borne by the Company, although they might with great propriety call upon Her Majesty's Government to relieve them from that charge."[56] At that point Pelly's most likely purpose was to curry favour with authorities who were then considering whether to renew the HBC's exclusive trading licence west of the Rocky Mountains.[57] In that objective, the company was successful, its licence being renewed in 1838 – four years before it had to be – for a further twenty-one years.[58]

Having concluded that a judicial officer with legal training was required at Red River, and that the company would be solely responsible for providing one, HBC officials chose the English model of a municipal "Recorder," which was appropriate in some respects but not in others. In England some boroughs had intermediate-level criminal courts that sat quarterly and were presided over by single judges called "Recorders." Recorders' courts heard appeals from courts akin to Red River's petty courts, and also had original jurisdiction over certain more serious crimes.[59] Although the General Quarterly Court of Assiniboia resembled recorders' courts in those respects, it differed from them in that it was a court of plenary jurisdiction, embracing *all* crimes, even of the most serious type, and all *civil* matters as well. The recorder contemplated for Red River would also differ sharply from English recorders in that he would not be a sole judge, as in England, but would sit as only one member, albeit an influential one, of a larger tribunal. His legal authority would derive solely from the HBC charter.

The search for the settlement's first recorder turned out to be easier than expected. The Governor and Committee thought that suitable candidates could be found in England; but George Simpson, who was in London at the time, told them he had someone from Lower Canada in mind, and asked them to delay advertising the position until he could approach the man in question.[60] Simpson's candidate – Scottish-born and -educated Montreal lawyer-journalist Adam Thom – was an extraordinary individual, whose appointment as recorder of Rupert's Land would have a massive impact on the General Quarterly Court and on the settlement. Some of that impact would be positive; much would not.

4

Judge without Experience, 1838–44

The first recorder of Rupert's Land, Adam Thom, was a man of many parts (scholar, journalist, lawyer); extraordinary capacities (courage, erudition, brilliance, imagination, energy); and crippling shortcomings (pettiness, arrogance, bigotry, foolhardiness). Recently called to the bar of Lower Canada, he had very little experience as a lawyer, and none as a judge. Author of numerous scathing editorial attacks on French Canadians and their culture – as well, it was said, of the Durham Report's anti-French passages – he was spectacularly ill-equipped to serve the chiefly francophone population of Red River.

Apart from a few problems caused by his prickly personality, however, Thom's early years at Red River were generally successful. The procedures he established for the General Court were effective; his insistence that Indians were subject to the same law as others was in line with similar trends worldwide; and his requirement that most General Court cases be tried by juries ensured the court's success. An astonishing product of Recorder Thom's first winter at Red River was a concise codification of English law for application to Rupert's Land. Among the earliest substantial codes of English law ever written, it was well conceived and competently drafted. Regrettably, it was never adopted. The settlement nevertheless benefited from his drafting of Assiniboia's everyday legislation.

Expansion and change continued apace, aided by a transformation of Rupert's Land's economy from subsistence living to entrepreneurship – a change exemplified by increasing Halfbreed involvement in the new buffalo robe trade and soon reflected in the dockets of Assiniboia's quarterly courts.

"A GENTLEMAN OF HIGH LEGAL ATTAINMENTS"

Born at Brechin, Scotland, on 30 August 1802 to the wife of a local merchant, Adam Thom[1] was educated at Aberdeen University, receiving a

Figure 4.1 Adam Thom, recorder of Rupert's Land from 1839 to 1854, was the first legally trained judge in British Northwest America, and contributed much to Red River's early judicial system; but his arrogance, irascibility, HBC partisanship, and francophobia nearly destroyed it.

master of arts degree in 1824. After teaching school in Scotland and England until 1832 he emigrated to Montreal, and there launched two careers simultaneously: articling in a lawyer's office[2] while undertaking, from January 1833, the editorship of a small newspaper. He was editor of a major newspaper, the *Montreal Herald*, by 1835, and was called to the bar of Lower Canada in 1837. A man of unusual intelligence and astonishing energy, Thom seems to have had no difficulty satisfying the requirements of both professions and was soon prominent among the conservative anglophone business elite of the city.

Intolerant in attitude and pontifical in style, Thom was notorious for editorials and letters to the editor strongly opposed to the cultural and political aspirations of the increasingly vocal and restive French majority of Lower Canada.[3] Those views, compatible with Simpson's own, may well have been what brought the younger man to the notice of the HBC's North American governor-in-chief. Perhaps they met at Montreal's Beef Steak Club, a businessmen's dining fraternity of which Thom became secretary in November 1833.[4] The Upper and Lower Canada rebellions of 1837–38, and the British government's subsequent appointment of Lord Durham as governor general of British North America with instructions to investigate their causes, gave Thom an official outlet for his francophobia. He applied for a position with Durham and was, in August 1838, appointed assistant municipal commissioner.

By that time, Adam Thom had also accepted a five-year appointment, commencing 1 May 1839, as recorder of Rupert's Land. George Simpson had made the fledgling lawyer a tentative offer on 5 January 1838,[5] a few months after testing his competence with questions about the *Cadien* case – the Mackenzie River massacre prosecution.[6] An annual salary of £500, plus free transportation to and from Red River and free lodging and board while he was there, was first proposed. Thom countered with a bid for a higher salary, and Simpson sweetened his offer a little by substituting an additional £200 annually for the free lodging and board. Moreover, he added, there would be an opportunity to practise law privately while at Red River, as long as it did not interfere with other responsibilities.[7] Thom accepted.

He would have been mad not to. A salary of £700 per annum, plus a private practice, was very handsome compensation for someone with almost no experience as a lawyer.[8] Nor would his official duties be unduly demanding. Simpson outlined them in his first letter: "In addition to the duties of your situation as Recorder of Rupert's Land, it would be necessary for you to act in the capacity of magistrate, likewise as councillor and legal advisor to the Company, and in such other duties as would not be derogatory to the appointment you would hold as Recorder."[9] The General Quarterly Court of Assiniboia sat for only a few days – often only one – every three months, and the Council convened less frequently than that. Thom's responsibilities as magistrate would involve little more than issuing an occasional warrant; and although he would be called upon regularly as in-house counsel for local HBC officials, there would be more than ample time to pursue private interests. One task, implicit in the title "Recorder of Rupert's Land," and intended by Simpson and the company to be performed by Thom, was to administer justice in HBC territory beyond Assiniboia. That could potentially have been quite time-consuming. The Council of Rupert's Land often dealt with legal problems, and occasionally held trials, at its annual meetings;[10] and Thom's presence at those meetings – usually held at a considerable distance from Red River – was expected. He contrived, however, to avoid ever attending distant meetings of the Rupert's Land council throughout his long residence at Red River.

The governor-in-chief's surprising initial confidence in this relatively untried lawyer had wavered slightly on one point only: Thom's ability and willingness to conduct trials in French. Simpson raised the matter forthrightly in both his January and April letters: "I presume you are qualified to express yourself with perfect facility in the French language, as that may in great measure be considered the language of the country, and without which you would not be adapted for the situation."[11] "About four fifths of our white and halfcaste population in the interior speak nothing but French. A knowledge of that language, and capability of speaking it with fluency, is therefore absolutely necessary, and without which you would not do justice to the appointment."[12] Thom's responses, if any, to those pointed statements are not known, but Simpson must have been satisfied. This was unfortunate, for Thom's inability or unwillingness to use French in the courtroom would eventually prove disastrous.

On 13 March 1839 the company's General Court formally created the position of recorder of Rupert's Land and, after Simpson's assurance that Thom was a suitable candidate, appointed him to that office for a five-year term. The Montreal lawyer was also made a member of the Assiniboia and Rupert's Land councils,[13] and at the same time Cuthbert Grant and Andrew McDermot were finally formally appointed to the Council of Assiniboia. Although the office of recorder was an entirely new institution, its powers were not novel, its judicial status being implicit in the recorder's membership in the two councils, both of which held adjudicative powers under the HBC charter.

Since Thom would not be required to depart for Red River until May 1839, he was able to devote the autumn of 1838 to co-authoring a paper on municipal government that would form part of Lord Durham's report. That work was so valued that Durham began using Thom as a spokesman. Then, in December 1838, he took Thom back to England to help prepare his final report. When Simpson learned of the recorder-to-be's interim assignment, he was delighted: "[I]t affords both the Governor and Committee and myself very great pleasure to learn that you are rendering your aid to Lord Durham in his very arduous duties, and ... thereby securing ... the patronage of that distinguished nobleman."[14] Simpson must have had a pretty good idea by then that he would agree with Durham's recommendations. How much influence Thom had on the contents of the Durham Report is not fully known, but its wholesale denigration of French Canadian culture certainly coincided precisely with his own views. If he did not pen them himself, he would certainly have rejoiced at such conclusions as: "[I]n any plan which may be adopted for the future management of Lower Canada, the first object ought to be that of making it an English province."[15]

Simpson promised Thom that any law books he would need in Rupert's Land had only to be asked for, and the company would ship them to Red River. In early January 1839, therefore, while Thom was still in England, he provided Simpson with a list of fifty-seven books, plus a request for the statutes of Upper and Lower Canada.[16] Many, if not all, of those authorities were eventually dispatched to the settlement.

NEW FACES AND FIRST IMPRESSIONS

When Governor-in-Chief Simpson's famed high-speed canoe flotilla left Lachine on his annual tour of inspection of HBC field operations in the early spring of 1839, its passengers included, besides Simpson and his usual staff and crew, Adam Thom and his wife, Anne,[17] a young Scot named John Black who was to serve as clerk of Thom's court, and the new governor of Assiniboia, Duncan Finlayson.

Duncan Finlayson was another career fur trader and chief factor, who had served the company since 1815 and had risen through the ranks without a blemish to his record. George Simpson's secret "Character Book" of 1832 described Finlayson as "[a] highly upright honourable correct man of good education and superior abilities to most of his colleagues. Has great influence with, and is much liked by, his equals, inferiors and the natives: Speaks Cree ... Firm, cool and decisive, one of our best legislators and most effective practical men, and his private conduct and character are models worthy of imitation; in short he may be ranked high among the most respectable and efficient men of his class."[18] The acuteness of that assessment would be borne out by Finlayson's five-year term as governor of Assiniboia. Alexander Ross remembered his regime warmly, rating Finlayson higher than almost anyone else mentioned in his Red River history.[19] One wonders what this quiet, tolerant man thought of his pompous, vociferous, bigoted judge as they travelled together through the rigours and splendours of the Canadian Shield. Thom could be charming, however, to those he considered his equals and obsequious to his superiors. There is no evidence that he and Governor Finlayson did not get along well.

Twenty-two-year-old John Black[20] had been engaged in Scotland to serve as court clerk and much more. When Simpson wrote to Thom in April 1838 to make the improved offer that the latter accepted, he asked whether Thom would be able to locate a "clerk accustomed to the routine of a lawyer's office in Canada, who writes French fluently, and who writes a good neat hand with dispatch and [is] qualified to draw up the papers accurately in legal form, and act as public prosecutor." The candidate must also be a "young unmarried gentleman of sober, steady, correct habits."[21] A suitable Canadian not having been found, young Black, who seemed to possess all those qualities, was found in Edinburgh and agreed to undertake, for £100 annually, not only the foregoing legal duties but also, when called upon, employment in the company's "stores, counting house, &c."[22] Despite his youth, and although he was not a lawyer, Black had learned much about the law during seven years in an Edinburgh solicitor's office. He was destined for distinguished, and far more than clerical, service to the General Quarterly Court and to the settlement generally.

The people of Red River – their leaders at least – knew that changes were in the wind. However, the first public announcement of Thom's appointment – "We have appointed Adam Thom Esq., a gentleman of high legal attainments, Recorder of Rupert's Land"[23] – seems to have been in a letter dated 20 March 1839 that was probably carried to the settlement in the same canoe flotilla that conveyed the recorder himself. But even if it had arrived in advance of Thom, it would have told the settlers little about their new judge. The Thoms, for their part, would have been only slightly better informed about what to expect of the remote community that would be their home for the next several years. Governor Simpson had attempted, in earlier correspondence, to paint the settlement in attractive hues: "[T]he country is salubrious – much the same as that of Lower Canada, [although] a few degrees colder in winter." As for social life, Simpson assured the newcomers, "[a]t Red River Settlement there is no want of society. [T]here is about 5,000 souls, one third of them Europeans and Canadians; and there are about 20 persons of respectability with whom you could associate."[24] The Thoms also had the advantage, of course, as they travelled west, of conversations with members of the canoe brigade who were familiar with Red River. Nonetheless, the contrast to Great Britain, and even to Montreal, must have been jolting.

Their first experiences, however, were probably reassuring. They were given immediate comfortable accommodation at Lower Fort Garry, and although that was intended only as temporary shelter while they found a home of their own, they would in fact remain there a long time. The governor-in-chief held high expectations for the "Stone Fort," now surrounded by high, nearly complete, defensive walls and bastions. He had told Alexander Christie the previous year, "The Lower Fort, I conceive, will in due time become the principal establishment for farming, warehousing, holding courts and councils &c., &c."[25] Although those expectations were never fully met – the court and council remaining at the Upper Fort – the Stone Fort did become a major Red River centre for the rest of the century. It and the surrounding pastoral areas provided a relatively genteel sanctuary from the uncouth bustle of the Forks for the new recorder and his wife.

Other parts of the settlement had also to be examined. The non-Indian population had reached 3,972 by 1838, occupying 641 homes and more than 3,800 acres of cultivated land. It was not a well-to-do community. Those 641 households employed only 89 servants in an era when most middle-class families depended heavily on domestic help. Although males and females were numerically almost equal, adults (over age twenty-one) totalled only slightly more than half the number of minors. And expansion was rapid: the total population had grown by 9.3 per cent since the 1835 census and would grow to 4,369 – a further 9.1 per cent increase – between 1838 and 1840.[26]

The newcomers were taken upstream to see the other areas for themselves: past the "Grand Rapids" at St Andrew's and the English Half-breed farms thereabouts, beyond the longer-established holdings of the Selkirk Settlers, to the bustling area of the Forks, where, on the east bank, the imposing new St Boniface Cathedral towered over the surrounding homes of francophone residents, and the recently renovated Upper Fort Garry stood on the opposite shore awaiting Adam Thom's assumption of judicial responsibilities.

The new recorder was sworn into office at the fort during a meeting of the Council of Assiniboia on 13 June 1839.[27] Those in attendance at the swearing-in must have been intensely curious as to what Governor Finlayson and the austere lawyer at his side could accomplish. Some were skeptical about Adam Thom from the first. Alexander Ross later summarized those initial misgivings:

> To let well alone has always been a maxim with us; but with this course some are not satisfied. In order to give a more legal tone to our judicial proceedings, and lend strength, as they supposed, to the arm of justice, the Company introduced a professional man into the colony this year, under the title of Recorder of Rupert's Land, and placed him as judge in Red River. ... [T]he appointment raised up a formidable host of objections ... [I]n place of the simple honesty which marked our proceedings hitherto, it has a tendency to substitute the quibbles and technicalities of law, which few but lawyers themselves comprehend. Besides this, a professional judge on the bench, without a professional lawyer at the bar, is an anomaly in judicial proceedings – not to mention that this high functionary is a paid servant of the Company's, drawing a liberal salary of £700 sterling per annum. In the nature of things, a paid servant must have a special eye to his employer's interest, above that of all others ... Mr. Thom being a Company's man, the people observed, "He cannot be the man for us"; and they added that as the Company had got a legal adviser, the people ought to have another, in order to keep the equilibrium of justice on a fair balance. "A lawyer on either side," said the people, "or no lawyer at all"; this was their creed; and whether law or no law, it was certainly common sense.[28]

Others, Ross said, objected to Thom because he could not speak French and was known to have been "no favourite of the French" in Lower Canada. But what Ross personally considered the "fundamental objection" was that "[a] man ... placed in Mr. Thom's position, liable to be turned out of office at the Company's pleasure, naturally provokes the doubt whether he could, at all times, be proof against the sin of partiality." "Such," he concluded, "was the commonsense opinion of the people on the arrival of their judge in 1839."[29] Ross was writing with the benefit of hindsight, of course, but his assessment has the ring of truth. Thom had a serious public relations hurdle to overcome even before he first sat with the General Quarterly Court.

COURT RULES AND NEW LAWS

He got right to work. In preparation for his first sitting, he drafted new rules for the courts, as well as some changes to the general local laws of the settlement, both of which the Council of Assiniboia enacted on 4 July 1839, only three weeks after his swearing-in.[30] Apart from the convoluted sentence structure to which Thom was sometimes prone, and an occasional whiff of unnecessary legalese, the changes were practical and useful.

Their content was highly miscellaneous. The sitting dates for the General Court were changed to the third Thursdays of February, May, August, and November every year, plus any special session thought necessary by the governor,[31] a pattern that would be generally followed in future years. The petty courts' criminal jurisdiction was restricted to offences carrying fines of less than £5, and cases "of doubt or difficulty," regardless of monetary value, could be referred to the General Court. All petty courts were required to keep written records of their proceedings, a commendable obligation eventually frustrated by the loss of most records. Other provisions dealt with default judgments in civil cases, conduct money[32] for witnesses and fines for those who did not show up, warrants, writs, and discretionary costs[33] to successful litigants.

Juries of twelve were required as fact-finders in the General Court for all criminal cases and civil cases involving more than £10. All land owners were made subject to jury duty, and the sheriffs were required to create lists of such persons and to choose jury panels[34] from those lists. Prisoners in the settlement jail who were "unable to maintain themselves" were required to be provided "a pound of pemmican a day, or ... an equivalent in other provisions." Councillor Reverend John Macallum was appointed coroner for Assiniboia – apparently the first such appointment ever. The perennial problem of making changes in the law known throughout a community that lacked a printing press[35] was addressed by requiring the senior magistrate of each district to be provided with copies of council minutes and to make them available for public inspection at the quarterly sessions of their respective courts. It was an impressive start to Recorder Adam Thom's Red River career.

THE RECORDER IN COURT, 1839–40

The loss of the first five years of Thom-era General Court records, and the fragmentary nature of available secondary evidence, leaves us only limited knowledge of the recorder's early experiences on the bench. What is known is nevertheless informative. Thom rated his own performance highly. In self-assessments written to HBC authorities in Montreal and London in 1840, he initially spoke of unexplained "doubts and difficulties" that had arisen;[36] but he was soon boasting of success.

His innovations, he said, "have inspired the public at large with implicit confidence in the Court of Governor and Council. This I hear from all quarters directly and indirectly."[37]

Thom's self-described "systematic establishment of trial by jury"[38] was unquestionably popular. To illustrate that fact, he told of persuading the victim of a brutal assault to abandon a lawsuit against his assailants in a petty court in favour of suing them in the General Court, where a jury later awarded him double the damages he would have received from the magistrates. The victim was delighted.[39] In fact, the general public had more confidence in juries than in "the Court" – which should have told the recorder something but apparently didn't.

Another widely approved aspect of Thom's reforms was his integration (as accused persons and civil litigants, though not as judges or jurors) of the Indian population into the judicial system that applied to everyone else, a topic to be addressed more fully at a later point.[40] However, the first case in which he appeared to do so also illustrates a personal trait – excessive legalism – that was causing him to be ridiculed by the community.

The trial of a twelve-year-old Indian boy for murder in November 1839 was a classic example of judicial pettifoggery. Twelve-year-old Henry Beardie and his friend William Bird were playing with bows and arrows near the latter's home when Henry shot an arrow in William's direction. It killed him. Henry had not intended to hit William, much less kill him, but a coroner's jury decided that the boy's fatal carelessness amounted to manslaughter and charged him with such.[41] Recorder Thom thought the act, if done by an older person, would have constituted murder, not just manslaughter. He may have been right – an English barrister thought he "probably" was[42] – but for Henry Beardie the distinction was irrelevant since a twelve year old's youth was a defence for *either* crime. The recorder nevertheless referred the matter to a grand jury – apparently Red River's first – which indicted the boy for murder. A trial – likely the settlement's first of an Indian – was then held, at which a petty jury acquitted Beardie because of his youth, as Thom had no doubt charged it to do.[43]

The boy was thus put through a double judicial ordeal, with a possible death sentence hanging overhead – just to demonstrate the fine legal distinction between murder and manslaughter – when all that was needed to dispose of the case lawfully and humanely was to stay the proceedings immediately on the basis of age. Some benefit did come from the petty jury's publicly "denouncing the dangerous practice of shooting arrows, which has for many years been so prevalent throughout the Settlement," but that denunciation could have been made by Thom himself or by a grand jury investigating safety in the settlement, without twice trying a child for a capital offence. Recorder Thom was proud of the *Beardie* case, explaining it at length in an 1845 grand jury charge he later published privately in Britain.[44] But his jurisprudential gymnastics struck the down-to-earth people of Red River as what Alexander Ross would later call "the quibbles and technicalities of law."[45]

The most outrageous example of Thom's arid legalism was described in his first account of his early judicial experiences.[46] He criticized the petty court magistrates who sat with him on the General Court bench ("my unprofessional brethren") for assuming that "the laws of this Kingdom," which the HBC charter made the basic law of Rupert's Land, meant *current* English law. This was wrong, he said, because, for reasons he never convincingly explained, the HBC charter referred to English laws in effect *on the day the charter was granted*: 2 May 1670![47] That interpretation would cause many future difficulties, not the least being how to determine, in the wilds of Rupert's Land, what the laws of England were over a century and a half earlier.It was a problem solely and unnecessarily conceived in the fecund brain of Adam Thom.

This criticism of the magistrates was not an isolated occurrence; Thom was constantly at odds with his judicial juniors, in whom he had no confidence and from whom he received no respect. Several of his legislative amendments were aimed at reducing the magistrates' authority. By imposing what he called "fixed and invariable rules of decision," he effectively reduced the powers previously exercisable by individual magistrates. When he reported to Simpson that Governor Finlayson had countermanded Alexander Ross's single-handed conviction and imprisonment on short rations of a young thief in defiance of the new rules, the recorder's account had a distinct tone of gloating.[48]

Thom claimed he considered public respect to be vital to the success of a legal system: "It is only by commanding the respect of the people that law can practically exist on Red River."[49] But he equated such respect with "dread of the law," which he asserted had increased after his amendments removed the prospect of magistrates exercising their discretion leniently.[50] The secret of his self-perceived success was boldness, he boasted. Winning the type of respect generated by a "dread of the law" on the part of "so simple and natural a ... society" as Red River required him to be bold, and never hesitate to make or enforce necessary laws through fear of "factious opposition."[51]

Although Adam Thom's boldness would certainly never fail him, it was actually losing, not winning, people's respect. Many of his energetic efforts were already attracting strong negative responses in the community. He had certainly achieved some significant successes, but for the most part his excessive legalism and maddeningly overbearing personality were befuddling and angering the general population, and alienating his judicial colleagues. Arrogant, stubborn, short-tempered, outspoken, and contemptuous of all he considered beneath him on the social scale (which included almost everyone of French heritage), Adam Thom was not troubled by his lack of popularity. He sometimes made fun of it, in fact, commenting to Simpson on one occasion that, having blamed him for many things beyond his control, critics "ought to have given me credit for the last year's abundant crop."[52]

RECORDER AS LEGISLATOR

Having demonstrated his legal drafting skills with the 1839 court reorganization legislation, Adam Thom was thereafter called upon to compose most amendments and new laws enacted locally while he remained at Red River.

He was far more than a mere draftsman. At the 8 June 1840 meeting of the Council of Assiniboia,[53] for instance, Thom proposed, as well as drafted, a package of resolutions relating to the sale of liquor to Indians; and when they encountered serious resistance from some councillors, his persistent debate persuaded a majority to adopt them. The sale of beer to Indians had been prohibited previously, with informers paid half the fines imposed. Thom did not consider that sufficient, and made several draconian "improvements." The new law covered all types of liquor, increased fines, entitled informers to nearly 100 per cent of the fines, and offered co-offenders immunity in return for informing. Indian purchasers of liquor could get their money back, as well as an informer's reward; and because Thom thought the magistrates too lax, all such prosecutions were to be tried by jury in the General Court rather than in the petty courts. One result of the amendments was that a Native to whom liquor was sold could – presumably after drinking it – accuse his or her supplier, testify for the prosecution, and receive a refund of the purchase price, along with all or most of the resulting fine.[54] As Thom later explained to Simpson, "My main object ... was to coax ... evidence from every quarter against the delinquents, and to present to their terrified imaginations every purchaser as an informer."[55]

A year later, on 25 June 1841, the recorder presented the Council of Assiniboia with a considerably more ambitious, if less controversial, legislative draft: a comprehensive revision and consolidation of the entire Laws of Assiniboia.[56] Regulations concerning fires, fences, trespassing animals, horse theft, hay harvesting, roads and bridges, distillation, sale of liquor to Indians, customs duties, maintenance of prisoners, police, courts, and the publication of laws were all refined and restated in a more complete form than ever before. That restatement included numerous substantive changes, although most were of relatively minor scope. Prisoners in the jail, whether for crime or for debt, would now all receive one pound of pemmican, plus water, daily at public expense, and would not be allowed to supplement the allowance from their own resources. Fines for every type of offence were to be shared with informers. Indians seeking refunds of the price of liquor sold to them would now have to sue for the amount – an unlikely prospect. And the publication of these local laws was no longer to be a responsibility of the petty courts alone: "That no person shall plead ignorance of these regulations, at least eight copies shall be fixed on pasteboard or wood, and distributed over the Settlement among such of the inhabitants as may be willing to take charge of them for the seasonable inspection of the public."

Some rudimentary rules for interpreting the laws were provided, including what future generations would call a "plain language" rule: "[T]he natural and obvious meaning [shall not] be set aside, either to punish or to screen offenders." The latter was an unexpected injunction from the pen of Adam Thom, who was capable of egregiously strained legal interpretations when they suited his purpose. The criminal jurisdiction of the petty courts, in which Thom had little faith, was reduced to breaches of local laws involving fines of less than £1. The recorder must have persuaded the council that magistrates could not be trusted with trials of common law crimes, or even of breaches of local laws if the offences carried penalties of £1 or more. The only change concerning the General Court, apart from giving it jurisdiction over *all* common law crimes, was that it would thereafter sit with a jury in *every* case.

Of the fifty-eight resolutions making up this new compilation of the Laws of Assiniboia, the most puzzling, and the one most productive of future confusion, was the first: "1. The following regulations shall apply to the whole of the District of Assiniboia, extending, in all directions, fifty miles from the forks of the Red River and the Assiniboine."[57] Since the HBC General Court in London had, in 1839, defined "District of Assiniboia" as "such portion of the territory granted to the late Thomas,

Earl of Selkirk ... as is now within the domains of Her Britannic Majesty,"[58] this new local "50 mile radius" definition must have referred to something different – something that came to be called the "Municipal District of Assiniboia." Its underlying purpose seems to have been to restrict any obligation on the part of settlement officials to extend police, court, and public works services to remoter parts of the former Selkirk grant, and it would sometimes, although not always, be so applied.[59]

The compilation was not without flaws. Several prohibitions failed to specify penalties, for example, and a provision repealing "all older resolutions" may have thrown out a few legislative babies with the bathwater. What, for instance, was the status of the previously enacted, but now unmentioned, laws about tavern licensing[60] and jury selection?[61] In places, Thom's draftsmanship was so labyrinthine that the citizens of a frontier settlement could not be reasonably expected to make sense of it. Despite such shortcomings, the compilation was a commendable achievement. It was minor, however, compared to two other quite astonishing pieces of legal research and writing that Red River's indefatigable recorder had already produced: a massive commentary on the laws relevant to Rupert's Land and an extraordinary codification of English law for use in Rupert's Land.

THOM'S LEGAL CODES AND "OBSERVATIONS"

Some historians have referred to the 1841 consolidation of the Laws of Assiniboia as Thom's "Code," but it was really nothing more than an improved compendium of local legislation. The recorder did, however, draft and propose enactment of two true codes, both of which were remarkable syntheses of, and attempted improvements upon, relevant principles of English common law and legislation for local application. They related, respectively, to criminal and civil law. In preparation for the composition of those codes, Thom produced an equally noteworthy and ultimately more useful memorandum of "Observations" about the law applicable to Rupert's Land.

Creation of the codes was not altogether a Thom initiative. Before leaving London en route to Red River in 1839, he had been instructed to turn his attention when he got there to "preparing a code of laws and regulations which you might consider applicable to the present circumstances of the country." Perhaps that is why he ordered so many law books to be sent to the settlement. In March 1840 Governor Simpson wrote to remind the recorder of that responsibility.[62]

But Thom had needed no urging. He spent much of the winter of 1839–40 researching and writing his lengthy background study "Observations on the Laws and the Judicature of Rupert's Land";[63] and on 29 May 1840, even before receiving Simpson's reminder, he sent his "Observations" to Simpson, requesting that he forward them to the HBC Governor and Committee in London.[64] He proposed that the document should, if approved by London, become the basis for the contemplated codification, to be prepared "with the advice and assistance of the Governor and magistrates of Assiniboia" and designed to "blend justice with mercy, temper law with equity, and reconcile the peculiar circumstances of Rupert's Land with the fundamental principles of the law of England." When Simpson's reminder letter arrived a few days later, Thom exulted, "It has gratified me to see that my labours have been merely anticipating the wishes of the Committee; and it has cheered me to think that I may now go forward without hindrance or delay."[65] He had probably already begun work on the *Penal Code*, which he completed on 18 July 1840[66] and sent off to Simpson eleven days later.[67] The *Civil Code* was finished on 15 October 1840.[68] All three of Thom's drafts were extraordinary documents that deserve more extensive commentary than is possible here. Only their essentials can be outlined.

The remarkably well-researched overview of Rupert's Land's legal landscape that Thom called his "Observations"[69] dealt, in fifty-seven handwritten pages, with the legal validity of the HBC charter and its geographic reach, the constitutional status of the company's proprietary domains, the complex relationship between English law and local laws of Rupert's Land, the applicability of those laws to the Aboriginal population, some of the bewildering consequences of Thom's absurd view that the applicable English law was almost 200 years out of date, the creative capacity of the common law, and scores of smaller but often significant questions. Although the document was fairly tightly structured, in twelve logically ordered sections, Thom's style shifted from passage to passage in accordance, perhaps, with his changing moods during that studious winter in the snowbound Stone Fort. Some passages were witty, even playful; others ponderous. The tone was magisterial at times; tendentious at others. The explanations ranged from pellucid to obscure. Thom's reasoning was sometimes impeccable; sometimes specious. The issues he chose to address varied in importance from fundamental to picayune.

A few of the more significant topics, and Thom's conclusions thereon, were the reception date of English law in Rupert's Land (2 May 1670);

whether Assiniboia courts had jurisdiction over Indians (yes); the criminal jurisdiction of petty courts (none because the HBC charter restricted such jurisdiction locally to the Assiniboia governor and council); whether the company could be a litigant in settlement courts (no because one cannot be a judge in one's own cause); and the power of the General Court to modify English law to better suit local circumstances (such power resides in the inherent creativity of the common law, but it would be unwise for practical reasons to exercise it). The latter point did not mean that Recorder Thom objected to tailoring English law to suit the conditions of Rupert's Land; he simply thought it would be better to accomplish that task legislatively than judicially, and he accordingly turned without further ado to the monumental job of drafting the criminal and civil legal codes he hoped the company would enact.

At the time Adam Thom undertook to codify the criminal and civil law of England for application to Rupert's Land, no such project involving common law principles had ever been successfully completed.[70] Some European civil law[71] had been codified, of course: France's *Code Napoleon* was almost complete after many years' effort by a commission of experts, though refinements were still being made; and a few German states had produced similar compilations. In Louisiana the noncriminal aspects of law had been codified in 1824, following the French model, and work on the criminal law was underway when Thom launched his project. But none of that involved "the laws of this Kingdom" – the common law and legislation of England. In British North America a massive proposal to codify united Canada's criminal law and procedure would be introduced in its legislature in 1850 but would never be proceeded with.[72] Work did not begin on Lower Canada's French-inspired *Civil Code* until 1857, and was not completed until 1866.[73] Extensive experimentation with common law codification by distinguished British legal scholars working for the Indian Law Commission had begun in 1834, but the resulting legislation was still years in the future. Although that commission had published a draft *Penal Code* in 1836, there is no indication that Adam Thom had access to it. As he sat down at his desk in Lower Fort Garry, on the banks of the Red River of the North, the recorder of Rupert's Land had nothing to guide him but the small library he brought from Montreal, his very limited experience as a lawyer, and his massive intelligence.

Thom's *Penal Code*,[74] written between late 1839 or early 1840 and 18 July 1840, was an elegantly structured and phrased, concise compendium of the essentials of English criminal law, "modified" in some respects to accord with Thom's perception of the differing conditions and needs of Rupert's Land, as well, in some instances, with his view of the common law's deficiencies.[75] Its ninety-six sections and seventeen explanatory notes are, unlike much of Thom's writing, relatively easy to read and understand. The modifications of English law he proposed for the Red River Settlement were few in number and not very radical. The most significant were simplifying the laws of larceny and breaking and entering; lowering the age of criminal responsibility from fourteen to seven if the child in question were proved mentally and physically capable of committing the crime; requiring clerics to assist police to suppress riots; and imposing more lenient punishments than in England.

Thom's *Civil Code*,[76] completed on 15 October 1840, just short of three months after he finished his *Penal Code*, was again concise – only forty-three sections in length, logically organized, and easy to read. It was accompanied, however, by two appendices of such prolixity and syntactical complexity that they would likely have left any Rupert's Land magistrate who tried to read them with serious intellectual indigestion. For the most part, the *Civil Code* dealt with procedural matters, addressing substantive law only in respect of a few aspects of the law of intestate succession.[77] In it Thom proposed a three-tier court system, consisting of a supreme court, superior court, and inferior court, to replace the existing structure of the general and petty courts. The jurisdiction of the inferior courts would be less extensive than that of the present petty courts. Juries, requiring only a majority of ten out of twelve members to decide cases, would invariably be employed in the two upper courts and could also be obtained in the inferior court if a party were willing to pay for the privilege. The courts would prepare written summaries of each party's position, and parties would be allowed to give evidence under oath, which was not possible under prevailing English law. The two appendices were learned essays on the law of evidence and a difficult legal concept known as domicile, of which only lawyers could make much sense.

REJECTION

Adam Thom's astonishing codification achievement was never adopted. London's initial response to his drafts – commendatory comments coupled with a cautious decision to postpone implementation for a year – was interpreted optimistically by Thom.[78] He was subsequently informed, however, in a surly letter from HBC secretary William G. Smith, that the company had decided not to proceed with codification. He should, instead, content himself with existing English law, "taking care to temper justice with mercy, and not to sentence anyone to such harsh judgments as may be called in question."[79] Spirited objections by the recorder failed to reverse that decision,[80] and subsequent attempts on his part to have all or part of the codes enacted locally were also unsuccessful.[81]

Why were Thom's codes so summarily and mean-spiritedly rejected by the company, given that it had requested them in the first place, that they were brilliantly composed in an amazingly short period of time, that the Council of Assiniboia had endorsed them, and that at least the *Penal Code* appears to have received an initially encouraging response from the Governor and Committee? It is highly likely that when the drafts were examined by the company's English legal advisors it was realized, as Thom must have known, that the HBC lacked the power to unilaterally amend either the common law of England or its own charter, that cooperation from the Crown and Parliament must therefore be sought, and that such cooperation was unlikely to be given. Another factor may have been the politely expressed but strong opposition of Assiniboia governor Finlayson to some of the codes' provisions.[82] But does any of that sufficiently explain London's complete about-face or the unpleasantly peremptory manner in which the entirety of the recorder's remarkable labours were rejected?

One plausible line of speculation is that London did not like some of Thom's "Observations." They were written before his codes and were originally intended to be seen by the Governor and Committee before the codes were submitted; but they did not in fact arrive in London until after both codes were in hand and the company's initial response to the *Penal Code* had been dispatched to Red River.[83] Could it be that after perusing certain of Thom's more uncomfortable "observations" – in particular his opinion that HBC courts could not entertain HBC litigation – the Governor and Committee were no longer disposed to look favourably upon the recorder's legal analyses and legislative efforts?

THE COURT, 1841–44

Although not much is known about the activities of the Quarterly Court of Assiniboia before November 1844, when the surviving court records commence, two partially recorded cases from the period 1841–44 are worthy of note.

Public Interest v. Atasawapah

At an HBC post somewhere in the Saskatchewan River territory, one day in early 1841, a young man by the name of Atasawapah – a Halfbreed – was severely provoked, and then physically assaulted, by an older fellow-employee – a Canadian called Flammond. The young man picked up a long fireplace poker and ran his tormenter through with it. Flammond died, and after the rivers were ice-free Atasawapah was brought, under arrest, to Red River for trial. He arrived in mid-June, between regular sessions of the court, while North American governor-in-chief Sir George Simpson (the knighthood was new) was preparing his annual report to London. Simpson added a paragraph saying that a special court sitting would be held for the case,[84] and later described the trial in his personal journal: "The first criminal case that has come before the Council of Assiniboia ..., the Recorder acting as their assessor, was tried during my stay, and at which I presided ... There was evidence of the deceased's having offered great provocation, [and] the jury therefore returned a verdict of manslaughter, and the Court sentenced the prisoner to one year's imprisonment with hard labor. Before quitting the Settlement, I dispatched him to York Factory ... there to undergo the term of his imprisonment."[85]

That account is interesting for several reasons. Why Simpson described it as the "first" criminal trial is difficult to understand, unless he meant that it was the first he had attended, the first potentially capital case, or perhaps the first unscheduled sitting of the court. His description of the recorder as an "assessor" was only partly accurate. In Roman and Scottish law an assessor sat with governors and lay magistrates at trials to assist them with questions of law and procedure, and the recorder of Rupert's Land certainly performed that role. But true assessors had no adjudicative function, whereas Adam Thom, as a member of the Council of Assiniboia, was a full-fledged and forcefully influential member of the court.[86]

Atasawapah's sentence, and the manner in which it was carried out, is also of much interest. Echoing, whether consciously or not, the assertion in Thom's "Observations" that North Americans felt the restriction of imprisonment more intensely than did the English, Simpson's journal entry went on to comment, "[S]o great an evil is confinement to persons of such roving habits as the Indians and Halfbreeds, that it is to them worse than death itself."[87] Exile from one's homeland to unfamiliar territory was also a very painful experience for many, as this case would demonstrate.

Whether the court's sentence included exile in this case, or Simpson simply took it upon himself to impose it afterward, is not known with certainty; but a letter from Simpson to Donald Ross and James Hargrave suggests, by attributing the imprisonment to the "sentence of the Court" but calling the exile a matter of "request,"[88] that the latter was the case.

There is plenty of evidence concerning the impact of both imprisonment and exile upon Atasawapah. Letitia Hargrave, who had come to York Factory about a year previously as the bride of its long-time chief factor James Hargrave, recorded the convict's arrival there in September 1841 in a letter to her father back in England: "We had to create a jail this year, the first there has been at York. The inmate is a Halfbreed ... found guilty of manslaughter and condemned to a year's imprisonment at York and banishment to Ungava on Hudson's Straits. I have not seen him, but they say he is a harmless gentle-looking boy. The poor creature was brought from Red River in irons and had not been changed, so that he was in a shocking state when he reached York."[89]

A little more than six months later, Mrs Hargrave reported to her father on how the prisoner had survived the winter: "The poor prisoner is still in gaol, and a miserable-looking object. He had a fine face when put in, but now looks like an old woman. He is ... very gentle, I don't think older than 19 at the most."[90] She also noted his release from prison and departure from York – not for home but for remoter regions still – in September 1842:

> The prisoner was released and sent off to Ungava, Hudson's Straits – in pity. He had never been farther than the length of his short fetters for a year, and when he got out he could scarcely walk, and had forgotten all his French. He came quite briskly to take leave, and shook hands with Joseph [her one-year-old son] and me, as if he had been a Methodist preacher. [Her husband, Chief Factor James] Hargrave[,] made a speech to him, explaining that it was from kind motives that he was not sent back to the plains, as the white people there would have annoyed him. He was satisfied at not going, but defended himself quite vehemently for killing the man, and if I

might judge him from his gestures, he would have had great pleasure in doing it again.[91]

Even if the dubious claim that Atasawapah was "satisfied" with his further exile were true, others were certainly not satisfied: "His friends on the Saskatchewan were much exasperated, and altho' they have settled down ... several of them declare that if he does not return safe, they will make *pemmican* of someone."[92] Governor Simpson continued, however, to insist that the exile be enforced. Almost two years after Atasawapah received his one-year sentence from the Quarterly Court of Assiniboia, Simpson wrote to the chief factor in whose territory the exiled man was working: "The man Atasawapah, who was sent from York with the intention of being forwarded to Ungava, must not on any account be allowed to return ... [T]ake especial care that he be not allowed to escape. While treating him with lenity, however, it ought to be borne in mind that he is a very dangerous character."[93]

What was there about this "very gentle" Halfbreed youth, driven to kill by the provocative behaviour of the deceased, that convinced Sir George Simpson he must serve his imprisonment at distant York Factory, where a jail had to be built especially for the purpose? And what so impressed him of the young man's continuing dangerousness that he inflicted what seems to have been intended as life-long unlawful exile to even remoter parts of the north? The only answer that makes sense is that the threat posed to the company and the settlement by Atasawapah lay in his very gentleness. The jury had reduced his murder charge to a manslaughter conviction because he had been severely provoked by his non-Aboriginal victim. Both Letitia Hargrave and her tough-minded chief factor husband found his conduct to be exemplary and spoke sympathetically of his situation. Glyndwr Williams tells us that "there were symptoms of impending [Halfbreed] eruptions" at Red River not long after his conviction,[94] pointing to an 1842 letter to Simpson from the normally unflappable Assiniboia governor Duncan Finlayson complaining of having to combat "so many conflicting opinions and passions" and deploring that "[t]he Halfbreed part of the population have already had too much of their own way and, perceiving the weakness of the Company to check them, are becoming daily more arrogant."[95] It appears, therefore, that Simpson and his advisors, knowing they were sitting on a powder keg at Red River that could perhaps be ignited by sparks of sympathy for a young man widely believed to have been wrongly convicted and harshly sentenced, decided to do everything in their power to remove him from view and to keep him that way for as long as possible.

Rothney v. Thom

The other trial of note involved the recorder himself as defendant.[96] When the Thoms came to Red River, they brought with them a young Scottish woman named Helen Rothney as a housemaid and companion for Mrs Thom. Her contract, for five years commencing 16 March 1839, entitled her to £24 a year, payable semi-annually but to be retained in safekeeping by Thom except for small sums to meet her immediate needs. About the second week of November 1842, a bitter argument took place between Helen Rothney and Anne Thom, probably triggered by the discovery that the girl was five months pregnant. Turned out of the Thoms' home without payment of the back wages being held on her account, Rothney sued the recorder in his own court. The trial took place in February 1843 before the governor of Assiniboia, the magistrate members of the court, and a jury. Although she would marry the father of the child she was carrying about a month after the trial, and he could have sued on her behalf if they had been married before the trial, Miss Rothney chose to face the court and her formidable former employer on her own.[97] She was nonetheless successful – more so, in fact, than she had expected to be. Although she had claimed only payment up to the date of her discharge, the court awarded damages for her entire five-year contract period.[98]

Almost immediately after this humiliating loss at the hands of his judicial colleagues, Adam Thom prepared and delivered to them an extraordinary "circular" castigating them for what he claimed were several errors in law and threatening to appeal.[99] The appeal threat was intriguing since there was nothing in the HBC charter or in the Laws of Assiniboia that suggested the possibility of appealing from a ruling of the General Quarterly Court of Assiniboia, and Thom knew this. Although his "Observations" pointed to the possibility of appealing to the Crown by an arcane process known as a writ of error,[100] he had acknowledged to Simpson that there was a "practical absence" of appeals.[101]

His threat to "appeal" the *Rothney* decision was not an empty bluff, however. The decision in favour of Helen Rothney was a jury verdict. Jury verdicts do not have direct legal force of their own. Before such a decision can be made binding on the parties, it must become the subject of a formal judgment by the court itself. Lacking the recorder to advise them about such technical niceties, the governor and magistrates had overlooked this formality in the *Rothney* case. So Thom took the legally correct position that since the proceeding was not complete until a judgment was issued it was still open to him to request the court to overturn the jury's verdict on the basis of the errors of law that his circular alleged.[102] Toward the end of the circular, Thom suggested that he was willing to drop his "appeal" in return for an agreed compromise; and the parties appear to have settled the dispute by his payment of wages earned up to the point of termination. Letitia Hargrave later reported that "the magistrates were indignant at her compromising."[103]

MATTERS NOT ADJUDICATED

Several events occurred during this period that could have resulted in proceedings before the General Quarterly Court but did not. In some instances, the reasons they did not do so tell us as much about the state of justice in the HBC empire as if the court had become involved.

Thomas Simpson's Death

The courier to whom Adam Thom entrusted the delivery of his "Observations" to London in 1840 had been Thomas Simpson, the governor-in-chief's cousin. Since the time, back in 1834, when he provoked a near-riot by striking a Halfbreed employee with a poker, Thomas Simpson had distinguished himself as an Arctic explorer for the company. After requesting authority to extend his explorations, and having received no response from London, the explorer had returned to Red River, determined to travel to England and press his proposal personally. He accordingly set off for the nearest US rail connection, initially joining a party of settlers heading in the same direction. The settlers moved too slowly for the impatient Simpson, however, and when the group was a day or two south of Pembina he engaged three guides, two of whom were Halfbreeds, to help him move on at a faster pace. Thomas Simpson never reached his destination. On 15 June, a week and a half after leaving Red River, his body was found on the prairie, along with those of two of his guides – one French Canadian and one Halfbreed. The circumstances of the deaths were never clearly determined. Strangely, word of the tragedy did not get back to Red River until October. The southbound settlers, having sent some of their number and the surviving guide to examine the scene of the killings and bury the dead, continued on to their destinations in St Peter's, St Paul, and elsewhere; and nothing was done to notify settlement authorities before they returned in the fall.[104]

Sir George Simpson chose to interpret that delay, together with some discrepancies in the affidavits of witnesses, as indicating a revenge killing by Halfbreeds still angry over the 1834 incident. His theory was that the two deceased guides were killed by Thomas Simpson in self-defence before the third man murdered him.[105] Sheriff Alexander Ross did not accept those suspicions. When news of the killings eventually reached Fort Garry, Ross was sent to investigate the matter as sheriff and magistrate. In doing so, he examined the witnesses under oath and travelled to the scene of the tragedy with a physician from the settlement. The surroundings were examined as thoroughly as the passage of four months permitted, and the bodies were exhumed and examined medically. Ross's finding was that Thomas Simpson, who had been acting aberrantly since before leaving Red River and had become increasingly irrational as the journey progressed, had shot the two guides under a delusion that they were plotting to kill him, and that when the third guide returned to the scene with others from the settlers' group the following day, Simpson took his own life.[106] No charges were therefore laid.

John McLoughlin's Killing

A year and a half later, a ship bearing Sir George Simpson moored at a small post called Fort Stikine in Alaska – Russian territory at the time. Simpson had been largely responsible, a few years earlier, for negotiating a treaty between Great Britain and Russia that ended competition from the Russian American Fur Company and authorized the HBC to operate in Alaska. The Stikine establishment had been placed under the charge of a rather junior company officer, John McLoughlin – the son of Dr John McLoughlin Sr, who headed HBC operations on the Pacific coast and was almost as legendary a figure in the company pantheon as Simpson himself. Aware that young McLoughlin's record of service was not exemplary, Sir George had come to see how he was handling this new and more demanding responsibility.

The first thing the governor-in-chief noticed as his ship approached Stikine was that its flags were at half-mast. They were in that state because the officer-in-charge, John McLoughlin Jr, had been shot dead by a company employee a few days prior to the ship's arrival. Simpson proceeded to take affidavits from those he considered reliable witnesses and quickly – too quickly – concluded that although McLouglin had unquestionably been shot by an employee, the killing was not culpable: "[I]t appears that Mr. McLoughlin's conduct and management during the past year were quite disgraceful; that he had become a slave to licentiousness and dissipation; that his treatment of the people was exceedingly violent and oppressive, and very frequently cruel in the extreme ... From [depositions taken] there was every reason to believe that the fatal shot was fired by a Canadian named Heureux, but under circumstances that, in my humble opinion, would in an English court of justice be pronounced a justifiable homicide."[107]

This report was dispatched to London at the first opportunity, and a copy was included in an extremely callous letter from Simpson to young McLoughlin's father.[108] Sir George also took the perpetrator, Urbain Heureux, on board his ship and delivered him, with copies of the depositions of witnesses, to Russian authorities in Sitka. He hoped, no doubt, that since the shooting had occurred on Russian territory, he could wash his hands of the affair. But although Simpson requested the Russian governor to deal with the matter "according to law," he added the proviso that "no measure should be taken that will affect the life of ... Heureux" until both the British and Russian governments were consulted.[109]

Dr McLoughlin, perhaps as much upset by the harshness of Simpson's letter as by the death of his son,[110] responded to the allegations angrily and energetically. He sent a colleague to Stikine to conduct a more thorough investigation than Simpson's, and dispatched the resulting voluminous evidence to London. That evidence effectively refuted the charges against McLoughlin Jr and strongly suggested an employee conspiracy to murder him. So persuasive was the evidence, in fact, that the Governor and Committee tentatively decided to request the British government to ask Russian authorities to hold a trial. Dr McLoughlin made the same request himself directly to the Russian governor at Sitka, delivering a second accused man to him as well. When Simpson got wind of these initiatives, he lobbied the Governor and Committee to change their minds, and seems to have succeeded.[111] In any event, the Russians refused to become involved, and in February 1844 the Sitka governor informed Simpson, "I regret very much not to be able to comply with the wishes of Mr. ... McLoughlin to keep the prisoners here any longer, because I am informed from St. Petersbourg that it is impossible to try them by the Russian laws, although the crime was committed on the

Russian territories, but not in presence of Russian authorities, or Russian subjects; and at the same time it is ordered to send them back by the first opportunity ... for which reason I have now delivered them to Mr. Mauson [Dr McLoughlin's agent]."[112]

Once the prisoners were under McLoughlin's control, he sent them, along with eleven witnesses and an interpreter, to Red River for trial by the Council of Rupert's Land at its annual convocation, due to be held there in June.[113] Simpson countered that move as well – with the help of the recorder of Rupert's Land. On 10 June, just prior to the council meeting, Simpson placed all of McLoughlin's documentation before Adam Thom, with the request that he peruse it "with your best attention in order that you may give your opinion in writing to be laid before the Council as to the proper courses to be pursued in reference to this perplexing subject."[114] Sir George was not disappointed with the recorder's analysis. As he later informed London, "[T]he Council, acting upon the opinion and advice of the Company's principal legal adviser in Rupert's land, ... declined taking any steps towards bringing the parties to trial."[115]

Dr McLoughlin, who was as stubborn a man as George Simpson, then insisted that the prisoners and witnesses be sent on to Canada, and they became, along with the packet of depositions, a part of Simpson's canoe entourage home. Before leaving Red River, Simpson wrote to the Russian governor of Sitka, thanking him for his assistance and assuring him that "the unfortunate occurrence ... is ... about to be submitted to our [Canadian] tribunals."[116] Simpson was not really willing for that to happen, of course; and when the party got to Canada he persuaded the attorney general that a prosecution would not be likely to succeed.[117] The jurisdiction of the Canadian courts was also far from clear, and although the attorney general was personally "very anxious to prosecute the case," Simpson's impression after the meeting was that a recommendation would be made for trial in England.[118] Such a recommendation appears to have been made, but the company refused, no doubt at Simpson's urging, to pay the transportation costs involved, and the matter ended there. "McLoughlin ... sadly realized that 'as it would cost to send the case to England, where alone it can be tried, at least ten thousand pounds,' he had to finish with it."[119] Although the consensus of both contemporary opinion and modern historians is that Dr McLoughlin's view of the case was correct,[120] the wishes of Sir George Simpson were not to be challenged.

Abitibi Massacre

Another category of unadjudicated wrongdoings involved situations left to be dealt with by traditional means. Sir George Simpson described such an incident, and its unofficial resolution, in a letter to London: "The establishment of Abitibi, heretofore so profitable, was less productive last season than usual, owing in some degree ... to an excitement arising from the murder in [the] course of the winter of eight members of one of their principal families at an encampment. Several weeks elapsed before the perpetrator of this foul murder was discovered ... But it was at length ascertained that the sole actor in this tragedy was a female of unsound mind, a member of the family, whose destruction by some of her own relatives restored tranquility."[121]

Windigo Killing

A more spectacular incident of the same kind, which occurred at Fort Severn on the Hudson Bay coast at about the same time, suggests that HBC policy in such matters was not always *entirely* passive. In some parts of that region, Native religious cults based on distortions of Christian beliefs and ceremonies had been on the rise,[122] and some unscrupulous "messiahs" had turned the trend to their own profit. James Hargrave, chief factor at York Factory, described one such situation to Simpson in December 1843: "[O]ne of my Indians, named Abishabis, ... set up for a prophet, and by his bold blasphemies had actually drawn after him almost all the natives on this coast between Churchill and Severn. These paid him tithes of clothing, arms and ammunition in such quantities that, from being one of the most worthless, idle and miserable among his countrymen, he found himself raised all at once to the rank of high priest of the tribe."[123]

Abishabis overreached, however, and when he demanded that a number of his followers also surrender their wives to him, his divinity began to be doubted. He soon then fell from favour altogether, and disappeared for a while. When he reappeared, he was thought to have been responsible for the horrible murder of five members of an Indian family. Cannibalism may have been involved in the crime, because he was thereafter feared as a human-flesh-eating "Windigo."[124]

Hargrave assured Simpson that he had instructed his officers in the area to adopt a hands-off policy in the matter: "I gave ... them strict injunctions that, as the affair was one entirely confined to the natives, they were on no account to take the murderer prisoner, or to allow any in the Company's service to take any part in the punishment of his crime." "But," he continued, "at the same time they were enjoined to (privately) excite the natives, especially the relations of the deceased, to do justice upon the homicide themselves." At first, that tactic did not work. When the suspect showed up at Severn, the local Indians "fled from him as an evil spirit ... crowding into the fort like a flock of sheep."

Although Hargrave said nothing about it in his letter, other accounts suggest that, in order to persuade the refugees to leave the fort, Abishabis was, contrary to Hargrave's orders, taken into custody by company officers.[125] Later, the prisoner somehow escaped, and Hargrave took up the story again at that point: "[A]t length one of ... [the local Indians] took heart ... and, in reply to some of his threats, knocked him on the head with a hatchet; after which the whole band of them ... dragged the body to an island and burned it – to secure themselves against being haunted by a 'Windigo.'" "My great aim through all this," Hargrave concluded, "was to ensure the execution of justice ... without involving the Company." Adam Thom's ideal that the rule of law should prevail uniformly throughout Rupert's Land had yet to be fully realized.

Dr McLoughlin's Violence

Nor was the company's laissez-faire attitude toward violence always restricted to the conduct of the Native population. In April 1844, before the rancorous affair of the Stikine killing had fully subsided, Governor Simpson received a complaint that the victim's father (and Simpson's nemesis), Chief Factor Dr John McLoughlin, had, while passing through Rupert's Land in 1838, beaten an employee so severely that the man died the following year. The governor-in-chief's response was to forward the complaint for investigation *by the alleged assailant McLoughlin himself,* saying that he was "leaving ... [the interrogation of witnesses] to be done by you should you consider such necessary."[126] Not surprisingly, Dr McLoughlin did not consider an investigation of his own behaviour to be necessary.

CHANGING TIMES

The early 1840s were a major economic watershed for Rupert's Land: a time of transition from the subsistence-living patterns that had prevailed since time immemorial to a market-dominated economy. The fur trade had always been part of a market economy, of course, but except in the days of intense HBC-NWC competition, bargaining power had been unequal. So far as HBC employees and suppliers, and Red River's settlers, were concerned, market competition had been relatively unknown. As Gerald Friesen puts it, "[N]ative and European co-operated peacefully for two centuries, between 1640 and 1840," in the western fur trade, but thereafter "the market economy and industrial capitalism re-created the entire region even as it had transformed England a century before."[127]

Gerhard Ens has described the major role the Halfbreeds, leveraging American competition, played in this process, and the effect the shift had on their way of life and their identity as a people.[128] The change was seen dramatically in the buffalo hunt, once of economic importance chiefly as the supplier of pemmican to the fur trade but now increasingly concerned with buffalo robes and tallow as well. The increasing proximity of American traders offered the Halfbreeds alternatives to the HBC as market outlets for their robes and other products – a risk to the HBC that was boldly illustrated by the 1843 establishment of Norman Kittson's trading post at Pembina, immediately south of the US border, and by the company's responsive reopening of a rival post at a nearby location on British soil.

These developments contributed much to the Halfbreeds' growing understanding of their significance as a people and to the HBC's growing concern about that metamorphosis of consciousness. Both Governor Simpson's overreaction to the possibility that Atasawapah's conviction and imprisonment would provoke retaliation by sympathetic kinsmen, and his belief that his cousin had been murdered by Halfbreed conspirators, were undoubtedly rooted in his realization that forces inimical to white hegemony were stirring.[129]

Not unrelated to those fears was Sir George's continuing concern that the settlement was getting too large. Seeing emigration as a way to relieve the pressure of population growth, and wanting at the same time to counteract the American immigration to Oregon that he considered a threat to company operations there, Simpson hired a young English Halfbreed named James Sinclair to lead an exodus of twenty-three Red River families to homesteads on the Columbia River.[130] A third bird he hoped to kill with that particular stone was the removal of Sinclair himself from the settlement for a time – Sinclair being an educated man and an independent trader with the potential to lead his people in directions Simpson did not want them to go. Although Sinclair's mission was successful, it would not be repeated for quite some time. The Oregon question was becoming a problem that could not be dealt with by such simple means. After returning to Red River, James Sinclair turned his full attention to commercial activities – to an extent that would soon place him seriously at odds with Sir George Simpson and the HBC.

As his term as governor of Assiniboia neared its conclusion, Duncan Finlayson decided he was unwilling to serve a second tour of duty. He had been unhappy for quite some time, and his concerns, like those of Governor-in-Chief Simpson, centred on Halfbreed discontent. As early as August 1842, Finlayson had informed Simpson, "I am heartily tired of this place ... where there are so many conflicting opinions and passions to combat." Moreover, he said, "The Halfbreed part of the population have already had too much of their own way, and, perceiving the weakness of the Company to check them, are becoming daily more arrogant in ... deportment."[131] When Finlayson moved on to another posting in November 1844, thoughtful observers in the settlement may have wondered whether – and how – his successor would be able to address the new Halfbreed self-awareness.

In the Canadas, the sequelae of the recent rebellions were being felt. Lord Durham's report had led to passage of the Act of Union of 1840,[132] welding the former colonies of Upper and Lower Canada into a single colony with unified governmental structures. As the consequences of that constitutional revolution worked themselves out, there would be major long-term implications for Rupert's Land. For the time being, though, Canada was preoccupied with its own concerns.

RECORDER UNFAZED

So was the recorder of Rupert's Land. The monumental legal change for which Adam Thom had hoped – adoption of the world's first large-scale codification of English law – had not occurred, but he did not seem disheartened by that setback. He appears, in fact, to have been generally quite content with his life at Red River.[133] The disdain with which he was now regarded by many of his colleagues on the court and council did not seem to trouble him; and the various economic, social, and political changes discussed above had little visible impact on the Thoms' tranquil existence at the Stone Fort. Although Adam and Anne lost their first child, a girl, shortly after her birth in May 1840,[134] they were blessed with a son in early 1844.[135] Also in 1844, Thom's Aberdeen alma mater awarded him an honorary doctorate of laws.[136]

There was plenty to occupy his time. As the company's resident legal advisor, he was asked from time to time for legal opinions on a variety of topics, such as the HBC's land rights in Oregon, its right to discipline absconding employees who sought refuge there,[137] and the issues arising from the shooting of young John McLoughlin. Even when he was not asked for legal opinions, Thom's rich imagination spontaneously generated questions he considered to be of interest, and he answered them without waiting to be asked. What were the company's rights in the McKenzie River region?[138] How strong, legally, was the HBC trading monopoly under the charter?[139] Would it be desirable to empower HBC officers, and clergymen other than Catholics and Anglicans, to solemnize marriages in HBC territories?[140] Did the bishop of Montreal have authority to ordain Anglican ministers in Rupert's Land?[141] Thom even took it upon himself to propose a tax on the pews of Protestant churches in order to offset the possible withdrawal of financial support from church organizations.[142] That most of his voluntary opinions encountered short shrift in London[143] does not seem to have troubled the self-assured Thom very much. Although it is doubtful that his private practice at Red River was ever very extensive, he was consulted by private clients from time to time. In June 1843, for instance, Simpson recommended that Thom provide advice to a beneficiary of an estate of which Simpson was the executor.[144]

Sir George made a globe-circling trip in 1841–42, and approached Adam Thom after his return to help him write a journal-based book documenting his travels. At first Thom felt obliged to decline because he had neither personal knowledge nor a sufficient library to acquaint himself with the areas in question,[145] but he was eventually persuaded to become a major ghost-writer of Simpson's book.[146] In the meantime, he had a book of his own to fill his days – a complex study of biblical prophecy that he hoped would make it possible to predict the end of terrestrial existence. When that task was completed at the end of June 1844, Thom sent the manuscript, which he described as "a marvellously curious treatise entitled 'Arithmetic of Prophecy,'" to Simpson with the request that the latter deliver it to a publisher in England.[147]

Adam Thom's first five-year contract expired in 1844. With Simpson's apparent support, he attempted to negotiate a higher salary for a second term[148] but failed.[149] When he was reappointed as recorder for another five years, it was on the same (very generous) terms as his first.

5

Recorder Thom at His Peak, 1844–48

With a chiefly Halfbreed population of about 5,000, the Red River Settlement was now a permanent, increasingly attractive, relatively stable community. The economy was healthy, and people got along reasonably well. The trauma of the Red River's first and only hanging, the heartbreak of drought, and the decimation of a vicious epidemic tended to unite the disparate population, and the arrival of a British military garrison brought further calm. Trouble was nevertheless brewing due to the determination of the Hudson's Bay Company to enforce its asserted trade monopoly more stringently than ever and Recorder Adam Thom's ham-handed efforts to assist.

The surviving records of the General Quarterly Court of Assiniboia begin with its November 1844 session, permitting the court's work to be more thoroughly observed than previously.

THE RECORDS ERA

The first of the extant continuous records of the General Quarterly Court of Assiniboia date from November 1844, and the series runs without break thereafter until the court was replaced by the Manitoba Court of Queen's Bench in mid-1872. Complete transcriptions of those records are available, along with annotations and commentaries, in volume 2 of this study. Earlier records existed at one time, probably dating back to the court's first sittings in 1835 or 1836,[1] but their fate is unknown. It was rumoured that during the occupation of Upper Fort Garry by Louis Riel's Provisional Government in 1869–70, a number of records were either hidden by HBC employees or disposed of by Riel supporters in the fort's well and never recovered.[2] If that is true, perhaps the first volume of the General Court records met a similar fate. Unfortunate as

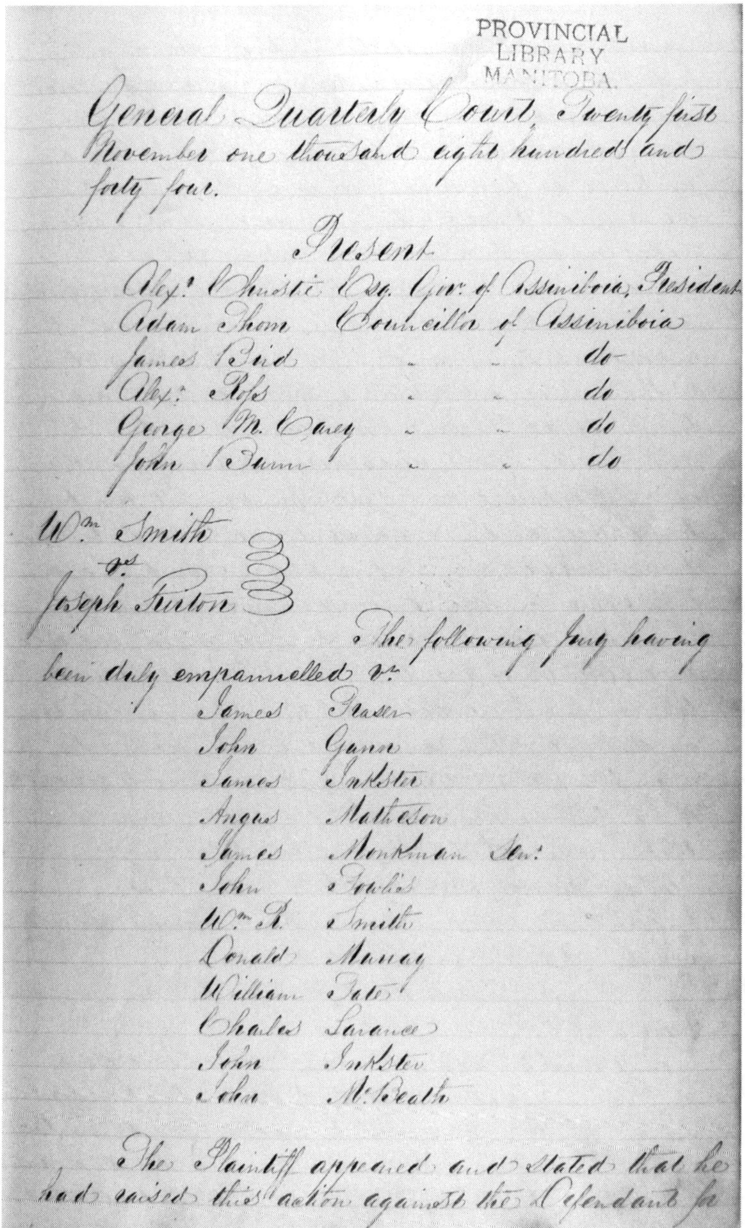
PROVINCIAL
LIBRARY
MANITOBA.

General Quarterly Court, Twenty first November one thousand eight hundred and forty four.

Present

Alexr Christie Esq. Govr. of Assiniboia, President
Adam Thom Councillor of Assiniboia
James Bird - - do
Alexr Ross - - do
George M. Cary - - do
John Bunn - - do

Wm Smith
vs.
Joseph Tirton

The following jury having been duly empannelled viz:

James Fraser
John Gunn
James Inkster
Angus Matheson
James Monkman Senr.
John Fowlis
Wm R. Smith
Donald Murray
William Tate
Charles Larance
John Inkster
John McBeath

The Plaintiff appeared and stated that he had raised this action against the Defendant for

Figure 5.1 Page of the General Quarterly Court of Assiniboia records.

that loss is, the intact survival of the records for the remaining twenty-eight years of the court's existence offers historians a unique opportunity to observe its operation and evolution through contemporary eyes, and to glimpse beyond the courthouse doors the slowly maturing society that brought its troubles through them.

THE SETTLEMENT

Red River had not changed much in the past few years, but its development since the arrival of the first Selkirk Settlers in 1812, and even since the settlement's reorganization in 1822, had been extensive. A population of some 5,000 was now spread along the Red and Assiniboine Rivers – from the French Halfbreed settlements on the White Horse Plains in the west and at St Norbert parish in the south to the Indian village of St Peter's in the north. Roughly 10 per cent of the settlement's population was of purely European origin, French or British, and another 10 per cent was Indian. The remaining 80 per cent was of mixed Aboriginal-European ancestry, about 30 per cent anglophone and 50 per cent francophone.[3]

The population tended to cluster ethnically. French-speaking, Roman Catholic enclaves flourished on the White Horse Plains, on the Red River south of the Forks, and most noticeably, near Bishop J.N. Provencher's imposing twin-towered riverside cathedral across from the mouth of the Assiniboine. The latter community was enriched, in June 1844, by the arrival of a group of Grey Nuns (Sisters of Charity) who, setting themselves up beside the cathedral, began almost immediately providing educational and medical services to the French population.[4] Facing the cathedral on the west bank of the Red and the north bank of the Assiniboine stood Upper Fort Garry, which, although the hub of the HBC's commercial activities and the seat of Assiniboia's government, was not a residential location for anyone other than company employees. Anglophone settlers were dispersed along the Red River north of the Upper Fort, chiefly on the west bank, and on the north side of the Assiniboine from a little below modern St James down to the Forks. Most were congregated around Protestant parish churches. About a half-mile north of the Upper Fort, where the overland trails of the Assiniboine and Red Rivers met, was a small scatter of buildings that would eventually form the nucleus of the future City of Winnipeg. Farther north, in an area that came to be known as St John's, was another anglophone community, and beyond that the original Scottish Selkirk Settlers and their descendants occupied farms in an area called Kildonan. The bulk of the English Halfbreeds lived below Kildonan in or near St Andrew's parish. Between the "Grand Rapids" at St Andrew's and the Indian settlement at St Peter's was Lower Fort Garry: the terminus for canoe and boat brigades, the relatively tranquil occasional residence of Governor-in-Chief George Simpson, and the home of Recorder Adam Thom and his family.

Farm fields were narrow and long, often extending 2 miles back from the rivers – with hay lands, both private and common, beyond.[5] The settlement's appearance had improved over the years, and probably looked very much at this time as it would to an American visitor seven years later: "[T]hese narrow farms ... [have] their dwellings and the farm outbuildings spread along the riverfront, with lawns sloping to the water's edge and shrubbery and vines liberally trained around them, and trees intermingled – the whole presenting the appearance of a long suburban village – such as you might see near our eastern seaboard, or such as you find exhibited in pictures of English country villages ... [There are] numerous windmills, some in motion, whirling around their giant arms, while others, motionless, are waiting for a 'grist.'"[6]

Agriculture and the HBC's operations were not Red River's sole economic pursuits. The twice-yearly buffalo hunt drew away a sizable proportion of the settlement's Halfbreed population every spring and fall in quest of meat, buffalo robes, and tallow. A year when a poor hunt and poor crops coincided was a bad year indeed. A growing number of settlers were also engaged in cartage work, conducting caravans of Red River carts[7] to St Peter's, St Paul, and other American centres for trade goods to stock the shelves of private shops and for other supplies. Such individual commercial intercourse with the United States was becoming a concern for the Hudson's Bay Company.

In the physical, economic, and legal senses, the community was making modest progress. In June 1845 the Council of Assiniboia authorized the establishment of a public ferry service across both rivers, the construction of a distillery,[8] and the creation of a Committee of Economy charged with finding ways to increase the settlement's prosperity. At the same meeting of the council, the local laws of Assiniboia were strengthened in several respects, especially in relation to causing or contributing to the intoxication of Indians; and a new bilingual procedure for publicizing new legislation was agreed upon.[9] Red River society seemed reasonably stable. It is true that a newcomer to the settlement in the summer of 1844 reported to his family back home that the place was rife with rumour; but he admitted that this was "usual in small communities."[10] Generally speaking, the inhabitants got along well with each other.

A lively letter from Dr John Bunn to a friend in early 1848 testifies to Red River's robust social activities, especially in winter.[11] It was, the doctor said, "Such a winter for wind, snowdrift and turbulence [as] would induce one to believe that the Devil himself 'rides on the whirlwind and directs the storm.'" Yet, despite "the mountains of drift in ... which we are entombed," there had been so many parties and balls that to describe them all would be a "task beyond the weakness of human nature." Merely to enumerate them would be a "Herculean labor." Bunn then painted a word picture for his friend of what he called "*the* ball," recently held, which, "like the feast of O'Rourke, 'T'will never be forgot by those who were there and those who were not'":

> The Lady Patroness [probably the governor's wife] was in full bloom, radiant in silk and gold ... The room was most tastefully decorated with stars ... [as well as] elegant festoons of evergreens ... The amusements commenced with Dr. Duncan's choir singing "God Save the Queen," ... and they further added to the enjoyment of the evening by occasionally interspersing choice songs and glees, which were sung in a style hitherto unheard by the echos of Rupert's Land. Polkas, gallops, waltzes, quadrilles, cotillions, country dances, reels, and jigs employed the heels and talents of the assembly. There were cards for the infirm and lazy, brandy and tobacco for the thirsty, and unremitting hospitality for all. At midnight there was an elegant supper consisting of all the delicacies nature and art could afford, to which ample justice was done. At its close, my memory expired: all became hiccough and happiness. Indistinct visions wrapt the senses in bliss, and a faithful version is lost to the world.

"But such frivolity cannot endure," Dr Bunn's letter concluded. "Next day brought headaches and reflections." And a few criticisms: "[T]he parsons ... railed at dancing as a damnable sin, which no lady would believe ... Papas may remonstrate, parsons may dispense brimstone by wholesale, but the girls will dance." As for himself, there was only one small regret: "I did fancy, now and then, [that] an odor [of perfume] from 'Araby the blest' would have been an agreeable addition to the charms of some. Women, God bless them, are lovely creatures, and would be angels if they did not perspire."

Not far below the jovial surface, however, elemental forces were shifting. The major economic and social transformation of Rupert's Land discussed earlier was underway.[12] And as in other parts of British North America, the slow ferment of political change had begun. In Canada, as we have seen, popular resistance to just such undemocratic governmental oligarchies as the HBC maintained at Red River had triggered Lord Durham's mission and the fusion of the Upper and Lower Canadian colonies, and was close to spawning responsible democratic government there.[13] Few doubted that the potential for similar resistance existed here too. Whether or not Frits Pannekoek is fully justified in saying that "Red River, taken as a whole, was a society ... of brittleness, whose parts were mutually antagonistic,"[14] it would not be long before that description was accurate.

GOVERNOR CHRISTIE'S COUNCIL

Alexander Christie was back as governor of Assiniboia, replacing Duncan Finlayson in 1844. A seasoned company officer widely respected for his management skills, probity, and good nature, Christie had been described in 1832 by Governor-in-Chief Simpson as "one of our best characters."[15] Alexander Ross would later call him "a kind urbane man," if a little too much wedded to company policy.[16] This was his second term as governor. During his first term, from 1833 to 1839, he had participated in the major restructuring that created Assiniboia's quarterly courts in 1835, and had presided over the General Quarterly Court until Adam Thom's arrival in the settlement.[17]

Christie's second appointment did not seem, at first, to herald any further change in Red River's governance. The faces he saw around the table at his first meeting with the Council of Assiniboia on 19 June 1844 were, for the most part, the familiar settlement patriarchs. All had been appointed by the HBC Governor and Committee on recommendation of the local company leadership, private residents of Red River having had no say in the matter. And certain segments of the community had been deliberately excluded. Although there was some representation from English Halfbreeds, the only francophone councillor was Bishop Provencher;[18] and the Indian population was completely unrepresented. There would be a few changes of individual councillors during the 1844–48 period, but the method of selection and the essential makeup of the council would not change.

To the extent that the council had a "left wing," it consisted of Andrew McDermot,[19] John Bunn,[20] Cuthbert Grant,[21] and Alexander Ross.[22] McDermot, a wealthy independent trader whom company officials never quite trusted, kowtowed to no one. Dr John Bunn, a native-born, Scottish-educated, mixed-blood physician who provided exemplary service to the settlement in medical, conciliar, administrative, and judicial capacities, was both conservative and conciliatory by temperament; but his basic humanity was sometimes at odds with official policy. Cuthbert Grant, the legendary Halfbreed leader whom Simpson had appointed "Warden of the Plains," at an annual stipend of £200, to ensure he refrained from free trading and kept his followers in line, was occasionally carried away by his out-sized personality, hot temper, taste for liquor, and passionate devotion to his people's interests. Grant acted as a kind of freewheeling deputy to Sheriff Alexander Ross, who, like McDermot, was a freethinker and could sometimes also be counted among the "loyal opposition." But even this minority of relatively liberal-minded councillors were appointees of the company. It is hard to tell whether, on occasion, they caused the enactment of more public-spirited laws than would otherwise have been passed, since council meetings were held in camera and, at this stage, its minutes rarely indicated dissent, or even suggested the course of debate.

SUPPRESSION OF FREE TRADE

Although the second Christie regime did not, therefore, seem portentous at the outset, the new governor had a special mission, and his efforts to carry it out, abetted by sly devices designed by the imaginative recorder, were soon creating turmoil. The HBC always claimed, despite consistent legal advice to the contrary, that the trading monopoly purportedly granted by its 1670 charter was lawful and legally enforceable; and whenever it detected or suspected competing operations, it moved to close them down.[23] From the time the Hudson's Bay and North West Companies fused in 1821 until the early 1840s, such threats of competition were relatively few. To eliminate challenges from the United States, Governor-in-Chief Simpson had reached an amicable noncompetition agreement with the American Fur Company, its major counterpart south of the 49th parallel.[24] Competition from the Alaska-based Russian-American Fur Company was nipped in the bud by an international agreement leasing the Alaska trade to the HBC. Closer to home, Simpson had transformed the company's greatest potential local rival, Andrew McDermot, into an ally for the time being by licensing him to trade with Indians on condition that he resell the furs solely to the company.[25]

But in 1843 an American trader, Norman Kittson, established a trading post at Pembina, just south of the US border, and was soon attracting considerable business from British territory, among both Indians and independent middlemen. It was largely to combat the Kittson threat that Simpson assigned Alexander Christie, known as a hard-nosed if straight-dealing fur trader, to a second stint as governor of Assiniboia.

Christie suspected, perhaps mistakenly at first, that Andrew McDermot and his business associate James Sinclair were behind much of the free trade on British soil, and he therefore terminated both McDermot's fur-trading licence and the company's freight-hauling contracts with both men. He also targeted a number of other so-called "petty traders," including Peter Garrioch, an impulsive young jack-of-all-callings and sometime colleague of Sinclair's, Garrioch's friend Peter Hayden,[26] an itinerant American trader named Joe Green, and local French Halfbreed Alexis Goulet.

After setting his sights on these independent businessmen, Christie requested the assistance of Adam Thom as the company's resident legal adviser. The energetic lawyer responded eagerly despite his undoubted awareness that the asserted monopoly was unlawful. In a series of letters to Christie in December 1844,[27] Thom reported having "concocted" several possible suppression measures. In addition to more orthodox techniques, such as prosecution of unmistakable violations and wide distribution of public notices prohibiting contravention of the company's monopoly, he called for a number of more devious approaches. He proposed sharply increasing the import duty on trade goods purchased in the United States, for instance, and suggested that possession of such goods should require a licence from the company – such licences to be voided by free trade activities. Garrioch and Green should be initially threatened with seizure of their US-purchased trading goods; but then (because of the dubious legality of seizure) they should be offered the option of selling the goods to the HBC at cost. In Green's case, Thom cynically observed, "The advantage of dealing with a foreigner is considerable. He can have, as an individual, no voice at Court,"[28] and US authorities would be unlikely to come to his aid. The use of company ships by independent traders such as McDermot and Sinclair to import goods from England should be permitted only on the condition that they not engage in free trading.

Thom's most imaginative ploy was a proposal that the company henceforth pay for furs with a new form of currency: Thom-designed HBC bills of exchange that could not be used to purchase trade goods in the United States because they would be payable at Red River in commodities rather than money. They would also be subject to periodic recall at any time for "registration," and would be nullified by fur trafficking on the part of the holder.[29] Thus, Thom assured Governor Christie, "Your ship, your courts and your currency render you absolute." Moreover, he promised, this could all be achieved "without needing the aid of a single policeman."[30] In that final assurance, he would be proven dramatically mistaken.[31]

Even as Recorder Thom was dreaming up these elaborate schemes, dissident petty traders were resolving to resist company pressures. On 19 December 1844 Governor Christie sent Sheriff Alexander Ross to seize what were thought to be illegal trade goods in the possession of Alexis Goulet.[32] Upon arrival at Goulet's premises, Ross encountered a large number of hostile French Halfbreeds, who had apparently gathered in support of Goulet and were eager to demonstrate their opposition to company restrictions. Although Ross managed to disperse the crowd, and to question Goulet about the provenance of the goods in question, he seems to have substituted discretion for valour by accepting that those goods were for Goulet's personal use.[33] During the winter of 1844–45, however, trade goods belonging to a petty trader called St Germain were confiscated, and tensions escalated again.[34]

When the Council of Assiniboia next met, on 3 April 1845, it learned from its frustrated collector of customs that several importers of American goods were refusing to pay the duty.[35] Peter Garrioch had vowed to "rot in jail" before he would pay, and Peter Hayden had threatened to shoot anyone who tried to seize his furs.[36] At the same meeting, the council may also have been informed of growing resistance by the magistrates who staffed the petty courts to enforcing unpopular restrictions on freedom of trade, since it was resolved, on the motion of Adam Thom, that henceforth "all questions of revenue or prohibition or licence, however inconsiderable may be the amount of the claim, shall be determined by the Governor and Council and a jury."[37] In that context, "Governor and Council" meant "General Court."

At three meetings held in quick succession in June 1845, the Council of Assiniboia enacted several of Thom's measures.[38] The final meeting modified the new import regulations slightly in light of the protests of Garrioch, Hayden, and their colleagues, but the changes did not mollify the protesters for long.

In July 1845 Sinclair and McDermot tried to sue the company in the General Quarterly Court for freighting fees they claimed it owed them. Simpson and Christie dodged the claim, very likely on Thom's advice, by taking the position that the court lacked juridical authority where HBC interests were directly at stake.[39] They do not appear to have noticed that it was a position difficult to reconcile with Thom's advice of using the court for enforcement of the company's alleged monopoly. Litigation having failed them, Sinclair and McDermot tried persuasion. Sinclair presented Christie with a list of questions about trading rights, underlying most of which was his assertion that, as a Halfbreed, he had an Aboriginal right to trade in furs.[40] McDermot wrote a long letter to the governor proposing an amicable resolution of his differences with the company.[41] Christie, at Thom's urging, refused to settle with either McDermot or Sinclair and pressed ahead on several fronts.[42] He attempted to seize the goods of American Joe Green,[43] and in order to compete aggressively with Kittson, he established two fur trade posts near the 49th parallel: one on British soil and the other, authorized by a licence from the American Fur Company, right under Kittson's nose at Pembina.[44] Early in 1846 Christie sent Co-Sheriff Cuthbert Grant to confiscate furs from Red River trader Peter Hayden, who began, as he warned he would, to take defensive measures. The tragic consequences of that decision included one of the General Court's strangest rulings: a 1 shilling fine for accidental manslaughter.[45]

The Halfbreed community, both French and English, was outraged by this harassment – and they were not alone. In February 1846 a large protest meeting was held at Andrew McDermot's house.[46] The potentially explosive anger of many of those present was fortunately channelled by Father Georges-Antoine Belcourt into a petition that would eventually find its way to authorities in Britain, being carried there by a disillusioned and, in Simpson's eyes, thoroughly reviled James Sinclair.[47] An earlier petition of similar substance, prepared by McDermot's nephew John McLaughlin, was dispatched to the American government.[48] But while the company's critics remained hopeful for some time that these petitions would sooner or later bring redress for their complaints, it was not to be.[49] The plaint addressed to American authorities encountered deaf ears and blind eyes.[50] The petition drafted by Father Belcourt and carried to England by James Sinclair was entrusted to former Rupert's Land resident Alexander Isbister, a lawyer and critic of the company, who took considerable time presenting it to the UK government. Only much later would the Colonial Office finally respond to the complaints –

by rejecting them.[51] In April 1846 the volatile Peter Garrioch decided that if he was going to be treated as a smuggler he might as well become one and, with a companion, conveyed a shipment of his and James Sinclair's furs to Norman Kittson at Pembina. Garrioch's often hilarious account of their adventures and misadventures along the way, entitled "The Pleasures of Smuggling," resides in the Archives of Manitoba.[52]

By then, Governor Christie's optimism about suppressing the free traders was drooping. He knew he lacked the enforcement personnel required to deal with what he believed to be widespread flouting of the company's claimed monopoly, and he did not seem hopeful of catching McDermot or Sinclair red-handed in the act of illegal trading. As for the courts, although Thom remained optimistic, Christie's view was gloomy:

> [H]ighly as I value our local courts for the general administration of justice, and sanguine as appear to be Mr. Thom's hopes of obtaining from a jury a favorable verdict, and from the magistrates an unanimous sentence in any prosecution that might be instituted for damages, I am yet clearly of opinion that, composed as the Court now is, it is not into the hands of the magistrates we should commit the ... interpretation of the Charter of the Honourable Company's rights ... [T]he assistance to be expected from the magistrates may be estimated ... from the fact that some of them ... have expressed a degree of reluctance amounting in my opinion to a fixed determination not to adjudicate in cases arising out of illicit fur trafficking.[53]

Three years later, however, Christie having moved to another posting, the responsibility for combatting free trade would fall to Chief Factor John Ballenden, who, with Thom's encouragement, called on the General Quarterly Court to enforce the trade monopoly. That monumental blunder would lead, in May 1849, to the court's most notorious session ever.[54]

EPIDEMIC

A deadly epidemic struck Red River in the summer of 1846. Eyewitness Alexander Ross described it vividly:

> In January the influenza raged, and in May the measles broke out; but neither of these visitations proved very fatal. At length, in June, the bloody flux began its ravages among the Indians of the White

> Horse Plains, and soon spread with fearful rapidity and fatal effect among the whites ... Hardly anything to be seen but the dead on the way to their last home; nothing talked of but the sick, the dying, and the dead ... From the 18th of June to the 2nd of August, the deaths averaged seven a day, or 321 in all; being one out of every 16 in our population. Of these, one-sixth were Indians, two-thirds Halfbreeds, and the remainder whites. On one occasion thirteen burials were proceeding at once. Many houses were closed altogether; not one of the family, old or young, being left in them.[55]

The colony was, Ross recalled, "overwhelmed with terror." The situation was made worse by simultaneous drought and crop failure; and it would be years before normalcy returned to the lives of some families.

POLICING AND THE SIXTH REGIMENT

Governor Christie's hopes for eventually controlling the free traders and restraining dissidents were pinned to the anticipated arrival in 1846 of a regiment of British troops. The military force he looked forward to welcoming to the settlement resulted from one of Sir George Simpson's more remarkable coups.

When Christie assumed the governorship of Assiniboia for the second time in 1844, Red River's policing arrangements were substantially the same as they had been since the governmental restructuring of 1835. Sheriff Ross commanded a force consisting of three sergeants and fifty-four privates.[56] The company contributed £100 annually to the force, but that was less than a quarter of its total cost. The remainder was paid from the settlement's public customs revenues. Membership in the force, which paid privates £6 annually, plus per diem fees, was considered something of a sinecure, and a petition in 1843 calling for a reduction in the number of police, and an annual rotation of membership "afin d'eviter les jalousies de ceux qui n'ont point de part à ce petit avantage,"[57] resulted in a decision to rotate one-half of the privates every two years, new members being chosen by ballot from householders under the age of fifty.[58]

Although the effectiveness of the Red River Volunteer Corps was often denigrated, it had its successes. In late 1844, for example, the community was shocked by a brazen burglary at Upper Fort Garry that netted the thief more than £400 from the company's cash box. According to a letter from schoolmaster John Macallum to a friend at York

Factory, "A veritable burglary was committed at Fort Garry malgré its high walls and strong gates, its jailor & jail. Of course the whole Settlement was in a commotion. There were ... anxious looks and pale features, for who would dare to perpetrate such an act but a strong body of Canadians?"[59] The Volunteer Corps was put on the case immediately, and a poster offering a £50 reward "for such information as may lead to the offender or offenders" was circulated.[60] The violated strong box was soon found, along with a ladder used to scale the fort wall. Suspicion fell on a man who had been seen leaving the settlement in the direction of Pembina, and police officers gave pursuit. The fugitive still being ahead of the officers when they reached the international boundary, where their writ ceased to have authority, they delegated the chase to private, reward-induced individuals in the United States, who apprehended the culprit at Red Lake. It was not possible to bring the fugitive back across the border for trial, but he was made to disgorge his loot, and all but a few shillings were recovered.[61]

By this time, however, the life expectancy of the police force was short. At the first Council of Assiniboia meeting attended by Governor Christie, on 19 June 1844, a small further reduction in membership – to fifty officers and men – was ordered.[62] Then, just a year later, the force was disbanded altogether and replaced by only fifteen constables, working under the supervision of the sheriff.[63] Why had so drastic a step been taken at a time when both Christie and Simpson, the latter of whom chaired this meeting, were concerned about the company's ability to enforce its alleged trade monopoly? There was some concern, at a time of rising tensions in the community, about the loyalty of the largely Halfbreed force.[64] Perhaps cost factors were also involved, although the only change in that respect was the increasing difficulty of collecting import duties. The main factor, however, was that Sir George Simpson was fairly sure by then that he had succeeded in arranging for a law enforcement body with which company officials would be much more comfortable.

The origins of the contemplated new arrangement lay, oddly enough, in Oregon.[65] The HBC had been operating in the Oregon Territory, south of the Columbia River, for quite some time, and it was concerned about steadily increasing American immigration to the area, as well as about intensified claims by the US government to jurisdiction over the area. James Sinclair's 1841 expedition to Oregon with a group of Red River emigrants had been aimed in part at strengthening British territorial claims there.[66] As the dispute between the two countries became more bitter, and the fear of war loomed larger, Sir George Simpson managed to involve himself on behalf of the British in a semi-official capacity. He sailed to England in late 1844 to discuss the situation with HBC and government officials, and on 4 April 1845 he reported to company governor Sir John Pelly that he had just met with Prime Minister Sir Robert Peel and a member of his cabinet and had been verbally authorized to spend, at public expense, up to £1,000 "in any measure I might consider advisable to take ... in reference to our claims in the Oregon Territory."[67]

A month later Simpson informed Pelly from Lachine that although he was personally convinced, as a result of consultations in New York and Washington on his way home, that the Oregon question "will be amicably adjusted," he was nevertheless hopeful that the circumstances would result in a military force being sent to Red River. Two officers assigned to assess the military prospects of the situation would be travelling with him (in the guise of civilian tourists) to Red River en route to Oregon, and he hoped "to be able to get the officers ... to report favourably on the practicability of conveying a few troops to Red River from Canada, where they are already much required for the preservation of good order, which the police of the Settlement are unable to maintain."[68] Simpson did indeed prevail on the officers, Lieutenants Henry Warre and Mervin Vavaseur, to assess and report immediately on the defence of Assiniboia in the event of an American incursion there. Their report made clear that they did not consider this task to fall within their orders, but that they undertook it "at the expressed desire of Sir George Simpson."[69] At the end of December, Simpson informed Christie in a confidential letter that there was "little doubt" the troops would be dispatched. He was anxious, however, that secrecy be maintained as long as possible: "[T]his letter is strictly confidential (to be communicated to no person except Mr. Recorder Thom) as, from the extraordinary character of the halfcaste population, there is no knowing how the intelligence that an armed force was about to be brought to the country might be received – the probability being that troublesome and disaffected persons might so construe it to the more ignorant as to lead to dangerous excitement."[70]

In the end Governor Simpson's gambit was successful[71] – too successful. Learning that almost 400 troops and family members of the Sixth Regiment, Royal Warwickshires, would be arriving from England via York Factory in the summer of 1846, the entire company establishment was thrown into disarray making arrangements to transport the massive influx from Hudson Bay to the settlement, and to accommodate them when they got there. To make matters worse, the epidemic was still savaging the settlement when the troops arrived. Under the lash of Sir George's determination, however – and at the cost of much inconvenience, including the displacement of Governor Christie and Recorder Thom from their comfortable Stone Fort homes – the task was accomplished.[72] Although enthusiastic military engineers proposed massive improvements to the fortifications of the upper and lower establishments that would have cost the company an appalling £80,000 to £120,000, Simpson eventually persuaded the army that strengthened fortifications would not be necessary.[73]

Although Simpson briefly lamented this sudden embarrassment of military riches, he was soon delighted with the change it brought to the community. As his reports to the Governor and Committee in London had always made perfectly clear, his desire for a garrison at Red River was based not on any real concern about external military threats but on the need to keep the peace locally – "to overawe ... the inhabitants of the Settlement ... [and] all the surrounding Indian tribes."[74] Not long after the troops were settled at Red River, Simpson was convinced this goal had been accomplished. The commanding officer, Colonel John F. Crofton, he observed, "shews every disposition to support the Company's officers, and if any attempt be made to infringe our rights under the Charter, I am quite satisfied he will act with promptitude. The presence of troops, however, will alone be sufficient to check the illicit trade."[75]

Alexander Ross, sheriff and commander of the settlement's former police force, confirmed in his history of Red River that the presence of the Sixth Regiment did in fact have precisely the influence Simpson predicted: "[T]he soldiers were a real benefit to us. From the moment they arrived, the high tone of lawless defiance and internal disaffection raised by our own people against the laws and the authorities of the place were reduced to silence. All those disaffected ... immediately sneaked across the boundary line."[76] In truth, by no means all – or even most – of the dissidents fled south.

The troops brought more than pacification to Red River. Their presence stimulated the local economy, and their officers enlivened the social scene. The intellectual life of the community was enriched by the establishment of the settlement's first public library, inspired by the example of the garrison library and realized with the material assistance of several officers.[77] But the regiment's effect on life in the settlement was not entirely benevolent. Adam Thom, writing to Governor Simpson in January 1847, deplored some aspects of the military influx: "Every second hovel is open to the soldiers ... becoming in its turn when the beer is in the way a common pot-house. In this neighbourhood four or five soldiers have, at different times, been found alone, lying on the frozen ground in a state of insensibility."[78] It was not long before Red River courts were being called upon to adjudicate soldiers' misadventures. The recorder, in the last-cited letter, mentioned his concern about the respective applicability of civil and military law,[79] and his difficulty obtaining access to the latter. Although those particular concerns were not very serious, the General Court would be faced in the months to come with one very troubling charge – attempted rape – against a member of the garrison.[80]

THE COURT

The composition of the General Quarterly Court of Assiniboia at its first session fully recorded in surviving documents – 21 November 1844 – was drawn from the same Red River aristocracy that composed the Council of Assiniboia. Every member of the court was a member of the council, and every councillor was appointed by the HBC Governor and Committee in London. There were seven places on the bench at that point. Besides Governor Christie and Recorder Thom, there were the presidents of the three petty courts in the settlement: James Bird, seventy-one-year-old major land owner and collector of customs; Captain George Carey, a retired military officer and former head of the settlement's failed experimental farm;[81] and Dr John Bunn, born on the shores of Hudson Bay to a Cree mother and a Scottish father, educated in Edinburgh, and now the community's physician and one of its most trusted public figures.[82] Red River's two sheriffs, Alexander Ross[83] and Cuthbert Grant, both of whom were also petty court magistrates, normally completed the panel, but Grant happened not to be present for that first session. The formal composition of the court did not change during the years covered by this chapter, except for the replacement of Governor Christie by Governor William B. Caldwell in 1848. Bird failed to sit at all during the final two years of the period, however, and Carey left the settlement after attending only two sessions in 1847.

The General Court confronted two difficult jurisdictional problems during these years. Especially challenging was the question of whether Rupert's Land – and therefore the court's authority – extended to the far northwest. When a man charged with murder at a trading post on the Mackenzie River was brought to the settlement for trial,[84] Recorder Thom produced an exacting legal-geographical analysis accepting jurisdiction over the area in question.[85] Other members of the court agreed, took custody of the accused man, and subsequently released him on bail. For reasons that are not altogether clear, no trial was ever held; but Thom's opinion left posterity an interesting examination of the court's geographic ambit.

The Sixth Regiment's arrival in 1846 raised a two-part jurisdictional issue: (1) to what extent were the troops subject to the settlement's courts, and (2) should the civilian courts apply military law when dealing with them? As for the first part, although both the General Court and the petty courts often tried soldiers,[86] no useful general explanation of the respective authority of Assiniboia and military tribunals seems ever to have been articulated. Recorder Thom later wrote, with respect to the Chelsea Pensioners, a group of part-time soldiers that replaced the Sixth Regiment, that they were "partly soldiers and partly citizens. How far they are citizens, and how far they are soldiers, we do not presume to decide; but clearly, so far as they are soldiers at all, they live under a law of their own."[87] One case seems to suggest that the decision as to whether civilian courts had jurisdiction over soldiers lay with the military commanding officer.[88]

The other subissue – the applicability of military law in settlement courts – was a matter of dispute between the recorder and certain magistrates. Thom, while taking pains to acquaint himself with the UK Military Act, and even to suggest to the commanding officer ways to improve military law for local application, strongly disapproved of its use in civilian courts, and refused to apply it in the General Court. But, he informed Governor Simpson, "[S]ome of our [petty court] wise men have been dabbling dangerously in the statute in question ... Captain Carey ha[s] been administering it, assuming a jurisdiction which did not belong to him, and mitigating a penalty which the Imperial Parliament alone could modify."[89]

Because the recorder had no legal authority over the petty courts, and had long since lost the respect of most magistrates, there was little he could do, directly, to prevent Carey and other petty court judges from "dabbling" in military law. The practice was never again mentioned, however, and was probably soon abandoned – perhaps after a quiet intervention by Governor Christie.[90]

While workable guidelines – whatever they might have been – for distinguishing between military and civil jurisdiction must have been agreed upon, social interaction between the military and civilian populations was unavoidable, with occasional unfortunate consequences. To reduce the incidence of such conflicts, the Council of Assiniboia enacted laws, in January 1847, imposing very heavy fines on civilians for encouraging or facilitating soldiers to abscond from duty or (with the exception of the HBC!) selling them intoxicating spirits.[91]

NEW PROCEDURES, FAIR AND UNFAIR

While Recorder Thom was riding high, he arranged the enactment of several new laws, most of which were calculated to facilitate liquor law and trade monopoly prosecutions – categories of litigation that were connected by the fact that free traders commonly traded liquor for furs. The decision to strip the lenient petty courts of their authority to adjudicate liquor prosecutions has already been mentioned.[92] The same meeting of the council resolved, on a motion of the recorder, that "[w]hereas, in the absence of written agreements, the best evidence is commonly to be found in the breasts of the parties themselves, ... [henceforth] in all cases coming before the General Court, the plaintiff may summon the defendant, or the defendant may summon the plaintiff as a witness."[93] This empowered plaintiffs and defendants in civil cases to examine each other under oath, contrary to the English practice, by which at that time parties' statements were unsworn and immune from cross-examination. That beneficial reform, which seems not to have been employed for several years,[94] was probably intended by Thom for use in HBC civil actions against free traders – although the trader in the only such action ever commenced gave his evidence without oath or, apparently, cross-examination.[95]

Other Thom-inspired procedural novelties enacted in 1845, not one of which would pass muster under today's Canadian Charter of Rights and Freedoms, were that: (1) A committee consisting of Thom, John Bunn, and Alexander Ross could examine parties privately before trial, and their report could be given as evidence to the jury with or without other evidence. (2) Intoxicated Indians were to be kept in jail until they either provided two sureties (a near impossibility) or agreed to prosecute the person who supplied the liquor, their evidence being "conclusive" against previously convicted or "reputed" offenders. (3) Evidence of a "general habit of violating the law" was indictable "without establishing any individual offence." And (4) anyone attempting to influence a prosecution witness in criminal proceedings was guilty of the crime charged (under an "implied confession" rationale) as well as of "tampering with the course of justice."[96] Thom's influence soon waned, however, and there is no evidence that any of those draconian measures was much employed.[97]

FIRST HANGING

Governor Christie's aforementioned favourable assessment of the ability of the settlement's courts to deal with "the general administration of justice" may have been influenced by the manner in which the General Quarterly Court dealt with a very difficult challenge in 1845.

Generally speaking, Red River authorities continued to pay little heed to lawlessness beyond the settlement. As a result of that policy, a chain of violent clashes on the prairie southwest of Assiniboia between Halfbreed and Saulteaux buffalo hunters from Red River and Pembina, on the one hand, and bands of rival Sioux, on the other, were ignored by Assiniboia authorities as they escalated, between 1840 and 1844, into major warfare. The culmination of those battles, in the latter year, was a decisive victory for the Red River combatants. Shocked by the scale of their losses, the Sioux made a peace overture, and an exchange of letters between them and Halfbreed leader Cuthbert Grant brought an end to the violence for the time being.[98]

There was a tragic sequel to the peace treaty, however, in the assassination not long afterward of a Sioux visitor to Red River by a local Saulteau. The killing took place just outside the walls of Upper Fort Garry, in plain view of numerous settlers. Because the act had threatened the safety of the settlement (the fatal bullet having, in fact, struck and killed a bystander as well as the intended victim), it could not be ignored by Fort Garry officials, and the General Quarterly Court was called upon to deal with the situation at a special session. Although that trial[99] – which resulted in Red River's first and only official execution – was conducted in a manner that was generally applauded within the settlement, it was heavily criticized in other circles.

NEW CLERK

The courts acquired a new clerk in October 1848. Former clerk John Black[100] had been increasingly employed in HBC commercial duties over the years, a career progression to which his marriage in 1845 to Governor Christie's daughter Margaret was undoubtedly related. When

Black was promoted to chief trader in 1848, it became imperative to relieve him of his clerical responsibilities to the courts and council. The clerical needs of the Assiniboia government had been expanding during the same period, and when the council appointed a replacement, it was as "Executive Officer," with a wide range of bureaucratic responsibilities.[101]

The man chosen to fill this hydra-headed role as Red River's first full-time civil servant was William R. Smith,[102] a well-respected resident who had come first to Rupert's Land as a sixteen-year-old HBC recruit in 1813 and had moved to the settlement with other redundant company employees after the merger of the HBC and the North West Company in 1822. Since then, Smith had farmed, worked as an Anglican catechist, and taught school. He would serve the community well for the next twenty years.

AN UNDERCOVER INVESTIGATION

More interesting than many of the cases that came before the General Quarterly Court during this period was one that did not. It involved Wesleyan Methodist missionary James Evans, best known to history for having devised and put to effective use a syllabic alphabet for the Cree and Ojibwa languages.[103] In 1840 Governor Simpson gave permission and assistance for Wesleyan missionaries to work among the Indians of Rupert's Land, and Reverend Evans made Norway House and the nearby Indian village of Rossville his base of operations. Although he quickly won the hearts of his Indian congregants, Evans's independent attitude and frequent criticism of HBC policies – especially his refusal to countenance work or travel on Sundays – angered Simpson. Concerned that the pastor was encouraging his followers to deal with free traders, the governor-in-chief began to withdraw privileges from him, and in 1845 he wrote to the Wesleyan Missionary Society requesting Evans's recall. By the end of that year, Simpson was confident the request would be met.[104]

Meanwhile, Evans encountered other setbacks. On a canoe trip in September 1844, he accidently shot and killed Thomas Hassell, a bright young Red River–educated Indian whom Evans employed as guide, interpreter, and acolyte. That tragedy struck the missionary hard, and he had not yet recovered from the shock of it when, in early 1846, rumours began to circulate that he had been taking sexual liberties with young Indian girls he sheltered in his home. Then the rumours were enlarged to suggest that Hassell's death might not have been accidental – and that Evans had become inappropriately close to Hassell's widow. To clear the air, Evans requested his assistant, Reverend William Mason, to conduct a trial of the allegations under church procedures. At the resulting proceeding, testimony was presented that would have been damning if believed. Although Mason found his superior not to be guilty of the charges against him, he also concluded that Evans had unwisely allowed himself to become too familiar with the girls in question. Moreover, the hearing transcript that Mason sent back to the Missionary Society, without Evans's examination or knowledge, contained hurtful parenthetical additions by Mason, and failed to note that some of the accusatory testimony quoted had been subsequently recanted.

In the summer of 1846 Mason had occasion to travel to Red River. He was in contact there with Sir George Simpson and other notables, and let drop in conservation the rumours concerning the death of Thomas Hassell. Although Simpson did not apparently pursue the matter with Mason before the latter departed the settlement, he decided, shortly thereafter, to institute an investigation. On 7 July 1846 he wrote two letters to Donald Ross, the HBC officer in charge of Norway House. The official one[105] instructed Ross, in his capacity as magistrate, to conduct "a thorough investigation" into Hassell's death, focusing on ten precisely phrased questions.[106] The first five questions concerned objective matters such as the relative positions of the parties in the canoe at the time of the shooting; the latter five sought to delve into the interpersonal relationships of Evans, Hassell, and their respective spouses. The second letter to Ross[107] was a personal one on the same subject. It began by noting that Evans would already have departed for England,[108] referred to him as a "worthless character," and emphasized what Simpson wanted Ross's investigation to focus on: "It is very desirable we should know whether any intimacy existed between Evans & Hassell's wife, & whether Hassell was aware of it; & if the wife be still alive, and within reach, I think you should get someone to question her closely respecting the intimacy, when it commenced, & how long it continued after Hassell's death."

That Simpson did not consider Ross's assignment to be an even-handed enquiry into the facts surrounding Hassell's death was also made clear by that second letter: "From some observations of Mason's ... which have come to my knowledge, it strikes me, as well as Mr. Thom & Mr. Christie, that Hassell's death was not accidental, but a deliberately planned murder." Not only, it seems, had Simpson and Christie already made up their minds on the basis of Mason's casual relaying of rumour; but so too had Recorder Adam Thom, before whom any homicide charge might well be expected to be tried! The prospect of a trial was not really on Sir George's mind, however. His plan, made clear in the opening paragraphs of the second letter, was simply to deter by blackmail an eventual return of Evans to Rupert's Land: "[I]n case he may keep his promise of visiting you at the expiration of two years, I think it is well we should be prepared to speak to him seriously on the subject of Hassell's death." As it turned out, there would be no need to spring the trap. After Evans's return to England, he was questioned by his superiors about the alleged improprieties with his young Indian congregants, and seems to have been completely exonerated. After that, he successfully fulfilled several public speaking engagements. But his health had been declining and, on 23 November 1846, James Evans suffered a sudden heart attack and died instantly.[109]

Sir George Simpson's role in this matter was clearly improper. In ordering the investigation he was exercising magisterial powers, and doing so for purposes of extortion was a gross violation of judicial authority. Thom's situation is a little more difficult to assess since the extent of his participation, the capacity in which it was performed, and his knowledge of Simpson's motives, are unknown. What is clear is that, once again, the recorder's divided commercial and public loyalties had placed him in a position that at least threatened his objectivity.

RECORDER THOM

Adam Thom was at the pinnacle of his power and influence at Red River at this point. Many of his schemes for suppressing the free traders had been adopted.[110] He dominated not just the General Court but the Council of Assiniboia as well, and he seems to have been high in the esteem of Governor Simpson. Although Thom might not have known it, Simpson suggested to the HBC Governor and Committee in 1846 that when Alexander Christie's term as governor of Assiniboia ended, the post should be filled by the commanding officer of British troops in the area or, failing that, "the next best that occurs to me would be to appoint Mr. Thom ..., in which case the office of Recorder would merge with that of Governor."[111]

Two pamphlets authored by Thom were published in England: one of them supporting the company's claims in Oregon;[112] the other refuting charges by an American pamphleteer that the company was abusing its monopoly in several respects.[113] His long-winded but informative 1845 charge to a Red River grand jury – which dealt among other things with the HBC's jurisdiction to administer justice throughout Rupert's Land and the applicability of the settlement's judicial process to Aboriginals – was published in England in 1848.[114] While the latter public documents were doubtless welcomed by Sir George Simpson, the literary project by which Thom must have earned the governor-in-chief's deepest gratitude was anonymous: the previously mentioned editing and substantial ghost-writing of Simpson's own book, *Narrative of a Journey Round the World*.[115] Considerable previous editorial revision by two others had not met with the "author's" entire satisfaction, and Thom, pressed by Simpson, agreed to try his hand, and brought the manuscript close to the form it bore when published in 1847. One scholar asserts, and the surviving correspondence seems to corroborate, that "much of the work on the book was done by Adam Thom" and one of the earlier editors.[116]

Thom also engaged in some private law practice. In January 1845, for example, he mentioned in a letter to Governor Simpson a legal problem he had encountered when acting on behalf of the estate of venerable fur trader James Sutherland, and claimed to have solved in a surprising manner. The problem was that Thom had prepared a will on Sutherland's instructions, but the old man had died before executing it. There was a previous will in existence, but Sutherland had altered some of its provisions without having the changes witnessed, and Thom thought those attempted changes would be considered by the courts to be invalid in themselves and possibly to invalidate the entire document. Ever resourceful, he hit upon "a mode by which, in my opinion, the unsigned draft may be held to be a good will," and he sent his solution to Simpson to be forwarded to London for approval.[117] Although the enclosure explaining how the inventive lawyer intended to accomplish this act of legal legerdemain seems to have been lost, the proposed solution probably lay in a passage from Thom's 1840 "Observations on the Law and Judicature of Rupert's Land,"[118] asserting that since the English Statute of Frauds – which among other things required wills to be written, signed, and witnessed – post-dated the HBC charter, it was not operative in Rupert's Land. On the same apparent authority, he claimed that the Sutherland estate should not have to pay the legacy duty required by contemporary English law.[119]

Thom's personal life appears to have been as fulfilling as his professional life. Although the arrival of the Sixth Regiment had expelled him from the quarters he and his family had been occupying at Lower Fort

Garry,[120] and his subsequent attempt to commandeer an unoccupied Anglican parsonage had come a cropper when the parson unexpectedly showed up,[121] he was eventually able to purchase a comfortable home on the banks of the Red River near the St Andrew's Rapids.[122] In the following year, he had the satisfaction of finally publishing in England the book about biblical prophecy into which he had been pouring much of his private energy since coming to Red River. Although his first manuscript, carried to England on his behalf by Sir George Simpson in 1844, had apparently been rejected, a revised version, with a new title, was subsequently published.[123] As his young son grew, Thom turned his attention to the boy's education; and reported in 1848 that he was spending "nearly half my time" teaching his four year old, as well as his housekeeper's son.[124] Life was good for Adam Thom.

About the only blot in the recorder's copybook at this point, so far as the governor-in-chief was concerned, was his failure to comply with Simpson's request to attend the annual meeting of the Council of Rupert's Land at Norway House in 1847.[125] This refusal did not appear to have immediate repercussions, but Sir George had a long memory. And whether or not he was aware of the fact – or cared – Thom had become persona non grata to a large segment of the Red River population. When Andrew McDermot wrote to Governor Christie in November 1845 in search of rapproachment with the company, he remarked, "There is not a man high or low ... but says that Mr. Thom is the cause of all the present evil in the Settlement."[126]

NEW COURTHOUSE AND JAIL

From about 1848 onward the General Quarterly Court would sit in new surroundings. The council had decided as early as July 1843 that "[i]t being found exceedingly dangerous and inconvenient to have the public gaol within the walls of Fort Garry, it was: Resolved ... That the present gaol be abandoned, and that a new building, to be erected on some suitable spot by the Hudson's Bay Company, be in future used for that purpose; the Honourable Company assuming possession of the present building, in lieu of that to be erected."[127]

When the council met next, almost a year later, to welcome Governor Christie back to Red River, little if anything had been done to implement this proposal. The resolution was therefore renewed, with the added direction that the new site be "within reach of the Fort guns."[128] Although both authorizing resolutions referred only to a "gaol," it seems to have been always understood that an adjoining courtroom would also be constructed.

Even after their construction, however, the new facilities were not immediately available to the General Court. A letter from Simpson to London on 23 July 1846, reporting on preparations under way to accommodate the Sixth Regiment, stated, "In addition to the foregoing accommodation, we intend making [available] our jail situated at the rear of the Fort, at a distance of 200 or 300 yards, which can be converted into a guardhouse or hospital, or applied to any other purpose for which it may be required for the use of the troops."[129] A map of Upper Fort Garry and its environs, drawn by members of the Sixth Regiment in July 1848, shows a largish structure west of the fort in the location described by Simpson. It is labelled "Garrison Hosp. & Jail."[130] The new building, although designed as a civilian courthouse and jail, was thus first occupied by the military, and was probably not surrendered to civil authorities until after the Sixth Regiment left Red River in 1848.

After it reverted to its intended use, Red River's citadel of justice served the settlement until 1870, when the District of Assiniboia was supplanted by the Province of Manitoba. Surrounded by a not-always-secure wooden palisade, the building was divided internally by a central corridor, with the courtroom on the right as one entered and the jail on the left.[131] The latter was overseen by a full-time jailer under the supervision of Sheriff Ross, whose many duties included being the "Governor of the Gaol."[132] As for the courtroom, a vivid word sketch was provided by Red River historian J.J. Hargrave, who first saw it in 1861 but whose description probably differs little from the original appearance:

> [T]he whole contents of the courtroom were formed on a very diminutive scale. A small bar partitioned off the portion of the room allotted to the accommodation of the general public from that set apart for the officials. At the back of the room rose the bench, approached by a couple of steps at each end, and so narrow that it was with considerable difficulty an ordinarily portly justice could squeeze his way out between the chairs of his brethren, when in session. Between the bench and the bar, almost the entire width of the space set apart for the officers of the Court was occupied by a little table covered with green cloth, at which presided ... [the court clerk] with his testament, his record book, a jug of cold water, and some tumblers arranged before him. Close to each other at the bar of the Court stood the dock and the witness box. On the left hand

> of the judge were arranged two rows of substantially constructed benches for the gentlemen of the jury.[133]

As an anonymous councillor pointed out in a letter to the editor of the settlement's newspaper about a year after Hargrave's foregoing description, space limitations were not the courtroom's only shortcoming: "The very imperfect ventilation of the courthouse has long been a subject of remark, but somehow or other nothing has ever been done to improve it. Even in summer, when windows and doors are thrown wide open, the air gets bad enough; but in winter, when all are closed and the stove is blazing away as fiercely as anybody likes to make it who has come in fresh from the outside cold, the atmosphere becomes intolerable."[134] Although cramped and stuffy, the courtroom was, along with the churches, put to a wide range of extrajudicial uses – from public meetings to theatrical performances – over the ensuing years. Even when serving its primary function, the new Red River courtroom would see its share of both high drama and low comedy.

6

Court Compromised, Recorder Dethroned, 1848–54

Long-sown seeds of trouble germinated, ripened, and burst. The next governor was a buffoon; the Sixth Regiment's efficient peacekeeping troops were replaced by a useless band of drunken troublemakers; the illegal fur trade monopoly of the Hudson's Bay Company met its end at the hands of an outraged public; and Recorder Adam Thom's insufferable behaviour brought his removal from the bench and ultimately from the Red River Settlement – though not before bringing the General Quarterly Court to its knees. While a stronger settlement, and a much better court, emerged from the crisis, in history's eyes the reputation of the latter would never quite recover.

THE SETTLEMENT

Red River continued to grow throughout the early 1850s. The population was approaching 6,000 in 1849, and would number nearly 7,000 when this chapter in the court's history closed. The roughly 650 homes and 4,000 cultivated acres that greeted Thom's arrival in 1839 had multiplied to over 800 homes and more than 7,000 acres before he left in 1854. The seven churches and twelve schools of 1849 had risen to nine and seventeen respectively by 1856; and watermills more than quadrupled in the same period.[1]

Three new anglophone enclaves sprang up along the Assiniboine River during these years. The most significant was at and around Portage la Prairie, where about twenty-five English Halfbreed families from the Parish of St Andrew's settled. Most were members of the Anglican congregation of Archdeacon William Cockran, a vigorous, rough-hewn Scot who had laboured prodigiously on behalf of both the Halfbreeds and the Indians of the settlement since arriving in 1825. Cockran examined

Portage la Prairie in 1851 and recommended it as a suitable site for an Anglican mission. A number of St Andrew's families moved there the following year, and the migration grew thereafter. As the presence of firebrand Peter Garrioch among the first contingent testifies, political dissatisfaction was a motivating factor for some. Reverend Cockran would move to the Portage himself in 1857.[2]

Portage la Prairie was at the southern terminus of the ancient canoe portage linking Lake Manitoba and the Assiniboine River. Although it offered excellent agricultural potential, Gerhard Ens has shown that the migrants from St Andrew's initially tended to be more attracted to trading and readier access to the buffalo plains than to farming.[3] The HBC opposed the creation of the new settlement and viewed it with great suspicion – as little more than an outpost for free traders. Over time, however, the Portage area became solidly agricultural, and its residents began requesting municipal services – police and courts in particular – from Red River authorities. Although some of the Portage homesteads may have been within the 50 mile radius of the Municipal District of Assiniboia established in 1841, others were not; and whatever the precise geographic situation might have been, the Council of Assiniboia refused, with London's concurrence, to extend its services to anyone in the area.[4] Interesting consequences would ensue.[5]

New Assiniboine communities closer to the Forks were St James, 2 miles upstream from Fort Garry, and Headingley, not far west of that. Anglican churches were established at those locations in 1853 by Reverend W.H. Taylor and Reverend G.O. Corbett respectively.[6]

Isolation remained a problem. Although the prospect of improved transportation and communication links was beckoning dimly from the south, it remained remote. The population of the entire Minnesota Territory, an area larger than the modern state, was only about 6,000 in 1850.[7] Although the Council of Assiniboia proposed in 1852 to supplement the infrequent HBC mail packets through Canada[8] and York Factory by a postal service to the United States, cost considerations put an end to that initiative.[9] A small private courier service to the United States began to operate in 1853,[10] but regular postal service to Pembina did not commence until 1855, and then only once a month.[11]

Isolation did not lessen conviviality. In the three days before Christmas 1851, the company store at the Upper Fort sold 600 gallons of rum, "besides brandy and wine."[12] But isolation did make more virulent the gossip endemic to all small communities. Red River hearsay "spreads over the whole Settlement," said an observer in 1844, "but by the time it reaches the most distant parts it has been so changed that no-one ... [can] recognize it."[13] An especially vicious strain of such gossip polarized much of the settlement in the first half of 1850, culminating in a sensational lawsuit for slander – one of the most notorious trials in the history of the General Quarterly Court – and Adam Thom's dismissal as recorder.[14]

In the spring of 1852 much of the settlement sustained another devastating flood.[15] Chief Trader John Black, who had been clerk of the court that sentenced the Saulteau assassin Capenessweet to death in 1845, described the scene surrounding Upper Fort Garry at the height of the flood: "From our upper storey windows not a spot of dry land was to be seen in any direction excepting – and it is a small exception – the bare summit of the little mound ... where the Saulteau was buried in '45."[16] Although the inundation was not quite as high, nor quite so prolonged, as the terrible flood of 1826, the substantial growth of the community in the intervening quarter-century meant that greater property damage was inflicted and more residents were displaced. Evacuation to higher ground was carried out efficiently, however, fewer areas were seriously affected than in 1826, and the waters receded relatively quickly. Only one life was lost, and crops were unusually good in the ensuing summer. Although the flood was certainly a disaster for some, the settlement as a whole recovered swiftly.

As Reverend Cockran's role in the exodus from St Andrew's to Portage la Prairie illustrates, the influence of the clergy throughout the colony was great. Three important new ecclesiastical leaders began their work at Red River between 1849 and 1854. Early in 1849 the Church of England declared Rupert's Land to be a bishopric, thanks in large part to a bequest from the will of wealthy former fur trader James Leith, who wished to see Christianity propagated among the area's Indians. The new Anglican bishop of Rupert's Land, Reverend David Anderson, arrived at the settlement that fall, accompanied by his formidable sister Margaret. A special meeting of the Council of Assiniboia, to which the bishop had been appointed, was called to welcome him to its number.[17] The Andersons, brother and sister, would figure prominently, and sometimes controversially, in Red River affairs in the years to come. Not long after their arrival, Margaret was up to her bustle in the alleged scandal from which the above-mentioned slander litigation arose; and in consequence the bishop found himself mired, before long, in a bitter dispute with the irascible Adam Thom.

The pioneer Roman Catholic bishop J.N. Provencher died in June 1853, being replaced, both as bishop and as a councillor of Assiniboia, by Reverend A.A. Taché, a talented, energetic, politically astute man who had been grooming for the position for the past several years – and who would make monumental future contributions to Red River, Rupert's Land, and Manitoba in a career that outlasted Assiniboia.[18]

The prayers of Red River's many Presbyterians, who had been making do with Anglican pastors while lobbying vigorously for a spiritual leader of their own, were finally answered with the arrival in September 1851 of Reverend John Black, whose influence on the rest of the expanding community would also be powerful and long-lasting.[19] Not long after his appearance, however, some of Black's parishioners may have entertained second thoughts about him. On New Year's Eve 1851 about 150 relatives and friends of Presbyterian Robert McBeath gathered to celebrate the marriage of his daughter. The other John Black (court clerk turned chief trader) described the event: "They had ate and drank to their hearts' content, and, with a fiddler on the spot all the time, were preparing for dancing out the evening when – behold – an admonitory letter from the minister ... constrained ... [McBeath] to interdict the trippers on the light fantastic toe; and there they sat the whole night, looking at one another and wondering, as many suppose, whether Mr. Black was quite orthodox."[20]

Conviviality did little to allay growing unrest. Those who had signed the 1845–46 petitions to American and British authorities[21] were becoming impatient awaiting responses. They knew that John McLaughlin had travelled to England after dispatching his petition to Washington, and that he and Alexander Isbister were pressing their cause there, but progress was imperceptible.[22] Meanwhile, continued harassment of free traders by company authorities at Red River, urged on by the combative recorder, fed festering public resentment and culminated, in May 1849, in an ugly riot at the Red River courthouse which marked the beginning of the end for Adam Thom's judicial career, and came close to destroying the Quarterly Court of Assiniboia.[23]

In the spring of 1851 a petition was circulated in the settlement calling for representative government.[24] The Halfbreed majority, encouraged by the effectiveness of their courthouse demonstration, and then by another historic victory over the Sioux at the battle of Grand Coteau in July 1851,[25] had become aware that it might possess the power to bring about permanent change in Red River's governance. Company officials were nervously alert to that growing awareness.

GOVERNOR CALDWELL

There would be no time when the public held the General Quarterly Court in lower esteem than between 1848 and 1854. In fact, most of the major political developments during those years were rooted, in one way or another, in controversial judicial proceedings.

The story is intertwined with the misadventures of the man whose unsteady hand was on Assiniboia's helm as this chapter opened. Major William B. Caldwell, a career soldier, arrived at Red River in September 1848 with a threefold responsibility: to relieve Alexander Christie as governor of Assiniboia; to command the force of retired British soldiers – "Chelsea Pensioners"[26] – that replaced the regular troops of the Sixth Regiment; and to report to the British government on the validity of recent complaints, notably those presented by Alexander Isbister.[27] Caldwell was the first governor for many years to be independent of the HBC's commercial operations, and his appointment ought therefore to have produced significant improvements in the settlement's governance.[28] It did not. Caldwell, who remained in office throughout the years covered by this chapter, was a blustering, oversensitive, unperceptive, indecisive incompetent, destined to fail in all three missions.[29]

The investigation of charges levelled at the HBC by disgruntled settlers, for which Caldwell was responsible solely to the British government, was conducted in early 1849 by means of a short questionnaire[30] directed to a handful of men Caldwell described as "upper class ... householder[s]," observing that "I know no portion of the inhabitants to be preferred to the upper class, either for intelligence or integrity,"[31] plus a report from an Anglican cleric who questioned residents of the Indian village on Caldwell's behalf and gathered unspecified "oral information from other sources."[32] The responses of the Indians, almost all negative to the HBC, were disregarded. A few of Caldwell's other informants were also at least partially critical of the company. They included Andrew McDermot, Alexander Ross, and possibly Bishop Provencher. Even the latter, however, had reason not to offend the company too seriously,[33] and most of the others consulted were on the payrolls of either the HBC or the Council of Assiniboia. Apart from the Indians, the only person Caldwell approached who was likely to have returned unrestrained negative responses if he had chosen to answer was James Sinclair, who had delivered the 1846 petition to Isbister in England; but he declined the opportunity to comment.[34]

When Peter Garrioch learned that the governor's investigation consisted of a meekly phrased questionnaire addressed to a few hand-picked residents, he sent Caldwell a pamphlet defending the company that Adam Thom had prepared in 1847,[35] interleaved with Garrioch's rebuttals to Thom's various assertions. The sincerity of Caldwell's efforts to assess public opinion can be judged by his response to that unsought contribution. Calling it an "unsolicited effusion" irrelevant to his enquiry, he returned it peremptorily the next day. Although, when doing so, Caldwell invited Garrioch to submit his personal grievances against the HBC, the latter's request for a copy of the questions put to the others, as a guide to formulating his own submission, was refused.[36] A letter of complaint about this high-handed and insulting rejection of Garrioch's overture later appeared in a London newspaper, along with the newspaper's own severe castigation of Caldwell's conduct.[37]

If further evidence is needed of the biased nature of Major Caldwell's investigation of his new employer, it can be found in his obsequious letter to the company's Governor and Committee enclosing a copy of his exculpatory report. The letter condemned Isbister's representations for encouraging "a spirit of discontent amongst the weak minded and ignorant" and attributed negative comments by residents of the Indian village to the influence of "evil-disposed persons ... [who] poisoned the minds of several Indians."[38] That an investigator responsible solely to the British government should have privately addressed the chief target of the investigation in so obviously partisan a manner illustrates Caldwell's abysmally poor judgment.

As commander of the settlement's protective forces, Major Caldwell's performance was no better. The much-lauded Sixth Regiment, which no one had expected to remain long, returned to England in 1848 and was immediately replaced by Caldwell's pensioners, a unit very different from the one it replaced. The company transported these retired soldiers and their families to Red River, granted them plots of land in the vicinity of the Upper Fort, and paid them on a per diem basis for what seems to have been minimal militia services. It also paid Caldwell, over and above his salary as governor, to be their commanding officer, and engaged a younger officer, Captain Christopher Vaughan Foss, to be the second-in-command. Caldwell and Foss never succeeded in making an effective unit of what Alexander Ross called their "motley squad" of pensioners. The contrast to the professional peacekeepers they replaced was dismaying. J.M. Bumsted has described them as "worse than useless" peacekeepers who occupied themselves with "precious little farming, and a good deal of heavy drinking."[39] A contemporary observer commented, "We have more trouble with the Pensioners than with all the rest of the Settlement put together."[40]

Court dockets soon reflected the latter fact. For example, a practice in which some pensioners engaged, to the great annoyance of magistrates, was having drunken altercations with each other and then applying to a magistrate for a "peace bond" ordering their adversaries to keep the peace on pain of either going to jail or forfeiting on the bond. Chief Trader John Black, now also a magistrate, described how he put a stop to the practice: "A few of the more turbulent had been repeatedly annoying me about getting each other bound over to the peace. They seemed to think I had nothing else to do ... So I *did* bind a fellow over ... [and] found an opportunity soon after of estreating his recognizance[41] of £10 to the Public Fund. He was obliged to pay it after an hour or two in one of the cells, and I have had no more applications for binding over to the peace!"[42]

When a large armed mob of hostile Halfbreeds and Canadians surrounded the Fort Garry courthouse in May 1849, intent on preventing the trial of petty trader Pierre Guilleaum Sayer on charges of violating the HBC charter's trade monopoly,[43] Major Caldwell did not dare to call out his ill-trained, ill-disciplined, and greatly outnumbered troops. It was Sheriff Alexander Ross who, single-handedly, persuaded the demonstrators to surrender Sayer for trial.[44]

And when, in August of the same year, a group of dissatisfied Indians, emboldened by the May uprising, left their employment as HBC boatmen and descended on the settlement exhibiting a "rebellious ... disposition," and Caldwell offered Ross "a sufficient number of Pensioners to support the police in capturing the delinquents," the sheriff declined the offer. Although he had only "about 11 policemen" under his command, Ross preferred to handle the perilous situation without the questionable support of Caldwell's men. After an attempt to negotiate through a clergyman friendly to the Indians failed, Ross got permission to spend a small sum of public funds recruiting a few Halfbreed buffalo hunters to accompany him and his men to the camp of the deserters. There they found the malcontents, their numbers now swollen by about forty supporters, engaging in war dances. Ross's account of the mission offers a vivid illustration of the sometimes nuanced nature of law enforcement at Red River.[45] The sudden appearance of the sheriff's party, accompanied by Halfbreed allies, caused the adult male rebels to flee their camp, discouraged that they could not count on Halfbreed support for their rebellion. Following that, and after "giving [those who remained at] the camp a good fright," Ross and most of his posse returned to Fort Garry, leaving only "three constables and the interpreter who, remaining behind, induced the Indians to call back all those who had fled, and recommended to the offenders to deliver themselves up to justice." The tactic worked. The next day, the surrendered leaders were brought before Ross, who in his magisterial capacity committed them to prison to await trial.[46] According to Caldwell, they were "kept some time in durance vile, and then discharged with an admonition from the magistrates."[47]

THE COURT

Major Caldwell performed as badly as General Court president as he did as investigator, troop commander, and governor. In fact, his failures in those other roles were sometimes linked to courtroom fiascos. Disdain for his administration began with the riot provoked by the *Sayer* trial in 1849,[48] following which he reported that although the settlement was "externally quiet," he was governing more "by sufferance than by authority."[49] By the end of 1850 Caldwell's inability to control Adam Thom in two further sensational court cases had lost him even that sufferance.

HBC *v. Sayer*[50]

The courthouse riot to which previous allusions have been made occurred in May 1849. John Ballenden, the HBC's chief factor at Red River, encouraged by Recorder Thom, decided to prosecute four freelance fur traders for violation of the company's alleged trade monopoly. Pierre Guilleaum Sayer and three others were arrested and their furs confiscated. Although the men were freed on bail pending trial, their furs were retained. Public outrage was widespread, especially among French Halfbreeds and Canadians. Rumours that Caldwell would call out his pensioners in force to protect the court caused upward of 300 armed and angry protesters to gather around the courthouse on the morning of the trial; and although the bloodbath that many feared was averted, the presence of the surrounding mob impacted the court's proceedings crucially. As the governor and court party pushed their way through massed demonstrators to gain access to the courthouse, hostility was palpable. Dark threats to the recorder's safety were heard.

And when the *Sayer* case was called, the crowd refused to surrender the accused men it sheltered.

It took several hours of intense negotiations outside the courthouse, while other trials proceeded within, before Sheriff Alexander Ross could persuade Sayer and his co-defendants to even enter the courtroom. When they did, it was with a delegation of supporters, led by James Sinclair and Peter Garrioch, who called themselves "delegates of the people." Before allowing the trial to begin, the delegation presented a petition alleging the illegality of the HBC fur trade monopoly, and raising various other long-standing grievances. When Recorder Thom informed them that "they could not be received in a court of justice" as "delegates of the people" but could make submissions to the next meeting of the Council of Assiniboia, Sinclair and his confreres reluctantly agreed to focus, for the time being, on the prosecution immediately at hand.

Five of the previously selected jurymen were challenged by James Sinclair as the defendants' counsel and replaced. But the evidence, including that of Sayer's own son, left no doubt that he had traded in furs. Although that trade was with other Halfbreeds, Sayer's claim to have had company permission to trade with compatriots was vigorously denied by prosecutor Ballenden; and Sinclair's challenge to the legal validity of the asserted monopoly was rejected by Recorder Thom. The jury had little choice but to convict and did so; but it recommended mercy by reason of Sayer's *belief* that his conduct was authorized.

Ballenden seized that straw to avert a violent conclusion to the trial, saying that the company, having established the legality of its monopoly in principle, would not seek any punishment, would not proceed against Sayer's three co-accused, and would give them all their furs back. This caused the demonstrators to think Sayer had been acquitted and that, as someone shouted, "Le commerce est libre!" Jubilation reigned. Although the popular assumption that the HBC trading monopoly had been broken was legally mistaken, in practice it unquestionably had; the company was never again willing to risk a bloody uprising in the interest of exclusive trade.[51]

The *Sayer* case also had other important consequences. The petition the court had declined to entertain was presented, less than two weeks later, to the full Council of Assiniboia, and it received serious attention. The minutes of that meeting summarized the objects of the petition as follows: "1st The immediate removal of Mr. Recorder Thom from the Settlement. 2nd The conducting of all judicial business through the medium of a judge who would address the Court in the French as well as in the English language. 3rd The rescinding of the existing law respecting all imports from the United States of America. 4th The infusion into the Council of Assiniboia of a certain proportion of Canadian and Halfbreed members. 5th A free trade in furs."[52]

The council's response dodged the essence of the first demand – Thom's removal being beyond its authority after all – but it bravely asserted that "the personal liberty of Mr. Thom must be held equally inviolable with that of every other citizen, and ... those attempting any infringement on the same must bear the consequences." The second demand drew a more encouraging answer. Thom having apparently agreed behind the scenes to speak in both languages when francophone interests were involved, the council promised that "such a line of procedure should be hereafter adopted." It also pledged to give "favourable consideration" to reducing the tariff on US imports, and to "make a recommendation" that the HBC appoint more Canadians and Halfbreeds to the Council of Assiniboia. As for free trade in furs, though, the response concluded, only Parliament could do anything.[53] A newspaper account of the council meeting, very likely authored by Peter Garrioch, provides an interesting counterpoint to the official minutes. After asserting that local authorities had failed to find even one man prepared to act as a special constable "to protect Mr. Thom," it went on to claim that "the poor councillors were so terrified" that "if anyone had asked for a sinecure in the moon it would have been granted." It scoffed at the significance of the concessions, however, saying they were worth no more than if "John Bull were to grant you the Isle of Cuba."[54]

Such pessimism turned out to be unjustified. Rhetorically, the company was always unyielding,[55] and some improvements were certainly slow to appear, but in time all five demands were met, either totally or substantially. Duties on US imports were immediately reduced to the same rate for English goods.[56] The court was soon making reasonable efforts to accommodate francophones, and even the unilingual English laws which, although not mentioned in the *Sayer* petition, presented a problem for the French-speaking population,[57] had French counterparts before long. Well before the end of the period covered by this chapter new francophone and Halfbreed appointees, including French Halfbreed leader François Bruneau, Alexander Ross's mixed-blood son William, and notably, James Sinclair's younger brother Thomas, were serving on the Council of Assiniboia.[58] And the size and determination of the mob that surrounded the Red River courthouse on 17 May 1849 ensured that the company's claim to exclusive trade was a dead letter from that day forward. Its ongoing battles with trade rivals were conducted thereafter by competition rather than litigation.

Such progress was insufficient to impress some of the colony's advocates for democracy, who, in March 1851, demanded unsuccessfully that "the people," with "the sanction of the Governor and Council of Assiniboia ... appoint twelve men from the different sections of the Settlement to form a House of Representatives."[59] Representative government was nevertheless perceptibly, if modestly, closer to realization by December 1854 than in January 1849, and the *Sayer* case can be thanked for that too.

And Adam Thom? The demand for Thom's immediate removal from the settlement was firmly rejected by both the Council of Assiniboia and company management in London;[60] and he remained at Red River for several years more. His long reign over the court and council soon ended, however. Shortly after the May 1849 council meeting, Sir George Simpson arrived on his annual tour of inspection, and the protesters promptly took their petition to him.[61] Hearing from them how passionate was the community's antipathy toward Thom, Simpson had a chat with the recorder, following which "Mr. Thom ... voluntarily offered to absent himself from Court and Council"[62] for a year. Inconveniently for the company, Thom's contract had just been renewed for a further five years.[63] Simpson thought, however, that if the unpopular recorder kept a low profile for a while passions would cool, the pressure for his deportation would diminish, and he might be able to resume his public duties. It was a vain hope.

Not everyone despised Adam Thom, and some colleagues were unhappy with even his temporary absence from the bench. Dr John Bunn, for example, a valued member of both the General Court and petty courts, submitted his own resignation, complaining that his position was "untenable" since Thom's absence "has deprived me of the only safe guide the country possesses. Who can point out the paths of law and justice without such guidance?"[64] Other magistrates followed his example. Fortunately, however, Bunn's resignation was temporary; he and others were soon persuaded to return to the bench.[65]

Governor Caldwell shared Dr Bunn's concerns. As president of the shrunken court, he bore the responsibility for providing the colony with an effective judicature, and it was not a role he found agreeable: "[A]lthough I am conversant in military courts and law, I am quite the reverse as regards civil law. The charging of the jury ... I shrink from, and feel unable to unravel the intricacies of, and to define, the law."[66] Simpson had advised the governor to consult with Thom about such matters,[67] but when he did so Thom petulantly declined.[68] Caldwell decided, therefore, that the best course would be to close the court until either London advised him otherwise or "the inconvenience ... led the people to feel their error, and ... [change their mind] regarding the Recorder." But when he made this proposal to the Council of Assiniboia he was nonplussed to discover that not only did most of its members share the public's opinion of Adam Thom,[69] but they also disagreed with Caldwell's view that court sittings should be deferred, unless absolutely necessary. They did vote to suspend the law of June 1837 *requiring* the courts to sit quarterly,[70] but in fact sittings continued almost uninterrupted. The General Court missed only the May and August 1850 sessions, and partially made up for that by a special sitting in July. As for the petty courts, which had lost other magistrates besides Dr Bunn, it was resolved that they should continue to be held "at the same time and place as heretofore," all of them chaired by the apparently indefatigable Alexander Ross alongside any two other council members.

Matheson v. Thom

When Adam Thom next set foot in the Fort Garry courtroom, in February 1850, it was as a litigant rather than as a member of the court.[71] He was sued for refusing to pay carpenter Hugh Matheson for building a veranda on the Thoms' home.[72] Although entirely satisfied with the workmanship, Thom thought he was being overcharged.

Both parties improperly approached Governor Caldwell privately in advance of the trial, but the governor correctly refused to speak to either; and at the trial Alexander Ross, who was the plaintiff's father-in-law, left the bench and sat in the audience. Apart from those proprieties, the hearing was a near-travesty from beginning to end. Although the official court record is much sparser than normal, disclosing only the names of the parties and the fact that Thom was victorious, a suppressed, fuller report of the case[73] reveals that Thom's condescension and high-handed tactics provoked angry outbursts from Magistrate Cuthbert Grant, echoed by matching ripostes from the suspended recorder. Governor Caldwell was unable to control either man.

Thom's defence – that he had no legal obligation to pay because Matheson had never submitted his account in writing – outraged most who heard it; but the pontifical lawyer managed to persuade the witless governor that the defence was correct in law. As Thom stomped out of the courtroom in triumph, without even waiting for the case to conclude formally, Alexander Ross protested from the audience that "there is neither law nor justice" to be obtained in the court. If any healing had occurred in Thom's ruptured relations with the community during his absence from the courtroom, the wound was torn open again. As for the bumbling Major Caldwell, the *Matheson* case confirmed his own self-assessment that he was an entirely incompetent court president.

Foss v. Pelly[74]

It was a third bizarre trial, however, that plunged Caldwell to the nadir of his gubernatorial career – and sealed the judicial fate of Adam Thom. That case was brought to the General Quarterly Court by the major's second-in-command of the Chelsea Pensioners militia – the dashing, hot-headed Captain Christopher Foss. A friendship had formed between Foss and Sarah, the vivacious wife of HBC chief factor John Ballenden. As the friendship blossomed, the colony's rumour mills ground out increasingly lurid accounts of questionable goings-on between the captain and the chief factor's lady. By mid-summer, rumours were so rife that Foss decided to sue some of the gossips in the hope of clearing the names of Sarah Ballenden and himself. Chief Factor Ballenden concurred. A special sitting of the General Court was accordingly declared, and before long almost the entire community was split, as in a colossal sporting event, between the supporters of the plaintiff and those of the defendants. The trial was one of the most acrimonious in the court's history.

Remarkably, Recorder Adam Thom was back on the bench for the occasion. The explanation for his reappearance did not reflect credit on anyone. Foss and the Ballendens had approached Thom, in his capacity as lawyer, for advice on how to suppress the rumours; and it was Thom who, after initial hesitation, recommended suing. Mrs Ballenden was of mixed-blood heritage, so when leaders of the Halfbreed community were asked whether they would oppose Thom's participation as recorder, they, knowing he supported her, raised no objection. To complicate matters further, Thom left the bench at one point during the trial, gave evidence from the witness box, and then returned to the seat of judgment. (Three other members of the court, Major Caldwell, Dr Bunn, and Sheriff Ross – as well as Court Clerk William Smith – also gave evidence.) The jury, after being charged at length by Recorder

Thom, deliberated long and returned a verdict awarding Captain Foss a staggering £300 in damages. Adam Thom had managed, with no apparent objection from President Caldwell, to be counsel, witness, and judge in a single case! For many, this was the final straw.

The Foss-Ballenden controversy did not end with the controversial judgment in July 1850. Foss had been recalled to England by the War Office, probably at the request of the HBC, and had promised that he would leave the settlement in October;[75] but he ended up staying until the following summer. As a result, perhaps, of the arrogant officer's continuing presence, the antipathies that had divided the settlement so sharply during the trial persisted until almost the end of the year.[76] John Ballenden had left the settlement on business shortly after the trial and was still absent when, in December 1850, evidence came to light that convinced most residents, including Adam Thom, that Foss and Sarah Ballenden were indeed lovers.[77] By the time Foss left Red River in disgrace in July, Mrs Ballenden was known to be pregnant.[78] Tragic though these developments were for John and Sarah Ballenden, they helped to ease Red River's social discord. Relations between Dr John Bunn and fellow councillor John Black provide a case in point. Once on the most cordial of terms, Bunn and Black were among the many who had been alienated by the case, Bunn having castigated Black and his wife for pointing the finger of shame at Mrs Ballenden, whom he had considered to be innocent. When the new revelations became public, the doctor wrote the chief trader a letter of abject apology,[79] to which the latter replied graciously that he was pleased "the breach is healed."[80]

ACTING GOVERNOR COLVILE

The company had decided some time previously that circumstances at Red River had deteriorated to the point where it was imperative for the governor-in-chief of Rupert's Land to reside in the settlement for a while once more in order to give stronger leadership than local authorities seemed able to provide. However, Sir George Simpson was personally unwilling to winter at Red River, his wife having refused to return. It was agreed, therefore, that Eden Colvile, the thirty-year-old son of HBC deputy governor Andrew Colvile, would be appointed as a co-governor-in-chief to act in Simpson's stead when necessary.[81] The younger man accompanied Simpson on his annual tour in 1848 to get a feel for the job, and spent 1849 supervising company operations on the west coast.[82]

In the summer of 1850 Colvile and his wife journeyed to Red River for an extended stay.

The moment this young new governor-in-chief arrived at the settlement on 11 August 1850, he faced a crisis. Immediately after stepping from his canoe at the Lower Fort, Colvile was handed a petition signed by the councillors of Assiniboia and 502 other settlers, requesting the removal of Governor Caldwell. Although most of the signatories were anglophones, there was little doubt that at least as large a proportion of the French-speaking community shared their views.[83] And the petition wasn't all. The previously loyal Alexander Ross, speaking for most of his fellow councillors, informed Colvile that they refused to sit on either the council or the court with Caldwell in the chair.[84] Socially as well, circumstances were, in Colvile's words, "unpleasant" and "ludicrous" in the tiny community cleaved by the *Foss* case: "For instance, today the [Anglican] Bishop & his [anti-Foss] sister were calling on us, & in the middle of the visit I heard a knock at the door, ... & found Mr. & Mrs. Ballenden [pro-Foss]. I had to cram them into another room till the Bishop's visit was over, but ... he had to pass through this room. It was altogether like a scene in a farce."[85] In sum, Colvile complained, "I am not on a bed of roses here."

Despite his inexperience, Eden Colvile dealt with the situation sagely. As pro tem governor-in-chief of Rupert's Land, he had the formal authority to override Governor Caldwell, but he chose persuasion over assertion. He convinced Caldwell that the only alternative to continued chaos during the several months before London could appoint a new council would be Colvile's temporarily assuming, with Caldwell's consent, "the presidency of the Court ... [and] Council," while the major retained his other gubernatorial functions.[86] Although Colvile considered Caldwell "the most unmitigated ass I ever had to do business with," he won the older man's approval for this compromise by "flattering his vanity a little."[87] He then turned his attention to Ross and the other councillors, rapping their knuckles for accusing the governor of "suspending the administration of justice" when their own resignations from the magistracy had given him little alternative. They had not displayed, he charged, "that conciliatory spirit with which alone the government can be satisfactorily carried on." Unless they agreed to his proposed compromise, he warned, "no new laws can be passed, and no existing laws administered. In a word, the colony will be in a state of anarchy."[88]

The councillors concurred, and assembled ten days later under the chairmanship of Eden Colvile, but with both Major Caldwell and Adam Thom present and participating, to begin the work of putting the machinery of government back together again.[89] About six weeks after that, on 16 October 1850, the council approved a detailed restructuring of the petty courts with a large new slate of magistrates, many of them Canadian or Halfbreeds, and with the formerly resigned magistrates as "ex officio presidents" of the courts. The jurisdiction of the petty courts was enlarged once more to include "all ordinary police cases," with no appeal to the General Court, plus all debt claims under £5, with an appeal for claims over £2.[90]

ADAM THOM IN LIMBO

The General Court, which had missed its regular sessions for May and August, sat again in November, with Governor Colvile presiding. Neither Caldwell nor Thom was present. It had been intended that the recorder should sit on that occasion, but, as Colvile later reported to Simpson, "Mr. Irlande alias Rielle [Louis Riel Sr] came to me about half an hour before the Court met to say that the people were determined to keep Thom out. As we had no preparations made for a row, the magistrates were all of opinion that it would be better for Thom to keep away; but if we have another Court in February I am clear for having him in, coute qu'il coute."[91] Before February arrived, Governor Colvile thought better of his determination to reinstate Thom. He probably realized by then that the Halfbreed resolve to keep the recorder out of the courtroom was simply too strong to resist. Or perhaps he had got wind of a resolution passed by the London Governor and Committee in December 1850 revoking Thom's commission as recorder.[92] By acting as counsel, witness, and judge in the *Foss* case, Adam Thom had at last reached the limits of even that insensitive body's patience.

Dismissing Thom altogether at this time would have been financially awkward for the company, because it had recently extended his contract to 1854. It accordingly proposed that his employment be continued, at the same generous salary, but as clerk of the courts and council rather than as recorder. It was undoubtedly hoped that Thom's pride would not allow him to accept the demotion, and would prod him to resign. But the defrocked jurist was a pragmatist where his personal interests were concerned and, "contrary to the expectation of all his friends," he agreed to remain in the settlement with reduced rank and diminished duties, so long as his remuneration was not affected.

Both Thom and the company reckoned without public opinion, however. As Colvile later explained to Sir George,

> With reference to Thom's new position, I am sorry to say that although he accepted the new appointment ... it has no way conduced to the peace of the Settlement, or contributed to rendering him more popular. Before the May Court I took the opportunity of seeing Rielle and others of the Canadian agitators, and explained to them the change in Thom's position, and that he was now servant of the Court instead of master as heretofore. They replied that in their opinion the people would not let him into Court even in the capacity of constable. And this proved to be the case, for I found the excitement so great among the French Halfbreeds that I believed if Thom had made his appearance he would have been maltreated.[93]

Colvile therefore advised Thom not to attend any future sittings of the courts. The former recorder's remaining contributions to the community during the three years he stayed on in the settlement as idle court clerk were almost entirely rendered behind the scenes. Since the Council of Assiniboia met in camera, Thom did continue to serve as *its* clerk until his departure from Red River. As will be seen, he also provided a valuable law reform service.

RETURNING TO NORMALCY

Eden Colvile chaired, and Caldwell was absent from, the February sitting of the General Court. While this ensured an orderly hearing, the company was nervous that Colvile's interim administration was giving the appearance of a usurpation of civil authority by the commercial organization. He was accordingly instructed to hand the reins back to Major Caldwell and did so at the next meeting of the Council of Assiniboia, on 1 May 1851.[94] Caldwell also presided over the General Court once more, at and after its May session, with Colvile sitting as a subordinate member. On the same bench on that occasion – his first as a member of that court – was Chief Trader John Black. The court's one-time clerk, and its future recorder, had risen considerably in Colvile's esteem since their first encounters.[95] Conspicuously absent from both the 1 May council meeting and the 15 May court hearings were Alexander Ross and Andrew McDermot, both of whom remained true to their resolve not to serve under Caldwell's leadership. Both also left their positions in the petty courts, and Ross resigned as sheriff and "governor of the gaol." To fill those vital posts, the council immediately appointed Ross's son William, thereby somewhat assuaging the father's feelings.[96]

That council meeting of May 1851 marked an auspicious new beginning for Red River's civil authority. In addition to the William Ross appointments, John Black was made president of the Upper District Petty Court in the stead of Ross senior, and an ambitious program of road improvements was undertaken, funded by an allocation of £500. A grant of £100 was also made, in equal moieties, to the Anglican and Roman Catholic bishops "for the purposes of education."[97] Dr Bunn proposed, for future discussion, that imprisonment for debts be abolished for sums under £2, and Reverend Cockran, newly appointed to council, gave notice of a motion to establish a public inspection system for weights and measures.[98] Very important from the legal perspective was the striking of a committee, consisting of Adam Thom, Reverend LaFlèche, and Dr Bunn, to prepare "a report on the state of the law."[99]

HBC authorities in London contributed somewhat to the aura of change by instituting a practice of directly appointing justices of the peace (JPs) for the colony under the authority of the company charter.[100] The post of justice of the peace is an ancient English magisterial office with the power of summons and arrest. The purpose of introducing JPs at this point is not clear, since those powers had long been exercised by locally appointed magistrates. Possibly, there was concern about the legality of local appointments; more likely, there was annoyance that the locally appointed Red River judiciary was displaying altogether too much independence. Another factor may have been that whereas locally appointed magistrates were paid for their services, justices of the peace traditionally were not. Whatever the intention, few of that first batch of newly designated JPs accepted their appointments,[101] and the Council of Assiniboia continued to appoint magistrates on its own authority. The pattern thereafter appears to have been that the London-appointed JPs became the senior members of the magistracy, serving as petty court presidents, issuers of court process (writs of summons, arrest, etc.), and members of the General Court.[102]

Despite Eden Colvile's hope "that by the canoes we may hear of a new Governor instead of Major Caldwell,"[103] the major remained in formal charge of the settlement for the remainder of the period under review, and he does not seem to have become any better at his job. Dr Bunn, writing to Simpson in August 1851, called the major "remarkably distinguished for maladroitness," said his "only defence against blunder is total inaction," and noted that he was "still the object of derision."[104] Somehow, however, Caldwell's ineptitude caused fewer problems in the later years of his tenure than at the beginning.

A partial reason for the improvement may have been that Captain Christopher Foss had been replaced as second-in-command of the pensioners (whose numbers were swollen by a second contingent in September 1850) by Captain Joseph Hill in September 1851.[105] Caldwell's new assistant made a good impression upon his arrival, and although the pensioners remained a blight on the settlement in many respects, they seem to have at least provided effective relocation assistance for the settlement during the 1852 flood – something for which Captain Hill was likely deserving of greater credit than Major Caldwell.

LAWS OF ASSINIBOIA REVISED

Adam Thom's final significant contribution to Red River was his revision, as the leading member of a Law Amendment Committee established by the Assiniboia council on 1 May 1851, of the Laws of Assiniboia. What Thom, "in conjunction with the Reverend LaFlèche and Doctor Bunn," was requested to do was to prepare "a report on the state of the law." Before the end of May, Thom had produced, with characteristic dispatch, much more than that. He had drafted a new consolidation of the settlement's local laws, cleansed of much obsolete legislation and substantively improved in several respects. Having obtained the approval of his fellow committee members for this revision, Thom read it to the council on 27 November 1851, with a view to its being considered at the next meeting.[106] The great flood of 1852 then interrupted all nonessential business, and council did not reconvene until 13 July 1852; but when it did so, the "revised Code of Municipal Regulations" was passed unanimously, with only a handful of minor amendments.[107]

Since Thom's compilation and revision of Assiniboia's laws in 1841,[108] only piecemeal changes had been made,[109] and an updated consolidation was greatly needed. This one was a marked improvement over the 1841 version. Although it embodied only one radical modification, there were a number of smaller but substantial and beneficial changes, as well as a welcome simplification of language. The latter was probably made at the behest of the two lay members of the Law Amendment Committee. This version was also shorter, containing only forty-six articles as opposed to the fifty-eight of the 1841 compilation. Typical of Thom products, this "simplified" consolidation was introduced by an elaborate preamble explaining the committee's approach (including its reasons for abandoning preambles!): "We have reduced the whole of the existing regulations within ... [a] very narrow compass ... This brevity we have attained partly by throwing aside all preambles[110] ... and partly by omitting all such regulations as would appear never to have been called into practical operation ... [W]e trust that we have been enabled to disencumber our Municipal Code of all those redundancies of language or enactment which inevitably spring from every man's overweening estimate of present interest and present feelings." The introductory explanation then rambled on to discussions of such matters as the limited legislative authority of local legislators, the desirability of ending imprisonment for debt, confusion about whose authority it was to issue marriage licences, and other matters. But the laws themselves were, as promised, spare and clear. Although this incarnation of the Laws of Assiniboia did not, like the last one, contain provisions concerning publication of its contents to the community, it appears to have been at least as well circulated as its predecessor. And now, for the first time, a French version, translated by committee and council member Father LaFlèche, was also made available.[111]

The laws on many matters – fires, trespassing animals, horse theft, haying, roads, and so forth – remained substantially unchanged. However, those on the vexed topics of intoxication of Indians and customs duties were made less complex and less severe, and the practice of fine-sharing with informers was finally abandoned. The police establishment was set at fifteen constables, each to be reappointed annually. And the governor was empowered to issue marriage licences and letters of administration for intestate estates. The enactment of future legislation by the Council of Assiniboia was required to pass two readings on different days. A public library was established.

The jurisdiction of the petty courts was extended to criminal charges carrying fines of less than £2 and to debt claims under £5, with appeals to the General Court if over £2. Parties to civil actions were authorized to examine each other on oath. Although imprisonment for debt was not abolished, it was no longer permitted at public expense: the creditor had to pay the debtor weekly, in advance, "the daily allowance of four pence," to be passed on to his jailer for food and water. Reflecting the increasingly agrarian nature of the settlement, the petty courts (but not the General Court) were permitted to adjourn at seeding time and harvest time.

The rule that English laws as of May 1670 applied in Rupert's Land was finally abandoned, and those of 20 June 1837 – the date of Queen Victoria's accession to the throne – substituted. As Thom's introduction noted, the laws of 1670 were, "independent of their inherent and essential inferiority, ... difficult, nay, generally speaking, impossible, to be ascertained ... in such a wilderness as this." As the settlement's only lawyer, he wrote, whenever asked for a legal opinion he must either close his eyes to the theoretically applicable law or "shock the common sense of the community with antiquated absurdities." That dilemma had been created by Thom himself, of course, in his absurd choice of 1670 as the reception date of English laws.[112] The substitution of 1837 as the date that would henceforth "regulate the proceedings of the General Court" did not dispose of the difficulty entirely. Apart from the obvious need to keep amending the date from time to time to keep Assiniboia's laws in step with England's, the word "proceedings" caused future problems. While Thom and his colleagues undoubtedly meant it to embrace everything the court was called upon to decide, it would be interpreted almost thirty years later to refer only to *procedural* matters,[113] creating much confusion about the status of substantive rights determined by litigation during those years.

The London Governor and Committee subsequently gave its "approbation" to the new compilation of laws.[114] The legal significance of that approval is not entirely clear. As pointed out previously,[115] although the Council of Assiniboia did not possess *explicit* legislative powers, it may well have held *implicit* law-making authority. Previous laws made by the council had been applied without approval of the London office, and previous company disapprovals of local laws had been couched as "suggestions." Yet this communication from London gives the impression that authorities there now considered their approval to be crucial; and Sir George Simpson claimed two years later that locally legislated changes in import duties "were not laws until confirmed at home."[116] Probably, the company's nervousness about growing populism at Red River caused it to adopt a narrower view than heretofore of the governing powers it had delegated to the Council of Assiniboia.[117] Was this newly vigilant approach legally defensible? It probably was, especially if treated – as seems to have been intended – as a power of veto rather than of compulsory advance approval.[118]

FAREWELL TO ADAM THOM

Apart from the legislative update project, the erstwhile recorder's final years at Red River were relatively idle. Prevented from carrying out his duties as court clerk, Thom continued to serve as clerk of the council, but that body met only six times while Thom held the position. He also remained the legal adviser to the company and the governor, but there is little evidence that he was called upon very often in those capacities either. Following the *Foss* case, Governor Caldwell was no longer willing to consult Thom.[119] And according to Colvile, the recorder was not at all missed in the courtroom: "I believe the Court gets on just as well without him."[120]

For so industrious a man, Thom's involuntary idleness must have been frustrating. However, contrary to what the company had probably hoped, that did not prompt him to leave the colony. Eden Colvile's assessment of the situation in July 1851 was that "Thom's plans, so far as I can judge, are to draw £700 a year from the concern as long as he can, at least until his boy Adam the second is old enough to go to school; and I believe there is no office you could give him that he would not accept, provided always that he got the same amount of pay."[121]

If Thom ever believed that public antipathy toward him would dissipate over time,[122] he was mistaken. Dr John Bunn informed Sir George Simpson in August 1851 that the former recorder "is as much as ever the object of bitter ... hatred" and "stands almost alone."[123] In large part, Thom contributed to his own pariahdom by increasing pettiness and irascibility on the fewer and fewer occasions when he found himself in the company of others. His one-time court clerk John Black, who had been at odds with Thom since at least the *Foss* trial, reported that during one council meeting, Clerk Thom insisted so "insolently" on taking part in the debate that Dr Bunn, normally a Thom sympathizer, had to remind him that he had no right to speak. At another meeting, Thom testily demanded the sole right to sign council minutes, to the exclusion of all council members.[124] And although he now had little personal use for the settlement's law library, he refused to share it with others. Even in church he made himself a nuisance with "loud, pompous, insulting" responses.[125]

In the Presbyterian congregation to which Thom then transferred his allegiance, however, he became an enthusiastic, active, and well-regarded member. In fact, the only Red River leader who now appeared to support Thom, and to advocate his return to office, was ironically the "Ruling Elder" of the Presbyterian congregation, Alexander Ross, who had been so critical of the recorder in the past.[126] But not even the support of Ross – himself no longer a friend of the administration – could do anything to restore the disgraced lawyer to public or official favour.

Much of Thom's abundant energy was now lavished on correspondence. There was, for example, a flurry of letters generated by a bitter feud with Anglican bishop Anderson over a sermon by the latter supporting the unsuccessful defendants in the *Foss* trial.[127] Another prolific correspondence – with Sir George Simpson – alternated between providing the governor-in-chief with news of the community and complaining about the way he had been treated by the company.[128]

Simpson, who generally addressed Thom in polite, even friendly, tones, finally lost his patience in December 1851, replying to two letters bemoaning the recorder's demotion with a broadside that would have demolished anyone lacking Thom's rhinoceros-like ego armour. After denying any responsibility for the demotion and claiming not to have even known about it in advance, Sir George began by refuting Thom's claim to have been selected because of his "more than ordinary success at the bar" and qualifications that fitted him "for the wilderness," as well as his contention that he had been injured in his future professional prospects by his service in distant Rupert's Land.[129]

Those points he responded to with a merciless barrage. Thom was actually chosen, Simpson said, because "you possessed all the legal knowledge requisite" and because "it was probable you would willingly accept ... [the position] as your prospects at the bar were not promising," since "your want of facility in public speaking was a serious drawback to your success." However, he continued, "you had not been long in the country when it was found that ... the selection was not, ... a happy one, ... [due to] your ignorance of the French language, your unfortunate temper, & your overbearing manner – these circumstances ... tending to render you exceedingly unpopular." This unpopularity had "the effect of seriously disturbing the peace, of impeding the administration of justice, and of bringing odium on the Company by maintaining you in office in opposition to the public voice. These facts are so notorious that it has been a subject of wonder to well-informed persons ... that the Governor & Committee did not restore harmony, as they no doubt might have done, by your removal." "Your case might be stated thus," he concluded:

> Here is ... the occupant of an important office, the duties of which, to the great injury of the public interests, he is unable to perform in consequence of his unpopularity, as proof of which he, in order to appease public clamour, for twelve months voluntarily abstained from the performance of his official duties, and which he has ever since been prevented discharging ... by threats of personal violence & the knowledge that the attempt to assume his functions would

> lead to a breach of the peace. This gentleman, whose services are thus entirely lost, is nevertheless in receipt ... of a handsome salary and allowance, for little more than the half of which there might be obtained from the Canadian bar a gentleman of high standing and experience, conversant with the French language, ... qualified to fill the appointment with credit to himself & satisfaction to the public. ... Petition after petition has been presented ... for the removal from office of the present incumbent, in which petitions it is alleged that his presence in the country, whether in or out of office, is disagreeable to a large majority of the inhabitants, and that the dislike of and desire to get rid of him have been the chief causes of the agitation and disaffection that prevail, having on one occasion actually lead to an armed resistance to the authorities.

"When the case is thus stated," the indictment wound up, "it must be admitted that the Company would have been perfectly justified in adopting even the extreme measure of removing you altogether from their service."[130] Typically of Simpson, however, the letter ended, "With an assurance of my continued regard."

Even though the governor-in-chief's cannonade made a strong case for Thom's immediate and complete dismissal, that did not happen. The company agreed, contrary to the wishes of the wintering partners,[131] to continue paying him until 31 May 1854. It even agreed, after some dickering, to purchase Thom's house for £500 – just a little less than he had paid for it and improvements.[132] After moving from the house in June, Thom and his family were housed and boarded at the Lower Fort at company expense until they could be transported home from York Factory at the end of the summer. Simpson instructed Black that the staff "must endeavour to make his last impressions of the service as little disagreeable as possible, and evince a disposition to oblige him & meet his wishes."[133] And Simpson remained willing to provide ongoing assistance with Thom's personal investments.[134]

The motivation for treating the former recorder so much more generously than he deserved was no doubt Simpson's concern that a dissatisfied and independent Thom could create damaging publicity in the United Kingdom.[135] Sir George clearly did not trust him – although, as he told Eden Colvile even before Thom left Red River, it would be difficult for the former HBC apologist to now reverse himself publicly: "Thom has already begun to shew the cloven foot, talking of that 'musty old piece of parchment, the Company's Charter' in the Council. He has committed himself in writing & print too often as the supporter of the Company's legal rights to be very dangerous, as if he now take an opposite view of the question people will set him down either for a very bad lawyer or a very great rogue."[136]

Adam Thom and his family departed Red River for York Factory in mid-August 1854,[137] and appear to have had an uneventful journey home. Contrary to Simpson's fears, the disgraced recorder made no attempt to betray the HBC thereafter. Consequences of his Red River escapades would, however, continue to plague the company and the settlement for years to come.

FURTHER FAREWELLS

John Black

The career of Chief Trader John Black, in contrast to that of the man he had come to Red River to assist as court clerk, was decidedly on the rise in the early 1850s, and in 1852, after the floodwaters had receded in the settlement, Black was rewarded with his first (and overdue) furlough. He and Mrs Black travelled to Lachine by canoe and to New York by rail. They enjoyed a "delightful passage" by swift steamship to England, and then moved on to Scotland where her parents had settled in retirement. It was a much-savoured vacation.[138]

The Blacks' situation darkened that winter, however. In late January 1853 he reported to Simpson that his wife had fallen seriously ill and that he might have to request an extension of his leave, failing which he might have to resign from the company.[139] Sir George's response, refusing a furlough extension, was unsympathetic: "[I]t would be unreasonable to suppose that ... family considerations could be made of paramount importance; ... when they come in conflict with duty, it is expected that they will give way. You are aware that I never allowed my family to interfere with my duties, having had occasionally to leave them for years at a time."[140] Reluctantly, Black decided against resigning and returned to duty, leaving his ailing wife in Edinburgh. It must have been difficult, upon arriving at New York and learning that Lady Simpson was dead, for Black to compose a sincere letter of condolence.[141]

Later that year, as reports reaching Red River of Mrs Black's deteriorating health grew bleaker, Black again requested leave, and was once more refused.[142] On Christmas Eve, anticipating the rejection of his most recent application for leave, John Black decided to act on his own authority. Turning his post over to a less experienced officer, he struck out for Lachine, en route to Britain.[143] Awaiting him at Lachine, however, was word of his wife's death. Distraught, Black wanted to proceed anyway, but Simpson persuaded him to return to Red River.[144]

The HBC Governor and Committee were incensed by Black's perceived dereliction of duty, and requested that the Council of Rupert's Land discipline him at its 1854 meeting – an order the council could hardly ignore.[145] A fine of £200 was accordingly imposed, and although Sir George tried to persuade him that the punishment would not affect his future career with the company,[146] John Black decided, after some hesitation, that he had had enough, and resigned his post.[147] He returned to the United Kingdom, and then moved to Australia. At his request, the company first reduced the penalty, and then rescinded it altogether, in order not to prejudice his future employment opportunities abroad.[148] It would be more than seven years before Red River heard anything more of this John Black. But he would be back.

Cuthbert Grant

The legendary Cuthbert Grant's influence among his former followers had declined due to the prominent role he was required by the company to play in the enforcement of its asserted trading monopoly. The *Sayer* case of 1849 demonstrated that the man who had signed himself "Chief of the Halfbreeds and Warden of the Plains" during the 1845 peace negotiations with the Sioux[149] no longer commanded the full and foremost allegiance of his people. That role had shifted to Louis Riel Sr and James Sinclair. At the next meeting of the Council of Rupert's Land, the title "Warden of the Plains" ceased to be recognized, and the associated annual stipend Grant had been receiving from the company for the past twenty-one years ceased to be paid.[150] His contributions to the joint Pembina–St Boniface–White Horse Plains buffalo hunts, which had once been almost indispensable, diminished as well. Grant took no part in the 1851 hunt, during which some 2,000 Sioux, abandoning the accord of 1845, attacked a much smaller group of Halfbreeds at Grand Coteau on the American plains and were decisively defeated by the Red River hunters, suffering many casualties. That battle became one of the proudest moments of the Halfbreed people, but their former icon was not even present.[151]

In 1853, at the age of sixty, Cuthbert Grant sought to reverse his failing fortunes by proposing to Governor Simpson that he be authorized (and bankrolled) by the company to trade on its behalf with Indians in competition with American free traders.[152] His letter suggested that the loan he sought to get the new business under way should be treated as a "composition in lieu of an annuity" to which he evidently considered himself entitled by reason of his many years of service to the company. The following year, after the apparent rejection of that proposal, Grant seems to have either renewed the annuity claim or sought reinstatement to his position as warden of the plains. Simpson temporized, "I am not prepared to give you an immediate reply to the points you have brought under my notice in reference to your salary as Warden of the Plains. The arrangement to which you refer was made thirty years ago, & although I have in my mind a general recollection of the terms, it is necessary to refer to documents not in my possession here [at Fort Garry]."[153] Although the governor promised to reply when he returned to Lachine, there was no need to do so. Grant had not been able to meet Simpson in person at Fort Garry because of serious injuries caused by a fall from a horse. On 15 July 1854 he died from those injuries.[154]

James Sinclair

A fourth figure who loomed large throughout the years covered by this chapter – James Sinclair – was also gone before they were over. Sinclair always claimed to have "been blamed more ... than I deserved" for assaults on the HBC fur trade monopoly, and to have "cared [little] about the free trade, provided I was let alone and fairly treated."[155] He made more than one conciliatory approach to the company,[156] and the breach was finally healed in 1850 by a request from Sir George Simpson that Sinclair examine and report on the state of company affairs in Oregon after the boundary settlement.[157] That mission led to Sinclair's leading a second convoy of settlers from Red River to Oregon in the summer of 1854; and after successfully completing that assignment, he resolved to remain in US territory. Tragically, he was killed only two years later by an Indian attack on a small Oregon settlement he was visiting.[158]

Sinclair's emigration from Red River did not have a significant impact on the settlement, since it came at a time when his leadership abilities were not greatly required. Cuthbert Grant was replaced soon after his death as both president of the White Horse Plains Petty Court and as a member of the General Court. And a new recorder of Rupert's Land was already in place.[159]

7

Scrutiny, Growth, Uncertainty, 1855–60

The best known event affecting the Hudson's Bay Company and the Red River Settlement in this half-decade was the 1857 enquiry of a Select Committee of the British House of Commons into the Hudson's Bay Company's stewardship of its North American territories. Despite receiving much criticism, the HBC *and the Assiniboia government emerged relatively unscathed from the ordeal, leaving the company in a strong position to begin negotiations for the eventual transfer of its lands and governmental responsibilities to Canada. But the shape of the colony's future remained indistinct.*

Meanwhile, those who had previously bungled Red River's governance and legal affairs left, and the egregious Chelsea Pensioners were replaced by a garrison of regular troops. When Red River's first newspaper began publication in 1860, its pages reflected new prosperity, new stability, and new leadership. In Recorder Adam Thom's place, until 1858, was a competent, thoroughly bilingual, barrister from Montreal and, thereafter, a man who lacked formal legal training but whose performance eclipsed those of the lawyers preceding him.

RECONSTRUCTION

The calamity-prone administration of Governor William B. Caldwell was still in office in Assiniboia when this period began. Although most settlers, of all perspectives and persuasions, would still have heartily agreed with the 1851 remark of the HBC's Donald Ross that "Caldwell is utterly unable to govern the Settlement,"[1] no replacement was in immediate sight. The petition demanding Caldwell's recall had not been supported by the company and had been ignored by the British government.[2] And although Caldwell's pensioners, the only protective force the colony had, were still "a great deal worse than useless,"[3] their commanding

Figure 7.1 Francis G. Johnson was a bilingual, legally skilled, and diplomatic recorder and governor whose laziness and soft scruples blemished his contributions and ensured that he was not fondly remembered.

officer had been recently promoted from major to lieutenant colonel. Reconstruction was nevertheless in train. Some changes of leadership had already occurred, and others would soon be in place. For the first time, moreover, the process of change was being monitored, prompted, and influenced by skeptical observers. The most searching scrutiny came from the UK Parliament.

PARLIAMENTARY ENQUIRY

The complaints laid before the British government by Alexander Isbister and others received a belated but widely publicized airing before a

Select Committee of the British House of Commons between February and June 1857.[4] Those complaints were not the sole, or even the principal, genesis of the enquiry. The immediate impetus was the looming expiration of the company's licence to operate west of the Rocky Mountains, an area beyond its chartered domains. Before deciding what to do when the licence expired, British authorities needed to know about the current state of the licensed territory. But the public was even more interested in the persistent complaints about the HBC's administration of Rupert's Land. And Canada, which was fast running out of arable land, had turned covetous eyes westward, making the possible Canadian annexation of Rupert's Land a hot topic of discussion. For those reasons – chiefly the latter one – the Select Committee was asked to scrutinize *both* the HBC's licensed and chartered territories.

Although Lord Palmerston's incumbent Tory government was generally friendly to the company, and the Select Committee's chairman, Colonial Secretary Henry Labouchere, was particularly so, the fate of the HBC's North American hegemony was not a matter of compelling importance to the government; and the committee's distinguished membership included powerful critics of the company and its commercial and governmental monopoly. There were, for example, the renowned Whig leader and former secretary of state for the colonies Lord John Russell and – even more notably – his brilliant colleague William Ewart Gladstone, a former colonial secretary, who was at the height of his famed rhetorical powers. Defenders of the HBC had their work cut out for them.

Much evidence critical of the company was presented to the Select Committee. Alexander Isbister, called early in the proceedings,[5] led the attack with an array of familiar complaints, based chiefly on the 1848 petition he had submitted to British authorities on behalf of discontented settlers, plus some criticisms of his own. Stating that his "chief object" was "to improve the condition of the native and half-caste Indians in the Red River Settlement,"[6] he was especially critical of inadequate educational opportunities for Indians.[7] He also contended that HBC payments to missionaries were "sops" intended to encourage the recipients to "shut their eyes to many matters which occur."[8] Briefly recalled on the final day of the hearing, Isbister presented a new petition from about 100 Red River residents requesting that Canada annex the settlement.[9]

Isbister's first appearance before the committee was immediately followed by that of Reverend G.O. Corbett, an Anglican pastor based at

Headingley, who complained that the company had discouraged the settlements and missions at Portage la Prairie and Headingley,[10] that schools were inadequately funded,[11] that the colony lacked representative government,[12] and that settlers' mail was being tampered with.[13] In later years, Corbett was convicted by Assiniboia's General Court of a very serious crime,[14] a prosecution he called retaliation for opposing the HBC before the Select Committee.

The witness who probably caused greatest concern to the company was William Henry Draper, a former premier of Upper Canada who currently held the office of chief justice of the Upper Canada Court of Common Pleas.[15] A highly respected jurist and statesman, Draper represented Canada before the committee; and his submissions[16] opposed the HBC's position in several important respects. He contended, for example, that the HBC charter granted the company less territory than it claimed, and that the trade monopoly it purported to grant was illegal. He revealed that he was currently seeking a reference to the Judicial Committee of the Privy Council to determine the boundary between Canada and Rupert's Land. And, of course, he pressed for Canadian annexation of such HBC territories as were suitable for settlement. Company operations should be confined, he urged, to northern areas where significant settlement was never likely to occur.

The witness who displayed the greatest personal animus toward the HBC was Andrew McDermot's nephew, John McLaughlin,[17] who had delivered the petition to the US government from disgruntled Red River settlers, and had been publicly castigating the company in England since then. Pro-HBC members of the committee, including Chairman Labouchere, came armed with questions to discredit McLaughlin, but that did little to undermine the plausibility of his charges about matters such as postal scrutiny, restrictive land deeds, the shipping embargo against free traders, currency restrictions, inadequate pay for Indians, and HBC control of the Council of Assiniboia.

McLaughin's most significant accusations, in the present context, concerned the administration of justice at Red River. His indictment of the legal system, and of Recorder Adam Thom in particular, was scathing – and in some respects unjustified. Although he accurately described the public's contempt for Thom, several of his specific claims were untrue. Twice, for example, he stated falsely that Thom had refused to be sued in the General Court,[18] and his comments about the 1845 *Capenesseweet* murder trial[19] were highly erroneous. "In a serious case of life or death," he asserted, "there were no means of defence for the prisoner, and on the merest circumstantial evidence he might be convicted."[20] But in the only "life or death" case that had yet occurred at Red River, the evidence was sworn testimony, far from circumstantial, by several members of a large crowd that had witnessed, in broad daylight, the unprovoked accused deliberately fire the fatal shot. Asked whether there was any doubt about who fired, McLaughlin implied that there was, stating untruly that another Indian had first been charged.[21] Questioned about whether a British statute allegedly requiring that capital cases be sent to Canada for trial (a complete misreading of the law in question) was known at Red River, he answered, "Perfectly well." And when asked why the settlers did not "remonstrate against ... [Capenesseweet's] execution," he replied, outrageously, that if they did so, "the Company would stop supplies."[22]

The allegations of McLaughlin and others about Red River justice caused at least one change in HBC strategy. Sir George Simpson, apparently no longer concerned about Adam Thom's "cloven hoof," had arranged for him to testify on the company's behalf,[23] but that never happened. Company officials wisely reconsidered the advisability of exposing the notorious former recorder to cross-examination by the likes of William Gladstone.

Understandably, the company counted on Sir George Simpson to be its most important witness, and in many ways he was. Appearing early in the proceedings, and testifying for almost two full days, Simpson provided a wealth of information about Rupert's Land and the HBC's North American operations.[24] But he was not an ideal witness. His manner, defensive and sometimes testy, was much less persuasive than his superiors had hoped. As historian Douglas MacKay puts it, "Thirty-seven years of absolutism had not fitted the Governor of the territories for a defensive role in a public investigation. The single great loyalty of his life was the Company, and suggestions that his management of affairs might have been better goaded him into indignant retorts."[25] Simpson encountered most difficulty over his assertion that "I do not think that any part of the Hudson's Bay Company territories is well adapted for settlement; the crops are very uncertain."[26] One committee member confronted him, twice, with passages from his book (largely ghost-written by Adam Thom and others), which contradicted that testimony.[27] This forced Simpson to concede at one point, "I do see ... I have overrated [in the book] the importance of the country for settlement,"[28] and to agree with Chairman Labouchere's suggestion that the book presented "too glowing a description."[29]

If Simpson did not succeed in winning the hearts and minds of the Select Committee, the company's other star witness came much closer to doing so. He was the Right Honourable Edward Ellice, a gregarious, wealthy, seventy-six-year-old businessman and major HBC shareholder. He was also a veteran member of Parliament and one-time cabinet minister. Ellice had been connected with the fur trade since 1803, when he went to Canada as a young man to join the XY Company, a Montreal-based rival to the North West Company his father had helped to finance. He remained with the NWC after it absorbed the rival, and was instrumental in engineering, at the request of Colonial Secretary Lord Bathurst, the amalgamation of the NWC and HBC in 1821. The length of his involvement in the fur trade thus exceeded even that of Sir George Simpson.

Ellice took the stand on the final day of the hearings, as the company's wrap-up witness. Being a member of the House of Commons himself, he was accustomed to the give and take of parliamentary proceedings and was much more adept than Simpson at parrying barbed questions. When, for example, a committee member began quoting a strongly anti-HBC statement from an 1815 NWC pamphlet Ellice had probably authored, hoping to lay a trap similar to that into which Simpson had walked, Ellice interrupted the questioner and adroitly spiked his guns: "I am not sure that I am not the author of that libel ... I have written many things as violent as that against the Hudson's Bay Company, and I suppose that parties who are engaged in a violent contest one with the other write a great many things which it would be very difficult to reduce to proof."[30] One imagines the elderly and personable gentleman speaking with a worldly chuckle.

But such sparring was incidental to Ellice's principal contributions to the enquiry. One of those was an authoritative overview of the past half-century of HBC history from the perspective of one who was centrally involved in the events described. For instance, on the vexed question of whether the Fur Trade Regulation Act of 1821 required certain cases from Rupert's Land to be tried in Canadian courts, as John McLaughlin and other critics insisted, Ellice explained carefully why that was not the case, adding when a questioner persisted, "I put in those clauses myself."[31]

Edward Ellice's most important function was to present the HBC's bottom-line position on the pivotal issues of Canadian annexation or Crown colonization of Rupert's Land. He took many by surprise. The proposition he offered was based on a proposal, startling on its face, that Sir George Simpson had made in confidence to HBC governor John Sheppard in August 1856:

> The Company's Charter, so far as exclusive right to trade goes, is almost a nullity, as we are unable to enforce its provisions. It is set at nought by the Americans and their Halfbreed allies in the country, but, notwithstanding the little benefit they derive from it, its possession subjects the Company to much odium, both in England and their own territories, as monopolists. I am inclined to think we should do almost as well without it as with it. I therefore ... [ask] whether it might not be advisable to make a merit of necessity by offering to Her Majesty's Government the voluntary surrender of the Charter on receiving compensation on some such basis as was allowed to the East India Company. Supposing the territory to be thrown open to all British subjects, the fur trade branch of the Company could still conduct the business as private subjects, and with their experience, organization and capital could put down the opposition in the legitimate way of trade, & practically have as much a monopoly as under the Charter. In fact that is the mode in which the business is now conducted.[32]

Initially, this radical idea was rejected by Sheppard.[33] Before long, however, it became the company's position – or at least the basis for its bargaining stance.[34] Although Ellice's testimony before the Select Committee did not directly reveal the company's willingness to surrender its charter if necessary, he nevertheless disclosed, without being asked, that the HBC would not resist Canadian annexation of some or all of its charter lands. Responding to a question concerning the uncertain boundary between Rupert's Land and the western edge of Canada, he stated, surprisingly, "But I take this question of boundary to be ... of no importance at all. If the Province of Canada requires any part of this territory, or the whole of it, for purposes of settlement, it ought not to be permitted for one moment to remain in the hands of the Hudson's Bay Company ... It would be much more for the interest of the Hudson's Bay Company to be upon a cordial and good understanding with the Government than to have any disputed question of right with respect to a certain quantity of land."[35]

When Chairman Labouchere, who had expected this turn of events,[36] broke in to ask for clarification, Ellice revealed a crucial condition of the offer:

> [Chairman:] You are of opinion that it would not be difficult to come to an arrangement by which the extension of Canada, by way of settlement, might be provided for, over any portion of the territory of the Hudson's Bay Company, which is adjacent to Canada, and adapted for such settlement?
>
> [Ellice:] Not only would there be no difficulty in it, but the Hudson's Bay Company would be too glad to make a cession of any part of that territory for the purpose of settlement, upon the one condition that Canada shall be at the expense of governing it and maintain a good police.[37]

Here was the crux of the matter: the governance of Rupert's Land was a difficult, thankless, and costly business; and if Canada wanted to annex the land, it must also take over that responsibility and expense. But Ellice said he doubted that Canada would be able to exercise that responsibility on its own:

> [Chairman:] What power do you conceive that Canada would have at present of governing, say the Red River and the country beyond the Red River?
>
> [Ellice:] I should say that it would be extremely difficult, and that Canada, upon a full consideration of the circumstances, and after a short experience, would entreat the Hudson's Bay Company to resume their government after they had made the experiment.[38]

"Annex if you wish," he seemed to be telling Canada, "but be prepared for very large governmental expenses, whether you govern yourselves or pay the Company to do it for you."

What was said publicly at the Select Committee's hearings was repeated, with greater elaboration and emphasis, in private by Ellice, Simpson, and other HBC leaders. Ellice was close to both his Whig colleagues on the Select Committee and to Chairman Labouchere – to say nothing of his own son, Edward Jr, also a member of Parliament, who sat on the committee. One historian has observed that the senior Ellice "employed customary behind-the-scenes legerdemain."[39] Simpson had been for years on very friendly terms with Chief Justice Draper,[40] Canada's principal representative at the hearings, and it would be hard to believe that frank and informal discussions did not also occur between them over brandy or port after adjournment of the Select Committee's sessions. Forthrightly expressed in those private communications, but not mentioned in the public sessions, was also the company's immovable demand for financial compensation in return for giving up its ownership of Rupert's Land. The sum proposed at that point was £1,000,000.[41]

When the hearings concluded on 23 June, it was obvious to all that the Select Committee had performed a monumental service to Rupert's Land and to Canadian history. In just fourteen days of gruelling public hearings spread over five and a half months and two parliamentary sessions, twenty-four witnesses had provided – in response to almost 7,000 questions and in a wealth of exhibits – an astonishingly rich record of Rupert's Land's past and present, together with a large array of proposals and prognostications for its future.

The committee lost very little time preparing its report. It met in camera on 20 July, less than a month after the last public hearing, to receive a proposed draft report from Chairman Labouchere and a list of alternative proposals from William Gladstone.[42] The latter's proposals, moved as an amendment to the chairman's draft, were considered first, and were defeated only after the chairman broke a tie vote of the committee.[43] Clause-by-clause consideration culminated, on 31 July, in adoption by a close margin of a considerably modified version of Chairman Labouchere's draft.[44] There was much common ground between the positions of the majority and minority. Both agreed that the HBC's exclusive licence and authority over territories west of the Rocky Mountains should not be renewed when it expired in 1859. With respect to Rupert's Land, both also agreed that the company should surrender ownership and governmental authority over Red River and other portions of the territory appropriate for settlement, doing so gradually as those areas were annexed by other authorities. The majority recommended that such annexations should be by Canada; the minority wished to leave open the possibility of a new Crown colony being established. Both groups were loath to see the many longstanding legal controversies concerning the scope of the charter and the company's legal rights thereunder submitted to formal adjudication, and urged negotiated solutions instead. And both scrupulously avoided the slightest criticism of the company's past administration of its territories, and any direct reference to compensating the company for the surrender of its lands.[45]

With the publication of the Select Committee's report, company authorities could breathe much easier. Their ownership of Rupert's

Land had been confirmed; and although their exclusive licence on the west coast would likely be terminated in two years, so would their troublesome governmental responsibilities there. Moreover, their established position in the region gave them a major headstart over future competitors. Support by the Law Officers of the Crown for disputed HBC charter rights was noted in an appendix to the report,[46] and although the Law Officers proposed confirmation of those rights by the Privy Council, and the company reluctantly agreed, the report downplayed the usefulness of judicial proceedings. Canadian annexation of some HBC territory was called for, but it was to be by negotiation based on "equitable principles," which the company insisted demanded a high level of compensation. And the HBC emerged from the enquiry entirely free from official criticism of its administration of its territories.

NEGOTIATION AND PROCRASTINATION

As for future arrangements, the only thing made certain by the Select Committee's report was that the HBC's exclusive trading licence west of the mountains would end in 1859. When that happened, the company politely refused to assist public authorities in governing the area, and continued to carry on business there more or less as in the past.[47]

The possibility that some or all of the legal disputes still cluttering the path to Rupert's Land's future would be referred to the Judicial Committee of the Privy Council hung in the air for a long while.[48] Even after the HBC announced in November 1858 that it "declined ... to be a consenting party to the trial of the validity of our Charter,"[49] the government kept the threat open.[50] But no hearing was ever ordered, and so, apart from the boundary question, which was eventually determined after Rupert's Land joined Canada,[51] the several legal uncertainties with which the charter was riddled remained forever unresolved.

It was widely expected following the Select Committee hearings that Canada would soon be gradually ingesting the settled and settlement-ripe portions of Rupert's Land. Even Sir George Simpson appeared confident that the committee's proposals would "form the groundwork for all future arrangements."[52] And negotiations with both Canadian and British authorities were indeed soon underway. The surrender, in 1858, of the East India Company's governmental powers to the British government after a mutiny against that company's authority suggested that the HBC's hegemony in Rupert's Land would shortly be extinguished as well.

The discussions progressed very slowly, however. That was due, in large part, to the company's firm insistence on heavy financial compensation.[53] There was also a growing concern on Canada's part about the cost of administering the HBC's vast territories. Those factors, coupled with a serious economic downturn, diminished Canada's appetite for immediate westward expansion,[54] and its political focus shifted away from western annexation for the time being. Although the UK government continued to discuss the Crown colony option, those talks grew desultory after the British, too, became afraid of the cost. "The Under-secretary for the Colonies said the other day in the House that the plan ... would involve a large sum for compensation," observed HBC governor Joseph Berens in early 1861. This did not discourage him, however, because "[t]his assertion looks as if they do not intend to rob us, as at one time they appeared to be inclined for."[55] So the company continued to play the slow game,[56] knowing that time was on its side.

And although nothing would emerge from the negotiations until after Canadian Confederation, both company and government used their continuation to excuse putting off major interim improvements to Red River's governance.

NEW COUNCILLORS

Minor adjustments were unavoidable, however. The fact that the HBC had escaped condemnation from the Select Committee did not mean the accusations of its many critics were entirely without effect. Even before the creation of the committee, gradual and grudging steps were being taken to respond to some of the complaints. The membership of the Council of Assiniboia was one of the matters addressed. As early as November 1852, the company's London secretary informed Assiniboia governor Caldwell that the company had appointed six new members, three of them Halfbreeds, to his council.[57] They were William Cowan, a young physician turned fur trader; Thomas Thomas, a company veteran; Robert McBeath, the farmer son of Selkirk Settlers; François Bruneau, a prosperous farmer and Halfbreed leader; Alexander Ross's eldest son, William, who had also replaced his father as postmaster and sheriff the previous year; and Thomas Sinclair, who seems to have been a farmer. Bruneau, Ross, and Sinclair were all of mixed-blood heritage, and the latter was a brother of James Sinclair, to whom Simpson and the company had been bitterly opposed for years. The six were sworn in as members of the council on 29 March 1853[58] and gradually took their seats on the General Court over the next few judicial sessions. McBeath, Bruneau, and Sinclair all served admirably for years to come. These were not radicals, but nor were they sycophants. Their appointment signalled the company's new appreciation of the need to assuage the discontent so widespread at Red River for so long.

Language remained an issue. Some French-speaking importers refused to pay the settlement's import tax, even after their trusted compatriot and new council member François Bruneau was appointed collector of duties; and when the governor of Assiniboia met with them to discuss the refusal, one reason they gave was that the French were still not adequately represented on the council. The governor asked London for more francophone appointments,[59] and in the fullness of time several of those suggested joined the Council of Assiniboia, starting with Pascal Bréland, Solomon Hamlin, and Maximilian Gendon.[60] Although the object of those appointments was somewhat frustrated by three new anglophone councillors being named several months later,[61] the move was nonetheless a further small step toward institutional recognition of the settlement's culturally diverse nature. Never, however, would an Indian be appointed to the council, or to any of the courts.

RECORDER JOHNSON

A new recorder was on the scene before this chapter opened. As Adam Thom and his family were preparing for the long canoe journey to York Factory and the voyage back to Scotland in the summer of 1854, Francis Godschall Johnson, a prominent thirty-seven-year-old barrister from Montreal, was preparing to travel to Red River from the east. Their paths did not cross; and if they had met, the men would have had little to say to each other, since two more greatly contrasting personalities than the first and second recorders of Rupert's Land would be difficult to imagine.

Sir George Simpson had searched long for a suitable replacement for the defrocked Thom. In May 1851 Eden Colvile offered confidential advice about several candidates Simpson was then considering, and ranked Johnson second of those with whom he was familiar. He nevertheless had reservations: "If my friend Frank Johnson had a little more steadiness & discretion I should prefer him, as he would keep everybody in good humour, save and except the parsons perhaps."[62]

Francis Johnson[63] had been born in England in 1817 to the wife of a peripatetic cavalry officer. Much of his schooling had been in France and Belgium, and he was thoroughly bilingual when he came to Lower Canada in 1834. After apprenticing with a Montreal judge, Johnson was called to the bar in 1839 and enjoyed early success as a barrister. Unusually eloquent in both English and French, Johnson was a popular choice to conduct jury trials. In addition to his courtroom prowess, he displayed a talent for legislative drafting, being appointed, only two years after his call to the bar, as secretary of the body charged with revising the *Statutes of Lower Canada.* He was just thirty years of age when, in 1847, he was appointed to the ranks of Queen's Counsel – the upper echelon of the barristers' profession. Although he lost that exalted rank temporarily two or three years later in consequence of his vigorous and prominent political opposition to the Baldwin-Lafontaine Reform government's Rebellion Losses Bill, the status was restored in 1853, just prior to his elevation to the bench of Rupert's Land.

Why had Eden Colvile hesitated to give so highly qualified a candidate his unqualified endorsement? And why did Simpson ignore those reservations? The answer to the first question is that Francis Johnson lacked altogether the serious-mindedness that his dour predecessor possessed in overabundance. Jovial, gregarious, quick, and witty, he could be unmindful of the hurt that brilliant repartee can inflict on others. His conviviality suggests partiality to drink, and there is some evidence of that.[64] Johnson was also financially irresponsible – a risky characteristic for one from whom absolute impartiality is expected. Sir George recommended Johnson as recorder with full knowledge of these characteristics – including the final one.

Simpson had known Johnson for several years. He had lent money to the young lawyer, in fact – and seems once to have foreclosed on his mortgage. On 28 November 1849 Johnson wrote Simpson a dejected letter that began, "I received this morning your note requiring payment of £18 interest on the obligation for £300 before Friday next," and confessed that "[h]arrassed & disappointed in every quarter, I am unable to pay even this small amount." Acknowledging that "I cannot ask for more delay," he concluded that "I may as well at once relinquish the property on which you are secured, & enable you to realize the amount by confessing judgment on the mortgage." In closing, he assured Simpson, "I shall always remember your kindness in advancing the money."[65]

Francis Johnson was still heavily in debt at the time of his appointment as recorder. A debt owed to senior HBC chief factor John Rowand (arranged by Simpson?) was mentioned in a letter to Johnson from company secretary Smith in June 1854;[66] and later that year, Simpson, who seems to have taken over the administration of Johnson's Montreal debts after he moved to Red River, informed the new recorder that there had been "sundry 'anxious enquiries'" from creditors, including a pressing one from "Torry, your wine merchant," and another from "Benny, who is really a decent man & should not be kept waiting for his money. The debt, moreover, is for your 'daily bread,' & as such usually considered by the world as more binding [than others]."[67] "If you would like me to arrange these two matters for you," Simpson concluded, "be good enough to write by the first opportunity." The impecunious recorder took up the governor's offer.[68] In placing Rupert's Land's judicial system in the hands of Francis Johnson, the governor could be reasonably sure that the recorder's independence would never get out of hand.

Simpson informed Johnson in late November 1853 that his appointment had been approved by the Governor and Committee.[69] The contract was somewhat more favourable to the company than Thom's had been, Johnson's annual stipend being only £500 and the appointment being for one year only, renewable annually at HBC pleasure. After the appointment was finalized, Johnson travelled to London to confer with company officials there (financing the trip by borrowing against his forthcoming salary).[70] He then proceeded to Rupert's Land by canoe from Montreal, arriving at Red River in time to sit with the General Court at its session of 17 August 1854.

It was not long before good things were being said about his performance as recorder. Governor Caldwell, for example, informed London in March 1855 that "Mr. Johnson's ability to charge the jury in both languages ... render the Canadians and French Halfbreeds more satisfied with the manner in which the law is administered."[71] He would continue to guide the court for the next four years, and it was largely to his credit that, for the most part, the controversies that had tarnished it since 1849 were avoided.

The court's dockets were small and infrequent, and Red River did not offer the energetic lawyer anything like the opportunities for diversion that Montreal had. As early as February 1855, Simpson, in Lachine, was reporting to London that he had heard the recorder was already bored: "Johnson, as was to be expected, finds the Settlement a dull residence."[72] He led as active a social life as frontier circumstances permitted, however, and found female companionship quickly. Johnson was a widower – the death of his wife in July 1853 had been one of his inducements to move west – and by mid-November 1854 the attentions he was paying to Miss Mary Mills, the daughter of the headmistress of the settlement's school for young ladies, were prompting rumours that a wedding was imminent.[73] Although those rumours proved to be premature, the couple continued to keep company and to be socially energetic. They finally married in March 1856[74] and then moved from the upper settlement, where Johnson had been living at Fort Garry, to the married quarters Adam Thom and his family had once occupied at the Lower Fort.[75]

Gallivanting was expensive, and Johnson seems to have been no better at keeping his finances under control at Red River than in Montreal. This caused Sir George Simpson, his concerned proxy at Lachine, to remark in January 1857, "I have written to Mr. Swanston to give you a further credit of £60 ... I observe what you say about the expense of living at Red River, but I do not agree with you in all particulars. The rate of living is ... [determined] by individual tastes and habits."[76]

Like Thom before him, Johnson acted as local legal advisor to the company, and was also free to supplement his income by private legal practice. Although little is known about his private practice, one assignment is worth mentioning. It was received, not long after arriving in the settlement, from Sir George Simpson himself. John Rowand, the longtime and very wealthy chief factor at Edmonton House, had died – not long after Johnson's own loan from Rowand was arranged. Sir George, who was one of the executors of the estate, wrote to Johnson in August 1854[77] to "request your professional services in connection with ... the three daughters, the principal legatees, who are at present boarding at the convent in Red River." Simpson's concern was that undue influence might be exerted on the young ladies to either take the veil themselves or give substantial portions of their large legacies to the Sisters of Charity. With a view to removing the girls from "the clutches of the nunnery,"[78] he and the girls' older brother, Dr John Rowand of Montreal, had devised what amounted to a kidnapping scheme.

The brother would come to Red River, ostensibly to "visit" his sisters, and induce them by some pretext to cross the river to Fort Garry. He would then immediately convey them to Montreal, where they would be beyond the Grey Nuns' influence. "It is not improbable," Simpson continued, that "difficulties may be thrown in his way unless the object he has in view be kept secret. Dr. Rowand will, therefore, consult both you and Mr. Ballenden as to the best ruse to be adopted." Since one of the "difficulties" contemplated would likely have been an application to the court to prevent the abduction, the propriety of this request, and of Johnson's agreeing to it, was highly dubious. The elder brother may have had authority as the girls' guardian to remove them from the convent, but a clandestine scheme, with the recorder's paid complicity, to preclude the court's involvement was surely unlawful.

Blessedly, the scheme went awry. Although Dr Rowand did journey to Red River, seems to have conferred with Johnson, and succeeded in inveigling his sisters to visit Fort Garry, the girls somehow found their way back to the convent, and their big brother returned to Montreal empty-handed. Simpson wrote to Johnson in November 1854, explaining these events, and also informing him that legal proceedings were underway in Lower Canada to frustrate the nuns' alleged intentions in another way. The Canadian court would be asked to delay distribution of estate assets indefinitely; and although the nuns might challenge those proceedings, "the suit may be run out till everybody is tired of the contest."[79]

On the bench, Johnson performed well, with few complaints on any hand, from his first session in August 1854 until he left the settlement in August 1858.[80] Because the court's caseload was surprisingly meager for most of that time, he had little to do, and he was certainly not a man who looked for work. Although Caldwell reported in March 1855 that "Mr. Johnson is revising our laws," that revision never saw the light of day.[81] Nevertheless, whatever Johnson did he did well. Unlike Thom, he was quite willing to travel to the hinterland, and visited Norway House twice for meetings of the Council of Rupert's Land: in the summers of 1855 and 1856.[82]

GOVERNOR JOHNSON

Governor Caldwell finally moved on in 1855. The Chelsea Pensioners' contracts expired on 1 June of that year, and the company had long since decided not to renew them. A War Office suggestion that they be induced to remain in the settlement was firmly declined.[83] Transportation was offered to those who wished to return to England; and Lieutenant Colonel Caldwell was perfunctorily informed that his appointments as military commander and governor would terminate on 1 June.[84] On 9 August, Caldwell was reported to be en route to York Factory with his family, in company with Captain Hill and furlough-bound Chief Factor John Ballenden and his daughter[85] – the lives of all of whom had been significantly altered by the *Foss* case in the General Quarterly Court of Assiniboia five years previously.

Caldwell was replaced as governor of Assiniboia by Recorder Johnson.[86] In return for an additional £200 annually, bringing his total stipend to the same salary – £700 – that Adam Thom had received as recorder, Johnson agreed to fill both posts.[87] He appears to have been as effective as governor as he was as recorder. Despite constant nervousness about the perennial grumpiness of much of the community, he never faced a major challenge. To avoid such, he relied heavily on an abundance of personal charm: "I laid down a rule when I came to RR to quarrel with no one; and though hard feeling has never in the history of the Settlement reached its present height, I am very politeful to them all, & they to me ... I won't let anyone quarrel with me, however much they may be so inclined." Although he remained apprehensive, the violence expected "at any moment" never manifested itself.[88]

It was Governor Johnson who, to appease importers who refused to pay import duties, recommended increasing francophone representation on the Council of Assiniboia.[89] Ordered by Simpson to do whatever he could to suppress or counteract anti-company agitation by activist William Kennedy, Johnson spoke publicly, and with some success, against Kennedy's claims without compromising the dignity of his office.[90] Asked to do everything possible to accommodate a visiting scientific expedition, he groused good-naturedly about the inadequacy of the dinnerware and other facilities available "in my lowly establishment"; but he promised to "beautify the state apartments," marshal "[a]ll the artistic talent available in the Settlement," and "sacrifice Gadona's ox" for the occasion.[91] His efforts managed to impress the visitors very favourably.[92]

Governor Johnson's proposals for changes of policy, and improvement of services affecting the settlement, met with less approval from London, however. The chaotic state of Assiniboia's land registry records concerned him, for example, as did uncertainty as to whether Aboriginal title to the land had ever been effectively extinguished: "The whole thing requires immediate and efficient attention, with a system of registration ... by an able public officer who, with nothing else to do, would find two or three years of hard work to set it all to rights and issue proper title deeds. There is a cry, too, about the title of the Company to the lands, on the ground that the Indians were never paid for them ... [O]ld Peguis, at Kennedy"s instigation, is talking very big, and many people believe him to be in the right."[93] London replied, in due course, that although the land records "are not in as satisfactory a state as could be desired ... at present it is not considered expedient to incur any additional expense in connection therewith."[94] Not a word was said about the uncertain extinguishment of Aboriginal title. Other of Johnson's concerns also received short shrift. His observation that US imports were excessive due to a paucity of competing goods in HBC stores was bluntly rejected; and his suggestion that better steps be taken to reduce the importation of American "ardent spirits" received a complacent reply.[95]

In fairness, it must be said that Johnson himself was no more diligent than he had to be in pursuing his duties as governor. He convened his council infrequently, and did little to institute reforms that were within his own power to bring about. When first appointed governor, for instance, he deplored the "total inadequacy of the means of punishment now at the disposal of the Court," and "the insufficiency of the jail regulations and the general treatment of criminals." He announced that he would bring before the council legislation for "adoption of stringent prison discipline and the imposition of a hard labour upon the convicts,"[96] but those topics were never broached to the council during Johnson's term of office.

Despite the light-hearted tone that marked most of his letters to Sir George Simpson, Johnson often conveyed to others a sense of personal hurt at being ignored in this isolated outpost. Writing to Simpson's private secretary, Edward Hopkins, in March 1857, for example, he said, "I have written 8 or 9 times to Sir George, & have had *one* letter, which came in one of Mrs. Johnson's. The private matters I wrote about ... have caused me great annoyance, and some insult, from ... [having] received no answer – but ... [t]he public concerns are much more important, & should receive a passing notice from the Committee when grouse-shooting is over."[97]

Johnson did not find Red River a congenial place to live. The settlement's infamous gossip offended him: "If I were to soil my pen with passing on half the foul gossip that reaches RR from every corner of the country, or even open my ears to its contamination, you would, I am sure, despise me as much as I should scorn myself."[98] A severe food shortage in the early months of 1857 prompted Johnson to remark to Simpson, "The people are living, or rather starving, on 'gold-eyes'[99] & there is not even enough wheat for seed." In his own case, he said that he and his family "live on the produce of my gun – at this season rather scanty and difficult of pursuit." He would not be able to invite a visiting expedition for dinner, he claimed, because "we have no dinner for ourselves."[100] He had previously described Lower Fort Garry, where he resided, as "a kind of penitentiary on the loose," surrounded by "snow and discontent."[101] And when he wrote to Simpson near the end of that year "from the gloom of our Arctic Christmas in a murky little den," he described the purpose of the leave of absence he had recently requested as being "to rescue my children from the contagion of surrounding ... barbarism."[102]

Little wonder, then, that after pondering the additional disincentive of Red River's high cost of living, and experiencing what he took to be a personal slight by Sir George Simpson during the latter's hurried annual visit to the settlement the following June, Francis Johnson impulsively tendered his resignation as both recorder of Rupert's Land and governor of Assiniboia.[103]

He offered to return to Red River temporarily until a successor could be appointed; and soon after he was back in Montreal, perhaps finding the prospects there less attractive than anticipated, he changed his mind altogether and sought to withdraw his resignation. Simpson got wind of this change of heart, and advised London not to agree: "With every good feeling towards Mr. Johnson, I must say that it would not be well to send that gentleman back to the country, as, although very talented, there is a levity, a want of steadiness, and (it is but proper that you should confidentially know) a want of truthfulness about him, which renders him less useful [than desired] in the offices ... [he held]."[104]

Francis Johnson was accordingly informed that his withdrawal had arrived too late to affect the situation.[105] His offer to return temporarily was ignored since the company had already decided, on Simpson's advice, that "a successor ... in the office of Recorder is [not] necessary immediately ... pending the negotiations at present in progress with the Government."[106] Few people crossed Sir George Simpson with impunity. Ever conscious, however, that disgruntled former officers could cause future trouble, Simpson proposed "that it might be a good policy ... to give Mr. Johnson a retaining fee on behalf of the Company." The former second recorder was therefore paid a retainer of 50 guineas a year for the next several years.[107]

GOVERNOR MCTAVISH

Until a new governor could be appointed, the ever-loyal Dr John Bunn agreed to fill in as acting governor,[108] but Red River's new chief factor, William McTavish – John Ballenden's replacement – was very soon performing that function.[109] McTavish was a seasoned, well-connected,

Figure 7.2 William McTavish, the last governor of Rupert's Land and of Assiniboia, was universally respected. When ousted by Louis Riel, his final message brought the Red River Settlement's disparate elements together sufficiently to permit the forging of a new province.

widely liked, universally respected company officer when posted to Red River, at Sir George Simpson's insistence, as chief factor in 1857. He and his brother Dugald, another company stalwart, were nephews of Simpson's great friend and HBC icon John George McTavish, and brothers of Letitia Hargrave, the wife of long-time York Factory chief factor James Hargrave. The fact that William was married to a mixed-blood daughter of Andrew McDermot, Red River's pillar of independence and sometime HBC nemesis, doubtless broadened his horizons. Tough but fair, self-effacing, serious-minded, and somewhat scholarly, McTavish was a prodigious worker despite a proneness to illness. Not long after his arrival at Red River, Governor-Recorder Johnson had reported to Simpson, "Mactavish works like a horse, and is quite ill from an influenza that is very prevalent."[110] Both characteristics marked the remainder of his career, which spanned most of the Quarterly Court's remaining years.

Appointed to the Council of Assiniboia while holding the commercial post of chief factor, McTavish soon found governmental responsibilities being thrust upon him too. After Johnson's departure in mid-1858, the day-to-day decision making for the colony seems to have devolved upon the chief factor, despite formal gubernatorial authority having been delegated by Johnson to Bunn.[111] And after Johnson's resignation was accepted later that year, William McTavish was formally appointed governor of Assiniboia.[112] At his first council meeting, on 9 December 1858, it was agreed that meetings would be held four times annually[113] – unheard-of frequency in past experience, and a token of the new governor's work ethic. William McTavish provided sound political leadership for the settlement until shortly before his death in 1870; and when he left the scene – with Fort Garry in the hands of a provisional government – it would be to the deep regret of both friends and adversaries.

ACTING RECORDER BUNN

Johnson's departure left the General Quarterly Court without a recorder once more – a situation that persisted for the remainder of the time under review in this chapter and beyond. In the meantime, the stalwart Dr John Bunn, having shown his aptitude for presiding over court proceedings during the Caldwell era, was pressed into service as acting recorder, and circumstances would conspire to prolong the assignment until 1862. After fulfilling that task without compensation or complaint for several years, Bunn eventually requested, and was granted, payment.[114] While that stipend was not likely as generous as those paid to Thom and Johnson, John Bunn performed the recorder's duties at least as well as the latter, and decidedly better than the former. When complaints about his lack of legal expertise reached an intensity that could not be ignored,[115] and the interminable negotiations between the HBC and the Governments of Canada and the United Kingdom remained deadlocked, Simpson was instructed to locate a suitable Canadian lawyer to fill the recorder's post.[116] He set about doing so with alacrity, confident he could take a new recorder with him on his annual tour of inspection in the spring of 1860. But the task proved much more difficult than anticipated.

The first hurdle was a delicate one. Simpson's instructions were to consult with Canada's attorney general and solicitor general because of their "intimate knowledge of all the members of the legal profession in

Figure 7.3 Acting Recorder John Bunn, MD, Red River's native-born, mixed-blood physician, filled numerous public offices with distinction, and proved that fine judges need not be lawyers.

the colony." He emphatically declined to do so, explaining that those politicians "would be sure to make a political job of it; and, to serve their own interests, would propose some adherent to their party – probably a French Canadian – who might be a tolerable lawyer & fluent speaker, but otherwise not the sort of person we would like in the position of Recorder. I would rather look around & select a man myself, and then refer to ... [them] for an opinion on his qualifications."[117] In subsequent letters, he was even more blunt, predicting that Attorney General Georges-Étienne Cartier would propose someone keen on "converting Red River into a French Canadian ... settlement"[118] and opposing "any French Canadians as, whatever their merits, their national predilections are indelible, and they are almost always the co-workers ... of the French priesthood."[119] Although Simpson considered several French-speaking lawyers of British descent to be suitable, they all proved to be unavailable, and even the reappointment of Francis Johnson began to seem an increasingly attractive option.[120] But by that time Sir George was preparing to leave Lachine for Red River, and it was too late to find someone for that year. He therefore adjourned the search until his return from the west, hoping that in the meantime success in the continuing discussions with government would render the search unnecessary.

THE SETTLEMENT

When Lieutenant Colonel Caldwell and his troops were recalled, fewer Chelsea Pensioners chose to return to the United Kingdom than had been anticipated or hoped. The HBC Governor and Committee nevertheless exulted in April 1856 that "all expense connected with the Pensioner Corps is now at an end."[121] The relief was fleeting because, although everyone knew a garrison of regular troops was needed, the chances of Red River's being assigned such seemed low. Although Simpson was characteristically pessimistic about the subject,[122] he continued to remind London of the settlement's military needs, and the company continued, in turn, to lobby the War Office and everyone else in government who would listen. Persistence was rewarded in July 1857 when company secretary Smith informed Assiniboia governor Johnson that help was on the way. A detachment of 120 members of the Royal Canadian Rifles had sailed the previous month from Montreal for York Factory en route to Red River.[123] The troops, under the command of Major George Seton, landed on the shores of Hudson Bay in August and departed in September for Red River,[124] where they were settled in by early November.[125] Governor Johnson reported in December, "The Fort resounds with warlike noises. The men are well conducted, & the officers quiet and unexceptional."[126]

Chief Factor (and governor-to-be) William McTavish had a somewhat different perception, noting shortly after the troops' arrival that they were "complaining about the cost of living,"[127] and later reporting that they "are perfectly orderly and comfortable, but grumbling very much."[128] Some officers had a mistaken impression, based on previous arrangements with the pensioners and a special "command allowance" paid to Major Seton in lieu of one he'd given up to come to Rupert's Land, that the HBC would supplement their military salaries. When others pressed for a bonus like Seton's, the company first refused, pointing out that it was not the men's employer;[129] but it eventually made concessions in order to maintain good relations with the garrison.[130]

Despite periodic talk of withdrawal, the troops were present in the settlement until the summer of 1861,[131] contributing significantly to the comparatively peaceful conditions that prevailed.

To say that these were times of peace does not mean they were times of contentment. Dissatisfaction, fed by uncertainty about the future, continued to smoulder in many quarters, and to be periodically fanned to flames by agitators. The most conspicuous local agitation occurred immediately before and during the public hearings in London. Captain William Kennedy, a former fur trader and a free trade advocate who had gained much attention leading one of Lady Jane Franklin's unsuccessful expeditions to the Arctic in search of her lost husband, returned to Red River in early 1857 to raise a petition protesting company rule and supporting Canadian annexation. He was ably assisted in this by respected settlement elder and company critic Donald Gunn. Governor-in-Chief Simpson, disturbed by Kennedy's mission, urged Governor-Recorder Johnson to do whatever he could to suppress it: "I look to you to keep him in order ... [by] such judicious, gentle measures as may appear to you most advisable to thwart his designs, and to act as antidotes to his doctrines of free trade, invalidity of the Charter, & so forth."[132] Johnson did his best to soften the impact of Kennedy's efforts by attending, and sometimes speaking out at, his public meetings.[133]

Overall, however, the petition was heavily supported, and when forwarded to Alexander Isbister for submission to the Select Committee it contained 575 signatures.[134] But, as it turned out, the petition was of little moment. It arrived in London too late to have much impact on the outcome of the public hearings, and as soon as the Select Committee issued its report, fickle public opinion moved on to other topics of interest.

The failure of Captain Kennedy's petition did not mean that Red River's discontent subsided. Saulteaux chief Peguis, the only surviving signatory to the 1817 Indian treaty with Lord Selkirk, wrote a letter asserting that the treaty was intended as a mere lease, rather than an outright grant, and had therefore not extinguished Aboriginal title. The letter found its way into the Select Committee's evidence[135] but received little official attention. Back at Red River in early 1860, however, it became the basis for a large meeting organized by the settlement's Halfbreeds, who claimed that they, too, as descendants of Indians, shared the allegedly unextinguished Aboriginal entitlement.[136] And in August of that year, no less a personage than Florence Nightingale entered the lists on behalf of the Natives of Rupert's Land, urging the Colonial Office to do something about the paucity of school and hospital facilities for Indians in the HBC's territories.[137]

There were other critics too. Governor Johnson lamented in June 1857 that the company had "no friends" in the settlement.[138] As long as the prospect of external governmental intervention persisted, local efforts to encourage such intervention were constant. Reverend G.O. Corbett was active after returning from his appearance before the Select Committee, publishing a pamphlet advocating Crown colony status for the settlement and drumming up significant local support for the proposal.[139] Donald Gunn continued, in Johnson's words, to "get up petitions to God knows what," and "the ecclesiastical element" was "secretly working on its own hook ... petitioning or remonstrating with somebody about something."[140]

Surprisingly, the ever-present restlessness did not interfere significantly with law and order. In August 1857, immediately after the London hearings and William Kennedy's visit, Governor Johnson feared that it might do so, warning that "if tranquility is to be preserved here, either the Canadian Government or the Colonial Office should pass a proclamation & have it sent here to me, exhorting the people to obey the laws as now administered, and disavowing any interference with the constituted authorities."[141] But less than four months later, he viewed the situation much more calmly. The anti-establishment activism of Donald Gunn and the local clergy was described in tones conveying more amusement than anxiety, and Johnson concluded contentedly that "[t]he Settlement is quite quiet, & the people [are] generally getting such absurd prices for what they sell that discontent is at a discount."[142] It remained that way for the next several years.

The detailed 1856 census that Sir George Simpson provided to the Select Committee[143] evidenced the comparative prosperity mentioned by Johnson: 8,300 acres under cultivation (up 2,000 acres since 1849); 19,155 head of livestock of all kinds (an increase of almost 6,400); and a total estimated value of dwellings, livestock, implements, and machinery of £111,536.[144] A steam mill was built right after the census.[145] The agenda of the Council of Assiniboia in these years was replete with projects for improving roads, bridges, and ferry services.[146] About the only negative development was that the Red River Academy closed its doors in 1859.[147]

While the local economy continued to experience periodic downturns due to unsuccessful buffalo hunts (1855), grasshopper infestations (1857 and 1858), and prairie fires (1860), and still lacked an external market for its agricultural produce, it was buoyed by burgeoning free trade, the presence of the Canadian Rifles, and a growing trickle of permanent and transient immigrants attracted by talk of pending governmental changes, the discovery of gold in the Fraser River in 1858, and the lure of limitless fertile prairie.

The immigration trickle was further stimulated by three scientific expeditions that arose, directly or indirectly, from the Select Committee's enquiry.[148] In 1858 Simon J. Dawson surveyed, on behalf of Canada, an all-British route from Thunder Bay to Red River, publishing an optimistic report in 1859. Although little came of Dawson's proposals for some time, he was eventually commissioned to construct a combined road and water route, which would be close enough to completion by 1870 to be used by Canadian troops sent to Manitoba to put down the Riel Resistance. Toronto-based naturalist Henry Youle Hind conducted two explorations in partial collaboration with Dawson.[149] One of the Hind expeditions, in 1857, focused on the Red River, including the settlement;[150] the other, the following year, concentrated on the Assiniboine and Saskatchewan Rivers. His findings were published in two volumes in 1860. The most ambitious expedition, sponsored by the Royal Geographical Society and the imperial government, was led by British explorer John Palliser between 1857 and 1860. It produced three volumes of reports dealing with the Lake Superior–Red River route (1859), the prairies (1860), and the Rocky Mountains (1863), plus, in 1865, a detailed atlas of the entire area.

Despite some misgivings about these alien probes, the company did its best to cooperate with them. During the Select Committee hearings in March 1857, for instance, Simpson wrote from London to urge Governor Johnson to give Palliser and his entourage "your personal kind attentions."[151] When the group arrived at the settlement, Johnson reported sardonically that "all is commotion & excitement. Every individual seems to expect that he is suddenly to be raised to fortune & eminence by the especial grace ... of the Canadian Government; and the wildest notions on all possible & impossible subjects seem to prevail. This will soon settle down, however, to the practical business of taking levels & procuring beef for the winter's subsistence."[152] The governor nevertheless ingratiated himself personally with Palliser and his colleagues, and Simpson later recorded that the expedition members "were pleased with the reception they met with in the country."[153]

Red River was still far removed from the rest of the world in 1855, but improvements in transportation and communication were either underway or in contemplation that would reduce the settlement's isolation dramatically by 1860. American settlement, with attendant railroads and telegraphs, was moving very rapidly closer to the 49th parallel. Minnesota's population would reach 172,000 by 1860.[154] In February 1855 a regular mail service to Pembina, and thence to everywhere, was established, Sheriff William Ross becoming Red River's first postmaster.[155] In 1858 the HBC began, on an experimental basis, to bring large quantities of its supplies to the settlement by way of the United States; and by the following year that was its preferred route.[156] On 9 June 1859 the first steamboat, *Anson Northup*, arrived at Red River from Minnesota,[157] and by the following summer, the HBC was running its own steamboat on the Red.[158]

THE *NOR'-WESTER*

In the autumn of 1859, two young Canadian journalists – William Coldwell and William Buckingham – trekked to Red River by ox cart, bringing with them a printing press upon which Rupert's Land's first newspaper would be printed. That December, the *Nor'-Wester* commenced biweekly publication from a building in the village that was beginning to form around the trail intersection now known as Portage and Main.[159] Coldwell and Buckingham opened Red River's first bookshop on the same premises the following year.

The publication of a newspaper at Red River gave both residents and the outside world vivid new views of each other. In the 14 September 1860 issue of the *Nor'-Wester*, for instance, a brief word picture of the settlement appeared that conveyed much more than any census data could:

> As one of the many signs of the progress of this Settlement, we may now fairly set down the very general building going on this season. At every turn we notice new houses rising. Above and below Upper Fort Garry – both on the Assiniboine and Red Rivers – a large addition has this year been made to the number of dwelling-houses, stores, barns, stables, and every other kind of building ... In many respects, the Settlement has made more progress since 1850 than ... during the previous thirty years; and we venture to say that the changes and improvements of '59 and '60 have been equal to those of the previous eight years. We are, manifestly, going ahead; the public pulse is beating faster. We had occasion, since our last issue, to perambulate most of the Settlement, and we were impressed by the improved style as well as the number of buildings. Two-storey houses, so rare a few years ago, are now quite common; and verandas and ornamenting of different kinds are coming into vogue. Another feature of the times is the large number of strangers now

Figure 7.4 William Coldwell, editor of the Red River Settlement's first newspaper, subjected the government and courts to public scrutiny, and left historians vivid and valuable supplements to the official court records.

among us. Old residents who, some years ago, knew every individual in the Settlement, say that now every second person they meet is a stranger.[160]

In the closing days of the period, however, the *Nor'-Wester* carried a long story recording a sad setback: "Disastrous Fire – Catholic Cathedral Burned! One Life Lost! The Bishop's Palace in Ashes! Loss £25,000."[161] The settlement's only really distinctive building, built by Bishop J.N. Provencher and made famous by American poet John Greenleaf Whittier's description of the tolling bells "that call from their turrets twain,"[162] had been totally destroyed, along with a library containing 5,000 books and, worse still, all the records of the diocese. It was a cruel loss, yet one which, architecturally, would be replaced before long under the energetic leadership of Bishop A.A. Taché. Another victim of fire that year was Red River's first steam mill,[163] but as with the cathedral, another would soon be built.

Not all parts of the community were open to the scrutiny of the press. Notably, the Council of Assiniboia denied representatives of the *Nor'-Wester* permission to attend its meetings.[164] Dissemination of public data was nevertheless increased significantly. The *Nor'-Wester* was provided with official council minutes, albeit long after the meetings they recorded; and Assiniboia's public accounts were made available for publication soon after their passage. This meant, for instance, that the salaries of most public officials and the cost of most public services became public knowledge for the first time. Citizens learned that the sheriff–jail governor was paid £30 annually, that other jail expenses, including the jailer's salary, prisoners' rations, and jail maintenance, ran between £30 and £40 a year, and that the presidents of the three petty courts were paid £10, and other magistrates £5, annually.[165]

An important function performed by newspapers is to provide a forum for public debate of controversial topics – something the seclusion of the Council of Assiniboia's meetings was clearly intended to discourage. The *Nor'-Wester* fulfilled its public forum function admirably, airing, and giving correspondents the opportunity to air, a wide range of issues. On the bedrock question of Aboriginal title, for instance, the paper published a copy of Chief Peguis's letter to the Select Committee challenging the validity of Lord Selkirk's treaty. That provoked a rebuttal by Andrew McDermot in the next issue, and probably led to the public meeting, at the new Royal Hotel[166] two weeks later, that supported Peguis's position and the Halfbreeds' first concerted assertion of Aboriginal claims as descendants of Rupert's Land's original inhabitants.[167]

The commencement of the first transatlantic telegraph service in 1858 promised the settlement and its newspaper eventual near-instantaneous communication to most parts of the globe. Although that particular service operated for only three weeks, and was not renewed for several years, its advent gave notice that as soon as the wire reached Red River, the settlement's isolation would be over.

THE COURTS

The courts were open to the press from the beginning, and the *Nor'-Wester*'s lively accounts of proceedings in both the general and petty courts, sometimes including verbatim testimony and banter between the bench and witnesses, offer a rich supplement to the official court records. The attention paid to proceedings in the petty courts in early issues provide, in fact, some of the best information extant about those ill-documented tribunals. For instance: "*Lower District Court*: The presiding magistrates at the usual sitting of this court on the 28th ult. were T. Sinclair, Esq., (Chairman), Donald Gunn, Esq., John Inkster, Esq., and Donald Murray, Esq. The 'civil cause' list presented a formidable array of names, over fifty suits having been entered, chiefly for small debts varying in amount from £3 to 10s. These the court speedily adjusted, and rose early."[168]

The *Nor'-Wester* reporter's shorthand notes of General Court trials sometimes gave readers the sense of sitting in the front row of courtroom spectators. In the first issue of the newspaper, for example, the account[169] of a civil suit by James Mulligan, a litigious former Chelsea Pensioner and well-known local character, included numerous exchanges between the plaintiff and members of the court and jury:

> The plaintiff submitted the witness to a severe cross examination, taking advantage of a brief pause in which, Dr. Bunn said:
>
> "Have you done harrowing this man, Mr. Mulligan?"
>
> Mr. Mulligan (with asperity): "Take care, sir – I want no such insinuations from you."
>
> Dr. Bunn (in a severely respectful manner): "I think *you* had better be careful, Mr. Mulligan."
>
> Mr. Mulligan (with rising anger): "It is not your witness, Doctor ... It does not become you, a justice of the peace, to insult those who come before you."
>
> Dr. Bunn (with provoking coolness): "... I submit to your rebuke, Mr. Mulligan." (Laughter)
>
> * * *
>
> Mr. Mulligan (with rising indignation): "I have never received justice in this court."

A Juryman: "You come here far too often."

Mr. Mulligan (overpowered by the painful reminiscences of bygone days): "It was so in Judge Johnson's time and it is so now ..."

Dr. Bunn: "It is not at all strange that a man who always loses never thinks that justice is done him ..."

Mr. Mulligan: ... [interrupts] ...

Dr. Bunn (quietly interrupting Mr. Mulligan): "You should show a little respect for the Court, Mr. Mulligan."

Mr. Mulligan (scornfully): "Respect indeed! You are on the strong side, whilst I, a poor man from the Old Country, is on the weak side. ... The Hudson's Bay Company sold my land twice over ... I am a great mote in the eyes of the Company."

The Governor [McTavish]: "Not at all, Mr. Mulligan. You are a very small mote indeed, I assure you." (Laughter)

Although his claim was dismissed for lack of evidence, the newspaper reported that "Mr. Mulligan marched out of court triumphant, if not victorious."[170]

Although judicial authority under the HBC charter resided in "the Governor and his Council," the entire membership of the Council of Assiniboia never sat on the General Quarterly Court.[171] That reality was demonstrated by a contrast between the council appointments made in March 1853 and those of June and September 1857.[172] Whereas the former group all served on the court, the latter were given no judicial responsibilities. Throughout most of the 1855–60 period, the membership of the court was uniform: the governor, the recorder if any, and petty court presidents Bunn, Bruneau, McBeath, and Sinclair.[173] At its September 1860 sitting, the General Court was expanded by the addition of Pascal Bréland, appointed to the Council of Assiniboia three years previously.

The sheriff was an officer vital to the effective operation of both levels of court: supervising the serving of court documents, arranging dockets, summoning jurors, selecting jury panels, and providing courthouse security. He was also central to the justice system in general: commanding the police, organizing prosecutions, and supervising the operation of the settlement's prison. When Sheriff William Ross died suddenly in May 1856, Dr John Bunn consented to add that large bundle of responsibilities to his existing duties as councillor, coroner, justice of the peace, and president of the Upper District Petty Court.[174] Bunn continued to hold all those posts even after taking on the role of de facto recorder of the General Court.

Although not many other changes affected the General Court's operations between 1855 and 1860, the council's 1857 motion that the court should never sit on Ascension Day – the holiday on which the *Sayer* trial had been held in a vain attempt to keep away Catholics sympathetic to the accused men – must have produced wry faces in some quarters.[175]

The most ambitious judicial initiative during these years was a plan to create a "Circuit Court," with civil and criminal jurisdiction, conducted by the recorder at Norway House. The idea surfaced at the annual Norway House meeting of the Council of Rupert's Land in June 1854, and received the blessing of the HBC Governor and Committee in their April 1855 general letter to senior company officers.[176] The 1855 meeting of the Rupert's Land council, at which Recorder Johnson was present,[177] resolved that the first session of the Circuit Court would be held the following June, and that any persons accused of committing crimes outside Assiniboia would be held in custody at Norway House pending trial.[178]

To accommodate those anticipated proceedings at Norway House, construction was begun on a new prison and a "recorder's house";[179] and when, in September 1855, three men were arrested for theft from company premises there, they were remanded – one in custody and two on recognizances – for trial by the "Recorder's Court" the following year.[180] When Recorder Johnson arrived at Norway House, in company with other HBC officers, for the June 1856 convocation of the Council of Rupert's Land, the construction was not yet complete, but the accused men, young Indians whose number had now increased to four, were on hand. The trial the following day, before the "Recorder's Court" and a jury, resulted in convictions and sentences of "two years' transportation from this District."[181]

Was the recorder's circuit court a lawful tribunal? It does not seem to have been considered an arm of the General Quarterly Court of Assiniboia; nor could it have been, since it had no connection to Assiniboia. The recorder's jurisdiction extended to all of Rupert's Land; but that fact alone would not have validated the court. Its sole possible source of legal legitimacy was the HBC charter, which authorized only courts consisting of governors and their councils. The validity of its decisions depended, therefore, on whether Governor Simpson and members of the Rupert's Land council took part in its proceedings – a matter about which the records are silent. On the one hand, the tribunal's name – "Recorder's Court" – and the construction of a special "recorder's house" might suggest that the recorder was expected to be present when a governor was not. On the other hand, the court convened in 1856 at the precise time when the governor and council were at Norway House. The question turned out to be academic (except for the four young Indians banished to the northern wastes at that session) because the circuit court never sat again after that one occasion in June 1856. Neither Francis Johnson nor any future recorder ever again exercised judicial functions while outside Assiniboia.

The cases heard by Assiniboia's General Court between 1855 and 1860 were unexceptional: nothing more noteworthy than the petty crimes and minor civil disputes that arose in the course of everyday life in any frontier community. There was also a strange reduction in judicial business – or at least in the number of court sessions – during much of Johnson's reign. In 1855, 1856, and 1857 the court sat just twice annually, returning to its normal pattern only during the last three years now under consideration. Whether Johnson was in some way responsible for the lull is not known, but he does seem to have had a lazy streak.

Sometimes inaction on the recorder's part was the best way to deal with a situation. Such was so with a case arising from a controversial arrest at Norway House on 27 September 1857 that threatened to become a cause célèbre at the November sitting of the General Court but never, thanks to Johnson's discretion, reached the court's docket. Although free trading in furs remained illegal in the view of the HBC – and according to the court's edict in the *Sayer* case – most company authorities tacitly acknowledged that the ruling was unenforceable as a practical matter. After 1849 many independent operators traded with Indians, and the company combatted those activities by commercial competition rather than prosecution. An exception to that new approach occurred the autumn of 1857, however, when Andrew McDermot's son-in-law Andrew G.B. Bannatyne took a small free-trading expedition to the north. When he and his party arrived at Norway House, they caught the attention of George Barnston, an old-school, blunt-minded fur trader who had succeeded Donald Ross as the head of that post. Offended by Bannatyne's blatant disregard for the company's claimed monopoly, Barnston, who like many senior HBC officers was a justice of the peace, ordered him arrested. Although Bannatyne had not yet done any trading, Barnston's arrest warrant charged him with having "the *purpose* of carrying on an illegal traffic with the natives for furs."[182]

After the arrest, which spurred threats of litigation by an intensely angry Bannatyne, Barnston placed his prisoner in the custody of fellow company veteran William Sinclair, to be conveyed back to Red River along with a contingent of newly arrived Canadian Rifles troops that Sinclair was transporting to the settlement. As soon as the brigade reached Red River, Recorder Johnson was presented with three documents: the arrest warrant, a covering letter from Barnston, and a very indignant letter from Andrew Bannatyne. The latter threatened to sue Sinclair as well as Barnston, and when the matter became public, "strong sympathies" for Bannatyne's cause were "expressed ... loudly."[183]

Johnson acted swiftly and skilfully. Seizing on Barnston's failure to send any affidavit evidence alleging illegal conduct on Bannatyne's part, he immediately ordered the prisoner's release, making it clear to everyone involved that there would be no prosecution.[184] He then wrote to Bannatyne to assure him that "there is ... nothing of which the authorities here can take legal cognizance," adding that "Mr. Barnston and Mr. Sinclair must be deemed to have acted on their own responsibility." He also undertook to pass Bannatyne's complaints on to the HBC Governor and Committee without delay. Although Johnson initially expected Bannatyne to sue someone at the November sitting of the General Court, that did not happen, and the public uproar soon died down.[185] While the tone of his official correspondence was restrained, Johnson's private letter to Simpson deplored the "indiscreet & blundering escapade of poor old Barnston's," which the recorder characterized as "commencing in violence, continuing in blunders, & resulting in ridicule."[186]

Although aftershocks persisted for months – including a mention in the British House of Commons[187] – Sir George Simpson managed the crisis with his usual finesse, ordering Barnston to stay away from Assiniboia in order to avoid the jurisdiction of the court there,[188] writing to Bannatyne's father-in-law, Andrew McDermot, to propose a quiet settlement,[189] and eventually paying the frustrated free trader £200 in compensation.[190] Whether the matter would have been disposed of so tidily if Adam Thom had been the recorder to whom Barnston's warrant was delivered is highly doubtful.

PASSINGS

Two giants departed life during these years.

Alexander Ross

Alexander Ross, who had played pivotal roles in the settlement's legal and governmental affairs before his break with Governor Caldwell, died at his Red River home, Colony Gardens, on 23 October 1856 at the age of seventy-three. His death came not long after the publication of his *Red River Settlement,* the book that would forever mark Ross as the settlement's proto-historian. In addition to that invaluable publication, and several children who contributed much to the future development of the community, Alexander Ross left two important earlier volumes on the history of the northwest fur trade.

Sir George Simpson

On 7 September 1860, at Lachine, death claimed Sir George Simpson, believed also to have been in his mid-seventies. Simpson's health had been erratic for quite some time, and his eyesight had declined to the point where he was no longer able to read or to write legibly. Despite bouts of illness, however, he remained in harness. He had set out early that summer, against medical advice, to pay his accustomed visit to Red River – this time by railroad, stagecoach, and steamboat – but he never reached his destination. Taken seriously ill at St Paul, he was forced to return home.[191] Even that admonitory experience failed to drive Simpson into retirement, however. After a brief recuperation, he threw himself into preparations for a spectacular HBC canoe demonstration on the Ottawa River in honour of the visiting Prince of Wales. The event was a great success, and Simpson was showered with praise for having organized it so well. Three days later, however, he suffered an apoplectic seizure like those he had suffered earlier in the year, and was dead within a week.[192]

An epoch was over.

8

Upheaval Abroad, Slow Progress at Home, 1861–65

Revolution engulfed the continent. American democracy was self-destructing. British Columbia, left rudderless after Hudson's Bay Company rule ended, was becoming a Crown colony. Canada, frustrated by years of political paralysis, was proposing a daring new constitutional adventure. To many at Red River, however, frustrated by the prolonged stare-down between the company and the British government over Rupert's Land's surrender, and by Canada's averted attention, their political future seemed distant.

In reality, change was closer than they imagined. And while some of the more restless launched hilariously unsuccessful democratic experiments, most were content with improved local government by a more competent and fractionally more representative Council of Assiniboia; and with a legal system guided by lay recorders whose performances generally surpassed those of their legally trained predecessors. When, in late 1865, the scrawny village at the crotch of the Portage and Red River Trails began to call itself the "Town of Winnipeg," it already possessed some features of what would become the first city in the Canadian west.

POLITICAL UPHEAVAL ALL ROUND

These were years of political reconstruction south, east, and west of Rupert's Land – developments that would soon impact the plodding negotiations over the HBC's chartered domains.

South of the 49th parallel, a fratricidal struggle was raging that permanently scarred American democracy. South Carolina seceded from the federal union in December 1860 in response to Abraham Lincoln's November election on a platform opposed to the expansion of slavery, and in February 1861 the southern Confederacy was formed. Lincoln became president in March, and war began the following month. From then until the Confederate army's surrender and Lincoln's assassination in April 1865, residents of Red River followed the bloody struggle in the pages of the *Nor'-Wester.* It may all have seemed remote to them, and immediate consequences were indeed few;[1] but long-range ramifications were just below the horizon. West of the Rocky Mountains, where the HBC had recently governed under licence from imperial authorities, the legislature of the new Crown colony of British Columbia held its first session in January 1864. It was a portent, some thought, of what Assiniboia's fate would be. Vancouver Island, a Crown colony since 1849 (administered by the HBC until 1858), would soon be absorbed by British Columbia.

The Canadians were at an impasse in 1861. While they had not abandoned their territorial ambitions in Rupert's Land, they were obliged by an economic downturn to shelve their annexation plans temporarily as a series of political impasses all but paralyzed their parliament and government. The 1840 Act of Union, which had fused predominantly English Upper Canada and predominantly French Lower Canada into a single governmental unit, was not working because the differing needs and interests of the two equally represented halves of the colony had produced legislative gridlock. Finally, in 1864, Opposition leader George Brown proposed an all-party coalition dedicated to breaking the perpetual deadlock by forming a larger federal union of British North American colonies. The result was the creation of a new government headed by John A. Macdonald and É.P. Taché, supported by Brown's Grits, with colonial confederation as its goal.

The benefits sought from federal union were numerous, interrelated, and strongly influenced by events to the south. For Macdonald and his colleagues, the immediate aim was to end the shotgun marriage of French and English Canada, permitting each to deal with local matters locally, and to share with other British American colonies the governance of issues of common interest. For the Atlantic colonies, the most pressing goal – an important matter for Canada too – was ending trade dependence on the United States. The predominantly north-south trade patterns prevailing in most British American colonies were threatened by the looming expiration of the British-American Reciprocity Treaty of 1854. It was therefore vital to improve trade among themselves.

Stimulating east-west trading patterns required new transportation facilities – chiefly railways. Railway links across British North America were also crucial to the defence of British possessions against a United

States made hostile by perceived British support of the Confederate cause – and soon to possess the world's largest unemployed army. And only a railway could connect the areas east of Lake Superior with the coveted HBC territories in the west and the new coastal colony of British Columbia. Railways of the extreme reach needed to unify British North America were hugely expensive – much more so than any of these economically underadvantaged colonies could individually afford. As a united and governmentally stable country determined to exploit the vast potential of northwestern North America, however, it might attract the interest of international money markets.

The matter was urgent. By the time Brown made his proposal in 1864, it seemed likely that the US civil war would be over soon, and that the United States would then turn its attention northward. The belief, first expressed in 1845 by American journalist John L. O'Sullivan, that "our manifest destiny is to overspread and possess the whole of the continent which providence has given us" was still widely held south of the border; and US secretary of state William H. Seward believed that destiny extended to "the icy barrier of the north."[2] By 1865 Prime Minister Macdonald was saying he considered invasion from the south to be imminent. The confederation project was accordingly launched and pursued with astonishing swiftness. On 30 June 1864, just two weeks after Brown's initiative, the new Canadian government requested permission to participate in a planned conference of Atlantic colonies about maritime union.[3] An invitation was cautiously proffered, conference arrangements were hastily expedited, and on 29 August key members of the Canadian cabinet set sail from Quebec for Charlottetown, Prince Edward Island, where the conference was to meet. They arrived on 1 September.

A week of conviviality and eloquence followed, at the conclusion of which agreement in principle was reached on a federal union of British North American colonies. The delegates further agreed to reassemble at Quebec in October to outline a constitution for the new federation. Although the work of the Quebec Conference was much more intense than it had been at Charlottetown, and the debate was more contentious, it produced a series of detailed resolutions from which the federation's ultimate constitution deviated little.[4] By the end of February 1865, the Canadian Parliament had thoroughly debated these resolutions and adopted them by a wide margin.[5]

The form of federalism outlined in the Quebec Resolutions differed markedly from that which had disintegrated in the United States. The proposed powers of Canada's central government would be stronger than they appeared to be south of the border; fewer rights and freedoms would be constitutionally guaranteed; the parliamentary system would be retained; and Canada would remain a British colony, albeit a little farther along the road to autonomy than most others. The new federation's "manifest destiny," moreover, would be explicitly inconsistent with that of the United States in the far northwest: the Quebec Resolutions contemplated the eventual inclusion of Newfoundland and British Columbia by mutual agreement; and, anticipating conclusion of negotiations over Rupert's Land, they added, "The Northwest Territory ... shall be admitted into the union on such terms and conditions as the Parliament of the federated provinces shall deem equitable, and as shall receive the assent of Her Majesty."

Events had proceeded with amazing speed to that point. Suddenly, however, they halted. The Quebec Resolutions were rejected by general elections in New Brunswick and Newfoundland, and by the legislature in Prince Edward Island. In Nova Scotia a beleaguered pro-confederation government dared not even present the plan to its legislature. The prospects for immediate British North American union were dark.

NEGOTIATING RUPERT'S LAND'S FUTURE

While this first push toward Confederation was under way, the tone and dynamic of the Rupert's Land discussions underwent subtle but significant change. In its 1861 general letter to senior field officers, the company reported that the colonial secretary had introduced a bill late in the previous session of Parliament to make southern Rupert's Land a Crown colony. The HBC's response was cautiously cooperative: "[W]e submitted such alterations and amendments as we considered necessary for the protection and preservation of the Company's rights," including "fair and reasonable compensation."[6] The bill died unenacted at the end of the parliamentary session, never to be reintroduced; and for the next two and a half years, both the Colonial Office and the company let sleeping dogs lie.

In the meantime, the HBC itself underwent a major metamorphosis. In early 1863 the company's shareholders, who had long ruled like patriarchs of a great family, sold their holdings to a new and much larger body of international investors. HBC stock began to trade on public markets, and a new governor and board of directors were elected.[7] Besides generating much suspicion and hostility among officers in the field, who were not consulted, these changes brought new "bottom-line" attitudes to the company's management. That policy shift was nourished by recent experience on the Pacific coast, where confusion between James Douglas's dual roles as the company's representative and governor of Vancouver Island had caused serious problems.[8]

The company's new Governor and Committee then decided to seize the initiative in its discussions with government, resolving in August 1863 that "the authority ..., executive and judicial, over the Red River Settlement and the south-western portion of Rupert's Land should be vested in officers deriving such authority directly from the Crown, and exercising it in the name of Her Majesty."[9] This resolution, along with a set of proposals for bringing the change about, was submitted forthwith to the Colonial Office. The ensuing negotiations became intense in the early months of 1864, and bargaining was hard. Although anxious to be relieved of all governmental responsibilities, the company was determined to retain its commercial opportunities, and to be well compensated for giving up its ownership rights. New HBC governor Sir Edmund Head commented in April 1864, "[I]t has not been easy to steer cautiously between frightening our shareholders by asking too little, and deterring the Government from treating with us at all by asking too much."[10]

At this point, the British government became aware that British North American colonial union, long a mere hypothesis, had become an active project; and its discussions with the HBC shifted to, and bogged down within, that framework. Queried in the House of Commons in mid-1865 about what had happened to the plan to place company lands under Crown control, Colonial Secretary Cardwell stated that the government had decided to accept the legality of the company's asserted charter rights, and was "hoping to induce the Canadian Government ... to undertake the government and settling of that territory."[11] In October 1865 the *Nor'-Wester* reported that Canada was unwilling to pay the price demanded by the company, which it considered exorbitant.[12] Clearly, therefore, the HBC would remain the governor of Rupert's Land for some time to come. But its heart was no longer in the role. Its annual letters focused thereafter almost exclusively on business, giving only token attention to the activities of the governor, council, or courts of Assiniboia.[13]

As Red River's residents realized that both company and government were indifferent to their needs, and saw Americans arriving in increasing numbers, popular sentiment grew more American in tone. The

Nor'-Wester remarked bluntly in February 1862 that "[t]he very peculiar system of government which prevails in this country bids fair to drive us into annexation to the United States. Even ... men born and brought up in the old country, and heretofore strongly British in their feelings and preferences, now join in the general outcry against the British connection ... What is the use – say they – of being connected with Britain when the connection is merely nominal?"[14]

GOVERNING IN THE MEANTIME

Whether or not the company liked the responsibility, it still had to govern its lands. So William McTavish remained not just the HBC's chief factor, but also governor of Assiniboia. And of Rupert's Land, London having written to McTavish two weeks after Sir George Simpson's death, reminding him that his 1857 appointment as acting governor of the entire charter territory in case of Simpson's incapacity had never been revoked. He was accordingly ordered "for the present" to do anything Simpson might have done that he considered "necessary for the proper carrying on of the business of the Company."[15] Workhorse McTavish undertook this onerous new responsibility, in addition to his already burdensome duties and in spite of less than robust health, without apparent complaint.

The London committee decided on Simpson's permanent replacement in early 1861, but did not announce the fact for quite some time. The choice had fallen on Alexander Grant Dallas, who was in charge of HBC operations on the west coast.[16] Elected to the committee in 1856 after a varied business career involving little or no North American experience, Dallas quickly won the confidence of the HBC's London leaders, and was commissioned in 1857 to improve the state of company operations on the Pacific seaboard. His report on James Douglas's less than successful performance in the dual role of Vancouver Island's governor and head of the HBC's Western Department undoubtedly influenced the company's diminished enthusiasm for colonial governance after 1863.[17] Before Dallas could take charge of the company's North American operations, he had to journey to London to report on the west coast situation and be instructed about his new responsibilities. That interlude, plus a two-month delay caused by the US Navy's seizure in late 1861 of the British mail ship *Trent*,[18] postponed his arrival at Red River until 18 May 1862.

Despite personal misgivings about mixing business and government, Alexander Dallas took his responsibilities as civil governor of Rupert's

Land seriously. About two weeks after arriving in the Red River Settlement, where he had been instructed to reside,[19] Dallas convened a meeting of the Council of Assiniboia. His position as senior governor allowed him to preside over that body if he chose, and he did so then and frequently thereafter. At that first meeting, the new governor-in-chief announced he had sold all his HBC stock, resigned his directorship, and was "anxious only to promote the best interests of the country."[20] His actions matched his words. In the two years he was based at Red River, Dallas chaired eleven of the fourteen meetings held by the Council of Assiniboia; and the three meetings he missed took place while he was either presiding over the Council of Rupert's Land at Norway House or conducting Simpsonesque tours of inspection to remote company posts.[21]

How good a civil governor was Alexander Dallas? One historian has credited him with early recognition of the need to deal with Aboriginal title and to provide better local government if "serious trouble" with Indians and Halfbreeds was to be avoided.[22] He abandoned the practice of making land grants conditional on undertakings not to trade in furs.[23] When, on several occasions, the settlement was visited by large numbers of destitute Sioux, fleeing US troops south of the border, Dallas dealt with them humanely but firmly, providing relief supplies but insisting that they move on. Most offers of "assistance" by US military authorities were politely refused.[24] As a result of his intimate knowledge of the west coast experience, Dallas also did his best to separate the HBC's governmental obligations from its business interests.

He was criticized by some for standing idly by on one occasion while a determined mob broke into the settlement jail and released a controversial prisoner, even though a group of volunteer special constables stood ready to defend the buildings upon his order; but the general consensus was that his avoidance of the risk of bloodshed was wise.[25] He is also said to have been unpopular with older officers,[26] but that is understandable given his close association with the new HBC management and its coldly commercial vision for the company's future. On balance, Governor Dallas performed well in a role he thought neither he nor any other company official should have been performing. It was not, however, a task he was willing to perform for long. Dallas tendered his resignation after a little more than a year,[27] leaving the settlement on 9 May 1864. Following his return to England, he was retained under contract for two years as a company consultant.

Dallas's resignation as governor-in-chief once more elevated William McTavish to that post. Although the arrangement was again intended to be temporary, McTavish would hold the position, along with the governorship of Assiniboia, until illness deprived him of the strength to carry on.[28] His appearance and demeanour during those years was captured by a travelling correspondent for *Harper's* magazine about 1860:

> [A] gentleman of Scotch birth or descent, [h]is figure is tall, and his head finely shaped, with a broad, high brow which ... gives you the impression of mental calibre. The wrinkles upon his forehead and face are such as care, not age, accounts for, and are set off by the Palmerston style of whisker and a heavy mustache, together with long sandy hair in which the streaks of gray are only beginning to appear. His manner has the quiet, well-bred tone oftener found among Englishmen than others, and his voice is low ... Energy, determination, and executive ability were ... obvious ... [and] his culture and tastes [were] confirmed by the books which we saw lying on the table and book-cases.[29]

The membership of the Council of Assiniboia remained virtually unchanged during the years discussed in this chapter, the only new member being John Dease, a Halfbreed trader in buffalo robes appointed in 1861.[30] He was an infrequent attender. Until 1865 councillors received no payment for serving as such, although many were paid for services in other public roles: governor, recorder, petty court magistrate, and so on. In March 1965 the council voted unanimously to change that situation: "[E]very councillor not receiving any salary for any other office shall be entitled to ten shillings a day for every day's actual attendance at Council."[31] It was another small step toward greater participation in government by nonestablishment settlers like John Inkster, who had moved the resolution.

The *Nor'-Wester* did not report Dallas's resignation until November 1864,[32] evidence of the secrecy in which governmental matters were still often cloaked. But if the *Nor'-Wester* had not brought fully open government to the settlement, its presence had certainly improved public awareness of what the council and the courts were doing. Newspaper accounts of cases in the General Court during this period were often better than those in the official court records, and the routine, if delayed, publication of council minutes provided at least a retrospective accounting of public affairs.

In November 1863 the *Nor'-Wester* listed Assiniboia's entire governmental establishment: one governor of Rupert's Land, one governor of Assiniboia, thirteen other councillors of Assiniboia, one recorder of Rupert's Land, five other justices of the peace (three of whom also sat on the General Court), eight other petty court magistrates (distributed among three courts), one sheriff–jail governor, one coroner, one clerk of council and court, one postmaster, four collectors of customs, four road superintendents, and nine constables.[33] Because some persons held more than one appointment, these fifty public positions were distributed among thirty-eight individuals. The 23 July 1864 *Nor'-Wester* issue printed Assiniboia's public accounts for the preceding year. Of a total £1,075 shown to have been spent in 1863–64, expenditures related to law and public order amounted to £378, or 35 per cent.[34] The legal category was made up of magistrates' stipends (£86), miscellaneous court expenses (£9), clerk's salary (£50), sheriff–jail governor's salary (£30), jailer's salary and rations (£33), prisoners' rations and medical expenses (£29), constables' stipends (£132), and jury and witness fees (£9).

RECORDERS AND COURTS

The sums expended on Red River's courts were repaid by what seems to have been general satisfaction with their performance, although a notorious conviction for attempted abortion in 1863[35] cleaved the anglophone population at least as sharply as had *Foss v. Pelly*[36] in 1850.

The pro tem services of Acting Recorder Dr John Bunn – the settlement's cordial, common-sense *pater familias* – had been guiding the court on a fair course ever since Francis Johnson's departure in 1858. Those services were finally recognized materially in February 1861 by a retroactive stipend,[37] a recognition that came none too soon. By the beginning of June, the universally respected and widely loved Dr Bunn was dead. He had conducted the May session of the court only a week previously, and his passing was altogether unexpected: "Before breakfast yesterday he was promenading on the river bank ... in the best of spirits, and seemingly in the best of health. When the [Upper Fort Garry] breakfast-bell rang, he went into his room, likely for toileting purposes, but went in the last time as a living man ... Mr. McTavish went to his rooms, and was appalled on finding him stretched on his bed, quite insensible ... Life was fast ebbing, and in less than an hour he was no more."[38] Bunn was thought to have been fifty-nine years of age at his death. Born in Rupert's Land and educated in Scotland, he had devotedly served Red River for most of his career: as physician and surgeon, coroner, councillor, acting governor, magistrate, acting recorder, and sheriff–jail governor. Few Red River elders, if any, were as widely and deeply mourned upon their passing.[39]

The search for a legally trained recorder had been long postponed by reason of Governor Simpson's other interests, illness, and death; and then by the need to fill his Gulliverian shoes. The *Nor'-Wester,* while praising Dr Bunn's locum tenens service at the helm of the court, had been sharply critical of this delay: "No organized community ... should be without a duly qualified legal adviser ... capable to give a correct opinion not only on general principles of law but on their varied and countless applications. When a nice point is decided by such a man the litigants are at once silenced into respectful acquiescence ...; but where a decision means simply an opinion or conjecture 'to the best of my judgment,' the losing party will never be satisfied, because he considers his own view as likely to be correct as that of his lay judge."[40]

With Bunn's passing, the search was finally reinstated, and by April 1862 a new recorder had been appointed and was on his way to Red River. The identity of the appointee was a great surprise to the settlement. Although a Canadian lawyer was initially sought,[41] that quest was abandoned when someone considered entirely suitable turned up fortuitously in London, and was appointed without further ado. He was former court clerk and chief trader John Black.[42] Following his discipline for leaving Red River without authorization to be with his dying wife, and his subsequent resignation, Black had moved to Australia with his sister. After initially farming in the Melbourne area, he had moved to Sydney and taken a senior post in the New South Wales government.[43] Returning to Britain in 1861 due to his sister's ill health just when the search for a new recorder was reinstated, he had little difficulty persuading the company that he was the man for the job.

Black was not a fully qualified lawyer. His formal legal training was limited to whatever he may have been taught as a law clerk in Scotland before coming to Red River as Adam Thom's first clerk. He had been a member of both the General Court and a petty court during his later years in the settlement, however; and according to HBC governor Joseph Berens, his government service in Australia had been "in an office somewhat similar, as regards adjudication, to the duties he will have to perform at the Settlement."[44] Moreover, Berens continued, "He knows the habits, manners, customs of the people ... and his ability, good sense and conciliating manners induce me to believe that he will fill the office with credit to himself and to the approval of all parties." Time would prove that assessment accurate.

Figure 8.1 John Black came to Red River as Adam Thom's clerk, rose to become one of its best recorders, and played a key role in bringing about Manitoba's provincehood.

Black's commission as "Chairman" of the General Court (a title chosen "to avoid any stigma of his not having been educated as a lawyer")[45] and justice of the peace, at £500 per annum, was issued on 14 April 1862.[46] He left London four days later in the wake of Governor Dallas, whom he met in New York and accompanied to Red River. Arriving in May, both men were welcomed by the Council of Assiniboia on 4 June. Black – described as "Recorder" and referred to almost invariably thereafter as that, or as "Judge Black," despite his carefully chosen official "Chairman" designation – conducted the next session of the General Court on 21 August.

Governor Dallas did not sit with the court at that or, indeed, *any* session, having decided to maintain an arm's-length relationship with the judicial process. This decision – doubtless a product of the new HBC management strategy of keeping commercial and governmental activities as distinct as possible – was understandable and probably beneficial. Assiniboia's Governor McTavish was told to follow suit, however, and *that,* from a legal perspective, might have been a fatal move. Because the court's only authority to administer justice was the judicial power the HBC charter gave to governors and their councils, the presence of a governor to validate judicial proceedings was imperative. One way to make up for the absence of both Dallas and McTavish from court sessions would have been to designate John Black as *acting* governor; and he was indeed issued such a commission in January 1865.[47] But what about the long period before that?

Possibly Governor McTavish had, of his own accord, delegated the powers of acting governor to Black at an earlier point. We do know that in June 1862, well before Black's first sitting with the court, McTavish empowered him to "assume charge of this establishment" during the governor's absence at Norway House.[48] Although that delegation might have applied only to McTavish's responsibilities as chief factor, it seems unlikely that as careful an administrator as William McTavish would have travelled to the far end of Lake Winnipeg without empowering someone at Red River to deal with governmental emergencies as well; and if he had done so Black would have been the obvious candidate. In March 1865, before Black's formal commission as acting governor arrived, he was described as such in correspondence.[49] So perhaps Recorder Black held sufficient pro tem gubernatorial power from the start to clothe the General Court with judicial authority under the HBC charter. In any event, nobody ever complained.

Black settled easily into his role as the court's sole presiding authority. The August and November sessions passed without significant incident, and the *Nor'-Wester* was unstinting in its praise of the new recorder.[50] His success owed much to Black's common-sense, patient, pedagogical style on the bench – savouring much more of the late Dr Bunn than of either Adam Thom or Francis Johnson. Black had given much thought to his approach, and had explained it in a letter to the *Nor'-Wester.* He would sometimes give legal advice from the bench, he said, assisting parties to settle disputes among themselves and thereby "avoid the costs and the delays and the animosities of litigation." But he thought it would be "utter absurdity" to suddenly apply "the rigid maxims of law ... to the settlement of suits among a community whose whole habits of thought and modes of transacting business are ... somewhat primitive and peculiar." In fact, Black asserted, it would be wise to avoid altogether the "artificialities" and "fictions" of law "which have too often stood in the way of real justice, and sacrificed the substance of essential right to the vain shadow of legal form." "So long as the ends of substantial justice are really attained," he concluded, "we ought not too eagerly to desire the introduction of subtle refinements and ingenious technicalities."[51] Recorder Black's guidance of the General Court over the ensuing seven years consistently reflected those attitudes.

The third session over which John Black presided – in February 1863 – presented challenges that would have tested the mettle of any jurist, however well seasoned. The principal case heard at that sitting, *R. v. Corbett*,[52] lasted nine days – the longest trial ever heard by the General Court. And, like *Foss v. Pelly* in 1850 (about which Black had unhappy personal memories), it divided the settlement's English-speaking population painfully. The salacious nature of the evidence titillated the prurient throughout, and far beyond, Assiniboia.

Reverend G.O. Corbett, a highly respected Anglican pastor resident in the settlement since the early 1850s, had in 1854 established a church to serve the new outlying community of Headingley. His parishioners were fiercely loyal. A well-known critic of the HBC since testifying against it at the 1857 parliamentary enquiry into its governance, Corbett was an advocate of Crown colony status for the settlement. But in early 1863 his bubble was burst by accusations of impregnating his serving girl and attempting to perform an abortion on her. When he was brought to trial before the General Court for breach of abortion laws, his supporters believed the charges had been trumped up in retaliation for his anti-company opinions and activities.

The *Corbett* trial brought to prominence twenty-eight-year-old James Ross,[53] the brilliant son of former settlement elder Alexander Ross. James had achieved great academic success at the University of Toronto, and had been back at Red River since 1858, serving as postmaster from 1859,[54] and as sheriff–jail governor since Dr Bunn's death in 1861.[55] All were positions that his late brother William had once held. James Ross was also a partner and co-editor of the *Nor'-Wester* by that time. He was already in the public eye due to those attainments, and his eloquent efforts as Reverend Corbett's defence counsel, reported by his own newspaper and the associated *Toronto Globe*, brought him even greater fame within and beyond the settlement.

Although litigants had often been represented by "agents" previously, Corbett's trial involved more and better-quality third-party advocacy than ever before. The late Dr Bunn's sons Thomas and John were retained as prosecutors by the Council of Assiniboa, and they performed skilfully. The defence team was ostensibly led by a formally trained lawyer, Red River's first: Frank Larned Hunt from Detroit. But although Ross was hired as Hunt's assistant, his performance far outshone that of his "leader," who in fact did next to nothing. The young man's five-hour closing address to the jury, undertaken at the last moment because Hunt failed to show up, was brilliant.[56] His work as agent in *Corbett*, and in several other court appearances, led Ross, less than a year later, to resign from the *Nor'-Wester* and open a law practice.[57] Not long after that, he would return to Toronto and undertake formal legal studies.

Notwithstanding James Ross's diligent efforts, his client was convicted. The voluminous evidence established overwhelmingly, in the eyes of the jury and impartial observers, that Reverend Corbett had indeed attempted unsuccessfully to terminate a pregnancy he had begun.[58] He was sentenced to six months' imprisonment. Recorder Black was subsequently commended by HBC governor Berens for having conducted the monster trial to the "general satisfaction" of all.[59] The *Nor'-Wester*'s assessment was even more laudatory: "We are more than ever impressed with the value to this Settlement of a man such as Mr. Black ... [He is] clear-headed, circumspect, astute and sound in judgment. He ... has given a respectability to the General Quarterly Court which, we venture to say, it never possessed before."[60]

For the remainder of this period, the court functioned smoothly. So juridically uneventful was the summer of 1864 that at the August sitting of the court, the sheriff announced a "maiden assize" – a session devoid of criminal prosecutions – and presented Recorder Black with a pair of white kid gloves to mark the occasion "in accordance with time-honoured usage on such occasions in English courts."[61]

Although this was, so far as is known, Red River's only observance of the white glove ceremony, it was not the first time the General Court had had an empty criminal docket. The May session was also a maiden assize, in fact. It appears that, simultaneously with Governor Dallas's departure that month, a decision was made to entrust the petty courts with a greater proportion of the criminal adjudication than previously. From May 1864 to May 1869, inclusive, eleven of the General Court's twenty-two sittings lacked any criminal prosecutions, and there was an almost fourfold reduction in the incidence of such cases, compared with the court's previous five sessions. Perhaps the 1863 *Corbett* case had diminished Black's appetite for criminal matters. Certainly both he and Governor McTavish understood the importance of assuaging the local magistrates' thirst for greater responsibility.

Civil dockets were expanding in both courts, however – especially in the case of commercial disputes – and multiple-day General Court sessions became more common. Regrettably, the court records became less informative than previously as to the facts of routine commercial litigation. In November 1864 the Council of Assiniboia increased the fees charged for issuing civil writs in the general and petty courts, the fees being split between the magistrate who issued the writ commencing a civil case and the constable who served it on the defendant. At the same time, it enacted that in future such fees, as well as procedural rules, would be for particular courts to determine themselves.[62]

In August 1865, in apparent response to concerns about the court's authority to supervise the care of orphans, the Council of Assiniboia resolved that "[i]t shall be lawful for the General Quarterly Court ... to issue letters for the guardianship of minors ... and ... empower the guardians to take and have the care of the persons and the management of the property of the minors ... subject always to the supervision and control of the Court."[63]

The courts and the entire community suffered a major loss in June 1865 with the death from typhoid fever of francophone leader and longtime public servant François Bruneau.[64] A prairie-born French Halfbreed, Bruneau was a successful self-made farmer. He first appears in the minutes of the Council of Assiniboia in 1843 as part of a French-speaking delegation seeking the creation of a distillery in the settlement.[65] The next time he came to history's attention was in 1849, as one of the Halfbreeds nominated by James Sinclair to serve on the *Sayer* jury. He was appointed to the Upper District (central) Petty Court in October 1850[66] and held judicial office thereafter, often on multiple courts, until his death. Commissioned as a member of the Council of Assiniboia and a justice of the peace in 1853, Bruneau first sat on the council in March of that year[67] and on the General Court in May.[68] He also held divers other public offices. The list of Assiniboia's functionaries published in the *Nor'-Wester* on 11 November 1863 shows François Bruneau as a member of both the council and the General Court, president of both the Middle (former Upper) District and White Horse Plains Petty

Courts, and superintendent of roads. He also served as a member of the 1862 Law Revision Committee,[69] and in 1864 he chaired a public meeting to discuss how to deal with an influx of destitute Sioux Indians.

A personal memoir by his son-in-law Johnny Grant described Bruneau's judicial style: "He was so big-hearted that a week or so before the ... court met, his house would be full of people asking advice. They got the advice and free board as well ... [H]e always tried to effect a settlement between litigants ... [H]e brought the two together, and in nine cases out of ten affected a settlement ... He explained the law to them and they would leave well satisfied and good friends."[70] While no doubt somewhat apocryphal, this account conveys convincingly both the tone of Bruneau's personal relations with litigants and the mediatory approach Red River courts generally adopted in civil matters.

François Bruneau's entry in the *Dictionary of Canadian Biography* concludes rather harshly: "He had served the authority of the HBC faithfully, without harming the interests of his Métis compatriots but also without contributing greatly to their political, social, or economic advancement."[71] Although he was certainly not a political activist, and chose to "work within the system," this seems an unfair assessment of a man who, in addition to much other public service, gave his people almost fifteen years of what the *Nor'-Wester* called "upright, sensible and just" adjudication in three different courts. His was probably the most extensive judicial contribution of anyone's in Red River's history. Bruneau was replaced on the court and council in February 1866 by Roget Goulet, whose work as surveyor and customs collector had been bringing him increasing prominence.[72]

REVISED LAWS

When "Recorder" John Black arrived at the settlement in June 1862, he found that its local laws had been recently consolidated and revised. A committee consisting of Governor McTavish and councillors François Bruneau and Thomas Bunn had been appointed in January of that year to draft the revision, and their recommendations had been debated, altered, and adopted at a special two-day meeting of the council.[73] In most respects, that new compilation followed Adam Thom's 1852 revision, with only minor amendments and elaborations. The growth and changing face of the settlement were reflected, however, in expanded and more complex customs laws, and in several new categories of regulations. The new laws concerned liquor-vendor licensing, absconding debtors, postal arrangements, surveyors, and employment contracts. Prisoners in the Red River jail became entitled to one pound of flour daily in addition to the previous ration of a half pound of pemmican and "water at discretion."

An important further legislative change – altering the date as of which English law was applicable to Rupert's Land – was made at John Black's behest in January 1864.[74] The laws that Adam Thom drafted in 1852 had changed that date from 1670 to 1837, when Queen Victoria ascended the throne.[75] That had concerned Black during the *Corbett* trial because the English statute under which Corbett was prosecuted had been enacted a quarter-century *later*.[76] He accordingly proposed, and the council enacted, an evergreen reception date: "[A]ll such laws of England, of subsequent date, as may be applicable ...; in other words, ... the existing laws of England for the time being, insofar as the same are known to the Court and are applicable to the condition of the colony."[77] This ended reception date concerns for the remainder of the court's existence.[78]

An important feature of the new revision was greatly improved accessibility. Thanks to the *Nor'-Wester*'s printing press, the 1862 compilation was both published in the newspaper itself and reprinted in pamphlet form for distribution throughout the settlement.[79] The days of posting new laws on church doors or placing them in the custody of local magistrates seemed to be over. It would not be long, though, before the enactment of unpublicized amendments created familiar problems.[80]

LAW ENFORCEMENT

Assiniboia's justice system had Achilles heels on both feet. One was the system's ownership by a potential litigant; the other was its inability to defend itself physically. Every effective legal regime requires a strong enforcement arm. This one lacked, throughout much of its history, sufficient resources to police its laws adequately. Whenever military muscle borrowed from British authorities was lacking, therefore, settlement officials were without the ability to enforce the law in showdown situations. That weak heel collapsed once more during the period under review.

The detachment of Royal Canadian Rifles garrisoned at Red River since November 1857 was withdrawn during the summer of 1861, and no replacements were seen for the next nine years. Red River's only official protection came from the sheriff and a police force "not exceeding twelve" constables.[81] Efforts to persuade the War Office to fill the military gap failed – in part, perhaps, because the politically sundered community sent two competing petitions on the subject to England. After Governor Dallas warned the Council of Assiniboia in October 1862 that a violent Sioux uprising south of the international boundary, and the US Army's massive response to it,[82] posed a serious threat of Sioux depredations against the settlement, Recorder Black drafted a petition to the Crown for settlers' signature.[83] But the *Nor'-Wester's* co-editor James Ross thought an HBC-blessed petition would benefit the company alone, and so not only withheld the newspaper's endorsement, but also circulated a rival petition. Both documents attracted considerable support. The upshot was that British authorities, already reluctant to help, used the lack of a common Red River position as an excuse for doing nothing.[84] And nothing was done locally to strengthen the settlement's protective forces. Even a proposed volunteer brigade to provide interim security was rejected by the Council of Assiniboia.[85]

The rebelliousness of James Ross the journalist soon undermined the career of James Ross the civil servant. At the time he denounced the council's troop petition, Ross was in its employ as sheriff–jail governor, postmaster, and frequent French-English translator in the courts. In fact, although he may never have known it, he had come within a hair of also being appointed to the Council of Assiniboia and the General Court – and thus holding all the public offices his father and older brother had collectively filled. On 2 September 1861 the HBC secretary wrote to Ross saying that his choice as sheriff and governor of the jail by "that portion of your fellow citizens who are best qualified to judge your qualifications" had prompted the Governor and Committee to confer the additional offices of councillor and justice of the peace upon him.[86] London took the precaution, however, of leaving the final decision to Governor McTavish, transmitting both Ross's new commissions and the foregoing letter to McTavish with discretion to pass them on to Ross or not.[87] McTavish opted to withhold the appointments since, by the time he received them from London, he was aware of Ross's comments in the *Nor'-Wester* opposing the company and favouring Crown colony status for the settlement. He was also privy to a long, arrogant, letter the intemperate young man had written to the Council of Assiniboia seeking increased compensation as postmaster.[88] The troop petition imbroglio settled the matter in McTavish's mind. At the next meeting of the Council of Assiniboia, on 25 November 1862, he accused Ross of "stirring up the people" and of conduct "incompatible with his position as an officer of government." He moved that "Mr. James Ross be removed from all his public offices from this day,"[89] and the motion passed unanimously.

Ross's replacement as sheriff and jail governor was Henry McKenney, a commercial dynamo who had arrived at Red River, just three years previously, on the first steamboat to reach the settlement.[90] Although some said he was only a few steps ahead of pressing creditors back in Canada, McKenney successfully launched a bevy of business ventures, including Rupert's Land's first hotel, the Royal, not long after his arrival; and he was sufficiently prominent by June 1861 to have been made a petty court magistrate.[91] At the time of his appointment as sheriff, McKenney was constructing a store at the intersection of the Portage and Fort Garry Trails – an establishment from which, along with the buildings of Andrew McDermot and one or two others, the famed corner of Portage and Main dates. Although a disputatious and litigious individual himself, Henry McKenney remained the settlement's chief law enforcement officer until shortly before Canadian troops arrived in 1870.

One of Sheriff McKenney's innovations was a book recording the results of civil cases in all courts from January 1863 to October 1869 inclusive – 783 cases in total. It demonstrated, among other things, that the General Court, which heard 189 civil and 29 criminal cases in the same period, handled only about one-third of the total civil caseload.[92] Although the precise number of criminal cases tried in the petty courts during that time is not known, the spotty evidence available indicates that their share of criminal adjudication was vastly greater than that of the General Court.

When, in April 1863, Assiniboia authorities faced their first threat of concerted violence, they had, at the outset, only Sheriff McKenney and his handful of constables to buttress the law. The threat was a sequel to G.O. Corbett's conviction and imprisonment for attempted abortion.[93] After Corbett had served about six weeks of his six-month sentence, his supporters petitioned for remission of the remainder of the sentence on compassionate grounds. Governor Dallas denied the request, and when it became clear that the petitioners were prepared to free their pastor forcibly if necessary, Sheriff McKenney assembled a sizable body of volunteer special constables. Realizing, however, that the protesters might well overpower even those reinforcements, and that blood would flow in any event, Governor Dallas declined to order armed resistance, and stood aside as the mob broke Corbett out of prison.[94] McKenney and his men arrested and imprisoned one of the leaders of that outrage, but he too was freed by an armed throng.

It had again been demonstrated, as at the *Sayer* trial in 1849, that Assiniboia's justice system lacked the ability to enforce its authority against an organized segment of the community determined to flout that authority. Fortunately, such situations were relatively rare.[95] The *Nor'-Wester*, consistent in its crusade against company government, suggested that resentment of the HBC was a major factor in the jailbreaks, and made an interesting prediction, prophetic as to event if not as to cause: "The moral of all this is that the government of the Settlement should at once be dissociated from the Company ... If it is to continue as heretofore, ... either anarchy will follow or provisional government will have to be set up by the people themselves."[96]

ABORIGINAL CONCERNS

The greatest perceived threat to the settlement from the paucity of law enforcement personnel came not from disaffected portions of the community itself but from the fear of incursions by the plains Sioux. Although other Aboriginal issues arose from time to time – a call by the British Aborigines Protective Society in early 1861 for the recognition of Aboriginal rights,[97] a local "Indian manifesto" issued about the same time by Chief Peguis and other Indian leaders demanding payment for cultivation of any land beyond the 2 mile strip granted to Lord Selkirk,[98] a quickly abandoned HBC demand in 1861 for rent from Half-breeds and others occupying land for which they had no formal legal title[99] – such matters were eclipsed by worrisome developments south of the border.[100]

Problems began, in the summer of 1861, with sporadic demands by American Indians for the payment of tolls from travellers along Red River's supply route from St Paul. That fall a settlement-bound steamboat on the Red River was seized and briefly held for ransom. Travel disruptions became much more serious in the summer of 1862, and the perceived dangers of random roadside attacks persisted for at least the next two years. A stagecoach passenger heading for Red River through Minnesota in 1864 described the precautions still being taken at the time: "From Sioux Center to Fort Ambercrombie the mail is guarded by six soldiers: two before, two behind, and one on either side. Otherwise the Indians would rob them and go off with the horses."[101]

Such measures were instituted after a bloody uprising by starving Sioux in the fall of 1862. Angered by the failure of US officials to deliver promised treaty benefits, Indians viciously attacked the white residents of several Minnesota communities. Swift and sanguinary retaliation by American troops dispersed the Sioux, both guilty and innocent, and for the next two years many sought refuge in British territory. In late December 1862 the first group of destitute Sioux exiles – about ninety of them – showed up at Red River, where they were given emergency supplies and temporary shelter in the courthouse. More groups straggled into the settlement in May and December 1863, January and February 1864, and – 3,000 in number – in August 1864. On each occasion, relief supplies were provided in modest quantities, and Governor Dallas and his aides persuaded most of the visitors to leave. When persuasion was not effective, other means were employed. On at least one occasion, US troops were permitted to pursue the fugitives;[102] on another, local Chippewas decimated a Sioux encampment;[103] and, according to one historian, a group of settlers led by A.G.B. Bannatyne drugged several Sioux chiefs and dragged them over the border on toboggans in January 1864.[104]

EXPERIMENTS IN DEMOCRACY

The English-speaking enclaves along the Assiniboine River were virtually ignored by settlement authorities, and alienation accompanied their growth. The jailbreaks of April 1863 were largely the work of settlers from St James and Headingley sympathetic to G.O. Corbett. He had been instrumental in establishing Headingley against the wishes of the HBC; and many residents there shared his antipathy for the company, heightened by resentment over the minimal assistance they received from authorities at the Forks. At Portage la Prairie, farther west along the Assiniboine, Archdeacon William Cockran and his neighbours were feeling even more isolated. While St James and Headingley were inside the 50 mile radius designated as the Municipal District of Assiniboia, and so recieved at least some services, most Portage homesteaders were beyond even that.

In May 1863, with Corbett illegally back in his Headingley home, ministering once more to his loyal congregants despite fugitive status and suspension by his bishop and missionary society, the two chief engineers of his escape – James Stewart and John Bourke – flushed with their success, proposed that Headingley, St James, and Portage la Prairie should secede altogether from HBC control and form a "provisional government" with a view to seeking status as an independent Crown colony.[105] They failed, however, to gain sufficient support from others in the proposed breakaway area, and the scheme was dropped. But in December of that same year the residents of Portage la Prairie decided to go it alone and met, at first, with more success than had Stewart and Bourke.

Under the leadership of Archdeacon Cockran, Portage settlers elected a governmental council and a court, both to function formally along the same lines as their Assiniboia counterparts, but to be more democratic in substance. The council members, seven in number, seem to have been nominated by the archdeacon's son, Reverend Thomas Cochrane, and were then elected to one-year terms by the populace at large. The chairman was Frederick A. Bird, and the vice chairman was John Garrioch – a younger and more prosperous brother of former free trader Peter Garrioch. The court, which was to meet quarterly as at Red River, consisted of all available council members, assisted by juries and a clerk.[106]

The first session of the court was held on 6 January 1864. The widow of James Whitford had sued one McBain for unlawfully occupying land inherited by her from her husband, and Chairman Bird duly issued a summons against the defendant. When the court convened, a jury was empanelled, with Peter Garrioch as foreman. Mrs Whitford's case was called, and she was sworn and lodged her complaint. Then her son-in-law, David Cusiter, stepped forward, announced he was her attorney, and stated that the wrong person had been sued! While it was true, he explained, that McBain was in possession of Mrs Whitford's property, that property had been wrongfully sold to McBain by her son Andrew; so it was Andrew who should have been the defendant. Andrew, who was in court, appeared quite willing to be sued.

Other supporters of the plaintiff – including jury foreman Garrioch, who was obviously in cahoots with Cusiter – vociferously urged Chairman Bird to permit the change of defendants. Why? How would it help Mrs Whitford to sue her own son – with whom she was clearly on friendly terms – rather than the person in actual possession of the land she claimed as hers? Evidently, it was hoped that this ploy would prevent McBain calling defence evidence. Andrew Whitford would admit his wrongdoing, but Cusiter would not ask the court for damages against him, requesting only a declaration that Andrew's mother owned the land. With such a declaration, McBain could be forced off the land, and would not likely sue Andrew for the return of his money because Andrew was penniless and not worth suing. The scheme had Peter Garrioch's thumbprints all over it.

Chairman Bird reluctantly acceded to the change of defendants, causing Vice Chairman John Garrioch to protest loudly against brother

Peter's "artful" manoeuvre. Bird then stepped down from the bench because he expected to be called as a defence witness, and John Garrioch took the chair. Cusiter called no evidence, however, relying on Andrew's unsworn admission of the sale from his seat in the audience, and merely made a submission to the jury. No defence evidence was called either, since McBain was no longer the defendant. Then, after a bitter altercation between the Garrioch brothers over an alleged will by the plaintiff's husband that turned out not to exist, John Garrioch delivered a pro-defence charge to the jury, which retired to consider its verdict. While it was deliberating, foreman Peter Garrioch returned to the courtroom, reported that one juror was stubbornly refusing to agree with the rest, and requested that the juror in question be replaced! Amidst loud objections that this would be improper, another juror stepped forward in support of the foreman's request, citing a personal precedent. Although "all was confusion and disorder" for a while, Chairman Bird, supported by three colleagues, eventually gave in again to the imperious Peter Garrioch and appointed a substitute juror. After that, according to McBain's later account, it was only "about forty seconds" before a now smiling Peter Garrioch was back to announce a verdict in favour of the plaintiff: "Andrew ... had no right to sell the land he got from his father." The jury foreman and his fellow Whitford supporters then trooped out of the courtroom in triumph.

They had overlooked something important, however. A jury verdict is not, at law, the court's formal judgment – and no judgment had been pronounced! In the three-month interval before the court's next sitting on 6 April, disgruntled Vice Chairman John Garrioch consulted with James Ross at Red River. Ross possessed a copy of William Blackstone's *Commentaries on the Laws of England*, which stated – among other relevant things – that a jury verdict could be disregarded until judgment was formally entered. Meanwhile, the plaintiff's friends, now also aware of their procedural oversight, moved to reopen the case at the April session of the court. It was placed at the end of the case list.

When the first regularly scheduled case was called at the April sitting, and the plaintiff came forward to state his claim, David Cusiter strode in front of him, demanding that the court must give formal judgment in the unfinished case before any new business was conducted. All he wanted was a judgment stating, "This land belongs to Mrs. Whitford," with no reference to the alleged wrongdoing of Andrew Whitford. Ordered by Chairman Bird to sit down and await his turn on the docket, Cusiter refused, and Peter Garrioch called out, "You are right, Mr. Cusiter."[107]

Another chaotic scene ensued, subsiding only when the chairman succumbed yet again to the plaintiff's insistent allies, and pronounced the judgment demanded.

As Cusiter and his apparently victorious party prepared to leave the courtroom, the court declared that the case was still open, and ordered them to remain until it came up again at the end of the list. When that time arrived, Bird once more vacated the chair, having again been summoned as a witness, and presiding vice chairman John Garrioch began the proceedings by reading *another* passage from Blackstone to the effect that judges may overturn jury verdicts that are contrary to law. Failing to realize that Bird's pronouncement of judgment had foreclosed that possibility, he challenged Cusiter to prove that the jury's verdict had *not* been illegal.

Cusiter had come prepared to prove his case all over again and began with a letter stating, "When the old man [Whitford] died, I was at his bedside, and heard him say: 'I leave all to my wife.'" John Garrioch interrupted, quoting yet another passage from Blackstone to the effect that the Statute of Frauds prohibited verbal wills.[108] All hell seems then to have broken loose. Peter Garrioch's own account probably captured the scene most accurately, despite self-serving embellishments: "[O]ne of the jurors, P. Garrioch (foreman) ..., sprang to his feet and said: 'Gentlemen, as a British subject I claim to be heard. We want justice here; there is no justice. That gentleman ... [his brother John] is not doing justice – he is acting in the two-fold capacity of judge and pleader.' In an instant, someone behind him ... cried out: 'Out with him,' and with him many others till the cry became general."[109] John, having no other recourse, left the bench, and the court adjourned. A few days later, a public meeting was held, chaired by brother Peter, at which John was replaced as councillor and magistrate. Whether the damage to the brothers' personal relationship was ever repaired is unknown, although they are thought to have been estranged in later years. Who ended up in possession of the land? Mrs Whitford was occupying it in February 1865, when Peter Garrioch published his final public statement on the subject,[110] and no further legal proceedings are known. In the absence of a legally valid will or land transfer, the land should have passed by law to the widow or the son, so substantial justice was probably served.

By then, in any event, the experiment in local government had collapsed, and the Council of Assiniboia had refused a request by John Garrioch and others to extend its jurisdiction to Portage la Prairie.[111]

More than two years would pass before another attempt was made to bring democratic government to the outrider settlement.

Although it is easy to poke fun at this attempt by untrained residents of a remote prairie community to administer justice among themselves, their efforts would likely have improved with practice if the experiment had lasted. Nevertheless, the comic-opera atmosphere that suffused the hearing of *Whitford v. McBain* bestows, by contrast, much credit on the relatively dignified proceedings and generally fair decisions of Red River's official courts.

The latter were certainly not free of criticism. The 15 February 1861 issue of the *Nor'-Wester*, for example, accused the Lower District (St Andrew's parish) Petty Court of "discreditable" conduct, but the behaviour criticized was only that both spectators and members of the court were observed smoking during the proceedings and that "persons in the room are ever and anon making remarks, giving opinions, and ... [being] listened to by the magistrates with due attention and patience."[112] This, it seems, was as bad as it got in settlement courts. Magistrate John Taylor was removed from the White Horse Plains Petty Court by the Council of Assiniboia on the recommendation of Governor McTavish "on account of certain acts of maladministration" in March 1863,[113] but that dismissal bore little resemblance to John Garrioch's sudden fall from judicial grace at Portage la Prairie.

THE SETTLEMENT

As if in response to the roiling political clouds upon which so much attention was centred at home and abroad, fate assaulted the settlement with a cruel succession of natural calamities: flood, pestilence, infestation, fire, drought, and famine. An hour before his death in the spring of 1861, Dr John Bunn was anxiously watching, from the banks of the Red River at Upper Fort Garry, the rise of a devastating flood which, although not quite so high as in 1826 or 1852, "drove all the settlers along the Red River north of ... [that fort] from their houses."[114] That autumn, prairie fires were especially destructive – and strangely beautiful. A *Nor'-Wester* account of the fires began with the writer's awe: "[O]ur vast level prairies have been overrun by magnificent fires, ... brilliant affairs at night ... [T]he flames roll and sweep majestically. There is something grand, something terrific – in fact something sublime – in them."[115]

The typhoid fever that carried away François Bruneau and his wife in June 1865 was part of a deadly epidemic that had arrived at Red

River the previous summer and was still wreaking havoc months after the Bruneaus' deaths.[116] The parching summer of 1864 that incubated the epidemic decimated the settlement's crops; and what was left was devoured by voracious grasshoppers. The latter "left the ground as bare as if it had been plowed ... They come in clouds, and almost obscure the light of the sun ... They ... come up against one with great force, like heavy hailstones."[117] Both drought and grasshoppers lingered for the next several years, with serious economic and human consequences. In March 1865 the Council of Assiniboia purchased seed grain from the company at cost for distribution to the needy;[118] and in May it prohibited large-scale fishing in the rivers so individual families could catch "their fair share of the fish."[119]

The drought also affected navigation. Steamboat travel had progressed, and the splendid new *International*, 137 feet by 26 feet, drawing only 27 inches of water fully loaded, and said to match "the finest floating palaces of the Mississippi," joined the vessels plying the Red in May 1862.[120] But low water in the following years caused frequent problems, grounding a steamboat in 1865 and creating many other disruptions.[121]

Despite low water, crossing the Red and Assiniboine was a constant concern. Although a ferry service had long existed over both rivers at the Forks, its quality was execrable. The loss of a cartload of goods to the Assiniboine's muddy waters in 1860 brought a lawsuit against the ferryman[122] but no improvement in service. The *Nor'-Wester* remarked in November 1865 that ice on the Assiniboine provided the first comfortable crossing since spring.[123] In summer, it claimed, one could cross only if "the boat was bailed out, the canoe not adrift, and the ferryman not drunk." Spring brought no change, just "one boat, rotten; one canoe, leaky and muddy; two assistants, small boys; and one ferryman, drunken."[124] Later, under new management,[125] a ferryboat disintegrated while crossing the Red, propelling "a horse and cart, a ferryman, a woman and boy, and a dog ... into the not very deep waters of that river."[126] "Till another boat is built," the newspaper lamented, "the crossing must be a tedious drag with oars."

The westward retreat of the buffalo accelerated in response to changing climate and increasing settlement; and annual hunts ceased to be major events. Whereas the 1862 hunt had involved more than 1,500 carts,[127] only about 150 participated in 1866.[128] Consequently, while the prospect of cheap homestead land was drawing new immigration from the east and the south, a westward emigration from former hunting communities like White Horse Plain and Portage la Prairie was equally evident.[129] And gold – in the Cariboo region, on the eastern slopes of the Rocky Mountains, and on the banks of the North Saskatchewan River – was drawing an adventurous migration across the prairies. During early 1862 alone, over 200 gold seekers passed through Red River, pausing just long enough to outfit themselves before heading farther west.[130]

In the main settlement, other changes were under way. The *Nor'-Wester* was under new management, with noticeable effect to its tone and quality. James Ross, who had replaced William Coldwell's original partner but was now out of favour with the settlement leadership, resold his interest to Dr John C. Schultz[131] and moved to Toronto to study law. Schultz, one of the most controversial figures of Manitoba history, came to Red River in 1861 in the footsteps of his half-brother, initial partner and later rival Henry McKenney. Practising as a physician-pharmacist although he never fully qualified as such,[132] Schultz also engaged in a wide range of business activities and, increasingly, in politics. The Coldwell-Schultz *Nor'-Wester* partnership lasted little more than a year. Coldwell sold out to Schultz and returned to Canada in 1865, following an unexplained fire that destroyed the newspaper building, all its contents, and Coldwell's adjoining bookstore.[133] Occurring in the middle of the night, the fire was not discovered in time to be extinguished by the settlement's first fire engine, acquired second-hand in 1862,[134] although Coldwell's nearby home was saved. The loss, Coldwell said, "is of course unmitigated by insurance, for hereabouts no such thing can be had."[135] The newspaper was back in circulation in little more than a month, operating from temporary premises and using an antiquated press and supplies borrowed from the Anglican clergy. A facsimile masthead had been hand-carved in wood by settler John Tait.[136] The experience discouraged Coldwell, however; and Schultz took over the entire operation in July. Although the *Nor'-Wester* continued to be published for quite some time, becoming a mouthpiece for Schultz's pro-Canadian views, its quality never again matched that of its Coldwell years.

Archdeacon William Cockran died at this home in Portage la Prairie on 1 October 1865, just days short of forty years after the rough-hewn cleric began his mission at Red River.[137] With his passing, added to G.O. Corbett's retreat to England and retiring Bishop David Anderson's replacement by Robert Machray,[138] Anglicanism in Assiniboia took on a new, more subdued, appearance. The Red River Academy, in decline for years, had closed its doors in 1859, and an attempt by S. Pritchard to establish another academy in 1863[139] was of short duration. The new

Anglican bishop, however, took immediate steps to create a new college – St John's – which accepted its first students in the fall of 1866.[140] For the Catholic students of Red River, St Boniface College continued to flourish. The settlement's library, which had operated on a subscription basis from the home of Court Clerk–Executive Officer William R. Smith, was judged in early 1862 to need reorganization, and a meeting of subscribers decided to split the library in two, placing one half in the home of James Ross near Upper Fort Garry and the other with Donald Gunn near Lower Fort Garry.[141] An "Institute of Rupert's Land" was formed to promote learning and culture in the settlement.[142]

And Red River was taking on a new appearance. A *Nor'-Wester* article in the summer of 1862, entitled "Times Changing," observed, "While our political system or governmental machinery remains the same ..., our social system is nevertheless greatly changed." Prosperous settlers were building elegant new homes of stone, not of wood, and shingling them with cedar rather than straw or mud. A new Roman Catholic cathedral was rising from the ashes of the old in St Boniface, and west of the Red a new Anglican cathedral was also under construction. Buggies had become popular, and cutters were replacing carioles in winter. Clothing was more fashionable than previously. In November 1864 a "Photographic Gallery" opened, "in which the likenesses are taken in the newest, cheapest and most durable style" on paper suitable for "the albums which are now coming into general use."[143] Bustle was in the air.

Not all change was desirable. Proliferating grog shops – cheap drinking establishments – were deplored as "an unmixed evil and a curse," and many hoped that a new licensing bylaw vesting increased discretion in the licensing magistrates would reduce their number.[144] In November 1862 the *Nor'-Wester* noted the presence in the settlement of "a class of unfortunate females who must be regarded as formal, professional, prostitutes."[145]

Subtle changes were observed, too, in how residents related to each other in business and personal matters: with growing caution and greater reliance on law. In May 1864 the *Nor'-Wester* observed that the General Court would require more than a week to dispose of all the cases on its current docket and commented,

> We are, surely, becoming a very litigious set of people. In the olden time ... [e]very man, apparently, believed his fellow to be honest until he found him out to be a rogue – which was very seldom. But now the reverse would almost appear to be the case. Then, bolts and

> bars were generally dispensed with, houses and lands were sold, and money loaned, ... without even a scrape of the pen between the parties. Now, we ... find ourselves doing pretty much as folks elsewhere do: using bolts and bars, having written contracts for everything, and withal getting [to be] such litigants that we have been "taking the law of each other" for five days this week and ... one or two extra sittings of the Court next week.[146]

As the trail intersection that became Portage and Main took on the appearance of a village hub, private and public rights in the area needed definition. By the early 1860s three settlers – Andrew McDermot, Henry McKenney, and William Drever – owned buildings in the immediate vicinity; and the boundaries of their respective properties and the adjoining public roads were uncertain. Settlement authorities surveyed the roads, concluding that one or more of Drever's buildings intruded onto the Portage Trail. Drever disagreed, and the upshot was a prosecution against him for "encroachment on public road" at the General Court's August 1863 sitting.[147] The evidence of historical usage being contradictory, Drever was acquitted. The Council of Assiniboia then decided to deal with the matter legislatively. It enacted, in July and November 1864,[148] a law decreeing that the Portage road ran across what William Drever considered to be his property; but it gave him eighteen years to remove any buildings that encroached on the public domain. The determination of private boundaries at Portage and Main was left to be resolved by extensive future litigation between Drever and McKenney.[149]

And as the settlement's centre of gravity shifted to Portage and Main, a new name was on people's lips. The masthead of John Schultz's *Nor'-Wester* on 2 October 1865 proclaimed, for the first time, that its place of publication was the "Town of Winnipeg."[150]

9

Confederation and Insurrection, 1866–69

Events moved swiftly during the final four years of Hudson's Bay Company hegemony. Canadian Confederation blossomed, and the fate of Rupert's Land was secretly settled in London. But the people of Red River demanded consultation before change; and, resisting premature Canadian incursions, the Métis formed an indigenous government to negotiate the territory's entry into Confederation and administer it until then.

While all that was happening, life went on in the settlement. Natural calamities occurred, the population grew, US railroads came closer, approaching telegraphs improved contact with the outer world, and Assiniboia's government, like a dying penitent, became yet a little more cooperative. When insurrection finally shut it down, the General Quarterly Court of Assiniboia was the last HBC *component to close.*

BREAKING ICE JAMS

In the spring of 1866, as ice on the Red and Assiniboine Rivers began to crack and shift, the political ice jams blocking British North American Confederation and the HBC's surrender of Rupert's Land also showed signs of breaking up.

After a brilliant beginning at the Charlottetown and Quebec Conferences in 1864, the Confederation project had stalled.[1] Although the Canadian Parliament had strongly endorsed the scheme in 1865, there was not nearly enough popular support for a unified British North America in either Nova Scotia or New Brunswick to allow those colonies to follow Canada's lead. A year later, however, the situation changed dramatically. Fuelled by American refusal to continue tariff reciprocity, the threat of Fenian raids from south of the border,[2] and fear that the victorious

Union army might move northward, pro-Confederation governments were elected in both Nova Scotia and New Brunswick in early 1866. Delegations from those colonies headed immediately to London to finalize Confederation plans before opposition forces gained the upper hand again. They hoped that British authorities could help them win modifications to the Quebec Resolutions, making them more palatable to Maritimers. Although the Canadian delegation delayed its departure for England, John A. Macdonald and his colleagues eventually got there in December, and agreement was reached before the end of the year on a scheme that varied little from what had been hammered out at Quebec. Although not as sweet a bargain as the maritime representatives had sought, it was the best they could get in the circumstances. Britain's legislative draftsman, working closely with Macdonald, put the plan into statutory language in early 1867, and the UK Parliament quickly enacted the British North America Act, fusing the joint Canadas into a federal union with the two largest Atlantic colonies. An order-in-council brought the new constitution into effect on 1 July 1867 – proclaiming it to be "a day of general rejoicing throughout the Royal Dominion."

There was little rejoicing in Rupert's Land. The issue of the *Nor'-Wester* announcing the long-awaited order-in-council commented, "Every mail which brings us news ... of the growing hope and faith of the Canadian people in their great political scheme, adds to our regret ... [L]ittle, if any, notice seems to be taken of us by the Home Government."[3] Sharply conscious of the US threat, the writer added, "If Canada owns the country, let Canada assume it before American influences shall have completed the change which is now ... in the minds of the [American] people." But Canada did not yet own the country. Before it could, there was a second ice jam to be broken: the transfer of Rupert's Land to the newborn Dominion.

The Canadian government, its impatience piqued by news that the United States had recently purchased Alaska from Russia,[4] tried to fast-forward the process in December 1867 with a week-long parliamentary debate on western expansion, culminating in a Senate-Commons joint address calling upon Britain to transfer Rupert's Land to Canada forthwith.[5] But, as the colonial secretary pointed out, the matter was not that simple. An act of the UK Parliament was required; and Parliament could not justly pass such an act without first compensating the HBC for surrendering a very large piece of North America.

The British government had initially proposed that "no present payment in money will be made," offering instead to provide vague future benefits, such as unspecified land reservations and "a share of the future proceeds of lands and precious metals."[6] Anyone familiar with the territory's value and the strength of the HBC's determination knew that proposal was futile, and negotiations reopened on a more realistic basis after its inevitable rejection. Now present were two Canadian representatives: Macdonald's closest cabinet colleague, Georges-Étienne Cartier; and William McDougall, the minister already marked as the surrendered territory's future governor. In early July 1868 the *Nor'-Wester* reported that the parties had "arrived at a basis for settlement said to be satisfactory to both the Company and the Government."[7] What broke the impasse was Canada's reluctant agreement to make an immediate cash payment in return for the surrender: not the £1,000,000 figure Edward Ellice had thrown out almost a decade earlier[8] but the nonetheless substantial sum of £300,000: the modern equivalent of more than $30,000,000.

Even after that agreement was reached, no one at Red River had any inkling of its terms – nor would they for a long time to come. Not even Governor William McTavish, although a company elder and the man chiefly responsible for the settlement's welfare, knew what was happening.[9] "Dame Rumour ... conquered all minds," said Winnipeg merchant and historian-to-be Alexander Begg. "Uncertainty bred fear, and fear bred a distrust of Canada, to which the majority ..., and particularly the Métis, were already too much inclined."[10] In the summer of 1869 some settlers sought to share in the uncertain future by staking claims to HBC reserve property in the no-man's-land between Upper Fort Garry and the "Town of Winnipeg."[11]

THE SETTLEMENT

Meanwhile, the world kept getting closer. US railroads and their companion telegraphs, no longer hampered by wartime priorities, had crossed the Mississippi, and were rapidly approaching the 49th parallel. Then, in August 1866, the *Nor'-Wester* announced, "Important News ... The Atlantic Cable Successfully Laid." The first cable, completed eight years previously, had functioned for only three weeks; but this one and its successors brought North America into permanent instantaneous contact with Europe and much of the rest of the world. While that was still not quite so for Red River, such contact was now only days, rather than weeks, away. *Nor'-Wester* subscribers began reading relatively fresh international news.

The Canadian government lost no time starting construction of a road and telegraph line between Thunder Bay and Red River. Work began in May 1867, and by the end of that summer, the first 6 miles were complete of what would be named the Dawson Trail in honour of the man who first surveyed the route.[12] The following autumn, construction of the western leg of the road commenced under the supervision of surveyor John Snow.[13] When Snow sought permission to begin work at Pointe de Chêne, a Métis community, Governor McTavish objected that Rupert's Land did not yet belong to Canada, but eventually relented, knowing the settlement needed the employment.[14] The project proceeded rapidly during the years under review, and by July 1869 nearly 400 men were working on it.[15] Many of those workers were Canadians, whose presence would alter Red River's demographic and political balance. Transportation works were under way within the settlement too. The Council of Assiniboia increased its works committees from four to ten in April 1867.[16] In 1869 it authorized an Assiniboine River ferry at Headingley and a pontoon bridge across the same river near the Forks.[17] The first plank sidewalks were tendered for Winnipeg's Main Street in September 1869.[18]

With increased traffic on settlement roads, accidents and injuries rose. On 24 February 1866 the *Nor'-Wester* carried a letter from "Aurica" deploring the "horrible practice of driving on either side, and even in the middle of the road," and proposing adoption of English rules of the road.[19] But no one had heeded Judge Black's identical recommendation in a legal action by a woman injured by a cariole two years previously,[20] and although the *Nor'-Wester* now urged making the rule law, nothing was done.

The Assiniboia government rarely heeded the *Nor'-Wester*'s advice, of course, and by now John Schultz's ownership of the newspaper had brought its influence with officialdom to a new low. Although Schultz turned over management of the paper to his friend and political ally Walter Bown, a dentist, in early 1868 and sold it to Bown later that year, its editorial policy continued to reflect Schultz's views. The council still denied *Nor'-Wester* reporters (and all other members of the public) access to its meetings; and by 1869 the paper had even ceased publishing official government announcements. Expansion of Red River's journalistic resources seemed imminent for a while. The *Nor'-Wester* announced, in September 1869, the looming advent of a competitor, which it professed to welcome.[21] William Coldwell, who had launched the *Nor'-Wester* with William Buckingham in 1859, was back, touting a new paper called the *Pioneer*. James Ross, who worked as a journalist in Ontario while studying for the bar, had also returned, and was to be Coldwell's partner. "Opposition is the life of business," the *Nor'-Wester* bravely affirmed, "and ... [b]oth papers will doubtless be adequately patronized." Red River was indeed now large enough to support two newspapers; but events were in train that would soon reduce, not expand, the settlement's access to news. In face of an armed Métis uprising,[22] the pro-Canadian, anti-French, *Nor'-Wester* published its last issue on 17 November 1869, and Coldwell and Ross never did launch their paper. Regular newspaper publication resumed in January 1870; but press freedom was seriously diminished for most of that year. Reading such newspapers as were available was made a little easier by the arrival of the Red River's first coal oil lamps in 1869.[23]

The environmental brutality of the past several years persisted.[24] Severe heat and drought killed crops, spawned prairie fires, decimated buffalo and fish populations, played havoc with river transportation,[25] and seriously depleted the normally plentiful berries and wildlife upon which the community customarily fell back in hard times. Late summer continued to breed grasshopper hordes. Then, in the early morning hours of 3 July 1868, the settlement experienced a devastating storm that the *Nor'-Wester* called both a "hurricane" and a "tornado." It lashed "our largest trees ... to and fro like reeds,"[26] destroyed crops, killed livestock, tore roofs from buildings, and lifted buildings from foundations. Among the buildings destroyed was a partially constructed Anglican church in which carpenters had been sleeping, one of whom "was crushed by falling timbers, and only survived for a couple of hours." The newspaper called the storm "the most serious ever witnessed in this country." That blow, followed by a grasshopper infestation, left the settlement staggering. At the end of September, Governor McTavish reported to London that "dread of scarcity" was causing "great numbers" to abandon the settlement to winter on the plains and the shores of Lake Winnipeg.[27] But the buffalo hunt failed again; and those who went fishing returned with nearly empty carts.[28]

The community rallied to assist those in the most desperate straits. The Council of Assiniboia provided £1,600 for relief supplies, the company added £2,000 more, and appeals for aid brought even greater financial assistance from Britain, the United States, and Canada. A Red River Co-operative Relief Committee,[29] chaired by Governor McTavish, distributed this assistance and made seed grain available in the spring to farmers whose crops had failed. Although the committee's work was later criticized for various reasons, its efforts prevented a dire situation becoming a disaster. In J.M. Bumsted's words, "[T]he relief activities had demonstrated that – in a crisis – the divided religious and racial communities of the Settlement could be brought together to pull for the common good."[30] Charity was not the sole source of famine relief. Work on the road from Lake Superior provided employment for some settlers, and in February 1869 ice fishing was successfully attempted, apparently for the first time. The memoirs of St Boniface resident Louis Schmidt recorded that "soon there was not a place left to run the nets; everyone was at it. It is near the mouth of the Assiniboine, a little up the Red, that the fishing was done. It was wonderful to see the quantity of the fish that was taken. It was a veritable providence."[31]

By the end of 1869 Red River was home to almost 12,000 settled inhabitants, composed of 5,757 French Halfbreeds, 4,086 English Halfbreeds, 1,565 whites, and 558 Indians. That population was distributed among twenty-six named communities,[32] the largest of which was St François Xavier on the White Horse Plain (1,843) and the smallest St Paul (5). Although Winnipeg could boast a mere 215 inhabitants,[33] in contrast to 819 across the river at St Boniface, it had become the heart of the settlement.

What was Winnipeg like at that point? We have an eyewitness account. Alexander Begg, a merchant whose meticulous journal of the events swirling around his premises on Main Street between mid-November 1869 and July 1870 has been an invaluable resource for historians of the period, left a sketch map of "the Town of Winnipeg" that depicted its forty-nine buildings in relation to the Upper Fort, the Red River, the intersection of the Portage Trail and Main Street (called King Street on the map), and three other short, as yet unnamed, streets between "King" and the Red that were beginning to give the village a shape.[34]

On the northwest corner of the main intersection, a stone's throw or two from Winnipeg's Anglican and Presbyterian churches, was the saloon of Hugh O'Lone, an American storekeeper driven from Portage la Prairie in 1866 by the unprosecuted depredations of a notorious Saulteau called Wolverine and some of his followers.[35] Another saloon and three hotels stood not far away. One of the hotels, operated by George Emmerling ("the Dutchman"), was famous for its two billiard tables. Directly across Portage and King from O'Lone's saloon was the studio of Ryder Larsen, a resident photographer soon to be indicted for murder.[36] Next door to Larsen on Main Street was the home and shop of Sheriff Henry McKenney. A block south of Portage, and slightly east of

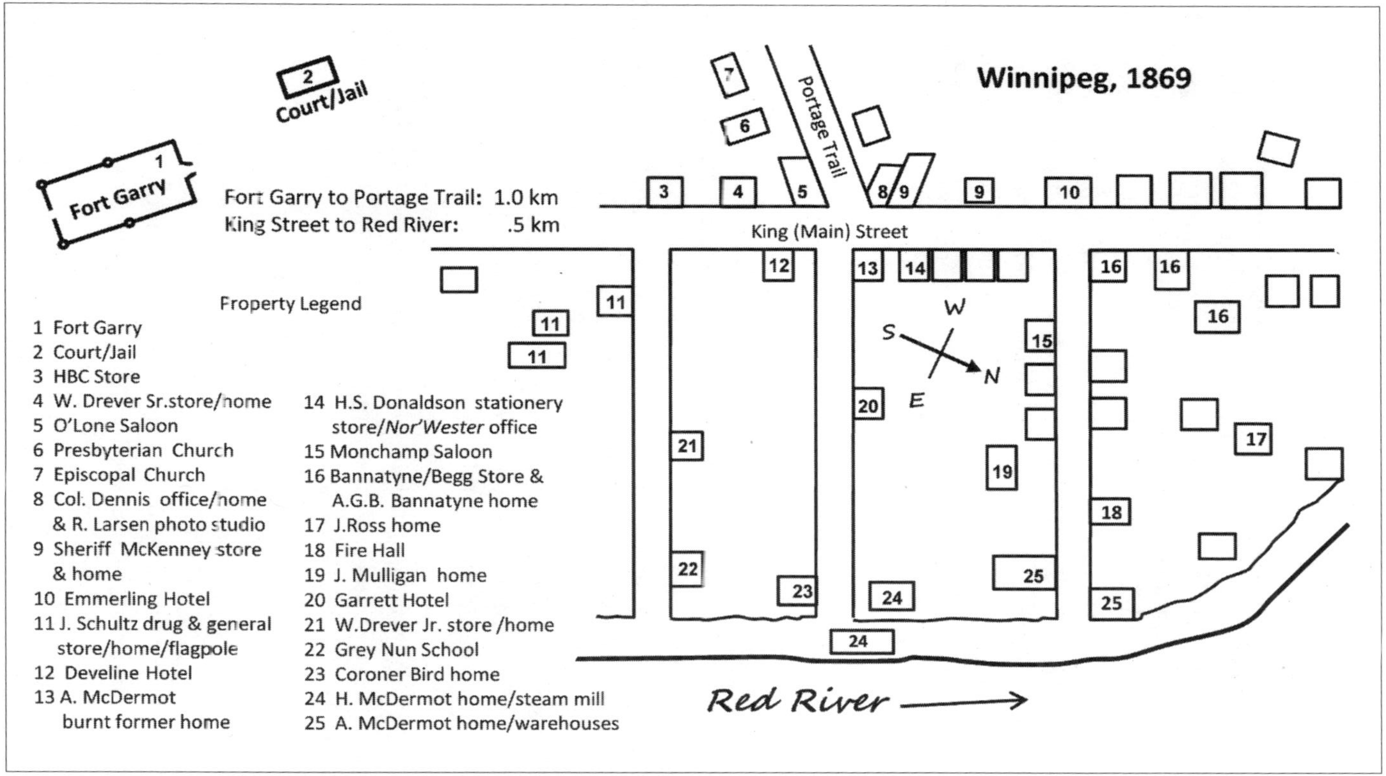

Winnipeg, 1869
Fort Garry
Court/Jail
Portage Trail
King (Main) Street
Fort Garry to Portage Trail: 1.0 km
King Street to Red River: .5 km
Red River
S
W
E
N
Froperty Legend
1 Fort Garry
2 Court/Jail
3 HBC Store
4 W. Drever Sr.store/home
5 O'Lone Saloon
6 Presbyterian Church
7 Episcopal Church
8 Col. Dennis office/home & R. Larsen photo studio
9 Sheriff McKenney store & home
10 Emmerling Hotel
11 J. Schultz drug & general store/home/flagpole
12 Develine Hotel
13 A. McDermot burnt former home
14 H.S. Donaldson stationery store/Nor'Wester office
15 Monchamp Saloon
16 Bannatyne/Begg Store & A.G.B. Bannatyne home
17 J.Ross home
18 Fire Hall
19 J. Mulligan home
20 Garrett Hotel
21 W.Drever Jr. store /home
22 Grey Nun School
23 Coroner Bird home
24 H. McDermot home/steam mill
25 A. McDermot home/warehouses

Figure 9.1

Main Street, was the compound of Dr John Schultz: three buildings, two of them brick – Winnipeg's first – and Schultz's famous soaring flagpole and "Canada" banner. No longer sure that residents of the village and the parishes north of it would continue shopping at the Upper Fort, the company now operated a retail store just across Main Street from Schultz's premises. North of the Schultz property and east of Main Street, scattered among various business establishments, a school, a steam mill, and a fire hall, were the homes of several men prominent in the court records: Andrew Bannatyne, Dr C.J. Bird, James Ross, Charles Garrett, James Mulligan, Alexander Logan, John Sutherland, and the venerable Andrew McDermot. McDermot had moved to a new home at the river end of the street now named for him; but the "burnt ruins" of his former home, which artist William Napier had painted before it burned, still stood, nearer Fort Garry – a reminder of the era that was ending.[37]

GOVERNING A RESTIVE COLONY

Consequences of the secrecy shrouding Canada's annexation of Rupert's Land would manifest themselves soon enough. In the meantime, the settlement was governed more or less as always. Particular faces around the governor's council table changed, but the general character of his council remained constant throughout this anxious period. Bishop David Anderson was replaced by Bishop Robert Machray; François Bruneau's death brought Roger Goulet, a younger, but almost as prominent and certainly as conservative, Métis. With few exceptions, these men were conscientious public officers, as anxious as anyone to see Red River's future settled satisfactorily, and as unhappy as everyone else to be kept in ignorance. They were cautious men, however, who respected authority and feared radical solutions. Although the fundamental interests of Assiniboia's leaders and its other settlers were similar, the rift that always divides the empowered from those who are not was hard to bridge.

Democratic impulses long evident beyond the council chamber were intensified by residents' exclusion from the process by which their futures were being determined in Ottawa and London. The first important manifestation of this swelling desire was engineered by the ever-more-prominent Dr John Schultz. Chief Factor James Clare, a member of the Council of Assiniboia, died suddenly in early 1867, and the council's March meeting received a letter from Thomas Spence, a Schultz acolyte,[38] enclosing petitions from all over the settlement requesting the doctor's appointment to the vacant position.[39] In the "ability and integrity" of Dr Schultz, the petitioners declared, they had "entire confidence," deeming him "a fit and proper person to represent our interests at the Council." Although the petitions and Spence's covering letter were politely couched, they did not disguise the petitioners' dissatisfaction with the incumbent government's unrepresentativeness. The method of selecting councillors was "partial" and "not subservient to the interests of the public," they complained; and granting their present request would "shew us that though it may not be in your power to secure to us direct representation, you desire to meet our views in so far as they are in accordance with your powers." The strength of the petition lay in both the number of its signatories – 605 – and the fact that the English and French communities were equally represented. A counter-petition, opposing Schultz's appointment, had also been circulated, but McTavish acknowledged that it attracted "but few signatories."[40]

When passing on both the pro- and anti-Schultz petitions to the company's head office, the governor's advice was initially equivocal: "My own opinion is that there are several here who have much better claims to the appointment, and whom I most certainly would recommend much before Dr. Schultz. Still, I am doubtful if the evils arising from his exclusion would not exceed those ... caused by his admission." His concern was rooted in the rapid growth of what was now being called the "Schultz Party." Spouting democratic rhetoric, the group opposed company government, advocated Canadian annexation, sneered at French and Aboriginal rights, and encouraged expansion of the anglophone population. Its members vociferously embraced the leadership of the tall, powerful, courageous, dynamic, ruthless physician-pharmacist-merchant-moneylender-journalist-politician whose premises and great "Canada" flag at the heart of Winnipeg had become the focal point of Canadian chauvinism and anglophone dissent.[41] Failing to appoint Schultz might lead to civil disobedience, McTavish feared.[42] Before long, however, he decided the cons of appointing Dr Schultz to the council outweighed the pros. Following publication of a *Nor'-Wester* article, probably by Schultz, "recommending that people refuse obedience to the laws," the governor concluded that "he cannot be admitted as a member of Council."[43] He did not anticipate serious consequences from ignoring the petition, suspecting that, despite its rhetoric, the doctor's party did not really want full-blown democracy until the Canadian population outnumbered the francophones.[44] Schultz was not appointed.

McTavish's letter went on to observe that "[t]here is, however, a pretty general feeling here that some change should be made in the government ... [M]ost of the councillors and justices of the peace ... are rather old; and ... [not] very well suited to deal with ... [recent newcomers to] the Settlement, although they did very well ... while they had none but Red River people to deal with."[45] Enclosed with the letter were ten recommendations of somewhat younger "Red River people" for council and justice of the peace appointments: Andrew Bannatyne, Dr Curtis J. Bird, Magnus Birston, John Bunn, Thomas Bunn, William Dease, William Fraser, William Inkster, James McKay, and John Sutherland.[46] "It is a large addition," the governor admitted, "but ... some additions ... are absolutely required. All the individuals mentioned in the list are sensible men, who have very considerable influence among their neighbours."[47] Those characteristics were undeniable, but at least one other stood out sharply too: although four of the ten were Halfbreeds, not one was French. The Schultz Party had been influential, both in that respect and in ensuring that all the nominees were "well suited to deal with" Canadian immigrants. The governor had not lost sight of francophone dissatisfaction; but the newcomers' wheels were squeaking louder than Métis carts at the moment. London quickly made all the recommended appointments.[48]

As it happened, the appointments – particularly as justices of the peace – were not all welcomed by the conferees. "I fear," wrote McTavish, "there will be some difficulty in getting the justices of the peace to accept their commissions, ... as they are unwilling to incur the trouble."[49] The problem was that the position of justice of the peace – an ancient and prestigious office – was both time-consuming and unpaid. In England it was generally accepted that the honour of official recognition was sufficient compensation for the sometimes onerous duties of the office.[50] At Red River, where JPs served as presidents of the petty courts, members of the General Court, issuers of warrants, and bearers of various other responsibilities, they were much less well-off financially than were their English counterparts; and there was little enthusiasm for demanding but unpaid obligations. A case in point was Andrew Bannatyne, one of the most prominent of those offered JP commissions, and a very practical man. Bannatyne was already serving as an ordinary petty court magistrate – a paid position – when informed he had been selected for promotion to justice of the peace. "Mr. Bannatyne ... plainly told me," McTavish grumbled, "that he would not act, as he now saw it would give him a great deal of trouble, and that since the Company had the government of the country, its officers should have the trouble and responsibility; but that as magistrate in the District Court he was willing to continue to act – that is, he would hold a paid office." Not everyone shared Bannatyne's attitude, however. Others were willing to accept the responsibilities he declined, and the Assiniboia government continued to function – undemocratically but responsively to popular concerns it couldn't ignore, and as effectively as straitened budgets permitted – until events beyond its control swept its authority away.

PORTAGE LA PRAIRIE

Impatience for improved governance was especially strong at Portage la Prairie, most or all of which lay just a little beyond the Forks-centred 50 mile radius of the Municipal District of Assiniboia, and was therefore denied access to even such sparse governmental services as were available elsewhere. After the failure of John Garrioch's efforts, four years previously,[51] to have Assiniboia annex the growing Portage community,[52] the only concession made to meet the area's needs was an 1866 trial-basis extension of postal services.[53] That situation was finally remedied in 1868; but it took three brutal deaths to bring about the change.

A violent affray in the spring of that year – killing two men and wounding a third – finally set the ponderous wheels of change in motion. On the afternoon of 28 May, nine Saulteaux men, led by a notorious individual known as "the Wolverine," entered a store operated by American newcomer Hugh O'Lone and two employees. The Indians demanded liquor and, when refused, attempted to steal some buffalo robes. Although beaten off by O'Lone and his employees, the intruders later returned with firearms. One employee was shot and later died; the other was stabbed with a knife. O'Lone returned the fire, killing one of the marauders and driving the others off, but not before they carried away much of his property.[54] Some months later, Schultz Party activist Thomas Spence induced O'Lone to report the attack to Governor McTavish at Red River and demand that something be done.

The governor was sympathetic but regretted that "as we are situated, it is particularly difficult to act,"[55] and merely referred the problem to London, where it was passed on to barrister Montague Bere for an opinion. Bere thought McTavish should have the culprits arrested and sent to Lower Canada for trial under the authority of the 1803 Canada Jurisdiction Act.[56] This highly impractical advice (involving, among other things, the conveyance of Mr O'Lone, an American citizen, to Montreal as a material witness) was not followed. Nor was anything else ever done about the crime. A year later, the *Nor'-Wester* raged that the Wolverine was still at Portage "threatening to rob and kill all and sundry who dare to dispute his sovereignty,"[57] and on 8 September 1868, well over two years after the event, the newspaper thundered that "absolutely nothing" had been done about the murder "and [that] one of the greatest rascals unhung is allowed to prowl around in the same section of the country, unwhipped by justice."[58]

The anger and frustration reflected in that outburst had already driven the residents of Portage la Prairie to attempt once more to govern themselves. Thomas Spence,[59] the man who accompanied Hugh O'Lone to Winnipeg to report the Wolverine's bloody attack, and who fronted the Schultz bid for appointment to the Council of Assiniboia, was a catalyst for anti-establishment dissatisfaction from the moment he settled at the Portage in early 1867. In February 1868 he and his neighbours declared independence, informing the British Colonial Office that the area's settlers, "who number over four hundred,"[60] had resolved unanimously to create a "self-supporting petty government in this isolated portion of Her Majesty's Dominions," with him as its president. He requested "favourable recognition" by Her Majesty's Government.[61] The territory over which Spence and his neighbours claimed authority stretched from Lake Manitoba to the US boundary and from "the boundary line of the jurisdiction of the Council of Assiniboia"[62] to the 100th parallel of latitude. Within that area, called New Caledonia at first, and then Manitoba or Manitobah, the settlers had elected a government that, Spence told London, had already imposed taxation, commenced construction of public buildings, made provision for the construction of roads and other public works, prepared to enter into Indian treaties, and begun to "carry out the laws."

Although the letter probably exaggerated what had been accomplished in the new government's first month, it had certainly imposed a duty on goods imported from Winnipeg and elsewhere – to the great annoyance of the HBC and at least some local settlers. One of the latter, a shoemaker name Macpherson, opposed the new levy so vigorously that Spence and his colleagues decided he must be tried for treason. In his secondary capacity as chief justice of the new republic, President Spence issued a warrant for Macpherson's arrest, and dispatched two freshly minted constables to apprehend him. Although that mission proved more difficult than anticipated, Macpherson was eventually "dragged before the tribunal[63] in a state of great excitement, his dishevelled hair, contorted visage and ragged clothes bearing strong testimony to the resistance he had offered to the minions of power." J.J. Hargrave's description continued: "The court ... had not proceeded far with its investigation when the house was surrounded by an excited mob of the prisoner's friends, who ... came to liberate him. The door flew open ... and a couple of men armed with pistols entered the chamber ... [and] turned to his judges, whom they attacked with such vigour and effect that, after a useless attempt at resistance, Governor and Council were ignominiously turned out of doors ... leaving their late prisoner and his friends in possession of the scene of action."[64]

This fiasco, added to the HBC's refusal to pay the demanded import duty, ensured that the proposed government headquarters could not be built. And when, in early summer, a letter arrived from Downing Street informing Spence that he and his colleagues had been "acting illegally in this matter" and "incurring grave responsibilities,"[65] the erstwhile president of Manitobah abdicated, and went off to the shores of Lake Manitoba to mine salt.[66]

But by the time Assiniboia authorities got around to extending the General Court's jurisdiction to Portage la Prairie, another killing had already occurred there. In June 1868 a man named Demarrais, while very drunk, harassed an older man, John McLean, as he was planting potatoes. Incensed by something McLean said in response, Demarrais ran to a friend's nearby home, obtained a rifle, fired the weapon in the direction of the McLean home, and then ran away. Three shots were then fired in the direction of the fleeing man, one of which wounded him severely. Demarrais died, probably from that wound, about a month later, and John McLean's son Alex was accused of firing the fatal shot.

By then, the company Governor and Committee in London, having pondered the question at great length, had agreed to "including the Settlement of Portage la Prairie within the [Municipal] District of Assiniboia"[67] and had instructed McTavish to arrange that "as you may consider most advisable under all the circumstances."[68] So when the Council of Assiniboia received a request in August 1868 from residents of Portage to "take cognizance" of the Demarrais shooting, it agreed to do so.[69] The recorder and governor travelled there, conducted a preliminary investigation, and decided that a trial was called for. Alex McLean was charged with manslaughter, and the case was placed on the docket of the General Quarterly Court.[70] The trial proved to be highly noteworthy – not just because it heralded closer ties between

Winnipeg and Portage la Prairie, but also because it featured a remarkable performance by the most extraordinary lawyer ever to appear in Assiniboia courts. It was a performance that strikingly illuminated the contrasts between the settlement's relaxed courtroom practices and those prevailing in more "advanced" adversarial arenas of the United States and Canada, and it severely rattled the normally unflappable Judge John Black.

LAW ENFORCEMENT

Although the 1866–69 period was marked by much unrest and disorder, it opened in relative tranquility. In February 1866 McTavish reported to London, "We are all quiet here. I think it is the quietest season I have seen at Red River – though there is a little agitation about representative government."[71] "Of course," he continued, this would last only "till some exciting question turns up, when some designing demagogue may aspire to the glory of martyrdom." The "designing demagogue" McTavish had in mind at that point was probably Dr John Schultz, but the Schultz threat never quite reached the level of seriousness prophesied at that point. An uprising that would do so, however, was only three and a half years in the future.

Those intervening years were not altogether free from violence and threats of violence. The Wolverine and McLean killings at Portage la Prairie have already been mentioned, and several other brutal incidents also occurred – both in Assiniboia and in greater Rupert's Land. The varied official responses to those events underline the paucity of law enforcement resources available.

Red River remained nervous about the uprooted Sioux, many of whom still roamed the Rupert's Land plains in destitute straits. When American military authorities requested, in March 1866, that the Assiniboia government do what it could to persuade these people to return to the United States and accept an offer of amnesty, the council heartily acted on the proposal, resolving to supply those who accepted the offer with provisions, an escort to Fort Ambercrombie, and someone to negotiate on their behalf.[72] Whether or not that initiative accomplished much, it did not prevent, about three months later, a visit by "a band of Sioux Indians, in disregard of the advices ... to keep away from the Settlement entirely, ... visiting [Upper] Fort Garry."[73] That event, involving about thirty Sioux, was altogether peaceable, and the guests soon began "quietly making their departure." They had proceeded only about a mile from the Fort, however, and were still in sight, when they were set upon by a war party of Saulteaux from the United States, and four of their number were killed. Although a hastily organized group of settlers raced to the scene and prevented further killing, they could not prevent the bodies of the dead being "horribly mutilated" by local Saulteaux bystanders.[74] The American assailants fled southward and were never apprehended.

That grisly incident spurred an emergency meeting of the Assiniboia council to plan protective measures against a possible retaliatory attack on the settlement by a much larger body of Sioux known to be massed nearby. "After mature deliberation" of the matter, the minutes record, "the Council unanimously resolved that ... the acting Governor [John Black] be empowered to collect from among the settlers a body of from fifty to one hundred mounted armed men to meet the Sioux on their way to the Settlement, and ... to take such measures for the preservation of the public peace and safety as might be deemed necessary."[75] Happily, it never became necessary to put those measures in force.

The Saulteaux attack on the Sioux would nevertheless have a further tragic consequence. As Governor McTavish later informed London, the mutilation of the victims' bodies by local Saulteaux generated "a very strong feeling against the Indians of the Settlement, and ... may lead to future acts of violence. Indeed, to this I attribute the death of an Indian whose abdomen was cut open by a Halfbreed within the walls of this Fort ... The Indian died of the wound, and the Halfbreed is now in gaol awaiting his trial for murder at the August Quarterly Court."[76] The resulting trial,[77] conviction, death sentence, commutation, and banishment would be the talk of the settlement for some time to come.

Although far from constant, the frequency and viciousness of intra-Indian violence in or near white settlements or trading posts was disturbing. In May 1867, for instance, a young HBC apprentice wrote to his family from the Touchwood Hills (in modern Saskatchewan) telling of a "great fight" that had taken place nearby between Cree and Blackfoot (Sioux) Indians, in which forty-six of the latter, of both genders and all ages, had been killed. The writer told in chilling detail of the cruelties inflicted on the victims' surviving families on that occasion, and then described a gruesome ceremony taking place just outside his door as he sat writing that evening: "The Indians are now dancing the scalp dance before the door, and making the most diabolical din imaginable. They have five scalps on poles, which they are flaunting about in great triumph."[78] The purpose of the macabre dance, he said, was to induce the traders to give the dancers tobacco as a form of bounty for having killed the Sioux with ammunition obtained from the HBC.

In February 1869 Governor McTavish informed London of an "outrage [that] took place at the White Horse Plain, close to the settlers' houses."[79] Two Saulteaux men from Minnesota, "who have been hanging about the Settlement all the autumn, lately murdered three Sioux women and two children" in their sleep "with their axes and knives." Another source added that the killers made no secret of their crime: "The two ... carried away the scalps ... and displayed the trophies to the settlers on their route, glorying in the infamy they had perpetrated."[80] The *Nor'-Wester* objected to the impunity accorded to the perpetrators of these crimes by law enforcement authorities. Under the headline "Indian Warfare Too Close," it complained that the killers "were allowed to take their leave without let or hinderance" and objected that while such conduct "may be all very well according to the ethics of savage warfare," it should not be permitted "in our very midst."[81] The writer acknowledged that the police had "no power to try a murderer"; but this was a mistaken view of both the law and the basis for the hands-off policy toward internecine Indian crime. The real reasons were the enormous cost of policing the boundless prairies and the risk of provoking collective retaliation against the white population. The HBC had long been attempting to shrink its governmental mantle, but was getting little help from British authorities. After the 1867 massacre of Sioux visitors by American Saulteaux, the company referred the matter to the UK government, but received only a formal acknowledgment in response; and its own sole assistance to the Assiniboia council was to approve a special local protective force *if* "discipline and control ... would be easily maintained," and the "necessary expense" were locally borne.[82]

Criminal violence by or against whites or Halfbreeds was, by contrast, considered to require at least some official involvement, no matter where in Rupert's Land it occurred. Two 1867 homicides from the Fort Edmonton area show, however, that there was no uniform response pattern. The first concerned two employees of a fur-trading party headed by Red River free trader and councillor William Inkster. The men in question, George Daniel and George Robertson, got into a fight during a year-end drinking binge. The first report received by Governor McTavish said Robertson "cleft the head of Daniel in twain with a large cast steel axe."[83] The governor ordered Edmonton chief factor W.J. Christie, who possessed magisterial powers, to investigate. When he had Christie's report, McTavish advised London that he was worried about conducting a trial at Red River because "both the men have many relations in the Settlement ... [and] in the event of the sentence of death being passed upon Robertson it could only be carried out either by the permission of the people generally or by using one portion of the Settlement to control the other."[84] He requested guidance, and was instructed that if the evidence indicated the likelihood of guilt Robertson should be sent to Canada for trial.[85] As it turned out, however, the governor did not find that necessary. When Inkster's party returned to Red River in the spring, McTavish interviewed witnesses to the killing, and decided that since Daniel had been pursuing Robertson with a gun when the latter struck him, "Roberston had a right to plead self-defence in justification of the deed." After determining that Inkster had no desire to proceed with the prosecution, Governor McTavish told London, "I took no further steps in the matter."[86]

The other Edmonton-area killing was handled very differently. On 12 January 1867, not much more than a week after having to deal with the Daniel axe death, Chief Factor Christie was urgently requested to advise the residents of St Albert, a few miles northwest of Fort Edmonton, how to deal with a fatal shooting there the previous day. The letter alleged that one Alexander Caracontier, dit Wakeras, shot his uncle Ignace Caracontier in the head "in cold blood." The victim was thought to have died instantly. Neither man had "tasted liquor, nor had they any quarrel of which we are aware."[87] Christie was asked to come to St Albert as quickly as possible to assist with the matter, he being the only nearby magistrate.

"We know," the letter added, "that whatever you may do in the present instance will be fully approved by those from whom you receive your authority, and will ... be a precedent to which we can refer on similar occasions so long as there is no regular court of justice established amongst us." The residents' intention was to call a meeting and "there to decide what must be done to the culprit." As the last word suggested, the writers had no doubt about the gunman's guilt at that point; and they stressed that "[t]here is no time to be lost. The guilty man must be taken at once, or he will evade all punishment." By the time Christie met with, and took depositions from, the people of St Albert the following morning, some of the urgency had dissipated, the accused man having absconded, but the situation remained serious. The settlers wanted to know whether Caracontier would, if captured, be sent to Red River and be tried and punished there. "If no steps are taken in the case," Christie reported, "they will likely take the law into their own hands and shoot, or otherwise make away with, the murderer, which *may* lead to the loss of other lives."[88]

Over the ensuing spring and summer, McTavish kept London informed of developments, which shifted from St Albert to the more distant community of Lac Ste Anne, from where Alexander Caracontier hailed. The man's own neighbours had "decided in [an informal local] council that ... [he] should be taken and tried for his life by leading men among the inhabitants of that settlement, and to carry out this plan they sent one of their number to apprehend the delinquent."[89] As more of the circumstances behind the shooting began to emerge, however, McTavish noted, "the great bulk of the Lac Ste. Anne's Halfbreeds are not so decided as they were about the necessity of taking vengeance on the murderer."[90] Ultimately, Caracontier's fate was determined by the man sent to arrest him: "[H]e was of opinion that the delinquent was justified in what he did, and declined to bring him to Lac Ste. Anne. He said that the man who was killed had, during the absence of her husband, criminal connection[91] with the wife of the accused, and that, moreover, two of his brothers-in-law were guilty in the same way."[92] Conjugal vengeance was no more a legally valid defence to a charge of premeditated murder then than it is today; but it is likely that if Caracontier had been arrested and tried by his Lac Ste Anne neighbours, or by a Red River jury for that matter, the verdict would have been the same as that of the vigilante constable who refused to apprehend him.

One final instance will round out this overview of law and order on the plains in the sunset years of company control. On the morning of 22 October 1867, Charles Favell, travelling with his wife and two Indian women through the Touchwood Hills, north of the Qu'Appelle Valley in what is now central Saskatchewan, came upon the body of Joseph Cadotte. The deceased had been shot in the chest at close range, and the surrounding terrain showed signs that a fight had taken place.[93] After reporting his discovery to the officer in charge of the HBC's Touchwood Hills post and starting back to the scene of the shooting with another company employee, Favell encountered one Alexis Pecheetoo, who said he had seen Cadotte and a companion a few days previously, encamped at the spot where the body was found. Pecheetoo supplied them liquor, he said, and when he left they were drinking and arguing about whether to terminate their hunting-trapping expedition. Cadotte wanted to quit, but his partner, François Matoney, did not. Matoney, whose gun holster was lying under Cadotte's body, was nowhere to be found; but news later reached the Touchwood Hills post that he had been observed heading for the Saskatchewan River, suffering from serious cuts and bruises. He claimed to have been "knocked senseless" by an unnamed assailant, and to have "only [been] prevented from being killed by pretending to be dead, or rather lying without motion."

Much of the foregoing information was hearsay, and only Favell's evidence was in a sworn deposition. When the Touchwood Hills post master was criticized for not investigating the killing personally, and for failing to take depositions from Pecheetoo and others, he said he had been busy at the time, and pointed out that he had subsequently arranged for Cadotte to be "decently interred" and for his widow and children to be transported free of charge to the widow's mother's home. "Further," he explained, "I did not at all consider myself bound to investigate matters more fully" because Cadotte was not an HBC employee, and "with the quarrels and murder of freemen ten miles from my establishment I have nothing to do."[94] The company's London authorities first proposed sending Matoney to Ontario for trial if apprehended, but later closed their file with the comment that "Matoney may have shot Cadotte in self defence ... [and that his] having quitted the neighbourhood bruised and wounded strengthens the correctness of that assumption."[95]

Although Red River's local policing arrangements were more effective than those prevailing on the prairies, a similar casualness and cost-consciousness was often evident. In February 1866, for example, Sheriff McKenney unexpectedly left the settlement on private business, forcing Governor McTavish to postpone a scheduled trip to England in order to fill in for him.[96] And when, early the following year, it was proposed by the governor to establish a small, permanent special volunteer police unit to deal with cattle theft and intra-Indian confrontations near white settlements, the Council of Assiniboia decided the scheme would "involve ... an expense which, with its present revenue, it could not afford." Instead, the council resolved only to make "a small addition" to the existing force, and to try to improve the efficiency of the existing constabulary.[97]

When residents of Winnipeg petitioned for two constables to patrol exclusively in their growing, and turbulent, neighbourhood, the council decided, after a year's delay, to grant them just one, although that new policeman turned out to be a significant addition. He was real estate speculator and former Chelsea Pensioner James Mulligan, a pungent personality already familiar to the courts as a litigant, who would serve conspicuously and well until the end of the company era.[98] By and large, the settlement police performed tolerably well despite limited numbers, even after Portage la Prairie joined the municipal fold. In outlying areas, though, their services were only provided on an as-needed basis. An urgent request from Portage residents in late 1868 that something be done about cattle thefts brought the rapid dispatch of a magistrate and twelve constables; but when local settlers declined to assist in the investigation, the councillors "expressed their surprise at the inaction and indifference of the petitioners" and cancelled the expedition.[99]

As the community grew, so did the responsibilities of the sheriff. In January 1869 Sheriff McKenney, who was paid £50 annually, resigned his position because of "the insufficiency of the remuneration." Governor McTavish was no friend of Henry McKenney personally; but at the meeting he quickly called to deal with the crisis, he sang the sheriff's praises, and persuaded the council to reappoint him at double his previous salary.[100] The *Nor'-Wester* professed to be outraged by this extravagance "[a]t this time of distress and famine among so many of our poor." Calling the position "almost a sinecure" and grossly minimizing the duties involved, the newspaper asserted that "a good efficient police constable is worth more ... than half a dozen of nothing-to-do sheriffs."[101] This unfair comment was almost certainly written by, or at the behest of, McKenney's half-brother and former partner, but now bitter enemy, John Schultz. Even after selling out to Walter Bown, the doctor exerted great influence over the newspaper's policies.

No one seems to have objected when the salary of elderly jailer Antoine Grouette was raised.[102] An increasing population and growing community unrest placed greater pressure on the jailer, and the incidence of jailbreaks was rising.

The most notorious of the jailbreaks occurred on 18 January 1868, when Dr Schultz's lively new bride, Agnes, and fifteen or twenty other Schultz supporters overpowered Grouette and a handful of special constables, freeing Agnes's husband from imprisonment for debt.[103] Schultz was never rearrested, because McTavish feared the consequences of trying to do so. After assembling 300 special constables, paid 10 shillings apiece, he thought better of confrontation with Schultz's liberators, and dismissed the special force.[104] He may have doubted their loyalty. "No government here, however popular," he explained to London, "would be effective in every emergency unless supported by troops."[105] This assessment probably overstated the case deliberately in order to induce the company and government to expedite the termination of HBC responsibility for Rupert's Land. In fact, public opinion firmly supported

McTavish and the council in this matter. In April, for example, a petition denouncing the Schultz jailbreak attracted 804 signatures; and when *Nor'-Wester* owner Bown refused to publish the petition a group of citizens led by Andrew Bannatyne threatened to imprison his printing press in the jail. Yet the governor's reports remained skeptical of public reactions: "[A]mong the population generally, any expression of opinion ... is perfectly worthless, as the great bulk of them will sign anything one day and the reverse the next."[106]

The next jailbreak occurred about five months later, when an American Saulteau known as Ogibbeway, sentenced to a year in prison for theft at the May 1868 assize,[107] was forcibly broken out by several compatriots. Although he and most of his liberators fled to freedom south of the border, one of the latter was captured and, according to the *Nor'-Wester*, "banished for 12 months from the Settlement." No official record of the banishment has been found. An apparent third jailbreak during this period involved James Stewart, a prominent and feisty resident of St James parish who had led the violent breakout of would-be abortionist G.O. Corbett in 1863, and experienced both incarceration and illegal release himself in consequence of that escapade. In its issues of 24 April and 15 May 1869, the *Nor'-Wester* recorded Stewart's recent conviction by the Middle District Petty Court. In the latter issue, Stewart – another outspoken disciple of Dr John Schultz – acknowledged ignoring a summons from the court. He could not comply with that order, he said, because it was issued by an HBC employee, not by "the public." He also claimed to have been unaware of the existence of the local law under which he was charged.[108] Having been "illegally taken and placed in the Hudson's Bay Company gaol," Stewart asserted, he was "liberated on the third day." The liberation was presumably illegal.

In the immediate aftermath of the Schultz jailbreak, the Council of Assiniboia revisited its earlier decision not to increase the settlement's law enforcement personnel, and resolved unanimously "[t]hat one hundred men be immediately sworn in as special constables to enforce ... [the court's judgment against Schultz], and that they or part of them be organized into a permanent force if considered necessary."[109] Less than a fortnight later, however, the governor reported that recruiting of the force was not going well. When he asked what to do, the council's response was tough: "That an order be issued by the Governor requiring *all* settlers to act as special constables, and to be in attendance at the courthouse on Monday next ... [when Schultz would be applying for a rehearing of the default judgment that had led to his imprisonment] at

12 o'clock to enforce the law."[110] How many citizens showed up is not known, but Schultz was never rearrested. Recorder Black, at McTavish's insistence, granted him a new trial,[111] at which the jury, on the basis of evidence that was probably perjured, reversed the decision against him.[112] The proposal for a permanent volunteer force was never followed up.

LAWS

Although the laws of Assiniboia did not change much during these years, there were a few noteworthy modifications.

In an effort to cope with a distressing level of public drunkenness, the liquor licensing regulations were tightened in November 1868, requiring, for example, that drinking establishments remain closed on Sundays and on Good Friday and Christmas Day.[113] Settlers probably chuckled when, shortly later, the company tripped over the new licensing laws. "At a District Court lately held in the Lower District," McTavish confessed to London,

> I regret to say that one of the Company's salesmen at the Lower Fort was sentenced to pay a penalty of £10, and the license under which he sold forfeited. It appears that the man had, in good faith, ... sold some liquor to a person, whom the Court afterwards held to be an Indian ... The case made some noise, and ..., on account of its being against the Company, was not unsatisfactory to a good many people; but I believe the Court, against any other party, would have modified its decision on account of the fault having been committed in ignorance. We have asked for a renewal of the license.[114]

He added that the company's licence to sell liquor at its White Horse Plains shop had also been cancelled by magistrates because of objections by nearby householders.

A longstanding doubt about the validity of Methodist marriages was swept away by an 1868 resolution stating, "[A]ny legally-ordained Wesleyan [Methodist] Minister labouring in the Settlement may validly solemnize marriages ..., and ... all registers of marriages, baptisms and burials kept by any legally ordained Wesleyan Minister shall be deemed legal and valid records."[115] The fact that this law was passed unanimously by a council that included both the Anglican and Catholic bishops shows that the volatile settlement agreed on some things.

Of even greater significance for marriage in Rupert's Land, where legally qualified clergy or other authorities were often unavailable to solemnize matrimonial unions, was an 1869 ruling of the Quebec Court of Appeal that "country" or "common law" marriages were legally valid in certain circumstances. In 1803, at Nelson House, Rupert's Land, a Cree woman named Suzanne married fur trader William Connolly by the "custom of the country." Although there was no authorized person to officiate, and no ceremony, both parties intended the union to be permanent, and it lasted for twenty-eight years, producing six children. When he retired from the fur trade in 1831, Connolly returned to Lower Canada, where he had been born, taking his family with him. But not long thereafter he met and married a white woman, eventually siring two more children by her. His first family was sent back to Red River, where Suzanne lived with the Grey Nuns until her death in 1862. Connolly provided some support to Suzanne during her lifetime, but when he died in 1864 his will left everything to his second wife and her children.[116] In a lawsuit launched by Suzanne's eldest son in the Superior Court of Quebec, the exclusion of the first family from the will was successfully challenged, and that decision was upheld by the Quebec Court of Appeal.[117] While the latter court did not claim that *all* "country marriages" were lawful, it did recognize the validity of "a marriage contracted where there are no priests, no magistrates, no civil or religious authority, and no registers" if it could be proved by "oral evidence, and ... the admission of the parties, combined with long cohabitation and repute." The reason this decision from Quebec, where civil law prevailed, was relevant to country marriages in common law jurisdictions like Rupert's Land is that under section 91(26) of confederated Canada's new constitution, the British North America Act, 1867, the essential legal elements of marriage were governed by federal, not provincial, law.

THE COURTS

At the seventeen assizes held between February 1866 and November 1869, the General Court entertained 156 cases, comprising a wide spectrum of civil and criminal litigation. The criminal charges included murder (2), manslaughter (1), infanticide (2), assault (5), burglary (1), and theft (many), along with a miscellany of arson, mutiny (from employment), fraud, failure to pay customs duties, selling liquor to Indians, and contempt of court. On the civil side, there were commercial and debt disputes (very many); claims about ownership and neglect of animals (also numerous); suits for trespass to land (several), for taking of personal property (2), for breach of personal contracts (3), for defective goods or defective workmanship (several), and for defamation (2); plus the issuance of guardianship orders and letters of administration for intestate estates. In the equivalent four-year periods beginning February 1844 and February 1856, the court had handled only 49 and 44 cases respectively. In other words, its workload had trebled in recent years, with a growing incidence of criminal cases. It seems likely that the pattern repeated itself for the petty courts also.[118]

The company's upper echelons, no longer interested in retaining its historic governorship of Rupert's Land, were trying very hard to keep the costs of governing as low as possible until relieved of the responsibility. They tried, for example, to shift the recorder of Rupert's Land's salary from the company' books to Assiniboia's – claming that only the settlers benefited from the court's work. That proposal was firmly rejected by the company's own Rupert's Land council, however, and London grudgingly agreed to continue paying the recorder.[119]

At the December 1868 meeting of the Council of Assiniboia, Recorder Black reported that William Smith, clerk of the courts and council for the past twenty years, was very ill, and quite unlikely to ever resume his duties.[120] After Black reminded it of "the carefulness and fidelity with which he had always performed his many, and often very arduous duties," the council granted the ailing former clerk a pension. Smith had been appointed president of the White Horse Plain Petty Court only about a year previously,[121] but his infirmities forced him to give up that responsibility too. As was feared at the time of his resignation, he did not survive long. On 14 May 1869 the man J.J. Hargrave called "the most remark-worthy man connected with the colony"[122] passed away.

Smith was replaced as petty court magistrate by the remarkable James McKay,[123] and Thomas Bunn was appointed clerk of the council and courts.[124] One of Dr John Bunn's two sons who had prosecuted G.O. Corbett in 1863, Thomas Bunn had since acted as agent for various litigants before the courts, and had sat on the Council of Assiniboia since January 1868. He surrendered his council seat six months later, probably in anticipation of soon succeeding Smith as clerk. Bunn would play an important nonpartisan, or at least ambiguous, role in the political upheavals soon to beset the settlement, and emerge as a respected public servant and one of the earliest members of the Manitoba bar.

The composition of the General Court changed little during these years. Every member of the May 1866 panel – John Black, Robert

McBeath, Thomas Sinclair, and Roger Goulet – was still in office at the time of the court's last sitting in November 1869. Only three judges participated in that final session (Black, McBeath, and Dr William Cowan),[125] the low attendance being doubtless attributable to the extraordinary circumstances prevailing at the time.

Recorder John Black, whose steadying presence on the court and loyal service as acting governor during McTavish's absences had long been a sheet anchor for the community, tendered his resignation in August 1868, to take effect a year later.[126] He had lost his taste for frontier life: "Red River is always doing something in an unpleasant way to distinguish itself," he complained. That remark alluded to the current grasshopper plague; had he known he was about to experience an infestation of American-style procedural objections in the *McLean* case, and then be deluged with political responsibilities, he might have used even stronger language. Requested to withdraw his resignation, Black declined;[127] but circumstances beyond anyone's control soon thrust upon him responsibility for one final, monumental, contribution to the Red River Settlement.

Prominent among the cases heard by the General Quarterly Court during the four years considered in this chapter were the following:

R. v. Demarrais

John Demarrais, a Métis, attacked and killed an American Saulteau named White Nail within the walls of Upper Fort Garry because of the latter's presumed association with those who had killed and mutilated visiting Sioux near Fort Garry not long before.[128] The trial attracted much attention, and family and friends of both the accused and the deceased were present in large numbers. The evidence of an unprovoked attack being undisputed, a guilty verdict and compulsory sentence of death were inevitable; and the mood was somber. Although known to be dangerous when drunk – as on this occasion – Demarrais was otherwise well liked by those who knew him. When the constable translating the proceedings was asked to inform the accused of the death sentence, he could not bring himself to do so, and a substitute interpreter had to be found.[129] The sentence being unpopular, a petition bearing upward of 350 names was got up calling upon the governor to commute it. McTavish did so, banishing Demarrais to New Caledonia.[130] Although even some of White Nail's relatives signed the petition, it was thought necessary to spirit the prisoner out of jail secretly when his banishment was implemented.

Recorder Black used the occasion of his address to the Demarrais grand jury to denounce eloquently the "appalling" public drunkenness now so common in the settlement, and so often linked to tragic events like White Nail's murder.[131] Go for a ride or a walk almost any day on almost any public road, Black challenged the jurors, and see "the victims of intemperance ... in almost every stage of drunkenness." "Things are verging to a crisis," he warned, and "it is high time you should lift up your voice in earnest denunciation against this gigantic evil." How the grand jury responded is not known.

Schultz versus the Justice System

The settlement was regularly entertained during this period by clashes between Dr John Schultz and Recorder John Black. Black, a stubborn man, tried hard to remain an immoveable object, but usually ended up yielding to the irresistible force of Schultz's outsized personality. Underlying these events were business disputes involving Schultz, his estranged half-brother Sheriff Henry McKenney, and an English wholesale merchant named Kew, who had supplied the brothers' partnership before it foundered. When a long-postponed action by Schultz against McKenney concerning division of the partnership assets was called at the May 1866 session of the General Court,[132] the doctor stood up and complained that "he could not obtain justice from the Court," which he claimed had been "intimidated and bullied" by McKenney in an earlier proceeding. An icily angry Judge Black "informed the Plaintiff that such language could not be permitted, and unless these words were retracted the Court could not listen to anything further from him." When Schultz refused to retract, Black called the next plaintiff's case.

Schultz had actions pending against four other persons at that sitting,[133] and when those cases were called the following day, the recorder reminded the doctor that he would not be allowed to proceed in person with those or future suits unless he withdrew his insults. He would be allowed, however, to sue through an agent. Schultz declined to either apologize or appoint an agent; so Black dismissed all his claims for want of prosecution. Governor McTavish felt the judge had gone too far, and HBC officials in London again sought the opinion of barrister Montague Bere. The latter criticized Black severely, and although the recorder fought back, he was eventually forced to relent. John Schultz's right to sue and speak for himself in the General Court was reinstated in February 1867.

When the English supplier Kew sued Schultz in the General Court shortly thereafter,[134] the doctor was absent from the settlement, and a large default judgment was entered against him. It was in response to Schultz's resistance to the court's enforcement of that judgment that Sheriff McKenney had imprisoned him, and it was from that imprisonment that the doctor's wife and friends had released him in the dramatic manner previously described.[135] Schultz now applied to Recorder Black for a rehearing of Kew's action, but Black dismissed the application on the ground that Schultz had previously ignored a notice of the action, absenting himself from the settlement instead. With public opinion supporting the doctor, a nervous Governor McTavish pressured Black to grant the new hearing after all. At that hearing,[136] Schultz produced a surprise witness, who testified – highly suspiciously but irrefutably in Kew's absence – that the account had long since been paid in full. So Kew's claim was dismissed. When Kew, in England, learned of the decision, he denied the witness's allegations under oath and applied to reopen the hearing once more. That application failed, however, because both Schultz's and Kew's Red River agents had agreed in advance to treat the first rehearing as final.[137] John Schultz had once more bested Red River's legal system. Governor William McTavish, chagrined about his unwitting contribution to what he became convinced was a fraud on the court and the plaintiff, subsequently sent Kew his personal cheque for the amount of the latter's loss.

R. v. McLean

Recorder Black's other nemesis was a remarkable legless American lawyer called Enos Stutsman.[138] Born in Indiana forty-two years previously with only a vestigial stump in place of legs, Stutsman had followed the American frontier westward, practising law, speculating in real estate, and dabbling in politics. His heroic leadership in defending a frontier settlement from Indian attacks had earned him the honorary title of "Colonel." He was currently based at Pembina, Dakota Territory, investigating international smuggling as a special agent of the US Treasury Branch, and was also a member of the Dakota Legislature. Stutsman was known in the Red River Settlement because his Treasury duties occasionally took him there, and because he was the only fully qualified lawyer within 500 miles of the settlement. It was he whom the McLean family of Portage la Prairie retained to defend their son Alex when he was tried for killing Francis Demarrais in 1868.[139]

Accustomed to the adversarial rough and tumble of US frontier courtrooms, with both sides represented by professional advocates and the judge restricted to a referee's role, Stutsman was, or professed to be, nonplussed by the Red River court's semi-inquisitorial style, with active participation by members of the bench and jury. Although his manner was polite – often obsequious – the attorney firmly challenged every procedure that differed from what he was familiar with, and soon the recorder, his self-confidence in tatters, was conceding every objection. McLean, whom the evidence clearly proved to be guilty of manslaughter, was acquitted. The *Nor'-Wester* chortled, and listed nine ways in which, based on Stutsman's successful objections, the trial had altered the General Court's procedures.[140] That did not prove to be so, however, because as soon as the US lawyer returned to Pembina, Black's court reverted to its past practices. Stutsman's brilliant victory had served only to demonstrate that adversarial advocacy cannot serve justice well unless both sides are represented by equally competent advocates. Several years would pass before the settlement's legal profession was numerous enough, and skilled enough, to make that generally possible. Red River had not seen the last of Enos Stutsman, however.

Corbett v. Dallas

John Schultz was not the only one to challenge the authority of Assiniboia's General Quarterly Court. G.O. Corbett, the Anglican pastor convicted in 1863 of attempting to abort his serving girl,[141] had returned to England in 1864, where his counsel devised a novel way of "appealing" his conviction to the courts of the mother country. He brought a civil action for false imprisonment in the English Court of Common Pleas against Alexander Grant Dallas, the governor of Rupert's Land at the time of Corbett's trial and imprisonment. Damages of £5,000 were claimed.[142] In order to garner evidence upon which the English court could adjudicate an occurrence on the other side of the Atlantic Ocean, Corbett's lawyers obtained an order for commissioned evidence, appointing four Assiniboians as commissioners – two for each party – to examine witnesses.

Due, probably, to Corbett's limited finances, the court order did not arrive at Red River until February 1869.[143] By that time, Maria Thomas, the prosecution's chief witness, was dead; one of Dallas's commissioners was too ill to accept the appointment; and the deadline for returning evidence was fast approaching. Examinations began, but one of Corbett's commissioners declined to act; and time ran out.[144] An extension was granted, and the process bumbled on; but the report submitted to England in September was incomplete, most of the plaintiff's witnesses still not heard from.[145] The reason the plaintiff's evidence was incomplete was that Corbett, likely having run out of money, had instructed his (as yet unpaid) commissioner to temporarily delay proceeding further. He later requested, and received, a second parcel of orders from the English court, including one to produce the General Court's records,[146] but the case was never brought to trial.[147] Because Corbett's pockets were not deep enough to conduct long-distance litigation, the legally intriguing question of whether English courts had the authority to challenge decisions of the HBC courts was never answered.

Public Interest v. Scott

The prematurely commenced Dawson road project ran into labour troubles in 1869. After two work stoppages, Superintendent John Snow refused to pay his men for time on strike, and a group of them threatened to throw him into a river unless he paid them then and there. In face of that threat, Snow paid his assailants but then travelled immediately to Winnipeg and laid criminal charges against them.[148] Four men were indicted for assault, two of whom were found guilty and fined £4 each. One of those convicted, perhaps the ringleader, was Thomas Scott, a man whose name, and whose opposition to the Métis uprising already in progress as he stood on trial, would be either revered or reviled in later years by followers of Manitoba history. The session at which Scott and his colleagues were tried was the court's final sitting as an HBC institution.

Probate, Guardianship, and Trusteeship

The workload of the General Court was expanded at the beginning of this period by adding the responsibility for guardianship and intestate succession. The power to appoint and supervise guardians for orphans and other minors without parents was bestowed on the court by the Council of Assiniboia in August 1865,[149] and two such orders were made in February 1866.[150] But when an attempt was made to apply one of those orders to property in Canada, the courts there refused to recognize the jurisdiction of Assiniboia authorities. Governor McTavish therefore proposed the creation of a special probate court with jurisdiction within HBC territories.[151] The company's response was again to seek a legal opinion from London barrister Montague Bere. That gentleman opined that such a court could probably be created under the authority of the HBC charter, although the collaboration of the Crown might also be required. In the meantime, he thought the ecclesiastical courts of England, operating under the authority of the Archbishop of Canterbury, would have jurisdiction.[152] The company cautiously applied to the colonial secretary for assistance;[153] but that correspondence became enmeshed in the general negotiations for the transfer of Rupert's Land to Canada,[154] and nothing ever came of McTavish's request. In the absence of assistance or instruction from England, the General Quarterly Court issued at least one more guardianship order,[155] and after the council empowered it in November 1866 to issue letters of administration for intestate estates,[156] it made at least two of those orders as well.[157] Other than those cases, doubts about the extraterritorial validity of Assiniboia orders seem to have discouraged efforts to seek them. Court Clerk Smith was lax in recording such orders, though, and it is possible that more were issued than appear in the court records.

Compounding the difficulties caused by the uncertain jurisdiction of Assiniboia authorities was the dilatoriness of company secretary William G. Smith, who administered the London-based assets of many of the estates and trusts involved. The funds of many, if not most, HBC employees and former employees were held in company accounts in London, and Smith looked after many of those accounts, apparently on a voluntary or fee-for-service basis. If the will of a deceased employee left money to family members, it was Smith who sent them the money, or invested it and paid debts, according to the terms of the will. But Smith's responses became tardy, and complaints piled up. Many of those complaints were directed to Governor McTavish, who was annoyed at being blamed for a situation he could not control. In December 1865 he wrote to another London-based HBC officer about the problem: "I wish you would stir up Mr. Smith, & get him to answer his correspondents here. They ... mob me, & think ... I am answerable for [his] shortcomings."[158] While he was last in England, McTavish continued, Smith "fairly deceived me, as he [falsely] assured me he had ... sent accounts to ... correspondents here whose claims I was pressing. I have written him every mail ... since my return, but cannot get an answer from him." A few days later, he told the same correspondent, perhaps tongue-in-cheek, "I mean to commence a daily series of letters to him, & recommend all his friends here to do the same, and ... send their letters unpaid ... If all follow my advice he will receive at least 50 letters weekly on his Red River business."[159] Although he probably did not carry that threat into effect, McTavish did keep up the pressure, with occasional success; but Red River beneficiaries rarely received satisfactory service.

The root problem came to light shortly after Assiniboia courts ceased to exist, when Smith wrote as follows to a beneficiary of a long-neglected Red River estate: "Dear Madam: You will be astonished to hear that I am a villain and a thief ... [Y]ou and many of my other friends may be hampered for money ... I have been mad for years past. My children go to beggary. I to prison. I can pay no more than that. I am no longer worthy of you."[160]

INSURRECTION

The political balloon burst in October 1869.

The winter of 1868–69 had been terrible for the poor of Red River, among whom the Métis[161] were disproportionately represented. Insult was heaped upon injury by a newly arrived Canadian poet and Schultz crony called Charles Mair.[162] In a letter to the *Toronto Globe*, Mair charged that the Métis were making undeserved claims on the Red River Famine Relief Fund. "The Halfbreeds," he claimed, "are the only people here who are starving. Five thousand of them have to be fed this winter, and it is their own fault – they won't farm."[163]

Mair's letter was skilfully refuted by one "L.R." in a letter to the Quebec newspaper *Le Nouveau Monde*. L.R. pointed out that the famine struck members of all segments of Red River society, and he tellingly criticized Mair for basing his assertions on pitifully inadequate evidence. "Be it said in passing, Mr. Mair," L.R. observed, "if we had only you as specimen of civilized men, we should not have a very high idea of them."[164] L.R. was almost certainly Louis Riel Jr, making his debut as spokesman for his people.

Another controversial remark in Charles Mair's *Globe* letter – an insulting remark about Halfbreed women married to prominent white men – provoked a more direct response from Annie Bannatyne, the mixed-blood daughter of Andrew McDermot and wife of Andrew Bannatyne. When she next encountered Mair, Mrs Bannatyne slapped his face and for good measure struck him a few blows with her riding whip.[165]

The resentment generated by such incidents fanned the embers of Halfbreeds' unease about their claims of Aboriginal title to the HBC lands soon to be devoured by Canada.[166] As time passed and federal authorities remained mum about their plans, those concerns mushroomed. On 29 July 1869 a public meeting of English and French Halfbreed leaders was held in the courthouse, and although the meeting was peaceful and ended inconclusively, there was general agreement by those present that the Indians and Halfbreeds had a legitimate claim to compensation for the land being transferred to Canada. There was also a proposal that Rupert's Landers should form their own government, but it attracted little support at that time.[167] Governor McTavish's report on the meeting ended ominously: "For the present, all is quiet again; but there is little doubt that if an opportunity occurs to make trouble, there are people here ready to take advantage of it."

Personally, McTavish was no happier about the situation than those at the public meeting. He had been expressing dissatisfaction for more than a year, and his gloom was magnified by worsening health: "If I continue to decline as I have lately, I will be nearly useless by the end of the outfit, and don't feel inclined to remain to be an object of pity."[168] Despite his threats of resignation, McTavish remained gamely at his post, but his pessimism persisted. And when, shortly after the Halfbreed public meeting, London instructed him to allow Canadian surveying to start before the legal transfer of ownership, his concern deepened. "I expect," he prophesied, "that as soon as the survey commences, the Halfbreeds and Indians will at once come forward and assert their right to the land, and possibly stop the work till their claim is satisfied."[169] Two weeks later, he informed London that Colonel J.S. Dennis had arrived with six surveyors, and that "[s]ome feeling has already been shewn by the ... [French] Halfbreed population, who appear to think that there can be no necessity for surveying their lands until they desire it themselves."[170]

As the survey work got under way in September, and was seen to involve the "American system" of sections rather than the river-lot pattern previously used in the settlement, distrust escalated despite Colonel Dennis's assurances that this was simply for descriptive purposes, and his promise that existing owners would get "proper deeds confirming their titles."[171] Even before the work began, a local informant wrote to Bishop A.A. Taché, then in Rome, that the project "has set the country on fire."[172]

Meanwhile, William McDougall, the governor-designate of Manitoba and the Northwest Territories, was approaching through the Dakota Territory with a carpet-bag administration in sixty overcrowded wagons, his progress being closely monitored by Métis scouts. He was expected at Pembina shortly. McDougall's instructions were to proceed immediately to Red River, and although his legal authority over Rupert's Land would not commence until the formal transfer of the territory – tentatively scheduled for 1 December – he was under orders, like Dennis's surveyors, to make an early start. And while instructed to make land available to newcomers, he had been told nothing about either Aboriginal rights or the preservation of existing land holdings.[173]

On 11 October a survey crew was running a line in St Vital parish from the principal meridian of longitude across the hay privilege land of Edouard Marion. André Nault, a cousin of Louis Riel Jr, was grazing cattle on Marion's land, and was probably also keeping watch for surveyors. Nault approached the crew, protested the trespass, and called for assistance from neighbours. A group of angry Métis, including Riel, arrived in short order, and halted the operation by standing on the survey chain. The crew, following Dennis's standing instructions for handling such confrontations, withdrew.[174]

The survey chain incident may or may not have been spontaneous; but the Métis had been preparing for some time to resist the premature occupation of Rupert's Land. Although the Halfbreed conclave in July had seemed inconclusive – a group led by Assiniboia councillor and reputed Schultz ally William Dease having urged moderation, while another, under John Bruce, demanded more radical action – the schism had caused the Bruce group to shake free from the conservatives, and to proceed independently.[175]

In October, five days before the surveying was halted, a letter to the St Hyacinthe, Quebec, *Courrier* was penned by "Two Métis Settlers of Red River" (author's translation), probably Riel and Bruce.[176] It announced that representatives from each of the settlement's French-speaking parishes had met to decide how to answer the Canadians' premature actions, and had passed five resolutions to the effect that (1) the Métis were loyal subjects of Queen Victoria, (2) they were "beholden" to the HBC for its past protection, (3) Snow and Dennis had "disregarded the law of nations in coming to carry out public work here in the name of an alien authority without paying any attention to the [HBC] authority today existing in the country," (4) the Métis were ready to submit to the transfer of governmental authority from the HBC to Canada, but "loudly proclaim" that by settling, working, and living on the lands they have assisted the HBC to open, they have acquired "indisputable rights in that country," and (5) the Métis would "do everything necessary to have the privileges accorded so liberally by the Crown of England to every English colony respected on their behalf" (author's translation).

Ten days after the encounter with Dennis's surveyors, the Métis Assembly decided that steps must be taken to prevent governor-to-be McDougall and his entourage entering the territory, and authorized the following order to be delivered to McDougall:

> Dated at St. Norbert, Red River, this 21st day of October, 1869
>
> Sir:
> The National Committee of the Métis of Red River orders William McDougall not to enter the territory of the North West without special permission of the above-mentioned Committee.
>
> By order of the President, John Bruce, Louis Riel, Secretary.[177]

The National Committee of Red River was now headquartered at St Norbert, a parish south of St Boniface and St Vital at the confluence of the Red and Sale Rivers. The committee met at the parish church there, and the local priest, forty-four-year-old Father Noel-Joseph Ritchot, became its spiritual, and probably tactical, guide. While Bruce was the nominal president, the committee's chief driving force was its twenty-five-year-old secretary, Louis Riel Jr. Just two weeks after penning its resolutions, the committee now had at its command many mounted and armed men, organized along the lines of the buffalo hunt and led by renowned hunter Maxime Lépine and his soon-to-be even more prominent brother Ambroise. Simultaneously with the McDougall blockade, a physical barricade was erected across the Fort Garry Trail at the Sale.

The Council of Assiniboia took longer than it should have to realize how serious the situation had become. On 19 October, two days before the Métis committee ordered McDougall to stay out of the territory, the council endorsed a fulsome letter of welcome to the governor-designate and his party. Governor McTavish knew that was a serious mistake. Riel had called upon him in his sick room on 13 October and told him precisely what was afoot, "knocking me up hopelessly for the remainder of the afternoon."[178] But although McTavish knew a majority of the settlement's population would oppose welcoming McDougall, his health had taken so serious a turn for the worse that he was unable to attend the council meeting and oppose the foolish message of greeting. By 25 October, however, four days after the injunction was issued and the barricade erected, council members were fully apprised of the circumstances, and they hurriedly met once more to try to deal with what they finally recognized as a monumental crisis.[179] Unrealistically thinking they could still influence events, they requested Riel and Bruce to attend.

Acting Governor Black pointed out that in adopting the address of welcome, the council had believed "the feelings of loyalty and welcome were ... shared by the great majority of the people," but that it now knew "a large party among the French population ... [appear] to be animated by a very different spirit." The Métis being intent upon keeping the Canadian representatives out of the country, Black continued, he had called this meeting "to see whether any, and what, measures could be adopted to prevent the threatened outrage." After the council expressed its unanimous "reprobation" of the Métis actions, it decided to try "by calm reasoning and advice" to induce the insurgents "to abandon their dangerous schemes." The Métis leaders were then invited to explain and justify their actions.[180]

Riel spoke for both men. In a long speech, the young Métis leader assured the council that his people were "perfectly satisfied with the present Government, and want ... no other." What they objected to was "any government coming from Canada without their being consulted in the matter." They were concerned that a large immigration would cause them to be "crowded out of a country which they claimed as their own," and they felt that "their existence, or at least their wishes, had been entirely ignored." Therefore, "they would never admit any governor ... not [appointed by] by the Hudson's Bay Company, unless delegates were previously sent with whom they might negotiate as to the terms and conditions under which they would acknowledge him." The Métis did not feel they were breaking the law, Riel explained, "but were simply acting in defence of their own liberty." And they considered themselves to be acting "for the good of the whole Settlement," French and English alike. If they encountered resistance from Schultz's Canadian Party, they were prepared for it, and "were determined to prevent Mr. McDougall from coming into the Settlement at all hazards."[181]

Council members tried to persuade Riel and Bruce that their views were "erroneous," their actions "highly criminal," and the consequences likely to be "very disastrous"; but Riel agreed only to pass on the council's views to the Métis committee. After he and Bruce left the room, the councillors anxiously debated the feasibility of taking up arms against the insurgents, concluding that "armed collision" between disparate "sections of the people who hitherto lived together in comparative harmony," with the probable involvement of Indians and "without a regular military force to fall back upon," would be a "sanguinary and protracted struggle ... full of possible mischief to the whole country," and could not be justified.[182]

The only action the council thought was left open to it was to try going above the heads of the Métis leaders. It therefore deputed two of its number, Roger Goulet and William Dease, to enlist some of the more "intelligent," "influential," and "respectable" members of the Halfbreed community to persuade the Métis already encamped near Pembina awaiting McDougall's arrival to disperse. Goulet, whose absence from the meeting had not been accidental, refused to participate, and most other "respectable" Halfbreeds, even some highly skeptical about the Métis committee's initiatives, had been persuaded by Father Ritchot that their wisest course was to remain aloof.[183] Dease attempted to carry out the council's instructions, but soon found he had no significant influence among the Métis.

In reality, if not in law, the HBC's 200 year reign as the governor of Rupert's Land had ended. Symbolic of that fact was the reaction of magistrate William Cowan to a legal complaint by a Canadian settler objecting to the St Norbert barricade.[184] Although the obstruction of the public highway was unquestionably illegal, Cowan did nothing. What could he do? When a truncated Council of Assiniboia next met, on 30 October 1869, it was only to be informed that the Dease mission had failed, and to approve a letter advising William McDougall to remain at Pembina for the time being. The council never met again under the auspices of the Hudson's Bay Company.[185]

When the McDougall party arrived at Pembina that same day, it was met by two formidable Métis scouts and presented with the foregoing order to remain on US soil. When, the following day, McDougall crossed the border in defiance of the order, and two members of his entourage proceeded on to St Norbert, they were all turned back by a force of armed Métis. Realizing that they might have to remain there for a while – perhaps even until December – McDougall and his party rented or built such temporary accommodations as tiny Pembina could provide. Even if those wretched quarters had been comfortable, Pembina was not a congenial town. The sympathies of local residents – mostly Métis themselves – were with the insurgents. And more than sympathy was involved. From McDougall's perspective, there were spies and suspected spies everywhere. He slept with a pistol beneath his pillow.[186]

Foremost among the US annexationists and purported Métis sympathizers at Pembina was lawyer, customs officer, and territorial politician Enos Stutsman.[187] As affable as he was devious, Stutsman had offered his services to Riel, as both legal advisor and scrutinizer of north-bound travellers for enemies to the uprising. Stutsman also began writing pro-Métis dispatches to American newspapers under a pseudonym. The Métis leader welcomed the lawyer's help, and gave the impression he was open to US involvement in the insurrection. That impression grew stronger after William B. O'Donoghue, a recent Irish American arrival at St Boniface, became one of Riel's closest advisors. Before very long, a St Paul newspaper would refer to Riel and Stutsman as possible future "Senators or members of Congress from the State of Winnipeg."[188]

Riel's next major move, on 2 November 1869, was to seize control of Upper Fort Garry. Governor McTavish was just finishing dictating a letter to London when a disturbance outside his quarters caused him to add a postscript: "As I close this letter, a party of one hundred of the malcontents have arrived and taken armed possession of Fort Garry under the pretext of defending it ... Mr. Riel alleges it is in danger. Guards are posted at each gate, and parade the platforms. They give assurance that nothing will be touched, and nothing taken. For what provisions they require they will pay in the name of the 'Council of Republic of Halfbreeds.'"[189] Riel's assurances were not honoured. A few days later, the insurgents broke into the fort's arsenal, seizing arms and ammunition. Other supplies were taken to provision the Métis troops, and Fort Garry's safe was eventually emptied of its cash. Repayment was promised but never made.

CONVENTION OF 24

Consonant with Riel's claim that the insurgents acted on behalf of everyone in the settlement, the Métis committee issued a public notice on 6 November 1869 extending "the hand of friendship" to residents of all the English parishes, and inviting them to send twelve representatives to meet with twelve from the French parishes at the courthouse on 16 November "in order to form one body with the above Council ... to consider the present political state of this country, and to adopt such measures as may be deemed best for the future welfare of the same."[190] When the notice was taken to the *Nor'-Wester* office to be printed for distribution throughout the settlement, editor Walter Bown refused. He was taken temporarily into custody, and his printing press and type were confiscated. Two printers were then engaged to print the notice under the supervision of James Ross, who would play a confusing double game throughout much of the ensuing crisis.[191]

Every parish in the settlement elected representatives to the bilingual conclave, which was called the "Convention of 24," and included many familiar faces. On the English side were Sheriff Henry McKenney, James Ross, saloon owner Hugh O'Lone, Dr. Bird, Maurice Lowman, Donald Gunn, George Gunn, John Garrioch, Robert and William Tait, Court Clerk Thomas Bunn, and, especially noteworthy, Henry Prince, who had succeeded his father, Peguis, as chief of the settlement's Saulteaux population. The Métis and French Canadian delegates were Patrice Bréland, Pierre Poitras, François Dauphinais, Pierre Léveillé, André Beauchemin, Pierre Parenteau Sr, Louis Lacerte, Baptiste Tourond, Jean-Baptiste Morin dit Perrault, Charles Nolin, and William B. O'Donoghue (an American Catholic fluent in French and wedded to the Métis cause). John Bruce and Louis Riel were the chairman and secretary respectively.

When the convention delegates straggled to the courthouse, they were greeted by cannonades from the fort and *feux de joie* from the firearms of about 150 armed Métis guarding the building. Although those noisy salutes were intended as friendly greetings, not everyone so interpreted them. Chief Prince remarked that among his people "it was customary to attend council without arms when peaceably inclined."[192] The first two days accomplished little beyond allowing both camps to let off steam. Riel and Ross eloquently dominated the debate on behalf of the French and English respectively.

Governor McTavish sent a message to the delegates which, after considerable palaver over its admissibility, was read by Sheriff McKenney.[193] It outspokenly condemned the "unlawful deeds" of the insurgents, and "the evils of anarchy and the horrors of war," concluding, "You are dealing with a crisis out of which may come incalculable good or immeasurable evil, and, with all the weight of my official authority and all the influence of my individual position, let me finally charge you to adopt only such means as are lawful and constitutional, rational and safe." Riel, whose calmness, diplomacy, and resourcefulness were impressive throughout, pounced upon, and made brilliant use of, those final words: "See what Mr. McTavish ... [writes]. He says that from the decisions of this assembly may come an inestimable good. Let us unite. The evil that is feared will not take place. See how he speaks. Is it surprising? His children are of mixed blood like ourselves."[194]

At the conclusion of the second day's debates, the convention adjourned to allow the General Court, in whose premises the meeting was being held, to conduct its regular November session. It would be the court's final sitting under HBC auspices. On the docket were an infanticide, the aggravated assault on John Snow by Thomas Scott and his cronies, and a civil appeal from a petty court decision. The appeal was not heard because of the appellant's absence. His letter explained that he was not present because of the insurgency: "[J]ustice cannot under existing circumstances be meted out." But Recorder Black would accept no such excuse and dismissed the appeal for nonprosecution, stating, "I cannot see why he should be so apprehensive of injustice ... [T]he Court sits here ... [able to] mete out to him all the justice and law to which he is entitled."[195] The fact that only two magistrates chose to join Black on the bench that day may however suggest that the appellant was not the only Red River resident who felt apprehensive about attending.

During the convention's adjournment, many meetings and discussions went on in delegates' home parishes. When it reconvened on 22 November, the debate was as unproductive as ever, and delegates expressed frustration. Enos Stutsman arrived in Winnipeg to advise the Métis sometime that day, and it may not have been coincidental that a breakthrough occurred on 23 November. During that fourth day of debate, Riel suddenly made a dramatic concrete proposal that many thought originated with Stutsman: that a provisional government be established to negotiate with Canada and to govern the settlement in the meantime. The English delegates, taken aback, requested an adjournment to seek their constituents' views about this radical proposal, and the convention recessed again – this time until 1 December. The parish debates began anew – more intensely. Riel participated in some of them and seemed, for a while, to favour a compromise: giving the Council of Assiniboia responsibility for day-to-day governance while the provisional government negotiated with Canada. Optimism was in the air. By 30 November, however, Riel was again insisting on an all-purpose provisional government, and attitudes hardened in both camps.

On 1 December, the day set to reconvene, the settlement was rocked by the news that would-be-governor William McDougall had crossed the international boundary during the night and proclaimed the surrender of Rupert's Land by the HBC to the Crown and its immediate transfer to Canada. McDougall declared that he was now in charge of the territory's government, and appointed Colonel Dennis "Conservator of the Peace."[196] Copies of the proclamation, smuggled into the settlement earlier, were being circulated. Enos Stutsman subsequently published a lampoon of the event:

> On the 1st instant, at the hour of 10 p.m., while the mercury indicated 20° below zero, and Old Boreas was on a bender, seven lonely pedestrians, fully armed and equipped, ... were seen stemming the blast, and ... [heading] in the direction of the oak post marking the international boundary, their brows contracted with firm resolve to do or die ... On nearing the boundary ... a charge was sounded, and, on double-quick, the brave little band dashed across the line into much coveted territory. Whereupon, the Dominion flag was unfurled, and, in defiance of the blinding storm and the inky darkness, Mr. McDougall ... assumed formal possession of the great Northwest Territory ... [and] returned in triumph to ... quarters on Uncle Sam's side of the national boundary.[197]

Humorous though it may have seemed, the event was to have very serious ramifications – but not those the governor-designate had contemplated.

The first consequence of McDougall's move was to bring the desultory Convention of 24 proceedings to a climax. After the proclamation was read and discussed at length on the afternoon of 1 December, Louis Riel announced, "If Mr. McDougall is really our Governor today, ... [h]e has no more to do than prove to us his desire to treat us well. If he guarantees our rights, I am one of those who will go to meet him in order to escort him as far as the seat of government."[198] James Ross then issued a challenge to be more specific: "What will we ask of him?" A hubbub ensued, during which many proposed demands were advanced and debated in disorderly fashion. Finally, the French proposed an adjournment, promising to return in two hours with a list of their demands. It was 4:00 PM. At 6:00 the convention was presented by Riel with the following document:

> List of Rights
>
> 1. That the people have the right to elect their own Legislature.
> 2. That the Legislature have the power to pass all laws local to the territory over the veto of the executive by a two thirds vote.
> 3. That no act of the Dominion Parliament (local to the territory) be binding on the people until sanctioned by the Legislature of the territory.

4. That all sheriffs, magistrates, constables, school commissioners etc., be elected by the people.
5. A free homestead and pre-emption land law.
6. That a portion of the public lands be appropriated to the benefit of schools, [and] the building of bridges, roads and public buildings.
7. That it be guaranteed to connect Winnipeg by rail with the nearest line of railroad within a term of five years; the land grant to be subject to the local Legislature.
8. That for the term of four years all military, civil and municipal expenses be paid out of the Dominion funds.
9. That the military be composed of the inhabitants now existing in the territory.
10. That the English and French languages be common in the Legislature and courts and that all public documents and acts of the Legislature be published in both languages.
11. That the judge of the supreme Court speak the English and French languages.
12. That treaties be concluded and ratified between the Dominion Government and the several tribes of Indians in the territory to ensure peace on the frontier.
13. That we have a fair and full representation in the Canadian Parliament.
14. That all privileges, customs and usages existing at the time of the transfer be respected.[199]

How had so thorough a compilation of demands, expressed in such good English, been produced in just two hours? Part of the explanation is that the Métis had been discussing and asserting their grievances for many years – at least since the *Sayer* case twenty years earlier. Not long after Stutsman first met with the Métis leaders, a full month before this final session of the Convention of 24, he sent the *St Paul Daily Press* a list of five demands, four of which were among the first six listed above. Some of the language was unchanged.[200] Another factor was that the highly articulate American lawyer was almost certainly present at the French caucus meeting to assist in drafting its manifesto.

When the meeting resumed, the List of Rights was discussed in detail, and to the probable amazement of the French, the English agreed with every item.[201] But when it was proposed that a delegation be sent to Pembina to meet McDougall and inform him that his entry to the territory was contingent on either agreeing to the demands on the strength of his own commission or obtaining legislation that granted them, "all the English refused to participate." At that point, Louis Riel's diplomatic veneer cracked: "Riel rises, and speaks hotly. 'Go,' he says, 'return peacefully to your farms. Rest in the arms of your wives. Give that example to your children. But watch us act. We are going to work and obtain the guarantee of our rights, and of yours. You will come to share them in the end.'"[202] The bilingual convention was over; action would now replace debate.

The first order of business was to deal with efforts by the Canadian Party and Conservator of the Peace Dennis to organize an armed counterinsurgency. Canadians hostile to the Métis regime had been gathering for some time at Dr John Schultz's unfortified compound, near Portage and Main and within easy range of the fort's cannons. They now numbered more than fifty, including some women and children. Although poorly armed and surrounded by Métis troops, they talked bravely of resisting the uprising. On 7 December the Métis decided to expel the Schultz group, by force if necessary. With Andrew G.B. Bannatyne and other Winnipeggers acting as mediators, the enclave was persuaded, over Schultz's objections, to surrender peaceably and be imprisoned – families and all – in Upper Fort Garry.[203]

Ever since his appointment as McDougall's conservator of the peace, Colonel Dennis, now ensconced at the Lower Fort, had been recruiting and training a resistance force. He had first met with Acting Governor John Black,[204] who lived nearby, to discuss declaring martial law. His initial target was to be the crippled Enos Stutsman.[205] Black counselled delay, however, and Dennis never did invoke martial law. He did call for volunteers[206] and managed, with the assistance of Captain Charles Boulton, to recruit a number of loyalists from Portage, Headingley, Kildonan, the lower settlement, and elsewhere. But he encountered so much reluctance to physical resistance – most notably from James Ross – that he eventually abandoned his efforts and departed the star-crossed colony with most of his surveyors.

PROVISIONAL GOVERNMENT

The immediate threat to the new regime having been effectively extinguished, the Métis lost no time before announcing their provisional government to the world. The very day Schultz's enclave surrendered, William Coldwell was engaged to print an eloquent and carefully reasoned "Declaration of the People of Rupert's Land and the North West," proclaiming the new regime's inception on 24 November 1869 and justifying its creation. Opening with the undeniable assertion that although subjects owe allegiance to their established governments, a people that has no government is "free to adopt one form of government in preference to another," the declaration

1 explained that the HBC, which had long ruled Rupert's Land under royal charter, had "surrendered and transferred" that authority to Canada in March 1869[207] without consulting the people affected;
2 claimed that "by transferring to a strange power the sacred authority confided to it" the company had freed "the people of Rupert's Land and the North West ... from all allegiance to the said Government"; and
3 announced that on 24 November 1869 "we, the representatives of the people" decided
   (a) to "refuse to recognize the authority of Canada";
   (b) to establish "a Provisional Government ... to be the only and lawful authority now in existence in Rupert's Land and the North West which claims the obedience and respect of the people"; and
   (c) to "hold ourselves in readiness to enter into negotiations with the Canadian Government as may be favourable for the good government and prosperity of this people."[208]

Only a lawyer – a very good lawyer – could have drafted that document. Its use of dates is of particular interest. The Provisional Government was said to date from 24 November – the day Riel, doubtless with Stutsman at his side, sold the idea of provisional government to his doubting Métis colleagues at a marathon caucus meeting.[209] That was a full week before the English delegates rejected the proposal and the French resolved to go it alone. More significantly, in light of the declaration's "abandonment" rationale, it was also a week before McDougall's proclamation purported to conclude the HBC's suzerainty.

Why had March been chosen as the date of Rupert's Land's surrender and transfer to Canada? Why not 1 December, when McDougall read the royal proclamation, or even 8 December, when the Provisional Government's declaration was issued? The reason was that many things were done by the insurgents before the latter dates that would have been unlawful if the former regime had still been in place. By selecting

March 1869, when Britain, Canada, and the HBC agreed to the transfer terms, it was undoubtedly hoped to establish that all existing governmental authority had been abandoned long before the people took power into their own hands. This was a dubious legal argument,[210] but it was the only one by which such acts as closing the highway, barring McDougall's entry, and seizing Fort Garry could possibly be legitimized.

On Friday, 10 December, two days after the formal announcement of the new government, the event was celebrated by festivities at Fort Garry. A flag bearing a fleur-de-lis and a shamrock (the latter recognizing the Irish sympathies of W.B. O'Donoghue, now Louis Riel's second-in-command) was raised, cannonades and small-arms volleys were fired, speeches were made, a band played, and "[t]hree cheers were given for the Provisional Government, three for the leaders, and three for the band – followed by three groans for [James] Mulligan, late chief of police, now a prisoner at Fort Garry."[211]

Meanwhile, at Pembina, the unease of the beleaguered governor-in-exile was increasing. Not only was Colonel Dennis's failure discouraging, but McDougall was beginning to fear that the bold proclamation he had hurled at the northern winds on 1 December might have been a mistake. Indeed it was. McDougall's expectation that Canada would become the owner – and he the governor – of Rupert's Land in December 1869 was unwarranted. That date had been only an estimate. His instructions were to await notification of the actual transfer before exerting any legal authority. Although the HBC had signed the deed surrendering Rupert's Land on 19 November,[212] it was contingent upon Canada's payment of the purchase price. Canada, shocked by news of the Métis uprising and unwilling to go further until peaceful possession of the territory could be assured, had postponed payment,[213] and the transfer process had shuddered to a halt. Thus McDougall's assertions that the territory was Canadian and that he was its governor were false. His authorization of Dennis's military actions was likewise unlawful.

When it learned of McDougall's premature and illegal actions, the Canadian government was understandably furious. Secretary of State for the Provinces Joseph Howe, the man chiefly responsible for bringing the northwest into Confederation, sent McDougall a frosty Christmas Eve reprimand for committing an "entirely illegal ... act," causing "grave consequences, ... [and] occasioning ... great anxiety" in Ottawa.[214] What troubled Howe and his colleagues most was that "if you were invested with the legal title to govern without being able to get into Rupert's

Land or exercise any authority, the revolutionary government would be strengthened by your weakness, & would in fact (the proclamation having superceded Governor Mactavish) be the only government in the territory until put down by force of arms."[215] An earlier cabinet memo signed by Prime Minister John A. Macdonald had voiced the same concern, pointing out that in "a state of anarchy and confusion ... a legal status might be given to any government de facto formed by the inhabitants for the protection of their lives and property."[216] The Métis Provisional Government was just such a de facto regime.

Howe's letter to William McDougall instructed him to "remain at Pembina until you can get peaceable access to Fort Garry." However, by the time the letter was received – indeed, even before it was written – McDougall had pulled up stakes and headed back to Ottawa,[217] sending McTavish a note telling him he was probably still in charge after all.[218]

LEGAL AND CONSTITUTIONAL CONSIDERATIONS

What was the legal status of the Provisional Government at that point? Governmental sovereignty over a territory has three components: physical possession, political control, and legal entitlement. By late December 1869 the first two – possession of and control over Rupert's Land – were both firmly in the hands of the Métis Provisional Government; but the legal entitlement to govern still belonged to the HBC.[219] Such situations of divided sovereignty are not uncommon, either historically or in modern times; and both international and domestic law deal with them similarly. After an insurrectionary usurpation of governmental power, the authority with the legal right to govern remains entitled, for a reasonable time, to re-establish possession and control if it can. If, however, the de facto regime can exercise exclusive and effective possession and control for a sufficiently long period of time that other regimes recognize its legitimacy, a new legality will displace that upon which the former government relied.

And even if the usurping regime is eventually driven from power, the laws it enacts and the governmental actions it takes while in power for the day-to-day welfare and good order of the population are considered legal.[220] So, while the long-range legitimacy of the government created by the Métis of Rupert's Land awaited the outcome of future events, its right and its responsibility to govern Rupert's Land in the meantime were clear.

BEGINNING TO GOVERN

The Provisional Government soon began to exercise that responsibility, although gradually at first. One of its earliest measures, after its military superiority was firmly established, came in response to a defiant *Nor'-Wester* extra edition on 17 November 1869. To suppress dissenting voices, it shut down both that newspaper and the gestating *Pioneer* that William Coldwell and James Ross were preparing to publish. *Nor'-Wester* owner Walter Bown soon fled the settlement.[221]

On 11 December, Andrew Bannatyne was appointed postmaster and judge (positions he had held previously),[222] and on 21 December, Bannatyne's partner Alexander Begg recorded that "Riel had the first case of judicial trial today. Mrs. Rodway against a near neighbour of hers, Mrs. Meeken, for assault."[223] Whether the case was tried by Bannatyne, Riel, or someone else is not known. Its outcome, announced three days later, was "damages all round: 10/ [shillings] to 20/ [shillings] each,"[224] whatever that meant. At an important meeting of the Provisional Government's assembly on 27 December 1869, a sweeping governmental reorganization took place, and other important measures were enacted.[225] Judicial arrangements were further altered by the appointment of Ambroise Lépine as "Adjutant," to administer justice with a council of three, one of whom was Bannatyne. That body was to meet twice monthly.

The most significant change was a major reshuffling of leadership positions. John Bruce having resigned as president "by reason of health,"[226] the fiction that Louis Riel had been merely the government's secretary ended with his election as president. François Xavier Dauphinais was made vice president, W.B. O'Donoghue became secretary-treasurer, and Louis Schmidt replaced his friend Riel as secretary of the Provisional Governing Council of Assiniboia. Other measures required existing liquor licences to be reconsidered by the Adjutant's Council, released twelve of the estimated sixty political prisoners held at Fort Garry,[227] and proclaimed that "All employees of the former government who purport to exercise their former authority will be punished for high treason."

More prisoners were released on 30 December, after trial by the Adjutant's Council.[228] When a Sioux band was reported approaching the settlement, a volunteer corps was organized to repulse them.[229] To finance the new regime, Riel first attempted to extract a loan from the HBC, and when McTavish refused that demand, the HBC safe was emptied of its entire contents: £1,090. The Métis troops were paid in merchandise from the company's stores at Upper Fort Garry and White Horse Plains.[230]

It was not yet a smoothly functioning or fully effective government. Persons importing goods into Assiniboia faced a chaotic situation, since they were required to pay import duties to the Provisional Government but were refused the legally required receipt of payment by Acting Governor Black because the Assiniboia government had not been paid.[231] And when, in late December, one Thomas Johnson was shot dead during a drunken melee in circumstances suggesting that Red River photographer Ryder Larsen had done the deed, no steps were taken to apprehend the suspect.[232] There were also huge political – and perhaps military – issues yet to be resolved: Would the Riel regime succumb to the blandishments of Enos Stutsman and other American annexationists? If so, how would the US government react? How, in either case, would the two-and-a-half-year-old Dominion of Canada respond to the crisis?

There was absolutely no doubt, however, as dawn illuminated the first day of 1870, that the Métis-led Provisional Government of Rupert's Land was in almost complete control of the HBC's former domains – and that the world was taking notice.

10

Governing Provisionally, 1870

When Canada and the world understood the seriousness of the Red River insurrection, the people of the region were courted by two suitors. Canada's first envoys discovered that ardent US annexationist Enos Stutsman already had Louis Riel's ear, and was using his strategic boundary location to screen would-be visitors to Red River, and to advocate American adoption. Those first Canadian emissaries could only assure settlers of Canada's good intentions; but the arrival of Donald A. Smith, with greater authority from Ottawa, prodigious negotiating skills, and a purse full of bribes, led to a Red River Settlement delegation being sent to Ottawa. The efforts of Stutsman and others to make Rupert's Land part of the United States' "manifest destiny" were trumped when, in May 1870, agreement was reached on terms of the area's entry into Canadian Confederation.

To deal with Canada, Red River's Provisional Government was enlarged and made more representative. While its delegates negotiated in Ottawa, it provided stable day-to-day government, including courts, until Canadian officials arrived in the fall. Tragically, it also executed a troublesome prisoner named Thomas Scott. That rash act not only dashed Riel's dream of personally passing the reins to the new administration; it also profoundly affected the future of prairie Canada and the Métis people.

EMISSARIES

It did not take Ottawa long to make soothing overtures to the angry Red River Settlement. On 6 December, Governor General Sir John Young issued a proclamation saying the "misguided" insurgents had acted from "misrepresentations." Assuring settlers that their "civil and religious rights and privileges will be respected," their "properties secured,"

Figure 10.1 Insurrection leader Louis Riel was chiefly responsible for the enactment and content of Manitoba's constitution, and then presided over an effective provisional government until Canadian authorities arrived.

and "all well-founded grievances" redressed, he offered an amnesty for all who peaceably dispersed and returned to their homes.[1] Shortly thereafter, three envoys were commissioned to travel to Red River as quickly as possible to assure residents of Canada's friendly disposition and sincere desire to bring the Hudson's Bay Company territories into Confederation on fair terms.

The first two of those ambassadors were old friends of the community.[2] Father Jean-Baptiste Thibault had served the Métis of Assiniboia for many years as parish priest and teacher. His co-emissary, Colonel Charles De Salaberry, had also lived and worked in the area, and was very well liked. Receiving a friendly reception upon their arrival, Thibault and De Salaberry conferred with Riel and the Provisional Governing Council of Assiniboia in January 1870. But when it became clear that they had no power to *negotiate* on behalf of Canada – no authority to do anything but express good wishes – their mission was politely dismissed by the rebels. Father Thibault seems, in fact, to have been persuaded by former colleagues, parishioners, and students that the insurgents' cause was just. Colonel De Salaberry, though gregarious, genial, and less impressionable, had no greater success deflecting his Métis friends from their resolve.

The Thibault–De Salaberry mission had been preceded by an informal December visit from Charles Tupper, a "Father of Confederation" and ally of Sir John A. Macdonald in the federal Parliament.[3] Tupper's visit was entirely unofficial. His daughter was married to Captain Donald Cameron, a member of William McDougall's entourage whose bombastic attempt to pass through the Métis barricade at St Norbert with a wagon full of the couple's personal belongings had caused the wagon to be confiscated and Cameron to be escorted back to Pembina. Because of their imprisoned possessions, the Camerons did not leave Pembina with McDougall; and Tupper journeyed there, and thence to Red River, to assist. At St Norbert he managed to befriend Riel's sister and, through her, to arrange informal meetings with her brother and others at Fort Garry. Although able to secure the release of the Camerons' property, Tupper did not – could not in light of the private nature of his visit – accomplish anything directly on the political front. He appears, however, to have been favourably impressed by the Métis leader and his cause, which might possibly have influenced future developments indirectly.

It was Canada's third official emissary, Donald A. Smith,[4] employing considerably more bold and ruthless tactics than his predecessors, who finally broke the impasse. Smith was a well-connected forty-nine-year-old HBC chief factor of surpassing abilities, currently directing the company's eastern Canadian operations from Montreal. His commission,[5] while not empowering him to negotiate formally, gave him much more authority than Thibault or De Salaberry. As "Special Commissioner to enquire into the causes, nature and extent" of the uprising, he was to examine "the causes of discontent and dissatisfaction alleged to exist," to explain "the principles on which ... Canada intends to administer the government" of the area, and "to take steps to remove any misapprehensions which may exist." Commissioner Smith was then to advise the federal government on "the best mode of quieting and removing such discontent and dissatisfaction; and ... the most proper and fitting mode for effecting the speedy transfer of the country and government ... to ... Canada, *with the general assent of the inhabitants.*"[6] Fearing, with good reason, that this commission might be confiscated if he brought it with him to Fort Garry, Smith left it at Pembina.

Upon arriving at Fort Garry in December, he was brought before President Riel and the Provisional Government's Governing Council, to whom he explained his mission, saying he would produce his commission only when he could display and explain it to "the people." The council, however, refused to negotiate or allow Smith to address "the people" until he acknowledged the legality of the Provisional Government, which he declined to do. That standoff rendered further discussion futile; and Smith was made, he said, "virtually a prisoner within the Fort."[7] Although allowed to reside in a company house, he was not permitted to leave the fort unless accompanied by a two-man Métis guard, a privilege he declined.

Donald Smith was not altogether isolated from "the people," however. On the contrary, he later reported that he "had frequent visits in the Fort from some of the most influential and most reliable men in the Settlement, who gladly made known to the people generally the liberal intentions of the Canadian Government." Moreover, during the two and a half weeks that this situation prevailed, Smith distributed more than verbal assurances. Although his commission and official report made no reference to the fact, Smith had authority to undermine Riel's support with bribes and promises of employment. These were especially attractive to some settlers, who, following Father Noel-Joseph Ritchot's advice, stood cautiously aside from the insurrection, assessing its likely success before committing their allegiance.[8] Although Smith's claim that, because of his secret efforts, "one after another of Riel's councillors seceded from him, and ... determined no longer to submit to his dictation," may have been exaggerated, his work contributed importantly to ending the Provisional Government's honeymoon.

There were other contributing factors too. One was the dilapidated state of the Red River jail. Although many "political prisoners" had been released upon promising not to resist the Provisional Government, hard-core Canadians like John Schultz, Charles Mair, and Thomas Scott refused to give that undertaking, and remained in custody. Those men – about forty in all – were moved to the six dank cells of the settlement's flimsy jail outside the fort's walls. On 9 January eight prisoners, including Mair and Scott, escaped, the latter joining a resistance force forming at Portage la Prairie.[9] The new regime's confidence was seriously undermined by that escapade, as well as by increasing defections, counterinsurgency preparations west and north of the Métis stronghold, and growing resentment toward US annexationists in the settlement. Smith thought the events of early January "had a marked effect on Riel, causing him to alter his tactics, and to profess a desire for an accommodation with Canada."

PUBLIC MEETING

Smith had nevertheless decided, after a 6 January meeting with Riel, that "no good could arise" from more discussions with the Provisional Government; face-to-face communication with the broader community was needed. And on 14 January, Riel conceded the point. Arrangements were accordingly made for Smith's credentials to be retrieved from Pembina and presented to a public meeting. An attempt by Riel's men to intercept Smith's messenger and seize the commission was foiled by a sizable posse of moderate Halfbreeds and French Canadians. On the other hand, Canadian emissary Father Thibault was now working to undo some of the effects of Smith's bribery.[10] The political situation remained volatile as the people of Red River sought a fair way to untangle the governmental snarl in which they found themselves.[11]

The public meeting opened on 19 January, the day after Smith's commission arrived. Although the weather was bitterly cold, a huge crowd – approaching 1,000 – showed up in the Fort Garry courtyard to hear Canada's representative.[12] Louis Riel began by proposing Thomas Bunn as chairman, and the crowd agreed. Recorder John Black was then selected as secretary. When Donald Smith nominated De Salaberry as translator, the colonel demurred, proposing Riel, who was chosen and performed the role well, distasteful though it must sometimes have been to him. As the meeting wore on – for five hours that first day – the crowd became impatient with Smith's droning recitation of legal documents. That may have explained a sudden shout from English Halfbreed John Burke demanding release of the remaining political prisoners. When Riel refused, and others echoed Burke's demand, Métis troops made their presence known. On that divisive note, the meeting adjourned until the next morning.

The mood seemed no better as the second session opened. Recorder Black, smarting from something Riel had said the first day, refused to continue as secretary. Not long after Andrew Bannatyne had replaced Black, however, the gloom lifted. The weather had improved somewhat;

translation was provided for the Indians present; John Burke apologized for his outburst; and a French priest's statement that friendship bridged the settlement's religious and ethnic rifts drew warm applause. After that, Smith, who had again been boring everyone with official quotations, suddenly started talking off the cuff, with apparent sincerity, about his personal view of the situation; and the audience cheered.

Louis Riel then made a decisive move, proposing a meeting of twenty French and twenty English representatives "with the object of considering ... what would be the best for the welfare of the country." The proposal was accepted, and as Donald Smith reported, "the English, as a body, and a large number of the French declar[ed] their entire satisfaction with the explanations given, and their earnest desire for union with Canada."[13] The meeting concluded with ovation-punctuated expressions of satisfaction by Father Ritchot, Anglican bishop Robert Machray, and Louis Riel. The young Métis leader, who spoke last, added a note of determination, however: "We are not yet enemies (loud cheers), but we came very near being so. As soon as we understood each other, we joined in demanding what our English fellow subjects, in common with us, believe to be our just rights (loud cheer). I am not afraid to say our rights; for we all have rights (renewed cheers). We claim no half rights, mind you, but all the rights we are entitled to. Those rights will be set forth by our representatives, and, what is more, gentlemen, we will get them."[14]

If Donald A. Smith's devious methods had made him enemies in the settlement, his courage, energy, persistence, and eloquence had accomplished more to dismantle the barriers to negotiation than his Ottawa masters likely thought possible. He could not have succeeded, however, without the good faith, good sense, and flexibility of Louis Riel and other influential figures, French and English, who shared the sense of community that still underlay Red River's divisions.

In the latter part of December, Enos Stutsman had intended to put down permanent roots in Winnipeg. Alexander Begg's journal for 20 December noted that the lawyer, "who is coming to reside amongst us," hoped to purchase, in partnership with American H.M. Robinson, the printing equipment abandoned by Walter Bown when the *Nor'-Wester* was closed down by Riel in November, and to publish "a newspaper in the interests of the French."[15] Two days later, Begg recorded that Robinson and Stutsman had instead purchased the equipment of William Coldwell's as yet unborn *Pioneer*, and had retained Coldwell's services as printer.[16] The new paper would be called the *New Nation*. Just three days after Stutsman's arrival on 10 January, however, Begg wrote,

"Colonel Stutsman begins to find his game about played out in the Settlement, and instead of remaining a month or two as he intended he has made up his mind to leave for Pembina tomorrow."[17]

What had happened? For one thing, the reputation of the too-smooth lawyer, already unpopular with many settlement residents, had plummeted farther by reason of a letter he had attempted to smuggle to Riel in late December recommending that Father Thibault not be admitted to the settlement.[18] In so proposing, Stutsman underestimated the respect with which Riel, and most Métis, regarded the venerable cleric. It is not clear whether the letter was ever read by Riel. Rather than placing it openly in an envelope, Stutsman had hidden it in a newspaper addressed to the president – probably to escape examination by Postmaster Bannatyne. It was discovered, however, and then copied and circulated. As for the original, Begg recorded that it "was found the other day inside the Fort – lying on the ground with the signature torn off. It seemed as if it had been used in the performance of a natural duty in which a man must necessarily place one hand behind him – directing it towards the end of his spine."[19]

The principal reason for the lawyer's retreat, however, was that he suddenly realized that the prospect of US annexation was virtually dead. His first intimation that the political winds had shifted came when he met his intended partner in journalism at George Emmerling's hotel in January. Robinson had brought out the first issue of the *New Nation* the previous day, and President Riel, angered by the paper's blatant support for US annexation, had administered a severe scolding to the astonished Robinson.[20] And when Stutsman himself called upon the Métis leader the following morning about "some very important business" that he wished to discuss in "strictly *private* conversation," he failed to receive the immediate welcome to which he was accustomed.[21]

Smith's undercover lobbying had accomplished much by that time, and the Provisional Government was on the verge of giving in to his demand to put Canada's case directly to the people of Red River. If popular enthusiasm for union with the United States had ever been as high as the settlement's American population believed, it had seriously shrunk in face of Canada's apparent contrition. When the US flag was flown over Emmerling's hotel on 12 January to mark the death of a former American secretary of war, it caused intense resentment among Red River's francophones.[22] On 13 January, Begg recorded his opinion that the "[p]oor Americans ... have played their hand too openly, and not too well." Although "[t]he American flag still flies at Emmerlings," he concluded, "[l]et it fly; it is doing good in rousing the French in opposition to anything like annexation to the States."[23] The next morning, Enos Stutsman began his long, cold journey back to Pembina. He seems never to have returned to Red River, and US annexation was never again a serious consideration, apart from a pathetic "Fenian Raid" instigated by W.B. O'Donoghue in 1871.

CONVENTION OF 40

The congress of forty French and English delegates proposed by Riel to discuss Donald A. Smith's representations and decide what to do next was warmly supported in the parishes. They elected their representatives in short order, and on 26 January (one day behind schedule due to a severe blizzard) the "Convention of 40." assembled in the courthouse to plot the settlement's fate.[24] Judge Black was chosen chairman at Riel's suggestion; French and English secretaries were chosen, as well as French and English translators; Smith's commission was read aloud; and after some delay caused by a few contested elections, the convention got down to business.

Riel was annoyed that the twenty francophones elected included Charles Nolin and two other Métis critical of the Provisional Government's policies and tactics. He was also unhappy to learn that the village of Winnipeg had elected Alfred H. Scott, a recent American immigrant, in preference to the more experienced and Métis-friendly Andrew Bannatyne. Relations among the delegates were nevertheless generally courteous and cooperative – friendly even, much of the time – and agreement was quickly reached on many points. Begg suggested that liquid refreshments may have contributed to the esprit de corps: "The refreshment room adjoining the council chamber where the Convention is sitting consists of the open air, and the bar [of] the snow banks in which innumerable bottles containing 'strong waters' are concealed, and from which the members regale themselves every now and again."[25] For the most part, however, the teamwork stemmed from a common desire to produce a negotiation agenda acceptable to Canada.

It was quickly agreed that the List of Rights upon which the Convention of 24 had agreed in November needed to be supplemented and revised. A drafting committee of three French and three English delegates, with no American representation, was accordingly struck. Coincidentally, perhaps, but nevertheless contributing to reduced tension, the star-spangled banner disappeared from Emmerling's hotel on the day the Convention of 40 first met.[26] On 29 January the drafting committee produced its proposed new List of Rights, and the parent body began straightaway to debate it. By the afternoon of 3 February, after five days' close scrutiny and debate, the convention agreed on twenty carefully phrased clauses.

It was time, most thought, to call in Donald A. Smith, who had declined to be present at convention meetings until its deliberations were complete. But when a motion to that effect was made, President Riel objected to doing so until an additional demand was considered: that Rupert's Land enter Confederation as a province rather than a mere territory as Canada proposed. This was an important point – on which Riel seems to have been outvoted in the drafting committee – and the convention agreed to postpone inviting Smith to attend until it was dealt with.[27] After the convention debated the point at length on 4 February, however, Riel was again in the minority. But when it was once more proposed to bring Commissioner Smith into the assembly, the stubborn Métis leader raised yet another demand, probably also rejected by the drafting committee: that the intergovernmental agreement of March 1869 for Rupert's Land's surrender to Canada be nullified.[28] After what Begg called a "stormy" discussion, that proposal was also defeated.[29] President Riel lost his temper at that point, and vowed to have his way in the end. In his pique he caused both the ailing Governor William McTavish and Chief Factor William Cowan to be placed under house arrest; and when Andrew Bannatyne protested, he found himself arrested too.

At the 7 February meeting of the convention, Donald A. Smith was in attendance. Explaining that he was not personally empowered to accede to the List of Rights, he proposed that the convention choose delegates to travel east and negotiate with Canadian authorities, offering the opinion that "all would be conceded by the Canadian Parliament." He promised that delegates' travel expenses would be paid by Ottawa.[30] The convention accordingly passed a unanimous resolution, moved by James Ross and seconded by Louis Riel, that since a "cordial reception" had been assured, the invitation should be accepted.[31]

SECOND PROVISIONAL GOVERNMENT

Discussion then turned to the more difficult question of governing the settlement while the negotiations were underway, and until Canada took charge. That debate raged for more than three days. Whereas the Métis insisted that the existing Provisional Government was appropriate, the English demanded representation therein. When someone pointed out that only the HBC was legally empowered to govern, Louis Riel scoffed, noting that no arrangements had been made for the courts' February sittings, and that no inquest had been held into the December shooting of Thomas Johnson.[32] A delegation was then sent to the guarded sick room of William McTavish for his views. The pain-wracked governor declared that although he was dying, he would not "delegate my power to anyone." He urged, however, "for God's sake to have any form of government which ... [will] restore peace and order."[33] McTavish's plea was heeded, and on 10 February the convention agreed on a revised Provisional Government with a "Council of 24": twelve French and twelve English. Each group chose its representatives as it wished, the English opting for another election, the French retaining their present members. Louis Riel remained president, with William O'Donoghue as treasurer, and Thomas Bunn and Louis Schmidt as secretaries. Most institutions, offices, and officeholders in place under the HBC regime were reinstated, with Sheriff Henry McKenney, Coroner C.J. Bird, Postmaster Andrew Bannatyne, and Customs Collectors John Sutherland and Roger Goulet all being restored to their former positions.

The courts were also reinstated, but in slightly altered form:

> The General Quarterly Court to be held same as before; five Petty Courts to be held as below:
>
> Lower Court – Parish of St. Andrews
> Middle " – Court House, Fort Garry
> Upper " – White Horse Plains
> Oak Point Court
> St. Anns do.[34]

The latter two courts were new, and there were some changes in the judiciary. James Ross replaced John Black as "Chief Justice" of the General Court,[35] and in the petty courts "all justices retain places except William Dease, who is supplanted by Norbert Larance."[36] Only a few of those measures were instantly implemented – most awaited confirmation and refinement by the yet-to-be-created legislative body – but it was a promising agenda.

Delighted with this apparent resolution of Red River's longstanding divisions, President Riel promised to free the political prisoners, starting with the immediate release of McTavish, Cowan, and Bannatyne. As at the inception of the first Provisional Government two months previously, celebratory firearm and cannon salvos shattered the icy air, supplemented this time by bonfires, and by fireworks originally acquired by Dr Schultz to welcome governor-to-be William McDougall. "Enthusiasm reigned everywhere," Begg wrote, and "a regular drunk commenced, in which everyone seemed to join ... till about four o'clock in the morning."[37] Although President Riel did not join in the general bacchanal, he did "drink a good horn of brandy" with Andrew Bannatyne upon the latter's release, in the hope of restoring good relations with an important Métis sympathizer.[38] The gesture succeeded.

All that remained was to choose Red River's delegation to Ottawa, elect English representatives to the new legislature, and release the remaining prisoners. The final session of the Convention of 40 accomplished the first task easily, selecting Father Ritchot for the French, Judge John Black for the English, and to the surprise and dismay of many, Alfred H. Scott for both the English and Americans of Winnipeg. Significantly, though they may not have realized it, the envoys were told to delay departure until after the new legislature met.[39] The English legislators were soon elected. The third task – setting political prisoners free – took longer, however, and had regrettable consequences. Sixteen prisoners were released on 12 February upon swearing to keep the peace. A number of others hesitated to take the oath,[40] but by 15 February most of the holdouts had signed and were set free. In the meantime, though, a foolhardy relief mission was under way.

COUNTERCOUP

Captain Charles Boulton, the second-in-command of Colonel J.S. Dennis's surveying crew, remained at Portage la Prairie after Dennis, allegedly disguised as a woman, fled. Also at the Portage were the escapees Charles Mair and Thomas Scott, attempting to organize an armed rescue of the remaining prisoners. Once a sizable group of settlers had signed up, Mair and Scott persuaded Boulton, against his better judgment, to lead the incursion; and on 10 February – the day the new Provisional Government was formed – a ragtag amateur army set out for the Forks, arriving at Headingley the following day.

When word of Boulton's expedition reached the Forks, he was advised by sympathizers in Winnipeg to remain at Headingley to see whether Riel would release the prisoners voluntarily, as promised. On the night of 14 February, however, with many prisoners still in custody, Boulton decided to attack in concert with another, larger assault force assembled at St Andrew's by Dr Schultz. The latter had escaped from the Upper Fort in January.[41] At 4:00 AM on 15 February, therefore, the Portage contingent, carrying ladders to scale the fort walls,[42] skirted quietly around Winnipeg to rendezvous with Schultz's men at Kildonan, a little to the north of the village.[43] An outraged Begg reported that "Prince's Indians are also there, and have torches prepared to set fire to Fort Garry."[44] By daybreak, Boulton and Schultz were planning their joint assault.

When the Provisional Government released its remaining prisoners later that day, however, the Canadians called off their attack, their mission having been accomplished peaceably, and Begg noted, "another danger to the Settlement had passed."[45] His relief was short-lived. A St Norbert Métis called Norbert Parisien, captured by the Canadians on 15 February, escaped the next day, shooting a popular young man named John Sutherland in the process. When recaptured soon afterward, Parisien was severely beaten. Both he and Sutherland subsequently died of their wounds – the first fatalities of the Red River uprising.

"The excitement now became great," Begg wrote. "Shops were shut, and such things as books and money were put in places of safety – as it was feared the English party ... would come up and attack Fort Garry. Women and children were sent out of the town in several cases – and all looked forward to a general fight commencing."[46] As hurried preparations were made to defend the Upper Fort and the St Boniface Cathedral across the river, Métis scouts were sent "in every direction." Riel sent a message to the would-be counterinsurgents, assuring them that his prisoners had indeed been released, under oath to keep the peace. He reminded them that representatives of all parishes had joined in the new Provisional Government, and warned them that he and his followers were prepared to defend themselves. Predicting that "horrible civil war" would be "the destruction of this country," he asked, "Who will now come and destroy the Red River Settlement?"[47]

Whether due to Riel's message, the common sense of the outnumbered, ill-provisioned, poorly armed raiders, or both, the counter-rebels announced that evening that they would disperse – but would retain possession of the Lower Fort. The next morning – 17 February – Captain Boulton and forty-seven of his men were spotted crossing the prairie from Kildonan to the Portage Trail. Although they were on their way home, they passed relatively close to Fort Garry, and some of their weapons were provocatively evident. Whether genuinely concerned that

Boulton's troops posed a threat or simply stung by their bravado, the Métis intercepted them, and Alexander Begg said "everyone expected a fight." However, Boulton surrendered peaceably and was imprisoned with all his men. Although relief was general, Begg was concerned that as a result of the escapade, there was again "a gulf between the two sides."[48]

EXECUTION: FEIGNED, THREATENED, ACTUAL

Although Begg's pessimism about future French-English cooperation would prove exaggerated in the long run, for the time being tension remained so high in some areas of the settlement that the Métis leadership felt it necessary to adopt a tougher stance toward their opponents. On the morning Boulton and his men were imprisoned, a rumour swept the settlement to the effect that William Gaddy, an English Halfbreed captive and former messenger for the Canadians, had been executed. Although Begg and others were skeptical, and the facts were never fully established, Gaddy was never again seen in the settlement. When he later turned up in the United States, it was concluded that Riel had feigned Gaddy's execution as a warning to others, and had then spirited him across the border.[49] The president may also have been bluffing when, on 18 February, he caused Captain Boulton to be tried by a drumhead court, and sentenced to death, for leading the counterinsurgency. He subsequently allowed himself to be persuaded by Donald A. Smith and others to grant Boulton a reprieve[50] in return for Smith's cooperation in convincing English parishes to participate in the new Provisional Government.[51]

But beneath the bluffing was stony determination on Riel's part to demonstrate the strength of his government. While debating Boulton's execution with Smith, Riel told him the Canadians "had laughed at and despised the French Halfbreeds, believing that they would not dare to take the life of anyone, ... [making it] impossible to ... establish order in the country. An example must therefore be made."[52] So the next time someone was condemned to death by a Métis court martial, Louis Riel refused to back away from the grim example he felt was needed.

Thomas Scott, a previous escapee reincarcerated as a leading member of Boulton's expedition, was making a nuisance of himself: disobeying and insulting his captors and inspiring some of his fellow prisoners to follow suit. Word of Scott's troublemaking had got abroad,[53] and soon after, matters having evidently escalated gravely, Begg reported,

> Thomas Scott, one of the prisoners, was condemned to be shot today at twelve o'clock. This was not believed at first ..., [but] when it became known that the lumber and nails had been procured for his coffin, people began to realize it ... [A] large crowd gathered around the side door leading to Fort Garry. Scott was then brought out – it is said he prayed as he walked. A bandage was then put over his eyes, and he knelt ... On a given signal, four of the guns fired (two missing fire), and Scott fell forward, pierced in four places. He was not yet dead, but struggled on the ground. The [French] Canadian [member of the firing squad] then went up and shot Scott – the ball from the revolver passed in at one ear and passed out at his mouth. The corpse was then put in a rough coffin, and placed in one of the bastions.[54]

What had brought about this tragedy? Why had Riel not intervened to prevent it, as he had for Gaddy and Boulton?[55] In those cases, the president had allowed himself to be dissuaded, but this time neither Donald A. Smith nor priests from St Boniface could move him.[56] What was different this time? The offensive conduct for which Scott was said to be punished did not, by any reasonable standard, justify the supreme penalty. He had allegedly been "rough and abusive to the guards, and insulting to [Riel]," and as a result other prisoners were following his example, making it "difficult to withhold the guards from retaliating."[57] But all prisoners were securely held, and Scott, already in irons, could easily have been isolated by solitary confinement. In no way could his offensive behaviour equal the seriousness of Charles Boulton's actions in leading a large military assault against the only effective government of the settlement. Why was Boulton reprieved and Scott not?

The real reason for killing Scott[58] must have been, as with Boulton's proposed execution, a perceived need to persuade both Canada and the local population that the Provisional Government of Assiniboia was a power to be reckoned with. "We must make Canada respect us," Riel told Smith,[59] echoing his earlier assertion of the need for an "example." When Smith objected that Scott would not provide much of an example, being "a rash, thoughtless man whom none cared to have anything to do with," Riel may have thought the very fact that Scott was not such a "fine fellow" like Boulton made him an expendable candidate for sacrifice. He concluded the interview with the words "He must die."[60]

John Milton called necessity "the tyrant's plea"; but many successful politicians, whether or not considered tyrants, are sometimes compelled by what they deem necessitous circumstances to do things they would consider unacceptable in other situations. Whether they get away with it when discovered depends on public opinion sharing their assessment of the need. In this case, while Riel may have accurately gauged the views of the local majority, he grossly underestimated the impact Thomas Scott's execution would have on Ontario voters and Ottawa politicians. John Schultz and Charles Mair, having escaped from the settlement in heroic circumstances, were already heading east to spread their outrage.

"PEACE REIGNS IN OUR MIDST"

It would be some time, however, before the consequences of Louis Riel's monumental misjudgment manifested themselves. In the meantime, there was much governing to do. Dr Cowan's home at Upper Fort Garry was commandeered as "Government House," and was furnished with items confiscated from Dr Schultz's premises.[61] Thanks in part to the efforts of Donald Smith, Anglican archdeacon John Maclean, and most of the Protestant clergy, the reluctant English parishes were persuaded to elect representatives to the new assembly, and Begg's journal for 26 February recorded that "[t]he whole Settlement has now joined the Provisional Government."[62]

The first meeting of the new Governing Council convened on 9 March; but even before that Louis Riel took some significant steps on the sole basis of his authority as president. For example, on 5 March – the day after Scott's death – he issued an order that "the Town of Winnipeg be ... hereafter the capital of the North West." He also defined the boundaries of the town, and revised the electoral representation that had been agreed upon for it by the Convention of 40.[63]

The next day, anxious to put the best possible spin on Scott's execution, the president ordered *New Nation* editor Henry Robinson to delay publication of the paper until its account of that event was officially approved.[64] Begg commented that the newspaper had become "the Government organ ... controlled completely by Riel."[65] And when the president stopped publication again on 18 March – being dissatisfied with a report of Bishop A.A. Taché's address to the new Provisional Governing Council – Robinson "resigned his position as editor ..., utterly disgusted with it."[66] The paper would resume publication two weeks later under the editorship of the more malleable Thomas Spence. While its political voice would thereafter remain consonant with that of Riel and his colleagues, the paper's journalistic qualities under Spence's editorship and Coldwell's paid professionalism were higher than the settlement had seen for quite some time.

The Governing Council, which now called itself the Legislative Assembly of Rupert's Land, endeavoured vigorously to restore normality, provide effective interim government, and begin revising local laws for future use. Never was there any doubt that the area's future lay with Canada, so long as the settlers' just demands were met; and there was now confidence on that score. When, early in its first session, the assembly received a visit from Bishop Taché, recently returned from Rome via London and Ottawa, its members greeted with cheers his assurances of Canada's willingness to accommodate local needs. The Provisional Government had been taking prisoners again, but when Taché proposed that half of them be released as a gesture of good will, Riel immediately agreed. According to Begg, Riel also said "he would give up his place willingly and joyfully as President as soon as a proper Governor came."[67]

By the time it prorogued on 26 March, that first legislative session had enacted laws to establish a military force of fifty, regulate the perennially troublesome hay privilege lands, pay members of the assembly, and provide for "administration of public justice." All former laws of Assiniboia were declared in force until amended, and former officeholders were reappointed. No courts were to be held, however, until after the second legislative session, more than a month later.[68] Between sessions, three legislative committees were to draft a constitution for Red River, examine the hay privilege fully, and revise the settlement's laws.

In early April, President Riel permitted the HBC's commercial operations to resume in return for certain benefits, including recognition of the Provisional Government, an immediate loan of £3,000 (plus £2,000 in future if needed) and £4,000 worth of supplies, governmental use of certain buildings, and putting HBC notes back in circulation.[69] Those terms being an "offer it could not refuse," the company agreed.[70] A few days later, a Riel proclamation[71] announced, "[T]he Government pardons all those whom political differences led astray only for a time[72] ... [P]ublic highways are open, and the Hudson['s] Bay Company can now resume business ... [P]eace reigns in our midst this day." The iron fist remained in the velvet glove, of course: "Public authority is now strong ... [and] the Government will treat with all the severity of the laws those who dare again to compromise the public safety." Concerned that Indians and others living beyond the bounds of Assiniboia might be incited to oppose the new Rupert's Land government, the president addressed a special proclamation to them, announcing that his regime "is today master of the situation ..., has ... succeeded in restoring order and pacifying the country ..., [and] has inaugurated very advantageous negotiations with the Canadian Government and with the Hudson's Bay Company." "We possess today ... almost half a continent."[73]

To symbolize the return to near-normal conditions, and to discourage those who still favoured US annexation, Riel decided on 20 April to replace the fleur-de-lis–shamrock flag of the Provisional Government with a Union Jack – a move that Begg thought caused the president's popularity to rise 50 per cent among the English. It was highly unwelcome, however, to Irish American William O'Donoghue, who ordered the Jack taken down as soon as he saw it. A temper tantrum on Riel's part got the British flag back up the pole; but the president did permit the former banner to be flown "under" that of the mother country. O'Donohue's supporters, lacking a second flagstaff, accordingly confiscated the one that had formerly borne the absent Dr Schultz's oversized "Canada" flag and erected it for their ensign within Fort Garry's walls. Since the Schultz mast was taller than the other, further controversy ensued; but both flags eventually fluttered in what the president considered a proper juxtaposition. The Union Jack's ropes were cut overnight by parties unknown, however; and it was 28 April before it was restored to its proper place of honour. Alexander Begg's wife's amused response to these solemn emblematic exercises was to run one of her shawls up a pole in front of the Begg home, causing a concerned scout to be "sent up from Fort Garry to see what it was."[74]

NEGOTIATING PROVINCEHOOD

The Provisional Government having brought "more confidence generally amongst the people"[75] at home, its next major task was to negotiate entry into Canadian Confederation on acceptable terms. Two of the settlement's three negotiators – Father Ritchot and Alfred H. Scott – were eager to be ambassadors (although Scott seemed to consider it little more than a lark); but the third man chosen, and the most credible with eastern authorities – Judge John Black – vacillated. On 16 February, five days after being named to the team, Black resigned, citing the ill health of his sister, with whom he lived.[76] Although many tried to persuade him otherwise, he had not withdrawn his resignation by 16 March – two days before Donald A. Smith was slated to return to Canada. The always persuasive Smith descended on Black that day, in company with Andrew McDermot's increasingly prominent son Henry;

and Colonel De Salaberry arrived later the same day, bent on the same mission.[77] Those visits tipped the scale, and it was announced on 19 March that the former recorder would be part of the delegation after all. He and his sister set off for Canada on 24 March, Ritchot and Scott having departed the previous day.[78]

The List of Rights agreed upon by the Convention of 40 was well known by Ottawa authorities. Donald Smith and other Canadian representatives had intimated, in fact, that most of those items were likely to be approved. But the list carried east by the Red River delegation differed markedly from the original.[79] Both lists contained twenty items,[80] and many of them, such as equal use of French and English in official communications and local ownership of public lands, were substantially similar. In several important respects, however, the two lists diverged. The most important additions were the two demands – provincial status and annulment of the HBC's surrender agreement – that Riel had failed to persuade the Convention of 40 to adopt. Another noteworthy change, though not included in the revised List of Rights, was a revised name for the new province. Although "North West Territories," "Rupert's Land," and "Assiniboia" had all been approved previously by the Provisional Government, Begg noted on 31 March, "It is rumoured that instead ... this is to be called the Province of Manitoba."[81]

These alterations and additions appear to have been made in secret. Certainly, the Legislative Assembly was never asked for approval. The journal of Alexander Begg, who was always remarkably well informed about settlement goings-on, and assiduous in recording them, contains only two other brief references to the changes. One, on 27 March, states, "It is said Reverend Mr. Ritchot has certain instructions entrusted to him in addition to the Bill of Rights which are not publicly known."[82] Begg had also noted on 21 March that "Riel is busy preparing the papers for the delegates to Canada,"[83] but there is no indication that he realized the president was clandestinely, and perhaps unilaterally, raising the stakes in Red River's pending poker game with Canada. An intention to do so must have been the reason Riel delayed the delegates' departure until after the Convention of 40 was replaced by the new Provisional Government, of which he was president.

What right had Riel to make those changes without consulting the peoples' elected representatives? While his conduct contrasted strongly with his democratic rhetoric, treaty negotiation has always been an executive function in most political systems. Certainly, he defied the Convention of 40 and kept the Legislative Assembly in the dark. But politics rarely ever involves either fair play or full disclosure. Besides, Louis Riel had given the Convention of 40 fair warning when it rejected his proposed amendments in February, stating that "the Convention had beaten him this time, but he would beat them yet."[84]

The Provisional Government's emissaries were preceded by others from the west.[85] William McDougall was back in his House of Commons seat, for instance, estranged from the government that had so severely reprimanded him for botching his attempted entry to Assiniboia, and determined to resist concessions to those who had barred his access. Commissioner Donald A. Smith presented his report to the government on 12 April.[86] Then came John Schultz and Charles Mair, whose provocative presence would have grave and lingering consequences. The arrival in Toronto of the latter eloquent refugees from Assiniboia caused the smouldering anger ignited by Thomas Scott's execution to flare fiercely. The pair harangued an outraged crowd of more than 10,000 in Toronto's market square on 7 April[87] and then carried their incendiary message to similar gatherings throughout Ontario. When the English Canadian press took up the chant to bring "murderer Riel" to justice, Sir John A. Macdonald and his cabinet knew that negotiating with the Red River delegates had become a vastly more challenging task than anticipated. Although it was not well known, the Canadian government already had a gun pointed at one side of its head by a British edict that the United Kingdom would not supply the troops and funds needed to dispatch a military expedition to the prairies unless Canada reached agreement with the Red River envoys. Now it faced an equally daunting threat from the other side: if they conceded too much to the insurgents, they could expect intense opposition at the polls.

Worried about possible vigilante violence against the Assiniboia delegates upon their arrival in Ontario, the Canadian government ordered Gilbert McMicken, the head of the Dominion Police, to meet Ritchot and Scott at the New York border and escort them safely to Ottawa. McMicken did so just four days after the monster demonstration in Toronto. Black, travelling on his own, proceeded via Detroit with no difficulty. The delegates' reception difficulties were not over, however. The day after getting to Ottawa, Alfred Scott was arrested and jailed overnight on the authority of a warrant issued by a Toronto magistrate charging that he and Ritchot had conspired in the murder of Thomas Scott. Father Ritchot surrendered himself the next morning, whereupon both men were released on bail. Some days later, a higher-level judge declared the Toronto warrant to be invalid; but a second warrant soon brought Ritchot and Scott back into the clutches of the Ontario courts. Only when a Crown attorney, pressured by federal authorities, dropped all charges against the men were they free to get on with their mission. Although not seriously harmed or hampered by this legal harassment, the Red River delegates had no illusions about their popularity.

Nor were their reception problems yet over. The Canadian government realized that it could not be seen to formally recognize and negotiate with representatives of a rebel regime. Yet its own commissioners had invited the delegation to Ottawa, and had even offered to pay their expenses. And the British government was demanding that the negotiations proceed. What to do? Sir John found a way – informing Parliament that the visitors were representatives of the *people*, not of the *government*, of the "North-West." When Ritchot demanded a written acknowledgment of the delegates' recognition, he received one describing his colleagues and himself as "delegates from the North-West to the Government of the Dominion of Canada"; and in keeping with the allegedly informal nature of the discussions, they were conducted at the private home of the prime minister's Quebec lieutenant, Georges-Étienne Cartier.

When bargaining finally got under way on 25 April, it proceeded swiftly. On the federal side, Cartier played the leading role, although Macdonald was usually present and active (only once "indisposed" due to drink). Although Judge Black was the most senior member of the western delegation and had the best rapport with the federal representatives, its leader was Father Ritchot, who exerted polite but unrelenting pressure throughout the meetings to gain what he and his colleagues had been instructed to achieve. Scott apparently contributed little. By 3 May an agreement had been reached on every demand that would ever receive legislative expression; and a draft Manitoba Act – the constitution of the new province – was introduced in the House of Commons that day. Although, as expected, the bill encountered much opposition, it ran the legislative gauntlet quickly, receiving royal assent on 12 May. It would come into force on the day the territory was transferred to Canada.

The Manitoba Act of 1870[88] provided for what was popularly dubbed the "Postage Stamp Province." It was a good deal smaller than greater Assiniboia, and Lilliputian compared to the balance of the former Rupert's Land. The latter expanse became a territory, known initially as the North-Western Territory, under federal jurisdiction. Manitoba was allocated four elected members and two senators in the Parliament of

Canada. The provincial legislature was bicameral, with a twenty-four-member elected Legislative Assembly and a seven-man appointed Legislative Council. English and French could be used in the legislature and courts, and both languages were required in the official documents of those bodies. The right to establish publicly funded denominational schools appeared to be guaranteed, and residents were assured ownership of all lands possessed by them before provincehood. The legislation promised 1.4 million acres of land "for the benefit of the families of the Halfbreed residents." In addition to those written constitutional guarantees, the Red River delegates were assured verbally that there would be an amnesty for those who had participated in the illegal uprising. The only obvious major failure of the western negotiators concerned ownership of public lands, which were to be federal, not provincial as in all other provinces. Although many of Canada's promises would be nullified or diminished over time by pettifogging legal interpretations and outright rejections, the agreement seemed at the time to be an extraordinary achievement. And when, back at Red River on 24 June, Father Ritchot reported to the Legislative Assembly of Rupert's Land, that body unanimously ratified the constitution of the fetal province, warmly praising the delegates' apparently successful efforts. Alexander Begg called it "the turning point in the affairs of the Settlement."[89]

On the previous day, in London, Queen Victoria had signed a proclamation[90] bringing the negotiations to legal fruition. After acknowledging the surrender of Rupert's Land to the Crown by the HBC, and payment of the agreed purchase price by Canada to the company, the proclamation formally transferred the territory to Canada, effective 15 July 1870. Although it was that proclamation and the Manitoba Act that gave it legal birth; Manitoba's real constitutional roots, democratically and politically speaking, lay in the deliberations of the Convention of 40, the Riel-amended List of Rights, the Ottawa negotiations, and ratification by Rupert's Land's provisional legislature.

GOVERNING

Although Manitoba sprang into legal existence on 15 July 1870, Canadian authorities would not arrive to take up their responsibilities until late August, and Father Ritchot told Riel that Canada expected him to govern in the meantime.[91] The president did not need to be asked. He had long dreamed of graciously handing over, to a legally and democratically legitimate lieutenant governor, the reins of a smoothly functioning local government. And the introverted, impecunious, miller's son was enjoying the trappings of leadership. His quarters in Dr William Cowan's former residence at Fort Garry, now fitted out with confiscated furniture William McDougall had intended for his viceregal home, were said to be "magnificent."[92] Convivial banquets, sometimes entertained by Father Dugas's boys' band,[93] eased the strain of his constant responsibility. He sometimes abused power, as when imprisoning a man "for speaking disrespectfully to the President";[94] and Alexander Begg disapproved of his "putting on so much style as he is now doing." But although Begg thought Riel "could not rule very long here,"[95] the president was determined to govern until Canada's lieutenant governor arrived. He almost did.

In point of fact, Riel and his colleagues had involved themselves in the day-to-day governance of the settlement almost ever since proclaiming the first Provisional Government on 8 December 1869.

They had begun with policing. The first concern of Riel's "Adjutant-General" Ambroise Lépine was to maintain a strong military arm to defend the insurrection from attack, but as that threat diminished, the army shrank, and the remaining soldiers shifted their role to providing routine police protection for the community. When, on 26 January 1870, "Jimmy from Cork" got drunk at the Fireman's Ball and became "boisterous," he was "put into jail at Fort Garry" by Riel's men.[96] On 23 March a troublesome individual – a Métis – was arrested for being drunk and disorderly at Fort Garry, and when five of the man's friends protested the arrest, they too were taken into custody.[97] Begg's description, a week later, of a saloon brawl in which a man was seriously injured, noted, "These rows will however be stopped shortly, as we are to have policemen in the town";[98] and by 3 April four such officers were on duty.[99] On 21 May, Begg wrote, "The police are active, and have made a number of arrests," concluding that "[t]aking it altogether, the Settlement has been more quiet this season than it ever was before in the shape of drinking and fighting."[100]

Riel's men were not always as competent policemen as the constables they replaced. On 14 June fugitive murder suspect Ryder Larsen[101] was spotted in town, and the Métis police moved to arrest him. But, Begg tells us, "as they went into the door he jumped out of the back window."[102] The Provisional Government did, however, improve upon the previous detention facilities. The notoriously insecure courthouse jail was replaced by one of Fort Garry's bastions as the settlement's prison, and the failure of an attempted jailbreak in July demonstrated the wisdom of that decision.[103] In respect of law enforcement, at least, the new regime was more effective than the old.

Although the office of sheriff was preserved, those appointed to it seem not to have performed the sheriff's traditional law enforcement responsibilities. When the 1869 uprising began, Sheriff Henry McKenney opted to support Riel and the US annexationists to whom Riel appeared sympathetic at that point.[104] He remained in Riel's good graces for some time thereafter, being appointed sheriff in February 1870.[105] How much work, if any, he did as such is uncertain, however, since law enforcement was the responsibility of Adjutant General Lépine. By May 1870 the prospect of American annexation was miniscule, and McKenney, like Enos Stutsman before him, must have realized he was backing a lost cause. Moreover, his business affairs were shaky: a Lake Winnipeg sawmill operation had failed, and creditors were pressing. He accordingly resigned as sheriff, shipped his sawmill machinery to Pembina, and established a new mill and store there. A few months later, he was chosen sheriff of Pembina County.[106]

Some time after McKenney's resignation as sheriff, the Provisional Government appointed Robert Tait, whom the *New Nation* called "a gentleman who has made himself popular among all classes by his obliging and social disposition," to the position.[107] That Tait was not appointed until late June, simultaneously with the opening of the courts and long after his predecessor left the settlement, supports the view that the Provisional Government looked to the sheriff for court-related services only, not for law enforcement. Tait's association with the Provisional Government did him no harm. His business career flourished after provincehood, and he soon became a justice of the peace.[108]

The fact that the Métis army was diminishing in numbers and assuming greater civil responsibilities did not mean it ceased entirely to have military duties. As the rivers cleared of ice in the spring of 1870, a need arose to monitor incoming traffic, and Begg wrote that "[s]oldiers for Pembina are on their way there in flat boats." He added on 13 May that "[a] number of men have been despatched by Riel to Pembina to act there as a guard."[109] On 10 June the Pembina contingent disputed the location of the 49th parallel with US troops, and were ordered by the Americans to move their operations farther north. On 24 June it barred a group of Canadian families on their way to Red River in a flatboat.[110]

While Lépine retained overall command of his dwindling army, an interesting addition was made to its officer corps in the person of Captain Norbert Gay, a colourful French military officer who showed up at Red River in January 1870, won Riel's confidence, and was eventually given military command of Fort Garry and put to work drilling the troops in martial skills. Although the men were clumsy in artillery exercises, they delighted the captain with their buffalo-hunt marksmanship from the backs of galloping horses.[111] Gay served Riel until almost the end of his regime, but departed hurriedly to serve his own country when he learned of the Franco-Prussian War.[112]

Reports and rumours of Indian violence continued to be received from Portage la Prairie, White Horse Plain, and even the Saulteaux village at St Peter's on the lower Red River, where residents were expressing resentment toward the Métis. Although well equipped to handle the situation militarily, the Provisional Government relied instead on the persuasive skills of James McKay, who had a strong rapport with Aboriginal people. McKay was appointed "Indian Commissioner" by Riel, and on 15 April 1870 the *New Nation* reported, "[T]hrough the influence of the Commissioner with the Sioux, a large party of them have left the country."[113]

Postal service was re-established early. Former Winnipeg postmaster (and Riel sympathizer) Andrew Bannatyne was the first previous officeholder requested – the fourth day the first Provisional Government existed – to resume his duties.[114] While control of the mails doubtless enhanced the rebels' powers of surveillance, renewed postal links benefited everyone. Another former officeholder whose essential public functions continued almost uninterrupted – albeit without Provisional Government sanction at first – was the coroner, Dr C.J. Bird. When the body of Thomas Johnson was discovered in late December, Dr Bird convened an inquest, and the jury decided that the deceased had been killed by Winnipeg photographer Ryder Larsen.[115] Bird was subsequently reinstated as coroner formally, but there seems to have been no interruption of his de facto service.[116]

By the spring of 1870 at least, the Provisional Government was also attending to public works. On 1 April, Alexander Begg remarked, "The French ... have been at work for some days on the floating bridge over the Assiniboine."[117] After yielding the governmental helm to Riel, John Bruce, a carpenter by trade, "remained on the governing Council, serving as Commissioner of Public Works. Under his direction, the ice on the Assiniboine River was cut away from the pontoons supporting the bridge so that the spring breakup of 1870 would not remove it. Repairs were made to other bridges."[118]

When a need for other forms of regulation arose, it was dealt with on an ad hoc basis. One example was a simple but forceful letter from Riel in February 1870 to (sheriff-to-be) Robert Tait, owner of a grist mill that had been closed since the Métis uprising: "Sir: You are hereby requested to run your mill, as the people are suffering from it. Yours, Louis Riel, President."[119] Another concerned professional services: "A French doctor ... has been compelled to stop practising by Riel on account of his being proved incompetent."[120] A third was the Provisional Government's response to the first report of the prairie smallpox outbreak that would later become a major challenge for Manitoba's fledgling authorities. Begg noted on 29 April that the government was taking steps to prevent contaminated buffalo robes being brought to the settlement,[121] the same target on which provincial/territorial authorities would later focus.

The final session of the second Provisional Legislature was impressively successful. The English and French segments of the assembly developed a grudging and cautious respect for each other, working together, day by day, to provide essential public services for their community, revising its laws, and ultimately ratifying the deal their delegates negotiated with the Canadian government. Any doubt as to the sincere desire on all sides to make the Provisional Government work would be dispelled by William Coldwell's verbatim transcripts in the *New Nation* of the polite, yet forthright, legislative debates. On the final day of that session, in late May 1870, for example, it was decided after much thoughtful discussion that those who held public office under the Council of Assiniboia, but had not been paid for their final months' services, should now be compensated, regardless of the individual's political stripes. The necessary funds were raised by collecting customs duties left unpaid when the HBC government collapsed.[122] Next, maintenance budgets were set, with more careful debate, for roads, bridges, and ferries throughout the settlement. And finally, with time running short, the Executive Council was authorized to resolve a number of important matters the assembly had been too busy to consider.[123]

The assembly's debates leave the strong impression of a hardworking, competent, politically divided but collegial group of legislators. They were at least as effective as the Council of Assiniboia – and were democratic to boot. Miss Black, the judge's sister, had watched the often raucous Manitoba Act debates in the Parliament of Canada, and remarked to Father Ritchot afterward how much more "well bred" were the proceedings she had observed in the Legislative Assembly of the settlement's Provisional Government.[124]

Even more impressive than their deportment was the quality of the work produced by the provisional legislators. Their consolidation of the

Laws of Assiniboia[125] offers a fine example. The assembly's first session had decided the laws needed to be updated, and had appointed a drafting committee to produce, with assistance of "Chief Justice" James Ross, a draft revision for adoption at the second session. Taking account of the numerous amendments made to the Laws of Assiniboia since their last consolidation and publication in 1862, but not stopping there, the committee proposed numerous revisions, which the second assembly scrutinized carefully before approving. While most of the changes were matters of detail, a few were substantial. For example, in place of the 1862 proscription of supplying liquor to "any person popularly known as an Indian, or any member of an Indian nation," the 1870 revision prohibited supplying it to "any unsettled or uncivilized Indian," recognizing that some members of the Aboriginal population were able to use intoxicants as responsibly as anyone else.[126] Overall, the Provisional Legislature's consolidation and revision of local laws was a workable experience-based body of common-sense rules for regulating the burgeoning, forward-looking frontier community Red River had become.

The one department of government that lagged markedly behind the others in returning to business as usual was the judiciary. Although both the Convention of 40 and the first session of the Provisional Legislature had called for the appointment of James Ross as chief justice and the reinstatement of most pre-uprising magistrates, the reopening of the courts was postponed – initially until the opening of the second session of the legislature in late April and eventually until late June. As it turned out, only the "District Courts" (former petty courts) would ever sit again.

One reason for postponing the opening of the courts seems to have been a desire to have the local laws brought up to date before judges were called upon to apply them. And after that there was a need to make numerous logistical arrangements, such as renting courtroom space, hiring court personnel, printing court forms, acquiring record books, and appointing magistrates (who, despite the initial wholesale reinstatement, ended up being engaged on a one-by-one basis, perhaps for reasons of patronage). There was no sheriff to supervise such details because, as we have seen, although Henry McKenney was reappointed to that post, he resigned and moved to Pembina without doing much, and his replacement, Robert Tait, was not appointed until just before the lower courts opened in late June.[127]

Those reasons for delay applied to both the Supreme Court (former General Quarterly Court) and the district courts; but there were additional factors affecting the senior tribunal, the most important being the complex and volatile character of James Ross. The chief-justice-designate had fallen out of favour with the Riel regime. Or perhaps it had fallen out of favour with him.

Ross had been the chief spokesman for the English during the debates of the Convention of 40, crossing verbal sabres with Riel on many occasions. Those duels engendered what seemed like mutual respect – perhaps just by Riel for Ross – and led to the latter's designation as chief justice. Ostensibly, Ross returned Riel's respect – to the outrage of many of his constituents.[128] When drunk, however – which Ross often was – the enigmatic journalist-lawyer often talked from the other side of his mouth, denouncing the Provisional Government and declaring that he would resign. While in his cups on one occasion, he claimed to have been playing "a double game."[129]

The latter remark was attributed to Ross just ten days after he was formally sworn in as chief justice and addressed the Legislative Assembly in that capacity. A week later, Riel wrote Ross to thank him for translating a document for the government, and asked him to "believe in my true respect for yourself."[130]

Less than three weeks after that, however, Begg's journal noted that "Riel, it appears, is averse to James Ross being on the Executive Council, and [has] proposed Mr. Bannatyne in his place."[131] Ross did not participate in Provisional Government affairs thereafter, either as chief justice or in any other capacity. That summer Begg reported his involvement in personal building projects;[132] and by August he was in Toronto, announcing to the press that he "never had anything to do with Riel's government."[133] The dismissal or defection of James Ross having left the new Supreme Court without a judge, it never sat.

How did the community get along without district (petty) courts for six months, and without a higher court for twelve? It was forced, to an extent not fully known, to make do with ad hoc informal adjudication. In fact, one of the regime's earliest instances of civil governance involved a trial held little more than a month after Riel seized power. In December 1869 a Mrs Rodway accused her neighbour Mrs Meeken of assault, and Alexander Begg reported on 21 December that "Riel had the first case of judicial trial to-day." On Christmas Eve he wrote, "The result of the trial of Mrs. Rodway v. Mrs. Meeken was damages all round: 10/ [shillings] to 20/ [shillings] each."[134] Nothing more is known of this little case, and questions abound. Did Riel himself sit in judgment? If so, was he alone? What did the award of damages mean:

that the defendant received, on balance, 10 shillings from the plaintiff? Or vice versa?

More significantly, one wonders, was this a one-of-a-kind trial, or were there others that Begg never heard of or did not bother to report? The only clue we have is Riel's complaint to former recorder John Black during the Convention of 40 debates in February 1870 that the next hearings of the General Court had not been announced.[135] Was he just making the rhetorical point that the HBC courts were now defunct? Or was he perhaps fed up with having to deal with private legal disputes? There certainly was a strong desire on all sides that courts be re-established.

Whether or not the Provisional Government directly tried any cases other than *Rodway v. Meeken*, another ad hoc procedure – arbitration – was at least occasionally employed. One such instance arose from a complaint against Charles Garrett, a familiar litigant in HBC-era courts, by a former employee named Parisien. An outspoken opponent of Riel, Garrett had been locked up as a political prisoner. While in jail, Garrett expected Parisien to be working assiduously on his behalf; but finding, upon release, that this had not been so, he refused to pay the man. Parisien then laid a complaint before President Riel, who ordered Adjutant General Lépine to deal with the matter. Lépine referred the case to arbitration by two private citizens – anglophone Andrew Bannatyne and francophone Onis Monchamp – and the arbitrators heard and decided the dispute the next morning.[136]

On 11 April 1870 Begg described another arbitrary civil legal process: "A man named Burr at the Portage being reported as about to leave for British Columbia with the intention of defrauding his creditors, a guard was sent up to attach his property, and he himself is to be brought down to answer the charges against him."[137] Burr was brought under escort to Fort Garry to be examined along with one of his creditors, Andrew Bannatyne. After being taken back to Portage to obtain his financial records, Burr was re-examined on 15 and 18 April. It is not known by whom the examinations were conducted, or what conclusion was reached, except that Burr's and his neighbour's denial that he intended to abscond seem to have been given credence.[138] One wonders whether the authorities would have been quite so vigilant if Bannatyne, a friend of the Provisional Government, had been the defendant instead of the claimant; or, indeed, if Parisien had been sued by Riel's enemy Garrett rather than vice versa.

While there is no firm evidence of the fact, there is reason to speculate that some HBC-era magistrates might, like Coroner Bird, have functioned on a consensual basis from time to time during this martial law period. Most magistrates were told, after all, by both the Convention of 40 and the first session of the Provisional Legislature, that their appointments would be renewed eventually; and interpersonal disputes requiring impartial resolution must have continued to arise during the settlement's long judicial freeze. When it was learned, in late March, that the normalization of the courts would be delayed, Begg noted "[s]ome considerable grumbling ... amongst the settlers."[139]

The community's increasingly urgent need for adjudication was underlined by a curious incident just two weeks before Begg's latter entry: "Thomas Sinclair Senior, petty magistrate under the old HBC rule, died last evening at about half past five o'clock, after a long and severe illness. His loss will be much felt. About half an hour before his death, a man called at his house, and insisted upon seeing him about a dispute. It was with difficultly that the man was prevented from seeing Mr. Sinclair, although he knew he was dying."[140] Would it be unreasonable to suppose that in other parts of the judicially deprived settlement other would-be litigants – especially those lacking rapport with or confidence in the insurgent regime – would also have approached trusted former adjudicators to resolve festering controversies? Might not clergymen have been similarly called upon?

When the Provisional Government's magistrates were finally appointed, their responsibilities commenced with their appointments, and some of them were required to exercise those responsibilities before the first full judicial sessions in late June. On 14 June, for example, magistrates Thomas Bunn, Andrew Bannatyne, and James McKay convened a preliminary hearing into the nonfatal shooting of Roderick Cook by George Raymond during what the *New Nation* called a "drunken affray." Evidence was given by both victim and accused, as well as by Dr Bird (concerning injuries) and an eyewitness to the shooting. The magistrates committed Raymond for trial at the next Supreme Court sitting and released him on bail.[141]

The *New Nation* reported only one full hearing of the new district courts – held by Bannatyne and two other magistrates at the courthouse. It is highly likely, however, that all or most of the other courts also convened about that time. The same issue of the newspaper announced that "the various magisterial commissions throughout the Settlement have been filled, and the legal business of the country will be conducted in future under the present regime with the same regularity as before any change in government." That one published district court report chronicles what seems to have been a quite routine session: "Several cases of petty debt were brought before the court, which did not occupy much time, the court adjourning at two o'clock till its next regular monthly sitting." There would never be a "next sitting" of that, or of any other, Provisional Government court, however, because that government ceased to exist before the scheduled date.

In late April 1870 President Riel had a chance to try his hand at international diplomacy. A delegation of Americans arrived, headed by former Minnesota governor William R. Marshall.[142] On its face, the visit was private, concerning a possible extension to Winnipeg of the US-based Northern Pacific Railway. Marshall represented railroad tycoon Jay Cooke, who, realizing that a Canadian line could not reach the northern prairies for a long time, was considering extending his rail network northward to Red River and beyond. Marshall was to report on construction conditions, as well as the political situation at Red River. And the political side of the mission involved more than passive observation.

Cooke was a swashbuckling entrepreneur who was considering organizing an incursion into Rupert's Land by the Fenian Brotherhood, an Irish American paramilitary organization that had recently been raiding Canadian territory in the east.[143] Louis Riel's confidante Louis Schmidt later revealed that when Marshall met with Riel the conversation included audacious offers of possible future military assistance to the Provisional Government: "The Americans ... renew[ed] their constant pressure upon us, in order to shake us from our British allegiance and draw us into the republic. Large sums of money were offered to Riel, as well as men and munitions to repel the Canadian troops in case they sought, in spite of us, to penetrate into the country."[144] As W.L. Morton has pointed out, it would have been more convenient for Cooke if his contemplated northern railroad extension could run over American rather than Canadian soil.[145]

Riel's response appears to have been as flexible as it had been to the suggestions of Enos Stutsman three or four months previously. While declining immediate acceptance, he was careful not to reject the offers, in case Canadian annexation should not occur. N.P. Langford, a member of Marshall's party, labelled the president's position "diplomatic and non-committal" and "a merit in him" as a leader.[146] The visitors nevertheless realized, on the basis of discussions with others in the settlement, that agreement between Canada and the Provisional Government was likely to occur, and that Mr Cooke would probably have to content himself with a northern rail extension on foreign soil.

Riel's strong personal preference, while keeping his options open, was to preserve the British connection. Nothing he is known to have said, and almost nothing he did, suggests otherwise. Schmidt took pains to refute the assertion of some that Bishop Taché was responsible for persuading Riel to reject the American option. "There is no doubt," he wrote, "that Bishop Taché gave his counsel ... But his Grace was preaching to the converted." The chief reason for the Provisional Legislature's swift and unanimous acceptance of Canadian annexation and for the concurrence by most settlers was that they shared what Schmidt called the president's "unchangeable fidelity, and even ... devotion, to England."[147]

How successful a governor was Louis Riel? Accolades from supporters and allies abound, of course, but the assessments of two of the president's opponents are even more telling. N.P. Langford, who might not be quite accurately called an "opponent" but did represent a competing interest in high-stakes negotiations, was deeply impressed by the skill with which Riel played the game and preserved his options, as well as by the energy and leadership he exhibited – admiring these qualities even as he was being taken in by them:

> Riel is about 28 years of age, has a fine physique, [is] of active temperament, a great worker, and I think is able to endure a great deal. He is a large man, with a high forehead (not broad), of very winning persuasive manners. And in his whole bearing energy and ready decision are prominent characteristics ... [I]n this fact lies his great powers, for I should not give him credit for great profundity. Yet he is sagacious, and I think thoroughly patriotic and ... incorruptible ...
>
> He ... said that he only desired to save his people from wrong, and to this end should do whatever was necessary. I could not but infer from this that, if Canada did not accept his terms, he would be in favor of [American] annexation; though from motives of policy he would not make his views known ... I cannot but think that Riel is secretly in favor of it, and will show his hand when the proper time comes ... With the people, and the country as a whole, ... [being] slow – 50 years behind our times – ... the influence of the leaders must be almost wholly *personal* ... [A] governor must be a hero to his valet de chambre, or he can be no hero at all ... [T]o such people, the untiring energy of Riel is a wonder: a something of which they stand in awe.[148]

The other arms-length witness to Riel's abilities – Captain William F. Butler – certainly was an opponent. Butler was a British military officer attached to the expeditionary force that would later expel Riel's government from Fort Garry. His account is a professional soldier's assessment of a grudgingly admired adversary: "It is almost refreshing to notice the ability, the energy, the determination, which up to this point has characterized all the movements of the originator and mainspring of the movement, M. Louis Riel. One hates so much to see a thing bungled that even resistance, although it border upon rebellion, becomes respectable when it is carried out with courage, energy and decision."[149]

Both Langford and Butler saw only fragments of Riel's work, of course. All historical spotlights, whether adulatory or damning, suffer from that shortcoming. When the focus is widened to illuminate as much as possible of what Riel and his colleagues actually accomplished during the nearly ten months they controlled north-central North America, what stands out most strikingly is not gallant or traitorous resistance, brilliant or brutal generalship, overdue or brazen cultural emergence, but competent government of a diverse and discontented population under very trying circumstances. When, in the vacuum left by Canada's blunders and the collapse of HBC rule, Riel assumed control, he understood that in doing so he undertook to provide sound government until normalcy returned. That responsibility was remarkably well fulfilled.

PASSAGES AND HARBINGERS

Although the months during which the Provisional Government literally "held the fort" waiting for Canadian authorities to take over were relatively uneventful, time did not stand still. Familiar figures passed from the scene; and events occurred that presaged major changes in the settlement's near future.

John Black

Former recorder John Black was already off the scene, having travelled on, after observing the Manitoba Act's passage in Ottawa, to retirement in Scotland. But he was not forgotten. While he and the other Red River delegates were negotiating provincehood with Cartier and Macdonald, Black was being discussed as a suitable candidate for the lieutenant governorship that McDougall's retreat had left open. The *New Nation* asserted in early May that Black "would indeed be the unanimous choice of the people of Red River – of all classes and creeds."[150] Two weeks later it reprinted an editorial from the *Hamilton Spectator* saying the recorder had been "agreeable to all and distasteful to none" and "exactly the Governor we need."[151] Whether Black was ever formally offered the position is not known; but the Colonial Office did ask him in August whether his resignation from the General Quarterly Court was final, presumably with a view to appointment to the Manitoba bench. Black confirmed his retirement unequivocally.[152] Thirty-one eventful years had passed since he had first travelled to the remote prairie settlement as clerk to Recorder Adam Thom, and he had no desire to return.

William McTavish

Also noteworthy was the departure of former governor McTavish. His resignation had been accepted with regret in March,[153] and Donald A. Smith was appointed in June to replace him as head of the company's North American operations.[154] On 17 May 1870 the seriously ailing fur trade veteran boarded the riverboat *International* with his family for his final journey out of the land where he had toiled with such great distinction all his adult life.[155] His hope was to spend the summer vacationing in the south of France, but it was not to be.

When he and his family reached New York, McTavish was interviewed at his hotel by an American journalist. The published account provides a shrewd assessment of the Red River population, an explanation of the uprising, and a vivid sketch of William McTavish in his final days:

> Governor Mactavish has a head like Henry Clay's, with enormous perceptive faculties. He is a gentleman of fine scientific culture and shrewd common sense ... [W]e found the Governor reclining in an easy chair, and evidently much overcome with the oppressive heat. Courteously saluting us, he said, with much effort: "Will you please make your inquiries as brief as possible, as I speak with great difficulty, and cannot hold a prolonged conversation."[156]
>
> Reporter: ... Perhaps it would be more agreeable to you to postpone the interview ...
>
> Gov. Mactavish: It is not likely that I shall ever be better, sir. Please to proceed.

McTavish declined at first to comment on the Red River insurrection, but his questioner was a skilled interviewer who, after pursuing innocuous topics for a while, slowly circled back to what he most wanted to know. This time his subject rose to the bait:

> Reporter: Were the Scotch inclined to be rebellious?
>
> Gov. Mactavish: No, nor were any of the inhabitants. The native population – the Halfbreeds – are peaceable. They are ignorant, but they are trustworthy, and are men of good common sense.
>
> Reporter: There does not seem to have been any material there for a rebellion, then?
>
> Gov. Mactavish: None at all. The Canadian traders who came up there were the only discontented persons. They were adventurers, with hardly a copper to rub, and no character. McKenney was one of them, and Schultz was another.

Schultz, the frontier elder explained, was "looked upon ... as a bad man" by most settlers, and when incoming Governor McDougall "took Schultz as his principal adviser," the choice "set the people against him." Then, after McDougall's gaffe with the toothless proclamation demonstrated that Canada had no legal authority over the area as yet, "The people said, 'The old government is wiped out, and there is no new government to put in its place, so we will have a provisional government.'" "They are a practical, honest, simple people," McTavish continued,

> and do not care a farthing for official dignity or the pomp and paraphernalia of government. What a man can't do in his shirt and trowsers out there he can't do at all. The robes of office won't help them a bit. There is nothing there for a ponderous governmental machinery to operate upon. The influence of the Governor and of the magistrates must be personal, and as pervasive as the atmosphere. If the people like and trust them, they will obey them, and not otherwise. When a judge that they trust makes a decision, they accept it as the law; but when a judge that they distrust makes a decision, they will not regard it as the law. Government is a practical thing out there, to be administered for the benefit, and to meet the wants of, the people ...

> Governor Mactavish, who had been animated during his statement, seemed overcome with exhaustion, and we took our leave.

William McTavish died shortly after his ship arrived at Liverpool.[157]

Waiting in the Wings

Awaiting events near Fort Alexander, having returned from Ottawa,[158] was Donald A. Smith, poised to take over McTavish's commercial responsibilities as the HBC's senior officer in North America. There were many other hints, also, of what was soon to happen. The settlement's English Canadians were much more in evidence than previously,[159] and francophones were becoming less assertive.[160] Work on the road from Lake of the Woods recommenced under the supervision of James McKay.[161] A spurt of new construction was observed at the settlement.[162] Although Dominion Day went surprisingly unobserved, Winnipeg's resident American population staged a boisterous Fourth of July celebration three days later.[163] Manitoba's first fully qualified resident lawyer (if one overlooks Recorders Thom and Francis Johnson and the dubious Frank Larned Hunt) appeared from Quebec, in the person of Joseph Dubuc.[164] A large number of Indians arrived in expectation of the Aboriginal treaty negotiations demanded by the final List of Rights.[165] And three Métis boatmen refused to return from Norway House to Red River, so apprehensive were they about what would soon happen there.[166]

ARRIVAL AND DISILLUSIONMENT[167]

Everyone but the Americans wanted British or Canadian troops at Red River. The HBC had been trying for years to persuade the UK government to provide military protection for the settlement once more; and it was the opinion of Anglican bishop Machray that the "sole reason" for the weakness of the Council of Assiniboia, which "was neither oppressive nor unpopular," had been that "it had no military or properly-organized police force."[168] The Canadian government believed troops were needed in case it had to fight for possession of the territory it had bought from the company. Many Ontarians, outraged by Scott's execution, hoped there would be such a fight. Ordinary Assiniboians, most of them British loyalists, felt a British military presence at Red River would forestall US annexation. The UK government, long concerned about allegations of oppressive treatment of Natives by the world's last major commercial government, had decided that offering Canada military assistance on condition that local agreement be reached would take the problem off their hands. And the Provisional Government of Rupert's Land was fully prepared – indeed eager – to transfer power peacefully to British or Canadian authorities, civilian or military, as soon as possible.

The military contingent agreed upon combined regular British troops with volunteer companies from Ontario and Quebec. The recruitment of volunteers in Ontario had been wildly successful; and although the response from Quebec was disappointing, the Ontario surplus was more than sufficient to complete the contingent. Colonel Garnet J. Wolseley, an ambitious British officer, was placed in overall command of the combined "expeditionary force." Since an all-British route was imperative, road builder Simon Dawson was retained in January to do whatever was needed to complete the route from Lake Superior – which he had surveyed and partially constructed years before – sufficiently to carry an army. That road, supplemented by long stretches of Aboriginal and fur trade waterways, brought Wolseley's force, sunburned and insect-bitten, to Red River before the summer was over.

On 30 June, just before the expedition pushed inland from Prince Arthur's Landing on the west shore of Lake Superior, Colonel Wolseley composed a reassuring proclamation "To the Loyal Inhabitants of Manitoba."[169] The message gave notice that he would be "stationing some troops amongst you" but hastened to add, "Our mission is one of peace, and the sole object of the expedition is to secure Her Majesty's sovereign authority ... Justice will be impartially administered to all races and all classes, the loyal Indians and Half-breeds being as dear to our Queen as any others of Her loyal subjects." The troops would be politically and religiously impartial, Wolseley promised, affording "equal protection to the lives and property of all races and of all creeds." They would maintain "the strictest order and discipline," respect private property, pay for all supplies required, and enquire promptly into all complaints of injury.

Copies of the proclamation were dispatched to persons considered to be reliable recipients in the settlement. The first copy received by Louis Riel reached him in a dramatic fashion. On the evening of 20 July, Begg's journal recorded, "The steamer International came in ... As it rounded coming into the Assiniboine from the Red River it touched the point nearest Fort Garry when Willie Drever and a stranger jumped off. The stranger disappeared mysteriously, and William Drever went home. Soon afterwards, ... Drever was arrested on account of the suspicious actions of himself and the stranger in thus jumping off the boat. The stranger, said to be one Butler or Baker, left some baggage on the boat."[170] Drever was a known Canadian sympathizer. The "mysterious stranger," as Begg subsequently labelled the other, was the above-mentioned Captain William F. Butler, a British officer sent to the settlement via the United States by Wolseley to scout the local scene, and then to proceed eastward to meet the advancing main party. After escaping whatever Métis guards were stationed near the steamer landing, Butler headed north and found his way to some sanctuary in the lower settlement.

Two days later, Riel was handed a copy of Wolseley's proclamation, apparently found among Butler's abandoned possessions. After reading it, and finding it very much to his liking, the president decided the document should be widely dispersed and arranged for it to be printed, both in the *New Nation* and as a separate broadsheet, supervising the printing process personally. He also invited Butler to call upon him.[171] The captain placed conditions on his willingness to meet with Riel: release Drever, give Butler back his confiscated luggage, and cease flying the Provisional Government's flag from the Upper Fort. He also insisted that Riel call upon him rather than vice versa. The president agreed to all but the flag demand (the British flag having fluttered above the insurgents' banner for quite some time already); and on 23 July, when the officer arrived at the Forks to collect his bag, Riel came to see him. It was not a very important meeting, but Riel was able to explain that he intended to hand over authority peacefully to the Canadians when they arrived. When Butler continued his journey eastward to meet and report to Colonel Wolseley, therefore, he had little reason to doubt Riel's peaceful intentions.

Although Riel's words of amity were unquestionably sincere, it is highly doubtful that Wolseley meant what he said when he claimed, "Our mission is one of peace." As they approached the settlement, his men became increasingly vociferous in their expressions of hostility to Riel and the Provisional Government. And their commander appears to have done little, if anything, to discourage their fervour. Riel, although holding to his resolve not to resist Wolseley's arrival, grew rapidly more nervous as, in late August, the troops entered the mouth of the Red River and were heard making menacing noises as they advanced southward.

The new lieutenant governor, Adams Archibald, was nowhere in sight despite Riel's having invited him long ago to receive the transfer of civil authority in advance of the troop arrival.[172] Nor had the promised amnesty ever arrived. And when Bishop Taché, who had rushed back to Ottawa to enquire about the amnesty's whereabouts, returned to the settlement on 22 August, he bore no more than verbal assurances that Wolseley's mission was friendly.

The president was receiving multiplying reports to the contrary. On the evening of 23 August, with the expeditionary force encamped somewhere between Lower Fort Garry and the Forks, Riel assembled his Executive Council and, after discussing the situation, gave orders that the Métis troops were not to be mustered. He and four others then proceeded northward on horseback, through darkness and heavy rain, to reconnoiter the bivouacked army. What they saw confirmed the scouting reports: Wolseley's men were in combat mode.

Returning to the Upper Fort about 1:00 AM, the president ordered his secretary, Louis Schmidt, to gather his papers and carry them to a place of safety. He then tried to sleep, but with little success. On the morning of 24 August, after a meagre breakfast that Riel's nervous stomach had trouble digesting, a supporter arrived on horseback with the news that the troops, now only a few miles distant, clearly intended to lynch him. Ordering the fort to be evacuated, Riel stayed on with William O'Donoghue until the others had gone, and then departed, leaving the gate open for the newcomers. After crossing the Red River, the two Provisional Government leaders paused at Bishop Taché's house long enough to tell his Lordship that he had been bamboozled by the Ottawa politicians. They then headed south, Riel to go into hiding[173] and O'Donoghue to seek, against Riel's wishes, assistance in the United States.

The reports of intended lynchings that caused Riel at the last moment to abandon his cherished dream of amicably transferring authority to Canada's representatives were accurate. Colonel Wolseley himself later acknowledged that he and his men were looking forward to "a fight" as "something that would cheer us." Discovering the fort to be empty was, he wrote, "a sad disappointment to the soldiers, who, having gone through so much toil in order to put down the rebellion, longed to be avenged upon its authors."[174] Wolseley's own intentions were no gentler: "Personally, I was glad Riel did not come out and surrender ... for I could not then have hanged him, as I might have done had I taken him prisoner when in arms against his sovereign."[175]

11

Provincehood, 1870–72

Factional violence darkened the first weeks of Canadian occupation. Despite those ugly incidents, Lieutenant Governor Adams Archibald and a handful of advisers cobbled together a rudimentary but effective administration. Their task would have been easier, however, if they had been allowed to adopt the Provisional Government's laws and institutions. Canada's responses to pressing problems were also politically selective: while Indian treaties were negotiated quickly, and compensation for the Provisional Government's opponents was promptly provided, the amnesty promised to Louis Riel's supporters was very slow in coming, and the Halfbreeds' constitutionally entrenched land guarantees were never fully honoured.

Archibald's government faced a menacing external crisis in 1871: imminent invasion by an apparently substantial army of "Fenians" organized by Riel's former colleague W.B. O'Donoghue. Although a pathetic tin-pot affair in actuality, it had serious consequences. On the positive side, the solidarity with which it was faced by most Manitobans – including Riel and the Métis – confirmed their fealty to Britain and Canada. Negatively, Archibald's public show of gratitude for Métis loyalty outraged anti-French militants, and seriously exacerbated tensions.

Those tensions probably delayed the granting of full responsible government to Manitoba; but there was in any case very much to do before a former corporate fiefdom could become a self-governing province. Creating and staffing numerous major and minor governmental organs, and producing a basic framework of laws, was laborious, time-consuming, and politically daunting work. Designing and staffing new courts took until the middle of 1872. Until then, the Hudson's Bay Company's General Quarterly Court and petty courts were temporarily resurrected, and former recorder Francis Johnson presided over the interim arrangements.

FIRST STEPS

If events had unfolded as President Riel had hoped, he would have surrendered his de facto authority to the constitutionally legitimate control of Lieutenant Governor Adams Archibald in person. But Archibald was under instructions to avoid direct dealings with the Provisional Government. He therefore ignored Riel's invitation, and delayed his arrival until 2 September 1870, eight days after Colonel Garnet J. Wolseley's hostile military expedition got there. That was unfortunate because Archibald and Riel would probably have worked well together. A "Father of Confederation" from Nova Scotia and secretary of state for the provinces in John A. Macdonald's first federal government, Archibald would prove far more understanding of and sympathetic to Halfbreed concerns than Macdonald and his Ottawa colleagues, who were under constant pressure from John Schultz's Ontario supporters. Archibald's sympathy, along with his impressive conciliatory skills, contributed greatly to fashioning a more fair and orderly transition to provincehood than might otherwise have been the case.

Before Archibald arrived, someone had to administer civil affairs, and Colonel Wolseley declined to do so. When, for example, the fugitive Ryder Larsen tried to surrender to Wolseley personally and face the murder charge against him, the colonel reportedly turned him away.[1] Rather than governing under his own authority, Wolseley proposed that Donald A. Smith, who had accompanied him to Red River and was the ranking company officer in Canada, assume civil authority until Archibald showed up. Although initially reluctant to accept responsibility, Smith allowed himself to be persuaded by Wolseley,[2] and appointed a few constables, placed hours-of-operation restrictions on drinking establishments, and prohibited the sale of liquor for off-site consumption. He issued these commands in his capacity as "President, Council of Northern Department" of the HBC.[3] Also attributable to Smith was a request to the HBC's London headquarters for vaccine to combat the spreading smallpox epidemic.[4]

Donald Smith's final official act was to issue, the day after Governor Archibald's appearance at Fort Garry on 2 September, a notice requesting the "gentlemen who constituted the Council of Assiniboia" to attend a meeting on the 6 September, at which Archibald's Manitoba and Northwest Territories commissions and oaths of office were read. An address of welcome by the former councillors was also delivered and replied to, and the governor was introduced to the councillors and others present.[5] A little less than half the members of the late council attended: Thomas Bunn, John Sutherland, Robert McBeath, William Fraser, Pascal Bréland, and Solomon Hamelin.[6] The next day, Archibald crossed to St Boniface, where a similar session was held; and by the 10 September he had visited every parish except the Indian settlement, to which he promised to travel shortly.[7]

A final public service rendered by Smith was a letter to the governor outlining various acts and threats of violence that had taken place on the plains in recent years and proposing the creation of a fifty-man constabulary, to be based at Edmonton immediately and duplicated at Fort Carlton the following year.[8] Although nothing was done about that proposal for a long time, Archibald did spring swiftly into action on many other fronts once he had taken the measure of his Manitoba constituency.

One of the first things the governor needed was an Executive Council. On 17 September he created a very small one, consisting of only Alfred Boyd, a thirty-four-year-old British-born merchant, who had been in the settlement for at least a dozen years and had served on the Convention of 40 in a vigorously pro-English fashion, and Marc-Amable Girard, a forty-eight-year-old lawyer very recently arrived from Montreal at Bishop A.A. Taché's behest to help Manitoba francophones protect their legal rights.[9] Girard, whom Archibald called "the nominee of the French party," was made provincial treasurer. Boyd, who became provincial secretary, was said to be "highly esteemed" by the English, and "not obnoxious to the French." A temporary clerk of the Executive Council and two justices of the peace, Robert McBeath and Solomon Hamelin, were appointed at the same time. With an Executive Council in place – albeit a miniature one – orders-in-council became possible, the first of which enjoined all citizens to keep the peace.

Threats to the peace were still in the air, due chiefly to a large Métis encampment at St Joseph, just south of the international boundary. Some of that group threatened the steamer *International* as it passed on the Red River. Others stopped a man travelling to Fort Garry by road, relieving him of $3.00 and ordering him to turn back.[10] Portage la Prairie residents felt vulnerable to possible attack from St Joseph due to their isolation from the main settlement. Archibald accordingly requested Colonel Jarvis, who took command of the military garrison when Wolseley returned to Canada, to station a troop detachment at the border,[11] and a post was established at the HBC establishment there (following a palaver with US officials over whether it was on British or American soil).[12]

The next order-in-council authorized a proclamation stating that the 1862 laws of "the late Province of Assiniboia" were still in effect. Included in those laws, it continued, were prohibitions against "supplying any Indian with intoxicating drinks," and after deploring extensive recent "quarrelling and rioting" among Winnipeg-area Indians, it reprinted the complete body of Assiniboia's 1862 liquor laws. Section 129 of Canada's constitution, which the Manitoba Act applied to the new province, continued the operation of "all laws ... in force ... at the Union" until repealed or revised by the appropriate federal or provincial legislature. But were the 1862 Laws of Assiniboia in force on 15 July 1870 when Manitoba entered Confederation? An act of the second session of the Provisional Legislature had repealed those laws and replaced them by updated and improved versions. A good case could therefore be made for saying that the "existing" laws were the more recent, and more democratically sanctioned, Riel-era laws rather than those of 1862. That would, of course, require acceptance that the second Provisional Government was a legitimate successor to the Council of Assiniboia, as there were plausible grounds for doing. There was absolutely no chance, however, that a Canadian government determined to reject any suggestion of the Riel regime's legitimacy would admit that its laws had ever been "in force." It is unlikely the possibility was even discussed.

The delicate matter of governmental and judicial appointments caused much consultation between Governor Archibald and local confidants – who probably included his executive councillors, both bishops, Donald A. Smith, HBC stalwart J.J. Hargrave, and perhaps one or two grizzled independents like Andrew McDermot and Donald Gunn. A large number of key appointments were announced on 27 and 30 September.[13] Many of them – often former Assiniboia officials – were expected; a few were not. No one was surprised by the reappointment of Coroner Dr Curtis J. Bird, by the replacement of seasoned roads superintendent Thomas Sinclair Sr with his well-regarded son, or probably, by the appointment as sheriff of the widely respected John Sutherland, whose son had been tragically killed in the Parisien affray in February. Archibald's choice of leaders for the new provincial police force must have furrowed some brows, however. Rather than promoting any former constables to those positions or following the usual convention of choosing from both major language groups, Archibald selected two officers from the recently arrived expeditionary force – both hopefully acceptable to the English because they were Canadians and to the French because they were francophones. The chief of police, Frank Villiers, was a universally respected officer; and his deputy, Louis de Plainval, was a colourful figure who sang opera rather well when off duty. Both performed creditably in creating and commanding Manitoba's first police force.

When it came to judicial appointments, there was an extraordinary similarity between Adams Archibald's choices and those of the Provisional Legislature. Not surprisingly, the governor opted to preserve the three Assiniboia petty court districts rather than the five established by the Provisional Government. But the new presidents of all three Manitoba courts had served in the Riel era, two of them as presidents. Five of the six Upper District petty court magistrates, three of five from the Middle District, and two of four from the Lower District had also done so. Of the total fifteen magistrates appointed by Archibald, thirteen are known to have served the Provisional Government as either JPs or magistrates (ten in the latter capacity). A further five men who served on the Provisional Government's courts were appointed by Archibald to be justices of the peace. The overlap might possibly have been even higher, since the personnel of only four of the five Riel-era courts are known.[14]

These figures are not cited to suggest that Archibald simply rubber-stamped most of the Provisional Government's appointments. Something more fundamental was at work – something that can be better understood by considering who served as JPs and magistrates *before* the insurrection. The paucity of relevant records unfortunately precludes compiling a complete list of those in office in 1869, but the full roster for the year 1863 is available. It discloses that, of the thirteen appointees common to Archibald's and the Provisional Government's lists, five were HBC-appointed JPs or magistrates *seven years previously*, and three more had held other Assiniboia public appointments. In other words, when choosing people to fill judicial and other public service positions, three very different selectors – an autocratic commercial enterprise, a democratically elected revolutionary legislature, and an appointed representative of an orthodox democratic government – all named not only the same *kind* of men (successful, respected, experienced, cautious, natural leaders) but also, to a surprising extent, the same *individuals.*

Two other points should be made about Archibald's choices. John Schultz's "loyal Canadians" were no better represented than they had been in the selections of the Provisional Government or of the HBC. And Governor Archibald gave one petty court seat to John Bruce, president of the first Provisional Government and a prominent official of the second. Bruce's appointment to the bench, coupled with the choice of two francophones to head the new police force, caused the Schultz Party to accuse Archibald of pro-French bias.

Perhaps for that reason, the recruitment of rank and file police officers leaned in the opposite direction. The first nineteen men appointed to the force included only four French.[15] The newspaper containing that information also printed an open letter from Provincial Secretary Boyd responding to critical petitions from five English parishes, and deploring the failure of the English to sign up as policemen: "The soldiers who are here were never intended to act as policemen ... With a view, therefore, to organize a police force, ... young men ... were asked to come forward and enroll themselves. They were offered ... wages higher than ... in any of the older provinces ... and yet ... not a man in any one of the parishes from which the petitions have come ... has offered ... to share in the indispensable work of protecting the public peace."

In the absence of sufficient volunteers, and it being too late in the year to attract recruits from other provinces, the government induced twelve soldiers to sign up as a "nucleus" for the new unit, and after that local recruits began to come forward. Within a fortnight the force consisted of thirty men and nine horses, and was steadily expanding.[16] "Much admired" blue uniforms with brass buttons had appeared, and the men were being "vigorously drilled by Captain Villiers, ... a magnificent drill instructor," twice a day. By that time, too, the force was beginning to provide protection for the settlement. In addition to routine constabular duties, police had destroyed numerous buffalo robes and other furs from areas infected by smallpox, and were watching for other contaminated imports.[17]

FACTIONAL VIOLENCE

It took a regrettably long time, however, before law and order was fully restored. For the first two or three months following Riel's expulsion, vigilante violence skulked the settlement's streets and trails. The community that Colonel Wolseley and his troops found themselves in on the sodden August morning of their arrival was riven by political, racial, linguistic, and religious antipathies. Lieutenant Governor Archibald reported to Ottawa two weeks after his arrival that "[t]here is very great uneasiness among the population. The French assert that they were promised an amnesty, and ... there can be no solid peace till that promise is fulfilled. The English ... declare that ... [no] peace can prevail till the principal actors in the late troubles are arrested and punished."[18]

While such tensions had long existed in the settlement, they had been magnified by events of the past nine months; and once it was clear that the "ins" and the "outs" had changed places, those few who had flown their dissenting colours boldly throughout – Dr John Schultz preeminent among them – were suddenly surrounded by eager "loyalist" acolytes.

In such conditions, the presence of an external military contingent like Wolseley's ought to have been vital to keeping the peace. Unfortunately, many of the peacekeepers shared the partisan passions of the Canadian loyalists, and violated the peace rather than preserving it. The troops who first liberated Fort Garry were British regulars who, if initially excited by the combat-conscious bloodlust Wolseley described, soon recovered their soldierly aplomb. But those professional troops withdrew, along with Wolseley himself, almost as soon as the situation was militarily stable. The force that remained consisted primarily of Canadian volunteers – the men, mostly from Ontario, who had signed up to avenge Thomas Scott's death and punish those traitors who, in their view, dared to oppose the British Empire. The situation was complicated by the Canadian government's divided loyalties. It had to satisfy voters in both Ontario and Quebec; and whereas Ontario supported Schultz and company, Quebec sympathized with the Métis. That fact, along with Archibald's personal preference for tolerance and reconciliation, resulted, as we have seen, in the exclusion of extremists of both stripes from positions of power in the new Manitoba government. When the loyalists realized they would not immediately be as officially victorious as expected, some turned to intimidation.

The first recorded grudge attack took place less than two weeks after the troops moved in – on the very day Governor Archibald first met the settlement's former leaders. Heading the assault was John Schultz, who had returned to Red River in Wolseley's wake expecting a hero's welcome, but had encountered a chilly official reception. The victim was the luckless Thomas Spence, erstwhile president of the "Republic of Manitobah" and current editor of the *New Nation*. In company with several armed thugs, Schultz broke into Spence's home, dragged him naked from bed, and horsewhipped him. Meanwhile, Schultz's confederates smashed the newspaper's printing press. The September 3 issue of the *New Nation* was its last. Although Schultz later claimed the attack was retaliation for an insult Spence directed to Mrs Schultz while her husband was in exile, there seems little doubt that political partisanship played a large role.[19]

At roughly the same time Spence was attacked, anonymous threats – happily unrealized – rumbled through the settlement that Thomas Bunn, clerk of the Provisional Legislature, and reputed Métis sympathizer Alexander Begg would be tarred and feathered. Constable James Mulligan, out of favour with both sides, was allegedly hauled through town tied to a cart and locked in the jail.[20] With none of the foregoing instances did official law enforcement agencies concern themselves.

The best known, best documented, and most tragic instance of retaliatory violence occurred on 13 September 1870, when Elzéar Goulet, a member of the Métis tribunal that condemned Thomas Scott to death, drowned after being chased into the Red River and stoned by a crowd that included at least two soldiers.[21] The tragedy began to unfold at Montchamp's saloon in Winnipeg about 3:00 that afternoon. A dozen or so soldiers and others were drinking there when one James Farquarson spotted Goulet talking to the proprietor. Farquarson, whom Archibald later called a "well known blackguard" and who had had more than one run-in with Louis Riel, asked Montchamp whether this was the man who had shot Scott. He was told "No," but someone confirmed Goulet's identity. A witness said Farquarson then called on others to "kill him."

Goulet fled in the direction of the river, pursued by several men, including two identified soldiers. The latter were temporarily called off by one of their officers, but rejoined the pursuers later. Goulet, unable to find a boat, threw off his coat and ran into the river. Stones and other objects were thrown at him as he tried to swim away. Farquarson apparently did not proceed as far as the river. After swimming some distance, Goulet disappeared beneath the water and drowned.

Governor Archibald had few resources with which to respond to this potentially explosive occurrence. There were no regular civil police as yet – just a handful of temporary constables – and the military could hardly be called in, given the soldiers' involvement. Not even an inquest was possible, because Coroner Bird was temporarily absent from the settlement. Archibald nevertheless acted swiftly, appointing Montreal barrister H.J.G. McConville, who happened to be visiting Red River, to act as special prosecutor and present the evidence to two magistrates for determination of whether a criminal prosecution should be commenced. Such preliminary hearings were customarily conducted by two magistrates, and those chosen were suitable: Solomon Hamelin, a middle-of-the-road, widely trusted Métis elder; and Robert McBeath, an experienced magistrate highly regarded by the English. Outraged French opinion was temporarily placated.[22]

McConville found the assignment onerous in the extreme. Many potential witnesses refused to cooperate, either from support for the vigilantes' actions or from fear of retaliation. And translators and clerks he hired suddenly quit – doubtless from external pressure. He was eventually able, acting personally as translator, clerk, and prosecutor, to locate several witnesses, question them before the magistrates, and instruct the latter on the relevant law. Hamelin proposed charging three men, but McBeath disagreed as to two of them. They concurred, however, in arresting the third, who appears to have been Farquarson. Because the evidence did not establish the man's name, McConville drafted a warrant leaving the name blank, to be determined later. His idea apparently was that a constable would get one of the witnesses to point out the man he saw pursuing Goulet. The constable, after so determining the man's name, would then fill in the blank and make the arrest. After reporting to Governor Archibald, McConville ceased to be involved. The governor, who did not like the proposed irregular arrest procedure, and may well also have been uneasy about the impact on the truculent Canadian population of *any* arrest, decided to lay the matter aside until he could consult the General Court judge temporarily assigned to Manitoba by the federal government, who had not yet arrived.

That judge was former recorder and governor Francis G. Johnson,[23] now a judge of the Quebec Superior Court, seconded to take interim charge of Manitoba's transitional courts. Unlike Archibald and McConville, Johnson did not act speedily on the Goulet matter. It was not until 7 December, long after Johnson's arrival in Winnipeg, that he produced his report. That report carefully summarized the evidence McConville had given the magistrates (the missing names having somehow been added) and concluded, "I think that the evidence, if any, is extremely slight to warrant a further investigation of the matter before a criminal court." The death never had further judicial consideration. "[T]he excitement," Johnson pointed out, "has since disappeared," and, as he knew, Ottawa was determined to keep it that way.

To say that Johnson summarized the evidence *carefully* does not necessarily mean it was *fairly* summarized. Without examining the original depositions, which are not available, one cannot be certain about that. Weaknesses in the prosecution's case were carefully emphasized, however. On the key question of whether Farquarson urged others to kill Goulet, Johnson remarked that only one witness said so, but he did not indicate whether anyone denied the statement. And when he said Farquarson was "positively sworn" to have stopped short of the river, he did not say whether anyone other than Farquarson himself so testified. On the question of how extensively Goulet was stoned, and with what effect – about which there has always been controversy – Johnson said, *directly*, only that someone called Campbell "threw something at him, which was seen to fall in the river," but he did not say whether other things were also thrown, by Campbell and/or others, with greater accuracy and injury. In fact, another of the judge's statements may *imply* that this was so: "[A]ccording to the medical and other testimony taken, no other *immediate* cause of death [than drowning] can be assigned, or has been suggested."[24] Why was the word "immediate" necessary? Its only purpose could have been to distinguish drowning from *contributing* causes, such as being chased into the river, not being allowed to return to shore, or being struck a nonfatal but debilitating blow to the head by a projectile.

The final noteworthy instance of partisan violence during this period took place in November, following a provincial election meeting at Poplar Point. It was a feisty gathering. One of the speakers, a Schultz crony named Dr James Lynch, accused the Archibald administration of being "corrupt and incapable." James Tanner, a sixty-year-old English Halfbreed, refuted these charges "in a speech," the newspaper reported, "that would have done honor to the House of Commons in England," moved a vote of entire confidence in Governor Archibald, and carried his motion three to one.[25] "But," the account continued, "the sad termination was to come. Mr. Tanner, on his way home, had not driven two hundred yards when some ruffians rushed towards his horse, waving their overcoats and throwing missiles, evidently to terrify the horse ... They succeeded ... for the horse started, poor old Mr. Tanner ... was thrown from the wagon, his skull was driven in, and he died on the spot."

That this was no mere prank gone wrong was indicated by the "gauntlet ... of clubs, stones and snowballs" launched against other government supporters immediately behind Tanner's wagon. "How long," the article demanded, "is this 'loyal rowdyism' to continue?" The verdict of Coroner Bird's inquest[26] was that the horse had been caused to bolt "willfully and maliciously by two persons unknown to this jury, thereby causing the death." The assailants being unknown, there was no prosecution.

In terms of law and order, then, the new administration got off to a poor start. By the end of 1870, however, Captain Villiers's Provincial Mounted Constabulary Force had matters somewhat better in hand.

CENSUS

Tabulating Manitoba's population was of high priority. By 1 October, Governor Archibald had divided the province into five census districts, appointed two-person bilingual enumeration teams for each, and issued instructions to the chosen enumerators.[27] The "primary object" of the census, the instructions said, was to determine how many were entitled to share the Métis land entitlement under the Manitoba Act – a "secondary object" being to record the province's complete population.[28] The results, published in mid-December, set the total provincial population at 11,943, distributed as previously described.[29] The populations of each of the province's twenty-six parishes and other communities were also listed, the largest being St François Xavier (1,843) and the smallest St Paul's (5). Winnipeg, with a population of only 215, compared to 819 for St Boniface, 330 for Headingley, and 1,321 for St Andrew's, clearly wielded an influence far beyond its numbers.

PROVINCIAL ELECTION

The provincial election was set for 30 December, and enthusiasm ran very high. A newspaper estimated the total number of eligible voters at 800,[30] adding, "[A]t the present moment there are at least 80 candidates in the field for legislative honors: one out of every ten." Although there were acclamations in several of the twenty-four constituencies, many seats were hotly contested, chiefly between supporters of the Archibald government and the Schultz Party.

Nomination meetings, though often unruly, heard considerable eloquent and informative oratory. James Ross, while not a candidate himself, was an especially prominent and effective pro-government speaker at several meetings. No doubt Ross hoped to cleanse the stains to his reputation caused by his double-dealing during the Riel months. His tone was usually good-natured and conciliatory, and his message urged forgiveness and progress: Archibald's goals.

Some of Ross's observations about the settlement's past governance still make interesting reading. Of the HBC's regime, which he had frequently criticized, he said,

> [W]e ... had a system of government under the Hudson's Bay Company which perhaps was not ... what we would like it to be, but a system which ... possessed many excellencies (cheers) ... I fought

> against the ... Company as a governing body ... [B]ut I want to say this about the old system – it was above reproach. (loud cheers) ... Logan, Bird, Bunn, Pruden, and others – were they not worthy representatives of the interests of Red River in their time? (cheers) ... During the reign of the Hudson's Bay Company substantial justice was always done in the country. (cheers).[31]

In an interesting debate with Sheriff John Sutherland at a nomination meeting in Kildonan, Ross contended that English delegates to the Convention of 40 did "the best that could be done at the time" to maintain "peace between the two sections of the people" and avoid "disaster." "We had either to yield or fight," he continued. "We thought anything was preferable to war, as this would be the utter ruin of the Settlement. (hear, hear) ... It was not a choice between good and bad; but a choice between bad and worse. (hear, hear)." When Sutherland accused the English provisional legislators of continuing to sit with the French "after that murder," Ross, who was not then a member, defended them by pointing out that both the Anglican bishop and Canadian commissioner Smith had urged the English parishes to send delegates and they all had done so. "Well, if they sent them," he concluded, "it is surely unfair now to blame those delegates for going – and unfair to upbraid them as associating with murderers. (Cheers)."[32]

The election results were highly favourable to the government.[33] Victories went to several carpet-bag lawyers from Quebec (Joseph Dubuc, Joseph Royal, Marc Girard, and H.J. Clarke), as well as to Alfred Boyd, Donald A. Smith, and many other government supporters. Riel's former secretary Louis Schmidt won by acclamation, though John Bruce was defeated by conservative Métis Pascal Bréland. The hardest-fought race was in Winnipeg, where Smith defeated John Schultz by seventy votes to sixty-three. The bitterness of that contest can be glimpsed in the newspaper comment that "[a]ll passed off quietly except in ... St. John's Division, in which there were 73 legitimate votes, and 163 were polled. The supporters of Dr. Schultz burned Mr. Smith in effigy."[34]

Electee Henry J. Clarke, QC, from Montreal, deserves a word at this point. He came to Manitoba with the encouragement of both George-Étienne Cartier and Bishop Taché in the apparent expectation of becoming provincial attorney general after the election.[35] That expectation was soon fulfilled, and Clarke, a talented and energetic lawyer and politician, would play a major role throughout Manitoba's formative years. But Governor Archibald found his mercurial personality very hard to take.

FIFTH ESTATE

Although the destruction of the *New Nation*'s printing equipment by Schultz's hooligans silenced that particular public voice, it was soon replaced. Only a week later, the *Manitoba News-Letter*, edited by prominent loyalist P.G. Laurie and published from quarters in Dr Schultz's "brick drug store," made its appearance. Its journalistic standards were low, and although promising not to be "a political party organ," it functioned as a Schultz mouthpiece for the next several months.

Fortunately for competent journalism and balanced public commentary, the *News-Letter* did not monopolize the newspaper scene for long. A second weekly, the *Manitoban*, began publication on 15 October from the *New Nation's* former premises in Andrew Bannatyne's building, using its repaired equipment. The publishers of the *Manitoban* were the seasoned William Coldwell and his new partner, Robert Cunningham. Their publication was soon Manitoba's leading journal. The *Manitoban* brought residents of the infant province accurate national and international news, local stories, and editorial comment of a moderate, if government-leaning, perspective until it merged in 1874 with the still extant *Manitoba Free Press*. Its professionalism was unmatched by its early rivals.

The repair of the *Manitoban*'s equipment was described in its first issue:[36] "[A] few weeks ago, the press with which the *Manitoban* is printed was made the subject of a piece of vandalism ... To repair the injury, we telegraphed to New York for a new lever; but meantime a few of the Ontario Rifles tackled the difficulty, and mastered it. Everybody said it could not be done, but it was ... In a very short time the whole thing was finished, and the press is now in comparatively good working order." Did the soldiers in question not realize that the publication whose birth they had hastened would soon be publishing liberal views sharply opposed to those of many of their comrades-in-arms? Or were these particular soldiers of a more moderate perspective?

On 2 September, before the *New Nation's* press was attacked, Louis Riel had written from hiding to Joseph Royal, a young lawyer-journalist-politician whom Taché had attracted to St Boniface from Montreal. The Métis leader urged Royal to claim the *New Nation*'s equipment and use it in the French interest: "[T]he National Committee of the Métis places it in your hands."[37] Royal replied that "the Government seized all the property of the *New Nation* on the pretext that they have a right to everything belonging to the Provisional Government,"[38] but he eventually launched an important French-language newspaper – *Le Métis* – in May 1871.

AND MUCH MORE

As 1870 drew to a close, Adams Archibald had good reason to congratulate himself. The four months since his arrival in this remote backwater, roiling with treacherous political cross-currents and riptides, had been extraordinary. In addition to establishing a reliable police force, reopening the courts, completing a province-wide census, and conducting a generally peaceful and politically successful first election, the governor and his colleagues had accomplished much more. Effective steps had been taken to contain the smallpox epidemic. The postal service, which Archibald had found intolerable in September,[39] was showing promise of improvement by the end of November.[40] Popular fears that the lawyers and judge from Quebec would import a French-style legal system were subsiding.[41] The HBC's chaotic land title records, made worse by a loss of documents under Provisional Government control,[42] were being organized by F.E. Molyneux St John, a versatile army officer turned journalist who had accompanied the Wolseley expedition and would play numerous useful governmental roles for the next several years. St John's land titles report was due on 3 January 1871.[43]

In his additional role as lieutenant governor of the Northwest Territories, Adams Archibald had blundered badly. Needing to move swiftly – especially in face of the smallpox threat – but lacking official documentation concerning his powers in the Northwest Territories, he had mistakenly assumed they were the same as for Manitoba. Acting on that assumption, he appointed councillors, issued orders-in-council, and took other urgent steps. In fact, he lacked the powers he purported to exercise, causing great concern in Ottawa and Winnipeg. The matter was quietly put right, however, and no one ever challenged the hard-pressed governor's unauthorized early steps.[44]

Before the year was out, Archibald also dealt with the local laws Manitoba inherited from Assiniboia.[45] Judge Johnson had been ordered to "enquire into and report on the state of the laws in the Province and the North West Territories,"[46] but the governor decided not to wait, and simply ordered the entire 1862 Assiniboia consolidation, followed by all post-1862 Council of Assiniboia amendments, to be reprinted.[47] No effort was made to integrate the amendments with the original text or improve the laws substantively. The excellent Riel-era consolidation, which did both, was completely ignored. While sad from rational and democratic perspectives, that oversight was politically unavoidable; the governor knew he could give no credit whatsoever to the Provisional Government's accomplishments.

It is not known how Adams Archibald celebrated New Year's Eve that year. But if he perhaps drank a little too much, who could blame him?

NOT QUITE RESPONSIBLE GOVERNMENT

Eighteen seventy-one brought many more moments when the lieutenant governor might have been tempted to indulge in a dram, but they were not always occasions for celebration. Successes still outnumbered defeats by a wide margin, but some were achieved at great political and personal cost; and before that year was over the political climate had decidedly changed.

By then, of course, Archibald was working with an elected Legislative Assembly, albeit one lacking independence and largely committed to his policies. His cabinet (Executive Council) was drawn primarily from that body. Fortunately for continuity's sake, Boyd and Girard were both elected. Reappointed to their previous cabinet positions, those ministers were joined by H.J. Clarke as attorney general of Manitoba and by Captain Thomas Howard, a vigorous young Wolseley expedition officer, as the minister of public works and agriculture. James McKay, not in the assembly but soon to be appointed to the Legislative Council (upper house), completed the expanded cabinet.[48] Clarke was a very active cabinet minister – certainly the most vocal – but although he is sometimes called Manitoba's first premier (as, too, is Alfred Boyd), Archibald did not recognize anyone as premier at that point. For the time being, he continued to lead the province personally, and met mounting criticism for doing so.

First scheduled for early February, the opening session of the Legislature of Manitoba was postponed until March. A few days before the opening, Governor Archibald appointed the Legislative Council's seven members, all of whom the cabinet endorsed unanimously. The upper house was astutely chosen to reflect the province's diverse demography reasonably well: two anglophones, two francophones, and one bilingual member; four Catholics (two English, two French) and two Protestants; four Halfbreeds (two English, two French); and three without Aboriginal blood. The Indian population, however, was not represented at all.[49] On the same day he announced the upper house, Archibald appointed

Molyneaux St John as its clerk and Thomas Spence as clerk of the Legislative Assembly. *Manitoban* publishers Coldwell and Cunningham were named Queen's Printers.[50]

One reason for not convening the legislature sooner was the need to find a place for it to meet. It required two separate but neighbouring chambers, with enough room for twenty-four members in the lower house, seven in the upper, and in both cases, attendant officers, press, and public. Andrew Bannatyne, who seemed always willing to help a good cause, offered space in his premises near Portage and Main, and hectic efforts transformed it into an appropriately august temporary venue for Manitoba's first legislature.

A large assembly chamber, created by combining two rooms, was entered through a door covered by green cloth. Dominating the room stood a raised speaker's chair, also draped in green, below which was a long clerk's table. To the speaker's right were ranged four desks for ministers and seats for the eleven other government members. On the opposite side were seats for the nine opposition members. There were desks for the press, and accommodation for about 100 other spectators. Next to the assembly door was another, clothed in red, leading to the Legislative Council chamber. About half the size of the other, it contained the lieutenant governor's red throne, a clerk's table, a large round table for the seven councillors, press desks, and seating for the public. On a floor above were offices for the speakers and clerks, as well as a smoking room for members.[51]

"In many respects," the *Manitoban* opined, "traditional models of parliamentary decoration have been so closely adhered to that but little difference is noticeable – except, perhaps, in the dimensions of the chambers themselves." But there were local touches too. Historian James Jackson noted that "[t]he mace, symbol of royal powers, was carved from a portion of the flagstaff of the Fort and the hub of a Red River cart."[52] When the first legislature finally convened on 15 March 1871, the *Manitoban* asked, "Who, two or three years ago, would have believed this a possibility? Accustomed only to the most primitive and patriarchal system of government, we have all at once the complete machinery of vastly more populous and wealthy communities ... [that] other provinces have reached only after long years of weary petitioning and agitation."[53]

After the assembly and the council chose Joseph Royal and James McKay as their respective speakers, work began on erecting a legislative framework for Manitoba. Preparation of the necessary bills had engaged

Archibald and his cabinet heavily since the beginning of the year, and likely contributed to the legislature's opening being twice delayed. Most of the bills – thirty-two out of the forty-seven enacted during the seven-week session – originated with the lieutenant governor himself.[54] All thirty-two carried with little opposition.[55] Attorney General Clarke was also intensely busy. While legislation establishing a judicial system had been Clarke's keenest personal concern, he also made major contributions to most government bills. Statutes of particular legal interest were An Act to Establish a Supreme Court in the Province of Manitoba; Frauds and Perjuries; Wills; Deeds by Married Women; Masters and Servants; Registration of Deeds; Administration of Intestate Estates; Police; Study and Practice of Law; Magistrates and Coroners; and Statutes of Manitoba. The *Manitoban*'s often verbatim reports of the debates on the details of these and other statutes contain much of interest – such as a chiding of Attorney General Clarke, a bachelor, for having overlooked widows in the class of persons entitled to share in intestate estates.[56] The government's estimates for the year 1871 were passed on 2 May (after a lengthy debate that the *Manitoban* called "somewhat discreditable" about the size of the lawmakers' own sessional indemnities). The total budget came to about $85,000 (including a last-minute increase in legislators' indemnities), the largest single item being $13,800 for the police force.[57]

On the afternoon of 3 May 1871, a 100 man contingent of the Ontario Rifles, complete with band, assembled on the rutted road in front of the makeshift legislature, while members of the assembly and council streamed into the building, many of them accompanied by ladies in fashionable garb. At 3:30 a carriage bearing Lieutenant Governor Archibald drew up, the troops presented arms, the band struck up "God Save the Queen," the artillery sounded a royal salute, and His Excellency proceeded to the tiny council chamber, where members of that house and their ladies awaited. When the governor was seated on the throne, the twenty-four assembly members were summoned in accordance with ancient parliamentary tradition and crowded in, "fill[ing] the chamber to its utmost capacity." Archibald pronounced royal assent for all but the four bills he had reserved, listened while assembly speaker Royal reported briefly on the work of the session, presented a congratulatory closing speech from the throne, and formally prorogued the legislature's first session.[58]

All involved had a right to be proud. Quite apart from what was accomplished, the work was done with surprising civility, considering the

Figure 11.1 Henry J. Clarke, Manitoba's first attorney general and government leader, shaped and oversaw enactment of the province's initial laws. He was effectively its first premier.

rawness of the community's political passions.[59] Even the debate over launching an official investigation of the "troubles of 1869–70" was characterized by a "spirit of moderation and kindness."[60] Prior to proroguing the session, the Legislative Assembly passed resolutions of thanks to Governor Archibald, as well as to Assembly Speaker Royal, whom the *Manitoban* reported, early in the session, to have "already won golden opinions for his ability, his impartiality, and his courteous, dignified bearing."[61] It was Attorney General Clarke, however, who had piloted the government's legislative agenda through the debates virtually unscathed; and both houses recognized his efforts by unanimous resolutions of praise.[62] The *Manitoban* went so far as to refer to Clarke as "Premier."

Behind the scenes, matters were not so rosy. Clarke and Archibald were often at odds. Knowing the ambitious lawyer aspired to a position on Manitoba's prospective superior court, the lieutenant governor warned the prime minister, to whom such appointments fell, that "[b]ad as he is where he is, he would be greatly worse on the bench," adding in a later letter that he had "seldom seen a man so void of ... discretion or common sense."[63] Clarke was anathema, moreover, to the never-to-be-overlooked loyalists. Although he was undoubtedly the most active and vocal member of the cabinet, and acted as government leader in the assembly, he could not be considered Manitoba's first minister in the full sense because Archibald was not yet willing to surrender the final say in governmental matters to the Executive Council. Not until 1874 would a later lieutenant governor inform Ottawa that "in forming the government I did so through the intervention of a Premier, thus introducing responsible government in its modern form."[64] For the remainder of the period considered herein, democracy was only partially attained in Manitoba.

MAKING GOVERNMENT WORK

If it wasn't fully democratic, the new administration was providing effective day-to-day governance.

In March 1871, for example, Governor Archibald learned from the province's customs collectors that some importers were refusing to pay duty, relying upon a legal opinion from a Montreal lawyer that only the Parliament of Canada could constitutionally impose such levies. Prominent among these scofflaws was a man called McArthur, who planned to resist with the help of "ten or a dozen men recruited from the taverns." Archibald quietly obtained a magistrate's warrant, and on his orders Captain Villiers staged a surprise dawn police raid on McArthur's premises, seizing his contraband imports before his toughs were out of bed.[65]

A few days later, Attorney General Clarke proposed to the Legislative Assembly steps to stabilize currency chaos that had prevailed in the settlement for years. Four different currencies were in common use: British pounds sterling, Canadian dollars, US dollars, and HBC promissory notes. Little agreement existed as to appropriate exchange rates for each. The pound, for example, was often exchanged in Winnipeg for $5.00 Canadian, when the official rate was only $4.87; so if the HBC received £1 for a Fort Garry sale, and spent that money in London, it gained a premium of 13 cents. While Clarke admitted that only Canada could legislatively regulate currency matters, he pointed out that since provincial government expenditures constituted a large component of the overall Manitoba economy, government spending and billing practices could significantly influence the situation. He therefore proposed that the province should deal exclusively in Canadian funds, with the expectation that others would follow suit. After much debate, the legislature endorsed the policy,[66] and Canadian money was soon in general use.

Implementing the new system of publicly funded Protestant and Catholic schools for which the legislature had provided was the government's largest task during the summer of 1871. It was carried out vigorously and well. A bicameral Board of Education, its members divided equally by religion, was appointed, with Joseph Royal and Molyneux St John as both joint secretaries of the board and secretary-superintendents of the Catholic and Protestant "sections" respectively. Sixteen Protestant and ten Catholic school districts were created, local trustees were elected for each, and teachers were hired and trained in time to make schooling available throughout the province by autumn.[67]

The provincial police force was fully operational by early summer 1871, with detachments at Winnipeg, Lower Fort Garry, and Portage la Prairie.[68] During the summer of 1871, too, the Archibald administration managed, without serious incident, to reinstitute the program of provincial land surveys that had triggered the 1869 insurrection.[69] In early September the provincial Board of Health, responding to an outbreak of typhoid fever thought to have been caused by dumping manure into rivers, rented a Winnipeg building for hospital purposes, thereby establishing the first, albeit temporary, hospital on the west side of the Red River.

FEDERAL ELECTION

Manitoba's first federal election took place on 2 March 1871. After a small panic caused by the election writs being temporarily lost in the still not very reliable mails,[70] voting took place on schedule.

The results shook the French-speaking, Halfbreed, and moderate populations. Although provincial government supporters Donald A. Smith and Pierre DeLorme were successful by comfortable margins in the constituencies of Selkirk and Provencher, strong opposition support was demonstrated in the other two federal ridings. Dr John Schultz won by a huge margin over young Colin Inkster in Lisgar; and Schultz's crony Dr James Lynch tied with English Halfbreed Angus MacKay in Marquette.[71] Lynch's strong showing testified to how rapidly the political landscape was changing. That area included a large Halfbreed enclave, and a knowledgeable observer had predicted only three months previously that "[i]f a Canadian came straight from paradise he could not get the Halfbreed votes in this parish."[72] Although Lynch would never sit in Ottawa, Schultz's victory gave him a parliamentary base from which he waged political war against Manitoba moderates until he was appointed lieutenant governor of the province in 1885.

In the two constituencies where the anti-Archibald vote was strong, the federal election was quite violent. The *Manitoban* expressed outrage about "rowdyism ... threats and intimidation" by Schultz supporters in Lisgar, where one poll was closed due to violence only twenty minutes after opening.[73] Joseph Dubuc reported to Riel a few days later that "things are boiling ... There has been violence at Portage ... Even the English say the country is in worse condition than ... ever."[74] North American polling places commonly saw hard drinking and partisan violence in the late nineteenth century, of course, and Archibald's official report of the election downplayed the problems: "On the whole, the elections were conducted quietly. Nothing could exceed the good order and propriety which distinguished the elections of Selkirk and Provencher. At the two polling districts of Lisgar, and at ... one of the polling districts of Marquette, there was some disorder, and perhaps some intimidation, but there was no open violence beyond what occurs at all elections ... [N]ot a blow was struck at any one of the ten polling places."[75] The election was a reminder, nevertheless, that efforts of Adams Archibald's government to encourage reconciliation were beginning to create a backlash in some quarters.

MAJOR ISSUES ADDRESSED AND IGNORED

Much was accomplished during the Archibald administration: not just the routine matters mentioned above, but some difficult major questions too. Other important issues, however – especially those of concern to former Provisional Government supporters – were either put aside for another day or simply ignored. To some this seemed ominous. Indians had gathered in considerable numbers in and near the settlement during the summer of 1870 hoping to negotiate with the Queen's representative over surrender of their Aboriginal title to the territory.[76] Their position was that the 1811 Selkirk Treaty was never intended by Indians as a permanent transfer of title, and that in any case Selkirk and his successors had not honoured the terms of the treaty. Governor Archibald lost no time meeting with Aboriginal representatives, but when he did, on 13 September 1870, he was only able to thank them for behaving "like good and true children" in not joining Riel, and to promise treaty discussions "as soon as possible."

It was not until over ten months later, on 27 July 1871, that Archibald met them – assembled 1,000 strong at Lower Fort Garry – for that purpose. This time the governor was accompanied by a team of federal negotiators under Wemyss Simpson, and by Manitoban James McKay. Archibald outlined the parameters of what the Great Mother was prepared to offer and then turned to Simpson and his colleagues to negotiate the details. The governor's personal involvement was not quite over, however. The Indians, having chosen their spokesmen, refused to begin discussions until Archibald removed "a cloud before them that makes things dark." The "cloud" was the fact that four Cree men were currently in jail for deserting their contracts as HBC boatmen – a criminal offence at the time.[77] Archibald replied that if the chiefs requested the men's release as a matter of "grace and favour," not of right, which they acknowledged, "Her Majesty would ... consent to their discharge," which she did. Simpson and his team were then able to negotiate satisfactory agreements with Indians in two separate conclaves: at Lower Fort Garry on 3 August (Treaty No. 1) and at Lake Manitoba on 25 August (Treaty No. 3). Between them, the two treaties dealt with the claims of the entire Indian population of Manitoba and much of the surrounding territory.

Although that would seem swift progress, given the complexity and seriousness of the issues involved, one impatient journalist objected to the ponderous deliberative process: "[T]hese prairie diplomats ... are in no hurry. They've spent the opening days smoking – no doubt awaiting inspiration from their Manitous."[78] Happily, tobacco was the only stimulant available. Law enforcement officers applied the liquor laws with the utmost stringency during the negotiations, and the results were salutary: "During the ten days of negotiations ... at the Lower Fort, not a solitary Indian appeared intoxicated, or with even the smell of liquor on him. Policemen were stationed in every saloon for miles round, and every precaution taken to prevent liquor coming into the camps. The only instance of drunkenness noticeable was ... that of a white man who ... fell asleep near an Indian tent. His flask, full, fell from his pocket, and an Indian picked it up and brought it to the police!"[79]

The victims of imprisonment, confiscations, and/or involuntary exile by the Provisional Governments, with John Schultz and Walter Bown in the van, lost no time lobbying the Canadian government for compensation, and the federal Treasury Board decided before the end of 1870 to pay any claims Recorder Johnson, acting as special commissioner, approved.[80] Rarely known for swift action, Johnson finally turned to the task in August 1871, submitting his report to Ottawa in December. He processed 173 applications for claims totalling $336,261, approving compensation for a very high percentage of the claimants but slashing the payment sums drastically. Only 26 per cent of the total amount claimed was awarded: $85,756 overall. Of that total, John Schultz received 37 per cent: $31,890.[81]

Johnson's awards were heavily criticized, both for their alleged stinginess and for what some perceived as favouritism toward Schultz and a few other claimants. He addressed the latter complaint during a final address to members of the Manitoba bar in May 1872, saying it involved a "misapprehension of law."[82] The statute under which he was commissioned authorized compensation for loss of property only, he pointed out, and "[n]o man received one farthing as damages for imprisonment ... in itself, or ... for his sufferings while in durance."[83] Not even Schultz received anything for imprisonment.[84] Schultz undoubtedly did lose considerable property, but, as Bumsted has noted, Johnson's willingness to accept claimants' own sworn affidavits as sufficient proof of loss "worked to Schultz's benefit."

In sharp contrast to the questions of Aboriginal rights and rebellion losses, the aching topic of amnesty for participants in the 1869–70 insurrection or the Provisional Governments remained unresolved until long after the years with which this study is concerned.[85] By 1875, when the Liberal federal government of Alexander Mackenzie announced a general amnesty for all but O'Donoghue, Ambroise Lépine, and Riel, it had ceased to be a matter of much political importance.

Fulfilment of the promise in section 31 of the Manitoba Act that 1.4 million acres of land would be selected by the lieutenant governor of Manitoba and divided "among the children of Halfbreed heads of families residing in the Province at the time" of provincehood lay even further – much, much, further – in the future than amnesty. Initially, Governor Archibald moved quickly to carry out that constitutional directive, submitting a plan for doing so to Ottawa before the end of 1870.[86] The federal government took over the task at that point, however, and, to deflect political protest from those opposed in principle to section 31, it developed a Dominion Lands Policy that delayed the process interminably, and gradually modified Archibald's straightforward approach in ways that ultimately subverted the purposes of the guarantee altogether.[87]

MIGRATIONS

Many Métis – realizing that their bishop and others had been hoodwinked about amnesty; knowing that their political leader was in hiding; sensing that their constitutional land guarantee was sinking out of sight in a political swamp; seeing Indians' Aboriginal rights, but not their own, recognized by treaty; believing that some of their loyalist opponents were being unduly compensated; and experiencing growing discrimination in parts of the settlement – gradually gave up the fight, cut their losses, and moved westward, where the plains still held traces of their old allure.

Métis migration to the northwest[88] had begun well before provincehood, and was fuelled by more than the social and political factors mentioned above; but those factors accelerated the process after 1870. As always, economics played a major role. The migrants tended to be the less affluent: families more dependent on the once-thriving buffalo robe trade than on more settled occupations like agriculture and commerce. Not only were the dwindling buffalo herds retreating westward, but more stringent import-export laws and US customs enforcement were making it difficult for any but major entrepreneurs to engage profitably in that trade from Manitoba. Farther west, where distances to the resource were shorter, and border surveillance was less thorough, smaller operations had better chances of success. Although the decision to pull up their Manitoba stakes would prove unfortunate for many migrating Métis, it was a plausible choice at the time. As Gerhard Ens has observed, "Hindsight alone confirms that the switch from peasant agriculture to the fur trade and domestic buffalo-robe industry would, over the long term, prove an unsuccessful strategy for adaptation to the new order in the west."[89]

Not only Métis were in motion. As they moved out, others were moving in, drawn from Ontario, and to a lesser extent from Quebec, by extensive newspaper advertising on the part of those with vested interests in expansion,[90] as well as by the newsworthy events of 1869–70. The Canadian government energetically encouraged and facilitated westward migration and was, as the *Manitoban* reported in April 1871, making arrangements "to convey immigrants through Canadian territory to the Northwest." It was proposed to adopt a combined water and wagon road route of travel. The fare for adults from Toronto to Fort William would be $5, half that for children under twelve. From Fort William to Fort Garry, the fares would be $25 and $12.50, with a liberal allowance of baggage. The whole fare from Toronto would be about half the price of Hudson Bay or US routes, and the time required for the journey would be just fifteen days. The government would provide "houses of shelter" along the way and ensure that "simple provisions could be obtained on the journey."[91]

Ottawa was also encouraging those who came to Manitoba with Colonel Wolseley to remain, offering "160 acres by pre-emption on the payment of one dollar per acre; another 160 acres as a homestead, without such payment, by continuing residence thereon for five years; and a third tract of 160 acres as a bounty or gift in consideration of ... military service, without actual residence thereon."[92] Rather unexpectedly, given the newspaper's general sympathy for the Indian and Métis populations, the *Manitoban* greeted that announcement, made long before the Indian treaties were negotiated, with the statement that "[w]e hold these rights as paramount to the Indian title. It is preposterous to propose that a mere roving privilege to hunt over half a continent, such as the savage tribes possess, should interfere with the sovereignty of Great Britain, much less should defeat the individual rights solemnly guaranteed to civilized occupants of the soil."[93] Actual and prospective immigration from the east, coupled with the probable settlement of many discharged troops, was yet another factor causing Manitoba Métis to move in the opposite direction.

Newcomers found suitable accommodations in short supply: "Boarding house and hotel keepers have more than they can undertake in the way of business in Winnipeg ... [S]ome of the newly-arrived strangers are hard-put to find bed and board."[94] And those looking to purchase land were dismayed by soaring prices: "Winnipeg land is 'going up' without any indications to where it will stop. For some lots, outside the probable limits of the town, £50 an acre is asked, and in other instances the figures named have been beyond the reach of anyone except a millionaire."[95]

When prosperity looms, lawyers are seldom far away, and the immigrants included several of that profession. In addition to the previously mentioned Dubuc, Royal, Girard, and Clarke, four others were advertising their services before 1871 was over: David M. Walker, John F. Bain, W.B. Thibodeau, and Rice M. Howard. On 30 December they assembled to elect the officers of a professional association they called the Bar

Society of Manitoba.[96] That body did not possess the powers of professional regulation normally exercised by such organizations, but it signified that a professionally trained bar was finally practising in Manitoba courts.

JAMES ROSS PASSES

Another lawyer – James Ross – also advertised in the *Manitoban* and appeared frequently before Manitoba's courts earlier in the year; but an obituary on 23 September 1871 announced that the multitalented thirty-six-year-old had made an unexpected migration of an entirely other kind.

After parting company with Riel and the Provisional Government in the spring of 1870, Ross had kept to himself for a while, pursuing personal interests and drinking much more than he should. In August, with the Wolseley expedition approaching, he had travelled to Ontario – ostensibly on business – making himself scarce until the political climate could be assessed. Preparing to come home in September, Ross worried about his likely reception, and urged his wife Margaret to prepare the ground:

> Tell [the Reverend] Mr. Black to say a good word for me ... All I did was to prevent bloodshed ... Try to see Cunningham, and tell him no more loyal man was in RR than me, but we had to give in to the French, for peace's sake ... You know I tried to act for the best last winter ... If I gave in to Riel, it was to prevent a massacre ... You know also what efforts I put forth to save Boulton's life, & ... that I never heard of the intention to kill Scott ... & you know how mad & grieved I was at the murder ... [G]et these views out in a prudent way. I opposed Riel until we found out Canada had not yet got the country, & until all the English clergy & people thought we had better give in ... [F]rom the time ... peace was secured I never went near the Fort for nearly four months ... Don't approve or encourage the violent measures being taken by Canadians against French Half-breeds and T. Bunn and Bannatyne. Don't for a moment encourage such a thing, for you will encourage a feeling to some extent against *me* too ... You ought to frown down by all means violence of every kind. Peace and quietness is what we want in the Red River above all else ... Poor, unhappy, distracted Red River. May it soon see better times![97]

After his return, Ross was active in much more than the practice of law. Although not a candidate himself, he played, as we have seen, a prominent and courageous role campaigning for government candidates in the provincial election. He hoped this would restore him to respectability "in the eyes of all quiet people," and expected some form of official recognition from Governor Archibald as a mark of that. When no such recognition was bestowed, he became bitter. Immediately after Archibald's appointments of Legislative Council members and legislative clerks were publicly announced, Ross wrote to him,

> I am ignored in all the appointments of office made under the new regime. I did not expect this – indeed, I think I had some reason to expect the contrary. It is not pleasant to trumpet one's self; but in a case of this kind I cannot well avoid "showing cause" for the disappointment indicated ... I took up the mantle left me [by father and brother], and in various offices of trust rendered the public good service for some years. A native of the country, speaking all the languages of the country, with all my relatives here, all my interests centred here, and with the family record indicated, I ... see a number of new men preferred who have not been here over a year or two in the country (some only a few months) and who have little or no stake in the country. With natural abilities & an education possessed by not very many in this Settlement, I see men of but little natural ability, and still less education and experience chosen ... I do not relish the turn of events ... [H]aving taken a leading part in guiding ... matters to a peaceful issue, I now receive only abuse & ingratitude ... Having laboured unceasingly since October, in private & public to convince people of the justice of the Government policy of conciliation, ... I naturally regret to find myself a loser on all hands ... I would have valued an appointment *far more* as an endorsement of my course last winter and this, than for its honor or its pay. Happily, I do not need office for the sake of its pay. I have been told ... that an objection ... urged to my appointment to office was that I am too fond of my wine. This has, no doubt, been exaggerated ... & possibly could be explained. In any case, if that is a valid objection, two – perhaps three – would not have been on the list ... published today.[98]

Archibald responded the same day with a conciliatory note asking Ross to call and discuss his concerns.[99] If that meeting ever took place, it would not likely have consoled Ross, who craved public, not private, redemption.

Despite having assured Margaret that he had repented of the "unworthiness" that had caused him to "forget my dignity & self-respect" in frequent drinking bouts, and that "God has brought me to my senses,"[100] renewed problem drinking continued after Ross's return, and contributed to a general undermining of his health. A pulmonary affliction finally carried him off. A long obituary in the *Manitoban*, undoubtedly written by his friend and one-time colleague William Coldwell, catalogued Ross's many accomplishments, mourned the dashing of his golden prospects, and attempted, in conclusion, to dissipate the cloud that still hung over his reputation at death: "Mr. Ross has suffered much obloquy on account of the actions he took during the troubles in Red River; but on all occasions, public and private, he was prepared to enter upon the subject, and we venture to say that no man who ever heard him explain his position can deny that all he did was with a single eye to the good of the country, with a clear perception of the results which have ultimately ensued."[101]

PROGRESS

The world was reaching out to Canada's new province. Railroads were still some distance away,[102] but were getting closer. The US Northern Pacific line, with a workforce of 4,000 men, was approaching Pembina at a rate of 2 miles a day, and that little border town was growing explosively as a result. The *Manitoban* reported in June 1871 that newcomers were "pouring into the country, and filling up the Red River Valley south of the boundary line." Such was "the immense number of freight and passenger teams on the road," the account continued, "that it looks like a grand procession from St. Cloud to Fort Ambercrombie."[103] Although the Canadian railway was not nearly so close, its exploration parties passed through Winnipeg that same summer.[104]

A new steamboat, the *Selkirk*, had joined the *International* on the Red River a little earlier in the year, and a newspaper description of her arrival conveys the excitement of the times:

> The *Selkirk* arrived at this port about 8 o'clock ... in the evening of the 13th, loaded down to the water's edge with freight and [about 100] passengers. She presented a most extraordinary appearance ..., having in tow a barge full of horses, her decks being thronged with

> passengers and every available space, even to the hurricane deck, being filled up with freight of every description. The fore part of her lower deck was piled up with wagon wheels to pretty nearly the height of the flag-staff, and the guards of the upper deck were so hung round with wagon boxes as to give her passengers the appearance of screening themselves behind barricades.[105]

The new arrivals, mostly from Ontario, seemed to the reporter to be of "the better class of Canadian farmers." Many had clearly come to stay, bringing with them "implements of husbandry of every description: and their life savings, said to be worth generally $500 to $2,000 apiece." Others were reconnoitring, "come to see this good land ... and come back again with other colon[ists] now awaiting their report as to prospects in Manitoba."

S.J. Dawson, chief engineer of the road and water route from Lake Superior to Winnipeg, visited in July, providing the *Manitoban* with an optimistic description of what he made seem like a project nearing completion. In the interests of accuracy, the newspaper appended a postscript outlining the complaints of a party of surveyors who had just travelled the route and who "tell a very doleful tale indeed, regarding this famous road."[106] Notwithstanding the postscript, an all-Canadian route from the east, passable for more than military expeditions, did now exist, and was under active improvement and heavy use.

On 16 September 1871 a much quicker and more comfortable means of travel to and from Winnipeg from the south was also announced: "On Monday night, another link ... with the world without was made ... by the arrival of one of Messrs. Blakely & Carpenter's stages, laden with ladies and gentlemen, right through from ... the terminus of the St. Paul and Minnesota Railway ... Now ... we are within five days' travel from ... a railway that can start us off to any part of the American continent."

On the communications front, an immensely important leap forward occurred on 20 November 1871, when Lieutenant Governor Archibald in Winnipeg and Governor General Lord Lisgar in Ottawa exchanged messages by telegraph.[107] Although that service would be somewhat unreliable for a while, the area was finally in instantaneous contact with the world most of the time. The postal service continued to be a source of frequent complaint, especially in regard to US treatment of Manitoba, but even that was improving.[108]

Less momentous forms of progress kept pace with transportation and communications: the first barbershop, operated by a member of the Ontario Rifles in his off-duty hours;[109] the new sport of velocipeding;[110] and Manitoba's first soda fountain in Dr Bird's drug store.[111]

The first novel by a Manitoba author made its appearance in April 1871. *Dot It Down,* by Winnipeg's merchant-diarist-historian Alexander Begg, was a tale of love and intrigue set in the Red River Settlement just prior to the Riel insurrection.[112] Although it offered no competition to better-known works of fiction published that year, such as George Eliot's *Middlemarch* or Lewis Carroll's *Through the Looking Glass,* it must have been read with great interest in many Manitoba homes, containing as it did accurately drawn local scenes, discussions of real local issues such as the political machinations of John Schultz's Canadian Party, and caricatures of several thinly disguised local personages. The villain was an obvious Schultz look-alike – a courageous thing for Begg to do in light of a pending libel action by Schultz against the *Manitoban*'s editors,[113] to say nothing of the horsewhipping Thomas Spence had sustained the previous fall.

Alexander Begg also published, that same year, his influential *The Creation of Manitoba: A History of the Red River Troubles,* based on the journal he kept during most of Riel's reign.[114] That book received a highly favourable review in the very popular *Illustrated Canadian News.* Remarkably, another book that would become a standard reference on early Manitoba history – J.J. Hargrave's *Red River*[115] – appeared that year also. Two new newspapers were launched in 1871: Joseph Royal's abovementioned French-language *Le Métis* in May; and the *Manitoba Liberal,* a short-lived, right-wing publication that replaced the *Manitoba Newsletter* in July. The *Liberal*'s editor, military officer Stewart Mulvey, would go on to play a prominent role on the English-Protestant side of public affairs in the months and years to come. In November 1871 the doors were opened at Manitoba College, an institution of higher learning from which the present University of Winnipeg eventually grew.[116]

Winnipeg's fire protection was markedly improved by the formation in April 1871 of the Nor'-West Engine Company No. 1, a volunteer organization. The HBC transferred its firefighting equipment to the new brigade, and "a number of gentlemen of the village ... promised to erect a fire hall." To guard against possible favouritism in firefighting services, its bylaws specified that "no member shall be allowed to introduce political subjects, or in any way allude to partyism, at any of the meetings."[117]

These new firefighting arrangements soon ended a long boycott of the fire-prone community by fire insurance companies.[118]

"FENIAN" RAID

One of Governor Archibald's most urgent challenges, and, it first seemed, one of his greatest triumphs, sprang from the only foreign military invasion the province has ever experienced.

"Viendront-ils? Ne viendrout-ils pas?" (Are they coming? Are they not coming?) asked an article in *Le Métis* on the 28 September 1871. "They" were invading troops thought to belong to the Fenian Brotherhood, the Irish American private army that had conducted several mostly unsuccessful incursions against targets in New Brunswick and Ontario in 1866 and 1870.[119] Ominous rumours of hostile gatherings south of the border had been drifting into Manitoba for some time, and were becoming insistent.

When W.B. O'Donoghue had parted from Louis Riel a little more than a year previously, it was with the intent, deplored by Riel, of seeking assistance from the United States.[120] Failing to win official support in Washington, O'Donoghue approached the Fenian Brotherhood, headquartered in New York. It would require only a small invading force to capture Fort Garry, he assured that organization's leaders, because the Métis could be counted on to renew their previous insurrection as soon as they knew that southern assistance was at hand. Although the brotherhood was sympathetic, it rejected the proposal. The optimism of 1866 and 1870 had largely dissipated, the Fenian treasury was no longer flush, and a ready supply of out-of-work Union army dischargees was no longer available.

O'Donoghue had nevertheless engaged the personal sympathies of several senior Fenian officers; and Generals John O'Neill and Thomas Curley, along with Colonel J.J. Donnelly,[121] accompanied him back to the northwest in their private capacities, with a view to raising funds and recruiting volunteers for an invasion of Manitoba. Along the way, O'Donoghue drew up a constitution for what he called the Republic of Rupert's Land, naming himself president and commander-in-chief. By summer's end, it was beginning to look as if their combined efforts might succeed. The *Manitoban* advised its readers on 30 September that, according to reports from St Paul, many strangers had been observed in the Irish hotels of that city hinting that "a considerable force" had been assembled and equipped, and that soon "a blow will be struck that will make the British lion howl."[122]

While the would-be invaders were making their preparations, Commissioner of Dominion Police Gilbert McMicken,[123] in far-away Ottawa, was also thinking about Manitoba. It was McMicken who had provided Provisional Government delegates Father Noel-Joseph Ritchot and Alfred H. Scott with safe conduct from the American border to Ottawa in 1870. Of more immediate relevance, McMicken had been instrumental in thwarting previous Fenian adventures in the east, and had been recently asked by Prime Minister Macdonald to move to Winnipeg and become the federal government's senior bureaucrat there. He was also to remain in charge of Dominion Police operations for the time being.

When McMicken heard about the suspicious activities of O'Donoghue, O'Neill, and company, he accelerated his relocation, hoping to reach Manitoba before the invaders did. A harrowing journey by special stagecoach from the end of rail, through massive prairie fires and a line of advancing invaders, brought him to Winnipeg on the evening of 2 October. McMicken advised Governor Archibald that the looming invasion was both real and imminent, although much smaller than the force of 500 to 2,500 men some rumours predicted.

Galvanized by that information, Archibald acted swiftly. The following day, Winnipeg's streets and other public places were festooned with copies of an urgent proclamation. It warned that "a band of lawless men, calling themselves Fenians," were poised at the border and preparing "to commit acts of depredation, pillage and robbery and other outrages upon the persons and property of our loving subjects," and called upon "all our said loving subjects, irrespective of race or religion or past local differences" to "RALLY ROUND THE FLAG!"[124] More specifically, the proclamation requested citizens to assemble in their parishes and select local officers to serve under experienced commanding officers the government would assign to supervise the necessary military training. "We are quite capable to repel these outlaws," the proclamation concluded, since they "can give no serious difficulty to brave men who have their homes and families to defend."

The call met with such an enthusiastic response, and recruiting proceeded so quickly, that by 5 October large numbers of settlers were under training, and several groups of mounted Halfbreed scouts had been dispatched to keep access routes to the province under surveillance.[125]

Late that night, scouts reported that the invaders had crossed the international boundary, and on the following day, "orders were issued to advance a body of [200] troops to meet the enemy." The weather being cold and wet, and most of the men inexperienced, it took that day and most of the evening to get the defence force across the Assiniboine River and in position to advance southward.[126] But the drenched and mud-caked bivouacked volunteers were mostly cheerful and keen to meet the enemy. Many of them must therefore have been disappointed to learn the next morning that the war was already over.

The invaders – only thirty-five or forty of them, it turned out – had indeed crossed the border early on the morning of 5 October. They armed themselves with rifles previously hidden under a haystack on the Canadian side, and proceeded to the Canadian customs house, where they took a prisoner, hauled down a Union Jack as a souvenir, and proceeded to the nearby HBC post. There, after informing the clerk in charge that he was a prisoner, O'Donoghue and his colleagues looted the store. While they were loading their booty into a wagon, however, a US cavalry force under Colonel Lloyd Wheaton galloped onto the scene, arrested several raiders, and chased the rest away. Although O'Donoghue escaped the first assault, he was pursued by some Canadian Halfbreeds, captured, and (to the subsequent chagrin of Canadian authorities) turned over to Colonel Wheaton, who confined him and the other prisoners on US territory. The invasion had thus ended very shortly after it began.[127]

The legal right of US troops to swoop down on the raiders on Canadian territory was dubious. Although Wheaton's men had been keeping an eye on the advancing Fenians for some time previously, they were probably not in "hot pursuit" when they crossed the border, and did not have advance permission from Canadian authorities.[128] Colonel Wheaton believed the HBC post to be on American territory, and carried that belief so far as to deny the still advancing force from Fort Garry permission to occupy and fortify the post, threatening to occupy the post himself if the Canadians persisted. As Archibald later explained to Ottawa, "Colonel Wheaton considers the post as within American lines for military purposes, though not for purposes of commerce, as the custom house is southward of the post ... Last winter we occupied the post with, as you will recollect, the consent of the US government."[129]

Realizing that pressing the point might create "international difficulties," and being thus denied the only suitable location at which to establish a border garrison, Lieutenant Governor Archibald ordered his defending army to return home – without so much as a glimpse of the enemy. While he did not share Wheaton's view about the location of the 49th parallel, he was grateful for the cavalry's swift action on this occasion, and therefore authorized any similar US actions that might be needed to prevent future hostile incursions. The disagreement as to the placement of the boundary line would later provide a plausible but ultimately unsuccessful defence to prosecutions of three Pembina Métis accused of assisting the "Fenian" foray.[130]

Colonel Wheaton turned over O'Donoghue and the other captured invaders to US civil authorities. A few days later, the prisoners were arraigned in a Pembina courtroom and defended by an attorney named Potter. Potter was assisted, from the spectators' seats, by Enos Stutsman – acting as what the newspaper called a "prompter." The charge was violation of US neutrality laws, and the prosecutor was Colonel Lloyd Wheaton. The proceedings turned quickly into what the *Manitoban*'s correspondent called a "screaming farce." Wheaton, clearly uncomfortable in the role of advocate, began by requesting adjournment until an important witness could be found; and defence counsel Potter responded with a stream of inanely facetious jibes at Wheaton, while "Stutsman laughed heartily at the want of common decency manifested by his puppet, and Colonel Wheaton sat with arms folded like the noble soldier he is, and paid no attention whatever to the insulting language."[131] Although that report did not say so, Wheaton's adjournment motion must have been granted, and the accused men were released on bail.

Following a long interlude, a regular US district attorney stayed the charges against the common soldiers involved on the ground that they were "obscure men ... misled" by their leaders. He brought O'Donoghue, O'Neill, Curley, and Donnelly before a grand jury in Pembina, however, on 21 February 1872. Although that jury returned indictments against all four, a procedural snarl necessitated a further adjournment, and O'Donoghue and Donnelly, the only accused men remaining on the scene, were again set free on bail. Warrants issued for O'Neill and Curley produced no arrests.[132] At that point, the trail of historical evidence grows cold. It is known that O'Donoghue and Donnelly were expected to be tried in September 1872,[133] but there is no indication that they were ever convicted – or even tried.

The only way the Fenian escapade could possibly have succeeded would have been with widespread participation by Manitoba Métis, and that could not have occurred without Louis Riel's concurrence. But Riel refused to have anything to do with the scheme.

Overtures were certainly made, the emissary appearing to have been the enigmatic Alfred Scott, former member of the Provisional Government's delegation to Ottawa, and an undoubted American sympathizer.

Scott travelled to Pembina in mid-July 1871, and wrote to Riel from there on 2 August that he "should like to meet you ... [I]t is a matter of great importance."[134] Riel was suspicious. Two versions of his reply, both dated 13 August, exist. The first, perhaps a draft, stated that "something serious objects to my meeting your desire." The other assured Scott that he could trust the bearer of Riel's letter to arrange an interview with Riel if it concerned "matters which regard only both of us." "If," however, Scott wanted to discuss "something of a higher importance," the messenger was to bring Scott's message in written form.[135] When Scott's written reply (regrettably unpreserved) went unanswered, he made one last attempt to meet the Métis leader in person: "From not answering your letter by my messenger I suppose you deem it of little importance. It is of utmost importance to you politically that I see and talk to you. Dare not write. There is a chance of your regaining your former position with firmer support."[136] That unmistakeable invitation to Riel to renew the Métis uprising with American assistance was as firmly shunned by the Métis leader as Scott's previous letters had been.

The Manitoba government had also been keenly interested in Louis Riel's intentions, and seems to have enlisted Bishop Taché's assistance at some time in September 1871 to determine Riel's position, and seek Métis support should the rumours of invasion prove to be true. Riel's first response was positive – but cagey. As for joining the Fenians, he was unequivocal: "[Y]ou can rest assured there is not the slightest danger of me or any one of my friends going with the Fenians. We dislike the Fenians, for they are condemned by our church, and ... I will have nothing to do with them."[137]

As for actively assisting the defenders, Riel was much more cautious at that point, telling Taché frankly, "You know perfectly well that my life is not safe. I may go to the front and fight against the Fenians, and I am sure to be killed by those behind me. So I am at a loss ... what can I do?" He had not altogether rejected the possibility of Métis assistance, however. Perhaps the concluding question mark indicated that he was angling for some quid pro quo.

At a secret meeting of Métis leaders convened at Riel's St Vital home on 28 September, a conclusion similar to that expressed in Riel's letter to Taché had been reached. Discussions were held between Governor Archibald and Father Ritchot that produced a guarantee that Métis who cooperated in the settlement's defence would be immune from prosecution. That assurance seems to have been accepted by the Métis leadership on 4 October. A draft letter from Riel to Ritchot the next day expressed the hope that their people would "rally and be inspired" by Archibald's proclamation,[138] and on 7 October, Riel wrote directly to the lieutenant governor, informing him that "[w]e appreciate what Your Excellency has communicated to Reverend Ritchot so we could aid during the exceptional situation. Several companies are organized and others are forming. Be assured that, without being enthusiastic, we have been devoted."[139]

By that time all the invaders had been either imprisoned or chased away by Colonel Wheaton and his men; but Archibald was no more certain of that fact than Riel was. Even knowing the initial raid had fizzled brought the governor only partial comfort, since it was far from clear that the enemy would not regroup and launch a second assault. "It was with great pleasure, therefore," Archibald informed Ottawa soon after, "that I received, on Saturday morning, the intelligence that the French Halfbreeds had rallied to the support of the Government."[140]

The governor's gratitude was no doubt enhanced by being informed on Sunday afternoon by Joseph Royal and Marc-Amable Girard that the Métis had followed up Riel's written assurance of support by assembling in St Boniface over 200 armed troops, about 50 of them mounted, in a demonstration of their readiness to serve the province. Would His Excellency be willing to inspect and speak to them? He most certainly would, and Archibald soon crossed the river, where he received a *feu de joie* from the men and an address of welcome from Girard. He replied with an expression of his pleasure at such loyalty from the French-speaking residents of the province, and then mingled and shook hands: "I spent some time in conversing with the crowd."[141]

At some point during his walkabout, Governor Archibald experienced what a modern counterpart might call an "uh-oh!" moment. "[A]mong the crowd," his report to Ottawa mentioned, "I had reason to believe there were some of the principal leaders of the movement of two years ago." One of those leaders was Louis Riel, although Archibald's report did not say so explicitly.

His tone turned defensive: "But when this large body of men were coming forward, under my proclamation, ... to rally the support of the Crown in a time of danger, it did not seem to me that that was the moment to inquire into the antecedents of any person in the assembly." A few days later, in a proclamation thanking Manitobans for their swift and wholehearted efforts to defend the province, Archibald attempted a public justification of his actions: "If among ... [the assembled Métis] there were – and I believe there were – some persons whose exceptional position might have led O'Donoghue to look for their support, it only adds to the value of the demonstration, and removes the last hope of the miscreants."[142]

This explanation did not help. Manitoba's "loyalists," and francophobes throughout Canada, were appalled that a viceregal representative had sought assistance from the Métis and – worse – had shaken the hand of the man they considered Thomas Scott's butcher. Adams Archibald had stumbled – badly. In early November 1871 John Schultz organized vociferous public meetings to protest the governor's alleged pandering to the French, and the Ontario press soon echoed the *Manitoba Liberal*'s hysteria.

POLITICAL SQUALLS

Three Métis from Pembina were accused of providing minor assistance to the raiders, and charged with "levying war against Her Majesty." Their trials in November 1871, which engaged all seven of the province's practising lawyers, are described below.[143]

While those trials were underway, an abrupt change occurred in the editorial policy of *Le Métis*, whose publisher, Joseph Royal, was a lawyer and the much-lauded speaker of Manitoba's first Legislative Assembly. On 23 November that newspaper, published as Royal was defending the alleged Métis "Fenians" in court, contained an editorial criticizing the Archibald government for having failed – especially in the months following the first legislative session – to improve relations between the province's Canadian and Métis populations.[144] The criticism was not levelled at Lieutenant Governor Archibald himself, but at his cabinet. Archibald, the editorial acknowledged, was personally responsible for most of the good things achieved during the past fourteen months, and could not be blamed for failing to accomplish single-handedly all that was required to be done. Dealing with every aspect of Manitoba's governmental needs was simply not possible for one man; the elected members of the ministry must therefore become much more involved in the vital work of reconciliation and governance. Was this not, in essence, a diplomatically expressed criticism of Archibald himself? Was it not an indirect demand for responsible government, which Adams Archibald, with Ottawa's support, was unwilling to institute or recommend?

The cabinet that *Le Métis* was criticizing for inaction had also been giving Archibald increasing difficulty. Attorney General Clarke, for one, was more difficult than ever to keep in line; and his independent, abrasive personality was riling some of his cabinet colleagues. Royal also thought Provincial Treasurer Girard, although French, was not sufficiently devoted to francophone interests. In fact, while criticizing the entire cabinet, Royal targeted Girard in particular.

Two days after the appearance of that editorial, Archibald submitted his resignation to Prime Minister Macdonald.[145] Whether or not the newspaper's criticism had triggered that decision, it had certainly not been the only cause. The irrational objections – from Ottawa and elsewhere – to Archibald's having sought Riel's assistance against the invaders, and having then thanked him for it, must have stung intensely. And those rebukes came on the heels of Ottawa's rejection of a proposal the lieutenant governor made concerning a group of Métis who returned from a prairie hunt to find eastern newcomers staking homestead claims to their land. In a private letter to Macdonald, Archibald accused the prime minister of not understanding the Manitoba situation at all.

Ottawa did not accept the resignation, however, even when Archibald renewed it in January 1872; so he agreed to remain in office for the time being. Royal's attacks on the government persisted nevertheless, and became more vitriolic after a bitter newspaper debate between defence counsel Royal and Attorney General Clarke over their competing roles during the "Fenian Trials."[146] In its final issue of 1871, *Le Métis* accused the cabinet of "notorious incompetence," and Girard of being "a traitor to his people."[147]

Marc-Amable Girard was appointed to the Senate of Canada in March 1872, and consequently resigned from the provincial cabinet. To the chagrin of Henry J. Clarke, Archibald appointed Joseph Royal to succeed Girard as provincial treasurer. This surprising appointment was due to Royal's strong influence among the French, along with Archibald's need to keep Clarke in line. Clarke, who considered Royal his rival as Manitoba's principal defender of French rights, was furious. But Governor Archibald had reached the end of his rope with Clarke, complaining to Macdonald in February, for example, that "[h]is indiscretions, which amount almost to madness, his utter disregard for the truth, his ignorance of the commonest principles of law, and his arrogance combine to make a compound of which I trust there are not many examples in the Dominion."[148] Clarke's political strength was too great to permit his dismissal; but adding Royal to the cabinet diluted Clarke's influence, gave the French a stronger voice in government, and – Archibald may have hoped – helped to keep both prima donnas in line.

More than cabinet feuding was troubling the provincial government. Finances were a serious concern, and the province became tardy in paying its debts. At least two court officers – Sheriff Sutherland and Court Clerk Bunn – complained of not being paid on time, and both eventually resigned their positions.[149] As will be seen, law enforcement was especially hard hit by financial restraints.[150]

STAYING ON COURSE

Adams Archibald remained at the helm of Manitoba's storm-tossed ship of state, doing his best to steer a middle course, until well after the period dealt with in this study. All things considered, it was an impressive performance.

When Alfred Boyd, the first member of the provincial cabinet, resigned due to business pressures in December 1871, Archibald replaced him with English Halfbreed John Norquay, an excellent choice with a distinguished premiership in his future.[151] Persistent requests by the governor for replacement troops after the expeditionary force withdrew brought a permanent garrison to the province.[152] Archibald's throne speech defence of his government's policies when the second session of the legislature opened in January 1872 met with hearty applause by most spectators.[153] The plaudits were louder still when the legislature prorogued five weeks later, having enacted another ambitious legislative program, largely initiated by Archibald. Twenty-nine bills had been passed, of which all but four received royal assent.[154] The twenty-five resulting statutes, when added to the forty-three enacted in 1871, completed a body of basic legislation sufficient to launch Manitoba into full-fledged provincehood – and to enable Archibald's successor, appointed late in 1872, to eventually grant the province full responsible government.

Of the four bills for which Lieutenant Governor Archibald reserved royal assent for the consideration of federal authorities (who declined to grant it), one calls for particular comment. The 1871 statute incorporating the Bar Society of Manitoba had been a compromise. Attorney General Clarke had wanted to create a law society based on the Ontario model, with legal authority to regulate its members. The lieutenant governor, however, had agreed only to a fraternal society being incorporated. At the 1872 session, the persistent Clarke persuaded the lawmakers that a law society with regulatory teeth was needed. Archibald, no less stubborn, reserved royal assent, explaining,

> This bill, even if the philosophy were sound under any circumstances, seemed to me premature. In a country like this, obstacles should not be thrown in the way of any person in good standing at the bar of any other Province to be admitted to the practice of law here ... But another important objection is the power given under this bill to the bar to regulate their own fees. Whether that is desirable in any stage of the history ... of a country, ... it would be a most dangerous power to extend to the bar of this Province in its present condition.[155]

The federal government agreed, and denied royal assent. The Manitoba bar would not gain self-governing powers until 1877.

LAW AND ORDER

Under the headline "Affray in Winnipeg," the *Manitoban* reported on 3 June 1871 that a few days previously "some 50 or 60 French Halfbreeds and soldiers engaged in a [street] fight in which fists, clubs, chairs, mud, and pieces of plank were freely used. Happily, the affair was one of only a few minutes' duration. Men were flitting angrily to and fro, flourishing weapons and grappling with each other, and had it not been that several of them were so drunk that they could hardly stand, a formidable riot might have occurred. The police were there, and two men were arrested: a French Halfbreed, and a Volunteer."[156] The brawl, which the newspaper described as "not very serious" in itself because "only one man was badly hurt," was attributed to the fact that "[t]here is much ill feeling between some of the French Halfbreeds and some of the Volunteers."[157] The writer noted that the ill feeling showed itself "when either or both are drinking. It has shown itself in several fights already, ... and we fear that if it is not stopped summarily the consequences may be of an alarming character ... The public peace must be preserved at all hazards."

But how could the passions that fuelled such breaches of the public peace be "stopped summarily" by a government as underresourced as Manitoba's? It was not just the Métis and the military who were at odds. Tension existed, at least in a collective sense, between Protestants and Catholics, anglophones and francophones, mixed-bloods and pure bloods, Americans and Canadians, and "loyalists" and "moderates." And few Indians were trusted by anyone else. Although the provincial police force had been put on a more professional footing than ever before, and was able to break up street fights like the above, its ability to deal with ethnic, religious, racial, or political violence on a large scale was little better than that of the sheriffs and constables of Assiniboia.

The force had other problems as well. In November 1871 a scandal arose over police handling of furs seized to stem the spread of smallpox.[158] Rumour had it that some furs had not been destroyed but had been secretly sold instead, to the personal gain of certain law enforcement officers. Attorney General Clarke took notice, and Police Chief Frank Villiers was suspended pending investigation by the sheriff. Deputy Chief Louis de Plainval took control of the force in the meantime. Due in part to the resignation of Sheriff Sutherland, that investigation was not completed until midsummer 1872, and when it was the results were inconclusive vis-à-vis Villiers. While there was no proof of his personal guilt, there had been "great irregularities," which Villiers had lacked "a business capacity" to deal with. His resignation was accordingly requested, and when it was not forthcoming, he was dismissed. Acting Chief de Plainval, always popular with the public, was confirmed in office, but the force had been tarnished.

Law enforcement problems were exacerbated by Manitoba's straitened financial circumstances. As the province's most expensive institution, the police force felt budget restraints heavily. When, in February 1872, Chief de Plainval was ordered by Attorney General Clarke to reduce spending, he was forced to reduce the size of the force from twenty-four to sixteen officers, despite the fact that those men were now spread over five detachments, St Norbert and Pointe du Chêne having been added to the previous three.[159] Regrettably, that cutback occurred just prior to a crime wave in the spring of 1872 caused by an infestation of cross-boundary hooligans.[160]

Whether reduced provincial spending on police protection contributed to an increase in the crime rate is impossible to tell from existing data. Two sets of rudimentary crime statistics for the Town of Winnipeg published in the *Manitoban* on 16 September 1871 and 15 April 1872 showed an increase in criminal charges laid between early November 1870 and mid-April 1871. Although the paper referred to a "per capita" increase, the rise can probably be accounted for by the growth of Winnipeg's general population during that period. There was a shift in *types* of charges: public drunkenness rose from 42 to 55 per cent of the total and theft from 11 to 18 per cent, while total charges against women fell from 14 to 0. So the police were getting busier as the law enforcement budget was shrinking; and offences commonly associated with transient populations, such as public drunkenness and theft, seemed to be on the rise.

Jail conditions remained a concern. Manitoba's first grand jury stated in its May 1871 presentment that "[o]n visiting the jail they found it entirely unsuited for the purpose for which it was used, and they recommended that prompt measures be taken for the erection of a jail and courthouse."[161] Although the grand jury failed to mention the fact, the jail – a new temporary facility housing the police office and a few tiny, unheated, unventilated holding cells – was not very secure. Two prisoners had escaped in February,[162] as did a man convicted at the current assize of an especially brutal assault on his wife.[163] Archibald moved swiftly, and as effectively as nearly empty provincial coffers permitted, on the jury's advice. He pointed out to Ottawa that the five men given lengthy sentences at the recent assize could not be housed in the jail because they would suffer or perish from cold in winter and suffocate in summer.[164] He proposed that a temporary federal penitentiary be established at Lower Fort Garry, where the HBC was willing to lease suitable accommodation, and he offered to make the necessary arrangements if assured "the expenses ... will be borne by the Government of Canada."

Under the 1867 British North America Act, Canada was constitutionally responsible for "penitentiaries," while the provinces were in charge of "reformatory prisons"; but the difference between penitentiaries and reformatory prisons was not explained. Prime Minister Macdonald, who was also Canada's attorney general, denied Archibald's request, asserting arbitrarily that penitentiaries were for imprisonments exceeding two years, and pointing out that Manitoba's only such prisoner had escaped.[165] Being in no position to challenge that interpretation in the courts, Archibald's government had no alternative but to lease the hoped-for "penitentiary" space at the Lower Fort itself as a provincially funded "reformatory prison." The grand jury selected for the November assize visited the new facility and found it quite satisfactory. "As for the lock-up in town," however, its recommendations continued, several improvements were urgently required.[166] When the latter measures were not taken, Police Chief de Plainval simply refused to keep prisoners in the cells overnight due to the risk of their freezing to death. Later, he had a physician certify in writing that the cells were "dangerous to human life."[167] The cash-strapped provincial government continued to ignore the problem, however, and satisfactory courthouse and jail facilities were not constructed in Winnipeg until 1873.

The escapades of the settlement's most notorious fugitive from justice, Ryder Larsen, continued to keep newspaper readers entertained throughout 1871. He was located, brought before the February assize, and charged with murder; but because the Crown was not ready to proceed to trial he was again released on bail.[168] Failing to appear at the May session, he was indicted on the murder charge, as well as one of larceny.[169] On 1 July the *Manitoban* offered its readers an illustration of how the smooth-talking former photographer so easily eluded the toils of the law:

> The famous Larsen ... has turned up again ... [S]ome children ... playing near ... Mr. Bourke's place, St. James, noticed a strange man take two horses from the prairie and tie them to a tree. Knowing the horses to be the property of Mr. Bourke, they ran and informed him of the fact. Mr. Bourke immediately proceeded to the spot with some neighbours ... Their first impulse was to bring him to town and give him in charge but, listening to his plausible promises of reformation and earnest prayers for "a chance," they foolishly allowed him to depart. The enterprising rascal went ... as far as Sturgeon Creek, where he secured two other horses, the property of a newly arrived Canadian, and made good his escape ... The police are on his track, and every effort will be made to bring him to justice.[170]

Although Ryder Larsen's name remained on criminal dockets for a long while, this was the last time he was seen in the settlement. The General Court's *civil* records nevertheless show that *someone* at Red River knew how to contact Larsen; for a civil claim against him was "settled," presumably through an agent, in November 1871.[171]

Law enforcement officers were still unable to deal effectively with vigilante and mob violence. On 21 December 1871, *Le Métis* reported, "A home invasion occurred, in truly odious circumstances, in the vicinity of St. Vital on December 8."[172] The invaded home was that of Louis Riel's mother, with whom the Métis leader and his sister had been living for some time. By diligence or luck, Louis was absent. "At about nine o'clock in the evening," the account stated, "a party of ten or fifteen men, armed with revolvers and faces masked, arrived at the residence ... Five of them entered at first, and demanded in English to be given accommodation for the night. They were told that, in view of the women being alone and the smallness of the house, they could not be put up." That ruse having failed, the five men left "after several insolent and indecent remarks." But, almost immediately, another contingent pounded on and kicked the door, and the women opened it again, fearing it would otherwise be broken down. This group of thugs took a different approach. They demanded entry "in the name of the Queen" and claimed to have a warrant for Riel's arrest. When his sister asked to see the warrant, "revolvers were exhibited" instead, and the intruders threateningly demanded to know Riel's whereabouts. When the women refused any information, the masked men searched the little house thoroughly and destructively, brandished their weapons a few more times, and left, their leader vowing "in a loud and menacing tone" that he would kill Riel "this very night" if he had to "search every house in the parish."

Although there was no doubt that the men were "loyalists," only one of them – a William Buchanan – was identified at that point. He was, according to *Le Métis*, arrested, brought before Magistrate Solomon Hamelin, and released on bail pending trial. Later, a Walter Davidson was also charged. But although both men were indicted at the May 1872 General Court assize for conspiracy to murder, they were never brought to trial.[173]

Matters did not soon improve. Gerhard Ens has described violence during the federal election riots of 1872: "Mobs, incited by Orangemen Cornish and Mulvey, invaded St. Boniface polls with bludgeons, and later smashed ... [the *Manitoban*'s] press. These outrages [were] sometimes supported by soldiers." And in March 1873 "Curtis Bird, an English Métis, and Speaker of the Assembly, was tarred for his opposition to a bill to incorporate the Town of Winnipeg."[174] The first of the riot leaders mentioned by Ens was a lawyer: Francis E. Cornish, recently arrived from London, Ontario, following professional, political, and marital setbacks there. Cornish was an experienced and talented barrister, but an unruly, violent, and bigoted – if roguishly charming – man, often at the centre of Manitoba's ethno-political mischief. When charges were laid against Cornish and other election-day rioters, he defended himself and them in court – retained, it was said, by his new friend and ally John Schultz.[175] The prosecutor was Joseph Dubuc, who, although an able counsel, lost every one of those cases because fear of reprisals deterred witnesses from testifying.[176] Dubuc himself then received a severe beating on the street outside the St Boniface courtroom at the hands of loyalist sympathizer John Ingram.[177] Although convicted of that assault, Ingram was lauded by many of the English-speaking population. Frank Cornish would be elected mayor of the newly incorporated City of

Winnipeg in 1874, and John Ingram would be hired as the city's chief of police.

THE COURTS IN TRANSITION

The transition from proprietary to provincial courts was lengthy and far from seamless. Until permanent courts could be created by the new legislature, it was necessary to rely temporarily, under section 129 of the constitution, on the courts extant when Manitoba became a province. As explained above, it can be persuasively contended that the second Provisional Government was lawful; in which case its laws and institutions should have been those so employed. Since Canada refused to accept the legitimacy of that government, however, the defunct courts of Assiniboia were resurrected. As we have seen, though, most of the same men sat in judgment anyway. We have also seen that the man chosen as recorder of the temporary "General Quarterly Court" of the province was former recorder and governor of Assiniboia Francis G. Johnson, borrowed from the Quebec Superior Court. Although he expected it to be a brief assignment, Johnson presided over seven judicial sessions: from November 1870 to May 1872 inclusive.

On 6 October 1870, not long after Thomas Bunn resumed his former duties as clerk of the General Quarterly Court (and Executive Council), the lieutenant governor proclaimed, "Our ... courts of justice are now open to suitors having any complaint or matter to bring before us therein."[178] Judge Johnson took his oath as recorder on 19 October,[179] and the first sitting of the born-again General Court occurred on 17 November.[180] Although the scene was in many respects familiar when the decrepit courthouse once more opened its doors for the dispensation of justice, there were a few changes. The recorder no longer sat with JPs and magistrates; he was alone on the bench. And, for the first time, there was a regular, professionally trained, prosecutor present: Henry J. Clarke, QC, soon to become Manitoba's first attorney general and the lieutenant governor's nemesis.[181]

That first session of the court[182] was surprisingly uneventful, given how little judicial activity there had been in the past year. An arrest warrant was issued for the still at-large Ryder Larsen, a stabbing case was remanded to the next session, an eight- or nine-year-old boy charged with shooting another boy was discharged due to his youth, and a motion to quash an 1868 civil judgment was adjourned.[183] One reason for the small caseload was that no criminal indictments could be preferred because no grand jury had been summoned, Judge Johnson being mistakenly of the opinion that grand juries could only be sanctioned by provincial legislation.[184] He had overlooked the legislation under which prior laws remained in force until replaced. Another possible reason for the slim docket was that a new way of dealing with civil claims was under consideration, and Johnson may have advised litigants to wait.

At that hearing, the recorder issued a stern warning to the volatile community: "[I]f there be any unruly spirits here who imagine that the law ... is to be over-ridden ... they will find, to their cost, that they are mistaken. I am obliged to say this ... [because] I have received information ... of lawless acts being contemplated by those who, of all others, have most reason to be thankful for their deliverance from recent trouble and the inauguration of the present state of things."[185] A clearer message to Dr Schultz and his loyalist followers would be hard to imagine; and it was repeated by prosecutor Clarke when the first Winnipeg sitting of the Court of Petty Sessions opened a few days later: "The public peace must be secured ... in Winnipeg, and in every corner of this Province of Manitoba, with as much certainty as it is maintained in front of Windsor Palace ... And restless and lawless spirits must learn ... that the day of mob law has passed away forever from this fair province, and that the law and order shall here prevail."[186]

At the latter hearing, with the venerable JP Andrew McDermot sitting alone on the bench (the requirement of multiple judges having been dispensed with for petty courts as well as for the General Court), another – and equally important – aspect of the rule of law was illustrated. A police officer – one Léon Hivet, described as "a respectable man" – was charged with being drunk and disorderly while on duty, and with throwing an overcoat at a superior officer when reprimanded. Technically, the latter charge was assault and battery. "[T]his man's offence is a very grave one," prosecutor Clarke said, "much more so than would be that of a civilian" because Hivet had "sworn to protect Her Majesty's subjects, and to maintain peace and order in this community." Although Clarke recommended, and McDermot imposed, the relatively light punishment of a $10 fine because the accused had pleaded guilty, he was subsequently dismissed from the police force. This case, and the newspaper prominence it received, demonstrated that everyone, regardless of position, was subject to the law.

The second session of the General Court was no busier than the first. Fortunately, the petty courts, which handled the lion's share of criminal cases and did not rely on grand juries to initiate prosecutions, remained operational.

Also active in Winnipeg, for about a week in January 1871, was a second round of evidence-gathering hearings in the English false imprisonment action by G.O. Corbett against one-time HBC North American governor-in-chief Alexander Grant Dallas in retaliation for Corbett's 1863 conviction for attempted abortion. An earlier round of hearings in that litigation had fizzled out, but the commission had now been renewed, and was being vigorously pursued by new personnel.[187] Corbett would later abandon the suit.

The first Manitoba Legislature created a new judicial system. Because of the rift between the attorney general and the lieutenant governor, it was not an easy process. Clarke had a more elaborate system in mind than had Archibald, and revised the governor's draft bill, which had called for a Supreme Court of only one judge, to create a three-judge tribunal. A dispute of major proportions ensued, at the conclusion of which, as with the Bar Society bill, the attorney general was obliged to accept the governor's original scheme.[188] Clarke's speech to the Legislative Assembly when introducing the Supreme Court bill[189] made no direct reference to his differences with Archibald. He even managed to sound pleased to be sponsoring the legislation he had been forced to accept. Two aspects of the bill would find particular favour with ordinary Manitobans, he boasted. One was that the court's processes were "as simple as possible" in both language and procedure. As for court procedures, "[T]he more simple the laws are made, the better for the people." The other point Clarke stressed was that the new court, like the old, would function solely on the basis of English laws and English legal principles. This assurance was designed to spike persistent loyalist complaints that Clarke and the other Quebec-trained lawyers were subjecting Manitoba to undue French influence.

The Supreme Court bill was thus enacted; but more than legislation is required to put a judicial system in place. Judges must be appointed, and under Canada's constitution, it is federal, not provincial, authorities who appoint judges at that level. The government of Sir John A. Macdonald ("Old Tomorrow") chose, for unknown reasons, to appoint no one for the time being. That meant the temporary General Quarterly Court had to be continued; and Judge Johnson travelled west again to conduct the May 1871 court session – with a large criminal docket that could no longer be postponed.

Even then, however, it took only two days for Johnson to deal with the ten criminal charges and one civil case.[190] The criminal docket was shortened somewhat because in three cases (two involving the elusive Ryder Larsen) the accused persons had absconded. The civil list was small due to elaborate new pretrial procedures which, despite the attorney general's boast of simplicity, slowed litigation considerably.[191] At the August 1871 sitting,[192] Judge Johnson was back once more, with a lighter criminal docket, but a heavier civil one. On that occasion he apologized to the grand jury for the inadequate temporary court facilities, explaining that there had not been time to fulfil the grand jury's request for a new courthouse and jail "this season." He acknowledged, however, that "the inconvenience of today would be an impossibility another season. Today we are enabled to proceed with open doors and windows; but in November next, with stoves lighted and doors and windows shut, it would be next to impossible to proceed. And before that time arrives, I hope we will have left so inconvenient a place."[193]

But when the recorder returned to Winnipeg in bitter November to open what would be an unusually demanding assize, he found that there were still no new facilities. His response was to open the court on the scheduled date and time in the old building, but to adjourn immediately until suitable accommodations were provided. A week later, proceedings resumed in a building previously used as a temporary hospital for cholera victims. In reporting these events, *Le Métis* asked, "When will we have a court of justice worthy of the name?"[194] Regrettably, the answer to that question would not be known until well after the General Quarterly Court ceased to exist. Following the first sitting, in October 1872, of the permanent court that replaced it – in the same temporary premises – the new chief justice would describe the experience to Prime Minister Macdonald: "Imagine ... a courtroom packed with people, one day so cold that I had to have a robe over my knees and a refreshing blast whistling past me, and afterwards stifling with the heat."[195] And that was only October.

Returning to the hospital-cum-courtroom in November 1871, the General Court's principal task was to deal with the "Fenian Trials,"[196] in which three Pembina Métis were accused of participating in O'Donoghue's incursion the previous month. The defendants were an aging and simple-minded man called Louison "Oiseau" Letendre and two younger men: André Jerome St Mathe and Isidore Villeneuve. There was only one other criminal case, in which the accused pleaded guilty, and a relatively light civil docket; but the court had its hands full with the Fenian cases. All seven of the province's courtroom lawyers took part: Attorney General Clarke and John F. Bain for the Crown and the rest for the defendants.[197]

The case placed Attorney General Clarke in a difficult political position. As a member of the provincial legislature and a frequent spokesman for the government, he had consistently defended the rights of Manitoba's francophone population. But, as attorney general, it was his duty to prosecute these three Métis men on charges that could cost them their lives. Many loyalists were concerned that Clarke would allow his sympathies to interfere with his duty, and it was rumoured that some spectators carried a rope to hang him if he failed to convict the alleged traitors.[198] Probably from professional integrity rather than fear, Clarke conducted the prosecutions vigorously, and with no evident restraint, despite sustaining undoubted political damage among the French as a result.

Defence counsel were hampered in their preparations by several serious obstacles: they were retained very shortly before trial; all the accused were francophones, and only two defence lawyers spoke French; the scene of the alleged crimes was a long way away; and that fact, coupled with the poverty of all three accused, precluded searching for eyewitnesses. The accused were not protected by their American citizenship because the legislation under which they were charged applied to aliens as well as to British subjects. The cases were nevertheless defended skilfully and tried fairly, with the result that two of the three accused, St Matthe and Villeneuve, were eventually acquitted. Letendre was convicted and sentenced to death, but, blessedly, his age and mental state, along with the minor nature of his role, brought an eventual reprieve from the governor general of Canada.

The lower courts were not yet affected by the federal government's tardy appointment practices. Although the 1871 legislation changed their names slightly from petty courts to petty session courts, their members continued for the time being to be considered provincial appointees, and in June 1871 the Manitoba cabinet revoked previous appointments and made new ones, mostly of the same people, to the newly structured courts.[199] In September the petty session courts began recordkeeping as such, employing in some cases the same record books their predecessors had used before being closed down by the November 1869 insurrection.[200]

Before the February 1872 sitting of the General Court, the as-yet-unimplemented 1871 court legislation underwent major amendment.[201]

Not only was the name "Supreme Court" changed to "Court of Queen's Bench," and the "Courts of Petty Sessions" to "County Courts," but, to Lieutenant Governor Archibald's probable annoyance, the Queen's Bench was also to have three members – a chief justice and two associate "puisne" justices – and to hear appeals with all three judges sitting "en banc." The Queen's Bench judges would also sit individually in the county courts. Federal authorities had come round to Attorney General Clarke's original views.

Macdonald's government continued, however, to procrastinate about actually appointing the judges it now agreed Manitoba required. Although the provincial cabinet urged Ottawa in March to appoint at least one judge immediately, and proposed Clarke for that position,[202] no appointment was made until fall. Recorder Johnson was accordingly obliged to preside over a very full agenda of the General Court in February 1872[203] and again at a final session in May.[204]

When Johnson left Montreal for that last Winnipeg sitting, it was in the expectation that he would remain for a considerable time, but in a different capacity. Lieutenant Governor Archibald had returned to the east, exhausted and jaded. Although the trip was described as a leave of absence, he had no intention of holding the viceregal post any longer than it took Macdonald to appoint a successor. The prime minister decided that Francis Johnson's long and varied experience in Assiniboia and Manitoba equipped him well to administer the problem-prone province, and Johnson accepted his invitation to become lieutenant governor, apparently on an interim basis, after the last sitting of the General Quarterly Court.

Parliament did not agree with the appointment, however. While Johnson was travelling westward, a debate took place in the House of Commons, during which the Opposition sharply criticized the fact that Johnson would be receiving a double salary – as both a Quebec judge and Manitoba's lieutenant governor (this likely being the chief attraction for the chronically cash-strapped Johnson); and Macdonald was forced to withdraw the offered appointment.[205] Having learned of this turn of fortunes as he passed through St Paul, Francis Johnson was a bitter man when he arrived in Winnipeg for his final tour of judicial duty there. And he faced an unusually crowded docket in Winnipeg – one that required almost two weeks to dispose of.[206]

Of greatest interest were two groups of politically charged cases that are almost invisible in the court records. The first group arose from an overreaction to the Fenian threat. While it was looming, someone accused two men – William Cosgrove and Edward Lennon – of communicating with the invaders. Lawyer John Bain, acting as a special constable, obtained warrants from magistrates Andrew Bannatyne and Robert Cunningham for the men's arrest and incarceration. After the Fenian crisis passed, Cosgrove and Lennon sued Bain, Bannatyne, and Cunningham for false imprisonment.[207] That was in February 1872. The claims were met with a procedural defence based on an English statute requiring advance notice of actions against public authorities. The emphasis placed on that technical defence suggests that there was not a strong substantive defence to the false imprisonment claim.

The plaintiffs admitted that no advance notice had been given in these cases, but argued that the statute in question was not applicable to this situation. At that point, someone – perhaps Judge Johnson – observed that there was not enough time left during that sitting to deal with all the legal and factual issues involved; and agreement was reached between counsel and the judge that Lennon's action would be adjourned until the May sitting. Cosgrove's action was summarily dismissed with his consent, but he was granted leave to commence a new action should he choose to do so. That arrangement allowed Johnson to get home promptly, gave counsel time to hone their legal arguments, and – perhaps not coincidentally – kept the dispute out of the public eye at a time when passions aroused by the "Fenian Raid" and its sequelae were still flaming.

At the May 1872 court session, the procedural question was argued, as agreed, in Lennon's case alone. Judge Johnson agreed with the defendants that failure to give advance notice defeated the action. The arguments and ruling were reported in the *Manitoban*,[208] whose editor was one of the defendants; but since the success of the technical defence prevented the factual coals being raked over in open court there was little public reaction. Cosgrove's action was reinstituted in April 1872,[209] doubtless after giving advance notice, but remained dormant until June 1873, when it was withdrawn without explanation. A quiet settlement arrangement seems to have been reached and adroitly executed, without arousing loyalist protests, to compensate the plaintiffs for being hastily and groundlessly prosecuted.

The other group of politically sensitive cases disposed of with very little publicity in May 1872 involved the December 1871 nighttime raid on the home of Louis Riel's mother by masked and armed loyalist hooligans.[210] Those cases were also kept off the February court docket, no doubt to forestall public demonstrations. But at the May assize three related draft indictments were placed before the grand jury for confirmation. The indictments charged two loyalists, William Buchanan and Walter Davidson, with separate offences of assault and battery and conspiracy to murder. The court record does not name the alleged *victims* of those crimes, as earlier records usually did; but there is little doubt that the assault and battery charges were brought by Madame and Mademoiselle Riel, and that the murder conspiracy charge was brought by Louis Riel.

Given that "assault" does not necessarily involve physical contact, but includes directly menacing another with a weapon, that charge had a reasonably good prospect of success. The likelihood was low, however, of convicting someone of conspiracy to murder who merely uttered a drunken threat to injure a person not present. Yet, inexplicably, the grand jury brought in a true bill on the conspiracy to murder charge, but not on the lesser ones. Then – more puzzling still – nothing further happened! Unlike most of the other cases in which true bills were returned that session, the Buchanan and Davidson prosecutions were never proceeded with.

What had happened? Attorney General Clarke had clearly stayed the cases, as all attorneys general have the discretion to do. As the Crown's representative, an attorney general, then as now, could stay proceedings without explaining why.[211] Clarke must have realized that a conviction of conspiracy to murder would be extremely unlikely to obtain and – more to the point – that even attempting to prosecute the case would risk a dangerous loyalist backlash. Why, then, had he put the charges to the grand jury in the first place? Perhaps he was ordered to do so by the lieutenant governor and cabinet – which now included Joseph Royal. And he probably expected to get an indictment for the threats to the women, which could be fairly safely prosecuted, but not on the far-fetched and incendiary charge of conspiracy to murder Louis Riel. When the grand jury reversed his expectations, he – and probably the cabinet – knew it would be foolhardy to proceed.

QUARTERLY COURT FAREWELL

The province's General Quarterly Court sat for the final time on 28 May 1872. As that day dawned, the only person who knew it would be the court's final day of sitting was Judge Francis Johnson.[212] Counsel arriving in the courtoom that morning with procedural motions to present or oppose might, however, have wondered why the shorthand reporter from the *Manitoban*, whom the judge had quietly asked to attend, was present on a day scheduled for only such routine matters. Attorney General Clarke knew the judge was anxious to get away soon, but Johnson had promised to remain at least long enough to deal with an important pending tenancy case. When the scheduled procedural business was complete, however, the reporter's presence was explained: Johnson proceeded to deliver a valedictory address.

"I avail myself of an opportunity, which will never occur again," he began, "to state to the profession some things which they and the public are interested in knowing. Certain proceedings took place in the House of Commons of Canada recently, which affected me personally. The nature of these proceedings was that of a vote or motion of censure against the Government for appointing me to the office of Lieutenant-Governor while holding the office of judge of the Superior Court of Lower Canada; and that proceeding resulted in my commission as Lieutenant-Governor being cancelled."[213] He then asserted that a Quebec law prohibiting "double-dipping" by judges of that province did not affect the legal validity of any of his judicial activities in Manitoba. After remarking that it would not be "becoming" for him to say anything further about his feelings concerning his treatment by the Government of Canada, but that he would do so at the "proper time and place," Johnson turned to his controversial awards of Riel Resistance compensation money, a matter dealt with above.[214] Then, following a few words of polite farewell by the judge, and an equally brief and laudatory response by Attorney General Clarke on behalf of the bar, the General Quarterly Court rose for the final time.

At 4:00 the next morning, Francis Johnson left Winnipeg by stagecoach,[215] hoping, as he had already informed the prime minister, "never again to visit these infernal regions."[216] Some of those he left behind may have shared – from an opposite perspective – the distaste Johnson apparently felt for his past associations with Manitoba.

Attorney General Henry Clarke, for instance, must have been biting his tongue when he told Johnson the previous day on behalf of the Manitoba bar that he would "always command their respect and good wishes."[217] Not only was Clarke annoyed by the judge's sudden departure before the business of the court was finished, but he and the government were also incensed by Johnson's refusal to perform a very important judicial assessment of alleged election irregularities assigned to him by statute at the 1872 sitting of the provincial legislature. The first provincial election had produced many complaints that unqualified persons had voted. More than half of those who cast ballots in Winnipeg were allegedly not entitled to do so, for example. The legislature decided a judicial evaluation was essential, but Clarke's repeated requests that Johnson carry out the task met with nothing but equivocation, avoidance, and broken promises from beginning to end of the judge's final visit to the province. Clarke sent an outspoken condemnation of Johnson's behaviour in the matter to the lieutenant governor, and Archibald, who shared the attorney general's concerns, passed the criticism on to Ottawa.[218]

Clarke was not alone in his distrust of the General Quarterly Court's last judge. Johnson's lifelong inability to manage his personal finances had caused numerous scrapes throughout his career, and had probably been at the bottom of Sir George Simpson's lack of respect for him. Lieutenant Governor Archibald complained to Macdonald in September 1871 that the judge risked tarnishing the public's perception of his judicial impartiality by accepting free room and board from the HBC while in Manitoba.[219] And Archibald's successor, Alexander Morris, told the prime minister in October 1872 that when Johnson left Winnipeg for the last time he reportedly took with him a sum of money entrusted to his safekeeping by one of his Winnipeg domestic servants.[220] Was that why the judge vanished so suddenly on the 4:00 AM stagecoach? Francis G. Johnson was intelligent, quick-witted, legally knowledgeable, charming, and a gifted speaker in both English and French. He was also self-centred, arrogant, improvident, lazy, and soft-principled. Over the years, he served long, and tolerably well, as recorder of Rupert's Land, governor of Assiniboia, and recorder of the provincial Quarterly Court. But Red River and Manitoba had deserved better.

SUCCESSORS[221]

Finally, in July 1872, the prime minister appointed a permanent judge for Manitoba. He was Alexander Morris, an Upper Canada–born, forty-six-year-old, physically ailing lawyer-politician – a cabinet colleague of Macdonald's – who had requested a judicial appointment where "the work would be light."[222] Little did he know what lay ahead. Despite what might seem unpromising portents, Morris performed creditably as Manitoba's first chief justice, and, a little later, as its second lieutenant governor and Canada's principal negotiator of western Indian treaties. Arriving in Winnipeg on 13 August 1872, he was sworn in the next day and called to the bar of Manitoba on 1 October. A week later, Manitoba's

Court of Queen's Bench sat for the first time, with Chief Justice Morris presiding. His two puisne colleagues, James C. McKeagney from Nova Scotia and Louis Bétournay from Quebec, were appointed later in the year, sworn into office in December, and first sat on 7 January 1873.

The petty sessions courts, which had not been seriously affected by the 1871 legislation, were very significantly impacted by the 1872 amendments. For one thing, their name was changed to "County Courts," a county structure having been created for the province. A very serious consequence of that change was that it transferred the appointment of the courts' members from provincial to federal jurisdiction, because section 96 of the British North America Act made the naming of the "Superior, District, and County Court" judges an exclusively federal responsibility. Nothing changed immediately, since the legislation preserved the existence of the petty sessions courts until the county courts were proclaimed in operation. As soon as Chief Justice Morris's appointment was announced in July, however, before he had even arrived in the province, and long before he had any colleagues to assist him, the county courts were proclaimed to exist. Two months later, as the consequences of that negligent premature act began to be realized, the provincial cabinet sent Ottawa an urgent dispatch pointing out that "this Province ... has been for the past two months without any Petty Courts," and that replacement county court judges had not yet been appointed.[223]

Matters got even worse when, very shortly after the appointments of McKeagney and Bétournay, but before they took their places on the bench, Alexander Morris was made lieutenant governor of Manitoba and the Northwest Territories, and another long search for a suitable chief justice began. But that was another era.[224]

12

Was Justice Served? 1835–69

The legal system whose operations are recorded in the pages of the General Quarterly Court of Assiniboia's records and related documents exhibited many roughnesses, shortcomings, and failures. It sought to achieve no more than "substantial justice between man and man."[1] *Was it a significantly less satisfactory justice system than those of Canada and England at the time – or now? The author thinks not.*[2]

What of the area's overall governance? Much injustice was experienced, especially but not exclusively by Aboriginal populations, at the hands of the area's corporate and early democratic governments. It is doubtful, however, that conditions were ever worse than, or even as bad as, those prevailing in other parts of the British Empire at the times in question. And a gradual, if incomplete and glacially slow, evolution toward more enlightened government can be discerned in the years reviewed. Justice was nevertheless more readily available from Red River's courts than from either its corporate or democratic governors.

"SUBSTANTIAL JUSTICE"

In November 1869 Judge John Black, whose experience with Red River justice went back thirty years, told a grand jury, "As far as possible, we have never allowed mere technicalities to stand in the way of substantial justice."[3] This was not an isolated observation. The term "substantial justice" was used frequently over the years to express the Red River Settlement's juridical desideratum.[4] Other terms were also used to express the same goal. Former Assiniboia governor William B. Caldwell, for example, told the 1857 parliamentary enquiry into Hudson's Bay Company governance, "I tried to do justly between man and man."[5] The object of this chapter is to consider how well that goal was achieved and to speculate about the differences, if any, between "substantial justice" and the goals of mature British-based legal systems.

COMPONENTS OF JURIDICAL SYSTEMS

What are the major components and characteristics of any effective justice system? First, there must be a body of laws: consistent and generally understood adjudicative norms by which peoples' behaviour and disputes can be judged. Needed next is an impartial judiciary: a body of arbiters capable of fairly applying the laws to particular situations. Since even competent and fair-minded arbiters are subject to error, the judiciary should be two-tiered, decisions of lower level tribunals being reviewable by higher ones. Most lawyers would say there must also be advocates to assist litigants to present their cases and ensure that all relevant factors are considered before judgment is rendered. Then enforcement machinery is needed: sheriffs, police, prisons, and so on, to coerce those unwilling to comply voluntarily with laws and judicial edicts. Finally, in all but totalitarian states, there must be a general acceptance of, and trust in, the foregoing components; or else the system would collapse for lack of compliance.

These are ideal requirements, of course. No real-life juridical structure has entirely satisfactory laws, invariably fair-minded adjudicators, uniformly competent and ethical lawyers, or completely efficient and humane enforcement agencies. Nor does any actual justice system enjoy the universal respect of those it serves. When assessing particular systems, one cannot reasonably expect more than substantial fulfilment of the ideal model.

COMPONENTS OF ASSINIBOIA'S JUSTICE SYSTEM

The adjudicative system operating at Red River between 1835 and 1869 included all the foregoing elements, although the strength of each waxed and/or waned over time. The general assessment for which this chapter aims will therefore entail considerable averaging and occasional comparison of not-quite comparable factors.

Laws

Laws were in place long before the Red River Settlement. The HBC's royal charter of 1670, which granted the company ownership of, a commercial monopoly within, and governmental suzerainty over north-central North America, stated that "within any of the ... lands or territories hereby granted ... all persons belonging to the said ... Company, or that shall live under them" should to be judged "in all causes, whether civil or criminal, according to the laws of this Kingdom."[6] The company and its local authorities could also make supplementary laws for local application within its territories, if such laws were "reasonable and not contrary or repugnant, but as near as may be agreeable to the laws, statutes or customs of this our realm."[7] That power to make laws with local application, as well as to adjudicate, was given to such governors and councils as the HBC appointed for particular localities within its domains.

After the 1821 merger of the Hudson's Bay Company and the North West Company concluded the bitter and bloody fur trade rivalry between them, a retirement community was established at the tiny settlement Lord Selkirk had established at the junction of the Red and Assiniboine Rivers almost a decade previously, and the area became the field headquarters for the new HBC's North American operations. The governmental needs of that community and the rest of Lord Selkirk's former Assiniboia territory were met by a new governor and council and other public officers.[8] Although few local laws were enacted before the early 1830s, they began to accumulate significantly about the beginning of the period with which this study is chiefly concerned.[9]

The historic meeting of the Assiniboia governor and council that created Assiniboia's quarterly courts was convened at Red River on 12 February 1835. Responding to suggestions from the HBC's North American governor-in-chief, George Simpson, the council adopted a number of important new laws relating to those courts, Assiniboia's new police force, and other matters. Thereafter, it produced a stream of legislation, steady if never profuse, to regulate local circumstances. By July 1839 a consolidation and revision of those local laws was required,[10] and further consolidations were enacted in 1852 and 1862.[11]

The fact that laws specifically applicable to Assiniboia existed was not in itself sufficient to satisfy the first component of an effective justice system. Were those laws appropriate to local circumstances? Were they understood and accepted by the local population? Were they compatible with English law? And was the general law of England sufficiently accessible and understood by the people of Assiniboia? There were problems from time to time in all these respects vis-à-vis both English law and the settlement's local laws, but in the author's opinion, none was fatal to their overall effectiveness.

Accessing the details of English law – whether common law or statutory – in the remote wilds of nineteenth century North America was difficult. Detailed legal knowledge was not required at Red River, however. All that was needed was an understanding of the basics sufficient to guide people in their interactions with one another, and to equip those who judged others' conduct to do so fairly and in substantial accordance with England's fundamental legal norms. Happily, there were at least two excellent books available at Red River at this time to provide that level of essential legal information: William Blackstone's *Commentaries on the Laws of England* and Richard Burn's *Justice of the Peace.*[12] The first provided an accurate overview of English law; the second was a thorough, clearly written, frequently updated procedural manual for magistrates in England and the British colonies. Although the Aboriginal population had much less opportunity than others to understand these laws and legal structures, those who lived in or had much contact with the settlement were not slow to learn their basics.

A potentially troublesome complication stemmed from Recorder Adam Thom's bizarre view of the vintage of applicable English laws. He contended that the HBC charter spoke as of the date of its enactment; and since that date was May 1670, no statutes enacted or modifications to common law made after that were, in his opinion, applicable within the HBC territories.[13] While neither Thom nor anyone else thought it made practical sense for the settlement's laws to be almost 200 years out of date, he nevertheless maintained that interpretation, in theory at least, until the reception date for English law was formally altered by local legislation. As a practical matter, however, Thom's interpretation made little difference. The nonlawyer magistrates who dealt with the bulk of the settlement's litigation in the petty courts, and who outvoted Thom on his own court, applied contemporary law in spite of him.[14] On one occasion he seems to have admitted doing so himself.[15]

The laws of greatest day-to-day significance to most settlers were those the Council of Assiniboia enacted to regulate purely local matters, and they generally suited the circumstances well. Their chief problem was being brought to the attention of residents in a community that, for most of the quarterly courts' existence, possessed neither newspaper nor printing press. Expedients employed to overcome that difficulty included tacking new laws to church doors, making copies available at the homes of local magistrates, and occasionally having the laws recited, like a sort of legal catechism, at the beginning of court sessions. One way or another, word got around the little community. And when it did not judges and juries were tolerant. Ignorance of the law never presented a serious problem at Red River.

Adjudicators

Red River also possessed a judicial structure. Between 1822 and 1835 that structure was quite rudimentary. The HBC-appointed governor and council of the area in question simply exercised their authority under the company's 1670 charter to administer civil and criminal justice. A serious challenge to that system came early, when the company's chief factor at Red River refused to acknowledge the jurisdiction of Assiniboia officials over activities of the company itself. But, after a period of uncertainty, the company's Governor and Committee in London resolved the matter in favour of the rule of law, and thereafter it was never denied that the company's commercial arm was subject to the authority of its governmental and judicial arms.[16] There were, to be sure, occasions when judicial authorities exhibited bias; but these were no more frequent than under major present-day legal systems, and were effectively offset by the juries and lay magistrates to be discussed below.

The next crisis for Assiniboia's justice system arose from the colony's growth. When Governor-in-Chief Simpson met the Council of Assiniboia in February 1835, he pointed out that Red River had outgrown its initial juridical arrangements, and proposed a more elaborate scheme. At his suggestion, the council created several judicial districts, each with a court of petty sessions, in which respected local magistrates adjudicated relatively minor criminal and civil matters; and a General Quarterly Court where the Assiniboia governor and council, expanded to include petty court magistrates, dealt with cases of greater importance and appeals from the petty courts. All courts sat quarterly, and more frequently when needed.[17] The appeal feature of these arrangements was deficient, in that there was no way to appeal from rulings of the General Court. In practice, however, this flaw rarely caused problems. Even in the case of petty courts, from which appeals were possible, they were rarely sought; and virtually all General Court decisions were based on jury verdicts – which are largely impervious to appeal even in modern practice.[18]

While the judicial arrangements enacted in 1835 functioned well, Governor-in-Chief Simpson felt the need for a judge with formal legal training. His search for such a judge led him to the remarkable fellow-Montrealer Adam Thom, who was appointed as recorder of Rupert's Land. That brilliant, well-educated, and prodigiously energetic man, although only one of several court members, rapidly became the principal figure on the bench: determining procedures, ruling on questions of law, instructing the sheriff and petty court magistrates, and charging juries. He also made several important contributions to the improvement of Red River's legal system. It was he who drafted both the first and second compendia of the settlement's local laws.[19] He established consistent procedures for court hearings. And, most important of all for the overall effectiveness of the system, Recorder Thom insisted that virtually all General Court trials be conducted before juries.

Despite those major accomplishments, Thom's judicial career was a disaster. His manner – arrogant and pontifical to all but those to whom he felt the need to be accommodating – was annoying to most with whom he dealt, in and out of the courtroom. His communicative style, both written and spoken, was so ponderous, pedantic, convoluted, and long-winded that those he addressed, including Governor-in-Chief Simpson, were often unable to determine his meaning. His temper, when aroused, was ferocious. Even more harmful was Adam Thom's bias. The anti-French attitudes he had honed to a lethal edge in Lower Canada brought him into great disfavour among the francophone majority of Red River. He refused to address French-speaking parties, witnesses, or jurors in their own language in or out of court.[20] When twice sued in his own court – first by a serving girl for arrears of wages and then by a carpenter whom he refused for petty reasons to pay, he used bullying tactics to achieve the results he desired.[21] And Thom's HBC loyalty led him to uphold from the bench tactics he himself had devised to suppress competition against the company.

Although the other factors steadily eroded public confidence in Recorder Thom from almost the moment of his arrival at Red River, it was his unremitting defence of the HBC's commercial monopoly that put him on a collision course with most of the community. The resulting confrontation at the *Sayer* free trade trial in May 1849,[22] in which a mob of armed demonstrators refused to let the proceedings continue except on their terms, was the worst violation of the rule of law in the history of Assiniboia's courts. And Thom's amazing swan song, in the multiple roles of counsel, witness, and judge in *Foss v. Pelly and Davidson*[23] the following year, brought perpetual ridicule to those courts in the estimation of some Canadian historians.

Fortunately, the story did not end in 1849–50. Thom was replaced as recorder by Francis G. Johnson, a bright, common-sense, young Montreal lawyer who, although flippant, lazy, and less than scrupulously principled, performed the responsibilities of recorder – and later of governor of Assiniboia – tolerably well. Before Johnson arrived in 1854, and after he left in 1858, the gap was filled, satisfactorily for the most part, by other Assiniboia governors, and later by two remarkably capable nonlawyer recorders. The first of the governors, Major (later Lieutenant Colonel) William B. Caldwell, was a bumbling fool who so dreaded the task that, fortunately, he relied on juries and the magistrates on the bench to make most decisions. The governor who replaced Johnson in 1858, and who remained in office until 1869, was William McTavish, a man who was everything Thom and Caldwell were not – wise, humane, down-to-earth, practical – and also, in sharp contrast to Johnson, an indefatigable worker.

Although McTavish performed well on the bench, he did not relish the judicial role and, like Caldwell, left as much of that work as he could to others, relying particularly heavily on Dr John Bunn. Besides being Red River's principal physician for many years, Bunn gradually became one of its most prominent governmental figures, serving, before his career was over, as coroner, petty court magistrate, councillor, collector of customs, sheriff, acting governor, and acting recorder. His sometimes stern, sometimes humorous, always fair-minded, exchanges with accused persons, litigating parties, witnesses, and jurors leave little doubt that "substantial justice" was indeed dispensed by the General Court under the doctor's humane leadership.

Dr Bunn's sudden death in the spring of 1861 brought erstwhile Court Clerk John Black back to the settlement and to the bench as acting recorder. Black was thoroughly familiar with both Red River and its courts. As the HBC governor remarked following the appointment, "He knows the habits, manners, customs of the people ... and his ability, good sense, and conciliating manners induce me to believe that he will fill the office ... to the approval of all parties."[24] He did. After announcing in the *Nor'-Wester* newspaper that his goal was to achieve "substantial justice,"[25] he proceeded to do so for the next seven years, with the approbation of most of the settlement's citizenry. Black's humiliating defeats at the hands of Dr John Schultz[26] and American attorney Enos Stutsman[27] did not significantly affect the widespread respect with which he was regarded by Assiniboians. Nor did they alter the informal but no-nonsense style with which he continued to conduct his court until its final session.

When assessing the quality of Red River justice from 1835 to 1869, it is important to remember that the General Court was only the tip of the judicial iceberg. Most of the settlement's adjudication was done in the petty courts, which consisted of community elders, designated magistrates, who lacked formal legal training but knew their neighbourhoods and their neighbours, and learned as much law as they needed to know by reading Burn and Blackstone. Some magistrates also sat with the General Court as judicial equals of the recorder and governor, and with the collective power to outvote them. While the General Court was seriously criticized from time to time, especially during Thom's tenure, there was widespread satisfaction with the petty courts. Given that after a few early changes – reducing four judicial districts to three and replacing single magistrates with panels of three – their structure remained largely unchanged, that they had consistently heavy caseloads, and that appeals to the General Court were exceedingly rare, there can be little doubt that Red River residents thought highly of their petty courts.

It should never be forgotten, either, that in the General Court the principal adjudicators were not the governor, the recorder, or even the magistrates, but the ordinary citizens who served on the mandatory juries. Adam Thom's most important contribution to Red River justice was to ensure that almost all cases in the General Quarterly Court were determined by the lay citizens – equally English and French where appropriate. A more effective instrument of "substantial justice" than the English jury would be hard to imagine, and that institution was vigorously active at Red River.

ADVOCATES

Enos Stutsman, the American lawyer whose objections so thoroughly disrupted the *McLean* manslaughter case in 1868, was by no means the first advocate to appear before the settlement's courts. From the beginning, the clerk of the court usually acted as prosecutor in criminal cases, although the clerk's other courtroom duties must have ensured that his advocacy was kept to a minimum; and William Smith – the man who served longest as clerk – appears to have had little taste or competence for prosecuting. From a quite early stage also, the courts permitted "agents" to examine and cross-examine witnesses, and to make representations, in support of any parties who requested such assistance. Of course, these were not trained advocates. Initially, they were merely family members or friends who agreed to help out. Over time, however, a few individuals began to appear as agents with unusual frequency and increasing competence. Some were paid for their services. In the 1863

Corbett prosecution for attempted abortion,[28] a particularly sensational and lengthy trial, two such advocates represented each side.[29] They were referred to as "counsel" and conducted themselves in the courtroom much as modern barristers would. After provincehood, two of the four were listed, along with several newcomers from Ontario, Quebec, and elsewhere, among the founding members of the Manitoba bar.[30]

Thus the availability of advocates, another requirement of just adjudication systems, existed at Red River, at least in the later years.

Law Enforcement

The importance of effective law enforcement arrangements was always recognized, but too often neglected. The first large-scale arrangements, legislated and implemented by the Council of Assiniboia in 1835, were ambitious. The resolution then adopted called for establishment of a "Volunteer Corps ... [of] ... 60 officers and privates, consisting of one commanding officer, one serjeant-major, 4 serjeants and 54 privates whose pay, amounting to about £400 per annum, shall be defrayed from the revenue arising on imports and exports, and who shall receive additional pay when employed as constables in private cases, and whose public duties shall be hereafter defined."[31] A force nearly that strong, led by Sheriff Alexander Ross, was maintained for ten years. After a while, however, its numbers began to diminish, no doubt for financial reasons; and in June 1845 it was completely disbanded, being replaced by a body of just fifteen constables working under the sheriff's direction.[32]

It was hoped that this reduced constabulary would be backed up by a body of imperial troops; and Governor Simpson did indeed persuade the British government in 1845 that the threat of war with the United States over ownership of the Oregon Territory somehow justified stationing a military garrison at Red River. In the summer of 1846 (after the Oregon crisis was over, it turned out), 400 troops and family members of the 6th Regiment, Royal Warwickshire Rifles, descended on the settlement,[33] ensuring peace and stability for the next two years.

After the inevitable withdrawal of that force, the HBC replaced it with a body of Chelsea Pensioners: soldiers retired from regular service on partial pensions for medical reasons, whom the company brought to Red River with their families, providing free land and small stipends in return for part-time service protecting law and order in the settlement. It seemed a "good idea at the time," as a later era would put it. In actuality, the pensioners proved to be, in the words of historian J.M. Bumsted, "worse than useless," occupying themselves with "precious little farming, and a good deal of heavy drinking."[34] A contemporary observer commented, "We have more trouble with the Pensioners than with all the rest of the Settlement put together."[35] It was the commander of the pensioners, Major W.B. Caldwell, in his other role as governor of Assiniboia, whose botched responses to the crises created by the *Sayer* and *Foss* cases in 1849 and 1850 almost brought Assiniboia's government to a complete standstill. He was no more effective in his military role than in his civil capacity.

The only significant changes in policing arrangements for the next several years were the appointment of a more effective Chelsea Pensioner second-in-command to replace the disgraced Captain Christopher Vaughan Foss[36] – and a deplorable further reduction of the constabulary: first to eleven and then to nine.[37] Finally, in late 1854, the company decided to disband the pensioners altogether.[38] Those relatively few who wished to return to Great Britain were transported home the following year, along with their commanding officer.[39] From early 1855 until late 1857, Red River's sole law enforcement personnel were the sheriff and nine constables. Luckily, there were no serious breaches of the peace during that period.

In November 1857, as a result of HBC pressure on the British government, a new military garrison was established in the settlement – this one a detachment of Royal Canadian Rifles from Quebec.[40] In December, Governor Johnson reported that "[t]he Fort resounds with warlike noises,"[41] and that garrison, without which Sir George Simpson contended "anarchy would prevail,"[42] remained in place until the spring of 1861.[43] It would be the last military presence in the settlement – apart from Louis Riel's substantial Métis force in 1869–70 – until after provincehood. There was talk from time to time of forming another volunteer militia like that which operated from 1835 to 1845, or of hiring more constables, but neither step was ever taken.

Despite Simpson's warning, anarchy did not prevail without a troop presence during those final eight and a half years. The courts functioned. Criminals were apprehended, tried, and jailed. Civil claims were adjudicated. Judgments were enforced. The streets and trails of the settlement were relatively safe. There certainly were occasions, however, when lawlessness exceeded acceptable bounds. Uncertainty about Rupert's Land's future, intensified by the highly public 1857 hearings of the Select Committee of the British House of Commons concerning the HBC's governance of its territories, did much to generate speculative immigration to the settlement, often by less-than-desirable newcomers, and that influx of strangers increased restiveness among longer-established residents concerning land rights and other matters. Excessive alcohol consumption, street rowdiness, and crime rates rose. Defiance of the law – on the part of even some considered to be community leaders – sometimes went unchallenged.

An instance of the latter type was a famous confrontation in January 1868 between the feuding half-brothers Dr John Schultz and Sheriff Henry McKenney. McKenney's seizure, in his official capacity, of goods from Schultz in satisfaction of a civil claim in which McKenney had a personal interest resulted, when Schultz resisted, in the latter's being imprisoned, and then released by an audacious jailbreak orchestrated by his wife. Governor McTavish lamented in a letter to London, "I consider it perfectly out of the power of anyone to carry out the law here without a suitable force on which authority can rely ... In one case of the infraction of laws ... [the sheriff] may, it is true, find people who will support him in punishing those who have broken it ... but in the next case ... will find his supporters on the former occasion arranged against him."[44] In that case, it was decided that since there was much public support for Schultz's position, it would be inexpedient to rearrest him or to charge the friends who broke him out of jail.

Although Sheriff McKenney's conduct was questionable in the foregoing instance, it was not typical. The settlement was generally fortunate in its sheriffs and other law enforcement personnel. Alexander Ross – fur trade veteran, prosperous settler, sometime scholar – filled the office from 1835 until 1850, when he refused to serve any longer under the outrageous Governor Caldwell. Resourceful, fair-minded, and fearless, Ross was widely respected in the settlement; and he accomplished his goals, more often than not, by persuasion rather than force. An excellent example of the Ross style was his defusing of a menacing demonstration of deserting Indian boatmen and their supporters in August 1849 by simply hiring a few Métis buffalo hunters to accompany him and his handful of constables to the scene. Peace was restored instantly.[45]

Alexander Ross was succeeded as sheriff by his son William, who served with apparent success until his sudden death in early 1856, at which point the versatile and universally respected Dr John Bunn took over. Bunn's death led to the appointment, in 1862, of another of Alexander Ross's sons: twenty-seven-year-old James. Exceptionally gifted though he unquestionably was, James Ross possessed remarkably little common sense, and his indiscreet attacks on the company and the

Assiniboia government in his capacity as part owner-editor of the *Nor'-Wester* incurred the wrath of Governor McTavish, resulting in his being relieved as sheriff and dismissed from other public offices in November of the same year.[46]

The successor of James Ross, who remained in office until the end of the HBC regime, was the aforementioned Henry McKenney, an energetic entrepreneur from Upper Canada. The McKenney years were sometimes turbulent. As uncertainty, and then impatience, about Rupert's Land's future brought many carpetbag adventurers (like the sheriff himself) to the settlement, long-time residents became suspicious and restive, and the company lost interest in governing. Litigation and lawlessness increased, and jailbreaks became more common. Although, as we have seen, McKenney's personal interests sometimes overlapped with his official duties, he seems, on the whole, to have done a creditable job with the limited resources available to him. More evidence of his day-to-day work and working methods has survived than for any other sheriff, and it reveals a methodical and generally careful approach to his duties.[47] He resigned in early 1870 to operate a sawmill at Pembina and become sheriff there, but returned to Winnipeg between 1874 and 1876, making a thoroughly unsuccessful bid for election as alderman, and then emigrated to the Oregon Territory, where he died a decade later. Governor McTavish's 1870 assessment of him as an "adventurer" who had arrived "with hardly a copper to rub, and no character,"[48] came close to the mark; but it omitted to mention valuable contributions that McKenney made to Red River's sadly malnourished law enforcement facilities.

For almost half the time under consideration – 1835 to 1849 – there were, in effect, two sheriffs of Assiniboia. When the Council of Assiniboia conferred that title on Alexander Ross in 1835, it was well aware that Métis leader Cuthbert Grant had, since 1828, held a similar office under the title "Warden of the Plains." While the chief purpose of Grant's appointment was political – to ensure that he would keep his people peaceable and loyal to the company – and was not renewed after the *Sayer* trial riot showed he had lost his influence over the Métis, Grant's legal authority as warden of the plains seems to have mirrored that of Sheriff Ross. Along with Ross, he was active from 1844 to 1849 attempting to suppress free trade activities;[49] and when William Ross replaced his father the formal appointment read, "That Mr. William Ross be appointed Assistant Sheriff with Mr. Grant."[50] Nevertheless, because Grant lived at White Horse Plain, a considerable distance west of the main settlement, and was a volatile, unpredictable individual, his involvement in day-to-day law enforcement activities was always limited.

Red River's sheriffs had multiple responsibilities. They directed the constables who investigated crime, arrested lawbreakers, and served court processes. In their magisterial capacity, sheriffs conducted preliminary investigations of alleged crimes and decided whether charges should be pressed. They attended and maintained order at sittings of the General Court, and ensured that their constables did so at the petty courts. They collected from defendants, and paid to plaintiffs monetary awards made in civil cases, and, where necessary, seized property in satisfaction of unpaid awards. As governors of the jail, sheriffs supervised the settlement's prison. Where possible and appropriate, they cooperated with military authorities in their efforts to maintain law and order. For the most part, those varied tasks were carried out effectively by the settlement's sheriffs and their subordinates.

In short, while Assiniboia's law enforcement measures left much to be desired, they served the purpose fairly well most of the time. Winnipeg residents are not much safer from crime in the twenty-first century than were the people of Red River.

Public Acceptance

The final requirement of an effective justice system is widespread acceptance by the community it serves. Was that so at Red River between 1835 and 1869? By and large, it was. The strongest evidence of such acceptance was the frequency – increasing steadily throughout the years in question – with which the community brought its disputes to the settlement's courts. It seems significant that the great bulk of court cases involved one person suing another, and that losing parties before the petty courts rarely appealed to the General Court.

The breakaway and generally anti-company settlement at Portage la Prairie, located just beyond an arbitrary 50 mile limit the Council of Assiniboia placed on its responsibilities, twice attempted to operate courts of its own, with farcical results both times,[51] and petitioned for access to Assiniboia courts for several years before the request was finally granted in 1868.[52] The failure of Portage to create effective indigenous courts can be blamed, by contrast with the main settlement's success, on insufficient public acceptance.

A strong indication of settlers' acceptance of the Red River legal system was the extent to which – albeit with occasional lapses – residents abided by court decisions, even when the colony's law enforcement authorities consisted of only a sheriff and a few ill-trained constables. It may even be instructive to consider the exceptions – situations in which constituted authority was resisted. Some of them, when examined carefully, turn out to be more illustrative than exceptional.

Consider the *Sayer* riot, for example. While it was, from the authorities' perspective, a plea bargain with many guns to the court's head, consider it from the demonstrators' perspective. Why did they bother to bargain? What did they have to gain? Pierre Guilleaum Sayer and his co-accused colleagues were safely under the protection of the mob, which had already proved the company powerless to enforce its fur trade monopoly. Why did those demonstrators not just walk away, as some of their number undoubtedly wanted to do? Surely it was because, as citizens of the settlement, they did not wish to break the back of an institution they valued. Much better to go through the form of a trial, and accept a toothless finding of guilt, than to destroy a court to which many resorted from time to time. It was not, after all, the General Quarterly Court as an institution to which the demonstrators objected; it was to Recorder Adam Thom, and his refusal to address francophones in French. Sheriff Ross doubtless assured the mob that their riot had already remedied that problem. Regarded in such a light, the willingness of Sayer's supporters to go through with the form of a trial was an affirmation, not a rejection, of the court's place in the community.

Think, too, about the Schultz jailbreak. That outrage was an undeniably serious violation of the law, and a clear demonstration of contempt for the legal system. Was it, however, an expression of contempt for *justice*? The jailbreakers would not have considered it such. They were not generally lawless men; most were respectable settlers who believed an *injustice* had been done, and who acted to rectify that perceived wrong. Most lynch mobs would claim the same excuse, of course. My point is not to justify what was done, but to ask whether it pointed to a general lack of support for Red River's judicial system on the part of the perpetrators. That is doubtful. If the jailbreakers believed, along with most of the settlement's governors, recorders, and magistrates, that the legal system's goal was to achieve "substantial justice" and also thought – as they had good reason to think in that case – that it was *unjust* for Sheriff McKenney to arrange the imprisonment of someone against whom he had a well-known personal animus while enforcing a judgment in which he had an undoubted personal financial interest, could they not plausibly be said to have acted *in support* of that system?

Even if it is not reasonable to claim that certain attacks on the juridical system can be explained in terms of its overall acceptance, it seems too clear for dispute that, *in normal circumstances*, most residents of the Red River Settlement accepted, supported, and participated in its juridical arrangements. Admittedly, however, there was one group – the Indians – about which that generalization cannot be plausibly made. Although many of them were prosecuted in the courts, and a very few of them sued or were sued civilly therein, the resident Cree and Saulteaux people had no say in the creation or administration of Assiniboia's laws or institutions. While that was also largely the case for the Halfbreed and white populations, the latter groups at least had some representation on the governing Council of Assiniboia, the courts, and, very significantly, the juries.

SUBSTANTIAL JUSTICE? SOME ILLUSTRATIONS

Most Red River judicial authorities sought "substantial justice." Did they succeed? Justice being a highly subjective notion, that question could now be answered conclusively only by averaging the responses of a statistically significant number of individuals, knowledgeable about settlement conditions, who have studied all the 600-plus General Court case reports and the sparse data that survive from the petty courts. The author believes that justice was substantially served. Lacking a statistically relevant group willing to review that evidence, however, I can only offer in support of that view a smattering of illustrative evidence. While it falls far short of proof, I hope it will be found suggestive, and perhaps persuasive.

Civil Cases

One of the most common types of civil case heard involved a defendant in possession of an animal, a horse or an ox, that the plaintiff claimed to be his. The frequency of such claims was a consequence of pasturing and wintering livestock on the open prairie. During the months on their own, animals wandered, grew, mated, foaled, injured themselves, and encountered wolves and poachers. They were often difficult to find and identify afterward; and A often ended up in possession of B's mare – or of a mare B thought was his. Litigation sometimes ensued. Numerous witnesses were called on both sides, most of them thoroughly versed on the physical characteristics and life history of their party's animal. The bench and jury then trooped out to the courthouse gate to examine the beast before rendering a long-pondered, vigorously debated decision. Were those decisions just? Perhaps not always; but the very number of such cases, along with the absence of appeals, strongly suggests that the community considered the process fair and worth pursuing.

Another very large group of civil cases involved commercial disputes of various kinds: between lenders and borrowers, suppliers and retailers of merchandise, importers and their carters, and so on. The verdicts are rarely surprising to modern readers of the evidence. What may be surprising to some is that only a very small fraction of that commercial litigation involved the HBC. In the twenty-five years of HBC-controlled General Court operations for which records exist, the company sued as plaintiff just six times, and was sued only once. All seven actions – including the one against the company – were successful, but as we have seen, the only really significant case, *Sayer*, resulted in only the emptiest of pyrrhic victories for the company. While a few additional cases were brought on behalf of the HBC in the names of individual company employees, there is simply no evidence, other than the *Sayer* debacle, of the HBC's using its courts to force its wishes on the people of Assiniboia. An attempt by an overzealous Norway House officer to do so in 1857, by arresting A.G.B. Bannatyne and sending him back to Red River in custody to face trial for free trading, was deftly foiled by Recorder-Governor Johnson,[53] and the company quietly compensated the irate Bannatyne for his inconvenience.[54]

The question of whether someone with a personal financial interest in the HBC's fur trade activities could sit in judgment of claims by or against the company arose relatively early and was decided in the negative. Prior to the August 1845 session of the General Court, entrepreneurs James Sinclair and Andrew McDermot, whose transportation contracts with the HBC had been cancelled because they were suspected of free trading, sought to sue the company for unpaid services. The court refused to entertain the claim, undoubtedly on Recorder Thom's advice, because no governor was available to preside over the case – Assiniboia governor Alexander Christie "being a party interested in the fur trade" and Governor Simpson, who was in the settlement at the time, being a company shareholder.[55] Although this was a plausible and commendable principle, there would be three subsequent occasions when "a party interested in the fur trade" *did* chair sessions of the court at which the HBC was a litigant.[56] It seems, therefore, that the "principle" applied in the 1845 case was simply an excuse devised to derail a particular claim against the company.[57] Contemptible although that ploy was, a single such instance is not sufficient to justify concluding that the court generally denied substantial justice in the very few HBC cases it heard.

Criminal Cases Generally

Turning from civil to criminal adjudication, we see a similar picture. The recorders' jury charges, which, after 1860, often appeared in the *Nor'-Wester,* leave little doubt that accused persons were, for the most part, treated fairly and in accordance with principles and procedures generally followed in Canada and England.

The Queen v. Joseph Armstrong and Owen Bourk[58] is illustrative. About midnight one September evening in 1865, James Mulligan, a former Chelsea Pensioner who was by then the settlement's best known – and very controversial – constable, looked out his window and saw a fire in his yard. Three large stacks of unthreshed wheat were ablaze, and a strong wind was blowing the flames toward his house. Although Mulligan and a neighbour saved the house, the wheat was destroyed – about 100 bushels in all. Found lying on the ground not far from the fire, in a very drunken condition, was one Owen Bourk. Accused by Mulligan of setting the fire, Bourk replied: "Yes! And three more. And you may go to Hell!" Prosecution evidence showed that the stove in the Mulligan house had been unused and cool for several hours before the fire started; that until ten or fifteen minutes before the fire began, Bourk had been drinking with Joseph Armstrong at a nearby house; that there was bad blood between Armstrong and Mulligan; that Bourk and Armstrong proceeded in the direction of Mulligan's house when they left the neighbour's; and that before doing so, Armstrong asked for, and was given, some matches "for his pipe." The accused men, represented by experienced "agent" Charles Garrett, established that some Indians had previously threatened to kill Mulligan and that about four hours before the fire began a passerby had seen three people in Mulligan's yard, carrying a light of some kind.

Judge Black's lengthy charge to the jury stressed the seriousness of the offence and the penalty, reviewed the evidence carefully, and explained both the usefulness and the risks of such circumstantial evidence. He concluded, according to the *Nor'-Wester,* that "'[u]nder all the circumstances, perhaps the jury might feel considerable doubt about the prisoners' guilt ... [and] if they had any reasonable doubt on their minds it was their duty to give the prisoners the benefit of it.'" The accused men were both acquitted,[59] following which Black tongue-lashed them for having been "roaming about drinking and behaving like anything but decent men" rather than "being in their beds before midnight." The case was a classic example of the common law's presumption of innocence properly applied in a case where one suspects the accused men were guilty.

Sentences of imprisonment for criminal convictions were typically much shorter at Red River than in England. Recorder Thom cited, early in his tenure, an example of the difference: "The girl who had committed house breaking and theft would have been liable in England, at the very least to a year's imprisonment, but here the year was reduced to ... two months."[60] There were many reasons for this discrepancy. One was that when it came to sentencing, the recorder was "but one of many co-equal colleagues" on the court, and could always be outvoted. Factors motivating the leniency of lay members of the bench, and often of the recorders themselves,[61] ranged from an awareness that Red River's prison had a limited capacity to a belief that those who lived in frontier areas prized their personal liberty more than English criminals, and were more severely affected by its loss.[62]

Capital Cases

"Capital cases" were those involving conduct which, if proved beyond a reasonable doubt, incurred the risk of hanging. The General Court dealt with just two types: homicide and rape.[63] Homicide included murder, manslaughter, and what would later be called "infanticide" (killing a newborn while under the influence of postpartum depression).

There were, in all, eighteen capital cases, involving twenty-one defendants, known to have been tried at Red River during the company era.[64] While only five of those cases (eight defendants) resulted in acquittals, just one of the thirteen convicts went to the gallows. Of the twelve who escaped death, ten were convicted of lesser, noncapital offences, three being reduced from murder to manslaughter, and four from rape to attempted rape or assault. The remaining two convictions – one involving infanticide and the other homicide of an adult – resulted in death sentences that were commuted by the governor to terms of imprisonment.

Vulnerable Persons

When considering the situation of vulnerable people, it is well to remember that this was the nineteenth century – and that the question is not whether they were treated well, but whether they were treated better or worse at Red River than in Canada or England.

Youth was a defence to criminal prosecution, but only for those below the age of fourteen. Thus a twelve-year-old boy who killed a friend with a bow and arrow in play was acquitted of murder.[65] And when two sisters, aged thirteen and fifteen, were charged with stealing money from the Lower Fort Garry shop, the younger sister was acquitted, while the elder was convicted.[66] Even for those under fourteen, however, youth was not a complete defence; it merely allowed the jury to find that a *particular* child lacked adult responsibility. So when a boy under fourteen mischievously set the prairie on fire, he was adjudged responsible as an adult and convicted under a local fire-prevention law.[67]

Age was also a factor when sentencing young offenders. In the case of the fifteen-year-old who stole from Fort Garry, for example, the sentence was only two weeks.[68] The case of the under-fourteen who started the prairie fire is interesting in this respect. Although Judge Black's charge to the jury recommended conviction, he also urged that it be for the lesser of two possible statutory offences, which carried a fairly mild punishment. When the jury convicted the boy of the more serious offence, Black arbitrarily reduced the legislated penalty by 50 per cent. Neither the objections of prosecutor James Ross nor the lack of any known legal authority to ignore the statutory terms prevented Black doing what he thought "substantial justice" required.[69]

The circumstances of needful elderly people without families to care for them must sometimes have been dire in an age before public assistance programs. This was so in London, Montreal, and Toronto, as well as at Red River. Although the settlement's courts had little occasion to consider such matters, the General Court records include one poignant series of cases, extending over a period of more than seventeen years,[70] that permit us to follow, if spasmodically and incompletely, the fortunes and misfortunes of such a person.

Nicholas Courtelle – an aging, perhaps confused, certainly difficult man – made an arrangement in the 1850s with the Grey Nuns (Sisters of Charity) of St Boniface to look after him for life in return for transferring his property to the convent. Unhappy with how that arrangement was working out, Courtelle sued the sisters in 1854. Although he lost the case, it was later agreed that he would leave the shelter of the convent, taking his property with him. He then entered another care agreement with one Louis Thébeault. Disputes with Thébeault led to litigation in 1859 and 1862, as well as to subsequent arbitration.

Courtelle nevertheless remained in Thébeault's care and employment until early 1866, when he once more sued in the General Court, winning a severance of the arrangement on terms more generous than had been awarded by two of the arbitrators but less so than the third's proposal. In the autumn of 1871, seventeen years after suing the Grey Nuns, Nicholas Courtelle had his fifth "day in court," in a similar suit against one Catherine Lacerte before the transition-period General Quarterly Court.[71] As in all but one of his previous actions, he was unsuccessful. It is not known what happened to Mr Courtelle thereafter; but it seems clear that the general courts of both Assiniboia and Manitoba dealt with his concerns at least as patiently, compassionately, and fairly, as any British or Canadian court might have.

Turning to cases with distinct impact on women, one finds much evidence of gender bias. Married women were not permitted to sue civilly, except in their husbands' names.[72] Although husbands could sue their wives' lovers for damages,[73] the reverse was not possible. Both judges and jurors were exclusively male; and because outright rape was a capital offence, few juries were willing to convict on that charge. Although all four rape-related prosecutions in Assiniboia's General Court – charged as either attempted rape or assault with intent to rape – resulted in convictions, the sentences were light, ranging from one to six months.[74] It is important, however, for the present purposes, to understand that in none of those respects did this court deviate markedly from its counterparts elsewhere in the British Empire.

Four cases of what would later be called infanticide came before the General Court between 1852 and 1869. The evidence in each case being very strong, all four resulted in convictions. In the first, which was prosecuted as murder, the court pronounced the mandatory death sentence, but Governor Caldwell commuted it to two years' imprisonment.[75] The other three were treated considerably more humanely, being prosecuted as, or reduced to, mere concealment of birth, and punished by imprisonment for three, six, and three months respectively.[76]

The only abortion-related case – against a high-profile clergyman convicted for attempting to terminate the pregnancy of a young woman in his employ[77] – was commenced by the girl's father and fully cooperated in by the victim herself. Although the accused's friends insisted that he was framed by the HBC and the girl's family, most objective readers of the evidence would probably agree that it overwhelmingly supported his conviction. The other well-known case arising from mistreatment of a female servant by her male employer was *Rothney v. Thom*,[78] in which a housemaid of the settlement's cantankerous first recorder, dismissed when found to be pregnant, successfully sued him for back wages he had refused to pay. While Thom ultimately browbeat the woman into settling for less than she had been awarded by his magistrate colleagues, that decision had been legally questionable in awarding more than the plaintiff claimed.

Sarah Ballenden, the chief factor's wife – who underwent prolonged and harrowing cross-examination, as well as exposure to searing counter-evidence concerning her personal conduct and morality, in the notorious defamation case of *Foss v. Pelly*[79] – is sometimes seen as a tragic victim of the court process. But she was a party to commencing the lawsuit, after all, hoping to cleanse the stain of gossip from her name. And the litigation resulted in an extremely generous award of damages (admittedly to her friend Captain Foss, who may or may not have shared the spoils of victory with her).

In none of these cases does it appear that the women in question received less than substantial justice as that concept was understood in nineteenth-century Assiniboia, Canada, or England.

How did the system treat Aboriginal people? The permanent Red River population included between 500 and 600 Cree and Saulteaux inhabitants most of the time the quarterly courts of Assiniboia were functioning.[80] From at least the time of Recorder Adam Thom's arrival in the settlement, they were considered to be subject to, and had access to, Red River's legal system.[81] If they were Christians, their evidence was sworn in the normal way; if not, they were "sworn in the Indian manner," which included an inquiry into their understanding of the need to be truthful, and of the consequences of failing to do so. Although they were rarely involved in civil litigation, there were a few instances of Indians being sued, and of their suing. It seemed to be assumed that they were ineligible for jury duty,[82] although the *Nor'-Wester* once claimed that "mixed juries" sometimes included Indians.[83] They were discriminated against statutorily by the law that prohibited selling liquor to Indians; but, interestingly, that law did not make either possession or consumption of liquor by Indians an offence. It targeted only their non-Indian suppliers, and actually provided a short-term boon for Indian imbibers by entitling them, after consuming the liquor, to get their money back from the vendor, as well as to share in fines as informers.

The incidence of neither prosecutions nor convictions of Aboriginal persons was significantly out of proportion to their overall numbers; and the punishments imposed upon them were not unusually severe, except – and it was a cruel exception – that banishment from the settlement was much more commonly imposed on Indians than on others. Even equal treatment often had a differential impact on Aboriginal convicts, of course, since most Indians accused of crimes, lacking the wherewithal or influence to raise bail, remained in custody pending trial.

The best known Aboriginal trial – one in which it is sometimes alleged that the accused was treated unfairly by reason of his race – was *R. v. Capenesseweet.*[84] The accused, a young Saulteau man, deliberately and without provocation shot a visiting Sioux to death, accidently also killing a man of his own tribe. It happened in broad daylight in front of a large crowd of settlers outside Upper Fort Garry. Capenesseweet was found guilty of murder on the basis of overwhelming evidence, and was sentenced to death in accordance with the mandatory English law of the time. Unlike the two other death sentences imposed by the court, however, that sentence was carried out. Capenesseweet was hanged from a scaffold above the gate of Upper Fort Garry only a few days after his trial.

Most criticisms of the case are due, in my opinion, to mistaken views of either the facts or the relevant law. It cannot be denied, however, that the case stands out from all other cases in the severity of the punishment imposed, that both the court and the jury were fully conscious of the gravity of the decision (being informed in advance that there would be no clemency if the accused were convicted), and that ethnicity was a factor. Do those facts suggest discrimination? Some think so; I do not.

The stern treatment of Capenesseweet reflected, rather, a profound concern for the safety of the settlement. Everyone was aware that if the killer were not hanged for assassinating a member of the visiting Sioux delegation, the settlement could soon expect a large-scale Sioux attack. While many might contend that such "public policy" factors ought not to affect legal decision making, such factors have always played a distorting role in adjudication, still do, and always will – even in the most advanced legal systems – when community peril or other matters of paramount public importance are perceived to be involved.[85]

It may be helpful to contrast *Capenesseweet* with two other cases in which Indian men were charged with killing other Indians that same year. In *Public Interest v. Keetchipiwaipasse*[86] the accused was observed severely beating his wife one evening. Both were drunk. Later that night, a man and woman were heard shouting in Ojibwa from the frozen Red River; and in the morning the wife's corpse was found on the river ice near a water hole. The husband, who led a nearby resident to the body, behaved suspiciously but did not admit guilt. An autopsy indicated that the cause of death was probably drowning, not beating. A grand jury indicted the husband for murder; but a petty jury, composed mostly of anglophones and including no Indians, acquitted the accused, as one might expect a modern jury to acquit on such inadequate and circumstantial evidence. After the acquittal, however, Recorder Thom directed the same grand jury to reconsider the matter as a case of assault, and an indictment on the lesser charge was returned. A second petty jury convicted, and the accused was sentenced to six months' solitary imprisonment.

In *Public Interest v. Newkesequeskik*[87] a Saulteau man fatally stabbed his older brother without provocation. Witnesses testified that the deceased was bad-tempered and had frequently berated the accused. On the morning of the stabbing, the older man had steadily criticized the younger for taking too long to prepare a dog for cooking. After hearing the evidence (translated to and from Ojibwa) of several witnesses, a mixed French-English jury convicted the accused of manslaughter, and the court imposed a sentence of twelve months' solitary confinement.

Two further cases deserve attention. One evening in late June 1860, Antoine Juando, a no-longer-young Indian, came to the home of James Armstrong – one of the many small groggeries with which the settlement was blemished – and was served liquor. Sometime later, outside, an inebriated Juando was being teased by a group of young people, including a young woman called Mary Park. Incensed by what was being said, Juando picked up a stick and began to chase Mary around the house. After two or three circuits, the woman also picked up a stick, and threw it at her pursuer. Struck on the nose, the man fell to the ground unconscious. No one paid him further heed until, a considerable time later, it was noticed that he was not breathing. A subsequent medical examination indicated that Juando's death was caused by apoplexy, from which the deceased was known to have suffered, and that the apoplexy could have been contributed to by intoxication and excitement, triggered by concussion from the blow that knocked him down. Mary Park was charged with, and acquitted of, manslaughter.[88] While the acquittal conformed to Dr John Bunn's charge to the jury, the doctor was distressed by the events leading to the tragedy. His charge sternly reprimanded Mary Park's male companions for not coming to the man's aid when they saw he was unconscious. To the accused, Bunn said after the verdict, "You are smiling. The Jury have brought in a verdict of Not Guilty, but remember that does not fully acquit you. You have escaped the consequences so far as man is concerned; but recollect that the all-seeing eye of God is upon you, and if you had any share in the death of the Deceased you will be punished ... hereafter."

About a year later, the court entertained two prosecutions, probably related, involving a recently arrived American merchant-tavernkeeper, Auguste Schubert, and his dealings with Indians of the Red River area. In September 1861 Schubert was visited by one Neecheegoose, a local Indian who claimed to represent a Pembina compatriot so severely beaten by Schubert that he could no longer support himself. Neecheegoose demanded compensation for the injured man. Schubert refused. A week later Neecheegoose returned with some thirty or forty others. The invaders filled the Schubert home-cum-tavern, terrified the family, and insisted on the payment of £50. When that was refused, the vigilantes altered their demand to an annual disability pension for the injured man, and Schubert reluctantly agreed to pay a pension of £3 per annum – as a matter of charity, he insisted, not of right. The invaders then claimed, and eventually took, a keg of whiskey for their own trouble.

When Schubert reported the incident to settlement authorities, Neecheegoose and a companion were charged with rioting and theft. In apparent retaliation, Schubert was reported to have sold liquor to an Indian, and was charged with that offence.[89] The riot-theft charges resulted in convictions and light sentences of imprisonment: one month for the leader, Neecheegoose, and two weeks for his colleague (plus, probably, two months in custody awaiting trial for both men). Schubert was acquitted on the liquor charge, despite plausible evidence of a scheme on his part to sell the liquor in the guise of a sham lawful transaction. It would be very surprising if the community did not consider "substantial justice" to have been done overall.

Everyone who considers these examples of Red River adjudication will form personal opinions about them. From the author's perspective, there is nothing in them – or in the records of the General Quarterly Court of Assiniboia generally – to suggest bias against the young, the elderly, women, or Aboriginals exceeding that to which British law and society were generally prone at the time.

CONCLUSION

One of the most astute – if not always the most objective – observers of Red River affairs was Alexander Ross, long-time resident, trader, scholar, and sheriff of the settlement. In Ross's opinion, the judicial system we have been examining was highly satisfactory in its early years: "During all this period they worked remarkably well, and gave general satisfaction, *without the aid of lawyers* ... [I]n no instance were the decisions of the magistrates questioned or disobeyed; no collision of interests or parties disturbed the peace. So much confidence was placed in the simple and straightforward course pursued, that the good will of the people always backed and strengthened the hands of justice."[90]

But note the words that Ross italicized. He was convinced that after the company sent lawyer Adam Thom to the settlement "to give more legal tone to our judicial proceedings," the system changed for the worse: "[I]n place of the simple honesty which marked our proceedings hitherto ... [Thom's appointment] has a tendency to substitute the quibbles and technicalities of law, which few but lawyers themselves comprehend. Besides this, a professional judge on the bench, without a professional lawyer at the bar, is an anomaly in judicial proceedings."[91] It must be remembered that Thom was still in office when those words were written. They describe the first recorder's style quite accurately. In spite of the important contributions he made to Assiniboia's judicial system, no man was less personally attuned to "substantial justice" than Adam Thom. But the recorders who succeeded him – certainly Bunn and Black, and even Johnson for the most part – exhibited a markedly less legalistic and more justice-oriented approach to their judicial function. And every recorder, including Thom, was subject to being outvoted by his lay magistrate colleagues on the court, as well as by the omnipresent juries.

Looking back at the Red River courts from 1835 to 1869 in terms of the essential elements previously identified, the following characteristics can be observed:

- reasonably accessible laws that combined the essentials of English common law and legislation with locally focused and locally enacted laws
- a two-tiered court system composed of recorders and governors who, except for Thom and Caldwell, were common-sense and humane; community-oriented lay magistrates; and in almost all General Court cases, juries that reflected the chiefly French-English linguistic makeup of the settlement[92]
- an absence, for the most part, of professionally trained lawyers, but a growing reliance on lay advocates
- policing that was sometimes inadequate but usually operated satisfactorily

- wide community acceptance of the system, except in a few cases of real or perceived injustice

In the author's view, that system exhibited, on balance, fair procedure, a satisfactory if unsophisticated knowledge of law, a full understanding of local conditions and community needs, compassion, and impartiality. All those characteristics appear to have usually prevailed, whether or not a legally trained recorder was on the bench. The latter three characteristics were chiefly attributable to trial by jury in the General Court, and to the use of three-member panels of magistrates in the petty courts. It is true, of course, that the system achieved no more than "*substantial* justice." That was all it ever sought to achieve. It aimed, and in my view succeeded, to "do justly between man and man."[93]

As one who practised law in Canada for more than fifty years, the author is convinced that "substantial justice" is both the highest and the lowest standard of fairness that *any* satisfactory juridical system can ever hope to achieve. And when I read the records of the quarterly courts of Assiniboia, I see a legal system that, albeit primitive, was no less effective in its essentials, and no less heedful of the rudiments of both law and fundamental justice, than the one within which I served.

GOVERNANCE IN GENERAL

It is also my view that the general governance of Red River and Rupert's Land was conducted appreciably less justly than the operation of the legal system.

This is not to say that either the Hudson's Bay Company or Canadian authorities governed with wholesale unfairness or gratuitous callousness in the years examined herein. The company's subjects, including the indigenous population, were generally treated with respect, and sometimes even with kindness. It was only good business to do so, and the inherent humanity of many fur trade personnel caused them to go further than self-interest required. If the company's reign were compared with those of analogous corporate dynasties, or of the British Empire itself, it would probably be rated favourably. And, over time, governmental arrangements in Assiniboia, if not in all of Rupert's Land, kept approximate pace with those of Great Britain as regards representativeness and proto-democratic developments. Canada too, when it took over, doubtless governed in a manner most Canadians considered satisfactory. Nor can it be denied that some governmental leaders of both the Hudson's Bay Company and Canada governed with genuine concern for the welfare of all their constituents. Lord Selkirk, Andrew Bulger, William McTavish, and Adams Archibald come immediately to mind in that respect.

But when account is taken of such egregious actions by the territory's political leaders – both corporate and democratic – as

- the company's conscious enforcement of an illegal trade monopoly for the better part of 150 years
- the consistent veil of secrecy cloaking most meetings of the Council of Assiniboia
- Sir George Simpson's cruel and illegal indefinite exile to Ungava of a young Métis convict in order to avoid arousing the sympathy of his compatriots
- Simpson's outrageous schemes to blackmail Methodist missionary James Evans; encourage Recorder Johnson to facilitate the kidnapping of a fur trader's daughters from a convent; and permit Dr John McLoughlin to investigate a murder charge against himself
- the Canadian government's refusal to abide by promises to take possession of Red River peaceably, to grant amnesty to Red River insurgents, and to protect Métis land rights in the new province
- the many other governmental travesties recorded in this study

it should be obvious that Red River's courts functioned, on the whole, a good deal more justly than did its governors. That, of course, is why distinct juridical systems exist.

Glossary

ACCOUNTING (DEMAND OR ACTION FOR): a request for a court order requiring that one party open his or her books or records to scrutiny by or on behalf of the other.

AFFIDAVIT: a written statement, made under oath or solemn affirmation, attesting to certain facts. It is sometimes called a written deposition (qv).

ANGLOPHONE: one whose first language, or usual mode of expression, is English. In Canada the term is most commonly used in contradistinction to francophone (qv).

APPEARANCE: a formally acknowledged presence in court by a party to litigation or by a party's counsel or representative, even if only for the purpose of seeking an adjournment.

ARDENT SPIRITS: distilled liquor (whiskey, rum, brandy, etc.). Although the sale of beer and wine was prohibited only to Indians in Assiniboia, the sale of whiskey and other "ardent spirits," without a licence, was absolutely prohibited in some areas at some times.

ARRAIGNMENT: an appearance (qv) of an accused person before a criminal court to plead guilty or not guilty to charges in an indictment (qv).

ASSAULT AND BATTERY: Strictly speaking, assault and battery are distinct wrongs. Whereas battery involves the application of physical force to the person of another without that person's express or implied consent, assault is an unconsented act, such as raising a fist or pointing a gun in a menacing manner, that creates a reasonable apprehension in the mind of that person that a battery is about to be inflicted. The term "assault" is often used alone, especially in the criminal context, to express either or both the above meanings.

ASSINIBOIA, COUNCIL OF: the body of men appointed by the Governor and Committee of the Hudson's Bay Company (qv) from time to time under the authority of the company's 1670 charter to govern the District of Assiniboia (qv) in collaboration with the governor of Assiniboia (qv).

ASSINIBOIA, DISTRICT OF: that portion of Rupert's Land (qv), centred on the Forks of the Red and Assiniboine Rivers, that was conveyed to the Earl of Selkirk by the Hudson's Bay Company in 1811 and was reconveyed to the company by Selkirk's estate after his death. A smaller area, extending 50 miles in all directions from the Forks and known as the Municipal District of Assiniboia, was created by the Council of Assiniboia (qv) on 25 June 1841. The settled portions of Assiniboia, comprising an area somewhat more far-flung and less regular in shape than the Municipal District, were commonly known, compendiously, as the Red River Settlement.

ASSINIBOIA, GOVERNOR OF: the man appointed by the Governor and Committee of the Hudson's Bay Company (qv) from time to time under the authority of the company's 1670 charter to govern Assiniboia (qv) in collaboration with the Council of Assiniboia (qv).

ASSIZE: court session. The General Quarterly Court of Assiniboia normally held four assizes each year.

ASSOILIZED: dismissed or absolved. It is a Scots law term, taken from "assoile" in French law, that was introduced to Assiniboia by Recorder Adam Thom to indicate the dismissal of a civil lawsuit.

ATTACHMENT: a court order (writ) to seize property of the defendant in satisfaction of a judgment or anticipated judgment in the plaintiff's favour. It was also referred to as "execution" and "fieri facias" (qv). If directed against land, the term "de terris" (qv) was added; if directed against personal property (goods), the added term was "de bonis" (qv). If no goods were recovered by the sheriff, the writ was returned to the court marked "nulla bona" (qv). See, for example, case 529, vol. 2, 630–1 (post-1870).

BARRISTER: a lawyer who represents parties as advocate in court proceedings, civil or criminal, and related matters. Barristers are often distinguished from solicitors, the latter being lawyers whose practice involves such noncurial matters as drafting legal documents, advising on legal problems, as well as preparation for litigation, and sometimes acting as advocates in lower-level courts and tribunals. In England the legal profession is formally divided into those two subprofessions; but in Canada, although the distinction is often observed in practice, most lawyers are officially entitled to practice as either, or as both, barristers and solicitors (post-1870).

BATTERY: See "assault and battery."

BILL OF COSTS: a list of litigation expenses for which one party, usually the successful one, claims reimbursement by the other. Before payment, the bill of costs is normally subjected to taxation (item-by-item scrutiny and approval or rejection) by an officer of the court (post-1870).

BILL OF EXCHANGE: an unconditional order in writing addressed by one person to another, signed by the drawer (signator), that requires the addressee to pay on demand, or at a fixed or determinable future time, a sum certain in money either to or to the order of a specified person or to the bearer of the document. Cheques (qv) and promissory notes (qv) are special forms of bills of exchange. All bills of exchange are "negotiable instruments" and, as such, are transferable ("negotiable") to any innocent transferee for value (called a "holder in due course") (qv).

BOB: slang for shilling. See "pound (sterling)."

BOWSMAN: the crew member of a York boat (qv) stationed in the bow to watch for, signal, and fend off approaching hazards. He was the second most senior member of the crew, after the steersman (qv).

BRINDLED: a term describing the appearance of an animal with indistinct dark markings on a tan or grey hide.

BUNG: a stopper or plug in a cask or the hole into which the stopper or plug was inserted.

BYRE: cattle barn.

CANADA, CANADIAN: These terms had bewilderingly numerous meanings over the years. Before 1840 there were two distinct British North American colonies called Canada: Upper Canada (now Ontario) and Lower Canada (now Quebec). In 1840 those colonies were united as the single colony of Canada by the UK Act of Union. Although that new united Canada had a unified legislature and executive government, it was divided for administrative and political purposes into Canada West (Ontario) and Canada East (Quebec), which divisions tended to retain, in common parlance, the old names of Upper and Lower Canada. In 1867 the UK British North America Act welded the united Canadas and the two maritime colonies of Nova Scotia and New Brunswick into a federation called Canada (or the Dominion of Canada). Those were the various formal uses of "Canada" and "Canadian." "Canadian" also acquired a number of informal meanings. Since the North West Company was based in Montreal and the Hudson's Bay Company head office was in London, "Canadian" often referred, in the early years, to any NWC officer or employee. Because very few people came to Rupert's Land from Upper Canada in those years, the term was also used to designate anyone from Lower Canada, particularly a francophone (qv), who did not have Aboriginal blood. In later years, however, growing numbers of immigrants came to Red River from Upper Canada (later Canada West and Ontario), and the expressions "Canadian" and "Canadian Party" shifted to that group.

CAPIAS AD RESPONDENDUM (WRIT OF): a court order that the defendant be arrested to ensure his or her appearance in court to answer the plaintiff's claim.

CAPOT (OR CAPOTE): a loose, rough coat, often hooded, usually worn by men.

CARIOLE: a light passenger sled or carriage drawn by horse or dogs.

CHAIN: a measurement of length. A surveyor's chain, consisting of 100 links, is 66 feet in length. See also "link."

CHALLENGE (JURY): See "jury challenges."

CHARTER: Unless the context indicates otherwise, the term "charter" refers herein to the royal charter of 2 May 1670 by which King Charles II of England granted the "Company of Adventurers of England trading into Hudson's Bay" (Hudson's Bay Company) ownership of, governmental authority over, and a (dubiously legal) trading monopoly within the vast expanse of north-central North America drained by Hudson Bay.

CHEQUE: a bill of exchange (qv) drawn on a bank and payable on demand.

CIVIL LAW: The term "civil law" has several meanings. Walker (1980) lists ten. The most common meanings in the context of this study are (1) that portion of the law that does not relate to criminal conduct; (2) law applicable to civilians, as opposed to that which applies exclusively to military personnel; (3) law administered by courts other than ecclesiastical tribunals; and (4) laws and legal systems rooted in Roman law, such as those of France, Quebec, and Scotland. When used herein in the fourth sense, the term is intended to be distinguished from "common law" (qv).

CLEMENCY: See "commutation, commute."

CLUBBER: someone who kept reluctant oxen in motion by prodding or striking them with a stick when they stopped.

COLONY: although this term is sometimes used herein to refer to any colony of Great Britain, reference to "the colony" designates the Red River Settlement (as does "the settlement").

COMMISSIONED EVIDENCE: When witnesses are out of the jurisdiction, a court may issue a commission authorizing a court or a designated person or persons in the foreign jurisdiction to examine those witnesses and to return a transcript of the examination. The best known example of such a commission involving the General Quarterly Court of Assiniboia arose in *Corbett v. Dallas* – an action in the English Court of Common Pleas that had the effect of challenging the General Court's decision in *R. v. Corbett* (case 238, vol. 2, 366) but was never completed.

COMMON: communal grazing land.

COMMON LAW: As English kings began, from the twelfth century onward, to centralize the country's governance, itinerant royal justices gradually developed, on a case-by-case basis, laws that were common to the entire realm. Unlike statutory law, which was enacted by Parliament from time to time, common law was unwritten, except to the extent that law reports published the judges' rulings and reasons for judgment. As Parliament became gradually more powerful over time, the principle of legislative supremacy became accepted, according to which statutes automatically overrule inconsistent provisions of the common law. Statute law has never fully displaced common law, however, and the laws of both England and its former colonies remain a mixture of legislatively enacted and judge-made components. The term "common law" has several meanings, the most significant of which, for purposes of this study, are (1) judge-made law, as distinguished from written legislative enactments; and (2) a legal system whose origins, like those of every Canadian province except Quebec, are rooted in the law of England. When used in the second sense, it is intended to be distinguished from civil law (qv) systems that are based on Roman law. See the entry for "common law" in Walker (1980). For Recorder Adam Thom's thoughts about the creative potential of the common law, see vol. 1, 66.

COMMUTATION, COMMUTE: The governor of Assiniboia and other HBC-appointed governors were endowed with some of the royal prerogative (qv) powers and immunities of viceregal governorships of British colonies. This authority included the power of mercy, by which penalties imposed by the courts could be commuted (i.e., altered, ameliorated, or expunged). Such commutation of penalties is sometimes called "remission" (as in case 58, vol. 2, 103, the first recorded instance of its use in Red River courts). In the United States it is referred to as "executive clemency."

COMPEARED: appeared in court. The *Oxford English Dictionary* (2nd ed.) defines "compeer" as "[t]o appear, ... esp. at a formal assembly," and notes a special usage in Scots law: "To appear in Court, as a Party to a cause." The use of the expression in the General Quarterly Court records in respect of the appearance of witnesses who were not parties probably reflects Recorder Adam Thom's Scottish background and his imperfect understanding of the word's precise meaning in Scots law.

COMPOUNDED: In a judicial context, "compounded" means settled by agreement between the parties or, in a criminal case, that the charges have been dropped.

CONDUCT MONEY: travel expenses and a per diem fee required to be paid to each witness subpoenaed for appearance at trial by the person who obtained the subpoena (qv).

COOPER: one who manufactures or repairs wooden barrels.

COSTS: an award made to one party to civil litigation, usually the successful one, against the other as reimbursement for the first party's litigation expenses.

COUNCIL OF ASSINIBOIA: See "Assiniboia."

COYOTE: See "wolf."

CRIMINAL CONVERSATION: a claim for damages (a civil claim despite the misleading term "criminal") by a husband against a man accused of adultery with the plaintiff's wife. This tort (qv) was abolished in most jurisdictions relatively recently.

CROSS, CROSSING: These words are used frequently in the court records to refer to crossing, or helping others to cross, from one side of the Red or Assiniboine River to the other, as in, "I crossed Mr. Smith" or "He crossed his ox." The latter statements signify that the person or animal in question was conveyed or driven over or through the water by someone else.

CROSS-EXAMINATION: examination of a witness in court by someone adverse in interest. See "examination in chief."

CURRENT (WHEN USED IN RELATION TO A DATE): the present month. Interchangeable with "instant" ("inst."). See also "ultimo (ult.)."

DE BONIS: related to personal property, as opposed to land. See "attachment" (post-1870).

DECERNED: gave judgment. "Decern" in Scots law means to decree or make a formal order, and its use in the court records might be attributable to Recorder Adam Thom's Scottish upbringing.
DECLARATION: a document that briefly set out the nature and basis of a plaintiff's claim. A lawsuit was commenced by filing the plaintiff's declaration with the court and serving (qv) the declaration on the defendant together with a writ of summons from the court ordering the defendant to appear in court on a particular day to respond to the claim. The declaration was later called a statement of claim (post-1870).
DEFAMATION: the tort (qv) of injuring another's reputation by a false statement, whether in written or otherwise permanent form (libel), or in verbal or otherwise transitory form (slander). Defences include truth, "privileged" status on the part of the defendant by reason of a right or duty to make the statement in question, and the right to express "fair comment" opinions about matters of public significance. Malice on the defendant's part defeats both of the latter defences.
DEMURRER: a defendant's response to a plaintiff's claim to the effect that even if all allegations in the declaration (qv) were proven, they would not establish a sufficient basis for the claim in law (post-1870).
DE NOVO: anew or afresh, as in bringing a new lawsuit.
DEODAND: The practice of specifying the value of the weapon used to kill someone – as in the *Capenesseweet* (case 6, vol. 2, 17) and *Newkesequeskik* (case 8, vol. 2, 31) indictments – was a hangover from an ancient common law rule called "deodand," which provided for an object or animal that caused someone's death, or the value of that object or animal, to be forfeit to the Crown, or to others such as the victim's family to whom the Crown might choose to award it. Although the practice was often criticized, and was eventually abolished after someone attempted to apply it to a locomotive, it remained a part of English law during at least some of the period covered by the court records. See Walker (1980, 351). Although there is no indication that deodand was ever invoked in any Red River case, the ancient fixation on the value of deadly weapons was sometimes reflected in the terminology of indictments.
DEPONED: testified or gave written evidence under oath or solemn affirmation. "Depone" is the Scots law equivalent of "depose," and its use in the court records might be attributable to Recorder Adam Thom's Scottish upbringing.
DEPONENT: one who gives evidence, written or oral.

DEPOSITION: the sworn or solemnly affirmed evidence of a witness. The term commonly refers to evidence given out of court for use in court proceedings, but the term is also sometimes used, as in the *Keetchipiwaipasse* indictment (case 4, vol. 2, 9) to refer to evidence given (deponed) in the courtroom. An affidavit is a written deposition.
DE TERRIS: relating to real property (land), not to personal property (goods). See "attachment" (post-1870).
DISTRICT OF ASSINIBOIA: See "Assiniboia."
DIT: called, or known as. The word introduces a nickname, and is applied sometimes to a person's surname, as in "Riell, dit L'Ireland" (case 77, vol. 2, #211), and sometimes to a given name, as in "Louison, dit Bonhomme" (case 365, vol. 2, #518).
EJECTMENT: a legal proceeding by someone who claims to have been deprived of the rightful possession of land ("ejected"). The proceeding seeks to regain such possession, and to be paid compensation.
EN BANC: a sitting of a court in which all available members of the court participate, as when Manitoba's first Court of Queen's Bench sat with its full membership for appellate purposes (post-1870). All of Assiniboia's courts sat en banc, but the term was rarely if ever used at that time because that was the *only* way they ever sat.
ENGLISH HALFBREED: See "Racial/Ethnic Identifiers" in the List of Conventions and Abbreviations.
ESTREAT: the process by which a recognizance (qv) is forfeited for default and converted to a debt owed to the Crown.
EXAMINATION IN CHIEF: examination of a witness in court by someone who is not adverse in interest to that witness. It is the opposite of cross-examination (qv).
EXECUTION: execution has several meanings, including signature of a contract, will, or other legal document; seizure of personal property or land in satisfaction of a judgment (see "attachment" and "fieri facias"); and the carrying-out of a death sentence or other judicial order.
EXECUTIVE CLEMENCY: See "commutation, commute."
EX PARTE: proceeding without the presence of a party to litigation. This occurs only when reasonable steps have been taken to notify the missing party of the proceedings, or in a situation of great urgency.
EXPENCES (EXPENSES): See "costs."
FAGGOT ROAD: a faggot road, later called a "corduroy road," was composed of logs (faggots) laid side-by-side across the right-of-way to assist passage over swampy or wet areas.

FARTHING: an English monetary unit valued at one-quarter of a penny (qv). See "pound sterling." The award of a farthing in damages by a court (sometimes called "contemptuous damages") signified the court's opinion that the plaintiff's claim, although legally valid, lacked moral merit.

FEE SIMPLE: the most extensive form of private ownership rights in land recognized by common Law.

FELONY: At common law, very serious crimes (murder, arson, rape, wounding, robbery, etc.) were classified as felonies and carried the consequence, in addition to other punishments, of forfeiture of the felon's property. Less serious crimes (including such relatively grave offences as riot and theft) were referred to compendiously as "misdemeanours" and did not carry that consequence. Neither the distinction nor the consequence has been part of English or Canadian law for many years.

FENIANS: The Fenian Brotherhood was an Irish American paramilitary organization that attempted to retaliate against Great Britain for what its members considered to be oppressive policies and actions vis-à-vis Ireland by attacking Britain's North American colonies. It conducted several mostly unsuccessful incursions against targets in New Brunswick and Canada/Ontario in 1866 and 1870. See Macdonald (1910) and R.B. Brown (2009). Neither of those sources deals with the 1871 Manitoba raid, which, although led by some Fenian leaders, lacked official support from the Fenian Brotherhood. That topic is thoroughly covered, however, in Howard (1952).

FEU DE JOIE: a discharge into the air of firearms to signify victory or celebration.

FIERI FACIAS: The writ (qv) of fieri facias (often abbreviated to fi. fa.) was an order of execution (qv) against property of the defendant to satisfy a judgment in favour of the plaintiff. It was also referred to as "attachment." If it was directed against land, the term "de terris" (qv) was used; if against personal property (goods), the term was "de bonis" (qv). If no goods were recovered by the sheriff, the writ was returned to the court marked "nulla bona" (qv). See, for example, case 529, vol. 2, 630–1 (post-1870).

FORKS: the junction of the Red and Assiniboine Rivers. See "Assiniboia, District of."

FRANCOPHONE: one whose first language, or usual mode of expression, is French. In Canada the term is most commonly used in contradistinction to anglophone (qv).

FRENCH HALFBREED: See "Racial/Ethnic Identifiers" in the List of Conventions and Abbreviations.
FULLING: a process of shrinking, and thereby thickening, woollen cloth by means of moisture, heat, and pressing.
GAOL: jail.
GENERAL COURT: In the context of the Hudson's Bay Company's organizational structure, the General Court was the annual November meeting of the company's shareholders. The term is also used herein as a short form of "General Quarterly Court of Assiniboia."
GOVERNOR AND COMMITTEE: the London-based governing body of the Hudson's Bay Company, consisting of a governor, deputy governor, and committee of seven shareholders, chosen or confirmed at the company's annual November General Court (qv).
GOVERNOR AND COUNCIL: the local governing body of Rupert's Land (qv) or of any designated area therein such as Assiniboia (qv). Local governors and councils, appointed by the Governor and Committee (qv), were empowered by the charter (qv) to govern and administer justice within their designated areas.
GOVERNOR OF ASSINIBOIA: See "Assiniboia."
GOVERNOR OF RUPERT'S LAND: See "Rupert's Land."
GRAND JURY: a body of citizens, between twelve and twenty-three in number, called together in the case of a serious crime to consider evidence against the accused person and determine whether that evidence was sufficient to justify trying that person, in which case the grand jury would return a "true bill," or "indictment," and the accused would be tried by a regular ("petty") jury composed of twelve persons other than those who served on the grand jury. The procedure originated in England, and does not appear to have been used in Scotland. It has been abolished in many jurisdictions, including Canada, where it was replaced by the preliminary enquiry. Trials for less serious crimes were commenced by information (qv).
GUINEA: a kind of "baker's dozen" pound sterling (qv) – a monetary sum equivalent to 21 shillings – in which lawyers were traditionally paid. There have never been official banknotes or coins in guinea denominations, and no guinea symbol is known to the author.
HALFBREED: See "Racial/Ethnic Identifiers" in the List of Conventions and Abbreviations.
HARD LABOUR: In the latter stages of the period examined in this study, convicted prisoners were sometimes sentenced to engage in hard labour while incarcerated. Although that was thought to add

stringency to the punishment, it was often welcomed by the prisoner as providing some relief from prison boredom. The most common form of hard labour seems to have been picking "oakum" (qv).

HBC: Hudson's Bay Company. See "charter."

HEARSAY EVIDENCE: evidence by a witness concerning what he or she was told by someone else rather than what he or she learned directly by means of his or her unaided senses. Hearsay is often rejected by courts because of its doubtful reliability. Double hearsay (what one was told that someone else was told) is especially problematic. Hearsay is not absolutely inadmissible, however, and is sometimes admitted subject to an admonition to treat it cautiously. Much hearsay evidence was admitted in proceedings before the General Quarterly Court of Assiniboia, often with no such warning as to its reliability. The famous marathon trial in *Foss v. Pelly & Davidson* in July 1850 (case 77, vol. 2, 136) provides many examples, including double and triple hearsay.

HOLDER IN DUE COURSE: a transferee for value of a negotiable instrument – bill of exchange (qv), cheque (qv), or promissory note (qv) – who has no knowledge of any defect in the transferor's rights at the time the transfer takes place. Such a transferee is entitled to payment of the instrument's face value regardless of any defence that might be available against the transferor. An example is provided by *Garret v. Gerald* (case 215, vol. 2, 343).

HOMICIDE: causing the death of a human being. Homicide may be either culpable or nonculpable. Culpable homicide includes murder (qv) and manslaughter (qv).

HUDSON'S BAY COMPANY: See "charter."

HUDSON'S BAY COMPANY GENERAL COURT: See "General Court."

HUDSON'S BAY COMPANY GOVERNOR AND COMMITTEE: See "Governor and Committee."

IGNORAMUS: defined by *Wharton's Law Lexicon* (14th ed.) as, "(We are ignorant). The word formerly written on a bill of indictment by a grand jury when they rejected it" (Wharton 1938). See "grand jury."

INDIAN: See "Racial/Ethnic Identifiers" in the List of Conventions and Abbreviations.

INDICTMENT: See "grand jury."

INFORMATION: the formal complaint, filed with a justice of the peace or magistrate, that commenced criminal proceedings in relatively minor criminal cases. More serious charges required an indictment (true bill) from a grand jury (qv).

INSTANT (INST.) (WHEN USED IN RELATION TO A DATE): the present month. Interchangeable with "current." See also "ultimo (ult.)."

INTERLOCUTORY MATTER OR MOTION: an interim proceeding, procedural in nature, occurring during the course of litigation.

INTERROGATORIES: If a party alleged that a plaintiff's declaration (qv) or a defendant's plea (qv) did not contain sufficient information, written questions, called interrogatories, could be served on the opposing party seeking clarification (post-1870).

JOIN ISSUE, JOINDER OF ISSUE: A plaintiff and defendant engaged in civil litigation are said to "join issue" at the point in the pretrial process where one party has asserted in writing and the other has denied in writing all the facts crucial to the issue in dispute. Sometimes, however, the expression "joinder of issues" was used in a different sense: to refer to the amalgamation of separate lawsuits involving the same parties and issues. It may, for example, have been used in that sense in cases 461 and 462, vol. 2, 583 (post-1870).

JP: justice of the peace (qv).

JURY: a group of men selected by the sheriff from a jury panel (qv) to adjudicate cases before the General Quarterly Court of Assiniboia as members of either a grand jury (qv) or a petty jury (qv). See also "mixed jury."

JURY CHALLENGES: The suitability of potential jurors may be challenged in two ways. If it is contended that a candidate for selection is disqualified for some specific reason (bias, mental or physical disability, etc.), a party may challenge that person "for cause," and the candidate will be removed if cause is proved. Parties are also allotted by law a number of "peremptory" challenges (varying in number from defence to prosecution, jurisdiction to jurisdiction, time to time, and situation to situation), which may be exercised without proof or designation of cause.

JURY PANEL: a list of property owners thought by the sheriff to be suitable for jury duty, from which the members of particular grand juries (qv) and petty juries (qv) were selected. Apart from being male, adult, and the owner of real property, no other formal qualification for inclusion on Assiniboia's jury panels is known; but no persuasive evidence has been found of the inclusion of Indians. No other racial, ethnic, or national exclusion seems to have been practised.

JUSTICE OF THE PEACE: a judge, similar to the magistrates who comprised the petty courts of Assiniboia but with greater powers, at least in later years, to issue warrants for arrest and imprisonment and other forms of legal process. The office is ancient, originating in the English Justices of the Peace Act of 1361, which remained in force throughout the HBC's entire reign over Rupert's Land. It is not clear, however, how many, if any, JP commissions were issued under the 1361 act for service in Rupert's Land. A later English statute, the Canada Jurisdiction Act of 1803, authorized the appointment of JPs for the "Indian Territories," and, despite disagreement about whether "Indian Territories" included Rupert's Land, JPs were appointed under that act from time to time to exercise jurisdiction in Rupert's Land. A third type of JP commission – issued by the Hudson's Bay Company on the sole authority of its own charter – was in use in Assiniboia by at least 1850, and continued to be used into the 1860s. The terms "justice of the peace" and "magistrate" were often used interchangeably, which is not surprising given that both JPs and magistrates sat side-by-side in the petty courts of Assiniboia. The offices differed legally, however, both in respect of the JPs' greater jurisdiction over the issuing of court processes, and in that they were unpaid (although the concurrent appointment of many JPs as petty court magistrates entitled them to the same remuneration in practice as their colleagues).

KNOCKED UP: exhausted. The term seems to have been used in reference to both humans and animals. There is no evidence in the court records or related documentation of the later meaning, when applied to women, of becoming pregnant.

LAW OFFICERS OF THE CROWN: the attorney general and solicitor general. Although ministers of the Crown, with departmental and political responsibilities, the holders of these offices were (and are) also expected to give objective, nonpartisan advice on important questions of public law. See Edwards (1964).

LEVEE: a public reception given by royalty or representatives of royalty, traditionally in the morning – "at rising" – hence the name.

LIARD: a distinctive grey colour of domestic animal.

LIBEL: See "defamation." Although the most common use of the word is as a form of defamation, another meaning refers to a written statement of the plaintiff's claim in a civil lawsuit. It was used in the latter sense in *Smith v. Kirton* (case 1, vol. 2, 3).

LINK: a standard unit of a surveyor's chain, 7.92 inches long. See also "chain."

MAGISTRATE: See "justice of the peace."

MALICE AFORETHOUGHT: premeditation.

MANSLAUGHTER: the unlawful killing of a human (homicide) (qv) that does not amount to murder because the perpetrator lacks malice aforethought (qv), acting instead under the impulse of sudden anger, provocation, negligence, etc.
MERCY: See "commutation, commute" and "royal prerogative."
MERINO: a fine-quality wool, used in high-quality fabrics.
MÉTIS/METIS: See "Racial/Ethnic Identifiers" in the List of Conventions and Abbreviations.
MIDDLEMEN: the crew members of York boats (qv), who occupied the six central positions and did the rowing.
MISDEMEANOUR: See "felony."
MIXED JURY: After the *Sayer* case in 1849 (case 68, vol. 2, 113) trials involving both anglophones (qv) and francophones (qv) were required to be heard by juries composed equally of French- and English-speaking persons. There is a suggestion in an 1861 *Nor'-Wester* account of a trial in the General Court that year that Indians were sometimes included in the mixture: "The mixed character of our population occasions something else besides the confusion of tongues. Juries have to be comprised of suitable representatives of the parties at the bar – suitable not only as to station or calling generally, but as to race and language, whether French, English or Indian" (NW611130). No other evidence of such a practice has been found, however.
MUNICIPAL DISTRICT OF ASSINIBOIA: See "Assiniboia."
MURDER: the unlawful killing of a human being (homicide) (qv) with malice aforethought (qv). Unlawful homicide without malice aforethought is manslaughter (qv).
NEGOTIABLE INSTRUMENT: See "bill of exchange" and "holder in due course."
NISI ("UNLESS" IN LATIN): a rule, order, or decree nisi is one that will take effect at some specified future time unless some specified condition is met or specified event occurs in the meantime (post-1870).
NOCE: a wedding celebration party.
NOLLE PROSEQUI: indicates a decision by the Crown that a particular matter is "not to be prosecuted."
NON COMPOS MENTIS: not of sound mind.
NON EST INVENTUS: This is a return (qv) made by a sheriff or constable unable to locate a person he has been ordered to arrest, or upon whom he has been ordered to serve a writ (qv).
NONSUIT: dismissal of a civil lawsuit, often without hearing from the defendant, on the ground that the plaintiff's claim or evidence, even if

entirely accepted on the facts, does not assert or establish a claim recognized by law. The term was often also used by the quarterly courts of Assiniboia to describe the dismissal of a claim simply because the defendant's evidence was accepted over that of the plaintiff.
NORTHERN COUNCIL: See "Rupert's Land, Council of."
NORTH WEST COMPANY: A Montreal-based fur-trading company that was the principal competitor of the Hudson's Bay Company (qv) until the two organizations merged in 1821 under the name of the latter.
NOTE OF HAND: a promissory note (qv) or bill of exchange (qv).
NOT PROVEN: a verdict, lying between "guilty" and "not guilty," that is possible in criminal prosecutions under Scots law. In terms of penal consequences, it has the same effect as a verdict of "not guilty"; but socially it signifies that while the court or jury does not consider the prosecution to have proved guilt beyond a reasonable doubt, as is required for conviction, it is not willing to say that the accused is innocent. Such a finding was not permissible under the law of England, which regulated legal proceedings in Rupert's Land, but it appears to have been made in case 112, vol. 2, 222.
NULLA BONA: a notation on the return (qv) of a writ of attachment (qv) indicating that no seizable goods were found. See "fieri facias" (post-1870).
NWC: North West Company (qv).
OAKUM: rope shreds used to caulk the seams of boats. A requirement to "pick oakum" – shred pieces of old rope – was a common form of "hard labour" (qv) imposed on prisoners.
OFFSET: a claim by the defendant offsetting that of the plaintiff in whole or in part. In modern practice, the term "set-off" is sometimes used to describe a countervailing claim arising from the same transaction upon which the plaintiff's claim is based, or a related one; whereas "counterclaim" refers to one that has a more distinct origin.
OSSINIBOIA: See "Assiniboia."
OUTFIT: A business year in the fur trade.
PAINTER: a rope used to secure or tow a boat.
PANNIKIN (VARIOUSLY SPELLED): a small metal drinking vessel.
PARK: A settler's "park" was the "infield" portion of the farm, closest to the house and outbuildings. It was used for the household garden and cereal crops. Animals usually grazed in the "outfield" area, beyond which was a "hay privilege." See Coutts (2000, 134).
PARTICULARS: If a defendant regarded the facts alleged in the plaintiff's declaration (qv) as insufficient to understand the nature or basis

of the claim, the defendant could, before pleading (replying) to the declaration, seek an order that further information ("particulars") be provided by the plaintiff (post-1870).

PEASE: peas.

PEMMICAN: a concentrated food consisting of ground dried meat, usually buffalo, melted fat, and sometimes dried berries. High in nutrition and easily preserved and transported, pemmican was the principal staple food of the fur trade.

PENCE: plural of penny. See "pound (sterling)."

PENNY: See "pound (sterling)."

PEREMPTORY CHALLENGE: See "jury challenges."

PETTY JURY: a body of twelve adults (male at all times relevant to this study) charged with determining, in senior courts (the General Quarterly Court and the Court of Queen's Bench in Assiniboia and Manitoba respectively), either the guilt or innocence of persons on trial for serious crimes or the respective entitlements and liabilities of parties to civil litigation. See also "grand jury."

PLEA, PLEADING(S): In civil litigation, a "pleading" is a preliminary written statement of a party's claim or defence. Prior to 1870 pleadings were not required in Assiniboia courts. Verbal statements sufficed. Following the creation of Manitoba in 1870, however, written pleadings became necessary. Defendants were required within a specified time after the receipt of the plaintiff's declaration (qv), or of particulars (qv) where ordered, to file and serve (qv) on the plaintiff his plea (later known as a statement of defence), which briefly outlined the defendant's side of the story and the reasons why, in the defendant's submission, the claim should be dismissed (post-1870).

POSSE COMITATUS: a group of private persons authorized by warrant or other lawful order to assist a sheriff or other law enforcement officer to carry out that officer's duties on a particular occasion. Literally, the expression means "power of the county."

POUND (STERLING): English currency was in common use at Red River during most of the period covered by this book, although other currencies occasionally showed up as well. The English units were the pound sterling, or "quid" (£); the guinea (qv); the shilling, or "bob" (/), of which there were twenty in every pound and twenty-one in every guinea; the penny (d) ("pence" in plural), of which there were twelve in every shilling; and the farthing, worth a quarter of a penny. In the court records, pounds, shillings, and pence are designated in various, sometimes confusing, ways, often separated by dots or slashes.

The convention adopted herein, unless the context indicates otherwise, is to express English currency sums as in the following example: £12.00.04 (12 pounds, 0 shillings, 4 pence). For a special use of the farthing in awards of damages, see "farthing."
PRAECIPE: a written request to a court for some action, such as issuing a writ or signing a judgment (post-1870).
PREMISES: foregoing circumstances.
PREROGATIVE: See "royal prerogative."
PRESCRIPTION: a process by which rights in relation to property may be acquired by virtue of the mere unchallenged possession or use of the property in question for a specified period of time. Although time periods varied considerably from situation to situation, twenty years was common for the acquisition of rights of way over real property at the time the quarterly courts of Assiniboia functioned.
PROSECUTE, PROSECUTION: Then, as now, the terms "prosecute" and "prosecution" were most commonly used to mean proceeding with a criminal charge. However, they were sometimes also used to mean pursuing a civil claim.
PROCESS: court process (as distinguished from court procedure, which refers comprehensively to all procedural regulations of the courts) comprises documents such as summons, arrest warrants, and papers that are required to be served upon a person or persons involved in court proceedings.
PROMISSORY NOTE: a form of bill of exchange (qv) consisting of an unconditional statement in writing, made by one person to another and signed by the maker, promising to pay on demand or at a fixed or determinable future time a sum certain in money to, or to the order of, a specified person or to the bearer of the document.
PROTHONOTARY: the chief clerical officer of the Court of Queen's Bench (post-1870).
PUBLIC INTEREST OR PUBLIC WELFARE: the designation of the prosecuting authority in criminal cases before 1864. After the Council of Assiniboia decided, on 7 January 1864, that proceedings in the courts should be regulated by the laws currently in force in England, "in as far as the same are known to the court and are applicable to the condition of the Colony," criminal prosecutions were commenced in the name of "The Queen," or Regina, a practice that had been occasionally followed before then as well.
PUISNE JUDGE: an associate justice; a member of a court other than the chief justice. Since chief justices are, generally speaking, merely

"first among equals," puisne justices possess the same powers as their chief justices, except for the administrative responsibilities entailed in, or special powers legislatively bestowed upon, the office of chief justice.

PUNCHEON: a large cask.

QC: abbreviation of Queen's Counsel (qv).

QUEEN'S COUNSEL (KING'S COUNSEL – KC – IN TIMES WHEN A MALE MONARCH IS ON THE THRONE OF ENGLAND): an honourary designation conferred by the Crown by letters patent upon certain senior members of the legal profession. In England only barristers (qv) are so honoured, but in Canada, where the profession is not formally bifurcated, lawyers who practise as solicitors (qv) are also eligible. Although originally restricted to lawyers retained by the Crown, the designation has long been conferred as well on lawyers who never act for the Crown – and even those who routinely act against the Crown.

QUEEN'S EVIDENCE: evidence given against someone with whom the witness has been associated in an alleged crime on condition that the witness will not be prosecuted in the same matter.

RECOGNIZANCE: a bond or promise made in court undertaking to perform or abstain from some action, such as to appear again in court, to keep the peace, to pay a sum of money, or to stay away from certain premises. See "estreat." See also the example in *Doherty v. Shepherd*, case 89, vol. 2, 186.

RECORD: The record was a compilation of documentation for a particular case: the declaration, demand for particulars, particulars, plea, etc. It was filed with a court by the plaintiff to signify that the case was ready to proceed to trial; or, as in case 503, vol. 2, 618, to inform the court that it would not be proceeding to trial because the parties had agreed to some other conclusion (post-1870).

RECORDER: a municipal-level judge of limited criminal jurisdiction in England and Wales at the time; a barrister sitting singly in a quarter sessions court. *Black's Law Dictionary* defines "Recorder," historically, as "[a] magistrate with criminal jurisdiction in some British cities or boroughs" (Garner 2004). For a fuller explanation of English and Welsh recorders, see Wharton (1938, 828, 847). The term was not used in Scotland. The recorders of Rupert's Land differed from the British model in that they were members of a multiple-member tribunal, which had plenary jurisdiction, both criminal and civil.

RED RIVER CART: a large wooden cart, held together mostly by rawhide, with two oversize concave wheels designed to traverse rough terrain and capable of doubling, with the wheels removed, as a boat when water had to be crossed. Drawn by pony or ox, and easily repairable in the wilds, it was the most common vehicle for long-distance transport over the prairie throughout most of the period under review.

RED RIVER SETTLEMENT: See "Assiniboia, District of."

REGINA (OR R.): Queen. See "public interest or public welfare."

REMISSION: See "commutation, commute."

REPLEVIN: a court order that goods the plaintiff claims were wrongfully taken by the defendant be seized and held until the right of possession can be determined by the court (post-1870).

RETURN: After serving a court document on someone or executing a warrant of attachment or arrest, the constable or other person who effected service or execution filed a report called a "return" with the court, certifying what was done. The term can also refer to the report of one who takes commissioned evidence (qv).

RIPARIAN RIGHT: the right of a person in possession of land bordering a river or other watercourse to make reasonable use of the water.

ROYAL PREROGATIVE: At one point in British constitutional history, most governmental power resided in the monarchy. Over time, much of that power was usurped by Parliament, which, by the mid-seventeenth century, had established its ultimate supremacy over the monarchy and all other governmental organs. There are some royal powers, however, that Parliament never chose to take away. That residue of monarchical authority, known collectively as the royal prerogative, includes the prerogative of mercy, under which representatives of the Crown may pardon or commute penalties imposed by the courts. See "commutation, commute."

RULE NISI: See "nisi."

RUPERT'S LAND: the vast territory in north-central North America, comprising the entire Hudson Bay drainage basin, that King Charles II granted to the Hudson's Bay Company by royal charter in 1670. See "charter."

RUPERT'S LAND, COUNCIL OF: the body of Hudson's Bay Company senior field officers created by resolution of the company's General Court (qv) on 29 May 1822 to govern Rupert's Land (qv) in collaboration with the governor of Rupert's Land (qv) under the authority of the company's 1670 charter (qv). Its members were appointed from time to time by the Governor and Committee of the Hudson's Bay Company. The governor and council (qv) normally met once annually, usually in June at Norway House, to conduct their business. Although often known as the Northern Council or the Council of the Northern District, the body is, for consistency, called the Council of Rupert's Land herein.

RUPERT'S LAND, GOVERNOR OF: the officer or officers appointed under that title by the Governor and Committee of the Hudson's Bay Company (qv) to govern Rupert's Land (qv) in collaboration with the Council of Rupert's Land (qv) under the authority of the company's 1670 charter (qv).

SEDUCTION: a common law action in tort (qv) entitling parents to sue men who made their unmarried daughters pregnant, and be awarded compensation for the loss of the daughters' domestic services during their confinement. A related action could be brought by employers of female domestic servants in similar circumstances.

SERVE, SERVICE (OF DOCUMENTS): formal delivery of court documents (notices, writs, warrants, declarations, etc.) to the persons affected.

SETTLEMENT: Although this term is sometimes used herein to refer to any settled community, "the settlement" designates the Red River Settlement (as does "colony").

SHILLING: See "pound (sterling)."

SIC ("SUCH" IN LATIN): an assurance that a word or expression quoted from a document or other statement is accurately quoted.

SLANDER: See "defamation."

SOLICITOR: See "barrister."

STEERSMAN: the man who steered a York boat (qv), by means of a long oar at the stern, and was for that reason the senior member of the crew, followed in seniority by the bowsman (qv).

STERLING: See "pound (sterling)."

STYLE OF CAUSE: the formal title of a civil or criminal case in the courts, such as *Smith v. Jones* or *The Queen* (often abbreviated *R.*) *v. Jones.* For an explanation of styles of cause in the courts of Assiniboia, see "public interest or public welfare."

SUBPOENA: a court order requiring a person to appear before the court as a party, a witness, or a juror. Literally, the word means "under penalty," and failure to obey the order without just excuse is punishable by fine or other punishment.

SUMMONS: a subpoena (qv).

SURETY: a person who provides a bond guaranteeing to the court that another person will fulfil bail conditions or be otherwise of good behaviour during a defined period of time.

TAXATION OF COSTS: A successful party to civil litigation, whether plaintiff or defendant, is entitled, in the court's discretion, to be paid his or her costs by the loser. That obligation can be made a court order if the court or one of its officials certifies that the claimed costs are legitimate. The examination and certification process is known as "taxation." It does not involve the payment of any tax. See "bill of costs."
TORO: an Anglicization of "taureau," which was "a strong bag made of buffalo rawhide sewn hair-side out, used as a container for 90 pounds of pemmican" (Avis 1967).
TORT: wrongful, but not necessarily criminal, conduct for which the victim may sue the perpetrator civilly for damages or other compensatory relief. Examples are trespass to the person (assault or battery) (qv), defamation (qv) (written libel or verbal slander), and, at the time the quarterly courts functioned, criminal conversation (qv) (sexual congress with another man's wife).
TRIPMEN: boat crews. See "York boats," "bowsman," "middlemen," and "steersman."
TRUE BILL: See "grand jury."
ULTIMO (ULT.) (WHEN USED IN RELATION TO A DATE): the month previous to the present one. See "instant (inst.)" and "current."
UNION JACK: British flag.
UT SUPRA: "as above" in Latin.
VACATION: the period of time between court sessions.
WOLF: The evidence in the court records refers occasionally to "wolves." Although there is no way of being certain, it seems probable that at least some of those references were to "prairie wolves," which are usually called "coyotes" today.
WRIT: court order. See particular types of orders, such as "attachment," "capias ad respondendum (writ of)," "fieri facias," "subpoena," etc.
XY COMPANY: The New North West Company, commonly called the XY Company after the markings it placed on its fur bales, was formed by former North West Company employees dissatisfied with the 1795 reorganization of the old firm. The new company operated in competition with both the HBC and the NWC until 1804, when it merged with the latter.
YF: the abbreviation for York Factory, marked or stamped, often in stylized form, on letters or packages bound for that destination.
YORK BOATS: Long wooden boats, based on a type used in the Orkney Islands, that were Rupert's Land's principal means of heavy-duty

inland water transport throughout the period of this study. York boats were from 34 to 42 feet in length, 9 feet wide amidships, and 3 feet in depth. They were capable, depending on size, of carrying from more than 2.5 to more than 5.5 tons of cargo. Each carried a crew of "tripmen," consisting of a steersman (qv), bowsman (qv), and six middlemen (qv). See Rich (1956, xl–xlii).

Notes

PREFACE

1 AM: B1/14. Napier appears to have been an officer with the Royal Canadian Rifles, a military detachment that arrived at Fort Garry in November 1857. His painting is reproduced on the cover of this book.

CONVENTIONS AND ABBREVIATIONS

1 See "Racial/Ethnic Identifiers" below.
2 Taylor (2005), prepared before the fourth volume was recognized for what it is, designates volumes A, B, and C as books 1, 2, and 3 respectively.
3 NW600328.

CHAPTER ONE

1 See generally Morton (1961); and Bumsted (2003b, 2008).
2 *The Royal Charter for incorporating the Hudson's Bay Company, granted by his Majesty King Charles the Second, in the 22d year of his reign, A.D. 1670*. See Oliver (1914, 135ff.).
3 Ibid., 136.
4 See generally Bumsted (1982, 2008).
5 Record Book A, District of Assiniboia. See Oliver (1914, 155).
6 Although "Assiniboia" designated the total area granted to Selkirk and all institutions of local government before Manitoba was created in 1870, the community was commonly known as the Selkirk or Red River Settlement.

7 Pemmican is a concentrated food consisting of ground dried meat, usually buffalo, melted fat, and sometimes dried berries. It is high in nutrition and easily preserved and transported.
8 Morton (1956, 45).
9 See "Racial/Ethnic Identifiers" in the Foreword.
10 Ibid.
11 Although the term "Canadian" could properly be applied to any NWC employee – or, indeed, anyone else – from Upper or Lower Canada, it most commonly then designated a francophone from Lower Canada who did not possess Aboriginal blood. See Glossary.
12 Morris (1880, 9–12, 299–300). Although treated as an extinguishment of Aboriginal title by Selkirk and the HBC, Indian and Halfbreed advocates later claimed that the treaty was a mere lease and that the rent had not been consistently paid (see vol. 1, 151, 163). The treaty was recognized by the General Quarterly Court of Assiniboia in *McDermot v. Fanyant et al.*, vol. 2, 52, case 25, February 1847. It was supplanted in 1871 by new treaties with the Government of Canada (Morris, 1880, 43, 313–20).
13 Although of considerable interest, that litigation lies beyond the scope of this study. See Bumsted (2008, 359–97).
14 The looming parliamentary bill that would become the Fur Trade Regulation Act in July 1821, and was sponsored by Colonial Secretary Bathurst, acted as both a carrot and a stick in negotiations between the companies.
15 Rich (1961, vol. 2, 385–99); MacKay (1966, 151–64).
16 1 & 2 Geo. IV, c. 66. The full title was *An Act for regulating the Fur Trade, and establishing a Criminal and Civil Jurisdiction within certain Parts of North America.*
17 The inadequacy of these resolutions, in themselves, is discussed in chapter 3 (25ff.).
18 Although that body was sometimes called the "Northern Council" thereafter, "Council of Rupert's Land" will be used herein. Although trials were conducted by the Rupert's Land governor and council from time to time, it would be the Assiniboia governor and council (later known, in its judicial capacity, as the General Quarterly Court of Assiniboia) that did most of the important judicial work in Rupert's Land.
19 See generally Galbraith (1976); and Raffan (2007).
20 Oliver (1914, 219–21).
21 Ibid., 221.
22 See generally Foster (1990a, 2005); Smandych and Linden (1996); and Baker (1996).

23 Oliver (1914, 150).

24 Baker (1996, 52–7).

25 HBCA: Albany Post Miscellaneous files, B.3/z/2, fo. 1–3 (1694–96).

26 HBCA: York Post Journal, 27 December 1715, B.239/a/2, fo. 76. Brown (1980, 12) points out that the HBC, unlike the NWC, "demanded both celibacy and chastity from its Bay employees," explaining that the only females to be found near the company's posts in the early years were Indian women, intimacy with whom, HBC officials feared, might damage trading relationships with their menfolk, create a drain on post provisions, risk espionage by rival French traders, and lead to disruptive "licentiousness."

27 AM: "Justice" Search File.

28 HBCA: B.177/a/5.

29 *Norway House Post Journal*, 23 March 1833, HBCA: B.154/a/23, fo. 49.

30 AM: "Justice" Search File.

31 This was James Bird, who ended up years later as a magistrate at Red River.

32 *Edmonton House Journal*, 19 October 1807, HBCA: B.60/a/7.

33 Oliver (1914, 150).

34 HBCA: A.39/1, fo. 5–8.

35 Draft Memorial to Attorney-General re judicial jurisdiction, 10 May 1806, HBCA: A.39/1, fo. 141.

36 Ibid.

37 The New North West Company, commonly called the XY Company after the markings it placed on its fur bales, was formed by former NWC employees dissatisfied with the 1795 reorganization of the old company. The new company operated in competition with both the HBC and the NWC until 1804, when it merged with the latter.

38 Morton (1939, 513).

39 43 Geo. II. c. 138. See the discussion of this legislation in the following section.

40 See Gibson and Gibson (1972, 6–14).

41 Macdonell to Selkirk, 31 May 1812 (Oliver 1914, 177–8). Knowing that the United Kingdom and the United States were on the brink of war at that time, Macdonell thought the British government might be willing to grant him military authority.

42 Nine others – company officers and members of the first Selkirk contingent – were also appointed magistrates under the 1803 act at that time. *Quebec Gazette*, 12 December 1811 (Oliver 1914, 176–7).

43 Oliver (1914, 178–83).

44 Ibid., 186–8.

45 The HBC denied the applicability of that statute to Rupert's Land. That view did not prevent its officers from relying upon it when it served their purposes to do so.

46 LAC: E1–1(4), 1176.

47 Selkirk to Macdonell, 13 June 1813 (Oliver 1914, 178).

48 The term "common law" has several meanings, the most significant of which, for purposes of this study, are (1) judge-made law, as distinguished from politically enacted written legislation, and (2) a legal system whose origins, like those of every Canadian province except Quebec, are rooted in the judge-made law of England. See Glossary.

49 For the many meanings of "civil law," see Glossary.

50 HBC reference of the draft code to barristers G. Holroyd and J. Scarlett, HBCA: A.39/3, fo. 28ff.

51 HBCA: E.8/8, fo. 116–168. The internal pagination (1–105) includes the verso sides of all folios, most of which contain comments on the draft code. The author is grateful to Dr DeLloyd J. Guth for bringing this document to his attention.

52 HBCA: A.39/3, fo. 28ff.

53 HBCA: A.8/1, fo. 20–3. Although some archivist gave the document an estimated date of 1819, the author has adopted a range of August 1814 to May 1815 because there is an internal reference to an event in the earlier month and the document was submitted, near completion, to counsel for comment in the latter one. HBCA: A.39/3, fo. 28ff.

54 Berens to Bathurst, 8 June 1815, HBCA: A.8/1, fo. 23(b)–25(b).

55 Ibid.

56 Unknown sender to Macdonell, June 1818 (Oliver 1914, 204–6).

57 Ostracized by the community.

58 Selkirk stressed the importance of doing so in 1813 (Oliver 1914, 179).

59 See vol. 1, 64–8. The governor of the HBC's Southern District, based at Moose Factory, promulgated a code-like document on 1 September 1815 that set out a schedule of disciplinary offences (i.e., mutiny, desertion, combination, disobedience, insolence, disrespect, and assaulting an officer) and the punishments that company employees who committed them could expect to receive (Oliver 1914, 1285–7). That did not purport to apply to anyone other than employees, however.

60 Bumsted (2003b, 9).

61 Oliver (1914, 135ff.)

CHAPTER TWO

1 Bumsted (2003b, 43–50). The problems, especially serious among the 1821 Swiss immigrants, were largely the fault of lax selection procedures and broken promises on the part of Selkirk's agents.

2 HBC Governor and Committee to Simpson, 27 February 1822 (Oliver 1914, 638).

3 HBC Governor and Committee to Simpson, 8 March 1822 (ibid., 639).

4 Bumsted (2003b, 43).

5 Oliver (1914, 1290).

6 Pannekoek (1991, 17).

7 Oliver (1914, 1290).

8 Minutes of HBC Northern Department (Rupert's Land) Council meeting, 20 August 1822 (ibid, 640).

9 MacLeod and Morton (1963, 86–7).

10 Ibid., 101.

11 Simpson to Andrew Colvile, 8 September 1821, quoted in Raffan (2007, 141–2). His view had not improved the following spring, when he described Red River as follows: "Take the colony all in all, and it is certainly an extraordinary place. The great folks would cut each other's throats if they could with safety. There is nothing like a social feeling among them, and the best friends today are the bitterest enemies tomorrow. Among the lower orders it is much the same: they have a certain feeling of pride, independence and equality among them which is subversive of good order in society. They are opposed to each other in little factions, and every man in the colony looks to his arms alone for safety and protection." Simpson to Andrew Colvile, 20 May 1822, quoted in Coutts (2000, 92). Simpson held generally pessimistic views of his fellow men.

12 Simpson to Andrew Colvile, 8 September 1821, quoted in Raffan (2007, 142). Raffan mistakenly identifies the target of these remarks as *Miles* Macdonell, the first governor of Assiniboia. For a scathing – and entertaining – description of Alexander Macdonell's administration, see Ross (1856, 64–8).

13 Oliver (1914, 1291). The books were William Blackstone's *Commentaries on the Laws of England* (1766), Richard Burn's *Justice of the Peace*, and Tomlin's *Law Dictionary*, all quite appropriate if they had been put to use.

14 Ibid., 219, reprints Bulger's commission, dated 27 March 1822. At this point, when Assiniboia was still owned by the estate of Lord Selkirk, the

governor was jointly appointed by the estate and the company, the latter's involvement being necessary to confer the powers of governor and council under the HBC charter upon settlement authorities. The company also agreed to contribute £200 annually to supplement what the estate paid the governor of Assiniboia. Governor and Committee to Simpson, 23 March 1823, AM: MG3, A5, fo. 20.

15 Oliver (1914, 219–21). See vol. 1, 8.
16 Bulger to A. Colvile, 25 July 1822 (ibid., 224).
17 Bulger to unknown recipient, 1822 (ibid.).
18 Bulger to A. Colvile [?], 8 September 1822 (ibid. 225).
19 Allen and Judd (2000).
20 Oliver (1914, 226n2), commenting on a reference in Minutes of Council of Assiniboia, 4 December 1822. The "attempted murder" involved an Indian pulling a knife during a scuffle with Governor Bulger, who had the man peremptorily imprisoned and flogged without trial. Bulger to A. Colvile, 7 December 1822, LAC: MG19, E5, fo. 407–9. See vol. 1, 30.
21 Bulger to A. Colvile, 14 December 1822, LAC: MG19, E5, fo. 423.
22 Oliver (1914, 240ff.), quoting Governor and Committee to Simpson, 21 May 1823.
23 Oliver (1914, 227–8) quotes the warrant. It is not known why Bulger expected his warrant to be honoured in the United States. The outcome of the case is unknown.
24 Ibid., 228–31.
25 Ibid., 231.
26 Governor and Committee to Simpson, 21 May 1823 (Oliver 1914, 240).
27 Bulger to Clarke, 23 April 1823 (ibid., 232). Although the Selkirk estate owned Assiniboia, the deed granting the land to Selkirk required the estate to make land available to retired employees in accordance with company directions.
28 Bulger to Clarke, 24 April 1823 (ibid., 233).
29 Minutes of Council of Assiniboia, 3 May 1823 (ibid., 235ff.).
30 Ibid.
31 Governor and Committee to Simpson, 21 May 1823 (ibid. 240–4).
32 Bumsted (2003b, 54).
33 Bulger's nemesis, Chief Factor Clarke, was transferred to a more remote and less sensitive post at about the same time.
34 Bumsted (1999a, 197).
35 G. Simpson to A. Colvile, 1 November 1823 (Oliver 1914, 258).

36 Martin (1898, 33); Public Notice Regarding Title Deeds, 20 January 1825 (Oliver 1914, 260). The register of land ownership would be first relied upon as evidence in the General Court in *McDermot v. Fanyant et al.*, case 25, vol. 2, 52.

37 Minutes of Council of Assiniboia, 4 May 1832 (Oliver 1914, 263–5).

38 See vol. 1, 26.

39 See vol. 1, 13.

40 Ross (1856, 76–7). Although the substance of Ross's report is likely correct, the words attributed to Pelly may have gained something in Ross's telling.

41 Court of Oyer and Terminer, Western District Assize, Upper Canada, 1822. The documents are held in Colonial Office Records, Public Records Office, London (PRO CO, 42/370, 25–42), and are partially published in Doughty and Story (1935, 175–7). See Smandych (2005); and Walters (1996).

42 Simpson to London, 10 August 1832, HBCA: A.12/1, fo. 418ff.

43 "[T]he [Indian] women and children," Simpson added, "were all [set] at liberty, being furnished with necessary supplies to enable them to provide for themselves."

44 Ross (1856, 83).

45 Ens (1996, 53).

46 Ibid.

47 Bumsted (2000, 78–84).

48 Ibid., 82.

49 Ibid., 59.

50 Ross (1856, 109).

51 Ibid., 110.

52 Although Simpson's presence in the settlement after 1833 would again be restricted to annual visits, his vast network of correspondents and the company's astonishing communications system ensured that he was seldom out of touch with developments there for very long.

53 Oliver (1914, 74).

54 Bumsted (2003b, 61–2); Pannekoek (1991, 87).

55 Ross (1856, 279–80).

56 Simpson (York Factory) to London, 21 July 1834, HBCA: D.4/100, fo. 3.

57 See vol. 1, 24.

58 See Ens (1996, 54–5).

59 The metaphor originated with Ross (1856, 167): "[T]he inflammable materials took fire, blazed out, and we had our first hostile demonstration of the Halfbreeds."

60 Simpson (York Factory) to London, 21 July 1834, HBCA: D.4/100, fo. 3.

CHAPTER THREE

1 "Burning Earth" or "Burnt Earth." This renowned Sioux leader later figured, indirectly, in an 1845 murder conviction that resulted in Red River's first and only hanging (case 6, August 1845, vol. 2, 17). See vol. 1, 100.

2 Simpson's concerns went beyond the Indian and Halfbreed factors. He also feared the disruptive consequences of the settlement's rapid population growth and proposed prohibiting future company retirees from settling at Red River unless they could afford to purchase at least 50 acres of land. The Council of Rupert's Land enacted that measure in 1835 (Oliver 1914, 723, res. 84).

3 Simson's letter was based on proposals set out in an undated, unsigned, draft petition for a new police force (HBCA: E.8/8, fo. 97ff.), which smacks of the style of Alexander Ross.

4 The size and financing of the proposed force would change somewhat before it was established. See vol. 1, 39.

5 Governor and Committee (London) to Simpson (Red River), 4 March 1835, HBCA: A.6/23, fo. 208b–209.

6 AM: MG2, B4–12.

7 See Oliver (1914, 266–74).

8 See Pannekoek (2000b).

9 See Klassen (2000).

10 This estimate exceeded official figures. The 1835 census for Red River showed a total non-Indian population of 3,679 (Oliver 1914, 74). Perhaps Simpson included the Indian population.

11 This was a probable reference to the Larocque-Simpson fracas and its aftermath, as well as to incidents arising from disputes over the price of pemmican.

12 Not everyone was so accepting. When twenty-three-year-old Peter Garrioch – school teacher, maverick, and free trade militant-to-be – heard about the council's decisions, he added up their total cost in his journal, deducted what he thought a proper police force ought to cost, and calculated that the difference would fund the purchase of a printing press – plus the salaries of a printer and printer's devil – with enough left over to finance the digging of 2 miles of ditches in the settlement. Journal of Peter Garrioch, 1835 (bound volume), AM: MG2, C38, title page.

13 The Council of Rupert's Land had approved the expenditure of £300 for the construction of the courthouse-jail and for "other public works in progress" at its meeting of 8 June 8, 1833 (Oliver 1914, 722).

14 This possibly refers to the governor of Assiniboia but more probably to the sheriff.

15 The districts were so bounded in the resolution but were not so named or so ordered. The names and order are from an undated document (AM: MG2, B4–7) believed to be an early sketch of Simpson's plan for the petty courts – but disputed by Oliver (1914, 270n1).

16 Cuthbert Grant, Robert Logan, James Sutherland, and James Bird.

17 AM: MG2, 734–7, B4–7. Might Ross have been its author?

18 The resolution also set out the fees for civil litigation: 3 shillings for warrants and 5 shillings for appeals to the General Court. Oliver (1914, 270) erroneously transcribes "magistrates" as "magistrate." The stipulation that the General Court meet at the governor's residence would apply only until the new courthouse was built.

19 Oliver (1914, 87).

20 Simpson to London, 10 June 1835, HBCA: D.4/102, fo. 23.

21 Ross (1856, 186).

22 Oliver (1914, 223).

23 Ibid., 290, resolution 14.

24 Ibid., 103–4, 274–5.

25 Ibid., 145, lines 40–146, line 1.

26 Another aspect of Christie's announcement worth noting is a reference to "*monthly* courts" (emphasis added). The council resolution called for both the general and petty courts to meet only *quarterly* (ibid., 228). Possibly, Christie's use of the word "monthly" was a slip of the pen; or perhaps it meant that the petty courts held their quarterly sittings on staggered months, ensuring that a court sat somewhere in the settlement every month of the year.

27 Executioner.

28 Ross (1856, 186–7).

29 Ibid., 187.

30 Oliver (1914, 278).

31 Ibid., 279.

32 Ibid., 280–1.

33 Governor and Committee to Council of Rupert's Land, 7 March 1838, HBCA: D.5/5, fo. 24.

34 Ross (1856, 222–3, emphasis in original).

35 Oliver (1914, 275–4).

36 Ibid., 263–5.
37 Ibid., 276.
38 Ibid., 284–5.
39 Ross (1856, 186).
40 Oliver (1914, 276–7).
41 Ibid., 280–1.
42 Simpson to Pelly, 1 February 1837, HBCA: A.8/2, fo. 46–50.
43 Simpson to London, 19 June 1835, HBCA: D.4/102, fo. 23.
44 Ross (1856, 162–5).
45 Ibid.,, 188.
46 Bumsted (2003b, 73); Pannekoek (1991, 90); Pelly to Palmerston, 24 May 1837, HBCA: A.8/2, fo. 57; Pelly to Glenelg, 17 November 1837, HBCA: A.8/2, fo. 60ff.
47 Oliver (1914, 763).
48 Simpson to Christie, 20 February 1838, HBCA: D.4/24, fo. 22.
49 HBCA: A.6/24, fo. 145–6. See also HBCA: A.39/7, fo. 16–40.
50 HBCA: D.4/23, fo. 43b–44b. The author is indebted to Dr DeLloyd J. Guth for drawing attention to this judicial odyssey.
51 HBCA: A.8/2, fo. 57b–59b, fo. 71–75.
52 HBCA: A.13/2, fo. 115–118. The "legality" in question, based on a mistaken assumption that the crime occurred west of the Rocky Mountains, was that Canadian courts lacked jurisdiction. Simpson to Pelly, 12 June 1838, HBCA: A.8/2, fo. 103–5.
53 Galbraith (1976, 155).
54 Ross (1856, 239).
55 Pelly to Glenelg, 10 February 1837, HBCA: A.8/2, fo. 40–5.
56 Pelly to Glenelg, 17 November 1837, HBCA: A.8/2, fo. 60–6.
57 Although the HBC charter lands did not extend beyond the mountains, the Crown had granted the company a time-limited trading licence there.
58 Bumsted (2003b, 74).
59 Wharton (1938, 828, 847).
60 Simpson to Thom, 21 April 1838, HBCA: D.4/23, fo. 151–2.

CHAPTER FOUR

1 See generally Bryce (1890, 1896); Stubbs (1967, 1–47); and Bindon (1972, 1981, 2000).
2 "Articling" refers to service under articles of clerkship, a form of apprenticeship for lawyers. In Lower Canada at the time, barristers were

required to apprentice for five years and then to write an examination. Since French civil law applied to noncriminal matters and English common law to crimes, lawyers needed to know both systems of law. See Lortie (1975–76); and Garneau (2009).

3 His best known diatribes were a series of open "Anti-Gallic" letters to Governor Lord Gosford, collected and published in pamphlet form in 1836. See Audet (1941).

4 Raffan (2007, 295); Bindon (2000).

5 Simpson to Thom, 5 January 1838, HBCA: D.4/23, fo. 84.

6 Simpson to Thom, 22 September 1837, HBCA: D.4/23, fo. 137.

7 Simpson to Thom, 21 April 1838, HBCA: D.4/23, fo. 151–2.

8 Simpson told Thom that his *Cadien* opinion was handled "with your usual ability," which might suggest Thom had done HBC work previously. Simpson to Thom, 22 September 1837, HBCA: D.4/23, fo. 137.

9 Simpson to Thom, 5 January 1838, HBCA: D.4/23, fo. 84.

10 Simpson's circular letter to participants at the 1836 meeting, for example, ordered them to "collect any evidence ... bearing on the case of Mr. Chief Trader Heron, who will be summoned to take his trial ... before the Council." HBCA: D.4/22, fo. 43.

11 Simpson to Thom, 5 January 1838, HBCA: D.4/23, fo. 84.

12 Simpson to Thom, 21 April 1838, HBCA: D.4/23, fo. 151–2.

13 Oliver (1914, 284–6).

14 Simpson to Thom, 6 October 1838, HBCA: D.4/25, fo. 5.

15 See Craig (1963, 151).

16 Thom to Simpson, 15 January 1839, HBCA: D.5/5, fo. 92. Unfortunately, the books were identified only by numerical references to an unidentified catalogue. Most would be shipped via York Factory, but Simpson promised Thom that "should you wish to have a few volumes with you they will be forwarded with the spring [canoe] packet." HBCA: D.4/24, fo. 1.

17 Née Blackford. She was Thom's second wife.

18 Williams (1975, 187). Williams adds that Simpson said in a private letter that "Finlayson is of a solitary turn of mind."

19 Ross (1856, 341–2). See also Friesen (2000).

20 See Dorge (2000a).

21 Simpson to Thom, 1 April 1838, HBCA: D.4/23, fo. 152.

22 London to Simpson, 20 March 1839, HBCA: A.6/25, fo. 30.

23 HBCA: A.6/625, fo. 34.

24 Simpson to unknown correspondent, 5 January 1838, HBCA: D.4/233, fo. 84. Simpson's snobbishness was a match for Thom's own.

25 Simpson to Christie, 20 February 1838, HBCA: D.4/24, fo. 20.
26 Oliver (1914, 74).
27 Ibid., 283–7.
28 Ross (1856, 223–4).
29 Ibid., 224–5.
30 Oliver (1914, 287–92).
31 The petty courts were set for successive Mondays in the same months.
32 Conduct money covered travel expenses and a per diem fee paid to each subpoenaed witness by the person obtaining the subpoena.
33 Discretionary costs were an award made to one party to civil litigation, usually the victor, by the other as reimbursement for the former's expenses.
34 A jury panel consisted of property owners thought by the sheriff to be suitable for jury duty, from which the members of particular grand juries and petty juries were selected. Apart from being male, adult, and propertied, no formal qualification for inclusion in jury panels is known, but it would be surprising if sheriffs did not exercise discretion in selecting reliable men.
35 Without reliable legal information, settlers sometimes fell back on scuttlebutt, myth, and other dubious sources. Thom told Simpson in 1845 about a scrapbook "of newspaper paragraphs" kept by elderly Magistrate James Bird that constituted "a code of laws" on the basis of which he contended, for instance, "that a husband has got a right to sell his wife, provided he put the halter round her neck, and so give livery and seisin [ownership and possession] of the freehold." Thom to Simpson, 27 March 1845, HBCA: D.5/13, fo. 343ff.
36 Thom to London, 29 May 1840, HBCA: D.5/5, fo. 283, at 284–5. He added that the court's caseload had been small since his arrival, mentioned indirectly having access to its pre-1839 records, and lamented the unavailability of a means to appeal its decisions.
37 Thom to Simpson, 27 July 1840, HBCA: D.5/5, fo. 293.
38 The key word here is "systematic." Thom did not bring trial by jury to Red River; a petty jury was used as early as April 1836 (Ross 1856, 186). However, they were not compulsory then. Thom's amendment made them compulsory in most General Court cases.
39 Thom to Simpson, 31 July 1840, HBCA: D.5/5, fo. 301–2.
40 See case 6, vol. 2, 17.
41 Coroner's juries, grand juries, and petty juries served distinct purposes but with some overlap between the first two. Coroner's juries, then as now, enquired into the cause of violent or unexplained deaths. A good example is found in HBCA: A.11/95, fo. 20–1, the record of an inquest

held on 17 May 1843 by Coroner John McCallum and a jury into the death of one Allan McMillan, found dead from a gunshot wound on the prairie. The coroner and jurors assembled at a home near where the body was found, examined six witnesses – including Dr John Bunn, who had performed an autopsy – and returned a unanimous verdict that "the deceased ... had committed suicide while labouring under insanity." Although not required to address culpability, they did at that time have the authority to lay formal charges. Grand juries chiefly determined whether persons accused of serious crimes should be brought to trial. If a grand jury found there was enough evidence to justify a trial, the accused was brought to court, where a petty jury determined guilt or innocence.

42 HBCA: A.39/5, fo. 87, 21 April 1840.

43 The verdict was in writing. University of Alberta Archives, Don Thompson Collection, item 76. The author thanks archivist emeritus Dr Merrill Distad for bringing this document to his attention. Although written jury verdicts were unusual – and still are – this is not the only known instance. See cases 103 and 105, vol. 2, 209, 212.

44 HBCA: D.5/13, fo. 270ff., FC 3207.99, pamphlet Z8, nos 35, 38.

45 Ross (1856, 223–4).

46 Thom to London, 29 May 1840, HBCA: D.5/5, fo. 283, at 284–5.

47 See vol. 1, 65.

48 Thom to Simpson, 31 July 1840, HBCA: D.5/5, fo. 301–2.

49 Thom to Simpson, 27 July 1840, HBCA: D.5/5, fo. 293.

50 Thom to Simpson, 31 July 1840, HBCA: D.5/5, fo. 301–2.

51 Thom to Simpson, 27 July 1840, HBCA: D.5/5, fo. 293.

52 Thom to Simpson, 31 July 1840, HBCA: D.5/5, fo. 301–2.

53 Oliver (1914, 293–5).

54 See, for example, case 9, November 1845, vol. 2, 34.

55 Thom to Simpson, 27 July 1840, HBCA: D.5/5, fo. 293ff.

56 Oliver (1914, 295–306). See vol. 1, 58–9.

57 The same provision defined "Settlement" as extending 4 miles from both banks of both rivers and 4 miles from the uppermost and lowermost permanent buildings.

58 Oliver (1914, 286).

59 In 1866, for example, Assiniboia authorities declined, despite considerable public pressure, to become involved in deadly depredations at Portage la Prairie by a notorious individual called "The Wolverine." See vol. 1, 209–10. Two years later, however, they agreed to prosecute another killing from Portage (case 414, vol. 2, 537).

60 Oliver (1914, 291, resolutions 22 and 23). A new tavern-licensing scheme was enacted on 19 February 1847 (ibid., 330–1).

61 Ibid., 290, resolutions 15, 16, and 17.

62 Simpson to Thom, 1 March 1840, HBCA: D.4/25, fo. 167.

63 HBCA: E.16/1, fo. 79. Although Thom later claimed that he did not begin to "contemplate" the "Observations" until early March 1840, it is likely that he started earlier, given the extent of what he produced in May. Thom to Simpson, 4 August 1842, HBCA: D.5/7, fo. 158a.

64 Thom to Simpson, 29 May 1840, HBCA: D.5/5, fo. 283–5.

65 Thom to Simpson, 3 June 1840, HBCA: D.5/5, fo. 286.

66 HBCA: E.16/1, fo. 26.

67 HBCA: D.5/5, fo. 297.

68 HBCA: E.16/1, fo. 1.

69 HBCA: E.16/1, fo. 79.

70 See "Codification," in Walker (1980). An impressive attempt had been made to draft a concise code for Assiniboia when it was still owned by Lord Selkirk, but it was ultimately abortive. See vol. 1, 15.

71 The term "civil law" has several meanings. See Glossary. The two most common meanings in the context of codification are (1) legal systems rooted in Roman law and (2) that portion of the law that does not relate to criminal conduct.

72 Baker (2008).

73 See "Civil Code," in *Canadian Encyclopedia* (2000).

74 HBCA: E.16/1, fo. 26ff.

75 Thom was not modest about his proposed improvements. In note 11, for example, he said, "I have endeavoured to make my definitions both more comprehensive and less redundant than those of Lord Coke." The *Commentaries* and *Reports* of Sir Edward (not Lord) Coke – who was solicitor general and attorney general for Queen Elizabeth I before becoming chief justice of the Court of King's Bench and one of the country's most erudite and courageous judges – were among the most influential expositions of the common law in existence.

76 HBCA: E.16/1, fo. 1ff.

77 Ibid., nos 40–3 and appendix B.

78 Thom to Simpson, 4 August 1842, HBCA: D.5/7, fo. 158b.

79 Smith to Thom, 19 March 1842, HBCA: A.6/25, fo. 172ff. The general tone of the letter was testy. It opened with a reprimand for charging the postage of certain communications to the company and included a criticism of Thom's "obscurely expressed" letters.

80 Thom to Simpson, 4 August 1842, HBCA: D.5/7, fo. 158b.

81 Compare the numerous proposed amendments enclosed in a letter from Thom to Simpson, 27 March 1845 (HBCA: D.5/13, fo. 343ff., at 347ff.) with the few that were eventually adopted (Oliver 1914, 318ff.).

82 Finlayson to Governor and Committee, 24 June 1840, HBCA: A.11/95, fo. 17.

83 Thom first dispatched his "Observations" (HBCA: D.5/5, fo. 285) to London in May 1840 via someone who died en route, and the letter was returned to Red River, where it was held for Simpson and relayed to London considerably later. Simpson to Smith, n.d., HBCA: D.4/58, fo. 161.

84 HBCA: D.4/109, fo. 22, no. 40.

85 HBCA: D.3/2, fo. 39.

86 See "Assessor," in Walker (1980). The reason Simpson bothered to explain the recorder's role in his personal journal was that he planned to publish it – a project with which Thom would eventually assist.

87 HBCA: D.3/2, fo. 39.

88 Simpson to Ross and Hargrave, 28 June 1841, HBCA: D.4/58, fo. 155.

89 Macleod (1947, 102).

90 Ibid., 115. As for the "hard labor" that the court had called for during his imprisonment, Mrs Hargrave's husband told a correspondent that he was "employed in picking oakum ... at which the poor creature works away very steady, and every Saturday delivers up his full weight by scale" (ibid., lxiii–lxiv). Oakum was shredded rope or hemp, used to caulk the seams of ships or boats. Shredding it was a common task for prison inmates.

91 Ibid., 119.

92 Ibid.

93 Simpson to Christie, 12 May 1843, HBCA: A.4/28, fo. 61. When dispatching Atasawapah to York Factory in the first place, Simpson wrote, "I have to request that the said prisoner ... be kept secure, whatever trouble, expence or inconvenience may be occasioned thereby, as it is highly important to the peace of the country that the ends of justice should be attained. I beg it moreover to be understood that the prisoner, after his liberation, is not to be permitted to return." Simpson to Ross and Hargrave, 28 June 1841, HBCA: D.4/58, fo. 155.

94 Williams (1973, xxvi).

95 Finlayson to Simpson, 10 August 1842, HBCA: D.5/7, fo. 192.

96 See Gibson (1990b, 30). Most of what is known about this case comes from a "circular" about it addressed to the magistrate members of the court by Thom on 21 February 1843, shortly after the trial (AM: MG2, B4–6, fo. 11).

97 The author has suggested elsewhere that the marriage might have been delayed to preclude a counterclaim by Thom against the father for having caused the Thoms' loss of their employee's domestic services (Gibson 1990b, 30).
98 Letitia Hargrave claimed that the court also awarded Rothney her travel expenses back to Scotland (Macleod 1947, 146), but there is no evidence of that.
99 AM: MG2, B4–6, fo. 11.
100 "Observations," HBCA: E.16/1, no. 71.
101 Thom to Simpson, 29 May 1840, HBCA: D.5/5, fo. 285.
102 Although unusual, the power of judges to reject jury verdicts on the ground that they are contrary to law is well established. Canada's most notorious example is probably *MacMillan v. Brownlee* – [1934] 62 *Canadian Criminal Cases* 159 (trial), [1935] 1 *Dominion Law Reports* 481 (Court of Appeal), [1937] *Supreme Court Reports* 318 (Supreme Court of Canada), [1940] *Appeal Cases* 802 (Privy Council) – in which the premier of Alberta was sued by his secretary for seduction. The jury verdict in her favour was rejected by the trial judge as being contrary to law, and although the verdict was eventually reinstated on appeal, the appellate courts did not deny the judge's power to do what he did.
103 Macleod (1947, 146).
104 They must have brought with them Thomas Simpson's mail packet, containing Adam Thom's undelivered "Observations."
105 George Simpson's "memorial" expressing his suspicions is quoted in Ross (1856, 226–7). His is not the only accusatory hypothesis. A biography of Sir George Simpson (Raffan 2007, 305–23) suggests that the governor-in-chief himself may have arranged to have his cousin done in!
106 Ross (1856, 228–33).
107 Williams (1973, 161). See generally Rich (1961, vol. 3, 712–17).
108 Williams (1973, 162n1).
109 Ibid., 164.
110 So thought the doctor's colleagues James Ermatinger (McDonald 1980, 253) and James Douglas (Rich 1961, vol. 3, xxxiii–iv).
111 Simpson to London, 21 June 1843, HBCA: A.12/2, fo. 170(a), no. 30, fo. 175(b), no. 46; Simpson to London, 28 July 1843, HBCA: A.12/2, fo. 207(a), no. 4. Apparently, Simpson felt that Heureux and the others should either be tried on the basis of his evidence alone or left to rot in the Sitka prison.
112 Etholine to Simpson, 14 February 1844, HBCA: D.5/10, fo. 169.

113 Rich (1961, vol. 3, 715), says they were sent to Norway House, but the Council of Rupert's Land met at Red River that year.

114 Simpson to Thom, 10 June 1844, HBCA: D.4/31, fo. 127.

115 Simpson to London, 24 August 1844, HBCA: A.12/2, fo. 449b. Thom (who was at that point negotiating with the company for an extension of his contract as recorder) would have had no doubt about what the governor wanted to receive from him. It would be unfair, however, to attribute his conclusions solely to undue influence. Although his reasons were not indicated, they were very probably based on the fact that the death occurred on foreign soil, which would be a perfectly valid reason for a court of territorially restricted jurisdiction to deny authority. Interestingly, however, no reference to this matter was included in the council minutes (Oliver 1914, 815–34).

116 Simpson to Etholene, 18 June 1844, HBCA: A.12/2, fo. 369.

117 Simpson to London, 24 August 1844, HBCA: A.12/2, fo. 449bb–450.

118 Ibid., fo. 450.

119 Rich (1961, vol. 3, 716).

120 Ibid., xxxiii–iv: "This episode is one of the least creditable in Simpson's career."

121 Simpson to London, 8 August 1844, HBCA: A.12/2, fo. 435. The HBC officer on the scene played what might be called a passive-aggressive role: "I would not allow them to shoot her at the House [post], when they enticed her away to an Indian tent that was in the woods. I told them that I would have nothing to do with her, but that they might do what they thought proper with her. I was certain that they were going to kill her; otherwise I would have encouraged them to do it." Fraser to Simpson, 4 March 1844, HBCA: A.12/2, fo. 296b (enclosure).

122 See Brown (1982, 2000).

123 Hargrave to Simpson, 11 December 1843, HBCA: A.12/2, fo. 295.

124 A Windigo was a kind of devil, thought to have supernatural powers and to have acquired that status by eating human flesh.

125 Hargrave's denial, later in the letter, that the company was involved in "conniving at his escape" seems to confirm, obliquely, that he was indeed in custody at some point.

126 Simpson to McLoughlin, 17 April 1844, HBCA: D.4/31, fo. 48–9. Simpson did, however, write to another HBC officer asking for additional information. Simpson to J.G. McTavish, 17 April 1844, HBCA: D.4/31, fo. 48. Might his failure to press the matter further be attributed to a realization that he had treated the doctor too harshly in the matter of his son's death? Or was this just a case of officer-class, or white, solidarity?

127 Friesen (1984, 4).

128 Ens (1996). Ens prefers the modern term "Metis," used without an accented *e*, to include both groups designated herein by the contemporary terms "French Halfbreed" and "English Halfbreed."

129 Simpson often expressed nervously negative opinions about the Halfbreeds. In a letter to London in June 1843, for example, he stated that although the settlement was currently tranquil, the population "are, nevertheless, very difficult of management, which is not to be wondered at when the variety of races and ignorance (the greater part of them but nominally removed from a state of barbarism) are considered." HBCA: A.12/2, fo. 180b. A month later, he reported that the situation was not as tranquil as could have been wished due to unreasonable demands "of the ignorant halfcaste population," who wanted to "legislate for themselves." He expressed hope, however, that "with good management" they "may be kept in order for a length of time, if proper means be taken, by encouraging emigration, to preventing any great increase in their numbers." HBCA: A.12/2, fo. 206b–207a.

130 See Lent (1963); and Spry (2000b).

131 Finlayson to Simpson, 10 August 1842, HBCA: D.5/7, fo. 192.

132 See *Revised Statutes of Canada 1985*, appendix 2, no. 4.

133 This is not to say that Thom admitted to being satisfied with his lot, then or ever. In January 1845, not long after being refused a salary increase, he grumbled to Simpson that "in a country where there is no one to consult, where an obsolete system of local law, which is arguably at variance with the habits of the many and the feelings of the few, embarrass one's every step ... the duties of ... [recorder and company counsel] have been proved by experience to be far more arduous and intricate than either ... [the HBC Governor and Committee] or myself anticipated from the beginning." Thom to Simpson, 2 January 1845, HBCA: D.5/13, fo. 10ff.

134 HBCA: E.4/1a, fo. 166 (baptism); AM: MG7, B4, no. 77 (burial).

135 HBCA: E.4/1, fo. 14.

136 Bindon (2000).

137 Simpson to London, 21 June 1843: HBCA: A.12/2, fo. 202ff.

138 While the area was not included in Rupert's Land by the charter, Thom thought the company had extensive, though not exclusive, rights there – including rights of judicature – under its Pacific coast licence. Thom to Simpson, 4 April 1842, HBCA: D.5/7, fo. 157ff. See *Re Calder*, case 49, August 1848, vol. 2, 77.

139 Thom was at his most enigmatic on that touchy subject: "I have found it less stringent in reality than I had conceived it to be. It seems to be essentially and permanently powerless against natives of any and every race, and temporarily and accidentally feeble even against others." Thom to Simpson, 4 April 1842, HBCA: D.5/7, fo. 157ff. Whatever the second sentence was intended to convey (perhaps it was expressed more clearly in the now missing full opinion, which the letter merely summarized), it didn't seem to promise much greater legal protection against free traders than the blunter opinions the company had previously received from other lawyers.

140 He recommended that the Governor and Committee so empower both "officers-in-charge and dissenting ministers," prospectively as well as retrospectively. Thom to Simpson, 4 April 1842, HBCA: D.5/7, fo. 157ff. Thom's opinion that only Anglican and Roman Catholic clergy could currently bring about lawful marriages was based on his view that the HBC charter imported English laws as of 1670, a time when only Anglican pastors were so empowered. Simpson to Thom, 30 June 1847, HBCA: D.4/36, fo. 62; Thom to Simpson, 28 July 1847, HBCA: D.5/20, fo. 51ff. If he were right, the impact would be especially significant for the congregants of Wesleyan Methodist missionaries, who had become active in parts of Rupert's Land. When word of the recorder's opinion got abroad, there was panic among some of those married according to Wesleyan rites and an offer was made by an Anglican pastor to remarry those affected. Evans to Ross, 26 April 1846, ABC: Donald Ross Collection, file 41, Add. MSS 635, letter 2.

141 This was a topic about which Thom held an especially strong negative opinion, expressed in at least three letters to Simpson: 4 April 1842, HBCA: D.5/7, fo. 157ff.; 26 October 1843, HBCA A.12/2, fo. 242b; and 9 July 1844, HBCA: D.5/12, fo. 28ff.

142 Thom to Simpson, 24 July 1844, HBCA: D.5/12, fo. 88ff.

143 See, for example, Smith to Thom, [illegible day and month] 1843, HBCA: A.6/26, fo. 52ff., in which the company declined to adopt Thom's suggestions regarding marriage law and colonial ordination – and then reprimanded him for an acrimonious dispute he had precipitated with Reverend John Smithurst, the Anglican missionary to the Indian village at St Peter's, over the legitimacy of Smithurst's ordination.

144 Simpson to Thom, 30 June 1843, HBCA: reel 3M20, fo. 69.

145 Thom to Simpson, 9 August 1842, HBCA: D.5/7, fo. 188–9.

146 Williams (1973, 192–5). See vol. 1,104.

147 Thom to Simpson, [illegible day] July 1844, HBCA: D.5/12, fo. 7. It was published in revised form in 1848. See vol. 1, 105.

148 Simpson to London, 1 December 1843, HBCA: A.12/2, fo. 269; Thom to Simpson, 8 July 1844, HBCA: D.5/12, fo. 20.

149 Thom to Simpson, 2 January 1845, HBCA: D.5/13, fo. 10ff.

CHAPTER FIVE

1 Recorder Thom referred to the existence of records predating his tenure in a letter to London on 29 May 1840. HBCA: D.5/5, fo. 283ff.

2 Martin (1898, 130). The well is undergoing archeological exploration as this is being written (Owen 2012, B3).

3 Figures are from the 1849 census, as reported by Pannekoek (1991, 17–18).

4 Bumsted (2003b, 87).

5 See generally the introductions in Morton (1961) and Rich (1956).

6 Alexander Ramsey, the governor of Minnesota Territory, was reporting on an 1851 visit to Red River, quoted in Bumsted (2003b, 119).

7 These were large wooden carts, held together mostly by rawhide, each with two oversize concave wheels designed to traverse rough terrain and drawn by oxen or horses. They were capable (with their wheels removed) of becoming boats when water had to be crossed.

8 The distillery was never built, but the prospect remained open for years, and related restrictions on the sale of whiskey were enforced in Red River courts. See *Public Interest v. McDermot,* case 18, vol. 2, 46, and the *Commentary* thereto.

9 Oliver (1914, 317–27). For a fuller description of the amendments, see *Public Interest v. Anderson,* case 9, vol. 2, 34.

10 Robert Clouston, in a letter quoted in Bumsted (2003b, 84).

11 John Bunn to Donald Ross, 12 March 1848, AM: MG1 D20–1, emphasis in original.

12 See vol. 1, 78ff.

13 See Schull (1971); Le Seur (1979); and Read (1982).

14 Pannekoek (1991, 14).

15 "George Simpson's Character Book, 1832," in Williams (1973, 180). An editor's footnote supports Simpson's assessment.

16 Ross (1856, 183).

17 See vol. 1, 33ff.

18 Cuthbert Grant, who was thoroughly bilingual, might also be considered francophone, although his mother tongue was English.

19 See Bumsted (1999a, 151).
20 See Stubbs (1967, 91ff.).
21 See MacLeod and Morton (1963).
22 See Bumsted (1999a, 214).
23 Bumsted (2003b, 97ff.). British legislation invalidated any monopoly not sanctioned by Parliament. See vol. 1, 19.
24 MacKay (1966, 225); Simpson to London, 24 May 1846, HBCA: A.12/3, fo. 62ff.
25 Spry (2000b).
26 The pursuit of Hayden would have tragic consequences. See case 10, vol. 2, 37.
27 Thom to Christie, 7–30 December 1844, HBCA: A.11/95, fo. 46–50. See also Thom's report to Simpson about several of these measures on 10 March 1845, ("Confidential"), HBCA: D.5/13, fo. 253ff.
28 This was legally incorrect. Aliens from countries friendly to Great Britain had standing in British courts to challenge wrongful treatment while on British soil (see "Alien," in Walker 1980).
29 This proposed "funny money" does not appear to have ever been approved by the company. However, when a major theft of currency and commercial paper from Upper Fort Garry occurred in November 1844, "Mr. Christie ... called in all the notes in the Settlement and had them registered" (Macleod 1947, 191; Poster, HBCA: A.11/95, fo. 44).
30 Earlier in the same correspondence, Thom said, "I am anxious to make the law, as such, vindicate its own supremacy without requiring the dubious aid of an ill [illegible word] police." He also claimed that his proposals relied "as little as possible on any extreme view of our legal rights," by which he seems to have meant that most of them (other than prosecution) would avoid the direct enforcement of charter rights. As a lawyer, he was well aware of the legally dubious nature of the HBC's asserted monopoly. Thom's stratagems were not the first legal devices by which the company attempted to suppress free trade. Restrictive covenants in settlers' deeds of land from the HBC were already in use. For example, Joseph Monkman's land deed, dating from before Christie's arrival, promised, among other things, that Monkman and his successors would not, without company permission, "carry on ... in any parts of North America any trade or traffic in ... any kind of skins, furs, or peltry, nor dressed leather." Report of Select Committee, House of Commons (UK), 1857, 371 (hereafter Select Committee Report).
31 See *Hudson's Bay Company v. Pierre Guilleaum Sayer*, case 68, vol. 2, 113.

32 Confiscation of furs or trade goods was the most provocative measure the company could adopt, and even the bold Adam Thom offered reasons "for dissuading Mr. Christie, as I had previously dissuaded his predecessor, from the seizure and confiscation of furs." Thom to Simpson ("Confidential"), 2 January 1845, HBCA: D.5/13, fo. 12ff.

33 Memorandum, Ross to Council of Assiniboia, 19 December 1844, AM: Ross Papers, MG2, C14, letter 1.

34 Christie to Simpson, 4 April 1846, AM: MG2, B4–10, fo. 70–9.

35 Oliver (1914, 314).

36 Thom to Simpson ("Private"), 27 March 1845, HBCA: D.5/13, fo. 343ff. For Garrioch's own pungent account of his relations with Customs Collector James Bird, see AM: Peter Garrioch Journal, MG9, A78–3, 28 March 1845 to 21 April 1845, 249–56.

37 Oliver (1914, 314). This change did not remove the magistrates from the process altogether since some of them were members of the General Court. It did, however, ensure that they would be under the watchful eyes of Governor Christie and Recorder Thom.

38 Oliver (1914, 315–27, 1303–5). The minutes of the earliest of these meetings, 10 June 1845, were not included in the regular collection of council minutes and turned up only later. The language of the resolutions passed on that occasion was much blunter than in the versions in the later, publicized minutes. For example, the term "fur trafficker" in the original became "public defaulter" in the published version. Moreover, the published minutes were stated to express only the "tenor" of the resolutions. Was the devious hand of Adam Thom at work here?

39 Simpson to Smith, 26 September 1845, HBCA: D.4/33 fo. 53b–54. The dispute would eventually be settled with the company. For a full discussion of the incident and its implications, see the *Commentary* to the August 1845 court session in vol. 2, 30ff.

40 Christie's response, undoubtedly penned by Thom, was arrogantly unhelpful. Both documents are reprinted in Lent (1963, 176–9).

41 McDermot to Christie, 30 November 1845, AM: MG2, B4–10, fo. 26. A previous letter, directed to Simpson over a year earlier, had been deliberately ignored by Sir George. Simpson to Christie, 2 December 1844, HBCA: D.4/32, fo. 79ff.

42 Simpson to Christie, 21 September 1846, HBCA: D.4/35, fo. 108ff.; Simpson to Christie, 26 November 1846, HBCA: D.4/36, fo. 123ff. In a letter to Simpson, Sinclair claimed to have reached a tentative compromise with Christie that Thom refused to countenance. Sinclair to Simpson, 4 June 1846, quoted in Lent (1963, 184–7). Thom's

description of the same occurrence, although different in tone, essentially corroborates Sinclair's assertion. Thom to Simpson ("Confidential"), 2 January 1845, HBCA: D.5/13, fo. 12ff.

43 Christie to Simpson, 4 April 1846, AM: MG2, B4–10, fo. 70–9.

44 Ibid.; Bumsted (2003b, 99).

45 *Public Interest v. Peter Hayden*, case 10, vol. 2, 37.

46 Christie's anger with McDermot for having hosted this meeting, and for his other acts of opposition to the company, may well have occasioned a strange special session of the court held for the sole purpose of prosecuting one of McDermot's sons for selling a quantity of whiskey without a licence. See *Public Interest v. James McDermot*, case 18, vol. 2, 46.

47 Simpson to Christie, 26 November 1846, HBCA: D.4/36, fo. 123ff.; Simpson to Barclay ("Confidential"), London, 24 December 1846, HBCA: A.12/3, fo. 396–7. In the latter communication, Simpson informed London authorities that, in his opinion, "Sinclair is, without exception, the most unprincipled man I ever had any dealings with in the Company's territories, & has, through misrepresentation and low cunning, very seriously injured the Company's interests. It is exceedingly desirable this man should be discouraged from remaining in the Settlement by withholding from him the usual facilities afforded to well disposed people."

48 McLaughlin continued on to England, where besides attempting to plead his uncle's case before HBC authorities, he made public allegations against the company that led to his being indicted for criminal libel. He fled the United Kingdom to escape prosecution, pursued by a bench warrant for his arrest that was forwarded to Sir George Simpson and carried by him to Red River. Although Simpson initially planned to pounce with the warrant when McLaughlin returned to the settlement, he never did so. The case was eventually decided in McLaughlin's favour, and the McDermot-Sinclair claims against the company ended up being settled. HBCA: A.39/7, fo. 121–40; A.12/2, fo. 49ff.; A.12/3, fo. 51ff., 345b.

49 See "The Colonial Office, Aboriginal Policy, and Red River, 1847–1849," in Bumsted (2000, 91ff.).

50 A 1929 enquiry by Dr Grace Nute of the Minnesota Historical Society determined that the petition was received by the secretary of state in October 1845, transmitted to the Indian Office and then to the secretary of war, returned to the Indian Office, and then apparently lost. Mereness to Nute, 28 December 1929, AM: MG9, A78–1, box 2, "Correspondence."

51 Bumsted (2003b, 107); Galbraith (1976, 193). Major W.B. Caldwell's report to the British government exonerating the company was not dispatched until March 1849. Caldwell to Grey, 22 March 1849, HBCA: A.11/95, fo. 238ff.

52 AM: MG9, A78–3.

53 Christie to Simpson, 21 April 1846, AM: MG2, B4–10, fo. 77–8.

54 *Hudson's Bay Company v. Pierre Guilleaum Sayer*, case 68, vol. 2, 113.

55 Ross (1856, 362–3). The precise nature of the disease is uncertain. Bumsted (2003b, 103) suggests that "bloody flux" was a form of dysentery caused by "some sort of extremely virulent flu strain."

56 Oliver (1914, 269, 12 February 1835; 303, 25 June 1841; 309, 3 July 1843). Prior to the latter date, the force also had a fourth sergeant and a sergeant major.

57 "In order to avoid the jealousy of those who had no access to this little benefit."

58 Oliver (1914, 309).

59 3 December 1844, quoted in Macleod (1947, 191n3).

60 Christie to London, 31 December 1844, HBCA: A.11/95, fo. 42, poster reproduced at fo. 44.

61 Ross (1856, 333–4). Ross places the incident in 1845, but archival documents leave no doubt that it was the previous year.

62 Oliver (1914, 311).

63 Ibid., 316–17, 16 June 1845.

64 Some of those who confronted Sheriff Ross when he came to seize the trade goods of Alexis Goulet had been off-duty police officers, and Recorder Thom was outraged when Ross "strove hard to screen" those men from punishment and dismissal for doing so. According to Thom, the sheriff showed favouritism when recruiting members of the force; and some policemen claimed they could not be punished for violating their oaths because "Mr. Ross had never sworn them in." Thom to Simpson, 28 April 1845, HBCA: D.5/13, fo. 464ff.

65 Discussions on the subject between the company and the UK government had a much longer history. See, for example, HBCA: A.13/2, covering negotiations from 1838 to 1846. It was not until the Oregon crisis, however, that military protection for Assiniboia became a real possibility.

66 See generally Lent (1963). Simpson also wanted to reduce the number of settlers at Red River.

67 HBCA: A.12/2, fo. 502.

68 Simpson to Pelly, 4 May 1845, HBCA: A.12/2, fo. 520.

69 Warre and Vavaseur (at Red River) to Colonial Office, 10 June 1845 (just a few days before the Council of Assiniboia disbanded the local Volunteer Corps), HBCA: A.12/3, fo. 149ff.

70 Simpson to Christie ("Confidential"), 29 December 1845, HBCA: D.4/33, fo. 255ff.; Simpson to Ross, HBCA: D.4/34, fo. 61ff.

71 The HBCA documentation is voluminous. The final stages can be observed at A.13/2, fo. 231–61.

72 Simpson to London, 23 July 1846, HBCA: A.12/3, fo. 204–8. The undoubted disruption and inconvenience that this displacement caused to Thom and his family was made worse, in the recorder's protocol-obsessed mind, by the fact that Governor Christie accorded the new military commander, Colonel John F. Crofton, second place – after himself – on the official list of councillors, a rank previously enjoyed by Thom. The recorder threatened to refuse to sign council minutes until the HBC Governor and Committee in London ruled upon the question. Thom to Simpson, 8 May 1847, HBCA: D.5/19, fo. 546ff.

73 Simpson to London, 28 October 1846, HBCA: A.12/3, fo. 346ff.; Simpson to London, 1 July 1847, HBCA: A.12/3, fo. 424ff.

74 Simpson to Pelly ("Confidential"), 23 July 1846, HBCA: A.12/3, fo. 204–8. In fact, the Oregon crisis had been settled by the time the troops arrived.

75 Simpson to Pelly ("Confidential"), 20 August 1846, HBCA: A.12/3, fo. 277b. See also Simpson to London, 14 September 1846, HBCA: A.12/3, fo. 345b.

76 Ross (1856, 364).

77 Thom to Simpson, [day illegible] January 1847, HBCA: D.5/19, fo. 31ff.; Thom to Simpson, 8 May 1847, HBCA: D.5/19, fo. 546ff. Sir George Simpson was displeased by this initiative: "I very much disapprove of the grant of £50 for the library." Simpson to Christie, 5 July 1847, HBCA: D.4/36, fo. 121ff.

78 Thom to Simpson, [day illegible] January 1847, HBCA: D.5/19, fo. 31ff.

79 Discussed in the following section.

80 *Public Interest v. Hogan*, case 35, vol. 2, 59.

81 Numerous attempts had been made over the years to stimulate agricultural development by means of subsidized farm projects. Lord Selkirk began the practice (Ross 1856, 77–8), and the company later followed his lead. None of the projects was successful. See Oliver (1914, 731); and HBCA: D.4/109, fo. 21(b), no. 38.

82 See Klassen (2000).

83 See Pannekoek (2000a).

84 See HBCA: A.11/95, fo. 232; and ABC: Donald Ross Collection, file 178, Add. MSS 635, letter 13.

85 *Public Interest v. Calder,* case 49a, vol. 2, 76.

86 The most notorious example was *Public Interest v. Hogan,* case 35, vol. 2, 59, in which a soldier was convicted of assault with intention to rape.

87 Preamble to Laws of Assiniboia (1852) (Oliver 1914, 371, obs. 5).

88 *Commentary* to *The Queen v. O'Brian,* case 203, vol. 2, 306.

89 HBCA: D.5/19, fo. 32.

90 The next governor of Assiniboia, Major William B. Caldwell, was an army officer. He later told a parliamentary committee that when he presided over the General Court, "I pretty m uch adopted the plan which is usual in our military courts, and instead of charging the jury ... I merely desired the clerk of the court to read the proceedings to refresh the memories of the jury, and I left them to decide the question." Select Committee Report, Q. 5504. There is nothing, however, to suggest that the substantive laws applied by the court, even during Caldwell's years, ever included more than the general laws of England and Assiniboia.

91 Oliver (1914, 328–9).

92 See vol. 1, 59, 63.

93 Oliver (1914, 314).

94 A case was heard on 16 February 1849 – *Smith v. Welsh & Turner,* case 59, vol. 2, 105 – in which the "Plaintiff," William Smith, gave evidence under oath. However, the record of Smith's testimony shows no sign that he was subjected to cross-examination, and both Welsh and Turner stood silent. The case was probably a miscaptioned criminal prosecution rather than a civil contest.

95 *Hudson's Bay Company v. Pierre Guilleaum Sayer,* case 68, vol. 2, 113.

96 Minutes of Council of Assiniboia, 3 April 1845 and 19 June 1845 (Oliver 1914, 314, 321, 322).

97 A witness at the 1857 enquiry into the affairs of the HBC by the Select Committee of the British House of Commons testified that to his knowledge the last of those devices was never resorted to. It is not known to what extent, if any, the others were used. See Select Committee Report, Q. 4899 and 4900.

98 Ross (1856, 324–33) tells the story of the peace agreement and quotes the remarkable correspondence that achieved it.

99 *Public Interest v. Capenesseweet,* case 6, vol. 2, 17. See the *Commentary* to that case and Gibson (2010b).

100 Dorge (2000a).

101 Oliver (1914, 348–9).

102 Hargrave (1871, 92–3, 208–12, 269). Although Smith was not formally appointed until 10 October 1848 and did not first sign the records as clerk of the General Court until 16 November 1848 (vol. 2, 96), there are indications (changed handwriting, phraseology, and spelling) that his clerical services may have commenced, on an acting or assisting basis, as early as August 1847 (vol. 2, 59ff.). It is possible, however, that some unknown third person filled in as clerk between May 1847, when Black seems last to have been involved, and November 1848. See the editor's note to the latter session in vol. 2, 89.

103 See Hutchinson (2000); and Shirritt-Beaumont (2001).

104 Simpson to Ross ("Strictly Confidential"), 29 December 1845, HBCA: D.4/34, fo. 61ff. An Anglican himself, although probably not a very passionate one, Simpson disdained, but tolerated, other religions – as long as they did not interfere with business.

105 Simpson to Ross, 7 July 1846, HBCA: D.4/35, fo. 57.

106 Evidently, Simpson was not aware that Ross had already, on the request of Evans himself, examined witnesses to the shooting and that they had exonerated the missionary (Shirritt-Beaumont 2001, 67–8; Macleod 1947, 191).

107 Simpson to Ross ("Private"), 7 July 1846, HBCA: D.4/35, fo. 58ff.

108 Evans had indeed received a summons from home in the form of a polite invitation to return to England for consultations, with no suggestion that he would not be returning to Rupert's Land. He was on his way with his wife to meet the ship at York Factory at the time Simpson wrote to Ross.

109 Thereafter, opined Norway House chief factor Donald Ross, "recollection and discussion" of the "disagreeable" allegations against Evans should, "as soon as justice to the living will permit, be buried in the oblivion of the silent tomb with the talented but unhappy man who gave rise to them." Ross to Mason ("Strictly Private and Confidential"), 20 April 1847, ABC: Donald Ross Collection, file 177, Add. MSS 635, letter 3.

110 An attempt by Thom to have the London Governor and Committee enact extensive changes to the Laws of Assiniboia, drawing in part on his ill-fated codes, was unsuccessful, however. Thom to Simpson ("Confidential"), 10 March 1845, HBCA: D.5/13, fo. 253ff.; Thom to Simpson ("Private"), 27 March 1845, HBCA: D.5/13, fo. 343ff. Among the rejected innovations were nine-man juries, several changes to the rules of evidence, and the creation of a governmental functionary called "Protector of Indians."

111 Simpson to London ("Confidential"), 23 July 1846, HBCA: A.12/3, fo. 204ff.

112 Hargrave (1871, 213).

113 HBCA: A.38/47, fo. 1ff., FC 3207.99, pamphlet. A later anonymous letter, probably from Peter Garrioch, to the editor of London's *Morning Chronicle* (published 3 October 1849, HBCA: A.71/8, fo. 24–9) indicated that although the pamphlet was printed in London, the company had decided against publishing it and accordingly had "suppressed" its circulation except within company circles.

114 HBCA: D.5/13, fo. 270ff., FC 3207.99, pamphlet Z8.

115 Williams (1973, 182).

116 Ibid., 189.

117 Thom to Simpson ("Private"), 1 January 1845, HBCA: D.5/13, fo. 7ff.

118 HBCA: E.16/1, fo. 80ff., no. 65(b)(i).

119 Thom to Simpson, 5 August 1845, HBCA: D.5/14, fo. 222. The story had two sequels. On the advice of an English solicitor, the company referred the problem, with documentation that included Thom's opinions, to the Queen's Advocate – a public officer charged with protecting the legal interests of children and other vulnerable people. The solicitor then, presumably at the advocate's suggestion, obtained probate of the *signed* will but only after obtaining the agreement of all beneficiaries to distribute the assets in accordance with the *unsigned* will. Slade & Co. to Smith, 6 June 1846, HBCA: A.36/12, fo. 253–4. While that eminently sensible practical solution *might* have been what Thom had recommended, it seems unlikely. Since the immediate beneficiaries were left only the income of the estate, the capital remained in the hands of the trustee – HBC secretary W.G. Smith – leading to a second sequel more than a quarter-century later, when Smith's embezzlements were found to have dissipated most of the funds. Smith to McTavish, c/o Bissett, 28 September 1872, HBCA: A.36/4, fo. 146–7.

120 Simpson to London, 23 July 1846, HBCA: A.12/3, fo. 204–8.

121 Bumsted (2003b, 85–6).

122 Thom to London, 2 July 1852, HBCA: A.11/95, fo. 472.

123 Thom (1848b). The new title was *Chronology of Prophecy: Tracing the Various Course of Divine Providence from the Flood to the End of Time in the Light as well of National Annals as of Scriptural Predictions.* The temptation to dismiss the book as an aberration of Thom's labyrinthine mind is weakened by an exhibit of manuscripts by Sir Isaac Newton indicating that the father of gravity also dabbled in speculative scholarship on a similar theme. *Globe and Mail*, 20 June 2007, A2.

124 Thom to Simpson, 28 November 1848, HBCA: D.5/23, fo. 356ff.

125 Simpson circular letter to Council of Rupert's Land, 18 September 1846, HBCA: D.4/35, fo. 53. Thom's absence was in part to blame for the council's inability to put an alleged thief on trial at that year's meeting. Simpson to London, 1 July 1847, HBCA: A.12/3, fo. 424ff.

126 AM: MG2, B4–10, fo. 26. Father Georges-Antoine Belcourt, who probably had a better understanding of French Halfbreed resentment and impatience at that time than any other white, would later tell Simpson, "Some of them ... would go and drown the judge, break the jail, cut off several of the first heads, and God knows what [other] excesses." Belcourt to Simpson, 29 December 1847, HBCA: A.13/3, fo. 241.

127 Oliver (1914, 310).

128 Minutes of the Council of Assiniboia, 19 June 1844, in ibid., 311.

129 Simpson to London, 23 July 1846, HBCA: A.12/3, fo. 204–5.

130 Warkentin and Ruggles (1970, 192). The original map is in the Archives of Manitoba.

131 See the description in Gibson and Gibson (1972, 50), from Bryce (1905).

132 Oliver (1914, 310).

133 Hargrave (1871, 213). His description probably exaggerates the space limitations somewhat. Other accounts suggest that the courtroom would accommodate about 100 people.

134 NW621104. Internal evidence indicates that this complaint may have come from recently appointed recorder John Black, who was about to chair his second session of the court – his first in winter conditions, when this complaint was published.

CHAPTER SIX

1 For 1839 and 1844, see Oliver (1914, 74); for 1849, see Ross (1856, 409); and for 1856, see Select Committee, House of Commons (UK) (1857, 363–5). The figures are approximations and include an estimated 500 settled Indians, who are not taken into account in all sources. Excluded is a population of about 1,000, which the 1856 census estimated for the largely French Halfbreed US community of Pembina, with which Red River remained closely connected.

2 Foster (2000).

3 Ens (1996, 111–14, and generally).

4 Governor and Committee to Colvile, 7 April 1852, HBCA: A.6/29, fo. 159.

5 See vol. 1, 190–4, for example.

6 Pannekoek (1991, 36).

7 Galbraith (1976, 188). Some American eyes were nevertheless turning to Assiniboia and the possibility of US annexation. See Bumsted (2003b, 118–19).

8 In 1847 Sir George Simpson authorized mail packets between Sault Ste Marie and Red River every second month, the cost to be shared equally by the company, the military garrison, and the settlers. See Simpson to Christie, 24 June 1847, HBCA: D.4/36, fo. 42ff.

9 Oliver (1914, 356–7).

10 Hargrave (1871, 100).

11 Oliver (1914, 98–9).

12 Black to Simpson ("Private"), 31 December 1851, HBCA: D.5/32, fo. 435ff.

13 Quoted in Bumsted (2003b, 84).

14 *Foss v. Pelly and Davidson,* case 77, vol. 2, 136. See vol. 1, 120ff.

15 Bumsted (2000, 84–7).

16 Black to Simpson ("Private"), 31 May 1852, HBCA: D.5/33, fo. 584ff.

17 Bumsted (1999a, 7; 2003b, 89); Barclay to Simpson, 13 April 1849, HBCA: A.6/28, fo. 46ff.; Oliver (1914, 354).

18 Bumsted (1999a, 244).

19 Ross (1856, 358); Black to Simpson ("Private"), 22 September 1851, HBCA: D.5/31, fo. 511ff. Uncertainty about the validity of marriages performed in Rupert's Land by Presbyterian clergy, which a legal opinion from Adam Thom did not altogether resolve, caused the Council of Assiniboia to enact, on 27 November 1851, that such marriages were valid (Oliver 1914, 385). Thom also looked askance at Wesleyan Methodist marriages. Thom to Simpson ("Private"), 28 July 1847, HBCA: D.5/20, fo. 51ff.

20 Black to Simpson ("Private"), 31 December 1851, HBCA: D.5/32, fo. 435ff. When such uncertainty among Presbyterians threatened to prompt Black's resignation, the HBC, which valued his nonpartisan leadership, paid him a personal stipend of £50 annually. Barclay to Simpson, 15 April 1853, HBCA: A.6/30, fo. 175ff.; Governor and Committee to Simpson et al., 5 April 1854, HBCA: A.6/31, fo. 1ff.

21 See vol. 1, 91.

22 The lobbying was not altogether unproductive. When a new governor of Assiniboia, William B. Caldwell, was sent out in late 1848, he lacked a prior HBC connection and was under orders to investigate local dissatisfaction on behalf of the UK government. The Colonial Office then referred the legality of the HBC charter to the Law Officers of the Crown

(attorney general and solicitor general), whose opinion favoured the company's position, but suggested seeking a confirmatory ruling from the Judicial Committee of the Privy Council, which never occurred. Governor and Committee to Simpson, 10 April 1850, HBCA: A.6/28, fo. 227. McLaughlin's efforts caused him to be prosecuted for criminal libel. HBCA: A.39/7, fo. 121–40, legal opinions; Barclay to Simpson ("Private and Confidential"), 12 April 1850, HBCA: A.6/28, fo. 234). But he was eventually acquitted "on a technicality" (Rich 1961, vol. 3, 546).

23 The case involved was *Hudson's Bay Company v. Sayer*, case 68, vol. 2, 113. See vol. 1, 115ff.

24 AM: MG2, B2–105 (petition); Bunn to Simpson, 4 August 1851, HBCA: D.5/31, fo. 219ff.

25 See Morton (1970).

26 "Chelsea Pensioners" were military personnel on medical pensions discharged from the Royal Hospital, Chelsea.

27 Governor and Committee to Caldwell, 7 June 1848, HBCA: A.6/27, fo. 276ff.; Simpson to Caldwell, 21 November 1848, HBCA: D.4/38, fo. 67–8; Caldwell to Governor and Committee, HBCA: A.11/95, fo. 213ff.

28 Red River's chief factor, John Ballenden, newly appointed himself, understood and applauded the importance of the change. Ballenden to London, 29 November 1848, HBCA: A.11/95, fo. 201ff.

29 See generally Morton (2000b). Morton is mistaken, however, in saying that Caldwell sat alone on the *Sayer* case.

30 It contained just five innocuous questions, not one of them so phrased as to likely draw a penetrating response. Anonymous letter (probably from Peter Garrioch) to editor, *Morning Chronicle* (London), published 3 October 1849, HBCA: A.71/8, fo. 24–9.

31 Caldwell to Garrioch, 15 March 1849, HBCA: A.11/95, fo. 242.

32 Caldwell to Lord Grey (Inquiry Report), 22 March 1849, HBCA: A.11/95, fo. 238ff.

33 One critic claimed Provencher refused to respond because "he could not give a favourable reply, and if he gave an unfavourable one the Company would starve his people if so inclined." Anonymous letter cited at note 30.

34 Sinclair abstained, it was said, because "the questions were not framed according to the commission from England." Anonymous letter cited at note 30.

35 Christie to London, 25 November 1847, HBCA: A.11/95, fo. 138–9. According to a later newspaper story, although the pamphlet had

been printed in London, the company decided against publishing it and suppressed its circulation except within company circles. How the letter writer obtained a copy is unknown. Anonymous letter cited at note 30.

36 Caldwell to Garrioch, 15 March 1849, HBCA: A.11/95, fo. 242.

37 Anonymous letter cited at note 30.

38 Caldwell to Governor and Committee, 28 March 1849, HBCA: A.11/95, fo. 236. Someone said the clergyman who gathered the Indian statements, HBC sympathizer Reverend John Smithurst, submitted only a selection of them, adding: "It was reported that he took only the depositions of such as were related to the Kennedy and Isbister family, so (as said) that it might appear an Isbister movement." Anonymous letter cited at note 30.

39 Bumsted (2003b, 106).

40 Ross (1856, 366), quoting Acting Governor Colvile.

41 A "recognizance" is a personal undertaking made under oath. A judge "estreated" on a recognizance when, having found that the person in question had violated the undertaking in some manner, he ordered that person to either pay the amount of the bond or go to jail. See Glossary.

42 Black to Simpson, 23 December 1851, HBCA: D.5/32, fo. 400ff. See case 89, vol. 2, 186.

43 See next note.

44 *Hudson's Bay Company v. Sayer et al.*, case 68, vol. 2, 113. See also the description in the next section.

45 Ross's report to Caldwell, dated 22 August 1849, is in the latter's report to London, 28 August 1849, HBCA: A.11/95, fo. 213ff., at 216.

46 The charge was probably desertion from employment, a criminal offence akin to mutiny at the time.

47 Caldwell to London, 26 January 1850, HBCA: A.11/95, fo. 306.

48 See the description below.

49 Caldwell to London, 26 January 1850, HBCA: A.11/95, fo. 306.

50 *Hudson's Bay Company v. Sayer et al.*, case 68, vol. 2, 113.

51 Ibid., *Commentary*.

52 Minutes of Council of Assiniboia, 31 May 1849 (Oliver 1914, 351–2).

53 Oliver (1914, 351–3).

54 Anonymous letter cited above.

55 Barclay to Caldwell, 29 November 1849, HBCA: A.6/28, fo. 137ff.; Barclay to Simpson ("Private and Confidential"), 12 April 1850, HBCA: A.6/28, fo. 234ff.

56 Minutes of Council of Assiniboia, 30 July 1849 (Oliver 1914, 353).

57 Ross (1856, 377).

58 Barclay to Simpson ("Personal & Confidential"), 12 April 1850, HBCA: A.6/28, fo. 234ff.; Barclay to Simpson, 19 November 1852, HBCA: A.6/30, fo. 63ff.; Oliver (1914, 389).

59 Unsigned copy or draft petition, dated 27 March 1851, AM: MG2, B2–105. Not much is known about this intriguing document. See Bunn to Simpson, 4 August 1851, HBCA: D.5/31, fo. 219–20.

60 Oliver (1914, 1, 352); Barclay to Caldwell, 29 November 1849, HBCA: A.6/28, fo. 137ff.

61 A previously cited letter described Thom's position revealingly and prophetically: "The people ... came to the decision to put Mr. Thom out of the Settlement, and gave him until the 5th [of June] ... to move. If not off by then, they would send him afloat in a canoe. Since then ... by the advice of a few sage heads they have determined to petition Sir George Simpson ..., and if ... Simpson does not comply they won't allow ... Thom to sit in the Court." Anonymous letter cited above.

62 Caldwell to Governor and Committee, 2 August 1849, HBCA: A.11/95, fo. 253–4.

63 His strenuous efforts to win a salary increase had been unsuccessful, however. Barclay to Thom, 4 April 1849, HBCA: A.6/28, fo. 16.

64 Bunn to Caldwell, 12 July 1849, HBCA: D.5/25, fo. 436.

65 Even before that, the public-spirited physician had agreed to replace the deceased Reverend John McCallum as the settlement's coroner (Oliver 1914, 355).

66 Caldwell to Governor and Committee, 2 August 1849, HBCA: A.11/95, fo. 253–4.

67 Simpson to Caldwell, 7 July 1849, HBCA: D.4/39, fo. 86–7. Simpson simultaneously asked Thom to cooperate. Simpson to Thom, 7 July 1849, HBCA: D.4/70, fo. 250.

68 Caldwell to Simpson, 2 August 1849, HBCA: D.5/25, fo. 434–5. Simpson subsequently *ordered* Thom to comply. Simpson to Thom, 23 November 1849, HBCA: D.4/40, fo. 55.

69 Caldwell to Simpson, 2 August 1849, HBCA: D.5/25, fo. 434–5.

70 Oliver (1914, 353–4).

71 This was the second time Thom was sued in his own court. See vol. 1, 72.

72 *Matheson v. Thom*, case 75, vol. 2, 132.

73 Unpublished report of *Matheson v. Thom*, HBCA: A.11/95. fo. 320–3.

74 *Foss v. Pelly & Davidson*, 16 July 1850, case 77, vol. 2, 136.

75 Colvile to London, 28 November 1850, HBCA: A.11/95, fo. 384.

76 Black to Simpson ("Private"), 29 November 1850, HBCA: D.5/29, fo. 282ff.

77 Colvile to Simpson ("Private"), 4 January 1851, HBCA: D.5/30; Rich (1956, 201–2); Black to Simpson ("Private"), 8 January 1851, HBCA: D.5/30, fo. 47ff.

78 Black to Simpson ("Private"), 26 July 1851, HBCA: D.5/31, fo. 140ff.

79 Thom to London, 1 January 1851, HBCA: A.11/95, fo. 403ff., enclosure.

80 Black to Simpson ("Private"), 8 January 1851, HBCA: D.5/30, fo. 47ff., enclosure.

81 Colvile's commission was delivered on 4 April 1849. Barclay to Colvile, 4 April 1849, HBCA: A.6/28, fo. 17.

82 Rich (1956, xcvi–xcvii).

83 Ibid., c (page 100 of the Introduction).

84 Colvile to Barclay, 26 August 1850, HBCA: A.13/4; Rich (1956, 26–8). The clergymen on the council had not joined in this refusal.

85 Colvile to Simpson ("Private"), 16 August 1850, HBCA: D.5/28; Rich (1956, 191–4).

86 Rich (1956, 26–8). Caldwell's support was lukewarm and wavering. At one point he attempted to organize a "counter-petition." Colvile to Simpson ("Private"), 19 September 1850, HBCA: D.5/28; Rich (1956, 197–8). He also tried to instigate a "counter-revolution" but was unsuccessful in this, as in most things. Bunn to Simpson, 17 September 1850, HBCA: D.5/28; Rich (1956, 604–5).

87 Colvile to Simpson ("Private"), 26 August 1850, HBCA: D.5/28; Rich (1956, 194–7). Colvile seemed to enjoy sharing his acerbic and usually accurate character assessments. The same letter called Thom's conduct in the *Foss* case "as unlike a judge as anything could be," describing him as "a clever man endowed with marvellously little judgment." Later he said of Caldwell, "Whether he was selected as being the tallest man in the army I do not know, but I can see no other qualification he possesses." Colvile to Simpson ("Private"), 19 September 1850, HBCA: D.5/28; Rich (1956, 197–8). In that letter he also called John Black "stupid as an owl." He would later recant.

88 Colvile to Barclay, 26 August 1850, HBCA: A.13/4; Rich (1956, 26–8).

89 Oliver (1914, 358–60).

90 Ibid., 360–3.

91 "Whatever it may cost." He added that the "stupid old Major" appeared to be in cahoots with Riel on this occasion. Ibid.

92 Barclay to Colvile, 6 December 1850, HBCA: A.6/29, fo. 17.

93 Colvile to Simpson ("Confidential"), 22 May 1851, HBCA: D.5/30; Rich (1956, 206–19).

94 Oliver (1914, 363). Colvile would remain in the settlement, however, as an *éminence grise* until after the 1852 flood.

95 Colvile had formerly considered Black "stupid as an owl." Colvile to Simpson ("Private"), 19 September 1850, HBCA: D.5/28; Rich (1956, 197–8). But he now said that Black had "agreeably disappointed" him by having "made himself much more popular with the community than I expected he would do – though he rather bores me with his long-winded and rounded periods." Colvile to Simpson ("Confidential"), 22 May 1851, HBCA: D.5/30; Rich (1956, 206ff.).

96 Oliver (1914, 364). Colvile reported to Simpson, "I managed to please old Ross by inducing the Council to name his son." Colvile to Simpson ("Confidential"), 22 May 1851, HBCA: D.5/30; Rich (1956, 206ff.).

97 After the Presbyterians objected to being overlooked in this grant, they were given an educational allowance as well (Oliver 1914, 387). These education grants would subsequently be criticized by the Governor and Committee in London. Barclay to Caldwell, 19 November 1852, HBCA: A.6/30, fo. 63.

98 Neither of these proposals was enacted, although a small improvement in the law of civil imprisonment was made in 1852 (Oliver 1914, 379).

99 Ibid., 363–6.

100 Dr John Bunn's commission as a justice of the peace is in AM: MG2, B4–7.

101 Colvile to Simpson ("Confidential"), 22 May 1851, HBCA: D.5/30; Rich (1956, 206ff.).

102 See "justice of the peace" in Glossary.

103 Colvile to Simpson ("Confidential"), 22 May 1851, HBCA: D.5/30; Rich (1956, 206ff.).

104 Bunn to Simpson, 4 August 1851, HBCA: D.5/31, fo. 219–20. See also Bunn to Simpson, 12 August 1852, HBCA: D.5/34, fo. 235ff.

105 Black to Simpson ("Private"), 29 September 1851, HBCA: D.5/31, fo. 542ff.

106 Oliver (1914, 369–79).

107 Ibid., 386–7.

108 See vol. 1, 63.

109 An attempt by Thom in 1845 to have the council enact extensive and somewhat radical reforms, such as jury decisions by majorities of nine, had failed. Thom to Simpson ("Private"), 27 March 1845, HBCA: D.5/13, fo. 343ff.

110 Thom had originally authored most of these preambles.

111 The French version is in Oliver (1914, 1325ff.). The only previous authorization of bilingual laws appears to be an 1845 council resolution

requiring that certain laws passed that day be copied "in both languages" so that they could be "read aloud and explained at the meetings of the General Court in November and February of each year" (ibid. 326).

112 See vol. 1, 65.

113 Report of Judge F.G. Johnson on Laws of Assiniboia, in *Journals of House of Commons of Canada*, vol. 14 (1880), 101, confirmed in *Sinclair v. Mulligan* (1886) 3 Man. LR; (1888) 5 MR 17 (Man. QB).

114 Barclay to Caldwell, 19 November 1852, HBCA: A.6/30, fo. 63ff.

115 See vol. 1, 40.

116 Simpson to Bunn ("Confidential"), 2 November 1854, HBCA: D.4/83, fo. 195ff.

117 The same explanation might account for its decision in the early 1850s to issue commissions for justices of the peace from London. See vol. 1, 125.

118 The letter expressing "approbations" of the revised laws went on to say that the company "do not disallow the grants for education ... but they wish it to be understood in future that no extraordinary application of the funds must be carried into effect without the previous sanction of the Governor and Committee." Barclay to Caldwell, 19 November 1852, HBCA: A.6/30, fo. 63.

119 Caldwell to London, 3 July 1852, HBCA: A.11/95, fo. 474.

120 Colvile to Simpson ("Private"), 17 December 1851, HBCA: D.5/32; Rich (1956, 247ff.). John Black observed in March 1852, "The only visible symptom of Mr. Thom's [continuing] connection with the Court was the bill of indictment [for a recent infanticide case], which in some way he had got to draw up, but which, with ... the Company's book of law forms, almost any body could have managed quite as well." Black to Simpson ("Private"), 25 March 1852, HBCA: D.5/33, fo. 340ff. This infanticide case was *Public Interest v. Heckenberger*, case 93, vol. 2, 191.

121 Colvile to Simpson ("Private & Confidential"), 14 September 1851, HBCA: D.5/31; Rich (1956, 221ff.).

122 For a possible behind-the-scenes ploy by Thom to have the court divided into two sections, one for the upper part of the settlement and one for the lower part, where Thom was arguably less unpopular, see the court records, 19 May 1853, vol. 2, 215.

123 Bunn to Simpson, 4 August 1851, HBCA: D.5/31, fo. 219ff.

124 Black to Simpson ("Private"), 23 December 1851, HBCA: D.5/32, fo. 400ff.

125 Ibid.

126 Bunn to Simpson, 12 August 1852, HBCA: D.5/34, fo. 235ff.

127 See, for example, Thom to Anderson, 19 August 1850, HBCA: A.11/95, fo. 347. Many similar and related missives exist.

128 Simpson received seven letters from Thom that year. Simpson to Thom, 10 December 1851, HBCA: D.4/44, fo. 79ff.

129 Simpson to Thom, 10 December 1851, HBCA: D.4/44, fo. 79ff. Simpson justified his paraphrase by calling Thom's writing style "so peculiar ... that in order to make my replies intelligible I must ... state the interpretation I put on your remarks."

130 Simpson went on to remind Thom that he had twice refused requests to attend meetings at Norway House. He also refuted claims by Thom that he had not been treated well concerning his living quarters at the Lower Fort.

131 Colvile to Barclay, 21 July 1852, HBCA: A.12/13; Rich (1956, 160).

132 Barclay to Thom, 19 November 1852, HBCA: A.6/30, fo. 68.

133 Simpson to Black ("Private"), 6 December 1853, HBCA: D.4/82, fo. 388ff.

134 Simpson to Thom ("Private"), 29 September 1854, HBCA: D.4/83.

135 Simpson's strategy in giving Thom so blunt a statement of the company's complaints against him was doubtless also to remind him of its ammunition for a potential counterattack.

136 Simpson to Colvile ("Private"), 25 February 1854, HBCA: D.4/22, fo. 627ff.

137 Ballenden to London, 16 August 1854, HBCA: A.11/96, fo. 16.

138 Black to Simpson ("Private"), 29 September 1852, HBCA: D.5/34, fo. 491ff.

139 Black to Simpson ("Private"), 25 January 1853, HBCA: D.5/36, fo. 119ff.

140 Simpson to Black, 19 February 1853, HBCA: D.4/46, fo, 22.

141 Black to Simpson, 8 March 1853, HBCA: D.5/37, fo. 454ff.

142 Simpson to Black, 21 December 1853, HBCA: D.4/47, fo. 36ff.

143 Memorandum signed by Black and Pelly, 24 December 1853, A.11/95, fo. 609.

144 Simpson to Colvile ("Private"), 25 February 1854, HBCA: D.4/22, fo. 627ff.

145 Governor and Committee to Simpson et al., 5 April 1854, HBCA: A.6/31, fo. 10, no. 30.

146 Simpson to Black ("Private & Confidential"), 12 August 1854, HBCA: D.4/83, fo. 30ff.

147 Simpson to Black, 6 January 1855, HBCA: reel 3M16, fo. 94.

148 Smith to Black, 20 January 1855, HBCA: A.6/31, fo. 175ff.

149 Ross (1856, 328).

150 MacLeod and Morton (1963, 137).
151 Ibid., 143–51; Morton (1970).
152 Grant to Simpson, 26 May 1853, HBCA: D.5/37, fo. 273.
153 Simpson to Grant, 29 June 1854, HBCA: D.4/48, fo. 68.
154 MacLeod and Morton (1963, 154).
155 Sinclair to McDermot, 19 March 1851, ABC: Sinclair Collection, reprinted in Lent (1963, 227).
156 As early as June 1846 he had written to Simpson hoping to "convince you that I have not from choice been placed in my present attitude as regards the supreme authority of this country" and to "return to more amicable relations." Central to the strained relations at that time, he suggested, was "Thom's personality." Sinclair to Simpson, 4 June 1846, reprinted in Lent (1963, 184–7).
157 Ibid., 221.
158 Ibid.. 285–6.
159 See vol. 1, 146.

CHAPTER SEVEN

1 Ross to Simpson ("Private"), 31 July 1851, ABC: Donald Ross Collection, file 180, Add. MSS 635, letter 25.
2 Barclay to Caldwell, 19 November 1852, HBCA: A.6/30, fo. 63ff.
3 Ross to Smith ("Private"), 23 August 1849, ABC: Donald Ross Collection, file 179, Add. MSS 635, letter 15.
4 Report of Select Committee, House of Commons (UK), 1857 (hereafter Select Committee Report).
5 Ibid., 120ff.
6 Ibid., Q. 2410.
7 Ibid., Q. 2469ff.
8 Ibid., Q. 2486ff.
9 Ibid., Q. 6094ff.
10 Ibid., Q. 2666ff.
11 Ibid., Q. 2849ff.
12 Ibid., Q. 2810. Corbett was not alone in this concern. Other clerics had called for the election of councillors in 1856. Simpson to London, 24 June 1856, HBCA: D.4/78, fo. 866.
13 Ibid., Q. 2880ff.
14 Case 238, vol. 2, 366.
15 Although the former colonies of Upper and Lower Canada were merged by that time, their courts retained their former designations.

16 Select Committee Report, 210–36.
17 Ibid., 262–85.
18 Ibid., Q. 4808 and 4986.
19 Case 6, vol. 2, 17.
20 Select Committee Report, Q. 4983.
21 Capenesseweet's brother was initially arrested with him as a possible conspirator but was later released and never charged.
22 Select Committee Report, Q. 5025 to 5029.
23 Simpson to Thom ("Private"), 17 February 1857, HBCA: D.4/52, fo. 123; Simpson to Thom, 30 March 1857, HBCA: D.4/52, fo. 138. Amazingly, Simpson never entirely lost his confidence in Thom. In 1859, advising HBC governor Berens as to a suitable representative of the company on an international commission to arbitrate claims arising from settlement of the Oregon dispute, he proposed that if his first choice were not available, "the Company's interests would be as safe in ... [Thom's] hands as in those of any other person I could name." Simpson to Berens ("Private"), 5 March 1859, HBCA: D.4/84A. See also Simpson to Berens, 22 January 1859, HBCA: D.4/84A, fo. 441ff. Thom was not appointed
24 Select Committee Report, 44–108.
25 MacKay (1966, 263).
26 Select Committee Report, Q. 716.
27 Ibid., Q. 773 and 818.
28 Ibid., Q. 774.
29 MacKay (1966, 263, 267).
30 Select Committee Report, Q. 5992.
31 Ibid., Q. 5889.
32 Simpson to Shepherd ("Private"), 2 August 1856, HBCA: A.7/2, fo. 33ff.
33 Shepherd to Simpson ("Private"), 1 September 1856, HBCA: A.7/2, fo. 38ff.
34 Shepherd to Labouchere ("Private"), 18 July 1857, HBCA: A.7/2, fo. 79ff.
35 Select Committee Report, Q. 5834.
36 Although a political adversary, Labouchere was one of Ellice's many personal friends. In late September and early October 1956, when the prospect of the enquiry was in the wind, Ellice wrote to Labouchere advising him in confidence of the company's position and challenging him bluntly: "Can this country or Canada ... govern the HB territory as satisfactorily without ... [the Company]? If they can, abolish it; if not, maintain it." Ellice to Labouchere, 1 October 1856, HBCA: A.7/2, fo. 52ff.

See also Ellice to Labouchere, 30 September 1856, HBCA: A.7/2, fo. 47ff.

37 Select Committee Report, Q. 5835. That condition was reiterated when Ellice later told the chairman that he thought the HBC would even be prepared to give up the Red River Settlement to Canada: "I have not the least doubt, although I have no authority to make statements upon this subject, that the Hudson's Bay Company would come to very easy terms to transfer the Red River Settlement to Canada, if Canada would only protect them and govern the country." Select Committee Report, Q. 5839.

38 Ibid., Q. 5838.

39 Colthart (2000).

40 Galbraith (1976, 195).

41 See, for example, Ellice to Labouchere, 30 September 1856, HBCA: A.7/2, fo. 47ff.

42 Select Committee Report, x–xii (Labouchere), xiv (Gladstone). Written proposals from committee member Christy (x11–xiv), although not discussed formally, figured in some of the subsequent deliberations of the committee.

43 Ibid., xiv.

44 Ibid., xvi.

45 As to compensation, the final report did say, however, that the territory should be ceded to Canada "on equitable principles" (ibid., 7). Failure of the government and the HBC to agree about what that meant would prevent an agreement being reached until 1869.

46 Ibid., 403.

47 Berens to Dallas ("Private & Confidential"), 22 October 1858, HBCA: A.7/2, fo. 109ff.; Fraser to Simpson, 15 July 1859, HBCA: A.5/34, fo. 227ff. The latter document instructed that although company officers "may pay cheerful obedience to such regulations as may be established by Her Majesty's Government, they have no concern in assisting or carrying out such regulations."

48 Labouchere to Shepherd ("Private"), 15 July 1857, HBCA: A.7/2, fo. 78ff.; Shepherd to Simpson ("Private"), 21 August 1857, HBCA: A.7/2, fo. 82ff.

49 Berens to Simpson ("Confidential"), 12 November 1858, HBCA: A.7/2, fo. 1.

50 The possibility of a reference, avoided by amalgamation in 1821, was still so strong in April 1860 that the HBC lawyers began preparing the company's case. Berens to Simpson ("Private"), 18 April 1860, HBCA: A.7/3, fo. 112.

51 Ontario won in an 1884 ruling of the Judicial Committee of the Privy Council. See Ontario, *Sessional Papers*, 1889, no. 60, "Proceedings ... respecting Western Boundary of Ontario, LAC: RG7, G21, no. 128, vol. 1.

52 Simpson to Johnson ("Private"), 21 October 1857, HBCA: D.4/53, fo. 100ff.

53 Simpson to Colvile ("Private"), 28 November 1857, HBCA: D.4/84.

54 Galbraith (1976, 199).

55 Berens to Dallas ("Private & Confidential"), 15 March 1861, HBCA: A.7/3, fo. 64.

56 Behind-the-scenes lobbying included naming a new company ship *Labouchere*. Berens to Dallas, 9 November 1860, HBCA: A.7/3, fo. 49–50.

57 Barclay to Caldwell, 19 November 1852, HBCA: A.6/30, fo. 63ff.

58 Oliver (1914, 389).

59 Johnson to London, 10 March 1856, HBCA: A.11/96, fo. 61ff.

60 Sworn in 19 September 1857 (Oliver 1914, 426).

61 Ibid., 423.

62 Colvile to Simpson ("Confidential"), 22 May 1851, reprinted in Rich (1956, 206–19).

63 See Stubbs (1967, 48–9).

64 In February 1856 Sheriff William Ross reported to his brother that, at a public meeting to consider ways to raise the settlement's moral condition, including a proposal to "drink less imported rum," Johnson had "said a few words on the different schemes, except the rum – too fond of it himself." Quoted in Stubbs (1967, 57).

65 Johnson to Simpson, 28 November 1849, HBCA: D.5/26, fo. 600. Whether Simpson foreclosed is unknown.

66 Smith to Johnson, 12 June 1854, HBCA: A.6/31, fo. 79ff.

67 Simpson to Johnson ("Confidential"), 2 November 1854, HBCA: D.4/83, fo. 184ff. Although Benny had offered to settle "cheap," Simpson suggested, in a rare kindly spirit, that "if he drops the interest it would be as much as can fairly be expected of him."

68 Simpson to Johnson, 22 September 1856, HBCA: D.4/52, fo. 28.

69 Simpson to Johnson, 29 November 1853, HBCA: D.4/46; Simpson to Black ("Private"), 6 December 1853, HBCA: D.4/82, fo. 391.

70 Simpson to Johnson, 5 January 1854, HBCA: D.4/47, fo. 43.

71 Caldwell to London, 12 March 1855, HBCA: A.11/96, fo. 36–7.

72 Simpson to Colvile ("Private"), n.d., HBCA: D.4/83, fo. 362ff.

73 Stubbs (1967, 53).

74 Ibid., 57, 58.

75 Simpson to Johnson, 12 February 1855, HBCA: D.4/50, fo. 18.

76 Simpson to Johnson ("Confidential"), 17 January 1857, HBCA: D.4/52, fo. 110ff.
77 Simpson to Johnson ("Confidential"), 12 August 1854, HBCA: D.4/83, fo. 7–8.
78 Simpson to Johnson ("Confidential"), 2 November 1854, HBCA: D.4/83, fo. 184ff.
79 Simpson to Johnson ("Confidential"), 2 November 1854, HBCA: D.4/83, fo. 184ff.
80 There was a personal squabble of some kind, however, between Johnson and John Swanston, a very senior fur trader then serving as the HBC's chief factor at Red River. Simpson wrote Johnson an avuncular letter urging "tact and forbearance" in the interest of presenting an appearance of "unanimity among ourselves ... out of doors." Simpson to Johnson ("Private"), 13 March 1857, fo. 131ff. See also Johnson to Simpson ("Confidential"), n.d., HBCA: D.5/43, fo. 490ff.
81 Caldwell to London, 12 March 1855, HBCA: A.11/96, fo. 36–7. Adam Thom's 1852 consolidation would remain in effect until 1862.
82 See vol. 1, 166.
83 Governor and Committee, annual general letter, 5 April 1854, HBCA: A.6/31, fo. 1ff., at para. 28.
84 Smith to Caldwell, 13 April 1855, HBCA: A.6/31, fo. 241ff.
85 Swanston to London, 9 August 1855, HBCA: A.11/96, fo. 44.
86 Although Johnson's commission as governor was not dispatched until November 1855, and he was not sworn in as such until 27 February 1856, he assumed his gubernatorial duties shortly after Caldwell's appointment expired on the basis of an appointment by Simpson as acting deputy governor of Rupert's Land. Governor and Committee, annual general letter, 17 April 1856, HBCA: A.6/32, fo. 47ff., at para. 25; Oliver (1914, 410).
87 Governor and Committee, annual general letter, 17 April 1856, HBCA: A.6/32, fo. 47ff.
88 Johnson to Simpson ("Confidential"), 23 May 1857, HBCA: D.5/43, fo. 490ff.
89 Johnson to London, 10 March 1856, HBCA: A.11/96, fo. 61–2. See vol. 1, 146.
90 See vol. 1, 158.
91 Johnson to Simpson ("Confidential"), 23 May 1857, HBCA: D.5/43, fo. 490ff.
92 See vol. 1, 160.

93 Johnson to Simpson ("Confidential"), 23 May 1857, HBCA: D.5/43, fo. 490ff., emphasis in original.
94 Smith to Johnson, 13 November 1857, HBCA: A.6/33, fo. 28ff. Systemic changes were to be deferred until the "future government of the Red River Settlement" was settled.
95 Johnson to London, 29 June 1857, HBCA: A.11/96, fo. 136ff.; Smith to Johnson, 13 November 1857, HBCA: A.6/33, fo. 28ff.
96 Johnson to Simpson, 6 June 1855, HBCA: D.5/40, fo. 289ff.
97 Johnson to Hopkins, 9 March 1857, HBCA: D.5/43, fo. 272ff., emphasis in original. In June he complained directly to the Governor and Committee. See Smith to Johnson, 13 November 1857, HBCA: A.6/33, fo. 28ff.
98 Johnson to Simpson ("Confidential"), 30 June 1857, HBCA: D.5/43, fo. 586ff.
99 This small local fish is now considered a delicacy in smoked form.
100 Johnson to Simpson ("Confidential"), 23 May 1857, HBCA: D.5/43, fo. 490ff.
101 Johnson to Simpson ("Confidential"), 9 April 1857, HBCA: D.5/43, fo. 368ff.
102 Johnson to Simpson, 18 December 1857, HBCA: D.5/45, fo. 481ff.
103 Johnson to London, 28 June 1858, HBCA: A.11/96, fo. 266; Johnson to Smith, 29 June 1858, HBCA: A.11/96, fo. 268–9.
104 Simpson to Berens ("Confidential"), 25 September 1858, HBCA: A.7/2, fo. 105–6.
105 Fraser to Johnson, 26 November 1858, HBCA: A.6/33, fo. 358.
106 Fraser to Simpson, 17 September 1858, HBCA: A.6/33, HBCA: fo. 291ff.
107 Fraser to Simpson, 22 October 1858, HBCA: A.6/33, fo. 338. In 1864 the company hired Johnson's son as apprentice clerk. Fraser to Johnson, 22 July 1864, HBCA: A.6/39, fo. 237–8.
108 Johnson to London, 25 September 1858, HBCA: A.11/96, fo. 201, 288.
109 Fraser to McTavish, 11 July 1861, HBCA: A.6/36, fo. 224ff.
110 Johnson to Simpson, 18 December 1857, HBCA: D.5/45, fo. 481.
111 Fraser to McTavish, 11 July 1861, HBCA: A.6/36, fo. 224–5.
112 Fraser to McTavish, 4 October 1858, HBCA: A.6/33, fo. 314. Since he remained chief factor while governor, McTavish was to receive an additional £200 annually for the dual responsibility. Deprived of that bonus for three years by clerical oversight, McTavish characteristically failed to tell anyone. Fraser to McTavish, 11 July 1861, HBCA: A.6/36, fo. 224–5.
113 Oliver (1914, 432–5).

114 Bunn to Simpson, 25 June 1860, HBCA: D.5/52, fo. 202ff.; McTavish to London, 5 February 1861, HBCA: A.11/96, fo. 219; Fraser to McTavish, 17 February 1861, HBCA: A.6/36, fo. 99ff.

115 McTavish to London, 23 December 1859, HBCA: A.11/96, fo. 399.

116 Fraser to Simpson, 17 February 1860, HBCA: A.6/35, fo. 32ff.

117 Fraser to McTavish, 9 March 1860, HBCA: A.6/35, fo. 37ff.

118 Simpson to Berens ("Private"), 16 March 1860, HBCA: D.4/84A, fo. 130ff. See also Simpson to Berens ("Private"), 23 March 1860, HBCA: D.4/84A, fo. 124ff.

119 Simpson to Berens ("Private"), 30 March 1860, HBCA: D.4/84A, fo. 114ff.

120 Fraser to McTavish, 9 March 1860, HBCA: A.6/35, fo. 37ff.; Simpson to Berens ("Private"), 23 March 1860, HBCA: D.4/84A, fo. 124ff.; Simpson to Berens ("Private"), 30 March 1860, HBCA: D.4/84A, fo. 114ff.

121 Governor and Committee, annual general letter, 17 April 1856, HBCA: A.6/32, fo. 47ff.

122 See, for example, Simpson to Shepherd ("Confidential"), 2 August 1856, HBCA: A.7/2, fo. 33ff.

123 Smith to Johnson, 3 July 1857, HBCA: A.6/32, fo. 331ff.

124 *Norway House Post Journal*, 26 September 1857, HBCA: B.154/a/63, fo. 11ff.

125 McTavish to London, 9 November 1857, HBCA: A.11/96, fo. 190.

126 Johnson to Simpson, 18 December 1857, HBCA: D.5/45, fo. 481ff.

127 McTavish to London, 9 November 1857, HBCA: A.11/96, fo. 190.

128 McTavish to London, 5 December 1857, HBCA: A.11/96, fo. 194.

129 Smith to Simpson, 17 February 1858, HBCA: A.6/33, fo. 78ff.

130 Governor and Committee, annual general letter, 16 April 1858, HBCA: A.6/33, fo. 130ff.; Governor and Committee, annual general letter, 18 April 1860, HBCA: A.6/35, fo. 92ff.

131 Governor and Committee, annual general letter, 17 April 1861, HBCA: A.6/36, fo. 101ff.; Fraser to McTavish, 17 May 1861, HBCA: A.6/36, fo. 159ff.

132 Simpson to Johnson ("Confidential"), 2 January 1857, HBCA: D.4/52, fo. 121ff.; Simpson to Johnson, 17 January 1857, HBCA: D.4/52, fo. 110ff.

133 Johnson to Hopkins, 9 March 1857, HBCA: D.5/43, fo. 272ff.; Johnson to Simpson ("Confidential"), 9 April 1857: D.5/43, fo. 368ff.

134 Select Committee Report, 437–9; Oliver (1914, 1305); Bumsted (2003b, 128–9).

135 Select Committee Report, 441–4.

136 NW600314.
137 Fraser to Simpson, 18 August 1860, HBCA: A.6/35, fo. 288ff.
138 Johnson to Simpson ("Confidential"), 30 June 1857, HBCA: D.5/43, fo. 586–7. Johnson did not seem too concerned about this, concluding, "I wish you pleasant breezes and shady treeses."
139 Pannekoek (1991, 147, 150–1).
140 Johnson to Simpson, 12 December 1857, HBCA: D.5/45, fo. 451ff.
141 Johnson to Simpson ("Private"), 22 August 1857, HBCA: D.5/44, fo. 162–3.
142 Johnson to Simpson, 12 December 1857, HBCA: D.5/45, fo. 451ff.
143 Select Committee Report, 363ff. A supplementary report prepared for the committee by Donald Gunn, discursive in style and decidedly anti-HBC in tone, appears at 381–3.
144 Comparative figures for 1849 were not given.
145 Spry (2000b). A wage claim in the General Court by a construction employee illuminates the difficulties of financing such projects. See case 160, vol. 2, 278.
146 See, for example, Oliver (1914, 417).
147 Governor and Committee, annual general letter, 18 April 1860, HBCA: A.6/35, fo. 92ff., no. 32.
148 Bumsted (2003b, 130–2).
149 Morton (1961, 29–82).
150 Hind's detailed map of the settlement in 1858 has been of great use to historians. See Warkentin and Ruggles (1970, 212).
151 Simpson to Johnson ("Private"), 13 March 1857, HBCA: D.4/52, fo. 131ff.
152 Johnson to Simpson, 9 September 1857, HBCA: D.5/44, fo. 264–5.
153 Simpson to Johnson ("Private"), 21 October 1857, HBCA: D.4/53, fo. 100ff.
154 Galbraith (1976, 188).
155 Oliver (1914, 409, 414).
156 Galbraith (1976, 201–2); Governor and Committee, annual general letter, 14 April 1859, HBCA: A.6/34, fo. 87ff.
157 Bumsted (2003b, 137).
158 Governor and Committee, annual general letter, 18 April 1860, HBCA: A.6/35, fo. 92ff. The company declined, however, to "become ... carriers" of US goods for Red River residents. Fraser to McTavish, 9 May 1860, HBCA: A.6/35, fo. 149ff.
159 Bumsted (2003b, 138).
160 NW600928.

161 NW601217.

162 The poem – Whittier's "The Red River Voyageur" – is quoted, and the cathedral and fire are described, in Bumsted (2003b, 143–6). Whittier, who never visited Red River, relied on the descriptions of others.

163 Spry (2000a).

164 Oliver (1914, 450–1).

165 NW600328, NW600628. The cost of the General Court continued to be borne by the company.

166 The Royal was the settlement's first hotel.

167 NW600214, NW600228, NW600314.

168 NW600614.

169 NW591228.

170 Case 178, vol. 2, 289.

171 There would not have been room for them all on the cramped bench if they had attempted to do so. The court's jurisdiction was never challenged on the ground that it sat with less than full council membership. Any such challenge would likely have failed for the same reason that, in British and Canadian constitutional practice, the sweeping legal powers of Her Majesty's Privy Council are exercised by a very much smaller informal "committee" thereof known as the cabinet.

172 See NW591228.

173 For the August 1857 session, however, Thomas Sinclair was temporarily replaced by council member John Inkster.

174 Oliver (1914, 420).

175 Ibid., 426. A full list of court holidays, including Ascension Day, was legislated in February 1860 (ibid., 455).

176 Governor and Committee, annual general letter, 9 April 1855, HBCA: A.6/3, fo. 219ff., no. 28.

177 *Norway House Post Journal*, 11–18 June 1855, HBCA: B.154/a/60, fo. 3–4.

178 HBCA: D.4/50, fo. 70–1, no. 23.

179 *Norway House Post Journal*, 11–18 June 1855, HBCA: B.154/a/60, fo. 3–4; and intermittently thereafter to 13 June 1857.

180 *Norway House Post Journal*, 17–18 September 1855, HBCA: B.154/a/60, fo. 15. A possible second trial was referred to in a June 1855 letter from Sir George Simpson to a Norway House official: "In the event of the death of Paulette Paul from the wounds inflicted by the man Patenaude, it would be proper to bring the latter to Norway House next summer for trial ... there by the Recorder in the month of June." Simpson to Sinclair ("Private & Confidential"), 28 June 1855, HBCA: D.4/50, fo.

67. Patenaude had not yet been captured at that point, and perhaps he never was, there being no evidence of his ever having been tried.

181 Select Committee Report, Q. 1145 and 1190; *Norway House Post Journal*, 13–16 June 1856, HBCA: B.154/a/62, fo. 12ff. Where the convicts were sent is not known, except that the latter document indicates they were initially taken to York Factory. Ungava seems a probable ultimate destination.

182 Johnson to London, 20 October 1857, HBCA: A.11/96, fo. 174ff., emphasis added. That document also describes several other of the facts related below.

183 Ibid.

184 The absence of affidavit evidence was not the only legal shortcoming. Barnston also failed to order imprisonment at Red River in the arrest warrant; and mere "purpose" was no crime in any event.

185 Johnson to London, 20 October 1857, HBCA: A.11/96, fo. 174ff.

186 Johnson to Simpson ("Private"), 4 November 1857, HBCA: D.5/45, fo. 196.

187 Smith to Simpson, 17 February 1858, HBCA: A.6/33, fo. 78ff.

188 Simpson to Johnson, 18 February 1858, HBCA: D.4/54, fo. 67–8.

189 Simpson to McDermot ("Private"), 21 January 1858, HBCA: D.4/84A, fo. 38ff.

190 Fraser to Simpson, 17 September 1858, HBCA: A.6/33, fo. 292.

191 Simpson to Berens ("Private & Confidential"), 1 June 1860, HBCA: D.4/84A, fo. 55ff.

192 Galbraith (1976, 203–6).

CHAPTER EIGHT

1 The company's General Letter of 16 April 1862 reported that the war was not affecting the St Paul supply route to Rupert's Land. HBCA: A.6/37, fo. 85ff., no. 13.

2 Quoted in Goodwin (2005, 122).

3 NW640713.

4 NW641121.

5 For a full and lively account of these events, see Creighton (1964).

6 Governor and Committee, General Letter, 17 April 1861, HBCA: A.6/36, fo. 101ff., no. 26.

7 Hargrave (1871, 296–300).

8 Lamb (2000).

9 Fraser to Dallas, 7 October 1863, HBCA: A.6/38, fo. 334–5.

10 Head to Dallas ("Private & Confidential"), 19 April 1864, HBCA: A.7/4, fo. 34–5.
11 NW650801.
12 NW651023. An accompanying *Nor'-Wester* editorial deplored this position.
13 See, for example, Governor and Committee, general letter, 27 April 1865, HBCA: A.6/39, fo. 478ff. Waning interest in government can be detected in earlier newsletters as well.
14 NW620205.
15 Berens to McTavish ("Private"), 28 September 1860, HBCA: A.7/3, fo. 40; Fraser to McTavish, 28 September 1860, HBCA: A.6/35, fo. 172ff. McTavish was to remain at Red River, however, Simpson's Montreal responsibilities being assumed by others.
16 Berens to Dallas ("Private"), 25 January 1861, HBCA: A.7/3, fo. 58–60.
17 Lamb (2000).
18 Fraser to McTavish ("Confidential"), 5 December 1861, HBCA: A.6/36, fo. 353ff.; Fraser to McTavish, 1 March 1862, HBCA: A.6/37, fo. 34ff.
19 Berens to Dallas ("Private"), 25 January 1861, HBCA: A.7/3, fo. 58–60.
20 Dallas's approach to the General Court was different. Although also entitled to preside over it, he declined to even attend its sittings. The consequences of that are discussed below.
21 NW620528.
22 Lamb (2000).
23 Berens to Dallas ("Private"), 24 February 1862, HBCA: A.7/3, fo. 84–6.
24 Governor and Committee, general letter, 5 March 1864, HBCA: A.6/39, fo. 65ff.
25 See the *Commentary* to case 238, vol. 2, 409.
26 Oliver (1914, 50).
27 Fraser to Dallas, 15 August 1863, HBCA: A.6/38, fo. 290.
28 James R. Clare relieved him of his commercial responsibilities as chief factor in late 1864. Clare to London, 14 November 1864, HBCA: A.11/97, fo. 262.
29 Reprinted in NW610315.
30 Oliver (1914, 68, 70). Roger Goulet was appointed in November 1865. Fraser to McTavish, 10 November 1865, HBCA: A.6/40, fo. 71. But he did not take his seat until January 1866.
31 Oliver (1914, 553).
32 NW641109. Before that he was said to be "visiting" England.
33 NW63111. At least one full-time employee was overlooked: jailer Antoine Grouette. Casual employees, such as road labourers, were also omitted.

34 NW640723. The sums quoted are rounded to full pounds. The total of £1,075 is somewhat misleading since the HBC always paid the salaries of the governor and recorder. The £100 salary of Executive Officer William Smith is divided equally between the law and nonlaw categories since he served both the governor and the courts. The figures for this year may have been distorted by the extraordinary expense of £288 for the relief of destitute Sioux visitors.

35 *Public Interest v. Corbett*, case 238, vol. 2, 366.

36 Case 77, vol. 2, 136.

37 Fraser to McTavish, 17 February 1861, HBCA: A.6/36, fo. 99ff.

38 NW610601.

39 See generally Stubbs (1967, 90–134); and Pannekoek (2000a).

40 NW610215.

41 One Canadian was expressly excluded. Although Francis Johnson was "very, very desirous" of returning to his old post, and was favoured by governor-designate Dallas, London authorities felt, as Simpson had, that he was "by no means a fit person to fill that office." Berens to Dallas ("Confidential"), 16 April 1862, HBCA: A.7/3, fo. 92ff. Canadian authorities thought differently; in July 1865 the *Nor'-Wester* reported Johnson's appointment to the Superior Court of Lower Canada. NW650704.

42 Berens to Dallas ("Confidential"), 16 April 1862, HBCA: A.7/3, fo. 92ff.

43 Stubbs (1967, 144); Hargrave (1871, 244). The latter says Black served as minister for lands in New South Wales.

44 Berens to Dallas ("Confidential"), 16 April 1862, HBCA: A.7/3, fo. 92–4.

45 Berens to Dallas ("Confidential"), 16 April 1862, HBCA: A.7/3, fo. 92–4; Fraser to Dallas, 1 August 1862, HBCA: A.6/37, fo. 257ff.

46 Fraser to McTavish, 17 April 1862, HBCA: A.6/37, fo. 107ff.

47 Fraser to McTavish, 25 October 1865, HBCA: A.6/40.

48 McTavish to London, 9 June 1862, HBCA: A.11/97, fo. 9; Black to London, 21 June 1862, HBCA: A.11/97, fo. 15ff.

49 Clare to London, 27 March 1865, HBCA: A.11/98, fo. 29.

50 NW620830.

51 NW620911.

52 Case 238, vol. 2, 366.

53 Smith (2000).

54 Oliver (1914, 442).

55 Ibid., 479.

56 MAN710923. See Bumsted (2000, 127–48).

57 NW631217. There were no formal requirements for doing so at that point. Ross's first case as agent might have been *The Queen v. O'Brian*, case 203, vol. 2, 318, in June 1860.
58 Although Corbett undoubtedly committed the acts of which he was accused, it is doubtful that he violated the relevant statute, which was enacted after the then-operative 1837 reception date of English law by Assiniboia. See vol. 2, 413.
59 Berens to Dallas ("Private & Confidential"), 6 May 1863, HBCA: A.7/3, fo. 164. Growing confidence in Black would soon lead to his being formally appointed acting governor of Assiniboia during periods of McTavish's absence. Fraser to Black, 5 January 1865, HBCA: A.6/39, fo. 362. From at least that point forward, any possible doubt as to the validity of court sessions held in the absence of the governor was removed.
60 NW630303. This comment was qualified by the observation that many of Corbett's supporters thought Black had sided unfairly with the prosecution. James Ross, who probably penned the piece, was after all both part owner of the *Nor'-Wester* and Corbett's counsel.
61 NW640818.
62 Oliver (1914, 548).
63 Ibid., 558.
64 NW650704. Bruneau's wife died two days later.
65 Oliver (1914, 307).
66 Ibid., 361.
67 Ibid., 389.
68 Court records, vol. 2, 215.
69 Oliver (1914, 485).
70 Ens (2008, 183).
71 Dorge (2000b).
72 Oliver (1914, 560).
73 Ibid., 485–502.
74 Ibid., 534–5.
75 Laws of Assiniboia (1852), s. 34 (ibid., 378). No change was made in Laws of Assiniboia (1862), s. 53 (ibid., 500).
76 Bumsted (2000, 238n4) says that although the statute was not specified in the indictment, it was clearly implicit. Black's charge to the jury was explicit. NW630512.
77 The amendment was not given retroactive effect to the *Corbett* case or other earlier situations.
78 Related problems arose during Manitoba's early years, however. *Sinclair v. Mulligan* (1886) 3 Man. LR; (1888) 5 MR 17 (Man. QB). See also Gibson and Gibson (1972, 159–60).

79 The pamphlet version is preserved in AM: MG14, C23. A long *Nor'-Wester* editorial had recently deplored the lack of accessible laws. NW611015.
80 See case 246, vol. 2, 430, reported in NW631125.
81 Laws of Assiniboia (1862), s. 32 (Oliver 1914, 494–5). The Laws of Assiniboia (1852) had a ceiling of fifteen constables.
82 See McGrady (2010, ch. 3).
83 Oliver (1914, 511–13); Hargrave (1871, 253–4); NW621104.
84 According to the HBC's 1863 general letter, the British government had decided, for the first time, that "they are not bound to defend a territory held by a great company under Royal Charter." HBCA: A.6/38, fo. 116ff. The ongoing Rupert's Land negotiations were doubtless a factor.
85 Fraser to Dallas, 21 May 1863, HBCA: A.6/38, fo. 204ff.; Oliver (1914, 515–17).
86 Fraser to Ross, 2 September 1861, HBCA: A.6/36, fo. 149ff.
87 Fraser to McTavish, 2 September 1861, HBCA: A.6/36, fo. 148.
88 Oliver (1914, 505–8).
89 Ibid., 514.
90 Reynolds (1969–70, 2000).
91 The *Nor'-Wester* opposed McKenney's appointment because "no magistrate should be a retail liquor dealer ... A magistrate is an officer of the peace, and the intimate connection between ... [liquor vendors] and breaches of the peace is too manifest to require elucidation." NW610615. A few months later, the newspaper attacked Magistrate McKenney for refusing to allow a constable to serve a summons on someone while on McKenney's own premises. NW611001.
92 AM: MG2, B4–3. These 783 cases are not the totality of civil litigation during the period but only those cases – generally where the plaintiff was successful – in which the sheriff was called upon to collect or administer the monies involved.
93 For a fuller account, see the *Commentary* to case 238, vol. 2, 409.
94 It would not have been a difficult task. The *Nor'-Wester* reported in August 1861 that part of the prison palisade had been blown down in a windstorm – not for the first time – and although repairs were made, the newspaper lamented that the structure was "too old to stand long." NW610801.
95 It would happen again in 1868, however, when Sheriff McKenney imprisoned his estranged half-brother, John Schultz, while enforcing a claim in which he had a personal interest. Schultz was soon freed by his redoubtable wife and a mob of supporters. See vol. 2, 218.
96 NW630512.
97 Bumsted (2003b, 142).

98 NW610415.

99 Ens (1996, 33).

100 The following account is largely from Bumsted (2003b, 166–8); Hargrave (1871, 266, 290–2, 313–18, 339–44); and Oliver (1914, 530–6).

101 Munro (2006, 11).

102 Oliver (1914, 535–6).

103 Dallas to Fraser, 5 and 10 May 1864, HBCA: A.12/43, fo. 216ff., 225ff. When a Sioux visitor was murdered in the settlement the previous winter, allegedly by local Saulteaux, Dallas lamented to London that "such is our weakness that we dare not stir the animosity of the Saulteaux by bringing the culprit to justice." Dallas to Fraser, 30 December 1863, HBCA: A.12/43, fo.156ff.

104 Bumsted (2003b, 168).

105 Pannekoek (1991).

106 This account is based on several *Nor'-Wester* items: NW640510, NW640531, NW640818, NW640916, and NW650206. The report chiefly followed is a letter in NW640916, which, although written on behalf of the defendant McBain, is the most detailed, and most plausible, of those available.

107 Although the defendant claimed Peter Garrioch was again the jury foreman, the latter denied this. NW650205. He certainly was foreman later in the day. NW640818.

108 Apparently, no one noticed that the same legislation required sales of land to be in writing, thereby invalidating Andrew's alleged (presumably) verbal sale to McBain as well.

109 NW640818. Although signed by two other jurors besides Garrioch, the letter's style was unmistakably his.

110 NW650206.

111 Oliver (1914, 538–9).

112 NW610215. Even that criticism was called "exaggerated" by a reader in the next issue. NW610301.

113 Oliver (1914, 518–19). Taylor's dismissal was seemingly a consequence of his behaviour in *Corbett*, case 238, vol. 2, 366.

114 Bumsted (2003b, 146). See also Bumsted (2000, 87–9).

115 NW611101.

116 Ens (1996, 110); NW651023.

117 Munro (2006, 81–2). Although written two years later, about a different part of the prairies, this matches descriptions of the Red River experience. See Hargrave (1871, 349–50).

118 Oliver (1914, 552–3).

119 Ibid., 555.
120 NW620528.
121 Bumsted (2003b, 179).
122 Case 190, vol. 2, 302.
123 NW641115.
124 NW650513.
125 NW650605.
126 NW650921.
127 Bumsted (2003b, 92).
128 Ens (1996, 120).
129 Ibid., 120–1.
130 Black to London, 21 June 1862, HBCA: A.11/97, fo. 15.
131 Peel (1974, 7, 13). Ross did not abandon journalism altogether. A year later he was an editor of the *Toronto Globe,* finding, like Adam Thom before him, that preparation for the bar could be combined with journalism. NW650704. He also worked for a while as an editor of the *Hamilton Spectator* (Smith 2000).
132 Bumsted (1999a, 223). He had partial medical training (Clark 2000a).
133 NW650330.
134 NW620806.
135 NW650330.
136 Peel (1974, 11); NW650330.
137 NW651002, NW651023.
138 Bumsted (2003b, 170).
139 NW630715.
140 Bumsted (2003b, 170–1).
141 NW620402. The Laws of Assiniboia were accordingly amended; in Oliver (1914) compare page 375 with pages 485–502. Ross's temporary move to Toronto probably did not affect this arrangement since his family remained at the settlement.
142 NW620305, NW620319.
143 NW620625, NW630722, NW641121.
144 NW640803.
145 NW621104.
146 NW640520.
147 Case 244, vol. 2, 426.
148 Oliver (1914, 545, 548–9).
149 The litigation began with case 328a, vol. 2, 497. See Reynolds (1969–70).
150 The newspaper may itself have been at least partially responsible for the name. In an article published almost a year previously, and headed

"A Name Wanted," it had proposed that the choice of an Indian name would be appropriate for reasons of "sweetness, significance, and as well a just debt to the vanishing tribes." It requested information from its readers "as to the Indian name of this place, both Cree and Saulteaux." Until something better was suggested, it concluded, "We have thought of 'Winnipeg' as being not inappropriate." NW641128.

CHAPTER NINE

1 See vol. 1, 173.
2 The Fenian Brotherhood, an Irish American paramilitary organization, conducted several, mostly unsuccessful, incursions into New Brunswick and Canada/Ontario in 1866 and 1870. See Macdonald (1910); and R.B. Brown (2009).
3 NW670713.
4 NW671214.
5 Bumsted (2003b, 172–5).
6 NW680613.
7 NW670704.
8 Ellice to Labouchere, 30 September 1856, HBCA: A.7/2, fo. 47ff.
9 A letter from London headquarters assured McTavish that his views were not "lost sight of," but it still kept him in the dark. Smith to McTavish, 18 July 1868, HBCA: A.6/42, fo. 283ff.
10 Morton (1956, 24).
11 NW690724.
12 Hargrave (1871, 418).
13 Ibid., 449–51.
14 McTavish to Smith, 26 December 1868, HBCA: A.12/45, fo. 140–1.
15 NW690724.
16 Oliver (1914, 579–80).
17 NW690522, NW690619.
18 NW6909231.
19 NW660224.
20 Case 250, vol. 2, 435. Was "Aurica" actually Judge Black?
21 NW690913.
22 See vol. 1, 229ff.
23 Begg (1894, vol. 2, 460).
24 See Bumsted (2003b, 168, 178–86; 2000, 149–61).
25 Low water levels beyond the settlement were probably also responsible for a mutiny by two boat crews that refused to make the trip from

Norway House to York Factory in 1867 and were successfully sued for the resulting losses (case 368, vol. 2, 519).

26 NW680704.

27 McTavish to Smith, 29 September 1868, HBCA: A.12/45, fo. 103.

28 McTavish to Smith, 27 October 1868, HBCA: A.12/45, fo. 113.

29 For the committee's minutes, see AM: MG2, B6.

30 Bumsted (2000, 160–1).

31 "Memoirs of Louis Schmidt," translated in Morton (1956, 460).

32 MAN701210 and MAN701210, reporting the 1870 census. The subsequently published official results were slightly higher.

33 Residents of Upper Fort Garry were enumerated with those of St James.

34 Morton (1956, 206–9). The accompanying illustration, based on Begg's map, identifies the following buildings that figured, either directly or because of their occupants, in events or cases dealt with herein: (1) Fort Garry, (2) combined courthouse and jail, (3) HBC Winnipeg store, (4) William Drever Sr's store and home, (5) O'Lone's Saloon, (6) Presbyterian Church, (7) Episcopal Church, (8) Colonel John S. Dennis's office and home and Ryder Larsen's photography studio, (9) Sheriff Henry McKenney's store and home, (10) George Emmerling's hotel, (11) John Schultz's drug store, general store, flagpole, and home, (12) Develine's hotel, (13) burnt ruins of Andrew McDermot's former home, (14) H.S. Donaldson's stationery store and the *Nor'-Wester* office, (15) Monchamp's Saloon, (16) A.G.B. Bannatyne and Alexander Begg's store and Bannatyne's home, (17) James Ross's home, (18) Fire Brigade engine house, (19) James Mulligan's home, (20) Charles Garrett's hotel, (21) William Drever Jr's store and home, (22) St Boniface Sisters of Charity School, (23) Coroner Dr Curtis J. Bird's home, (24) Hy. McDermot's home and steam mill, and (25) Andrew McDermot's new home and warehouses.

35 See vol. 1, 209.

36 Case 455, vol. 2, 579.

37 See cover illustration.

38 A recent arrival, Spence was a keen Canadian annexationist (Peel 2000c).

39 McTavish to Smith, 12 March 1867, HBCA: A.12/44, fo. 268ff.; Oliver (1914, 573).

40 McTavish to Smith, 12 March 1867, HBCA: A.12/44, fo. 268ff.

41 See generally Clark (2000b); and Bumsted (2000, 163–77).

42 McTavish to Smith, 5 March 1867, HBCA: A.12/44, fo. 265ff. He had noted previously that increasing taxation would be difficult without

increasing the council's representativeness. McTavish to London, 22 August 1866, HBCA: A.12/44, fo. 161ff.

43 McTavish to Smith, 18 April 1867, HBCA: A.12/44, fo. 296ff.

44 Clark (2000). Note that "Canadian" now meant something antithetical to its earlier meaning of "francophone from Lower Canada."

45 McTavish to Smith, 18 April 1867, HBCA: A.12/44, fo. 296ff.

46 McTavish to Smith, 29 April 1867, HBCA: A.12/44, fo. 300ff.

47 McTavish to Smith, 18 April 1867, HBCA: A.12/44, fo. 296ff. Of Dease and Inkster, the plaudits were cooler, but it was felt that "their admission to Council cannot do any harm." McTavish to Smith, 29 April 1867, HBCA: A.12/44, fo. 300ff.

48 Fraser to McTavish, 15 June 1867, HBCA: A.6/41, fo. 214ff.

49 McTavish to Smith, 15 September 1867, HBCA: A.12/44, fo. 326ff.

50 See Eddy (1963); and Moir (1969).

51 See vol. 1, 193.

52 For a glowing description of the area, see NW680915.

53 Oliver (1914, 560–1).

54 Hargrave (1871, 392–3); Opinion of Montague Bere, 13 May 1867, HBCA: A.39/7, fo. 340ff.

55 Deposition of Hugh Francis O'Lone, 12 February 1867, quoting Opinion of Montague Bere, 13 May 1867, HBCA: A.39/7, fo. 340ff.

56 Opinion of Montague Bere, 13 May 1867, HBCA: A.39/7, fo. 340ff.

57 NW670525.

58 NW680808.

59 Peel (2000c).

60 This figure referred to the total population, not just to those attending the organizational meeting.

61 Oliver (1914, 873–4). Spence also sought recognition from Canada (Peel 2000c).

62 This boundary was difficult to identify since the Municipal District of Assiniboia was circular, and greater Assiniboia included the entire area claimed.

63 The Council of Manitobah, in its newborn judicial capacity, convened in temporary quarters until it had collected the tax revenues required to finance construction of the council building and the combined courthouse and jail.

64 Hargrave (1871, 429–30). Another account says, "A brawl ensued, shots were fired into the ceiling, the oil lamp was overturned, and the court sitting ended" (Peel 2000c).

65 Oliver (1914, 877–8).

66 Hargrave (1871, 445).

67 Smith to McTavish, 15 February 1868, HBCA: A.6/42, fo. 81ff. There had never been any legal impediment to extending governmental services beyond the Municipal District of Assiniboia, since both the council and the court were created to serve all of Assiniboia, as defined in Lord Selkirk's grant.

68 Smith to McTavish, 2 May 1868, HBCA: A.6/42, fo. 168ff.

69 Oliver (1914, 587).

70 Hargrave (1871, 445). The case was tried at a special session of the court in September (case 414, vol. 2, 537).

71 McTavish to Fraser, 13 February 1866, HBCA: A.12/44, fo. 127ff.

72 Oliver (1914, 563–4).

73 Ibid., 567; Hargrave (1871, 396).

74 McTavish to London, 31 July 1866, HBCA: A.12/44, fo. 155; Hargrave (1871, 396–7).

75 Oliver (1914, 567–8).

76 McTavish to London, 31 July 1866, HBCA: A.12/44, fo. 155.

77 Case 325, August 1866, vol. 2, 491.

78 Munro (2006, 78–9).

79 McTavish to Smith, 2 February 1869, HBCA: A.12/45, fo. 168.

80 Hargrave (1871, 465–6).

81 NW690122.

82 Governor and Committee, annual circular letter, 16 April 1867, HBCA: A.6/41, fo. 126ff.

83 Christie to McTavish, 2 January 1867, HBCA: A.12/44, fo. 369ff.

84 McTavish to Smith, 26 February 1867, HBCA: A.12/44, fo. 261ff.; McTavish to Smith, 9 April 1867, HBCA: A.12/44, fo. 280ff.

85 Fraser to McTavish, 13 April 1867, HBCA: A.6/41, fo. 121ff.

86 McTavish to Smith, 15 September 1867, HBCA: A.12/44, fo. 326ff.

87 St Albert residents to Christie, 12 January 1867, HBCA: A.12/44, fo. 312.

88 Christie to McTavish, 13 January 1867, HBCA: A.12/44, fo. 310, emphasis in original.

89 McTavish to Smith, 15 September 1867, HBCA: A.12/44, fo. 326ff.

90 McTavish to Smith ("Private"), 6 August 1867, HBCA: A.12/44, fo. 318ff.

91 Adultery.

92 McTavish to Smith, 15 September 1867, HBCA: A.12/44, fo. 326ff.

93 Campbell to McTavish, 30 October 1867, HBCA: A.12/44, fo. 397–9; Munro (2006, 87).

94 Finlayson to Campbell, 25 November 1867, HBCA: A.12/45, fo. 15.

95 Smith to McTavish, 15 February 1868, HBCA: A.6/42, fo. 81ff.; McTavish to Smith, 31 March 1868, HBCA: A.12/45, fo. 27; Smith to McTavish, 11 April 1868, HBCA: A.6/42, fo. 132ff.
96 McTavish to Fraser ("Private"), 28 February 1866, HBCA: A.12/44, fo. 138ff.
97 Oliver (1914, 570, 574–6).
98 Ibid., 565; Hargrave (1871, 417–18).
99 Oliver (1914, 600–2, 604).
100 Ibid., 602–3.
101 NW690205.
102 Oliver (1914, 566).
103 The story is told more fully in the *Commentary* to case 354b, May 1868, vol. 2, 530.
104 Hargrave (1871, 427).
105 McTavish to Smith, 3 February 1868, HBCA: A.12/45, fo. 8; McTavish to Smith, 18 February 1868, HBCA: A.12/45, fo. 9–10. See also McTavish to Smith, 20 January 1868, HBCA: A.12/45, fo. 3–5.
106 McTavish to Smith, 28 April 1868, HBCA: A.12/45, fo. 55–6. The printing press incident led indirectly to a slander claim against Bown at the next session of the General Court. See the *Commentary* to case 403, vol. 2, 534.
107 Case 351, vol. 2, 507.
108 The only recently enacted law of the settlement was a revision of the liquor licensing laws in November and December 1868 (Oliver 1914, 591, 596).
109 Ibid., 583.
110 Ibid., 584, emphasis added.
111 McTavish to Smith, 18 February 1868, HBCA: fo. 9–10.
112 Case 354c, vol. 2, 566.
113 Oliver (1914, 591–6). See Recorder Black's moving grand jury address concerning public drunkenness, quoted in the *Commentary* to *Queen v. Demarrais,* case 325, August 1866, vol. 2, 491.
114 McTavish to Smith, 1 December 1868, HBCA: A.12/45, fo. 128–9. The Lower District Petty Court trial that convicted the HBC salesman was probably chaired by long-time company critic Donald Gunn.
115 Oliver (1914, 595). Council agreed in 1866 that the Presbyterian Church could receive all marriage licence fees paid by members of that congregation, a privilege that the Anglicans and Roman Catholics had long enjoyed (ibid., 568). Although not mentioned in the council minutes, that privilege was probably now extended to the Methodists.

116 Peel (2000c); Brown (2001).

117 *Connolly v. Woolrich and Johnson* (1869), in *La Revue Légal* (Montreal), vol. 1, 253–400. An appeal to the Judicial Committee of the Privy Council was commenced but then withdrawn when the parties reached a settlement.

118 The petty courts had certainly been busy. Sheriff's Book, 1863–71, AM: MG2, B4–2; Sheriff's Lower District Court Record Book, 1868–72, AM: MG2, B4–6.

119 Governor and Committee, annual circular letter, 2 May 1866, HBCA: A.6/40, fo. 224ff. The same attempt was made with regard to the stipend paid to the bishop of Rupert's Land – with the same result.

120 Oliver (1914, 598).

121 Ibid., 568.

122 Hargrave (1871, 92). The same author describes Smith's varied career at 208–12.

123 A Métis guide, fur trader, and jack-of-all-trades trusted by whites, Halfbreeds, and Indians alike, McKay was only in his late thirties but already had an almost legendary reputation. He would participate importantly in Manitoba's transition from company territory to province (Turner 2000).

124 Oliver (1914, 598).

125 Cowan came to Red River as a physician to the Chelsea Pensioners in 1848. After marrying a local woman, he took a commercial position with the company, rising by 1867 to the rank of chief company officer at Fort Garry. He was appointed to the Council of Assiniboia in 1853 and to the court in November 1866.

126 Black to Smith, 5 August 1868, HBCA: A.11/98, fo. 247. It was promptly accepted. Smith to Black, 6 October 1868, A.6/42, fo. 345.

127 Cowan to Smith, 27 March 1869, HBCA: A.12/45, fo. 217ff.

128 See vol. 1, 213.

129 Hargrave (1871, 398).

130 NW660824.

131 NW671214.

132 Case 280d, vol. 2, 483.

133 Cases 313, 314, 315, and 316, vol. 2, 484ff.

134 Case 354a, May 1867, vol. 2, 510.

135 See vol. 1, 218.

136 Case 354b, May 1868, vol. 2, 530.

137 Case 354c, May 1869, vol. 2, 566.

138 See generally Gibson, Gibson, and Harvey (1983).

139 Case 414, September 1868, vol. 2, 537.
140 NW680929, NW681017.
141 Case 238, February 1863, vol. 2, 336.
142 McTavish to Fraser, 10 September 1864, HBCA: A.12/44, fo. 15ff.
143 McTavish to Smith, 2 February 1869, HBCA: A.12/45, fo. 168.
144 Hargrave to Smith, 17 April 1869, HBCA: A.12/45, fo. 251–2.
145 McTavish to Smith, 21 September 1869, HBCA: A.12/45, fo. 290ff.
146 Smith to Cowan, 6 March 1870, HBCA: A.6/45, fo. 234ff.; Smith to Cowan, 20 May 1870, HBCA: A.6/44, fo. 12ff.; MAN710128.
147 J. McTavish to London, 3 August 1870, HBCA: A.11/99, fo. 224–5.
148 NW691026; case 454, vol. 2, 573.
149 Oliver (1914, 559).
150 Cases 300b and 309, vol. 2, 482.
151 McTavish to Fraser, 22 January 1866, HBCA: A.12/44, fo. 105ff. Although "probate" strictly refers to proving the authenticity of wills, probate courts often also supervise testate and intestate estates, as well as guardianships.
152 Opinion of Montague Bere, HBCA: A.39/7, fo. 336–9. Of course, invoking the aid of the archbishop's court would not be feasible for Red River's Roman Catholic majority.
153 Cardwell to Head, 5 April 1866, HBCA: A.13/15, fo. 49.
154 Head to Cardwell, 6 April 1866, HBCA: A.13/15, fo. 51–2; Cardwell to Head, 16 April 1866, HBCA: A.13/15, fo. 56.
155 Case 310b, May 1866, vol. 2, 488.
156 Oliver (1914, 569, 602).
157 Cases 422 and 423, November 1868, vol. 2, 533.
158 McTavish to Fraser ("Private"), 12 December 1865, HBCA: A.12/44, fo. 81ff.
159 McTavish to Fraser ("Private"), 19 December 1865, HBCA: A.12/44, fo. 79ff.
160 Smith to "Miss McTavish" (Clifton), 28 September 1872, HBCA: A.36/4, fo. 146–7. No other direct evidence of Smith's defalcations is known to the author.
161 The moment when "French Halfbreeds" began to call themselves "Métis" is difficult to pinpoint. Some undoubtedly used the term well before the uprising about to be described brought it into general use, but this seems as good a point as any to adopt it herein. In more recent times, "Métis" has also been applied, sometimes without an accented *e*, to the group called "English Halfbreeds" in this book. Since that usage was rarely, if ever, heard at the time, it is not adopted here; and

"Halfbreed" continues to be used where the French and English mixed-blood populations are referred to collectively.

162 Mair came west as paymaster of the Dawson road construction crew.

163 Morton (1956, 398).

164 Ibid., 401.

165 Bumsted (1996, 42), quoting from a letter by Alexander Ross Jr.

166 The Indians also worried about their Aboriginal entitlements, of course. Saulteaux chief Peguis expressed their concerns. The Halfbreeds were better organized to take action, however.

167 McTavish to Smith, 10 August 1869, HBCA: A.12/45, fo. 282–3.

168 McTavish to Smith, 9 June 1868, HBCA: A.12/45, fo. 74ff. An "outfit" was a fur trade business year. See also McTavish to Smith, 28 April 1868, HBCA: A.12/45, fo. 8ff.; and McTavish to Smith, [day unknown] April 1868, HBCA: A.12/45, fo. 55ff.

169 McTavish to Smith, 10 August 1869, HBCA: A.12/45, fo. 280.

170 McTavish to Smith, 24 August 1869, HBCA: A.12/45, fo. 284–5.

171 NW690831.

172 Morton (1956, 409).

173 Oliver (1914, 878–80).

174 Morton (1956, 46); McTavish to Smith, 12 October 1869, LAC: RG6, C1, vol. 12, fo. 1043 (AM: reel M22).

175 The story of the insurrection from this point is well told in Siggins (1994, 98ff.).

176 Morton (1956, 411). Bruce was described as president and Riel as secretary of the "Assembly" to which the letter referred (Siggins 1994, 101).

177 Siggins (1994, 106).

178 McTavish to Smith ("Private"), 13 October 1869, HBCA: A.12/45, fo. 310–2.

179 Oliver (1914, 615–18).

180 Ibid.

181 Ibid.

182 Ibid., 618.

183 Siggins (1994, 103).

184 Morton (1956, 53), citing Parliament of Canada, *Sessional Papers*, 1870, vol. 12, page unknown. Colonel Dennis also complained to Cowan about the closing-down of his survey; but the magistrate declined to prosecute that act too, saying, "it would be best ... [to proceed] by persuasion rather than by force." NW691025. His persuasion was also of no avail.

185 Oliver (1914, 619).

186 LAC: Macdonald Papers, MG271, C6, vol. 1, 40779.

187 Gibson, Gibson, and Harvey (1983, 97–148).
188 Ibid.
189 McTavish to Smith, 2 November 1869, HBCA: A.12/45, fo. 313–17.
190 Oliver (1914, 888–9).
191 Morton (1956, 164).
192 Ibid., 172. He also complained about not being allowed to speak.
193 Ibid., 167ff.
194 Ibid., 422. This was Riel's rendition. As both convention secretary and chief spokesman for his party, his hands were full, and he appended a note to the minutes: "I cannot very well write and take note of the discussion, seeing that I am obliged to speak all the time ... But what I have written is always the sense, and almost always the terms, of what was said in French." Like Bannatyne, McTavish was married to a mixed-blood daughter of Andrew McDermot.
195 *Commentary* to case 452(b), vol. 2, 576.
196 Morton (1956, 93–5, 213–14); Oliver (1914, 893, 896–9).
197 *Daily Press* (St Paul), 21 December 1869.
198 Morton (1956, 427). Again, this is a translation of Riel's own notes, written after the event.
199 Ibid., 209–10.
200 *Daily Press* (St Paul), 1 November 1869. See Gibson, Gibson, and Harvey (1983, 120).
201 Morton (1956, 428).
202 Ibid., 428. Riel's after-the-event notes may well have polished this transcript of his outburst.
203 Ibid., 215–18.
204 Dennis to McDougall, 2 December 1869, LAC: RG6, C1, vol. 6 (AM: reel M22).
205 "Should we succeed in getting hold of ... [Stutsman], I shall put him in a strong room ... under the charge of my friend Prince, the Indian Chief, and his warriors until he may be delivered by some due, but we shall hope tedious, course of law."
206 Morton (1956, 214).
207 The lengthy tripartite negotiations reached agreement on the terms for Rupert's Land's transfer to Canada in March.
208 Morton (1956, 218–20).
209 Ibid., 426.
210 It was dubious because the March agreement was simply a tripartite contract to do certain things – pay money to the company, surrender possession to the Crown, and transfer control to Canada – *at a future*

date. It made no *immediate* governmental changes. There was a later time – December 1869 – when the termination of both the HBC's legal right to govern and its physical power to do so coincided to create a constitutional vacuum that justified establishing a grassroots provisional government, but the insurgents were already guilty of several legal violatons by then.

211 Mulligan, who had resisted early actions of the insurgents, was imprisoned with Schultz and his coterie.

212 Morton (1956, 67).

213 Macdonald to Rose, 26 November 1869, LAC: Macdonald Papers, vol. 101; Morton (1956, 450–4).

214 Howe to Archibald, 24 December 1869, LAC: RG6, C1, vol. 12 (AM: reel M22). The conduct of Colonel Dennis was subjected to even more scathing criticism, and Acting Governor Black was praised for refusing to invoke martial law.

215 The "if" was important. Because the territory had *not* been surrendered to the Crown and transferred to Canada as McDougall's proclamation had asserted, he was *not* "invested with the legal title to govern." The HBC retained the legal right to govern, but it had lost the physical ability to do so.

216 Morton (1956, 453), citing Parliament of Canada, *Sessional Papers*, 1870, vol. 12, 141–4.

217 Ibid., 75.

218 McDougall to McTavish, 16 December 1869, LAC: RG6, C1, vol. 12 (AM reel M22).

219 The HBC's entitlement to govern was subject to such property and self-government rights as flowed from Aboriginal title.

220 Gibson and Lercher (1986).

221 Peel (1974, 23, 25).

222 Morton (1956, 227).

223 Ibid., 236.

224 Ibid., 239.

225 Ibid., 255–6.

226 Bruce had indeed been seriously ill but was recovering by this point. Although he had certainly been more than a figurehead, and may well have been originally considered a more suitable president than the younger, less well-known, mercurial Riel, the latter had emerged as the real leader, and Bruce was not wholly in accord with his approach. Bruce remained a member of the Provisional Governing Council but not a prominent one. See Ronaghan (2000).

227 Morton (1956, 228).
228 Ibid., 246.
229 Ibid., 247–9. It turned out that force was not needed, the visitors being persuaded by James McKay, Louis Riel, and a handful of others to leave peaceably.
230 Morton (1956, 455–7).
231 Ibid., 230.
232 Ibid., 233–5. The case would haunt those charged with administering justice until the creation of Manitoba courts. See cases 455a, 455b, 455c, 455d, vol. 2, 579, 584, 585, and 597. It is of some interest, incidentally, that despite the injunction against HBC functionaries exercising their former authority, a coroner's inquest was held into Johnson's death, presumably in accordance with the longstanding procedures prevailing before the insurrection (Morton 1956, 235). Riel's later taunt to Dr Bird that no inquest had been held (ibid., 301) was mistaken.

CHAPTER TEN

1 Oliver (1914, 900–1).
2 Siggins (1994, 131).
3 Ibid., 130–1.
4 Reford (2000). Smith arrived on 27 December, preceded the previous day by Thibault and followed by De Salaberry on 6 January.
5 Oliver (1914, 907–8).
6 Emphasis added.
7 Smith's report, 12 April 1870 (Oliver 1914, 920).
8 Siggins (1994, 134–5).
9 Ibid., 135–6.
10 Oliver (1914, 922–3); Siggins (1994, 137–8).
11 Smith admitted that "a majority of those who had seceded from Riel were again on friendly terms with him" (Oliver 1914, 923).
12 Most of the following account is based on Morton (1956, 265–77). See also Siggins (1994, 139–42).
13 Oliver (1914, 924).
14 Morton (1956, 276).
15 Ibid., 234.
16 Ibid., 236.
17 Ibid., 259.
18 Ibid., 242.
19 Ibid., 253.

20 Ibid., 256.
21 Stutsman to Riel, 11 January 1870, AM: Riel Papers, no. 20, emphasis in original.
22 Morton (1956, 259).
23 Ibid.
24 Ibid., 285. The conventions and subsequent proceedings are reported there and in the *New Nation.*
25 Ibid., 294. Sometimes social lubricants detracted from the quality of debate: "James Ross spoke a little too much today and had to be stopped – he had drunk a little too much" (ibid., 293).
26 Ibid., 287.
27 Ibid., 295.
28 Ibid.
29 Ibid., 296.
30 Ibid., 299.
31 Ibid., 300.
32 A coroner's inquest *was* held into Johnson's death (ibid., 235).
33 Ibid., 301.
34 Ibid.
35 This was not an aspersion on Black, who had resigned as recorder long ago and would soon perform a much more important service for the settlement.
36 Ibid., 302–3. The Métis considered Dease an enemy.
37 Ibid., 303.
38 Ibid.
39 Ibid., 304–5.
40 Ibid., 306.
41 Riel declared Schultz an exile whom anyone was at liberty to shoot (ibid., 304).
42 Ibid., 303–8.
43 The only Canadian combatants absent from Kildonan were a few left to defend their Lower Fort stronghold.
44 Ibid., 312.
45 Ibid., 308–9.
46 Ibid., 311.
47 Ibid., 312n.
48 Ibid., 315.
49 Ibid., 313n. Smith told Joseph Howe on 12 April 1870 that Riel had pardoned Gaddy but had kept him in custody until he escaped on his own (Oliver 1914, 933).
50 Morton (1956, 316–17).

51 Ibid., 319.
52 Smith's Report to Howe, 12 April 1870 (Oliver 1914, 929).
53 Morton (1956, 376).
54 Ibid., 328. Other accounts differ a little in detail but not in substance. See "Thomas Scott's Body," in Bumsted (2000, 3–10).
55 See "Why Shoot Thomas Scott? A Study in Historical Evidence," in Bumsted (2000, 198–209).
56 Oliver (1914, 931–2).
57 Ibid., 932.
58 Sheer anger cannot be ruled out, of course.
59 Oliver (1914, 932).
60 Ibid., 933.
61 Morton (1956, 306–7).
62 Ibid., 323. Some elections remained to be held.
63 Ibid., 329.
64 Ibid., 331. The published account was accurate but devoid of editorial comment. NN700304.
65 Morton (1956, 334).
66 Ibid., 339.
67 NN700402. Seventeen prisoners, including Captain Boulton, were released the next day (Morton 1956, 337).
68 NN700402. The reason for the delay is not known. Perhaps Chief Justice James Ross, who later claimed to have been double-dealing, was stalling for time.
69 The company ceased circulating its notes, the settlement's chief currency, when the crisis began, and the use of specie also declined. Begg wrote on 14 March, "It is astonishing how little silver and gold is now in circulation – it seems as if people have been hoarding it up since our troubles commenced. Some ... [merchants] have had to issue cheques ... for change" (Morton 1956, 336). The first company note was issued in April (ibid., 353); by 18 April, Begg was saying, "Money is a little more plentiful" (ibid., 359).
70 NN700402.
71 Riel proclamation, 7 April 1870 (Oliver 1914, 918–19).
72 The pardons came with the condition that they "submit to the Government" and "discountenance or inform against dangerous gatherings."
73 NN700415. This was not Riel's first bid for Aboriginal support. On 23 March he had a short proclamation printed, addressed to Indians, informing them that the Provisional Government's demands of Canada

included the conclusion of treaties between Canada and the Indian tribes of Rupert's Land (Pannekoek 1991, 28).

74 Morton (1956, 360–5).

75 Ibid., 345.

76 Ibid., 311, 320.

77 Ibid., 337–8.

78 Ibid., 340, 342. Captain Boulton travelled with the Blacks.

79 Compare the original (ibid., 291–5) with the final version (Oliver 1914, 915–18).

80 Item twelve of the original list, concerning a local military force, had eventually been removed, however (Morton 1956, 293).

81 Ibid., 348. The choice was not final at that point. On 19 April, Riel gave the delegates a choice between "North-West" and "Manitoba" (Manitoba Culture, Heritage and Recreation 1984c).

82 Morton (1956, 345). The only item he then mentioned was that Canada should pay the Provisional Government's expenses. On 31 March he noted a rumour about the name change (ibid., 348).

83 Ibid., 341.

84 Ibid., 296.

85 Much of what follows draws upon Bumsted (1996, 171–91).

86 Compare Morton (1956, 339) with Oliver (1914, 919–36).

87 See the *Toronto Globe* report of the meeting (Morton 1956, 510ff.).

88 33 Vict., c. 3 (Canada).

89 Morton (1956, 384).

90 *Rupert's Land and North-Western Territory Order*, 23 June 1870 (UK), reprinted in appendices to *Revised Statutes of Canada 1970*, 257–77.

91 Schmidt memoire (Morton 1956, 477).

92 Morton (1956, 358).

93 See, for example, ibid., 338.

94 See, for example, ibid. 356–7.

95 Ibid., 359.

96 Ibid., 287.

97 Ibid., 342.

98 Ibid., 349.

99 Ibid., 350.

100 Ibid., 374.

101 Larsen was accused of shooting another man in a drunken affray. See case 455a, vol. 2, 579.

102 Morton (1956, 380). If Larsen, perhaps Red River's first resident photographer, had been apprehended, he might possibly have shed light on

an unusual recent crime: photographic counterfeiting of HBC currency. See NN700527; and Smith to D.A. Smith, 8 July 1870, HBCA: A.6/44, fo. 65ff.

103 Morton (1956, 373, 389).

104 Report of Major J. Wallace, enclosed in W. McDougall (Pembina) to J. Howe (Ottawa), November 1869, AM: RG6, C1, vol. 12, fo. 1074; Reynolds (2000).

105 Bumsted (1999a, 161).

106 Reynolds (1969–70); Reynolds (2000).

107 NN700624.

108 Royal to Howe, Despatch No. 16, 8 October 1870, LAC: unpaginated documents, RG6, C1, vol. 27 (AM: reel M24).

109 Morton (1956, 369, 370–1).

110 Ibid., 379, 384.

111 Ibid., 370, 374–5; NN70527; NN700603; NN700708.

112 Schmidt memoire (Morton 1956, 478). See also ibid., 383.

113 NN700415.

114 Morton (1956, 227).

115 Ibid., 233–5. Riel later accused Bird of *not* holding an inquest (ibid., 301). See also NN700107; and the *Commentary* to case 455a, vol. 2, 579.

116 He was not paid, however, for inquests held before his reappointment.

117 Morton (1956, 349).

118 Ronaghan (2000).

119 Huel (1985, 56).

120 Morton (1956, 348). Many years later Riel's secretary, Louis Schmidt, gave a less clear-cut account: a commission of three physicians was appointed to examine the man, an elderly francophone named Pillard; but Pillard refused to cooperate and continued to practise (ibid., 468, 475). The fact that the commissioners were also the complainants, and were all English, may have affected the situation.

121 Ibid., 365.

122 The collection of unpaid duties began on 29 June 1870 (ibid., 386).

123 NN700527. The executive met every Thursday (Morton 1956, 386).

124 Bumsted (1996, 184).

125 Published in NN700520.

126 Compare section 18 of the 1862 law (Oliver 1914, 489) with section 1 of the 1871 "Liquor Laws" (NN700520).

127 Morton (1956, 383); NN700624.

128 Ibid., 308.

129 Ibid., 324, 350. Begg thoroughly disliked Ross, however.

130 Huel (1985).
131 Begg's journal, 29 April 1870 (Morton 1956, 364).
132 NN700708.
133 *Manitoba News Letter*, 18 September 1870.
134 Morton (1956, 236, 239).
135 Ibid., 301.
136 Ibid., 322–3. Begg did not disclose who won.
137 Ibid., 355. Except for his initials – F.H. – nothing more is known about Burr.
138 Ibid., 357, 359.
139 Ibid., 346.
140 Ibid., 342.
141 NN700617. An account in Morton (1956, 380–1, 384) is less detailed and probably less accurate. Raymond was never brought to trial (Taylor 2005).
142 See the Introduction to Morton (1956, 127–8); and Louis Schmidt's recollection of the visit (ibid., 476–7).
143 Cooke to H.D. Cooke, 14 April 1870, Pennsylvania Historical Society: Cooke Papers (ibid. 128).
144 Ibid., 476.
145 Ibid., 128.
146 Ibid., 502.
147 Ibid., 477. A contributing factor may have been the sudden recall of Winnipeg's US consul in mid-March due to the pending disclosure of his efforts to promote US annexation (ibid., 337–8).
148 Langford's report to J.W. Taylor, 10 July 1870, emphasis in original (ibid., 520–1).
149 Siggins (1994, 171), quoting from Howard (1952, 133). A far less flattering picture is found in the account by a Toronto journalist of his detention by, and interview with, Riel in January 1870 (Morton 1956, 488ff.). Some of Butler's other references to Riel were also less respectful than the words quoted.
150 NN700506.
151 NN700520.
152 Black to Colonial Office, 23 August 1870, LAC: RG6, C1, vol. 16, AM: reel M22.
153 Northcote to McTavish ("Private"), 12 March 1870, HBCA: A.7/4, fo. 44–5.
154 Smith to D.A. Smith, 16 June 1870, HBCA: A.6/44, fo. 36.
155 Morton (1956, 372).

156 NN700716, reprinted from *Sun* (New York), 25 June 1870.
157 Northcote to D.A. Smith ("Private"), 11 August 1870, HBCA: A.7/4, fo. 147–8.
158 "He and Mr. Hardisty [his right-hand man] are going round to Norway House, not deeming it safe to come near the Settlement" (Morton 1956, 381). After meeting with the HBC Northern Council at Norway House, they returned to Fort Alexander.
159 "It is strange to note how men who kept shady during the late troubles now come forward to claim their reward from the Canadian Government" (ibid., 358).
160 "It is very noticeable that there is no boasting nor riding over others shown by the French since peace reigned" (ibid., 369).
161 NN700730.
162 NN700708.
163 Morton (1956, 386–7). The peaceful state of the settlement at that point was illustrated by the Americans having been lent a cannon from the Fort by Riel's soldiers to add a sonic dimension to their festivities.
164 Ibid., 380–2. Dubuc would figure prominently in Manitoba's early public life.
165 "A large number of Indians are in. Riel has given them presents" (ibid., 390).
166 HBCA: B.154/a/69, fo. 43.
167 This section draws heavily on Bumsted (1996, 192ff.).
168 Morton (1956, 502).
169 Ibid., 392–3.
170 Ibid., 391.
171 Ibid., 392.
172 Ibid., 385–6. It was later disingenuously alleged that Archibald's party had lost its way.
173 Riel initially hid at St Joseph, a Métis community south of the border. Sara Riel to Madame Riel Sr, 31 August 1870, AM: MG3, D1, Riel Papers, Calendar, series 1.
174 Morton (1956, 564).
175 Bumsted (1996, 217).

CHAPTER ELEVEN

1 Recollection by a Red River resident of a conversation with Larsen, August 1870, MAN711216. He would never be tried. See case 455a, vol. 2, 579, and other hearings referred to therein.

2 "Smith said he gave way to Wolseley in order that life and property would be protected." Joseph Dubuc to Louis Riel, undated archival paraphrase in English, AM: MG3, D1, Riel Papers, Calendar, series 41.

3 HBCA: A.11/99, fo. 250. Even if that made him a charter "Governor," he acted without a council.

4 Smith (London) to D.A. Smith (RR), 20 October 1870, HBCA: A.6/44, fo. 147ff.

5 Oliver (1914, 620–1).

6 HBCA: A.11/99, fo. 255. Missing, for political or personal reasons, were James McKay, John Inkster, Maxmillian Genton, William Dease, Roger Goulet, Magnus Burston, and Henry Fisher.

7 Archibald to Howe, 10 September 1870, LAC: RG6, C1, vol. 16 (AM: reel M22). On 17 September he met large groups of Indians at St Peters and the Lower Fort. Archibald to Howe, 17 September 1870, LAC: RG6, C1, vol. 16 (AM: reel M22).

8 D.A. Smith to Archibald, 9 September 1870, HBCA: A.11/99, fo. 262. Smith acknowledged that such protection would benefit the HBC as well as others. His summary focused on greater Rupert's Land rather than the local scene, and so overlooked a vicious stabbing in Winnipeg about a week before his report that "dreadfully mutilated" a woman with life-threatening injuries. NN70903. The perpetrator seems never to have been apprehended.

9 Girard had accompanied Taché to Manitoba in late August. NN700827. With them was Joseph Royal, another Montreal lawyer who would make a large impact on Manitoba's early history.

10 The traveller was later given his money back and allowed to proceed.

11 Archibald to Howe, 21 September 1870, LAC: RG6, C1, vol. 16 (AM: reel M22).

12 Ibid., enclosures. Riel's troops had lost the same argument with the Americans, but with help from Ottawa, the Jarvis contingent was more successful.

13 Archibald to Howe, 8 October 1870, LAC: RG6, C1, vol. 17 (AM: reel M22).

14 For Archibald appointments, see Archibald to Howe, 8 October 1870, LAC: RG6, C1, vol. 17 (AM: reel M22). For those of the Provisional Government, see MAN701111.

15 MAN701015.

16 MAN701029.

17 D.A. Smith to London, 24 September 1870, HBCA: A.11/99, fo. 289b.

18 Archibald to Howe, 17 September 1870, LAC: RG6, C1, vol. 16 (AM: reel M22).

19 MAN701112, quoting *Ottawa Citizen*; MAN701015.

20 Bumsted (1996, 222).

21 The following account is based chiefly on Archibald to Howe, 7 December 1870, LAC: RG6, C1, vol. 16 (AM: reel M22), and on enclosed summaries of witness depositions. As for Farquarson, see Bumsted (1999, 80). Archibald's first report is in Archibald to Howe, 17 September 1870, LAC: RG6, C1, vol. 16 (AM: reel M22).

22 "The excitement ... was very considerable, but I believe it is now beginning to subside." Archibald to Howe, 31 September 1870, LAC: RG6, C1, vol. 16 (AM: reel M22).

23 See vol. 1, 146ff.

24 Emphasis added.

25 MAN701203.

26 MAN701210; Archibald to Howe, 6 December 1870, LAC: RG6, C1, vol. 18 (AM: reel M22).

27 MAN701015.

28 MAN701022.

29 See vol. 1, 159ff. See also MAN701210 and MAN701224.

30 Females, Indians, everyone under twenty-one, and anyone who did not own property of a specified value were disqualified. Even so, the estimate was low.

31 MAN701105. On another occasion, Ross said the HBC governed with "the most respectable and capable men in the Settlement" and "administered substantial justice between man and man." MAN701112.

32 MAN701112.

33 MAN710104.

34 Unidentified newspaper clipping, HBCA: A.11/99, fo. 326.

35 MAN701112; Clark (2000a).

36 MAN701015.

37 Riel to Royal, 2 September 1870, AM: MG3, D1, Riel Papers, Calendar, series 1, archival paraphrase.

38 Dubuc to Riel, 6 September 1870, AM: MG3, D1, Riel Papers, Calendar, series 1, archival paraphrase.

39 Archibald to Howe, 29 September 1870, LAC: RG6, C1, vol. 16 (AM: reel M22).

40 MAN701119.

41 MAN701203.

42 D.A. Smith reported to London that "nothing could be more unsystematic and irregular," adding, "The whole thing, in short, is a tangled web

to unravel, which will be very difficult, if not entirely impossible." Smith to London, 10 October 1870, HBCA: A.11/99, fo. 296.

43 St John to Archibald, 3 January 1871, AM: Finding Aid, M781, no. 164, Archibald Papers Calendar.

44 Archibald to Howe, 22 October 1870, LAC: RG6, C1, vol. 12 (AM: reel M22); Howe to Archibald, [day unknown] November 1870, AM: Finding Aid, M781, no. 69, Archibald Papers Calendar; Howe to Archibald, 17 November 1870, LAC: RG6, C1, vol. 12 (AM: reel M22); Archibald to Howe, 9 December 1870, LAC: RG6, C1, vol. 18 (AM: reel M22).

45 Archibald to Howe, 10 December 1870, LAC: RG6, C1, vol. 18 (AM: reel M22).

46 Meredith to Archibald, 16 September 1870, AM: Finding Aid, M781, no. 23, Archibald Papers Calendar. See also Canada, *Journals of the House of Commons*, vol. 14, 1880, 101.

47 Archibald to Howe, 10 December 1870, LAC: RG6, C1, vol. 18 (AM: reel M22).

48 MAN710114.

49 Archibald to Howe, 11 March 1871, LAC: RG6, C1, vol. 20 (AM: reel M23)

50 MAN710311.

51 MAN710218.

52 Jackson (1970, 113).

53 MAN710318.

54 Archibald granted royal assent to forty-three of the forty-seven, reserving four bills (concerning railways and telegraphs) for the consideration of the federal government, as the constitution authorizes the lieutenants governor to do.

55 Archibald to Howe, 6 May 1871, LAC: RG6, C1, vol. 20 (AM: reel M23); Clark (2000a).

56 MAN710415.

57 MAN710506.

58 MAN710506.

59 Archibald to Howe, 6 May 1871, LAC: RG6, C1, vol. 20 (AM: reel M23).

60 MAN710429.

61 MAN710318.

62 MAN710506.

63 Clark (2000a). "[Archibald] has been sadly bothered with his Attorney-General." Johnson to Meredith, 7 June 1871, LAC: RG6, C1, vol. 21 (AM: reel M23).

64 Clark (2000a). The premier was Marc-Amable Girard; the lieutenant governor was Alexander Morris.

65 Archibald to Howe, 24 March 1871, LAC: RG6, C1, vol. 20 (AM: reel M23).
66 MAN710401.
67 MAN710624; MAN710715; MAN710722; MAN710826.
68 See Gibson and Gibson (1972, 68–9, 87–90).
69 MAN710722. This is not to say it was easy. One surveyor received a letter stating, "Would like to know why you act like a surveyor on my property. The Government gave me no advice that there was to be a survey, ... and I give you no permission." The letter was signed "Louis Riel." AM: MG3, D1, Riel Papers, Calendar, series 1 (archival translation).
70 MAN710211; MAN710225; Archibald to Howe, 4 March 1871, LAC: RG6, C1, vol. 18 (AM: reel M23).
71 Archibald to Howe, 4 March 1871, LAC: RG6, C1, vol. 18 (AM: reel M23). Parliament prorogued before the Lynch-MacKay tie could be resolved, and Lynch declined to run again. MacKay was elected in 1872.
72 Gunn to Ross, 23 November 1870, AM: Ross Papers, MG2, C14, letter 455.
73 MAN710304.
74 Dubuc to Riel, 5 March 1871, AM: MG3, D1, Riel Papers, Calendar, series 1 (archival translation).
75 Archibald to Howe, 4 March 1871, LAC: RG6, C1, vol. 18 (AM: reel M23).
76 Morris (1880, 25–43, 313–20); MAN710729; MAN710805; MAN710812.
77 Although there is no record of those convictions, they were probably connected to the conviction of one Daniel Budge by magistrates McDermot and Bannatyne on 12 June 1871. MET710615.
78 MET710803.
79 MAN710812.
80 Treasury Board to Howe, 29 April 1871, LAC: RG6, C1, vol. 20 (AM: reel M23).
81 Bumsted (1996, 228–30). Ottawa added $2,000 for the parents of Thomas Scott.
82 MAN720601.
83 "[I]n the instance of laborers and mechanics," he admitted, he had decided that "their property was their time and labor and skill, and compensated them according to the amount which they were earning at the time," but that was not the favouritism complained about.
84 This assertion is difficult to reconcile with some of the categories of compensation listed in Bumsted (1996, 229).
85 See the summary in ibid., 230–41.

86 Archibald to Howe, 20 and 27 December 1870, LAC: Department of Interior Records, RG 15, vols 228 and 229, files 1/1871 and 796.

87 The literature is massive and politically bifurcated. Well-known expositions of the left-wing and right-wing positions are, respectively, Sprague (1988) and Flanagan (1991). The portion of Canada's Royal Commission on Aboriginal Peoples (1996) dealing with that and related subjects (vol. 4, 199–386, to which this writer contributed) was sympathetic to the Métis position. A lawsuit launched in 1981 by a Manitoba Métis organization took until 2013 to produce a declaration by the Supreme Court of Canada that "the federal Crown failed to act with diligence in implementing the land grant provision set out in s. 31 of the *Manitoba Act* in accordance with the honour of the Crown." *Manitoba Métis Federation v. Canada* 2013 SCC 14. The court having ordered no specific remedies, it was not known as this book went to press whether and how the Crown's honour would compensate in the twenty-first century for its failure in the nineteenth century.

88 The most authoritative study of this subject is Ens (1996, esp. 139–71).

89 Ibid., 173.

90 See Distad (2005, 62–71).

91 MAN710408.

92 MAN710429.

93 Ibid.

94 MAN710506.

95 MAN710513.

96 MAN711230. The organization was incorporated by statute. S.M. 1871, c. 10.

97 James Ross to Margaret Ross, 17, 24, and 29 September 1870, AM: Ross Papers, MG2, C14, letters 443, 446, and 447. This compression of remarks from three long letters perhaps exaggerates Ross's concerns somewhat.

98 Ross to Archibald ("Private"), 11 March 1871, AM: Ross Papers, MG2, C14, letter 465.

99 Archibald to Ross ("Private"), 11 March 1871, AM: Ross Papers, MG2, C14, letter 466.

100 James Ross to Margaret Ross, 29 September 1870, AM: Ross Papers, MG2, C14, letter 447.

101 MAN710923. See also MET710921.

102 MAN710325.

103 MAN710624.

104 MAN710722.

105 MAN710617.
106 MAN710729.
107 MAN711209.
108 Archibald to Howe, 6 May 1871, LAC: RG6, C1, vol. 20 (AM: reel M23); MAN711223.
109 MAN710218.
110 MAN710422.
111 MAN710902.
112 *"Dot It Down": A Story of Life in the North-West* (Begg 1871b) was reprinted in facsimile by the University of Toronto Press in 1978.
113 MAN710211; case 461. The defendants counterclaimed against Schultz in case 462. See vol. 2, 583. Both cases were apparently settled.
114 MAN710909; Begg (1871b).
115 Hargrave's *Red River* (1871) was reprinted in 1977 by Friesens Printers, Altona, Manitoba.
116 MAN711104.
117 MAN710408.
118 That situation, condemned by the *Manitoban* in August (MAN710819), was first addressed by forming a local fire insurance company (MAN710930), followed quickly by expressions of interest from foreign insurers (MAN711014; MAN711118).
119 See Macdonald (1910); and R.B. Brown (2009). Neither source deals with the Manitoba raid, but that topic is thoroughly covered in Howard (1952).
120 Stanley (2000).
121 The authorities are about equally divided over whether Curley or Donnelly was the general.
122 MAN710930.
123 Betke (2000); Gibson and Gibson (1987).
124 Archibald to Howe, 5 October 1871, LAC: RG6, C1, vol. 23 (AM: reel M24).
125 Archibald to Howe, 7 October 1871, LAC: RG6, C1, vol. 23 (AM: reel M24).
126 For a colourful account of the exercise, and the enthusiastic recruiting sessions of the preceding days, see MAN711007.
127 MAN711007; MAN711014. See also the court records of the resulting prosecutions and the related *Commentary* for cases 483, 484, and 485, vol. 2, 599ff.
128 They are sometimes said to have had such authorization – they would be given it in future – but that seems inconsistent with the next source cited.

129 Archibald to Howe, 9 October 1871, LAC: RG6, C1, vol. 23 (AM: reel M24).

130 Cases 483, 484, and 485, vol. 2, 599ff.

131 MAN711014.

132 Thornton to Dufferin, 8 August 1872, LAC: RG6, C1, vol. 28 (AM: reel M24). In a letter to Riel enclosed in one from John Bruce to Riel, Reverend Simon at St Joseph stated, "Everything is quiet here. The prisoners have been freed, Colonel Wheaton is detested by everyone. General O'Neill and Curley have left for St. Paul. O'Donoghue and Donnelly are here, and still smile at their adventure. O'Donoghue said he was content to see the Métis reconciled to the Government. A certain Canadian from Fort Garry came to get him as having been taken prisoner on British soil, but Colonel Wheaton said he had nothing more to do with that." Simon to Riel, 30 October 1871, AM: MG3, D1, Riel Papers, Calendar, series 1, no. 117 (archival translation).

133 Thornton to Dufferin, 8 August 1872, LAC: RG6, C1, vol. 28 (AM: reel M24).

134 Scott to Riel, 2 August 1871, AM: MG3, D1, Riel Papers, Calendar, series 1, no. 106.

135 Riel to Scott, 13 August 1871, AM: MG3, D1, Riel Papers, Calendar, series 1, nos 108, 109.

136 Scott to Riel, [day and month unknown] 1871, AM: MG3, D1, Riel Papers, Calendar, series 1, no. 110.

137 Quoted in Siggins (1994, 204), from Taché deposition in Report of Select Committee, House of Commons (UK), 1874.

138 Riel to Richot (draft), 5 October 1871, AM: MG3, D1, Riel Papers, Calendar, series 1, no. 113 (archival translation).

139 Riel to Archibald, 7 October 1871, AM: MG3, D1, Riel Papers, Calendar, series 1, no. 114.

140 Archibald to Howe, 9 October 1871, LAC: RG6, C1, vol. 23 (AM: reel M24).

141 Ibid.

142 MAN711014.

143 See vol. 1, 331ff.

144 MET711123. See also MET711130.

145 Pryke (2000).

146 MET711130; MAN711209; MAN711216; MET711221; MAN711230.

147 MET711228.

148 Archibald to Macdonald, 28 February 1872, LAC, Macdonald Papers, 78146. Detailed newspaper accounts of Clarke's eloquent assem-

bly speeches and his skilled courtroom performances suggest that Archibald seriously underestimated the attorney general's legal ability.

149 AM: Executive Council Minutes, 14 December 1871, 28 December 1871, 7 March 1872. Sutherland, appointed to the Senate, would probably have resigned in any case. His replacement as sheriff was Edward Armstrong. Bunn was replaced as court clerk by Thomas Barton.

150 See vol. 1, 324.

151 MAN711216.

152 Cabinet Report, 13 October 1871, LAC: RG6, C1, vol. 23 (AM: reel M24); MAN711028; MET711102; MAN711118; Howe to Archibald, 3 April 1872, LAC: RG6, C1, vol. 236 (AM: reel M24).

153 Pryke (2000).

154 Archibald to Howe, 21 February 1872, LAC: RG6, C1, vol. 25 (AM: reel M24).

155 Archibald to Howe, 14 April 1872, LAC: RG6, C1, vol. 25 (AM: reel M24). Archibald also reserved royal assent for a bill giving land surveyors a similar power to regulate their profession.

156 MAN710603.

157 The Canadian government did nothing to assuage that ill feeling when it disclosed, in response to a House of Commons request, that it had kept no documentation concerning the Elizear Goulet drowning and related violence or other complaints of undisciplined conduct by the volunteers. House of Common Debates, 10 April 1871, LAC: RG6, C1, vol. 20 (AM: reel M23).

158 Gibson and Gibson (1972, 87–8).

159 Plainval to Clarke, 23 February 1972, LAC: Manitoba Mounted Constabulary Force Letterbook, letter 34.

160 Begg (1894, vol. 2, 107). See also Archibald to Howe, 1 July 1871, LAC: RG6, C1, vol. 21 (AM: reel M23): "[T]here are in the Province at this moment some twenty American deserters from the Pembina [US Army] Garrison, several of whom, since they came here, have been guilty of criminal offences, and all of whom are a most undesirable addition to our population."

161 MAN710527.

162 MAN710225 (supplement). That breakout might have been from an Upper Fort bastion.

163 Archibald to Howe, 27 May 1871, LAC: RG6, C1, vol. 21 (AM: reel M23). This was case 471, vol. 2, 586.

164 Archibald to Howe, 18 May 1871, LAC: RG6, C1, vol. 21 (AM: reel M23).

165 Minister of Justice Report, 14 June 1871, LAC: RG6, C1, vol. 21 (AM: reel M23).
166 MAN711125.
167 12 December 1871 and 13 February 1872, LAC: Manitoba Mounted Constabulary Force Letterbook, letters 24 and 30.
168 Case 455b, vol. 2, 584. The *Manitoban* defended the bail decision. MAN710225.
169 Case 469, vol. 2, 586. Larsen had apparently escaped from custody before the hearing. MAN710506. A later report claimed he was spotted on the road to Pembina on 20 May. MAN711216.
170 MAN710701.
171 Case 556, vol. 2, 642.
172 MET711221 (author's translation). See also Siggins (1994, 206–7).
173 See vol. 2, 609.
174 Ens (1996, 145).
175 Archibald to Macdonald, 25 September 1872: LAC, Macdonald Papers, 78230.
176 Morris to Macdonald, 10 October 1872, LAC: Macdonald Papers, 113840.
177 MET721012.
178 MAN701015.
179 MAN701022.
180 MAN701119.
181 MAN701112; Clark (2000a).
182 See vol. 2, 579ff.
183 See ibid.
184 Note in Sheriff's Book, 1863–71, 18 November 1870, AM: MG2, B4–2; MAN701119. That was not Johnson's only questionable ruling. In a requested report on the state of the law in Assiniboia at the moment it entered Canada, he adopted Adam Thom's original view that English law as of 1670 still applied, sidestepping by a sterile literal interpretation the legislation expressly enacted by the Council of Assiniboia to avoid that nonsensical conclusion. Canada, *Journals of the House of Commons*, vol. 14, 1880, 101.
185 Ibid.
186 MAN701126.
187 MAN710128. Attorney General Clarke, in his personal capacity, represented Dallas in this round.
188 Archibald to Cartier, 26 May 1871, LAC: Macdonald Papers, 77897.
189 MAN710325.

190 See vol. 2, 584ff.
191 See ibid., 615ff.
192 See ibid., 567ff., 618ff.
193 MAN710819.
194 MET711118.
195 Morris to Macdonald, 5 November 1872, LAC: Macdonald Papers, 113883.
196 Cases 483, 484, and 485, vol. 2, 599ff.
197 Ibid. Girard, although a lawyer, seems never to have practised in the courts.
198 See Begg (1894, vol. 2, 96).
199 MET710629.
200 See, for example, Lower District Court: County of Lisgar Court of Petty Sessions Record Book, 1868–72, AM: MG2, B4–6.
201 Archibald to Howe, 21 February 1872, LAC: RG6, C1, vol. 25 (AM: reel M24); Gibson and Gibson (1972, 91–2).
202 Clarke had undoubtedly lobbied his cabinet colleagues. Archibald sent Ottawa the suggestion without immediate comment. Archibald to Howe, 16 March 1872, LAC: RG6, C1, vol. 28 (AM: reel M24). But he warned Macdonald in May, "Bad as he [Clarke] is where he is, he would be greatly worse on the bench" (Pryke 2000).
203 See vol. 2, 605ff.
204 See ibid., 608ff.
205 Gibson and Gibson (1972, 93); MAN720001.
206 See vol. 2, 608ff.
207 Cases 578 and 579, vol. 2, 649, 650. Cosgrove had sued earlier (case 553, November 1871, vol. 2, 641) but had not proceeded with that action. These cases do not appear in volume C of the court records, which no longer noted civil cases, but they are noted in volume D.
208 MAN710525.
209 Case 655, vol. 2, 676.
210 Cases 499, 500, and 502, vol. 2, 609. See the earlier discussion of the incident in vol. 1, 326ff.
211 See Edwards (1964, 177).
212 Archibald to Howe, 24 June 1872, LAC: RG6, C1, vol. 27 (AM: reel M24), enclosure.
213 MAN720601.
214 See vol. 1, 305ff.
215 Archibald to Howe, 24 June 1872, LAC: RG6, C1, vol. 27 (AM: reel M24), enclosure.

216 Johnson to Macdonald, 7 May 1872, LAC: Macdonald Papers, 157573.
217 MAN720601.
218 Archibald to Howe, 24 June 1872, LAC: RG6, C1, vol. 27 (AM: reel M24), enclosure.
219 Archibald to Macdonald, 12 September 1871, LAC: Macdonald Papers, 77952.
220 Morris to Macdonald, 5 October 1872, LAC: Macdonald Papers, 113838.
221 Gibson and Gibson (1972, 94–103).
222 Morris to Macdonald, 18 May 1871, LAC: Macdonald Papers, 113776. See also Talbot (2009); Friesen (2001); and Morris (1880).
223 Archibald to Howe, 30 September 1872, LAC: RG6, C1, vol. 28 (AM: reel M24), enclosure.
224 For the story of the next century of Manitoba's legal history, see Gibson and Gibson (1972); and for a more recent overview, see Jewers (2013).

CHAPTER TWELVE

1 James Ross, quoted in MAN701112.
2 This chapter is based on a paper presented to a Rupert's Land Colloquium, Winnipeg, Manitoba, 19–22 May 2010. It deals primarily with the years when Assiniboia and the quarterly courts were HBC responsibilities.
3 NW691201.
4 For other examples, see Gibson and Gibson (1972, iii). The author thanks Lee Gibson for drawing the frequent use of such expressions to his attention.
5 Report of Select Committee, House of Commons (UK), 1857, 301, Q. 5438 (hereafter Select Committee Report).
6 Oliver (1914, 150, lines 9–13). "This Kingdom" was England.
7 Ibid., 145, lines 1–9, lines 40–146, line 1.
8 Ibid., 219–21.
9 Ibid., 267n3, identifies a package of legally binding obligations, appended as conditions to settler land grants in November 1823, as well as general regulations dated May 1832. The latter prefaced what Oliver (ibid., 267n1) called "the first Minute Book of the Council of Assiniboia."
10 Ibid., 288–92.
11 Ibid., 373–9 and 485–502, respectively.

12 Copies of both books were available at Red River at least as early as 1822 (ibid., 1291).

13 Adam Thom, "Observations on the Law and Judicature of Rupert's Land," HBCA: E.1b/1, fo. 80, no. 47.

14 Thom to London, 29 May 1840, HBCA: D.5/5, fo. 283–5.

15 Thom to Simpson, 31 July 1840, HBCA: D.5/5, fo. 301–4.

16 Oliver (1914, 240–4).

17 Ibid., 266–74.

18 One convicted criminal attempted a sort of appeal by suing Red River authorities in the English Court of Common Pleas for the common law tort of false imprisonment for having been locally convicted and jailed for a crime, but that attempt was later abandoned. See vol. 1, 226ff.

19 A much more extraordinary achievement – one of the world's first extensive codifications of common law – failed to win HBC approval. Simpson to London, [date unknown], HBCA: D.4/58, fo. 161–2.

20 Two letters from Simpson during the appointment negotiations had informed Thom that facility in French was an indispensable condition of employment. Simpson to Thom, 5 January 1838, HBCA: D.4/23, fo. 84; Simpson to Thom, 21 April 1838, HBCA: D.4/23, fo. 151.

21 *Rothney v. Thom,* [day unknown] February 1843, AM: MG2, B4–6; *Matheson v. Thom,* case 75, February 1850, vol. 2, 132.

22 *HBC v. Sayer,* case 68, vol. 2, 113.

23 Case 77, July 1850, vol. 2, 136.

24 Berens to Dallas, 16 April 1862, HBCA: A.7/3, fo. 92–4.

25 NW620911.

26 Cases 280 and 313, vol. 2, 462ff., 484. HBCA: A.39/7, fo. 329; A.6/40, fo. 372, 377, 380; A.6/41, fo. 76, 149; A.39/7, fo. 327.

27 *The Queen v. McLean,* case 414, September 1868, vol. 2, 537.

28 *The Queen v. Corbett,* case 238, February 1863, vol. 2, 366.

29 One of them – the least active of the four – professed to be a fully qualified American attorney, but his incompetent performance put that claim in doubt.

30 *Manitoba Directory, 1877–1878,* 104. One of them, Thomas Bunn, had in the meantime served for several years as court clerk.

31 Oliver (1914, 271–4).

32 Ibid., 316–17.

33 Simpson (Lachine) to Pelly (London), 4 April and 4 May 1845, HBCA: A.12/2, fo. 502 and 520; Simpson (Red River) to London, 23 July 1846, HBCA: A.12/3, fo. 204–080.

34 Bumsted (2003b, 106).

35 Ross (1856, 366), quoting Acting Governor Colvile.
36 Colvile to Barclay, 17 December 1851, HBCA: A.12/13.
37 Caldwell to London, 8 August 1854, HBCA: A.11/96, fo. 11.
38 London to Simpson, 28 November 1854, HBCA: A.6/31, fo. 159.
39 Swanston to London, 9 August 1855, HBCA: A.11/96, fo. 44.
40 McTavish to London, 9 November 1857, HBCA: A.11/96, fo. 190.
41 Johnson to Simpson, 18 December 1857, HBCA: D.5/45, fo. 481.
42 Simpson to Berens, 30 July 1858, HBCA: A.7/2, fo. 95.
43 London to McTavish, 17 April 1861, HBCA: A.6/36, fo. 101.
44 McTavish to Smith, 20 January 1868, HBCA: A.12/45, fo. 3.
45 Ross report, HBCA: A.11/95, fo. 216–17.
46 Oliver (1914, 514).
47 A surviving record indicates that the sheriff's office during McKenney's term was a busy and efficient place. AM: MG2, B4, reel 389.
48 NN700716.
49 MacLeod and Morton (1963).
50 Oliver (1914, 364).
51 See *Republic of Manitobah v. Macpherson* treason trial (Peel 2001c); and the trial reported in NW640510.
52 The request was finally granted for *The Queen v. Alexander McLean*, case 414, September 1868, vol. 2, 537.
53 Johnson to London, 20 October 1857, HBCA: A. 11/96 fo. 174–85.
54 Johnson to London, 20 October 1857, HBCA: A.11/96, fo. 174–9.
55 Simpson to Smith, 26 September 1845, HBCA: D.4/33, fo. 53–4.
56 Case 36, August 1847, vol. 2, 65 (Christie); case 199, December 1860, vol. 2, 312 (McTavish); case 203, May 1861, vol. 2, 318 (McTavish).
57 The HBC eventually settled their claims, however. Select Committee Report, Q. 4818 to 4821.
58 Case 296, November 1865, vol. 2, 469; NW651211.
59 A jury reached a similar conclusion, five years earlier, in a case of theft where circumstantial evidence of guilt had been equally strong. That case involved theft from HBC premises, however, and might have reflected jury bias against the company. *The Queen v. Daniel O'Brian*, case 203, (heard June 1860 but mistakenly reported in May 1861), vol. 2, 318.
60 Thom to Simpson, 4 August 1842, HBCA: D.5/7, fo. 157, at 158–9.
61 In his "Observations on the Law and Judicature of Rupert's Land" (HBCA: E.16/1, fo. 80, 92), Thom himself observed that English punishments for offences against property were "altogether too severe" and that applying them in Rupert's Land "would amount to judicial cruelty."

62 George Simpson told London in 1841, "So great an evil is confinement to persons of such roving habits as the Indians and Half Breeds that it is to them worse than death itself." HBCA: D.3/2, fo. 39.

63 A third group – treason and related offences – is not relevant here, no such case having been tried during the HBC regime, although there was one in 1871 (case 485, vol. 2, 599).

64 That number includes just one case from the period 1835–44, from which very few records have survived.

65 *Jury Verdict re Henry Beardie*, 20 November 1839, University of Alberta, Don Thompson Collection, item 76. Recorder Adam Thom's pettifoggery insisted on a charge of murder, even though a coroner's jury recommended manslaughter, and Thom admitted the boy's youth was a defence to either charge. HBCA: D.5/13, fo. 270Bff., nos 35, 38.

66 *The Queen v. Catherine and Mary Daniel*, case 173, December 1859, vol. 2, 287.

67 *[Constable] John Bruce v. Robert Mulligan*, case 252, February 1864, vol. 2, 439; NW640308.

68 The girl might also have served some time in jail awaiting trial, but if so it could not have been long because the trial was held only a few weeks after the offence.

69 The *Nor'-Wester* seemed to approve the "spirit of leniency and consideration" that underlay Black's initiative, but thought "the precedent is not a very safe one" and called on the Council of Assiniboia to provide a statutory basis for such sentencing discretion. NW640308. That was never done.

70 Case 122, August 1854, vol. 2, 236; case 162, June 1859, vol. 2, 279; case 230, August 1862, vol. 2, 359; case 304, February 1866, vol. 2, 478; case 524, November 1871, vol. 2, 627.

71 Case 524, vol. 2, 627.

72 A married woman could also sue indirectly by means of a male "champion" allegedly doing so on her behalf, as in *Foss v. Pelly*, case 77, July 1850, vol. 2, 136.

73 See, for example, *Smith v. Kirton*, case 1, November 1844, vol. 2, 3.

74 The most egregious example was a four-month sentence for attempted rape of an eight year old. *The Queen v. Bunn*, case 242, May 1863, vol. 2, 421.

75 *Public Interest v. Heckenberger*, case 93, February 1852, vol. 2, 194.

76 *Public Interest v. Duncan*, case 116, February 1854, vol. 2, 226; *The Queen v. Linklater*, case 321, August 1866, vol. 2, 488; *The Queen v. Saunders*, case 453, November 1869, vol. 2, 572.

77 *The Queen v. Corbett*, case 238, February 1863, vol. 2, 366.

78 February 1843, AM: MG2, B4–6. See also Gibson (1990b, 30).
79 Case 77, July 1850, vol. 2, 136.
80 Pannekoek (1991, 18) states, on the basis of the 1849 and 1871 censuses, that there were 537 in 1849 and 560 in 1871 – a drop of from 5 to 10 per cent of the total population.
81 Matters occurring more than 50 miles from Upper Fort Garry were usually ignored, however, whether their impact was solely upon the other Aboriginals, as when Saulteaux attacked a Sioux encampment on Lake Manitoba in 1864 (NW640510), or upon white settlers, as when a Saulteau known as "the Wolverine" and some followers raided a Portage la Prairie store in 1867, killing a clerk (NW670525; NW690219).
82 Thom to Caldwell, 10 March 1849, HBCA: A.8/6, fo. 36.
83 NW611130.
84 Case 6, August 1845, vol. 2, 17. See also Gibson (2010b).
85 See Gibson (1990a, 2010b).
86 Case 4, February 1845, vol. 2, 9. Thom's charge to the grand jury was later published – probably in heavily edited form. HBCA: D.5/13, fo. 270ff., FC 3207.99, pamphlet Z8.
87 Case 8, November 1845, vol. 2, 31.
88 Case 193, December 1860, vol. 2, 306. See also NW600714; and NW610201.
89 Case 212, November 1861, vol. 2, 338; case 213, November 1861, vol. 2, 341. See NW611130.
90 Ross (1856, 222–3, emphasis in original).
91 Ibid., 223.
92 Although juries were not available in the petty courts, panels of lay magistrates produced similar results.
93 William B. Caldwell, quoted in Select Committee Report, 301, Q. 5438.

Bibliography

Aitken, Alex. 2003. *Sarah Ballenden.* Novel. Kingston, ON: Artful Codger.

Allen, Robert S., and Carol M. Judd. 2000. "Bulger, Andrew H." In *Dictionary of Canadian Biography Online.* Toronto and Laval: University of Toronto Press and Presses de l'Université Laval.

Audet, Francis-J. 1941. "Adam Thom (1802–1890)." *Mémoires de la Société Royale du Canada,* ser. 3, vol. 35: 1.

Avis, Walter S., ed. 1967. *A Dictionary of Canadianisms on Historical Principles.* Toronto: W.J. Gage.

Backhouse, Constance. 1981. "Shifting Patterns in Nineteenth Century Canadian Custody Law." In David Flaherty, ed., *Essays in the History of Canadian Law,* vol. 1, 221. Toronto: Osgoode Society.

– 1983. "Nineteenth Century Canadian Rape Law: 1800–94." In David Flaherty, ed., *Essays in the History of Canadian Law,* vol. 2, 200. Toronto: Osgoode Society.

– 1991. *Petticoats and Prejudice: Women and Law in Nineteenth Century Canada.* Toronto: Osgoode Society.

Baker, G. Blaine. 2008. "Strategic Benthamism: Rehabilitating United Canada's Bar through Criminal Law Codification, 1850–54." In J. Phillips et al., eds, *Essays in the History of Canadian Law,* vol. 10, 257. Toronto: Osgoode Society and University of Toronto Press.

Baker, Howard Robert. 1996. "Law Transplanted, Justice Invented: Sources of Law for the Hudson's Bay Company in Rupert's Land, 1670–1870." MA thesis, University of Manitoba.

– 1999. "Creating Order in the Wilderness: Transplanting the English Law to Rupert's Land, 1835–51." *Law and History Review* 17: 209–46.

Begg, Alexander. 1870. *Alexander Begg's Red River Journal and Other Papers Relative to the Red River Resistance of 1869–1870.* Ed. W.L. Morton. Toronto: Champlain Society, 1956.

– 1871a. *The Creation of Manitoba, or A History of the Red River Troubles.* Toronto: Hunter, Rose.

– 1871b. *"Dot It Down": A Story of Life in the North-West.* Novel. Reprint, Toronto: University of Toronto Press, 1978.

– 1894. *The History of the North-West.* 3 vols. Toronto: Hunter, Rose.

Betke, Carl. 2000. "McMicken, Gilbert." In *Dictionary of Canadian Biography Online.* Toronto and Laval: University of Toronto Press and Presses de l'Université Laval.

Bindon, Kathryn M. 1972. "Journalist and Judge: Adam Thom's British North American Career, 1833–1854." MA thesis, Queen's University.

– 1981. "Hudson's Bay Company Law: Adam Thom and the Institution of Order in Rupert's Land, 1839–54." In David Flaherty, ed., *Essays in the History of Canadian Law,* vol. 1, 43. Toronto: Osgoode Society.

– 2000. "Thom, Adam." In *Dictionary of Canadian Biography Online.* Toronto and Laval: University of Toronto Press and Presses de l'Université Laval.

Blackstone, Sir William. 1765–69. *Commentaries on the Laws of England.* 4 vols. Facsimile reprint, Chicago: University of Chicago Press, 1979.

Blanchard, Jim, ed. 2002. *A Thousand Miles of Prairie.* Winnipeg: University of Manitoba Press.

Boorstin, Daniel J. 1941. *The Mysterious Science of the Law: An Essay on Blackstone's Commentaries.* Reprint, Boston: Beacon, 1958.

Boreskie, Thomas G. 2000. "Corbett, Griffith Owen." In *Dictionary of Canadian Biography Online.* Toronto and Laval: University of Toronto Press and Presses de l'Université Laval.

Bowsfield, Hartwell. 2000. "Rolette (Rollette), Joseph." In *Dictionary of Canadian Biography Online.* Toronto and Laval: University of Toronto Press and Presses de l'Université Laval.

Brown, Jennifer S.H. 1980. *Strangers in Blood: Fur Trade Company Families in Indian Country.* Vancouver: UBC Press.

– 1982. "The Track to Heaven: The Hudson's Bay Creek Religious Movement of 1842–3." In W. Cowan, ed., *Papers of the 13th Algonquin Conference,* 55. Ottawa: Carleton University Press.

– 2000. "Abishabis (Small Eyes)." In *Dictionary of Canadian Biography Online.* Toronto and Laval: University of Toronto Press and Presses de l'Université Laval.

– 2001. "Partial Truths: A Closer Look at Fur Trade Marriage." In T. Binnema, G.J. Ens, and R.C. MacLeod, eds, *From Rupert's Land to Canada,* 59. Edmonton: University of Alberta Press.

– 2004. "The Wasitay Religion: Prophecy, Oral Literacy, and Belief on Hudson Bay." In Michael Harkin, ed., *Reassessing Revitalization: Perspectives from*

North America and the Pacific Islands, 104. Lincoln: University of Nebraska Press.

Brown, R. Blake. 2009. "'Stars and Shamrocks Will be Sown': The Fenian State Trials, 1866–7." In Barry Wright and Susan Binnie, eds, *Canadian State Trials*, vol. 3, 35. Toronto: Osgoode Society.

Brown, Stephen R. 2009. *Merchant Kings: When Companies Ruled the World, 1600–1900*. Vancouver: Douglas and McIntyre.

Bryce, George. 1882. *Manitoba: Its Infancy, Growth, and Present Condition*. London: Sampson Low, Marston, Searle, and Rivington.

– 1885. "The Old Settlers of Red River: A Paper Read before the Manitoba Historical and Scientific Society, 26 November 1885." *Manitoba Daily Free Press*, 3 December 1885.

– 1890. "The First Recorder of Rupert's Land." *Manitoba Historical Society Transactions*, ser. 1, no. 40: n.p.

– 1896. "Worthies of Red River: Adam Thom – Judge and Philosopher." *Winnipeg Free Press*, [day and month unknown] 1896. Reprint in HBCA Library: 920.07127 Bry.

– 1900. *The Remarkable History of the Hudson's Bay Company*. Toronto: William Briggs.

– 1905. "Illustrated History of Winnipeg." *Winnipeg Free Press*, 21 June.

Bumsted, J.M. 1982. *The People's Clearance, 1770–1815*. Edinburgh and Winnipeg: Edinburgh University Press and University of Manitoba Press.

– 1996. *The Red River Rebellion*. Winnipeg: Watson and Dwyer.

– 1999a. *Dictionary of Manitoba Biography*. Winnipeg: University of Manitoba Press.

– 1999b. *Fur Trade Wars: The Founding of Western Canada*. Winnipeg: Great Plains.

– 2000. *Thomas Scott's Body and Other Essays on Early Manitoba History*. Winnipeg: University of Manitoba Press.

– 2001. *Louis Riel v. Canada: The Making of a Rebel*. Winnipeg: Great Plains.

– 2003a. *Reporting the Resistance: Alexander Begg and Joseph Hargrave on the Red River Resistance*. Winnipeg: University of Manitoba Press.

2003b. *Trials and Tribulations: The Red River Settlement and the Emergence of Manitoba, 1811–1870*. Winnipeg: Great Plains.

– 2008. *Lord Selkirk: A Life*. Winnipeg: University of Manitoba Press.

Campbell, Marjorie Wilkins. 1957. *The North West Company*. Toronto: Macmillan.

– 1962. *McGillivray Lord of the Northwest*. Toronto: Clarke, Irwin.

Canada, Royal Commission on Aboriginal Peoples. 1996. *Report of the Royal Commission on Aboriginal Peoples*. Ottawa: Minister of Supply and Services Canada.

Canadian Dictionary/Dictionaire Canadien (Concise). 1962. Toronto and Montreal: McClelland and Stewart.

Canadian Encyclopedia. 2000. Toronto: McLelland and Stewart.

Clark, Lovell. 2000a. "Clarke, Henry Joseph." In *Dictionary of Canadian Biography Online.* Toronto and Laval: University of Toronto Press and Presses de l'Université Laval.

– 2000b. "Schultz, Sir John Christian." In *Dictionary of Canadian Biography Online.* Toronto and Laval: University of Toronto Press and Presses de l'Université Laval.

Colthart, James M. 2000. "Ellice, Edward." In *Dictionary of Canadian Biography Online.* Toronto and Laval: University of Toronto Press and Presses de l'Université Laval.

Colvile, Eden. 1849–52. *Eden Colvile's Letters, 1849–1852.* Vol 19. Ed. E.E. Rich. London: Hudson's Bay Company Record Society, 1956.

Cooper, Barry. 1988. *Alexander Kennedy Isbister: A Respectable Critic of the Honourable Company.* Ottawa: Carleton University Press.

Coutts, Robert J. 2000. *The Road to the Rapids: Nineteenth-Century Church and Society at St. Andrews Parish, Red River.* Calgary: University of Calgary Press.

Craig, Gerald M., ed. 1963. *Lord Durham's Report.* Toronto: McClelland and Stewart.

Creighton, Donald. 1964. *The Road to Confederation.* Toronto: Macmillan.

Dauphinais, Luc. 1991. *Histoire de Saint-Boniface.* St Boniface, MB: Édition du Blé.

Distad, Merrill. 2005. "Print and Settlement in the West." In Fiona Black and Yvan Lamonde, eds, *The History of the Book in Canada,* vol. 2, *1840–1918,* 62. Toronto: University of Toronto Press.

Dorge, Lionel. 2000a. "Black, John." In *Dictionary of Canadian Biography Online.* Toronto and Laval: University of Toronto Press and Presses de l'Université Laval.

– 2000b. "Bruneau, François-Jacques." In *Dictionary of Canadian Biography Online.* Toronto and Laval: University of Toronto Press and Presses de l'Université Laval.

Doughty, A.G., and N. Story, eds. 1935. *Documents Relating to the Constitutional History of Canada, 1819–1928.* Ottawa: King's Printer.

Driscoll, Heather Rollason. 2001. "A Most Important Chain of Connection: Marriage in the Hudson's Bay Company." In T. Binnema, G.J. Ens, and R.C. MacLeod, eds, *From Rupert's Land to Canada,* 81. Edmonton: University of Alberta Press.

Eddy, J.P. 1963. *Justices of the Peace.* London: Cassell.

Edwards, J.L.J. 1964. *The Law Officers of the Crown.* London: Sweet and Maxwell.

Ens, Gerhard J. 1996. *Homeland to Hinterland: The Changing Worlds of the Red River Metis in the Nineteenth Century.* Toronto: University of Toronto Press.

– ed. 2008. *A Son of the Fur Trade: The Memoirs of Johnny Grant.* Edmonton: University of Alberta Press.

Ermatinger, Francis. 1818–53. *Fur Trade Letters of Francis Ermatinger, 1818–1853.* Ed. Lois Halliday McDonald. Glendale, CA: Arthur H. Clark, 1980.

Evatt, H.V. 1987. *The Royal Prerogative.* Sydney: Law Book Company.

Fitzgerald, James Edward. 1849. *An Examination of the Charter and Proceedings of the Hudson's Bay Company with Reference to the Grant of Vancouver's Island.* London: Trelawney Saunders.

Flanagan, Thomas. 1991. *Métis Land in Manitoba.* Calgary: University of Calgary Press.

Foster, Hamar. 1989. "Sins against the Great Spirit: The Law, the Hudson's Bay Company, and the Mackenzie River Murders, 1835–1839." *Criminal Justice History* 10: 23–76.

– 1990a. "Long Distance Justice: The Criminal Jurisdiction of the Canadian Courts West of the Canadas, 1763–1859." *American Journal of Legal History* 34: 1–48.

– 1990b. "Mutiny on the *Beaver*: Law and Authority in the Fur Trade Navy, 1835–1840." *Manitoba Law Journal* 20: 15–45.

– 1992a. "Forgotten Arguments: Indian Title and Sovereignty in Canada Jurisdiction Act Cases." *Manitoba Law Journal* 21: 343–89.

– 1992b. "Killing Mr. John: Law and Jurisdiction at Fort Stikine, 1842–46." In John McLaren, Hamar Foster, and Chett Orloff, eds, *Law for the Elephant, Law for the Beaver: Essays in the Legal History of the North American West,* 147. <Complete?> Regina and Pasadena: Canadian Plains Research Centre and Ninth Judicial Circuit Historical Society.

– 1993. "Conflict Resolution during the Fur Trade in the Canadian North West, 1803–1859." *The Advocate* 51: 871–7.

– 1996. "British Columbia: Legal Institutions in the Far West, from Contact to 1871." *Manitoba Law Journal* 23: 293–340.

– 2005. "Law and Necessity in Western Rupert's Land and Beyond, 1670–1870." In Louis Knafla and Jonathan Swainger, eds, *Laws and Societies in the Canadian Prairie West, 1670–1940,* 57. Vancouver: UBC Press.

Foster, Hamar, Benjamin L. Berger, and A.R. Buck, eds. 2008. *The Grand Experiment: Law and Legal Culture in British Settler Societies.* Vancouver: UBC Press and Osgoode Society.

Foster, J.E. 2000. "Cockran, William." In *Dictionary of Canadian Biography Online*. Toronto and Laval: University of Toronto Press and Presses de l'Université Laval.

Friesen, Gerald. 1984. *The Canadian Prairies: A History*. Toronto: University of Toronto Press.

– 1996. *River Road: Essays on Manitoba and Prairie History*. Winnipeg: University of Manitoba Press.

– 2000. "Finlayson, Duncan." In *Dictionary of Canadian Biography Online*. Toronto and Laval: University of Toronto Press and Presses de l'Université Laval.

Friesen, Jean. 2001. "Morris, Alexander." In *Dictionary of Canadian Biography Online*. Toronto and Laval: University of Toronto Press and Presses de l'Université Laval.

Galbraith, John S. 1976. *The Little Emperor: Governor Simpson of the Hudson's Bay Company*. Toronto: Macmillan.

Garneau, Jean-Philippe. 2009. "Civil Law, Legal Practitioners, and Everyday Justice in the Decades Following the Quebec Act." In C. Backhouse and W. Pue, eds, *The Promise and Perils of Law: Lawyers in Canadian History*, 129. Toronto: Irwin.

Garner, Bryan A., ed. 2004. *Black's Law Dictionary*. 8th ed. St Paul, MN: West.

Gibson, Dale. 1990a. "The Real Laws of the Constitution." *Alberta Law Review* 28, no. 2: 358–83.

– 1990b. "A Scandal at Red River." *The Beaver* 70, no. 5: 30–8.

– 2001a. "Company Justice: Origins of Legal Institutions in Pre-Confederation Canada." In D. Guth and W. Pue, eds, *Canada's Legal Inheritances*, 247. Winnipeg: Faculty of Law, University of Manitoba.

– 2001b. "Development of Federal Legal-Judicial Institutions in Canada." In D. Guth and W. Pue, eds, *Canada's Legal Inheritances*, 450. Winnipeg: Faculty of Law, University of Manitoba.

– 2010a. "Doing Justice at Red River." In *Papers of the Rupert's Land Colloquium, 2010*. CD. Winnipeg: Centre for Rupert's Land Studies, University of Winnipeg.

– 2010b. "The First Hanged Was Indian: Capital Punishment in the Quarterly Court of Assiniboia." In *Papers of the Rupert's Land Colloquium, 2008*. CD. Winnipeg: Centre for Rupert's Land Studies, University of Winnipeg.

– 2013. "Louis Riel as Governor." In *Papers of the Rupert's Land Colloquium, 2012*. Compact disk. Winnipeg: Centre for Rupert's Land Studies, University of Winnipeg.

Gibson, Dale, and Lee Gibson. 1972. *Substantial Justice: Law and Lawyers in Manitoba, 1670–1970*. Winnipeg: Peguis.

– 1987. "Who Was Gilbert McMicken and Why Should Legal Historians Care?" Paper presented at the conference Canadian Law in History, Carleton University, Ottawa, 1987.

Gibson, Dale, with Lee Gibson and Cameron Harvey. 1983. *Attorney for the Frontier: Enos Stutsman.* Winnipeg: University of Manitoba Press.

Gibson, Dale, and Kristin Lercher. 1986. "Reliance on Unconstitutional Laws: The Saving Doctrines and Other Protections." *Manitoba Law Journal* 15: 305–31.

Giraud, Marcel. 1986. *The Métis in the Canadian West.* Trans. George Woodcock. Lincoln and London: University of Nebraska Press.

Glazebrook, G.P. de T., ed. 1947. *The Hargrave Correspondence, 1821–1843.* Reprint, New York: Greenwood, 1968.

Goodwin, Doris Kearns. 2005. *Team of Rivals: The Political Genius of Abraham Lincoln.* New York: Simon and Schuster.

Gray, John Morgan. 1963. *Lord Selkirk of Red River.* Toronto: Macmillan.

Gressley, Gene M. 1972. "Lord Selkirk and the Canadian Courts." In J.M. Bumsted, ed., *Canadian History before Confederation,* 294. Georgetown, ON: Irwin-Dorsey.

Gunn, Donald. 1880. *History of Manitoba from the Earliest Settlement to 1835.* Ottawa: Maclean, Roger and Co.

Guth, DeLloyd J. 1994. "The Traditional Common Law Constable: From Bracton to the Fieldings to Canada." In R. Macleod and D. Schneiderman, eds, *Police Powers in Canada,* 5. Toronto: University of Toronto Press.

Hargrave, J.J. 1871. *Red River.* Ed. Helen Doherty. Altona, MB: Friesens, 1977.

– 1821–43. *The Hargrave Correspondence, 1821–1843.* Ed. G.P. de T. Glazebrook. 1947. Reprint, New York: Greenwood, 1968.

Hargrave, Letitia. 1838–52. *The Letters of Letitia Hargrave.* Ed. Margaret Macleod. New York: Greenwood Press, 1947.

Harring, Sidney L. 2005. "'There Seemed to Be No Recognized Law': Canadian Law and the Prairie First Nations." In Louis Knafla and Jonathan Swainger, eds, *Laws and Societies in the Canadian Prairie West, 1670–1940,* 92. Vancouver: UBC Press.

Healy, W.J. 1967. *Women of Red River.* Centennial edition. Winnipeg: Peguis.

Hill, Robert B. 1890. *Manitoba: History of Its Early Settlement, Development, and Resources.* Toronto: William Briggs.

Howard, Joseph Kinsey. 1952. *The Strange Empire of Louis Riel.* New York: Houghlin Mifflin.

Huel, Raymond, ed. 1985. *Collected Writings of Louis Riel.* Vol. 1, *1861–1875.* Edmonton: University of Alberta Press.

Hutchinson, Gerald M. 2000. "Evans, James." In *Dictionary of Canadian Biography Online.* Toronto and Laval: University of Toronto Press and Presses de l'Université Laval.

Jackson, James A. 1970. *The Centennial History of Manitoba.* Winnipeg and Toronto: Manitoba Historical Society and McClelland and Stewart.

Jewers, Gerald. 2013. *Manitoba Justice: A History of Manitoba Law and Lawyers.* Winnipeg: Jewers.

Klassen, H.C. 2000. "Bunn, John." In *Dictionary of Canadian Biography Online.* Toronto and Laval: University of Toronto Press and Presses de l'Université Laval.

Knafla, Louis. 1986. "From Oral to Written Memory: The Common Law Tradition in Western Canada." In Louis Knafla, ed., *Law and Justice in a New Land,* 1. Toronto, Carswell.

– 2005. "Introduction: Laws and Societies in the Anglo-Canadian North-West Frontier and Prairie Provinces, 1670–1940." In Louis Knafla and Jonathan Swainger, eds, *Laws and Societies in the Canadian Prairie West, 1670–1940,* 1. Vancouver: UBC Press.

Koenig-Sheridan, Erika. 2003. "'Gentlemen, this is no ordinary trial': Sexual Narratives in the Trial of the Reverend Griffith Owen Corbett, Red River, 1863." In Jennifer S.H. Brown and Elizabeth Vibert, eds, *Reading beyond Words: Contexts for Native History,* 2nd ed., 365. Peterborough, ON: Broadview.

La Forest, G.V. 1969. *Natural Resources and Public Property under the Canadian Constitution.* Toronto: University of Toronto Press.

Lamb, W. Kaye 2000. "Dallas, Alexander Grant." In *Dictionary of Canadian Biography Online.* Toronto and Laval: University of Toronto Press and Presses de l'Université Laval.

Lent, D.G. 1963. *West of the Mountains: James Sinclair and the Hudson's Bay Company.* Seattle: University of Washington Press.

Le Seur, W.D. 1979. *William Lyon Mackenzie: A Reinterpretation.* Toronto: Macmillan.

Lordon, Paul. 1991. *Crown Law.* Toronto: Butterworths.

Lortie, Léon. 1975–76. "The Early Teaching of Law in French Canada." *Dalhousie Law Journal* 2, no. : 521–32.

MacBeth, R.G. 1897. *The Selkirk Settlers in Real Life.* Toronto: William Briggs.

McCusker, John J. 2001. "Comparing the Purchasing Power of Money in Great Britain from 1264 to Any Other Year ..." Economic History Services, Miami University, http://www.eh.net/hmit/ppowerbp.

Macdonald, J.A. 1910. *Troublous Times in Canada: A History of the Fenian Raids of 1866 and 1870.* Toronto: Johnston.

McDonald, Lois Halliday, ed. 1980. *Fur Trade Letters of Francis Ermatinger, 1818–1853*. Glendale, CA: Arthur H. Clark Co.
McGrady, David G. 2010. *Living with Strangers: The Nineteenth-Century Sioux and the Canadian-American Borderlands*. Lincoln and Toronto: University of Nebraska Press and University of Toronto Press.
MacGregor, J.G. 1966. *Peter Fidler: Canada's Forgotten Surveyor, 1769–1822*. Toronto: McClelland and Stewart.
MacKay, Douglas. 1966. *The Honourable Company: A History of the Hudson's Bay Company*. 2nd ed. Toronto: McClelland and Stewart.
McLaren, John, A.R. Buck, and Nancy E. Wright, eds. 2005. *Despotic Dominion: Property Rights in British Settler Societies*. Vancouver: UBC Press.
Macleod, Margaret, ed. 1947. *The Letters of Letitia Hargrave*. New York: Greenwood.
MacLeod, Margaret, and W.L. Morton. 1963. *Cuthbert Grant of Grantown*. Toronto: McClelland and Stewart.
Manitoba Culture, Heritage and Recreation. 1984a. *Captain William Kennedy*. Winnipeg: Historic Resources Branch.
– 1984b. *Georges-Antoine Belcourt*. Winnipeg: Historic Resources Branch.
– 1984c. *The Origin of the Name Manitoba*. Winnipeg: Historic Resources Branch.
– 1984d. *Pascal Bréland*. Winnipeg: Historic Resources Branch.
– 1984e. *Pierre Falcon*. Winnipeg: Historic Resources Branch.
Manitoba Library Association. 1971. *Pioneers and Early Citizens of Manitoba: A Dictionary of Manitoba Biography from the Earliest Times to 1920*. Winnipeg: Peguis.
Martin, Archer. 1898. *Hudson's Bay Company Land Tenures*. London: Clowes.
Merk, Frederick. 1968. *Fur Trade and Empire: George Simpson's Journal, 1824–25*. Cambridge, MA: Harvard University Press.
Mitchell, Estelle. 1980. *Les Soeurs Grises de Montréal à la Rivière-Rouge, 1844–1984*. Sherbrooke, QC: Méridien.
Moir, Esther. 1969. *The Justice of the Peace*. London: Pelican.
Morice, A.S. 1908. *Dictionnaire Historique des Canadiens Métis*. Quebec: n.p.
Morris, Alexander. 1880. *The Treaties of Canada with the Indians*. Toronto: Belfords, Clarke.
Morton, A.S. 1939. *A History of the Canadian West to 1870–1*. Toronto: University of Toronto Press.
– 1944. *Sir George Simpson*. Toronto: Dent.
Morton, W.L., ed. 1956. *Alexander Begg's Red River Journal and Other Papers Relative to the Red River Resistance of 1869–1870*. Toronto: Champlain Society.
– 1961. *Manitoba: A History*. Toronto: University of Toronto Press.

– 1970. "The Battle at the Grand Coteau, July 13 and 14, 1851." In Donald Swainson, ed., *Historical Essays on the Prairie Provinces*, 45. Toronto: McClelland and Stewart.

– 1980. *Henry Youle Hind, 1923–1908*. Toronto: University of Toronto Press.

– 2000a. "Bunn, Thomas." In *Dictionary of Canadian Biography Online*. Toronto and Laval: University of Toronto Press and Presses de l'Université Laval.

– 2000b. "Caldwell, William Bletterman." In *Dictionary of Canadian Biography Online*. Toronto and Laval: University of Toronto Press and Presses de l'Université Laval.

Munro, K.D., ed. 2006. *Letters of Willie Traill, 1864–1894*. Edmonton: University of Alberta Press.

Newman, Peter C. 1985. *Company of Adventurers*. Markham, ON: Viking.

– 1987. *Caesars of the Wilderness*. Markham, ON: Viking.

Nigol, Paul C. 2005. "Discipline and Discretion in the Mid-Eighteenth Century Hudson's Bay Company Private Justice System." In Louis Knafla and Jonathan Swainger, eds, *Laws and Societies in the Canadian Prairie West, 1670–1940*, 150. Vancouver: UBC Press.

Oliver, E.H., ed. 1914. *The Canadian North-West: Its Early Development and Legislative Records: Minutes of the Councils of the Red River Colony and the Northern Department of Rupert's Land*. Ottawa: Government Printing Bureau.

Owen, Bruce. 2012. "Upper Fort Garry Well Worth Exploring." *Winnipeg Free Press*, 20 August, B3.

Pannekoek, Frits. 1991. *A Snug Little Flock: The Social Origins of the Riel Resistance, 1869–70*. Winnipeg: Watson and Dwyer.

– 2000a. "Bunn, John." In *Dictionary of Canadian Biography Online*. Toronto and Laval: University of Toronto Press and Presses de l'Université Laval.

– 2000b. "Ross, Alexander." In *Dictionary of Canadian Biography Online*. Toronto and Laval: University of Toronto Press and Presses de l'Université Laval.

Peel, Bruce. 1974. *Early Printing in the Red River Settlement, 1859–1870*. Winnipeg: Peguis.

– 2000a. "Connolly, Suzanne." In *Dictionary of Canadian Biography Online*. Toronto and Laval: University of Toronto Press and Presses de l'Université Laval.

– 2000b. "Falcon, Pierre." In *Dictionary of Canadian Biography Online*. Toronto and Laval: University of Toronto Press and Presses de l'Université Laval.

– 2000c. "Spence, Thomas." In *Dictionary of Canadian Biography Online*. Toronto and Laval: University of Toronto Press and Presses de l'Université Laval.

Promislow, Janna. 2004. "Towards a Legal History of the Fur Trade: Looking for Law at York Factory, 1714–1763." LLM thesis, York University.

Pryke, K.G. 2000. "Archibald, Sir Adams George." In *Dictionary of Canadian Biography Online.* Toronto and Laval: University of Toronto Press and Presses de l'Université Laval.

Raffan, James. 2007. *Emperor of the North: Sir George Simpson and the Remarkable History of the Hudson's Bay Company.* Toronto: HarperCollins.

Read, Colin. 1982. *The Rising in Western Upper Canada, 1837–8.* Toronto: University of Toronto Press.

Reford, Alexander. 2000. "Smith, Donald Alexander." In *Dictionary of Canadian Biography Online.* Toronto and Laval: University of Toronto Press and Presses de l'Université Laval.

Reid, John Philip. 1994. "Principles of Vengeance: Fur Trappers, Indians and Retaliation for Homicide in the Transboundary North American West." In Tina Loo and Laura McLean, eds, *Historical Perspectives on Law and Society in Canada,* 14. Toronto: Copp Clark.

Reynolds, George F. 1969–70. "The Man Who Created the Corner of Portage and Main." *Manitoba Historical Society Transactions,* ser. 3, no. 26: 5–40.

– 2000. "McKenney, Henry." In *Dictionary of Canadian Biography Online.* Toronto and Laval: University of Toronto Press and Presses de l'Université Laval.

Rich, E.E., ed. 1938. *Journal of Occurrences in the Athabasca Department by George Simpson, 1820 and 1821, and Report.* Toronto: Champlain Society.

– ed. 1956. *Eden Colvile's Letters.* Vol. 19, *1849–1852.* London: Hudson's Bay Company Record Society.

– 1961. *Hudson's Bay Company, 1670–1870.* 3 vols. New York: Macmillan.

Ronaghan, N.E. Allen. 2000. "Bruce (Brousse), John." In *Dictionary of Canadian Biography Online.* Toronto and Laval: University of Toronto Press and Presses de l'Université Laval.

Ross, Alexander. 1856. *The Red River Settlement: Its Rise, Progress, and Present State with Some Account of the Native Races and Its General History to the Present Day.* Reprint, Edmonton: Hurtig, 1972.

Rothney, G.O. 2000. "Girard, Marc-Amable." In *Dictionary of Canadian Biography Online.* Toronto and Laval: University of Toronto Press and Presses de l'Université Laval.

Schull, Joseph. 1971. *Rebellion: The Rising in French Canada, 1837.* Toronto: Macmillan.

Select Committee, House of Commons (UK). 1857. *Report on the Hudson's Bay Company.* London: House of Commons.

Shirritt-Beaumont, Raymond M. 2001. "The Rossville Scandal, 1846: James Evans, the Cree, and a Mission on Trial." MA thesis, University of Manitoba and University of Winnipeg.

Shortt, A., and A.G. Doughty. 1918. *Documents Relating to the Constitutional History of Canada.* Ottawa: King's Printer.

Siggins, Maggie. 1994. *Riel: A Life of Revolution.* Toronto: HarperCollins.

Simpson, George. 1820–21. *Journal of Occurrences in the Athabasca Department by George Simpson, 1820 and 1821, and Report.* Ed. E.E. Rich. Toronto: Champlain Society, 1938.

– 1841–42. *Simpson's Letters to London.* Vol. 29, *1841–42.* Ed. Glyndwr Williams. Winnipeg: Hudson's Bay Record Society, 1973.

Smandych, Russell. 2005. "The Exclusionary Effect of Colonial Law: Indigenous Peoples and English Law in the Canadian West to 1860." In Louis Knafla and Jonathan Swainger, eds, *Laws and Societies in the Canadian Prairie West, 1670–1940,* 127. Vancouver: UBC Press.

Smandych, Russell, and Rick Linden. 1996. "Administering Justice without the State: A Study of the Private Justice System of the Hudson's Bay Company to 1800." *Canadian Journal of Law and Society* 11, no. 1: 21–61.

Smandych, Russell, and Karina Sacca. 1996. "From Private Justice to State Law: The Hudson's Bay Company and the Origin of Criminal Law Courts in the Canadian West to 1870." In Alvin Esau, ed., *Manitoba Law Annual, 1996,* 1. Winnipeg: Faculty of Law, University of Manitoba.

Smith, W.D. 2000. "Ross, James." In *Dictionary of Canadian Biography Online.* Toronto and Laval: University of Toronto Press and Presses de l'Université Laval.

Sprague, D.N. 1988. *Canada and the Métis, 1869–1885.* Waterloo, ON: Wilfrid Laurier University Press.

Spry, Irene M. 2000a. "Inkster, John." In *Dictionary of Canadian Biography Online.* Toronto and Laval: University of Toronto Press and Presses de l'Université Laval.

– 2000b. "Sinclair, James." In *Dictionary of Canadian Biography Online.* Toronto and Laval: University of Toronto Press and Presses de l'Université Laval.

Stanley, George F.G. 1963: *Louis Riel.* Toronto: Ryerson.

– 2000. "O'Donoghue, William Bernard." In *Dictionary of Canadian Biography Online.* Toronto and Laval: University of Toronto Press and Presses de l'Université Laval.

Stonechild, Blair, and Bill Waiser. 1997. *Loyal Till Death: Indians and the North-West Rebellion.* Calgary: Fifth House.

Stubbs, Roy St George. 1967. *Four Recorders of Rupert's Land.* Winnipeg: Peguis.

Talbot, Robert J. 2009. *Negotiating the Numbered Treaties: An Intellectual and Political Biography of Alexander Morris.* Saskatoon: Purich.

Taylor, Ken. 2005. "District of Assiniboia General Quarterly Court Finding Aid." Archives of Manitoba, MG2, B4–1.

Thom, Adam. 1848a. *Charge Delivered to the Grand Jury of Assiniboia, 20 February 1845.* London: Couchman.

– 1848b. *Chronology of Prophecy: Tracing the Various Course of Divine Providence from the Flood to the End of Time in the Light as well of National Annals as of Scriptural Predictions.* London: Longman.

Turner, Allan R. 2000. "McKay, James." In *Dictionary of Canadian Biography Online.* Toronto and Laval: University of Toronto Press and Presses de l'Université Laval.

Van Kirk, Sylvia. 1974–75. "'Destined to Raise Her Caste': Sarah Ballenden and the Foss-Pelly Scandal." *Manitoba Historical Society Transactions,* ser. 3, no. 31: n.p.

– 1980. *"Many Tender Ties": Women in Fur Trade Society, 1670–1870.* Winnipeg: Watson and Dwyer.

– 1986. "'The Reputation of a Lady': Sarah Ballenden and the Foss-Pelly Scandal." *Manitoba History,* no. 11: 4–11.

Walker, D.M. 1980. *The Oxford Companion to Law.* Oxford: Clarendon.

Walters, Mark D. 1996. "The Extension of Colonial Criminal Jurisdiction over the Aboriginal Peoples of Upper Canada: Reconsidering the *Shawanakiskie* Case (1822–26)." *University of Toronto Law Journal* 46, no. 2: 273–310.

Warkentin, John, and Richard I. Ruggles. 1970. *Historical Atlas of Manitoba.* Winnipeg: Manitoba Historical Society.

Wharton, J.J.S. 1938. *Wharton's Law Lexicon.* 14th ed. Ed. A.S. Oppé. London: Stevens and Sweet & Maxwell.

Williams, Glyndwr, ed. 1973. *Simpson's Letters to London.* Vol. 29, *1841–42.* Winnipeg: Hudson's Bay Record Society.

– ed. 1975. *Hudson's Bay Miscellany.* Vol. 30, *1670–1870.* Winnipeg: Hudson's Bay Record Society.

Index

Page numbers in italics refer to photographs and maps. For use of racial and ethnic identifiers, such as Halfbreed and Indian, see the discussion on pages xix–xx. Unless otherwise stated, Council refers to the Council of Assiniboia, and General Court refers to the General Quarterly Court of Assiniboia. RR refers to Red River Settlement. Case numbers in parentheses refer to cases in volume 2 of this work.

2015 Patrons of the Osgoode Society

Blake, Cassels & Graydon LLP

Chernos Flaherty Svonkin LLP

Gowlings

McCarthy Tétrault LLP

Osler, Hoskin & Harcourt LLP

Paliare Roland Rosenberg Rothstein LLP

Torys LLP

WeirFoulds LLP

The Osgoode Society is supported by a grant from the Law Foundation of Ontario.

The Society also thanks the Law Society of Upper Canada for its continuing support.

Publications of the Osgoode Society for Canadian Legal History

2015 Susan Binnie, Eric Tucker, Barry Wright, eds., *Canadian State Trials: Volume IV, War Measures and the Repression of Radicalism 1914–1939*

Lori Chambers, *Adoption in Ontario: A Legal History*

David Fraser, *Honorary Protestants: A Socio-Legal History of the Jewish School Question in Montreal*

Dale Gibson, *Law, Life, and Government at Red River*

Volume 1: Settlement and Governance, 1812–1872

Volume 2: General Quarterly Court of Assiniboia, Annotated Records, 1844–1872

2014 Christopher Moore, *The Court of Appeal for Ontario: Defining the Right of Appeal 1792–2013*

Dominique Clèment, *Equality Deferred: Sex Discrimination and British Columbia's Human Rights State, 1953–1984*

Paul Craven, *Petty Justice: Low Law and the Sessions System in Charlotte County, New Brunswick, 1785–1867*

Thomas Telfer, *Ruin and Redemption: The Struggle for a Canadian Bankruptcy Law, 1867–1919*

2013 Roy McMurtry, *Memoirs and Reflections*

Charlotte Gray, *The Massey Murder: A Maid, Her Master, and the Trial that Shocked a Nation*

C. Ian Kyer, *Lawyers, Families, and Businesses: The Shaping of a Bay Street Law Firm, 1863–1963*

G. Blaine Baker and Donald Fyson, eds., *Essays in the History of Canadian Law: Volume XI: The Canadas*

2012 R. Blake Brown, *Arming and Disarming: A History of Gun Control in Canada*

Eric Tucker, James Muir, and Bruce Ziff, eds., *Property on Trial: Canadian Cases in Context*

Shelley Gavigan, *Hunger, Horses, and Government Men: Criminal Law on the Aboriginal Plains, 1870–1905*

Barrington Walker, ed., *The African-Canadian Legal Odyssey: Historical Essays*

2011 Robert J. Sharpe, *The Lazier Murder: Prince Edward County, 1884*

Philip Girard, *Lawyers and Legal Culture in British North America: Beamish Murdoch of Halifax*

John McLaren, *Dewigged, Bothered, and Bewildered: British Colonial Judges on Trial*

Lesley Erickson, *Westward Bound: Sex, Violence, the Law, and the Making of a Settler Society*

2010 Judy Fudge and Eric Tucker, eds., *Work on Trial: Canadian Labour Law Struggles*

Christopher Moore, *The British Columbia Court of Appeal: The First Hundred Years*

Frederick Vaughan, *Viscount Haldane: The Wicked Step-father of the Canadian Constitution*

Barrington Walker, *Race on Trial: Black Defendants in Ontario=s Criminal Courts, 1850–1950*

2009 William Kaplan, *Canadian Maverick: The Life and Times of Ivan C. Rand*

R. Blake Brown, *A Trying Question: The Jury in Nineteenth-Century Canada*

Barry Wright and Susan Binnie, eds., *Canadian State Trials, Volume III: Political*

Trials and Security Measures, 1840–1914

Robert J. Sharpe, *The Last Day, the Last Hour: The Currie Libel Trial*

2008 Constance Backhouse, *Carnal Crimes: Sexual Assault Law in Canada, 1900–1975*

Jim Phillips, R. Roy McMurtry, and John Saywell, eds., *Essays in the History of Canadian Law, Vol. X: A Tribute to Peter N. Oliver*

Gregory Taylor, *The Law of the Land: Canada=s Receptions of the Torrens System*

Hamar Foster, Benjamin Berger, and A.R. Buck, eds., *The Grand Experiment: Law and Legal Culture in British Settler Societies*

2007 Robert Sharpe and Patricia McMahon, *The Persons Case: The Origins and Legacy of the Fight for Legal Personhood*

Lori Chambers, *Misconceptions: Unmarried Motherhood and the Ontario Children of Unmarried Parents Act, 1921–1969*
Jonathan Swainger, ed., *The Alberta Supreme Court at 100: History and Authority*
Martin Friedland, *My Life in Crime and Other Academic Adventures*

2006 Donald Fyson, *Magistrates, Police, and People: Everyday Criminal Justice in Quebec and Lower Canada, 1764–1837*
Dale Brawn, *The Court of Queen's Bench of Manitoba 1870–1950: A Biographical History*
R.C.B. Risk, *A History of Canadian Legal Thought: Collected Essays*, edited and introduced by G. Blaine Baker and Jim Phillips

2005 Philip Girard, *Bora Laskin: Bringing Law to Life*
Christopher English, ed., *Essays in the History of Canadian Law, Vol. IX: Two Islands, Newfoundland, and Prince Edward Island*
Fred Kaufman, *Searching for Justice: An Autobiography*

2004 John D. Honsberger, *Osgoode Hall: An Illustrated History*
Frederick Vaughan, *Aggressive in Pursuit: The Life of Justice Emmett Hall*
Constance Backhouse & Nancy Backhouse, *The Heiress versus the Establishment: Mrs. Campbell's Campaign for Legal Justice*
Philip Girard, Jim Phillips & Barry Cahill, eds., *The Supreme Court of Nova Scotia, 1754–2004: From Imperial Bastion to Provincial Oracle*

2003 Robert Sharpe and Kent Roach, *Brian Dickson: A Judge's Journey*
George Finlayson, *John J. Robinette: Peerless Mentor*
Peter Oliver, *The Conventional Man: The Diaries of Ontario Chief Justice Robert A. Harrison, 1856–1878*
Jerry Bannister, *The Rule of the Admirals: Law, Custom, and Naval Government in Newfoundland, 1699–1832*

2002 John T. Saywell, *The Law Makers: Judicial Power and the Shaping of Canadian Federalism*
David Murray, *Colonial Justice: Justice, Morality and Crime in the Niagara District, 1791-1849*
F. Murray Greenwood and Barry Wright, eds., *Canadian State Trials, Volume Two: Rebellion and Invasion in the Canadas, 1837–1838*
Patrick Brode, *Courted and Abandoned: Seduction in Canadian Law*

2001 Ellen Anderson, *Judging Bertha Wilson: Law as Large as Life*

Judy Fudge and Eric Tucker, *Labour Before the Law: Collective Action in Canada, 1900–1948*
Laurel Sefton MacDowell, *Renegade Lawyer: The Life of J.L. Cohen*
2000 Barry Cahill, *The Thousandth Man: A Biography of James McGregor Stewart*
A.B. McKillop, *The Spinster and the Prophet: Florence Deeks, H.G. Wells, and the Mystery of the Purloined Past*
Beverley Boissery and F. Murray Greenwood, *Uncertain Justice: Canadian Women and Capital Punishment*
Bruce Ziff, *Unforeseen Legacies: Reuben Wells Leonard and the Leonard Foundation Trust*
1999 Constance Backhouse, *Colour-Coded: A Legal History of Racism in Canada, 1900–1950*
G. Blaine Baker and Jim Phillips, eds., *Essays in the History of Canadian Law, Vol. VIII: In Honour of R.C.B. Risk*
Richard W. Pound, *Chief Justice W.R. Jackett: By the Law of the Land*
David Vanek, *Fulfilment: Memoirs of a Criminal Court Judge*
1998 Sidney Harring, *White Man's Law: Native People in Nineteenth-Century Canadian Jurisprudence*
Peter Oliver, *Terror to Evil-Doers: Prisons and Punishments in Nineteenth-Century Ontario*
1997 James W. St.G. Walker, *Race, Rights, and the Law in the Supreme Court of Canada: Historical Case Studies*
Lori Chambers, *Married Women and Property Law in Victorian Ontario*
Patrick Brode, *Casual Slaughters and Accidental Judgments: Canadian War Crimes and Prosecutions, 1944–1948*
Ian Bushnell, *The Federal Court of Canada: A History, 1875–1992*
1996 Carol Wilton, ed., *Essays in the History of Canadian Law, Vol. VII: Inside the Law – Canadian Law Firms in Historical Perspective*
William Kaplan, *Bad Judgment: The Case of Mr. Justice Leo A. Landreville*
Murray Greenwood and Barry Wright, eds., *Canadian State Trials, Volume I: Law, Politics and Security Measures, 1608–1837*
1995 David Williams, *Just Lawyers: Seven Portraits*
Hamar Foster and John McLaren, eds., *Essays in the History of Canadian Law, Vol. VI: British Columbia and the Yukon*
W.H. Morrow, ed., *Northern Justice: The Memoirs of Mr. Justice William G. Morrow*

Beverley Boissery, *A Deep Sense of Wrong: The Treason, Trials, and Transportation to New South Wales of Lower Canadian Rebels after the 1838 Rebellion*

1994 Patrick Boyer, *A Passion for Justice: The Legacy of James Chalmers McRuer*

Charles Pullen, *The Life and Times of Arthur Maloney:The Last of the Tribunes*

Jim Phillips, Tina Loo, and Susan Lewthwaite, eds., *Essays in the History of Canadian Law, Vol. V: Crime and Criminal Justice*

Brian Young, *The Politics of Codification: The Lower Canadian Civil Code of 1866*

1993 Greg Marquis, *Policing Canada's Century: A History of the Canadian Association of Chiefs of Police*

Murray Greenwood, *Legacies of Fear: Law and Politics in Quebec in the Era of the French Revolution*

1992 Brendan O'Brien, *Speedy Justice: The Tragic Last Voyage of His Majesty's Vessel Speedy*

Robert Fraser, ed., *Provincial Justice: Upper Canadian Legal Portraits from theDictionary of Canadian Biography*

1991 Constance Backhouse, *Petticoats and Prejudice: Women and Law in Nineteenth-Century Canada*

1990 Philip Girard and Jim Phillips, eds., *Essays in the History of Canadian Law, Vol. III: Nova Scotia*

Carol Wilton, ed., *Essays in the History of Canadian Law, Vol. IV: Beyond the Law – Lawyers and Business in Canada 1830–1930*

1989 Desmond Brown, *The Genesis of the Canadian Criminal Code of 1892*

Patrick Brode, *The Odyssey of John Anderson*

1988 Robert Sharpe, *The Last Day, the Last Hour: The Currie Libel Trial*

John D. Arnup, *Middleton: The Beloved Judge*

1987 C. Ian Kyer and Jerome Bickenbach, *The Fiercest Debate: Cecil A. Wright, the Benchers, and Legal Education in Ontario, 1923–1957*

1986 Paul Romney, *Mr. Attorney: The Attorney General for Ontario in Court, Cabinet and Legislature, 1791–1899*

Martin Friedland, *The Case of Valentine Shortis: A True Story of Crime and Politics in Canada*

1985 James Snell and Frederick Vaughan, *The Supreme Court of Canada: History of the Institution*

1984 Patrick Brode, *Sir John Beverley Robinson: Bone and Sinew of the Compact*

David Williams, *Duff: A Life in the Law*

1983 David H. Flaherty, ed., *Essays in the History of Canadian Law, Vol. II*

1982 Marion MacRae and Anthony Adamson, *Cornerstones of Order: Courthouses and Town Halls of Ontario, 1784–1914*

1981 David H. Flaherty, ed., *Essays in the History of Canadian Law, Vol. I*